Japanese
Kanji
AND
Kana

A COMPLETE GUIDE TO THE JAPANESE WRITING SYSTEM

WOLFGANG HADAMITZKY & MARK SPAHN

D0061487

TUTTLE Publishing

Tokyo | Rutland, Vermont | Singapore

The Tuttle Story: "Books to Span the East and West"

Most people are surprised to learn that the world's largest publisher of books on Asia had its beginnings in the tiny American state of Vermont. The company's founder, Charles E. Tuttle, belonged to a New England family steeped in publishing. And his first love was naturally books—especially old and rare editions.

Immediately after WW II, serving in Tokyo under General Douglas MacArthur, Tuttle was tasked with reviving the Japanese publishing industry, and founded the Charles E. Tuttle Publishing Company, which thrives today as one of the world's leading independent publishers.

Though a westerner, Charles was hugely instrumental in bringing a knowledge of Japan and Asia to a world hungry for information about the East. By the time of his death in 1993, Tuttle had published over 6,000 books on Asian culture, history and art—a legacy honored by the Japanese emperor with the "Order of the Sacred Treasure," the highest tribute Japan can bestow upon a non-Japanese.

With a backlist of 1,500 titles, Tuttle Publishing is more active today than at any time in its past—inspired by Charles' core mission to publish fine books to span the East and West and provide a greater understanding of each.

Published by Tuttle Publishing, an imprint of Periplus Editions (HK) Ltd.

www.tuttlepublishing.com

Copyright © 2012 by Wolfgang Hadamitzky and Mark Spahn

Third edition, 2011
Second edition, 1997
First edition, 1981
German language edition published in 1979 by Verlag Enderle GmbH, Tokyo; in 1980 by Langenscheidt KG, Berlin and Munich

Library of Congress Cataloging-in-Publication Data for this title is available.

ISBN 978-4-8053-1116-5
ISBN 978-4-8053-1222-3 (for sale in Japan only)

Third edition
15 14 13 12 11   5 4 3 2 1   1111MP

Printed in Singapore

Distributed by

North America, Latin America & Europe
Tuttle Publishing
364 Innovation Drive
North Clarendon, VT 05759-9436 U.S.A.
Tel: 1 (802) 773-8930
Fax: 1 (802) 773-6993
info@tuttlepublishing.com
www.tuttlepublishing.com

Japan
Tuttle Publishing
Yaekari Building, 3rd Floor, 5-4-12 Osaki
Shinagawa-ku, Tokyo 141 0032
Tel: (81) 3 5437-0171
Fax: (81) 3 5437-0755
sales@tuttle.co.jp
www.tuttle.co.jp

Asia Pacific
Berkeley Books Pte. Ltd.
61 Tai Seng Avenue #02-12
Singapore 534167
Tel: (65) 6280-1330
Fax: (65) 6280-6290
inquiries@periplus.com.sg
www.periplus.com

TUTTLE PUBLISHING® is a registered trademark of Tuttle Publishing, a division of Periplus Editions (HK) Ltd.

Table 2. Basic Rules for Writing by Hand

Stroke direction

1.	Horizontal strokes from left to right	一
2.	Vertical or slanting strokes from top to bottom	├ ＼ ノ く し
3.	A stroke may change direction several times	コ ヲ ア し ム 辶 そ

Stroke order

a.	From top to bottom	二 工 こ テ
b.	From left to right	川 竹 い ル
c.	Middle stroke before short flanking side-strokes	小 当 水
d.	Horizontal stroke before inter-secting vertical stroke	十 土 七 ま ナ
e.	X-forming strokes: from upper right to lower left, then from upper left to lower right	文 父 攵
f.	Piercing vertical stroke last	中 申 車 半 聿 平 手
	If the vertical middle stroke does not protrude, upper part, then middle stroke, then lower part	里 壬
g.	Piercing horizontal stroke last	女 子 母 舟

These handwriting rules for the stroke direction and order apply to kana as well as kanji. For a more-detailed explanation of kanji writing rules, see the summary on pages 46–48.

Table of Contents

List of Tables

Preface

Fourteen years after it was last revised, this standard work of the Japanese writing system has been expanded and completely updated. The main part of the book now lists 2,141 kanji (formerly 1,945). In addition, with its 19 tables, it presents a fresh, modern design.

A feature of this handbook is its double usefulness as both a textbook and a reference work. It serves beginners as well as those who want to look up individual kanji via the three indexes. And the many tables provide a quick overview of all important aspects of the Japanese writing system.

The information is so organized and presented – the pronunciation of each character is spelled out in roman letters – as to allow easy entry into the Japanese writing system for beginners and those who are learning on their own, providing the background anyone needs to know to become able to read Japanese without constantly looking up one kanji after another.

All the information about the hiragana and katakana syllabaries and the kanji is based on the official orthography rules of the Japanese government. The 2,141 kanji listed in the main part of this book include the 2,136 characters of the "Revised List of Kanji for General Use" (改定 常用漢字表, 2010) as well as five further kanji that were dropped from the official list that was in effect up to 2010.

This work is divided into three parts:

1. Introductory chapters
A general introduction to transliteration is followed by a presentation of the two sets of phonetic characters, the hiragana and the katakana (called collectively the kana). Then comes a section devoted to punctuation. Next is a general introduction to the world of the ideographic characters, the kanji: how they arose, how they are put together, how to write them, how to read (pronounce) them, what they mean, how to find them in a character dictionary, and tips for how to learn them effectively.

2. List of the 2,136 Jōyō Kanji
The bulk of the book is made up of the official list of the 2,136 Jōyō Kanji. The order of presentation is based on pedagogical principles, proceeding from simple, frequent kanji to those that are more complex and occur less often. Within this general framework, characters that are graphically similar are presented together in order to call attention to their similarities and differences in form, reading, and meaning.

Each head-kanji is set in a modern, appealing font, and is accompanied by: its running identification number from 1 to 2141, how it is written (stroke by stroke) and its stroke-count; its readings and corresponding meanings; its handwritten form and variants; its structure and graphic components; its radical; and its location in more-comprehensive character dictionaries.

Under each head-kanji are listed up to five important compounds with reading and meaning. These compounds are made up of earlier-listed characters having lower identification numbers

(with only a few exceptions). So working through the kanji in the order they are presented in this book will make it easier for you to build up a vocabulary while reviewing what you have learned before. Each compound is labeled with the numbers of its constituent kanji, for quick review lookup.

In all, the kanji list and compounds contain a basic Japanese vocabulary of over 12,000 words.

3. Indexes

Each of the 2,141 characters in the kanji list can be looked up via three indexes at the end of the book: by reading, by stroke-count, and by radical.

Acknowledgments
The revision of this book is owed primarily to Mr. and Mrs. Rainer and Seiko Weihs, who prepared and proofed all the data in their usual competent, patient, detailed way and produced the typographically complex work you hold in your hands. The quality of the data was considerably improved by the many additional suggestions of Mrs. Vera Rathje and Mrs. Violaine Mochizuki. To all of them we express our heartfelt thanks.

Buckow, Germany, August 2011   Wolfgang Hadamitzky
                                                www.hadamitzky.de
West Seneca, New York, USA, August 2011   Mark Spahn

Further study aids and dictionaries by the authors on the Japanese writing system

A Guide to Writing Japanese Kanji & Kana. Books 1, 2. 1991
Writing templates for the kana syllabaries and the kanji 1 to 1945.

Kanji in Motion. (KiM) 2011
Game and tutorial program. Trains the user for rapidly recognizing and reading all kana and Jōyō Kanji.

KanjiVision. (KV) 2012
Web-based Japanese-English character dictionary. Contains about 6,000 head-kanji and 48,000 multi-kanji compound words. Search options: by grapheme (up to six per character), reading (in romanization or kana), meaning, stroke-count, and kanji (copied from other sources).

Introduction

Japanese is written in a mixture (called *kanji-kana majiri*) of three types of symbols, each with its own function:

1. **Kanji**
   These ideographic characters, adopted from the Chinese language, are used for conceptual words (mainly nouns, verbs, and adjectives) and for Japanese and Chinese proper names.

2. **Hiragana**
   Written with hiragana are the inflectional endings of conceptual words as well as all words, mostly of grammatical function, that are not written in kanji.

3. **Katakana**
   Katakana are used to write foreign names and other words of foreign origin, and to emphasize individual words.

Besides kanji, hiragana, and katakana, one often finds in Japanese texts the same roman letters and Hindu-Arabic numerals as in English; for example, the semigovernmental radio and television broadcasting corporation 日本放送協会 *Nippon Hōsō Kyōkai* is abbreviated *NHK* (the letters are pronounced as in English), and in horizontal writing, numbers are usually written with Hindu-Arabic numerals rather than with kanji.

There has never been an independent, purely Japanese system of writing. Around the seventh century the attempt was first made to use Chinese characters to represent Japanese speech. In the ninth century the Japanese simplified the complex Chinese ideographs into what are now the two sets of kana (hiragana and katakana). Each of these kana syllabaries encompasses all the syllables that occur Japanese, so it is quite possible to write exclusively in kana, just as it would be possible to write Japanese exclusively in romanization. In practice, however, this would hamper communication due to the large number of words that are pronounced alike but have different meanings; these homophones are distinguished from each other by being written with different kanji.

Japanese today is written either in vertical columns proceeding from right to left or in horizontal lines which are read from left to right. The traditional vertical style is seen mostly in literary works. The horizontal European style, recommended by the government, is found more in scientific and technical literature. Newspapers use both styles: most articles are written vertically, headlines and advertisements appear in both styles, and radio and television program listings are laid out horizontally.

Handwritten Japanese may be written either vertically or horizontally. For writing practice it is recommended that the beginner use either manuscript paper (*genkō yōshi*), which has space for either 200 or 400 characters per page, or the practice manuals that accompany this text. There, each kana, and each kanji from 1 to 1945, is presented twice in gray for tracing over, followed by empty spaces for free writing.

Whether handwritten or printed, the individual characters are written separately one after another; the characters of a single word are not strung together, nor are any blank spaces left between words. Here the conventions governing the use of kanji and kana for different types of words aid the reader in determining where one word ends and the next begins.

All the characters within a text are written in the same size; there is no distinction analogous to that between capital and lowercase letters.

As with roman letters, there are a few differences between the printed and handwritten forms, which sometimes makes character recognition difficult for the beginner. In order to familiarize the student with these differences, each of the 2,141 kanji presented in the main section of this book and in the practice manuals appears in three ways: in brush form, in a model handwritten form, and in printed form. Within the printed forms of kanji, there are various typefaces, but the differences between them are usually insignificant.

In handwriting (with brush or pen), three styles are distinguished:

1. The standard style *(kaisho)*, which is taught as the norm in school and is practically identical to the printed form. All the handwritten characters in this volume are given in the standard style.
2. The semicursive style *(gyōsho)*, a simplification of the standard style that allows one to write more flowingly and rapidly.
3. The cursive style or "grass hand" *(sōsho)*, which is a kind of calligraphic shorthand resulting from extreme simplification according to esthetic standards.

Kaisho   Gyōsho   Sōsho

And in practice, several frequently occurring characters are sometimes used in greatly simplified forms which are not officially recognized; for example, the characte 門 is sometimes simplified to 门, 曜 to 旺, and 第 to 才.

And let it be noted that there is also a Japanese shorthand intended for purely practical rather than artistic purposes.

Since the 1980s Japanese has been written less often by brush, pencil, and pen, and more often by keyboard. But even if your goal is simply to be able to read, and the need to eventually write Japanese by hand seems slight, writing practice is still worthwhile, because it familiarizes you with the characters, fixes them in your mind, and gets you to notice details that can help in recognizing characters and being able to look them up in a character dictionary. And perhaps writing practice will stimulate an interest in calligraphy, one of the oldest of the Japanese arts.

Romanization

Writing Japanese with the same roman letters as in English presents no problems; the Japanese language can easily be transliterated using only 22 roman letters and two diacritical marks.

So why haven't the Japanese adopted such an alphabet to replace a system of writing which even they find difficult? The answer lies in the large number of homophones, especially in the written language: even in context it is frequently impossible to uniquely determine the sense of a word without knowing the characters it is written with. Other rational as well as more emotional considerations, including a certain inertia, make it very unlikely that the Japanese writing system will undergo such a thorough overhaul.

In 1952 the Japanese government issued recommendations for the transliteration of Japanese into roman letters. Two tables (on pages 12 and 13) summarize the two recommended systems of romanization, which are both in use today and differ only slightly from each other:

1. The *kunrei-shiki rōmaji* system
   Patterned after the Fifty-Sounds Table in which the kana syllables are arranged, the initial consonant sound of all five syllable in each row is represented uniformly with the same roman letter, regardless of any phonetic variation associated with the different vowel sounds.

2. The *Hebon-shiki rōmaji* system
   This romanization system too follows the kana characters. The *Hebon-shiki* was developed by a commission of Japanese and foreign scholars in 1885 and was widely disseminated a year later through its use in a Japanese-English dictionary compiled by the American missionary and philologist James Curtis Hepburn (in Japanese: *Hebon*). In Hepburn romanization the consonant sounds are spelled as in English, and the vowel sounds as in Italian.

The Japanese government romanization recommendations of 1952 favor *kunrei-shiki rōmaji*, but explicitly allow the use of *Hebon-shiki rōmaji*, especially in texts for foreigners. The Hepburn system allows an English speaker to approximate the original Japanese pronunciation without the need to remember any unfamiliar pronunciation rules, and is therefore less likely to lead a non-Japanese into mispronunciation. A good illustration of this is the name of Japan's sacred mountain, which is spelled *Fuji* in the Hepburn system but misleadingly as *Huzi* in the *kunrei* system. That is why the transliterations in this book are spelled with Hepburn romanization.

The following transliteration rules are taken from the official recommendations. The examples as well as the remarks in parentheses have been added.

1. The end-of-syllable sound ん is always written *n* (even when it appears before the labials *b*, *p*, or *m* and is phonetically assimilated to *m*: *konban, kanpai, kanmuri*).
2. When needed to prevent mispronunciation, an apostrophe ['] is inserted to separate the end-of-syllable sound *n* from a following vowel or *y*: *man'ichi, kon'yaku*.

3. Assimilated, or "stretched," sounds *(soku-on)* are represented (as in Italian) by double consonants: *mikka, massugu, hatten, kippu: sh* becomes *ssh, ch* become *tch,* and *ts* becomes *tts: ressha, botchan, mittsu.*
4. Long vowels are marked with a circumflex [^] (this does not correspond to the kana orthography), and if a long vowel is capitalized, it may be doubled instead. (In practice the simpler macron [ˉ] has become prevalent: *mā, yūjin, dōzo.* The lengthening of *i* and (in words of Chinese origin) of *e* is indicated by appending an *i: oniisan, meishi* (but: *onēsan*). In foreign words and names written in katakana, the long vowels *i* and *e* are written with a macron if in the original Japanese they are represented by a lengthening stroke [ー]: ビール *bīru,* メートル *mētoru,* ベートーベン *Bētōben* (but: スペイン *Supein,* エイト *eito.*)
5. For the representation of certain sounds there are no binding rules. (Short, sudden broken-off vowels at the end of a word or syllable – glottal stops, or *soku-on* – are denoted in this book by adding an apostrophe: *a', are', ji'.*)
6. Proper names and the first word of every sentence are capitalized. The capitalization of substantives is optional: *Ogenki desu ka? Nippon, Tōkyō, Tanaka, Genji Monogatari, Kanji* or *kanji.*

The only real problem in romanizing Japanese text, in which there are no spaces between words, is in deciding where one word ends and the next begins. Basically, it is recommended that independent units thought of as words should be written separately: *Hon o sagashite iru n desu.* Hyphens serve clarity by separating word units without running them together in a single word: *Tōkyō-to, Minato-ku, Tanaka-san.* For sake of legibility, compounds made up of four or more kanji should be partitioned into units of two or three kanji each: 源氏物語 *Genji Monogatari,* 海外旅行 *kaigai ryokō,* 民主主義 *minshu shugi.*

But we will refrain from any further discussion of proper romanization, which in any case is just a side-issue in a work whose aim is to get the learner as soon as possible to the passive and active mastery of the original Japanese text.

Table 3. Transliteration (Hepburn romanization)

			Fifty-Sounds Table		
	あ ア a	い イ i	う ウ u	え エ e	お オ o
k	か カ ka	き キ ki	く ク ku	け ケ ke	こ コ ko
s	さ サ sa	し シ shi/si	す ス su	せ セ se	そ ソ so
t	た タ ta	ち チ chi/ti	つ ツ tsu/tu	て テ te	と ト to
n	な ナ na	に ニ ni	ぬ ヌ nu	ね ネ ne	の ノ no
h	は ハ ha (wa)	ひ ヒ hi	ふ フ fu/hu	へ ヘ he (e)	ほ ホ ho
m	ま マ ma	み ミ mi	む ム mu	め メ me	も モ mo
y	や ヤ ya	—	ゆ ユ yu	—	よ ヨ yo
r	ら ラ ra	り リ ri	る ル ru	れ レ re	ろ ロ ro
w	わ ワ wa	ゐ*ヰ* i	—	ゑ*ヱ* e	を ヲ wo
	*obsolete				ん ン n
g	が ガ ga	ぎ ギ gi	ぐ グ gu	げ ゲ ge	ご ゴ go
z	ざ ザ za	じ ジ ji/zi	ず ズ zu	ぜ ゼ ze	ぞ ゾ zo
d	だ ダ da	ぢ ヂ ji/zi	づ ヅ zu	で デ de	ど ド do
b	ば バ ba	び ビ bi	ぶ ブ bu	べ ベ be	ぼ ボ bo
p	ぱ パ pa	ぴ ピ pi	ぷ プ pu	ぺ ペ pe	ぽ ポ po
	a	i	u	e	o

Supplementary Table

—	—	—
きゃ キャ kya	きゃ キャ kyu	きょ キョ kyo
しゃ シャ cha/sya	しゅ シュ shu/syu	しょ ショ sho/syo
ちゃ チャ cha/tya	ちゅ チュ chu/tyu	ちょ チョ cho/tyo
にゃ ニャ nya	にゅ ニュ nyu	にょ ニョ nyo
ひゃ ヒャ hya	ひゅ ヒュ hyu	ひょ ヒョ hyo
みゃ ミャ mya	みゅ ミュ myu	みょ ミョ myo
—	—	—
りゃ リャ rya	りゅ リュ ryu	りょ リョ ryo
—	—	—

ぎゃ ギャ gya	ぎゅ ギュ gyu	ぎょ ギョ gyo
じゃ ジャ ja/zya	じゅ ジュ ju/zyu	じょ ジョ jo/zyo
—	—	—
びゃ ビャ bya	びゅ ビュ byu	びょ ビョ byo
ぴゃ ピャ pya	ぴゅ ピュ pyu	ぴょ ピョ pyo
ya	yu	yo

The Kana Syllabaries
Origin

The characters (kanji) in Chinese texts brought into Japan via Korea beginning in the fourth century gradually came to be adopted by the Japanese for writing their own language, for which there was no native system of writing. The characters were used phonetically to represent similar-sounding Japanese syllables; the meanings of the characters were ignored. In this way one could represent the sound of any Japanese word. But since each Chinese character corresponded to only one syllable, in order to write a single multisyllabic Japanese word one had to write several kanji, which frequently consist of a large number of strokes.

Hiragana

To simplify this bothersome process, instead of the full angular style *(kaisho)* of the kanji, a cursive, simplified, derivative style *(sōsho)* was used. In addition, the flowing and expressive lines of the *sōsho* style were felt to be better suited for literary notation. Toward the end of the Nara period (710–794) and during the Heian period (794–1185) these symbols underwent a further simplification, in which esthetic considerations played a part, resulting in a stock of phonetic symbols which was extensive enough to represent all the sounds of the Japanese language. This was the decisive step in the formation of a purely phonetic system for representing syllables. These simple syllable-symbols, today known as hiragana, were formerly referred to as *onna-de*, "ladies' hand," since they were first used in letters and literary writing by courtly women of the Heian period, who were ignorant of the exclusively male domain of Chinese learning and literature and the use of Chinese characters. But the hiragana gradually came to prevail as a standard syllabary.

The hiragana syllabary in use today was laid down in the year 1900 in a decree for elementary schools. Two obsolete characters were dropped as part of orthographic reforms made shortly after World War II. As a result, today there are 46 officially recognized hiragana.

The now-obsolete kana that were dropped by the above decree, and which were derived from different kanji, are called *hentai-gana* (deviant-form kana).

Katakana

The katakana symbols were developed only a little later than the hiragana. While listening to lectures on the classics of Buddhism, students wrote in their text notations on the pronunciation or meaning of unfamiliar characters, and sometimes wrote commentaries between the lines of certain passages. Doing so required a kind of note-taking shorthand.

This practice resulted in the development of a new phonetic script based on Chinese characters, the katakana syllabary. Each katakana is taken from one component of a *kaisho*-style Chinese character corresponding to a particular syllable. This makes the katakana more angular than the hiragana, which are cursive simplifications of entire kanji. In a few cases the katakana is only a slight alteration of a simple kanji: チ (千), ハ (八), ミ (三).

Since katakana were closely associated with science and learning, for a long time these angular phonetic symbols were used only by men.

As with the hiragana, the final form of the katakana in use today was prescribed in 1900 in a decree for elementary schools. And the number officially recognized katakana is today 46, the same as for hiragana.

A kana takes on not just the form of the kanji from which it is derived, but also its adopted Chinese pronunciation, called its *on* reading. Three kana are exceptions: in チ (千 *chi*), ミ (三 *mittsu*), and と/ト (止 *tomaru*), the pronunciation comes not from the *on* reading of the kanji, but from the first syllable of its native-Japanese *kun* reading.

The pronunciation of a word written in kanji that the reader might not know how to read can be specified by marking the kanji with little kana, usually hiragana. These annotation kana for indicating pronunciation are called *furigana*. In horizontal writing they are written above the kanji, and in vertical writing they are written to the right of the kanji (for examples, see page 32).

The derivation tables on the following two pages show which kanji each kana is derived from.

Table 4. Hiragana Derivations

あ	安	い	以	う	宇	え	衣	お	於
a	105	i	46	u	1027	e	690	o	4h4.2
か	加	き	幾	く	久	け	計	こ	己
ka	722	ki	897	ku	1273	ke	340	ko	371
さ	左	し	之	す	寸	せ	世	そ	曽
sa	75	shi	0a2.9	su	2070	se	252	so	1450
た	太	ち	知	つ	川	て	天	と	止
ta	639	chi	214	tsu	33	te	141	to	485
な	奈	に	仁	ぬ	奴	ね	祢	の	乃
na	947	ni	1727	nu	2118	ne	4e14.1	no	0a2.10
は	波	ひ	比	ふ	不	へ	部	ほ	保
ha	677	hi	812	fu	94	he	86	ho	498
ま	末	み	美	む	武	め	女	も	毛
ma	305	mi	405	mu	1071	me	102	mo	287
や	也			ゆ	由			よ	与
ya	0a3.29			yu	364			yo	548
ら	良	り	利	る	留	れ	礼	ろ	呂
ra	321	ri	329	ru	774	re	630	ro	1396
わ	和	ゐ	為			ゑ	恵	を	遠
wa	124	i	1881			e	1282	o	453
ん	无								
n	0a4.24								

The number or (for non-Jōyō-Kanji) descriptor below each kanji tells where its entry can be found in this book or in the kanji dictionaries by Spahn/Hadamitzky.

Table 5. Katakana Derivations

ア 阿 a　2d5.6	イ 伊 i　2a4.6	ウ 宇 u　1027	エ 江 e　840	オ 於 o　4h4.2
カ 加 ka　722	キ 幾 ki　897	ク 久 ku　1273	ケ 箇 ke　1570	コ 己 ko　371
サ 散 sa　781	シ 之 shi　0a2.9	ス 須 su　1531	セ 世 se　252	ソ 曽 so　1450
タ 多 ta　229	チ 千 chi　15	ツ 川 tsu　33	テ 天 te　141	ト 止 to　485
ナ 奈 na　947	ニ 仁 ni　1727	ヌ 奴 nu　2118	ネ 祢 ne　4e14.1	ノ 乃 no　0a2.10
ハ 八 ha　10	ヒ 比 hi　812	フ 不 fu　94	ヘ 部 he　86	ホ 保 ho　498
マ 末 ma　305	ミ 三 mi　4	ム 牟 mu　4g2.2	メ 女 me　102	モ 毛 mo　287
ヤ 也 ya　0a3.29		ユ 由 yu　364		ヨ 與 yo　548
ラ 良 ra　321	リ 利 ri　329	ル 流 ru　247	レ 礼 re　630	ロ 呂 ro　1396
ワ 和 wa　124	ヰ 井 i　1255		ヱ 恵 e　1282	ヲ 乎 o　0a5.17
ン 尓 n　0a14.3				

The number or (for non-Jōyō-Kanji) descriptor below each kanji tells where its entry can be found in this book or in the kanji dictionaries by Spahn/Hadamitzky.

Order

Table 1 (inside the front cover) shows the usual "alphabetical" order of the hiragana and kataka-na syllable-characters. It is based on Indian alphabets which, like the Devanagari alphabet to-day, order their syllables according to their articulatory phonetics. Around the year 1000 people in Japan began to arrange the Japanese syllables and syllable-characters, which had been in use since early in the Heian period, into a sequence according to their pronunciation following the Indian example. The result was the so-called Fifty-Sounds Table *(gojū-on-zu)*, a syllabary in which every syllable is assigned a character. Of the 46 characters in all, 40 are arranged in groups of five each that belong together phonetically; five are arranged in corresponding slots in this arrangement, and one lies outside this arrangement. The table appears in two formats: with the named groups arranged either in vertical columns (Table 1), or in horizontal rows (Tables 4 and 5, pages 16 and 17).

In the vertical arrangement, the characters in the Fifty-Sounds Table begin with the right column and are read from top to bottom. Thus the Japanese syllable alphabet begins *a, i, u, e, o; ka, ki, ku, ke, ko, ...* The five characters in each column *(dan)* are arranged according to their vowel sounds, in the order *a-i-u-e-o*, and the ten characters in each row *(gyō)* are arranged ac-cording to their initial consonant sound, in the order *ø k s t n h m y r w*. (This is sometimes memo-rized as *a-ka-sa-ta-na, ha-ma-ya-ra-wa* in the sing-song musical rhythm of do-re-mi-fa-so, so-fa-mi-re-do.) This systematic ordering makes it easy to memorize the Japanese *aiueo* alphabet.

The end-of-syllable sound *n* lies outside the scheme of the Fifty-Sounds Table, because purely Japanese words do not use this sound. The *n* was not tacked on to the Fifty-Sounds Table until Chinese characters and their pronunciation made their way into the Japanese language.

The Fifty-Sounds Table can be written in either hiragana or katakana. The two kana sylla-baries have no symbols in common (although their *he* characters へ and ヘ are nearly indistin-guishable), but they denote the same sounds in the same order.

Let it be noted that the major writing systems of the world arrange their characters by any of three different principles. The European alphabets are based on the oldest Semitic alphabet, which is ordered according to meaning and pictorial similarity; the Arabic alphabet is ordered according to the form of its characters; while the Devangari alphabet of India, with which San-skrit and Hindi is written, is ordered according to the sounds of the characters. Despite their fundamental differences, the three basic alphabet systems have some commonalities, includ-ing putting the vowel *a* at the beginning of the alphabet.

Two diacritical marks make it possible to represent beginning-of-syllable consonants that cannot be represented by the unmodified kana. Thus the "muddied", that is, voiced sounds *g, z, d,* and *b* (called *daku-on*) are denoted by putting a mark [ˋ], called a *daku-ten* or *nigori-ten*, on the upper right of the corresponding unvoiced kana. And the "half-muddied" sound *p- (handaku-on)* is denoted by putting a mark [˚], called a *handaku-ten* or *maru*, on the upper right of the corresponding *h-* kana.

Combinations of kana are used to represent some sounds, most of which were adopted

from Chinese. One-syllable "twisted" sounds (*yō-on*: consonant + *y* + *a, u* or *o*) and "assimilated" sounds (*soku-on:* unvoiced doubled consonants, or glottal stop) are written with two kana, the second of which is written smaller; and the one-syllable combination *yō-on* + *soku-on* is written with three kana, the last two of which are written smaller.

The assimilated sounds do not appear in the usual syllabary tables. Shown here are a few examples of how they are spelled and romanized.

あっ アッ	あっか アッカ	あっきゃ アッキャ
a'	*akka*	*akkya*

かっ カッ	かっか カッカ	きゃっか キャッカ
ka'	*kakka*	*kyakka*

In Japanese, alphabetical order – also known as dictionary order or lexical order – is based on the Fifty-Sounds Table (see Table 3, pages 12 and 13). But with any alphabet of characters that have variants, when alphabetizing a list of words, we need tie-breaking rules to decide which of two words comes first when they differ only by length (e.g., *china* vs. *chinaware*, あな vs. あなば), by diacritical mark (*resume* vs. *résumé*, はり vs. ばり vs. ぱり), by character-size (*china* vs. *China*, かつて vs. かって), or, in Japanese, by the hiragana/katakana distinction (これら vs. コレラ). One solution (others are possible) is given in Table 6, in which the alphabetical order proceeds down the columns, taking the columns from right to left. Table 7 gives examples of words sorted into kana alphabetical order, taking the columns from left to right.

One way to get a different alphabetical order from any set of characters is to arrange them in a "perfect pangram," in which every character occurs just once. For example, the 26 letters of the English alphabet can be rearranged into the odd sentence "TV quiz jock, Mr. PhD, bags few lynx." And something similar happened with the kana during the Heian period: they were arranged into a Buddhist poem, called the Iroha from its first three kana. Its first characters イロハニホヘト are used today for labeling items in sequence, such as subheadings, items in a list, or the musical keys A to G. The Fifty-Sounds Table contains 46 kana, but the Iroha contains 47, because it includes the two now-obsolete kana ゐ *(w)i* and ゑ *(w)e*, and lacks the kana ん *n*.

This Iroha poem is reproduced line by line on page 22, along with a translation.

Romanized Japanese can be alphabetized as in English, and this is done in Japanese-foreign language dictionaries.

Table 6. Alphabetical order of the syllables of the Fifty-Sounds Table and supplementary table

ン	ワ	ラ	ヤ	マ	ハ バ パ	ナ	タ ダ	サ ザ	カ ガ	ア
		リ		ミ	ヒ ビ ピ	ニ	チ ヂ	シ ジ	キ ギ	イ
		リャ		ミャ	ヒャ ビャ ピャ	ニャ	チャ	シャ ジャ	キャ ギャ	
		リュ		ミュ	ヒュ ビュ ピュ	ニュ	チュ	シュ ジュ	キュ ギュ	
		リョ		ミョ	ヒョ ビョ ピョ	ニョ	チョ	ショ ジョ	キョ ギョ	
		ル	ユ	ム	フ ブ プ	ヌ	ツ ヅ	ス ズ	ク グ	ウ ヴ
		レ		メ	ヘ ベ ペ	ネ	テ デ	セ ゼ	ケ ゲ	エ
	ヲ	ロ	ヨ	モ	ホ ボ ポ	ノ	ト ド	ソ ゾ	コ ゴ	オ

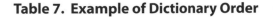

Table 7. Example of Dictionary Order

あ	あいかぎ	あいぎん
ア	あいき	あいく
ああ	あいぎ	…… …
アー	あいきどう	あち
アート	あいきゃく	あつ
ああら	アイキュー	あっ
あい	あいきょう	あつい
あいか	あいぎょう	あつか
あいが	あいきわ	あっか
あいがえし	あいきん	あつかい

The above table shows by a few examples the order in which words spelled with kana appear in dictionaries and in listings given in **aiueo** order. Note that these are not the only possible order-determining rules. Some reference works list a small-size kana before its full-size counterpart: ゃ before や, ゅ before ゆ, っ before つ. Some dictionaries handle the katakana vowel-lengthening mark ー (called **chōonpu** or simply **bō**) by ignoring it, as a hyphen would be ignored in English-language alphabetization, while other dictionaries take it as coming either just after or just before (アー before アア, キュー before キュウ) the preceding vowel it lengthens. And words in which **zu** and **ō** are correctly spelled with づ and おお are sometimes alphabetized as if spelled with ず and おう, respectively.

Table 8. The Iroha Syllable Order

い i	ろ ro	は ha	に ni	ほ ho	へ he	と to
ち chi	り ri	ぬ nu	る ru	を (w)o		
わ wa	か ka	よ yo	た ta	れ re	そ so	
つ tsu	ね ne	な na	ら ra	む mu		
う u	ゐ (w)i	の no	お o	く ku	や ya	ま ma
け ke	ふ fu	こ ko	え e	て te		
あ a	さ sa	き ki	ゆ yu	め me	み mi	し shi
ゑ (w)e	ひ hi	も mo	せ se	す su		

The Iroha (Japanese: *iroha-uta*) was composed as a mnemonic poem in which every kana of the syllabary occurs only once. (Translation by Basil Hall Chamberlain, 1850–1935)

iro ha nihoheto	Though gay in hue,
chrinuru wo	the blossoms flutter down also,
waka yo tare so	Who then in this world of ours
tsune naramu	may continue forever?
uwi no okuyama	Crossing today
kefu koete	the uttermost limits of phenomenal existence,
asaki yume mishi	I shall no more see fleeting dreams,
wehi mo sesu	Neither be any longer intoxicated.

Writing

The two kana syllabaries are the best first step toward mastering the Japanese writing system, because:

a. They are limited in number (46 hiragana, 46 katakana).
b. They are simple in form (one to four strokes each).
c. There is a one-to-one correspondence between sound and symbol (except for two characters, which each have two readings).
d. Each syllabary encompasses all the sounds of the Japanese language, so that any text can be written down in kana (as is done in books for small children).

It is debatable which set of kana should be learned first. Hiragana occur far more frequently, but katakana are used to write words of foreign origin, including English words the beginner might recognize from their Japanese pronunciation.

The following two principles govern the sequence and direction in which to write the strokes of a kana (as well as of a kanji):

1. From top to bottom
2. From left to right

In Tables 9 and 10, the small numbers at the beginning of each stroke indicate the direction in which each stroke is written, the sequence in which the strokes are written, and how many strokes the kana consists of:

し コ い イ

Japanese is handwritten not on lines but (even for adults) in a printed or at least imaginary grid of squares. In learning how to write, it is recommended that from the beginning you use Japanese manuscript paper *(genkō yōshi)* or the practice manuals that accompany this book. Tracing over the gray-tone characters in the practice manuals is the quickest way to get a feel for the proper proportions of each character:

あ	あ	あ									
い	い	い									
う	う	う									
え	え	え									
お	お	お									

Table 9. How to Write Hiragana

あ	い	う	え	お
か	き	く	け	こ
さ	し	す	せ	そ
た	ち	つ	て	と
な	に	ぬ	ね	の
は	ひ	ふ	へ	ほ
ま	み	む	め	も
や		ゆ		よ
ら	り	る	れ	ろ
わ				を
ん				

Table 10. How to Write Katakana

ア	イ	ウ	エ	オ
カ	キ	ク	ケ	コ
サ	シ	ス	セ	ソ
タ	チ	ツ	テ	ト
ナ	ニ	ヌ	ネ	ノ
ハ	ヒ	フ	ヘ	ホ
マ	ミ	ム	メ	モ
ヤ		ユ		ヨ
ラ	リ	ル	レ	ロ
ワ				ヲ
ン				

25

Orthography

Modern kana orthography *(gendai kanazukai)* reflects pronunciation closely. This section explains, with examples, the most important orthographic rules.

The long vowels *(chō-on) ā, ii* and *ū* are represented by appending あ, い, or う:

ああ	*ā*	Ah! Oh!
お**かあ**さん	*okāsan*	mother
いいえ	*iie*	no
お**にい**さん	*oniisan*	elder/older brother
ゆうがた	*yūgata*	evening
すうがく	*sūgaku*	mathematics

Long *ē/ei* is written

in words of Japanese reading *(kun)*, with an appended え:

ねえ	*nē*	indeed, right?
お**ねえ**さん	*onēsan*	elder/older sister

in words of Sino-Japanese reading *(on)*, with an appended い:

ていねい	*teinei*	polite
きれい	*kirei*	pretty; clean

Long *ō* is normally represented with an appended う:

どうぞ	*dōzo*	please
おは**よう**	*ohayō*	Good morning.

In some cases, however, お is appended instead of う:

おおい（多い）	*ōi*	numerous
おおきい（大きい）	*ōkii*	big
オオカミ	*ōkami*	wolf
おおやけ（公）	*ōyake*	public, official
こおり（氷）	*kōri*	ice
とお（十）	*tō*	ten
とおい（遠い）	*tōi*	far
とおる（通る）	*tōru*	go along/through, pass
ほ**のお**（炎）	*honō*	flame
も**よお**す（催す）	*moyōsu*	sponsor

These historically based spelling exceptions need not concern you too much, because these words are usually written with kanji in such a way (shown in parentheses) that the problem does not arise.

In the transliteration of foreign words into katakana, long vowels are denoted by a lengthening stroke (ー):

コーヒー	*kōhī*	coffee
ビール	*bīru*	beer
ボール	*bōru*	ball
ダンサー	*dansā*	dancer
エスカレーター	*esukarētā*	escalator

But:

エイト	*eito*	eight
スペイン	*Supein*	Spain

The voiced sounds (*daku-on*, "muddied" sounds) g-, z-, d-, and b- are denoted with a pair of short diagonal strokes *(nigori)* on the upper right corner of the corresponding unvoiced character, and the "half-muddied" sound *(handaku-on)* p- is similarly denoted with a small circle *(maru)*:

が ガ	ざ ザ	だ ダ	ば バ	ぱ パ	
ga	*za*	*da*	*ba*	*pa*	etc.

The "twisted" sounds *(yō-on)*, which do not have characters of their own either, are denoted with two kana; the first is taken from the *i* column, and the second from the *ya* row. The second kana is written smaller to indicate that the sounds of the two characters are merged into a single syllable:

きゃ キャ	きゅ キュ	きょ キョ	
kya	*kyu*	*kyo*	
ぎゃ ギャ	ぎゅ ギュ	ぎょ ギョ	
gya	*gyu*	*gyo*	etc.

Assimilated sounds *(soku-on)*, that is, those sound that are represented in romanization by a doubled consonant, are denoted by a small っ/ッ before the consonant sound:

れっしゃ	*ressha*	train
じっぷん	*jippun*	ten minutes
ロケット	*roketto*	rocket

Short, broken-off vowels at the end of a word or syllable (final glottal stops, *soku-on*) are likewise denoted by a small っ/ッ:

あっ	*a'*	Oh!
ジッ	*ji'*	(an *on* reading of the kanji 十 for ten)

The sounds *ji* and *zu* are usually written じ/ジ and ず/ズ:

ま**じ**め	*majime*	serious, sober
ま**ず**い	*mazui*	bad-tasting
ラ**ジ**オ	*rajio*	radio
ジャズ	*jazu*	jazz

But づ and ぢ are used

a. when the preceding syllable (of the same word) is the same character without the *nigori* mark:

つ**づ**り	*tsuzuri*	syllable, spelling
つ**づ**く	*tsuzuku*	continue
ち**ぢ**む	*chijimu*	shrink

b. when the syllable つ or ち is voiced to *zu* or *ji* in a compound word:

かな**づ**かい（かな＋つかい）	*kanazukai*	*kana* orthography
き**づ**かれ（き＋つかれ）	*kizukare*	mental fatigue
はな**ぢ**（はな＋ち）	*hanaji*	nosebleed

Sometimes the spelling rules in a. and b. are not followed, and *tsuzuri* and *hanaji* appear, and are alphabetized in dictionaries, under the spellings つずり and はなじ rather than つづり and はなぢ.

The syllables *e*, *o*, and *wa* are written え/エ, お/オ, and わ/ワ when part of a word:

いい**え**	*iie*	no
な**お**	*nao*	further, still more
わたし	*watashi*	I, me
エネルギー	*enerugī*	energy
オペラ	*opera*	opera
ワシントン	*Washinton*	Washington

But the same three sounds are written へ/ヘ, を/ヲ, and は/ハ when they represent postpositional "auxiliary words" (*joshi*):

わたし**は**	*Watashi wa*	I [subject]
はがき**を**	*hagaki o*	the postcard [direct object]
ポスト**へ**いれた。	*posuto e ireta.*	put into the mailbox.
また**は**	*mata wa*	or
こんにち**は**	*konnichi wa*	Hello.

The word 言う "say" is pronounced ゆう (*yū*) but written いう (*iu*).

Table 11. Important Katakana Combinations
(in ABC alphabetical order)

	a	e	i	o	u
c		che チェ			
d			di ディ		
f	fa ファ	fe フェ	fi フィ	fo フォ	
g	gwa グァ				
h		hye ヒェ			
j		je ジェ			
k	kwa クァ	kwe クェ	kwi クィ	kwo クォ	
s		she シェ			
t			ti ティ		tu トゥ
ts	tsa ツァ	tse ツェ		tso ツォ	
v	va ヴァ	ve ヴェ	vi ヴィ	vo ヴォ	vu ヴ
w		we ウェ	wi ウィ	wo ウォ	
z			zi ズィ		

Small-written katakana vowel symbols are used to represent foreign sounds that do not other-wise occur in Japanese. This table shows the most frequent katakana syllables in which such a small vowel occurs.

The common rōmaji-to-kana text editors also accept the following variant transliterations for the following katakana combinations:

ディ *dhi*, クァ *qa*, クェ *qe*, クィ *qi*, クォ *qo*, ティ *thi*, トゥ *twu*, ウォ *who*, ズィ *zuxi*.

Usage

The following rules outline how the two syllabaries hiragana and katakana are used.

Hiragana are used to write
a. all types of words other than nouns, verbs, and adjectives:

よく	*yoku*	well, often
たぶん	*tabun*	probably
この	*kono*	this, these
あそこ	*asoko*	there
かなり	*kanari*	quite, considerably
まだ	*mada*	still, (not) yet
だけ	*dake*	only
へ	*e*	to

b. nouns, verbs, and adjectives in certain cases (as when a formerly used kanji has become obsolete):

ことわざ	*kotowaza*	proverb
さん	*-san*	Mr./Mrs./Ms. …
する	*suru*	do, make
できる	*dekiru*	can, be able
きれい	*kirei*	pretty
うれしい	*ureshii*	happy

c. inflectional endings of words written with kanji:

行く	*i-ku*	go
行かない	*i-kanai*	not go
白い	*shiro-i*	white
祭り	*matsu-ri*	festival

Hiragana used for writing word endings (*gobi*) are called *okurigana*. Sometimes not just the word's inflectional ending but also part of its stem (*gokan*) is written in hiragana:

新しい	*atara-shii*	new
大きい	*ō-kii*	big
食べる	*ta-beru*	eat
幸せ	*shiawa-se*	happiness

Katakana are used to write

a. foreign-derived words:

ビル	*biru*	building
ビール	*bīru*	beer
テーブル	*tēburu*	table

b. foreign words and foreign proper names (except Chinese and some Korean proper names, which are written in kanji):

アメリカ	*Amerika*	America
ドイツ	*Doitsu*	Germany
パリ	*Pari*	Paris (France, not Texas)
シェークスピア	*Shēkusupia*	Shakespeare

c. names of plants and animals (especially in a scientific context):

ネズミ	*nezumi*	mouse, rat
セミ	*semi*	cicada
マグロ	*maguro*	tuna
サクラ	*sakura*	cherry tree (the species)
タンポポ	*tanpopo*	dandelion

but:

犬	*inu*	dog
桜	*sakura*	cherry tree
みかん	*mikan*	satsuma orange, mandarin

d. some female given names:

エミ	*Emi*
マリ	*Mari*

e. onomatopoeic words such as animal cries and other sounds; children's words; exclamations:

ワンワン	*wan wan*	bowwow
ニャーニャー	*nyā nyā*	meow
ガタガタ	*gata gata*	(rattling sound)
トントン	*ton ton*	(knocking sound)
ピューピュー	*pyū pyū*	(sound of the wind)
アレ／アレッ	*are/are'*	Huh?!
オヤ／オヤッ	*oya/oya'*	Oh!

f.　colloquialisms and slang:

インチキ	*inchiki*	trickery, flimflam, crooked
デカ	*deka*	police detective

g.　words and proper names that are to be emphasized:

もうダメだ	*mō dame da*	Too late!
ナゾの自殺	*nazo no jisatsu*	a mysteeerious suicide
トヨタ	*Toyota*	Toyota (company name)
ヨコハマ	*Yokohama*	Yokohama (city name)

The limited usage of katakana makes them stand out and often lends them a certain weight. This high visibility, which is often made use of in advertising, has somewhat the same effect that italics and capital letters have in Western languages.

Both hiragana and katakana are used to show the pronunciation of kanji, like this:

一つ	*hitotsu*	片
平仮名	*hiragana*	仮 katakana
漢字	*kanji*	名

These small kana, written either above or below the kanji in horizontal writing and to the right of the kanji in vertical writing, are called *furigana* or *rubi*.

In transliterating individual kanji, katakana are used for Chinese-derived *(on)* readings, and hiragana for native-Japanese *(kun)* readings:

人　ジン、ニン、ひと　*JIN, NIN (on), hito (kun)*　person

In transliterating foreign words and proper names, the basic rule is that the katakana should follow as closely as possible the pronunciation of the original (usually English) word. But despite a general trend toward unification of the transliteration rules, some foreign words and names are rendered into katakana in more than one way:

ベット	*betto*	bed
ベッド	*beddo*	bed
ダーウィン	*Dāwin*	Darwin
ダーウイン	*Dāwin*	Darwin

For many foreign sounds there is nothing in the traditional Japanese sound and writing system that corresponds. These non-Japanese sounds are represented by many new combinations of traditional katakana and diacritical marks (see also Table 11 on page 29):

フィリピン	*Firipin*	the Philippines
ダーウィン	*Dāwin*	Darwin
ヴィーン	*Vīn*	Vienna (Ger. Wien)
ジュネーヴ	*Junēvu*	Geneva (Fr. Genève)
デュッセルドルフ	*Dyusserudorufu*	Düsseldorf
ティー	*tī*	tea
クォータリー	*quōtarī*	quarterly (publication)

For many words, an approximation using only the katakana in the Fifty-Sounds Table is preferred over a more-exact reproduction of the original pronunciation:

バイオリン	*baiorin*	violin
ビタミン	*bitamin*	vitamin
チーム	*chīmu*	team
ラジオ	*rajio*	radio
ベートーベン	*Bētōben*	Beethoven

The consonant *l* (ell), which does not occur in Japanese, is represented by *r-*:

ホール	*hōru*	hall
ラブレター	*raburetā*	love letter

The kana repetition symbols *(kurikaeshi fugō)*
If within a single word the same kana occurs twice in a row, the second occurrence can be replaced with the kana repetition symbol, thus:

あゝ	*ā*	Ah! Oh!
かゝし	*kakashi*	scarecrow

This repetition symbol may also be used with a *nigori*:

ほゞ	*hobo*	almost, nearly
たゞし	*tadashi*	but, however

The repetition symbol for two syllables is used only in vertical writing:

いろく	*iroiro* various	わざく	*wazawaza* on purpose

Punctuation

There are no compulsory, uniform rules for the usage and nomenclature of the various punctuation marks *(kugiri fugō* or *kutōten)*, and this chapter is but an attempt to present in a systematic way a uniform terminology and practical explanation of Japanese punctuation as it is used today.

In general, a punctuation mark is given the same amount of space as any other character; that is, on *genkō yōshi* (Japanese manuscript paper), an entire square is used even for a punctuation mark. However, a pair of successive punctuation marks like 「『 or 。」 is written in a single space, the *tensen* (ellipsis) is written three dots per space, and some punctuation marks (see examples under 4, 5, 10, and 11 below) extend over several spaces.

Some punctuation marks take different orientations or forms depending on whether the writing is vertical or horizontal:

⌐	→ 「」	⌐	→ 『』	„″	→ " "
◡	→ ( )	≋	→ (( ))	∫	→ ~
ひ、 る、	→ ひる	よ る|	→ よる

The examples are listed in "backwards" Japanese style, in vertical columns read from right to left from page 38 to page 35. The example sentences 14 and 15 are written in columns but illustrate what commas and periods look like in horizontal writing; to read them, tilt your head 90 degrees to the right (or just tilt the book).

Table 12 presents a summary of the most important punctuation marks and what they are called in Japanese.

The *wakiten* side-dots (example 10) in vertical writing are replaced in horizontal writing by *nakaten* dots placed over the characters, and the *wakisen* (example 11) in vertical writing is replaced in horizontal writing by underlining *(andārain)*:

15	14	13	12	11	10
，	・	！	？	│	⁝
a. はい、そうです。	a. 平成23.9.4	a. 「ちがう、ちがう、ちがうぞ！」	b. 「きのう見に行った？」 a. 「ええ？ なんですって？」	b. 次の傍線を引いた語について説明せよ。そう考えられる。 a. 名辞は、単一の名詞から成ることもあり、あるいは長い名詞句から成ることもある。人はパンのみにて生くるものにあらず。	c. ぴんからきりまである。 b. ひるという言葉は、 a. まず、句点は文の終わりにつける、というのが……

10. *Wakiten*

These "side-dots" are similar to italics in that they highlight words and phrases (a), words which for some reason are written in kana instead of the usual kanji (b), and slang, dialect, and other types of unconventional words (c).

11. *Wakisen*

Use of these "side-lines" is similar to underlining to draw the reader's attention to certain phrases (a) or words or parts of words (b) (similar to 10a).

12. *Gimonfu*

Even questions in principle end with a *maru*. The question mark is to be used only when it would otherwise be unclear whether the sentence is a statement or a question.

13. *Kantanfu*

As in English, the exclamation point indicates emotional intensity and should be used sparingly.

14. *Piriodo*

In horizontal writing the period is used as a delimiter between the year, month, and day in dates.

15. *Konma*

The comma can be used in horizontal writing instead of the *ten* (see 2).

No.	Mark	Ex.	Example
9	〜	a.	一〜三時間　四月〜六月　東京〜大阪
8	（　）	d.	（一）（イ）（a）
8	（　）	c.	（田中）
8	（　）	b.	（第二回）（完）（終）（続く）
8	（　）	a.	和独辞典（平成二十三年刊）
7	" "	a.	これは有名な"月光の曲"です。
6	『　』	e.	彼は「人生に大切なのは『努力』ということだ」と言った。
6	『　』	d.	「母も『よろしく』と申しております。」
6	「　」	c.	漢字の読み方は「音」と「訓」との二つがある。
6	「　」	b.	国歌「君が代」
6	「　」	a.	See 1c, d, 2c, 4a, 5a–c, 12a, b, 13a.
6	「　」	d.	第一章　序説……………一頁
6	「　」	c.	「ごめんね、由美ちゃん。」「……」

6. Kagikakko or kagi

These quotation marks correspond to the quotation marks of English, in quoting direct speech (a) or in citing a word or phrase (b, c).

Futaekagi

These double quotation marks are used inside *kagi* pairs, for quotations within quotations (d, e).

7. In'yōfu

Quotation marks of this type are often used today instead of *kagi*, especially in the sense of "so-called".

8. Kakko

These parentheses are used in vertical writing to enclose explanatory information of all kinds (a–c), and in horizontal writing to enclose numbers or letters to label the sections and subsections of a long text (d).

9. Namigata

This wavy punctuation mark is used, like a hyphen is used in English, between the starting and ending points of a "from … to …" range. When read aloud, it is usually pronounced *kara*, "from".

5	4
⋮	│
b. 「それもそうだけど……」 **a.** 「それからね……いやいや、もうなんにも申し上げますまい。」 **f.** 中野区中央五─六─十四 **e.** 三─五週間 **d.** 上野─新橋、渋谷─銀座、新宿─日比谷の電車	**c.** 汽車は、京都──名古屋──東京と、走っていった。 **b.** もうひとりの人─背の高い男─が大声で言った。 **a.** 「それはね、──いや、もうやめしょう。」 **g.** ジョン・F・ケネディ **f.** 八・五％ **e.** 昭和五二・九・四 **d.** 大阪・京都、東京へ旅行した。

4. *Nakasen*

This dash mark indicates that a sentence or thought has been broken off while still incomplete (a) (cf. 5a, b); sets off explanatory information inserted into a sentence (b); has the meaning "between … and …" when used for distances (c, d) or "from … to …" when used for timespans (e); and separates the *chōme* and *banchi* numbers in addresses, where it is pronounced *no*.

5. *Tensen*

This string of centered dots is used like the ellipsis […] in English. It denotes that a sentence or thought remains uncompleted (a, b) (cf. 4a); indicates the trailing off of the voice at the end of an utterance (b); denotes silence in a conversation (c); and is used to form connection lines between headings and page numbers in a table of contents or the like (d).

Mark		Example sentences
1	○	a. 日本は島国です。 b. どうぞ、こちらへ。 c. 「どちらへ。」 d. 「おおい、田中君。」
2	、	a. はい、そうです。 b. ただ、例外として、…… c. 「行きますか」と、彼はきいた。 d. 見ましたか、今朝の新聞を。 e. 大きな、めがねをかけた男。 　 but: 大きなめがねをかけた男。 f. 二・三日 g. 二、三三〇円
3	・	a. りんご・なし・みかんなど b. 田中・大平会談 c. 米、英・独と協商 　 but: 米英独三国

1. *Maru*

This little circle corresponds to the English-language period at the end of a sentence (a, b). Even questions (c) and exclamations (d) often end with a *maru*.

2. *Ten*

Like the comma in English, the *ten* indicates a pause to clarify the structure of a sentence (a)–(e) (e: "a big man wearing glasses", "a man wearing big glasses"); separates successive numbers (f: *ni-san-nichi*); and divides numbers of four or more digits into three-digit groups (g: *nisen sanbyaku nijū en*).

3. *Nakaguro* or *nakaten*

This centered dot is used to separate words that go together (a–d); to separate the year, month, and day when citing a date (e: read *nen* and *gatsu*); to indicate a decimal point (f); and to separate the component words of foreign phrases and names written in katakana (g).

Table 12. Punctuation Marks

(For explanations and examples, see pages 38–35)

1.	2.	3.	4.	5.	6.	7.
。	、	•	|	⁝	「 」 『 』	" „
句点 マル（丸）	テン（点） 読点	ナカテン（中点）	ナカセン（中線）	テンセン（点線）	カギカッコ フタエカギ（二重かぎ）	引用符
Maru *Kuten*	*Ten* *Tōten*	*Nakaten*	*Nakasen*	*Tensen*	*Kagikakko* *Futaekagi*	*In'yōfu*

8.	9.	10.	11.	12.	13.	14.	15.
（ ） ⸤⸥ ◯	〜	⁝⁝	|	？	！	・	，
カッコ（括弧）マルガッコ フタエガッコ（二重括弧） ヨコカッコ	ナミガタ（波形）	ワキテン	ワキセン	疑問符	感嘆符	ピリオド	コンマ
Kakko Marugakko *Futaegakko* *Yokokakko*	*Namigata*	*Wakiten*	*Wakisen*	*Gimonfu*	*Kantanfu*	*Piriodo*	*Konma*

The Kanji
Brief Historical Outline

The oldest known Chinese characters date back to the sixteenth century B.C., but their number and advanced form indicate that they had already gone through a development of several hundred years. Like the Egyptian hieroglyphics, the earliest Chinese characters started with simple illustrations, which during the course of time became increasingly abstract and took on forms better adapted to the writing tools of the time.

These characters, along with many other elements of Chinese culture, came to Japan by way of the Korean peninsula beginning in about the fourth century A.D., and since the Japanese had no writing of their own, the Chinese characters soon came to be used for the Japanese language as well.

At first these monosyllabic Chinese characters were used purely phonetically, with no reference to their meaning, to represent similar Japanese syllables:

久 尔   *ku-ni*   country

This method enabled one to write down any word, but a single multisyllabic Japanese word required several Chinese characters, each consisting of many strokes.

A second method soon developed: the characters were used ideographically, with no reference to their Chinese pronunciation, to represent Japanese words of the same or related meaning:

国   *kuni*   country

Both methods are used in the *Man'yōshū*, Japan's oldest collection of poetry, dating from the eighth century. Here, words denoting concepts are written with the corresponding Chinese characters, which are given the Japanese pronunciation. All other words, as well as proper names and inflectional endings, are represented phonetically by kanji which are read with a Japanese approximation to their Chinese pronunciation. The characters used for this latter, phonetic function are called *Man'yōgana*. The kana syllabaries developed from these characters after great simplification (see pages 14–17).

For centuries, kanji, hiragana, and katakana were used independently of one another, and the number of symbols in use and their readings kept growing. Toward the end of the 1800s, after the Meiji Restoration, the government as part of its modernization program undertook to simplify the writing system for the first time.

The latest major writing reform came shortly after World War II:

1. In 1946 the number of kanji permitted for use in official publications was limited to 1,850 *Tōyō Kanji* (increased to 1,945 *Jōyō Kanji* in 1981 and to 2,136 *Jōyō Kanji* in 2010); of these, about 900 were selected as *Kyōiku Kanji* to be learned in the first six years of schooling.

2. The *on* and *kun* readings of the *Tōyō Kanji* were limited in number to about 3,500 (increased to over 4,000 *Jōyō Kanji* readings in 1981, and to 4,394 readings in 2010).
3. Many kanji were simplified or replaced by others easier to write.
4. Uniform rules were prescribed for how to write the kanji (sequence and number of strokes).

The print and television press strives to follow these and other government recommendations concerning how Japanese is to be written. A knowledge of the set of characters treated in this book will therefore be sufficient for reading Japanese newspapers without time-consuming reference to a character dictionary. To be sure, this assumes mastery of a vocabulary of at least 10,000 Japanese words, most of which, including proper names, consist of two or three kanji. This is an important reason for learning kanji not in isolation but always in the context of multi-kanji compounds.

Since 1951 the government has from time to time published a supplementary list of kanji which, together with the *Jōyō Kanji*, are permitted for use in given and family names. Some of the characters in this list of kanji for use in personal names *(Jinmei-yō Kanji)* are traditional kanji that were replaced with a simpler form in the reform of 1946 and for a time were therefore no longer allowed, even though many families preferred to write their names with traditional, unsimplified characters. According to Japanese law, only the kanji and readings that appear in these two lists may be used in given and family names. The first list of personal-name characters, which was issued in 1951, included 92 kanji; the latest list, issued in 2009, includes 985.

An average educated Japanese is familiar with about 3,000 kanji. Today roughly 6,000–7,000 characters are used in written Japanese, including technical and literary writing. The monumental Chinese-Japanese character dictionary *Dai Kan-Wa Jiten* (1955–60, in 13 volumes), by the Japanese linguist and Sinologist Tetsuji Morohashi and colleagues, lists about 50,000 kanji and over 500,000 compounds, although most of them are obsolete and of merely historical interest, having been used only in China.

From Pictures to Characters

Most characters are built up from a limited number of basic elements according to principles that are easily grasped. How these elements are put together determines the meaning, and often the pronunciation, of a kanji, and therefore familiarity with the most important elements and their use will make it easier to understand and memorize the 2,141 kanji in this book as well as those not included here.

Chinese characters can be divided according to their origin and structure into three groups: pictures (pictographs), symbols (ideographs), and picture combinations (composed characters).

1. **Pictographs**

   The first characters developed from simple illustrations of objects and phenomena of daily life. Even in the abstract form used today, the object depicted can often still be recognized:

山	*yama*	mountain (three towering peaks)
木	*ki*	tree (trunk with branches)
田	*ta*	field, paddy (square plot of land with ridges/furrows)

   There are only a few pictographs that are used today as independent characters. But they serve as building blocks for almost all the other characters.

2. **Ideographs**

   For abstract concepts, characters were invented that indicate meaning in only a few strokes (*on* readings in uppercase, *kun* readings in lowercase):

一	*ICHI*	one	上	*ue*	above
二	*NI*	two	下	*sita*	below
三	*SAN*	three	中	*naka*	middle

3. **Composed characters**

   To increase the stock of word signs, characters already available were put together in new combinations.

   At first two or three pictographs with the same or similar meanings were combined into a single new character (logogram):

林	*hayashi*	woods	(木 tree + 木 tree)
森	*mori*	forest	(木 tree + 木 tree + 木 tree)
明	*akarui*	light, bright	(日 sun + 月 moon)

In other cases, the Chinese took the reading of one part of a newly created compound character as the reading of the entire characters (phonologogram):

理	*RI*	reason

The pronunciation-indicating part is in this case the character 里, whose reading is *ri*. Over 90 percent of all kanji are combinations constructed according to this principle. In most cases the pronunciation-indicating part (which often also contributes to the meaning) appears on the right, and the meaning-indicating part on the left.

Thus the phonologograms can be classified into six groups, corresponding to the position of the component indicates pronunciation (**P**) and of the component indicates meaning (**M**):

M on left,	**P** on right:	銅	*DŌ*	copper	(金 metal + 同 *DŌ*)
P on left,	**M** on right:	歌	*KA*	sing	(欠 yawn + 可 *KA*)
M on top,	**P** on bottom:	花	*KA*	flower	(艹 grass + 化 *KA*)
P on top,	**M** on bottom:	盛	*SEI*	fill	(皿 dish + 成 *SEI*)
M outside,	**P** inside:	園	*EN*	garden	(囗 enclosure + 袁 *EN*)
P outside,	**M** inside:	問	*MON*	ask	(口 mouth + 門 *MON*)

The 17 structures

The number of basic elements (graphemes) from which a kanji can be assembled is limited, and so is the number of patterns they form. There are basically 16 kanji structures that occur with any frequency. All other structures are denoted in this book by a square containing three dots. These structures, listed approximately in decreasing order of their frequency, are:

In the *Jōyō Kanji* list of this book, the structure of each kanji is given along with its radical and graphemes.

When you learn a new kanji you should take note of its structure and components (graphemes), and as you build up you kanji vocabulary, you will encounter more and more often structures and graphemes you have seen before. Understanding how kanji are put together will not only make it easier and more fun to learn them well enough to write them from memory, but will also make it quicker to look up kanji and compounds in electronic character dictionaries.

Readings

When Chinese texts were introduced into Japan, the Japanese adopted not only the Chinese characters but their readings as well. In being adapted to the Japanese phonetic system, the Chinese pronunciations were modified. For example, the distinction between the four tones of Chinese was ignored. (This is one reason for the large number of homophones in Japanese.) Later, Chinese characters were used to represent Japanese words of identical or similar meaning and were given Japanese readings. This explains why most kanji have both Chinese-derived *(on)* and native-Japanese *(kun)* readings.

And a given character might have two or three different on readings, because it was adopted from the Chinese language of different historical eras and different regions (dialects). Different *kun* readings for the same kanji, on the other hand, are accounted for by different nuances and parts of speech, as in 煙 *EN, kemuri* = smoke, *kemu(ru)* = to smoke, smolder, *kemu(i)* = smoky.

In prescribing the *Jōyō Kanji* the government limited not only the number of characters recognized for general use but also the number of officially authorized readings. Of the 2,136 *Jōyō Kanji* listed in this book, 1,240 have both an *on* and a *kun* reading, 823 have only an *on* reading, and 78 have only a *kun* reading. The kanji that have only a *kun* reading consist almost entirely of characters (called *kokuji*) that were created by the Japanese in imitation of the Chinese pattern. The character 働, meaning "work," is the only *kokuji* to which a pseudo-*on* reading is attached; its *on* reading is *DŌ*, and its *kun* reading is *hatara(ku)*.

By convention, when it is necessary to distinguish between *on* and *kun* readings, an *on* reading is spelled with katakana or uppercase roman letters, and a *kun* reading is spelled with hiragana or lowercase roman letters.

Whether a word is to be read with an *on* or a *kun* reading can be determined in most cases by the following criteria:

1. One-character words are read with their *kun* reading:

人	*hito*	person
口	*kuchi*	mouth
日	*hi*	sun; day

But:

本	*HON*	book
一	*ICHI*	one

2. Single characters and compounds with *okurigana* are pronounced with a *kun* reading:

一つ	*hitotsu*	one
見出し	*midashi*	headline
話し合う	*hanashiau*	talk together, converse

3. Compounds without *okurigana* are to be read with an *on* reading:

見物	*KENBUTSU*	sight-seeing
人口	*JINKŌ*	population

But:

出口	*deguchi*	exit

Family names are usually read with a *kun* reading:

田中	*Tanaka*		鈴木	*Suzuki*
山田	*Yamada*		坂本	*Sakamoto*

But:

本田	*HONda*		加藤	*KATŌ*

The characters composing a given multi-kanji compound word are generally read either all *on* or all *kun* and are transcribed with lowercase roman letters or hiragana. (The representation of *on* readings by uppercase letters in the above examples was just to make them stand out.)

Some compounds have two, and in rare cases three, different readings:

明日	*myōnichi, asu*	tomorrow
一日	*ichinichi, ichijitsu*	one day
	tsuitachi	the first of the month

Kanji that are used together with other characters exclusively
(a) to convey the meaning of a word, disregarding the usual readings of the kanji; or
(b) as phonetic symbols, disregarding the meanings of the individual kanji,

are called *ateji*.

(a)	大人	*otona*	adult
	お母さん	*okāsan*	mother

This group of "convey meaning, ignore pronunciation" *ateji* also includes the above readings *asu* for 明日 and *tsuitachi* for 一日.

(b)	出来る	*dekiru*	can, be able
	独逸	*Doitsu*	Germany (Deutschland)

The kanji repetition symbol 々 (*kurikaeshi fugō*), which is not itself a kanji, has no reading of its own; it is read like the kanji for which it stands:

人々 (for 人人)	*hitobito*	people
山々 (for 山山)	*yamayama*	mountains

Rules for Writing Kanji

At least at the beginning, reading practice should be supplemented by writing practice. Repeatedly writing an individual character together with compounds in which it occurs will help fix it in your mind and give you confidence in reading. And writing is the best way to master stroke-counting, which is indispensable for looking up kanji in a character dictionary or via the stroke-count index at the end of this book. Writing the most complex kanji will present no difficulties once you know how to apply the writing rules to the limited number of elements that make up any kanji. The main challenge is active writing: reproducing from memory a kanji you already can recognize.

A good way to get a feel for the correct length, direction, and relative position of the constituent strokes of a kanji is to practice writing with either Japanese manuscript paper *(genkō yōshi)* or the writing practice manuals that supplement this book.

The small sequential numbers at the beginning of each stroke in the following examples and in the main part of the book indicate, as with the kana, the direction in which each stroke is to be written and the order in which the strokes of a kanji are to be written; the last number gives the total number of strokes in the kanji.

Table 2 in the preceding section summarizes the most important rules for writing kanji.

1. Stroke direction

Horizontal strokes are written from left to right:

Vertical or slanting strokes are written from top to bottom:

An exception is the combination of a short slanting down-stroke followed by a short slanting up-stroke, as in the radicals *sanzui* 氵, *nisui* 冫, and *yamaidare* 疒 and in 求 and similar kanji:

A stroke may change direction several times:

2. Stroke order

a. From top to bottom:

二 工

b. From left to right:

川 竹

c. Middle stroke before short flanking side-strokes:

小 当 水

But:

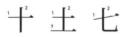

d. With intersecting strokes, horizontal before vertical:

十 土 七

Exceptions:

田 王 隹

e. With X-forming strokes, from upper right to lower left, then from upper left to lower right:

父 文 夊

f. A piercing vertical stroke is written last:

If the vertical middle stroke does not protrude above or below, the sequence of strokes is: upper part, then middle stroke, then lower part:

g. A piercing horizontal stroke is written last:

女 子 母 舟

h. First the vertical stroke, then the short horizontal stroke that adjoins it on the right:

上 正 足 走

i. First the left and upper part of an outer enclosure:

国 回 匡 同 司 内 風

But:

区 医

j. A lower-left enclosure is written last:

進 直

These stroke sequence rules should suffice; explaining every detail of the officially prescribed stroke-sequence rules would bloat this book, which explicitly presents the stroke sequence of every *Jōyō Kanji* anyway.

The kanji repetition symbol 々 *(kurikaeshi fugō)*, which is not itself a kanji, is written as follows:

The character 々 stands for a repetition of the immediately preceding kanji, and is read like the kanji for which it stands:

一々	*ichiichi*	one by one; every single thing
人々	*hitobito*	people
山々	*yamayama*	mountains
国々	*kuniguni*	countries, every country
島々	*shimajima*	(many) islands

The repetition symbol is not used when the same kanji occurs in sequence just by coincidence:

民主主義	*minshu shugi*	democracy ("democratic" + "ism")

Character forms

The rules described on the two preceding pages are for writing characters by hand with a conventional writing implement like a pencil or pen. In practice, however, there are as many variations in writing as there are in other written languages – variations in handwritten forms and printed fonts that can make it difficult for learners to recognize and read kanji.

In this book we cover only the standard, non-calligraphic script taught in schools and seen in books and newspapers. But to point out the slight differences within this standard, all the kanji listed in the main part of this book appear in three styles: the head-kanji as a model for copying (with the strokes labeled with little numbers to indicate in what direction and order they are to be written), a handwritten form, and, in the compounds, a standard printed form. The length and orientation (horizontal, vertical, slanting) of the strokes should be noted as well as the direction and sequence in which they are written.

When counting strokes, be aware that printed kanji sometimes appear to be written with a different number of strokes than the number they are actually written with by hand. In particular, the following components have the following stroke-counts:

了 (1), 子 (2), 阝 (2), 辶 (2), 比 (4), 夊 (4), 臣 (7)

The following list gives examples of the most frequently occurring variations from the norm. The first three characters in each row are the standard taken as correct: a handwritten form, a printed form with serifs, and a sans-serif printed form. The fourth is in a calligraphic script, the fifth is a common handwritten form, and the sixth is in cursory handwriting. The number at the beginning of each line is the sequence number of the variant stroke, and the number at the right is the identification number of the kanji in this book.

Length of stroke

(1) 雨 雨 雨 雨 雨 雨　　**30**　　(likewise 雲 646, etc.)

(1) 天 天 天 天 天 天　　**141**

(1) 戸 戸 戸 戸 戸 戸　　**153**　　(likewise 所 153, 戻 1304, etc.)

(1) 商 商 商 商 商 商　　**418**

(1) 無 無 無 無 無 無　　**93**

Direction of stroke

(1) 言 言 言 言 言 言 **66** (likewise 語 67, etc.)

(1) 安 安 安 安 安 安 **105** (likewise 字 110, etc.)

(1) 立 立 立 立 立 立 **121** (likewise 六 8, 方 70, 文 111, 高 190, 広 707, 玄 1289, etc.)

(1) 主 主 主 主 主 主 **155** (likewise 注 358, etc.)

(1) 社 社 社 社 社 社 **308** (likewise 礼 630, etc.)

(1) 良 良 良 良 良 良 **321** (likewise 食 322, etc.)

(6) 第 第 第 第 第 第 **408** (likewise 等 578, etc.)

(4–6) 終 終 終 終 終 終 **466** (likewise 紙 180, etc.)

(3) 化 化 化 化 化 化 **254** (likewise 北 73, 死 75, 能 386, 考 550, 老 552, 比 812, etc.)

(3) 集 集 集 集 集 集 **442** (likewise 進 443, etc.)

(5) 令 令 令 令 令 令 **850** (likewise 冷 851, etc.)

(3) 含 含 含 含 含 含 **1317**

Down-stroke with a hook at the end sweeping to the upper left

(2) 木 木 木 木 木 木 **22** (likewise 本 25, 村 191, 架 768, etc.)

(4) 米 米 米 米 米 米 **224** (likewise 来 69, 料 319, etc.)

(10) 第 第 第 第 第 第 **408** (likewise 弟 409, etc.)

(4) 糸 糸 糸 糸 糸 糸 **242** (likewise 終 466, 系 930, etc.)

(3) 特 特 特 特 特 特 **282** (likewise 株 754, etc.)

Curved stroke

(4)	六 六 六 六 六 六	8	(likewise 分 38, 外 83, 公 126, 船 377, etc.)
(5)	央 央 央 央 央 央	352	(likewise 美 405, 奥 484, 検 540, 漢 565, etc.)
(10)	家 家 家 家 家 家	165	(likewise 録 546, 求 737, 像 753, 隊 809, etc.)
(4)	返 返 返 返 返 返	448	(likewise 経 557, etc.)
(5)	青 青 青 青 青 青	208	(likewise 通 150, 育 246, 有 265, 背 1338, 骨 1340, etc.)
(1)	子 子 子 子 子 子	103	(likewise 了 941, 承 972, etc.)
(4)	手 手 手 手 手 手	57	
(5)	空 空 空 空 空 空	140	(likewise 商 418, 深 545, 陸 678, etc.)
(4)	令 令 令 令 令 令	850	(likewise 冷 851, etc.)
(2)	心 心 心 心 心 心	97	(likewise 必 529, etc.)
(2)	人 人 人 人 人 人	1	(likewise 火 20, 欠 384, 入 52, 込 790, etc.)
(4)	込 込 込 込 込 込	790	(likewise 進 443, etc.)

Touching strokes or gap left between strokes

(12–13)	楽 楽 楽 楽 楽 楽	359	(likewise 果 496, 条 573, 栄 736, etc.)
(1–2)	又 又 又 又 又 又	1700	(likewise 文 111)
(3–4)	月 月 月 月 月 月	17	(likewise 日 5, 田 35, 目 55, 耳 56, 当 77, 理 143, 門 161, 進 443, 酒 526, 恵 1282, etc.)
(1–2)	立 立 立 立 立 立	121	(likewise 玄 1289, etc.)
(3–4)	不 不 不 不 不 不	94	(likewise 否 1316, etc.)

Crossing strokes

(2–3) 女 女 女 女 女 女   102 (likewise 好 104, 安 105, etc.)

Number of strokes

(2) 比 比 比 比 比 比   812 (likewise 皆 596, etc.)

(4) 衣 衣 衣 衣 衣 衣   690 (likewise 依 691, 表 272, 裏 273, etc.)

(3) 公 公 公 公 公 公   126 (likewise 育 246, 流 247, etc.)

(3) 茶 茶 茶 茶 茶 茶   251 (likewise 花 255, 薬 360, etc.)

Position of stroke

(3) 北 北 北 北 北 北   73 (likewise 背 1338, etc.)

Lexical Order

Looking up Japanese words requires two kinds of dictionaries. If you know how a word is pronounced, you can look it up easily in a dictionary arranged in *aiueo* alphabetical order. Otherwise you will need a character dictionary to look up how a kanji or multi-kanji compound is read and what it means. But how is it possible to alphabetize symbols? Lexicographers have tried in vain to put Chinese characters in a logical order in which every character has its own unique and easy-to-find place.

For some 2,000 years the most common system for arranging kanji in reference works has been a system involving "radicals." This is based on the recognition that kanji are built up from an "alphabet" of a limited number of graphic elements according to which the characters can be sorted. But unlike the linear arrangement of the letters of a word in a Western language, these kanji elements are arranged two-dimensionally within the character, in so many different positions that it is very difficult to come up with an order of positions that could apply to any kanji. Moreover, the number of different basic graphic elements is considerably greater than the number of letters in a Western alphabet.

The following pages and tables explain the system of radicals by which characters are to be found in older and newer character dictionaries, as well as the development of this system from the earliest Chinese reference works to modern electronic character dictionaries.

The oldest character dictionary, the *Shuowen jiezi*
The oldest surviving dictionary is the *Shuowen jiezi* (in Japanese, the *Setsumon kaiji*), which dates from the year 121 A.D. This is not strictly a dictionary in the modern sense but rather a collection of 9,353 characters whose analysis and organization into 540 categories was meant to support the theories of the scholar Xu Shen concerning the history of writing and language. At the beginning of each of these 540 groups is a character that, in the opinion of the author, expresses a meaning that is common to all the characters in that group. He called these characters *bushou* 部首 (literally, "group heads," called *bushu* in Japanese and "radicals" in English). This idea of organizing complex characters according to one of their constituent elements was taken up by lexicographers in China and later in Japan, was further developed, and was put into practice in countless dictionaries. There has been no serious alternative to this basic idea of radicals.

The classic *Kangxi zidian*
In 1716 there appeared, at the behest of the Chinese emperor Kanxi (in Japanese, *Kōki*), a character dictionary called the *Kangxi zidian* (in Japanese, the *Kōki jiten*). This work, after which all subsequent character dictionaries were modeled, classifies 47,035 characters under 214 radicals, some of which were not among the 540 "group heads" of the *Shuowen jiezi*. Since the *Kangxi zidian* was oriented to word origins, for most characters the meaning-bearing part of the character was taken as its radical, as in the *Shuowen jiezi*. But this creates the problem that

in order to look up a character, you first have to know something about what it means. In this sense the *Kangxi zidian* lagged behind older dictionaries that set a character's radical according to its position within the character, without requiring any etymological foreknowledge about it. Despite this, the wide use of this dictionary was soon assured by its abundance of information as well as the money and power of the emperor. The radicals are arranged in increasing order of their stroke-count, and the characters under each radical are similarly arranged in increasing order of their total stroke-count. Table 14 on pages 58–59 presents a list of these traditional 214 radicals.

Monolingual Sino-Japanese character dictionaries
Almost all modern monolingual character dictionaries *(Kan-Wa jiten)* for Japanese users make use of a more- or less-modified form of the 214-radical system. Most characters that were simplified and lost their traditional radical in the writing reforms after 1946 are listed under a different constituent element. A set of radical-determining rules that goes beyond the general rule according to which the meaning-indicating part of a character is its radical, is as rare as the example of the *Kangxi zidian*. But to help locate a kanji in a character dictionary you will usually have a readings index *(on-kun sakuin)*, and sometimes also a stroke-count index *(sōkaku sakuin)*.

Japanese-English character dictionaries
Andrew N. Nelson: Japanese-English Character Dictionary. Rev. ed. 1997.
The most comprehensive and popular character dictionary since its first edition in 1962. About 6,000 head-kanji organized according to the 214-radical system. Before its revision in 1997 it was organized according to the position within the character of the 189 radicals it made use of.

Mark Spahn, Wolfgang Hadamitzly: The Kanji Dictionary. 1996
Sorts its almost 6,000 head-kanji according to the position in the character of the 79 radicals it uses. Another feature is that every compound can be looked up under each of its constituent kanji. An online version is available since 2012 under the title KanjiVision. Head-kanji and compounds can be investigated under any of the constituent graphemes.

How to use the lookup indexes
Each of the 2,146 kanji in the main part of this handbook can be looked up via any of the three indexes at the end of the book: by its reading, its radical, or its stroke count. Thus this book functions not only as an explanatory handbook but also as a character dictionary of the *Jōyō Kanji* and the multi-kanji compounds listed under them.

The number to the right of each kanji entry in the indexes is the kanji's identification number telling where it will be found in the main part of this book.

1. Index by Readings
The alphabetically arranged Index by Readings is the easiest to use when you know one of the readings of the desired kanji. Look up the kanji by its *kun* reading, if you know it. Oth-

erwise you might have to scan through a long list of kanji having the same *on* reading, like the 46 kanji listed under *KAN*.

Kanji with the same *on* reading are divided into groups each having the same pronunciation-indicating component, which is usually on the right side of the kanji (see page 43). Example: *KI* 己 忌 紀 起 記. At the end of each group are kanji that contain this component and thus could also be looked for in this group, but which have a different reading. These kanji are listed in parentheses, with their actual reading given where their identification number would be.

2. Index by Radicals

If you do not know any reading of the kanji you are trying to find, try the Index by Radicals, which arranges the characters according to the 79-radical system of the character dictionary by Spahn/Hadamitzky. This system is made up of two parts: a table of radicals (Table 18, back endpaper), and rules for determining the radical of a kanji (Table 19, inside back cover).

The 79 radicals in Table 18 are arranged in increasing order of stroke-count, within the same stroke-count by their usual position within a kanji (left, right, top, bottom, enclosure, elsewhere), and within the same position by how frequently they occur (most common first).

The rules in Table 19 for determining a kanji's radical are a step-by-step checklist to decide which of two or more radical-candidate components of a kanji is actually its radical. For example, if both the left part and the right part of a kanji are listed in the radical table, the left part is its radical, according to the rule "left before right."

Having determined the radical, you look up the kanji in the Index by Radicals, in which the radicals are arranged in the same order as in the radical table. Under each radical, the characters are listed in increasing order of stroke count.

3. Index by Stroke Count

If no reading of a character is known and it seems too troublesome to determine its radical, you can find the character in the Index by Stroke Count, which lists all the characters in this book in increasing order of stroke count, sub-ordered by radical.

Table 13. The 79 Radicals (with variants) (page 57)

This table presents an overview of the 79 radicals and their variants. (Table 18 without variants is on the back endpaper.) Variants in the narrow sense are forms of a radical that depart more or less strongly from the normal form. Which form a radical takes depends on where in the kanji it occurs (e.g., compare radical 4k on the left in 性 and on the bottom in 怒). This table shows variants that are similar to the normal form or differ from it only by having more or fewer strokes.

With one exception, the 79 radicals are a subset of the 214 traditional radicals. They are arranged in increasing order of stroke-count, and their number-letter descriptors (like 2a for the radical 亻) consist of the radical's stroke-count and its position in the group of radicals of the same stroke count. The radicals are arranged in the Index by Radicals according to these descriptors. The radical descriptor is the first part of the descriptor (like 2a5.10 for 作) that identifies each kanji listed in character dictionaries that use the 79-radical system. Experience has verified that a smaller number of radicals (79 instead of 214) makes it simpler and faster to look up a character.

Table 14. The 214 Traditional Radicals (pages 58–59)

This table lists the 214 traditional radicals and their variants in the traditional order, which is still in use today.

Table 15. The Most Important of the 214 Traditional Radicals (page 60)

This table contains a selection of the most important of the 214 traditional radicals, arranged by their position within the character (shown by crosshatching). Each radical is accompanied by its Japanese name and two kanji as examples.

Table 16. The 214 Traditional Radicals and Their Meanings (pages 61–64)

This table lists the meaning of each of the 214 radicals. Some 80 of them occur both as meaning-indicating components of kanji and as independent kanji, and occur frequently enough that it is worthwhile to remember their meaning.

Table 17. The 80 Graphemes (without variants) (page 65)

This table, which mostly coincides with the 79 radicals, lists 80 graphic elements from which any kanji can be composed. It functions as a "control panel" for the online character dictionary KanjiVision: To find a kanji or a compound, just pick, by clicking or typing on the digital grapheme keyboard, any two or three graphemes contained in what you are looking for. Two examples:

1. Suppose you want to look up the kanji 東 *higashi*, east. Click or type the graphemes 日 and 木.
2. To find the compound 日本語, click or type 日 for the first character, and 言 and/or 口 for the third character. The number of hits fitting your description can be narrowed down by providing further information about a grapheme's position (left, top, etc.) or frequency (e.g., three graphemes 木 for 森).

Other electronic character dictionaries with similar functions still use 214 radicals, which cannot all be displayed on a small screen.

Table 13. The 79 Radicals (with variants)

2	亻 a	人 (a)	𠆢 (a)	氵 b	冫 (b)	孑 c	了 (c)	阝 d	卩 e	刂 f	丿 (f)
	刀 (f)	力 g	又 h	冖 i	亠 j	艹 k	十 (k)	𠂉 m	卜 (m)	夂 n	丷 o
	八 (o)	八 (o)	厂 p	辶 q	辶 (q)	㢟 (q)	冂 r	冂 (r)	几 s	匚 t	
3	氵 a	水 (a)	永 (a)	氺 (a)	土 b	士 (b)	扌 c	手 (c)	口 d	口 (d)	女 e
	巾 f	犭 g	犬 (g)	弓 h	彳 i	忄 (4k)	彡 j	艹 k	宀 m	⺍ n	小 (n)
	⺌ (n)	屮 o	耂 p	夂 (4i)	广 q	尸 r	辶 (2q)	夂 (4i)	弋 (4n)	匚 (2t)	口 s
4	木 a	月 b	日 c	火 d	灬 (d)	礻 e	示 (e)	王 f	玉 (f)	牛 g	方 h
	水 (3a)	手 (3c)	犬 (3g)	攵 i	夊 (i)	夂 (i)	欠 j	心 k	忄 (k)	忄 (k)	灬 (d)
	戸 m	戶 (m)	戈 n	弋 (n)							
5	石 a	立 b	立 (b)	目 c	禾 d	衤 e	衣 (e)	玉 (4f)	罒 f	罒 g	皿 h
	氺 (3a)	示 (4e)	疒 i								
6	糸 a	米 b	舟 c	虫 d	耳 e	竹 f	竹 (f)				
7	言 a	貝 b	車 c	𧾷 d	足 (d)	酉 e					
8	釒 a	飠 b	食 (b)	𩙿 (b)	隹 c	雨 d	雨 (d)	雨 (d)	門 e	鬥 (e)	
9	食 (8b)	𩙿 (8b)	頁 a	**10**	馬 a			**11**	魚 a	鳥 b	

A table of the 79 radicals without variants is found on the back endpaper.

Table 14. The 214 Traditional Radicals

(numbers in parentheses denote variants of the radical)

1	一 1	丨 2	丶 (2)	丶 3	丿 4	丿 (4)	一 (4)	乙 5	し (5)	し (5)	亅 6	
2	二 7	亠 8	人 9	亻 (9)	𠆢 (9)	儿 10	入 11	八 12	丷 (12)	丷 (12)	冂 13	冂 (13)
	冖 14	冫 15	几 16	凵 17	刀 18	刂 (18)	力 19	勹 20	匕 21	匚 22	匚 (22)	匸 23	十 24
	十 (24)	艹 (24)	卜 25	卜 (25)	卜 (25)	卩 26	厂 27	厶 28	又 29	辶 (162)	阝 (163)	阝 (170)	
3	口 30	囗 31	土 32	士 (32)	土 (32)	士 33	夂 34	夊 (34)	夊 35	夕 36	大 37	大 (37)
	女 38	子 39	宀 40	寸 41	小 42	丷 (42)	尢 43	尸 44	屮 45	山 446	川 47	巛 (47)	工 48
	己 49	巾 50	干 51	幺 52	广 53	廴 54	廾 55	弋 56	弓 57	彐 58	彑 (58)	彡 59	彳 60
	忄 (61)	扌 (64)	氵 (85)	犭 (90)	犭 (94)	艹 (140)	辶 (162)	阝 (163)	阝 (170)				
4	心 61	小 (61)	忄 (61)	戈 62	戈 (62)	戸 63	戶 (63)	手 64	扌 (64)	支 65	攴 66	攵 (66)
	文 67	斗 68	斤 69	方 70	无 71	旡 (71)	日 72	曰 73	月 74	木 75	欠 76	止 77	歹 78
	加 (78)	殳 79	毋 80	母 (80)	比 81	毛 82	氏 83	气 84	水 85	氵 (85)	氺 (85)	火 86	灬 (86)
	爪 87	爫 (87)	父 88	爻 89	爿 90	丬 (90)	片 91	牙 92	牛 93	牜 (93)	犬 94	王 (96)	疋 (103)
	礻 (113)	冈 (114)	耂 (125)	月 (130)	艹 (140)								
5	无 (71)	毋 (80)	比 (81)	氺 (85)	牙 (92)	玄 95	玉 96	王 (96)	瓜 97	瓦 98	甘 99	生 100
	用 101	田 102	疋 103	正 (103)	疒 104	癶 105	白 106	皮 107	皿 108	目 109	矛 110	矢 111	石 112

示 113	ネ (113)	內 114	禾 115	穴 117	立 (122)	罒 (138)	加 (145)	ネ

6	竹 118	𥫗 (118)	米 119	糸 120	缶 121	网 122	罒 (122)	羊 123	羊 (123)	羽 124	老 125	耂 (125)

而 126	耒 127	耒 (127)	耳 128	耴 (128)	聿 129	聿 (129)	肉 130	月 (130)	臣 131	自 132	至 133	臼 134

舌 135	舛 136	舟 137	舟 (137)	艮 138	艮 (138)	色 139	艸 140	艹 (140)	虍 141	虫 142	血 143	行 144

衣 145	ネ (145)	西 146	襾 (146)	豸 (152)	𤴓 (157)

7	臣 (131)	舛 (136)	見 147	角 148	言 149	谷 150	豆 151	豕 152	豸 153	貝 154	赤 155	走 156

足 157	身 158	車 159	辛 160	辰 161	辰 (161)	辵 162	辶 (162)	邑 163	阝 (163)	酉 164	釆 165	里 166

麦 (199)

8	金 167	長 168	門 169	阜 170	阝 (170)	隶 171	隹 172	雨 173	青 174	非 175	食 (184)	斉 (210)

9	面 176	革 177	韋 178	韭 179	音 180	頁 181	風 182	飛 183	食 184	𩙿 (184)	首 185	香 186

10	韋 (178)	馬 187	骨 188	高 189	髟 190	鬥 191	鬯 192	鬲 193	鬼 194	鬼 (194)	竜 (212)

11	魚 195	鳥 196	鹵 197	鹿 198	麥 199	麻 200	麻 (200)	黃 (201)	黒 (203)	亀 (213)

12	黃 201	黄 (201)	黍 202	黑 203	黒 (203)	黹 204	歯 (211)

13	黽 205	鼎 206	鼓 207	鼠 208

14	鼻 209	齊 210	斉 (210)

15-17	齒 211	歯 (211)	龍 212	竜 (212)	龜 213	亀 (213)	龠 214

Table 15. The Most Important of the 214 Traditional Radicals
(arranged by their position within a character)

hen		偏			言	gonben	語	話		耂	oikanmuri	者	老
亻	ninben	体	住		貝	kaihen	財	貯		雨	amekanmuri	雲	電
冫	nisui	次	冷		車	kurumahen	転	輪					
口	kuchihen	味	呼		金	kanehen	鉄	針		**ashi**		脚	
土	tsuchihen	地	場		馬	umahen	駅	験		儿	hitoashi	先	免
女	onnahen	好	始							心	kokoro	想	悪
弓	yumihen	引	強		**tsukuri**		旁			灬	rekka/renga	無	照
彳	gyōninben	役	御		刂	rittō	別	制		皿	sara	盗	盟
阝	kozatohen	防	院		力	chikara	助	効		貝	kogai	貨	負
忄	risshinben	性	情		卩	fushizukuri	印	却					
扌	tehen	持	招		彡	sanzukuri	形	彫		**kamae**		構	
方	katahen	放	旅		阝	ōzato	都	郡		冂	dōgamae	円	同
日	hihen	明	曜		攵	nobun	故	政		匚	hakogamae	区	医
木	kihen	林	村		斤	onozukuri	新	断		囗	kunigamae	国	四
氵	sanzui	海	池		欠	akubi	歌	欧		戈	hokogamae	戦	成
火	hihen	畑	灯		殳	rumata	段	殺		行	gyōgamae	街	術
牛	ushihen	物	特		隹	furutori	難	雑		門	mongamae	間	問
犭	kemonohen	独	犯		頁	ōgai	類	顔					
王	ōhen	理	現							**tare**		垂	
目	mehen	眼	眠		**kanmuri, kashira**		冠			厂	gandare	原	厚
矢	yahen	知	短		亠	nabebuta	交	京		尸	shikabane	局	居
石	ishihen	砂	破		八	hachigashira	分	公		广	madare	広	庁
礻	shimesuhen	社	礼		冖	wakanmuri	写	冠		疒	yamaidare	病	痛
禾	nogihen	和	私		宀	ukanmuri	家	安					
米	komehen	粉	精		艹	kusakanmuri	花	茶		**nyō**		繞	
糸	itohen	続	約		癶	hatsugashira	発	登		廴	ennyō	建	延
月	nikuzuki	胴	服		穴	anakanmuri	空	窓		辶	shinnyō/-nyū	進	返
舟	funehen	般	航		罒	amigashira	買	罪		走	sōnyō	起	超
衤	koromohen	初	裸		竹	takekanmuri	筆	答					

Table 16. The 214 Traditional Radicals and Their Meanings
(classical order according to stroke-count groups)

— 1 —

1	一	one; (horizontal stroke)
2	丨	(vertical stroke)
3	丶	(dot stroke)
4	丿	(diagonal stroke)
5	乙	No. 2, B
6	亅	(vertical stroke with hook)

— 2 —

7	二	two
8	亠	lid, top; up
9	人, 亻	man, human being
10	儿	legs, human being
11	入	enter
12	八	eight
13	冂	enclose
14	冖	cover
15	冫	ice
16	几	table
17	凵	container
18	刀, 刂	knife, sword
19	力	power
20	勹	wrap
21	匕	spoon
22	匚	box
23	匸	conceal
24	十	ten
25	卜	oracle
26	卩	stamp, seal

27	厂	cliff
28	厶	private, I
29	又	again; hand

— 3 —

30	口	mouth
31	囗	border
32	土	earth
33	士	man; scholar
34	夂	follow
35	夊	go slowly
36	夕	evening
37	大	large
38	女	woman
39	子	child, son
40	宀	roof
41	寸	inch
42	小	small
43	尢	lame
44	尸	corpse
45	屮	sprout
46	山	mountain
47	川	river
48	工	work
49	己	self
50	巾	cloth
51	干	dry; shield
52	幺	young; slight
53	广	slanting roof
54	廴	move

55	廾	folded hands	86	火, 灬	fire
56	弋	javelin	87	爪	claw, nail
57	弓	bow (in archery)	88	父	father
58	彐, 彑	pig's head; hand	89	爻	mix
59	彡	hair-style; light rays	90	爿, 丬	split wood (left half)
60	彳	step, stride	91	片	split wood (tight half)
			92	牙	fang, canine tooth
			93	牛	cow
			94	犬, 犭	dog

— 4 —

61	心, 忄, 㣺	heart
62	戈	spear
63	戶, 户	weapon; door
64	手, 扌	hand
65	支	branch
66	攴, 攵	strike, hit
67	文	literature
68	斗	(unit of volume)
69	斤	ax
70	方	direction
71	无	not
72	日	sun; day
73	曰	say
74	月	moon; month
75	木	tree, wood
76	欠	lack
77	止	stop
78	歹	decompose
79	殳	lance shaft
80	毋	mother; not
81	比	compare
82	毛	hair
83	氏	family, clan
84	气	breath, air
85	水, 氵	water

— 5 —

95	玄	darkness
96	玉, 王	jewel
97	瓜	melon
98	瓦	tile
99	甘	sweet
100	生	be born, live
101	用	use
102	田	rice paddy
103	疋, ⻊	roll of cloth
104	疒	sickness
105	癶	outspread legs
106	白	white
107	皮	skin, hide
108	皿	bowl, dish
109	目	eye
110	矛	halberd
111	矢	arrow
112	石	stone
113	示, 礻	show; altar
114	禸	footprint
115	禾	grain
116	穴	hole
117	立	stand

— 6 —

118	竹, ⺮	bamboo
119	米	rice
120	糸, 糸	thread
121	缶	earthen jar
122	网, 罒	net
123	羊	sheep
124	羽, 羽	feather
125	老	old
126	而	and also
127	耒	plow
128	耳	ear
129	聿	writing brush
130	肉, ⺼	flesh, meat
131	臣	retainer, minister
132	自	self
133	至	arrive, reach
134	臼	mortar
135	舌	tongue
136	舛	contrary, err
137	舟	ship, boat
138	艮, 艮	stop; hard
139	色	color
140	艸, ⺾	grass, plant
141	虍	tiger
142	虫	worm, insect
143	血	blood
144	行	go
145	衣, 衤	clothing
146	西	cover; west

— 7 —

147	見	see
148	角	horn; corner
149	言	speak, say
150	谷	valley
151	豆	bean
152	豕	pig
153	豸	badger; reptile
154	貝	shell, mussel; money
155	赤	red
156	走	run
157	足	foot, leg
158	身	body
159	車	vehicle, wheel
160	辛	bitter
161	辰	(5th zodiac sign); 7–9 A.M.
162	辵, 辶	advance, move ahead
163	邑, 阝	community
164	酉	wine jug; bird
165	釆	separate
166	里	(2.44 miles); village

— 8 —

167	金	metal, gold
168	長	long
169	門	gate, door
170	阜, 阝	hill
171	隶	capture
172	隹	small bird
173	雨	rain
174	靑, 青	green, blue
175	非	wrong; non-

— 9 —

176	面	face; surface
177	革	leather

178	韋	leather
179	韭	leek
180	音	sound, noise
181	頁	head; page
182	風	wind
183	飛	fly
184	食	food, eat
185	首	head
186	香	scent

— 10 —

187	馬	horse
188	骨	bone
189	高	high
190	髟	long hair
191	鬥	fighting
192	鬯	herbs
193	鬲	tripod
194	鬼	demon

— 11 —

195	魚	fish
196	鳥	bird
197	鹵	salt
198	鹿	deer
199	麥	wheat
200	麻	hemp

— 12 —

201	黃	yellow
202	黍	millet
203	黑, 黒	black
204	黹	embroider

— 13 —

205	黽	frog
206	鼎	3-legged kettle
207	鼓	drum
208	鼠	rat, mouse

— 14 —

209	鼻	nose
210	齊, 斉	alike

— 15 —

211	齒, 歯	tooth

— 16 —

212	龍, 竜	dragon

— 17 —

213	龜, 亀	turtle
214	龠	flute

Table 17. The 80 Graphemes (without variants)

1	一 1	丨 2							
2	亻 3	二 4	冫 5	孑 6	阝 7	力 8	又 9	匕 10	亠 11	十 12
	 13	 14	 15	儿 16	厶 17	厂 18	辶 19	冂 20	
3	氵 21	土 22	扌 23	口 24	女 25	巾 26	犭 27	弓 28	彳 29	夕 30
	彡 31	艹 32	宀 33	大 34	小 35	屮 36	寸 37	工 38	彐 39	尸 40
4	木 41	日 42	月 43	火 44	礻 45	王 46	牛 47	方 48	攵 49	斤 50
	心 51	戈 52								
5	石 53	立 54	目 55	禾 56	衤 57	罒 58	皿 59	疒 60		
6	糸 61	米 62	舟 63	虫 64	耳 65	竹 66				
7	言 67	貝 68	車 69	足 70	酉 71					
8-11	金 72	隹 73	雨 74	門 75	頁 76	食 77	馬 78	魚 79	鳥 80	

Tips on Learning Kanji

Kanji-learning is like running, and learning all 2,141 kanji in the main part of this book is like running a marathon, while sporadic learning is like running a sprint or taking a walk: the longer the distance to be covered, the more it pays to develop a strategy for reaching your self-imposed goal in the surest and quickest way. The following tips should help you reach your goal faster.

1. Learn the kanji in order

You will have the best lasting success if you learn the kanji in the order in which they are presented. They start from the simplest and most common and proceed to those that are more complex and less frequently encountered. And the up to five compounds introduced with every kanji are made up only of kanji that have been introduced before. If you were to learn the kanji in some other order, you would have to look them up via one of the three indexes at the end of the book.

2. Prioritize

Much information is listed with each kanji. Focus on what is important for you. This will almost always include the readings and meanings of a kanji, but you need not learn everything about a kanji all at the same time and with the same intensity.

3. Take many sips, not one big gulp

The characters will stick in your mind much sooner and more lastingly if you spend a few minutes at a time two or three times a day learning them, rather than devote a solid hour per week. If you write down the kanji you are currently learning on a piece of paper or copy them to a mobile device, you will have something on you that you can review in any otherwise idle moment.

4. Learn things together

The appearance, readings, and meanings of a character go together and reinforce each other, and should be learned together. Associating these pieces of information with each other will make it easier to recall this knowledge later.

5. Be aware of the structure and components of kanji

When learning a new kanji, take a few seconds to look at its structure and components. You will soon notice that you keep seeing the same graphemes mostly in the same positions, like 氵 (water) on the left side in 池 (pond), 海 (sea), and 港 (harbor), or 艹 (plant) on the top in 花 (flower), 草 (grass), and 茶 (tea). In this way even the most complicated kanji will no longer seem like a scary tangle of arbitrary strokes.

6. See kanji as pictures

The simpler characters are mostly recognizable as stylized pictures of objects or creatures, and the more-complex characters as simply combinations of them, so you may find it useful to mentally break up a kanji into its pictorial components, with maybe a mnemonic story to help fix the kanji in your mind.

7. Don't overload yourself

With kanji that have several readings, it can make sense to learn at first only one *on* reading and one *kun* reading, or to limit yourself to those readings you have seen elsewhere. Trying to take in too much information all at once can detract from concentrating on what is important. But with each reading you should learn the corresponding meaning.

8. Learn compounds with known kanji

Compounds are important as mini-context for going beyond the acquisition of individual characters. They will increase your vocabulary while getting you to review previously learned kanji.

9. Write the kanji

Before beginning to write a kanji, take a look at its structure and components and its meanings and readings. You will then better understand what you are writing and why it is to be written as described. As you write the kanji, try also to write a word – more precisely, a reading and meaning – to associate with it, as you would when vocabulary-building in your own language. This will help you fix the character in your memory and recognize it upon seeing it again.
When you feel you can reproduce the kanji from memory, write the compounds in which it occurs with the readings you have learned.

10. Highlight as you learn

Highlight with a colored marker the readings, meanings, and compounds that you want to concentrate on during a first pass, or that you have already learned. On subsequent passes, use a different color. This will distinguish the new from the old as you learn it. And if you like to work with copies of pages, copy the pages before you mark them up.

11. Review, and train yourself to read quickly

In modern Japan, text will not always sit still and wait for you. Street signs, subtitles in movies and Internet videos, captions on TV news programs, and even karaoke lyrics, rush by too fast to think them over, much less look up characters in a dictionary.
One possibility for reviewing and developing the ability to quickly recognize all the kana and kanji in this book is the game and tutorial program "Kanji in Motion" (KiM). The object is to make as fast as possible a connection between characters swirling on a screen and the corresponding readings and meanings shown on the side. A demo version is available on the Internet.

Explanation of the *Jōyō Kanji* Entries

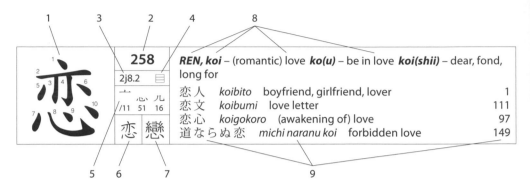

1. The kanji in brush form, with little numbers showing stroke order positioned at the beginning of each stroke.

2. Running number identifying the kanji in this book (here, 258).

3. Descriptor (2j8.2) of the kanji in character dictionaries using the 79-radical system. It consists of a radical designation (2j, for ⼗), followed by the residual stroke count (8 = total stroke count 10 – the 2 strokes of the radical), then a decimal point followed by a sequential number (2).

4. Structure of the character (for a list of the different structures, see page 43).

5. Up to three graphemes (graphic elements of characters according to the online character dictionary KanjiVision) included in the kanji, with grapheme number (see the table of graphemes on page 65). A slash appears before the grapheme number (/11) if the first grapheme is the same as the radical in the printed character dictionaries that use the 79-radical system.

6. The kanji in pen form *(pen-ji)*.

7. Variant of the kanji (usually an obsolete form).

8. Readings and meanings of the kanji, with *on* readings in uppercase italics, *kun* readings in lowercase italics, *okurigana* in parentheses, and rare or specialized readings in square brackets. As in the official *Jōyō Kanji* list, the first reading given is the one by which the kanji is alphabetized (in *aiueo* order); this is usually the kanji's most frequent *on* reading. Readings with the same meaning are listed together *(REN, koi)*.

9. Example compounds and expressions in which the kanji is used, with transliteration, meaning(s), and cross-reference numbers to the entries for the other characters in the compound. The compounds are made up only of kanji that appear earlier and that you will have already studied if you learn kanji in the order presented in this book. In the few cases in which a kanji of a compound has no cross-reference number, it is not among the *Jōyō Kanji*.

The *Jōyō Kanji* List

人	**1** 2a0.1 ☐ イ /3 人	**JIN, NIN, hito** – human being, man, person アメリカ人　*Amerikajin*　an American 100人　*hyakunin*　100 people 5、6人　*go-rokunin*　5 or 6 people あの人　*ano hito*　that person, he, she 人々、人びと　*hitobito*　people
一	**2** 0a1.1 ☐ 一 1 一	**ICHI, ITSU, hito(tsu), hito-** – one 一ページ　*ichi pēji*　one page; page 1 一々　*ichi-ichi*　one by one; in full detail 一つ一つ　*hitotsu-hitotsu*　one by one, individually 一人　*hitori*　one person; alone　　　　1 一人一人　*hitori-hitori*　one by one, one after another　1
二	**3** 0a2.1 ☐ 二 4 二	**NI, futa(tsu), futa-** – two 二人　*futari, ninin*　two people　　　　1 一人二人　*hitori-futari*　one or two people　2, 1 二人ずつ　*futarizutsu*　two by two, every two people　1 二つずつ　*futatsuzutsu*　two by two, two at a time 二人とも　*futaritomo*　both people, both (of them)　1
三	**4** 0a3.1 ☐ 二 一 4 1 三	**SAN, mit(tsu), mi(tsu), mi-** – three 三人　*sannin*　three people　　　　1 二、三人　*ni-sannin*　two or three people　3, 1 三キロ　*san kiro*　3 kg; 3 km 三つぞろい　*mitsuzoroi*　three-piece suit 二つ三つ　*futatsu mittsu*　two or three　3
日	**5** 4c0.1 ☐ 日 /42 日	**NICHI** – day; (short for) Japan　**JITSU, hi, -ka** – day 一日　*ichinichi, ichijitsu*　1 day　　　　2 　　*tsuitachi*　1st of the month 二日　*futsuka*　two days; 2nd of the month　3 三日　*mikka*　three days; 3rd of the month　4 二、三日　*ni-sannichi*　two or three days　3, 4
四	**6** 3s2.2 ☐ 口 儿 /24 16 四	**SHI, yot(tsu), yo(tsu), yo-, yon** – four 四人　*yonin*　four people　　　　1 四日　*yokka*　four days; 4th of the month　5 三、四日　*san-yokka*　three or four days　4, 5 三、四人　*san-yonin*　thre or four people　4, 1 四つんばい　*yotsunbai*　(on) all fours
五	**7** 0a4.27 … 丁 一 14 1 五	**GO, itsu(tsu), itsu-** – five 五人　*gonin*　five people　　　　1 五日　*itsuka*　five days; 5th of the month　5 四、五日　*shi-gonichi*　four or five days　6, 5 四、五人　*shi-gonin*　four or five people　6, 1 三々五々　*san-san go-go*　in small groups, by twos and threes　4

六	**8** 2j2.2 ☐ 亠 儿 /11 16 六	**ROKU, mut(tsu), mu(tsu), mu-, [mui-]** – six	
		六人　*rokunin*　six people	1
		五、六人　*go-rokunin*　five or six people	7, 1
		六日　*muika*　six days; 6th of the month	5
		五、六日　*go-rokunichi*　five or six days	7, 5
		六つぐらい　*muttsu gurai*　about six	

七	**9** 0a2.13 ☐ 一十 12 七	**SHICHI, nana(tsu), nana-, [nano-]** – seven	
		七人　*shichinin*　seven people	1
		七日　*nanoka*　seven days; 7th of the month	5
		七メートル　*nana mētoru, shichi mētoru*　seven meters	
		七五三　*shichi-go-san*　festival day for 3-, 5-, and 7-year-olds (Nov. 15)	7, 4

八	**10** 2o0.1 ☐ ソ /16 八 八	**HACHI, yat(tsu), ya(tsu), ya-, [yō-]** – eight	
		八人　*hachinin*　eight people	1
		八日　*yōka*　eight days; 8th of the month	5
		八ミリ　*hachi miri*　8 mm	
		八グラム　*hachi guramu*　8 grams	
		お八つ　*oyatsu*　afternoon snack	

九	**11** 0a2.15 ☐ 一十 12 九	**KYŪ, KU, kokono(tsu), kokono-** – nine	
		九人　*kyūnin, kunin*　9 people	1
		九日　*kokonoka*　9 days; 9th of the month	5
		九ドル　*kyū doru*　9 dollars	
		九ユーロ　*kyū yūro*　9 euros	
		九九　*kuku*　multiplication table	

十	**12** 2k0.1 ☐ 一十 /12 十	**JŪ, JI', tō, to-** – ten	
		十人　*jūnin*　ten people	1
		十日　*tōka*　ten days; 10th of the month	5
		二十日　*hatsuka*　20 days; 20th of the month	3, 5
		十四日　*jūyokka*　14 days; 14th of the month	6, 5
		十八日　*jūhachinichi*　18 days; 18th of the month	10, 5

円	**13** 2r2.1 ☐ 冂 亠 /20 11 円 圓	**EN** – circle; yen **maru(i)** – round	
		一円　*ichi en*　one yen	2
		二円　*ni en*　two yen	3
		三円　*san en*　three yen	4
		四円　*yo en*　four yen	6
		十円　*jū en, tō en*　ten yen	12

百	**14** 4c2.3 ☐ 日 一 /42 14 百	**HYAKU** – hundred	
		百人　*hyakunin*　100 people	1
		八百円　*happyaku en*　800 yen	10, 13
		九百　*kyūhyaku*　900	11
		三百六十五日　*sanbyaku rokujūgonichi*　365 days	4, 8, 12, 7, 5

千	**15** 2k1.2 ☐ 十 丨 /12 2 千	**SEN, chi** – thousand	
		一千　issen　1,000	2
		三千　sanzen　3,000	4
		八千　hassen　8,000	10
		千円　sen en　1,000 yen	13
		千人　sennin　1,000 people	1

万	**16** 0a3.8 … 一 一 14 1 万　萬	**MAN** – ten thousand　**BAN** – many, all	
		一万円　ichiman en　10,000 yen	2, 13
		百万　hyakuman　1 million	14
		一千万円　issenman en　10 million yen	2, 15, 13
		二、三万円　ni-sanman en　20,000-30,000 yen	3, 4, 13
		万一　man'ichi　(if) by any chance, should happen to	2

月	**17** 4b0.1 ☐ 月 /43 月	**GETSU, tsuki** – moon; month　**GATSU** – month	
		一月　ichigatsu　January	2
		hitotsuki　one month	
		一か月　ikkagetsu　one month	2
		一月八日＝1月8日　ichigatsu yōka　January 8	2, 10, 5
		月ロケット　tsukiroketto　moon rocket	

明	**18** 4c4.1 ☐☐ 日 月 /42 43 明	**MEI, a(kari)** – light, clearness　**aka(rui), aki(raka)** – bright, clear　**a(keru), aka(rumu), aka(ramu)** – become light　**a(ku)** – be open　**a(kasu)** – pass (the night)　**a(kuru)** – next, following　**MYŌ** – light; next	
		明日　myōnichi, asu　tomorrow	5
		明くる日　akuru hi　the next/following day	5

曜	**19** 4c14.1 ☐ 日 隹 ヨ /42 73 39 曜	**YŌ** – day of the week	
		日曜（日）　nichiyō(bi)　Sunday	5
		月曜（日）　getsuyō(bi)　Monday	17, 5
		曜日　yōbi　day of the week	5

火	**20** 4d0.1 ☐ 火 /44 火	**KA, hi, [ho]** – fire	
		火曜（日）　kayō(bi)　Tuesday	19, 5
		9月4日（火）　kugatsu yokka (ka)　(Tuesday) September 4	17, 5

水	**21** 3a0.1 ☐ 氵 /21 水	**SUI, mizu** – water	
		水曜（日）　suiyō(bi)　Wednesday	19, 5
		水がめ　mizugame　water jug/jar	
		水かさ　mizukasa　volume of water (of a river)	

木	**22** 4a0.1 ☐ 朩 /41 木	**BOKU, MOKU, ki, [ko]** – tree; wood

木曜（日）　*mokuyō(bi)*　Thursday　　　　　　19, 5
三木　*Miki*　(surname)　　　　　　　　　　4
八木　*Yagi*　(surname)　　　　　　　　　　10

金	**23** 8a0.1 ☐ 釒 /72 金	**KIN, KON** – gold; metal; money **kane** – money **[kana]** – metal

金曜（日）　*kin'yō(bi)*　Friday　　　　　　　19, 5
月・水・金　*ges-sui-kin*　Monday, Wednesday, Friday　17, 21
金メダル　*kinmedaru*　gold medal
金ぱく　*kinpaku*　gold leaf/foil
金もうけ　*kanemōke*　making money

土	**24** 3b0.1 ☐ 土 /22 土	**DO, TO, tsuchi** – earth, soil, ground

土曜（日）　*doyō(bi)*　Saturday　　　　　　　19, 5
土木　*doboku*　civil engineering　　　　　　22
土人　*dojin*　native, aborigine　　　　　　　1
土のう　*donō*　sandbag

本	**25** 0a5.25 ☐ 朩 一 41 1 本 本	**HON** – book; origin; main; this; (counter for long, thin objects) **moto** – origin

日本　*Nihon, Nippon*　Japan　　　　　　　　5
日本人　*Nihonjin, Nipponjin*　a Japanese　　5, 1
本日　*honjitsu*　today　　　　　　　　　　　5
ビール六本　*bīru roppon*　six bottles of beer　8

大	**26** 0a3.18 ☐ 大 34 大	**DAI, TAI, ō(kii), ō-** – big, large **ō(i ni)** – very much, greatly

大金　*taikin*　large amount of money　　　　23
大きさ　*ōkisa*　size
大水　*ōmizu*　flooding, overflow　　　　　　21
大みそか　*ōmisoka*　New Year's Eve
大人　*otona*　adult　　　　　　　　　　　　1

小	**27** 3n0.1 ☐ �␣ 35 小	**SHŌ, chii(sai), ko-, o-** – little, small

小人　*kobito*　dwarf, midget　　　　　　　　1
　　　shōjin　insignificant person; small-minded man
　　　shōnin　child
大小　*daishō*　large and small; size　　　　　26
小金　*kogane*　small sum of money; small fortune　23

中	**28** 0a4.40 ☐ 口 丨 24 2 中	**CHŪ** – middle; (short for) China **-CHŪ, -JŪ** – throughout, during, within **naka** – inside, midst

日本中　*Nihonjū, Nipponjū*　all over Japan　　5, 25
一日中　*ichinichijū*　all day long　　　　　　2, 5
日中　*nitchū*　during the daytime　　　　　　5
　　　Nit-Chū　Japanese-Chinese, Sino-Japanese

風	**29** 2s7.1 几 虫 丨 /20 64 2 風	**FŪ, [FU]** – wind; appearance, style **kaze, [kaza]** – wind

風水　*fūsui*　wind and water; feng shui　21
風土　*fūdo*　natural feature, climate　24
日本風　*Nihon-fū*　Japanese-style　5, 25
中風　*chūbū, chūfū*　paralysis, palsy　28
そよ風　*soyokaze*　gentle breeze

雨	**30** 8d0.1 雫 /74 雨	**U, ame, [ama]** – rain

風雨　*fūu*　wind and rain　29
大雨　*ōame*　heavy rain, downpour　26
小雨　*kosame*　light rain, fine rain　27
雨水　*amamizu*　rainwater　21
にわか雨　*niwakaame*　sudden shower

下	**31** 2m1.2 下 丨 14 2 下	**KA, GE, shita, moto** – lower, base **shimo** – lower part **sa(geru), o(rosu), kuda(su)** – lower, hand down (a verdict) **sa(garu)** – hang down, fall **o(riru)** – get out of, get off (a vehicle) **kuda(ru)** – go/come down **kuda(saru)** – give

下水　*gesui*　sewer system, drainage　21
風下　*kazashimo*　leeward side, downwind　29

上	**32** 2m1.1 上 一 /13 1 上	**JŌ, [SHŌ], ue** – upper **kami, [uwa-]** – upper part **a(geru)** – raise **a(garu), nobo(ru)** – rise **nobo(seru), nobo(su)** – bring up (a topic)

水上　*suijō*　on the water　21
上下　*jōge*　high and low, rise and fall; volumes 1 and 2　31
上り下り　*nobori-kudari*　ascent and descent, ups and downs　31

川	**33** 0a3.2 几 丨 16 2 川 巛	**SEN, kawa** – river

川上　*kawakami*　upstream　32
川下　*kawashimo*　downstream　31
小川　*ogawa*　stream, brook, creek　27
ミシシッピー川　*Mishishippī-gawa*　Mississippi River
中川　*Nakagawa*　(surname)　28

山	**34** 3o0.1 山 /36 山	**SAN, yama** – mountain

山水　*sansui*　landscape, natural scenery　21
火山　*kazan*　volcano　20
下山　*gezan*　descent from a mountain　31
山々　*yamayama*　mountains
山本　*Yamamoto*　(surname)　25

田	**35** 5f0.1 田 /58 田	**DEN, ta** – rice field, paddy

水田　*suiden*　rice paddy　21
田中　*Tanaka*　(surname)　28
本田　*Honda*　(surname)　25
山田　*Yamada*　(surname)　34
下田　*Shimoda*　(city on Izu Peninsula)　31

畑	**36**	***hata, hatake*** – cultivated field
	4d5.1	田畑　*tahata*　fields　　　　　　　　　　　　　　　　35
	火　田	みかん畑　*mikanbatake*　satsuma orange orchard
	/44　58	小畑　*Obata*　(surname)　　　　　　　　　　　　　　27
	畑	

刀	**37**	***TŌ, katana*** – sword, knife
	2f0.1	日本刀　*Nihon-tō*　Japanese sword　　　　　　　　5, 25
	力	大刀　*daitō*　long sword　　　　　　　　　　　　　26
	8	小刀　*shōtō*　short sword　　　　　　　　　　　　27
	刀　釖	*kogatana*　knife, pocketknife
		一刀　*ittō*　a sword/blade; (a single stroke of a) sword　2

分	**38**	***BUN*** – portion ***BU*** – portion, 1 percent ***FUN*** – minute (of time/arc) ***wa(keru), wa(katsu)*** – divide, share, distinguish ***wa(kareru)*** – be separated ***wa(karu)*** – understand
	2o2.1	
	ソ　力	十分　*jūbun*　enough, sufficient, adequate　　　　12
	/16　8	*jippun, juppun*　10 minutes
	分　分	十分の一　*jūbun no ichi*　one tenth, 10 percent　12, 2

切	**39**	***SETSU, [SAI], ki(ru)*** – cut ***ki(reru)*** – cut well; break off; run out of
	2f2.2	大切　*taisetsu*　important; precious　　　　　　　26
	十　力	一切れ　*hitokire*　slice, piece　　　　　　　　　　2
	12　8	切り上げ　*kiriage*　conclusion; rounding up; revaluation　32
	切	切り下げ　*kirisage*　reduction; devaluation　　　　31

国	**40**	***KOKU, kuni*** – country
	3s5.1	大国　*taikoku*　large country, major power　　　26
	口　王　丶	万国　*bankoku*　all countries, world　　　　　　16
	/24　46　2	六か国　*rokkakoku*　6 countries　　　　　　　　8
	国　國	四国　*Shikoku*　(one of the 4 main islands of Japan)　6
		中国　*Chūgoku*　China; (region in western Honshū)　28

寺	**41**	***JI, tera*** – temple
	3b3.5	国分寺　*Kokubunji*　(common temple name)　　40, 38
	土　寸	山寺　*yamadera*　mountain temple　　　　　　　34
	/22　37	寺田　*Terada*　(surname)　　　　　　　　　　　35
	寺	

時	**42**	***JI, toki*** – time; hour
	4c6.2	四時二十分＝4時20分　*yoji nijippun*　4:20　6, 3, 12, 38
	日　土　寸	一時　*ichiji*　for a time; 1 o'clock　　　　　　　2
	/42　22　37	*hitotoki, ittoki*　a while, moment
	時	時々　*tokidoki*　sometimes
		日時　*nichiji*　time, date, day and hour　　　　　5

間	**43** 8e4.3 □ 門 日 /75 42 間	**KAN, KEN, aida** – interval (between) **ma** – interval (between); a room

時間　*jikan*　time; hour　42
中間　*chūkan*　middle, intermediate　28
人間　*ningen*　human being　1
間もなく　*mamonaku*　presently, in a little while, soon

生	**44** 0a5.29 □ 土 仁 22 15 生	**SEI, SHŌ** – life **i(kiru), i(keru)** – be alive **i(kasu)** – bring (back) to life, let live **u(mu)** – give birth to **u(mareru)** – be born **ha(eru), ha(yasu)**, **o(u)** – grow **nama** – raw **ki-** – pure

人生　*jinsei*　life, human life　1
一生　*isshō*　one's whole life　2

年	**45** 0a6.16 … 仁 十 一 15 12 11 年	**NEN, toshi** – year

生年月日　*seinengappi*　date of birth　44, 17, 5
三年生　*sannensei*　third-year student, junior　4, 44
五年間　*gonenkan*　for 5 years　7, 43
年金　*nenkin*　pension, annuity　⌐Sept. 4, 2011　23
2011年9月4日　*nisenjūichinen kugatsu yokka*　7, 5

以	**46** 0a5.1 … 亻 丨 丶 3 2 2 以	**I-** – (prefix)

以上　*ijō*　or more; more than; above-mentioned　32
三時間以上　*san jikan ijō*　at least three hours　4, 42, 43, 32
以下　*ika*　or less; less than; as follows　31
三つ以下　*mittsu ika*　three or fewer　4, 31

前	**47** 2o7.3 ⊞ ソ 月 力 /16 43 8 前	**ZEN, mae** – before, in front of, earlier

以前　*izen*　ago, previously, formerly　46
前もって　*maemotte*　beforehand, in advance
人前（で）　*hitomae (de)*　before others, in public　1
分け前　*wakemae*　one's share　38
二人前　*nininmae, futarimae*　enough for two people　3, 1

後	**48** 3i6.5 ⊞ 彳 夂 厶 /29 49 17 後	**GO, nochi** – after, later **KŌ, ushi(ro)** – behind **ato** – afterward, subsequent, back **oku(reru)** – be late, lag behind

以後　*igo*　hereafter; since then　46
前後　*zengo*　approximately; front and rear　47
明後日　*myōgonichi*　day after tomorrow　18, 5
その後　*sono go*　thereafter, later

午	**49** 2k2.2 … 十 仁 /12 15 午	**GO** – noon

午前　*gozen*　morning, a.m.　47
午後　*gogo*　afternoon, p.m.　48
午前中　*gozenchū*　all morning, before noon　47, 28
午後四時　*gogo yoji*　4:00 p.m.　⌐afternoon　48, 6, 42
午前も午後も　*gozen mo gogo mo*　both morning and　47, 48

先	**50** 3b3.7 ☐ ⼟ ⼉ ｜ /22 16 2 先	**SEN, saki** – earlier; ahead; priority; future; destination; the tip

先日　*senjitsu*　recently, the other day　5
先月　*sengetsu*　last month　17
先々月　*sensengetsu*　month before last　17
先生　*sensei*　teacher　44

今	**51** 2a2.10 ☐ 亻 一 /3 1 今	**KON, KIN, ima** – now

今日　*konnichi, kyō*　today　5
今月　*kongetsu*　this month　17
今年　*kotoshi*　this year　45
今後　*kongo*　after this, from now on　48
今ごろ　*imagoro*　about this time (of day)

入	**52** 0a2.3 ☐ 亻 3 入	**NYŪ, hai(ru), i(ru)** – go/come/get in, enter **i(reru)** – put/let in

入国　*nyūkoku*　entry (into a country)　40
金入れ　*kaneire*　cashbox; purse, wallet　23
日の入り　*hi no iri*　sunset　5
入り日　*irihi*　setting sun　5

出	**53** 0a5.22 ☐ 凵 冂 36 20 出	**SHUTSU, [SUI], da(su)** – take out; send **de(ru)** – go/come out

出火　*shukka*　outbreak of fire　20
出入り　*deiri*　coming and going (of people)　52
人出　*hitode*　turnout, crowds　1
日の出　*hi no de*　sunrise　5

口	**54** 3d0.1 ☐ 口 /24 口	**KŌ, KU, kuchi** – mouth; oral; speak; job; beginning

人口　*jinkō*　population, number of inhabitants　1
入(り)口　*iriguchi*　entrance　52
出口　*deguchi*　exit　53
川口　*kawaguchi*　mouth of a river　33
口出し　*kuchidashi*　meddling, butting in　53

目	**55** 5c0.1 ☐ 目 /55 目	**MOKU, [BOKU], me, [ma]** – eye, (suffix for ordinals)

一目　*ichimoku, hitome*　a glance　2
目上　*meue*　one's superior/senior　32
目下　*meshita*　one's subordinate/junior　31
　　　mokka　at present
三日目　*mikkame*　at the 3rd day　4, 5

耳	**56** 6e0.1 ☐ 耳 /65 耳	**JI, mimi** – ear

耳目　*jimoku*　eye and ear; attention, notice　55
中耳　*chūji*　the middle ear　28
耳たぶ　*mimitabu*　earlobe

手	**57** 3c0.1 ☐ 扌 /23 手	**SHU, te, [ta]** – hand	
		上手 *jōzu* skilled, good (at)	32
		下手 *heta* unskilled, poor (at)	31
		手本 *tehon* model, example, pattern	25
		切手 *kitte* (postage) stamp	39
		小切手 *kogitte* (bank) check	27, 39

足	**58** 7d0.1 ☐ 𧾷 /70 足	**SOKU** – foot, leg; (counter for pairs of footwear) **ashi** – foot, leg **ta(ru), ta(riru)** – be enough, sufficient **ta(su)** – add up, add (to)	
		一足 *issoku* 1 pair (of shoes/socks)	2
		hitoashi a step	
		手足 *teashi* hands and feet, limbs	57
		足下に *ashimoto ni* at one's feet; (watch your) step	31

身	**59** 0a7.5 ☐ 月 丨 43 2 身	**SHIN, mi** – body; one's person	
		身上 *shinjō* strong point; personal background	32
		shinshō one's fortune, property	
		出身 ...*shusshin* (be) from ...	53
		前身 *zenshin* one's past life; predecessor	47
		身分 *mibun* one's social standing; identity	38

休	**60** 2a4.2 ☐ 亻 木 /3 41 休	**KYŪ, yasu(mu)** – rest; take the day off **yasu(meru)** – give it a rest **yasu(maru)** – be rested	
		休日 *kyūjitsu* holiday, day off	5
		休火山 *kyūkazan* dormant/inactive volcano	20, 34
		一休み *hitoyasumi* short rest; a break, recess	2
		中休み *nakayasumi* take a break	28

体	**61** 2a5.6 ☐ 亻 木 一 /3 41 1 体 體	**TAI, TEI, karada** – body	
		身体 *shintai* body	59
		人体 *jintai* the human body	1
		五体 *gotai* the whole body	7
		大体 *daitai* gist; on the whole, generally	26
		風体 *fūtai, fūtei* (outward) appearance	29

自	**62** 5c1.1 ☐ 目 丨 /55 2 自	**JI, SHI, mizuka(ra)** – self	
		自分 *jibun* oneself, one's own	38
		自身 *jishin* oneself, itself	59
		自体 *jitai* one's own body; itself	61
		自国 *jikoku* one's own country	40
		自らの手で *mizukara no te de* with one's own hands	57

見	**63** 5c2.1 ☐ 貝 68 見	**KEN, mi(ru)** – see **mi(eru)** – be visible **mi(seru)** – show	
		一見 *ikken* (quick) glance	2
		先見 *senken* foresight	50
		見本 *mihon* sample (of merchandise)	25
		見出し *midashi* heading, headline	53
		見分ける *miwakeru* tell apart, recognize	38

	64	**BUN, MON, ki(ku)** – hear, heed; ask **ki(koeru)** – be audible	
聞	8e6.1	見聞　*kenbun*　information, observation	63
	門 耳	風聞　*fūbun*　hearsay, rumor	29
	/75　65	聞き手　*kikite*　listener	57
	聞	聞き入れる　*kikiireru*　comply with	52

	65	**SHU, to(ru)** – take	
取	6e2.2	取り出す　*toridasu*　take out; pick out	53
	耳 又	足取り　*ashidori*　way of walking, gait	58
	/65　9	聞き取る　*kikitoru*　catch, follow (what someone says)	64
	取	日取り　*hidori*　appointed day	5
		取り上げる　*toriageru*　take up; adopt; take away	32

	66	**GEN, GON, -koto** – word **i(u)** – say	
言	7a0.1	言明　*genmei*　declaration, definite statement	18
	言	一言　*ichigon, hitokoto*　a word, brief comment	2
	/67	一言二言　*hitokoto futakoto*　a word or two	2, 3
	言	小言　*kogoto*　a scolding; complaints, griping	27
		言い分　*iibun*　one's say; objection	38

	67	**GO** – word **kata(ru)** – talk, relate **kata(rau)** – converse	
語	7a7.6	言語　*gengo*　language, speech	66
	言 口 亠	日本語　*nihongo*　Japanese language	5, 25
	/67　24　14	国語　*kokugo*　national/Japanese language	40
	語	中国語　*chūgokugo*　Chinese language	28, 40
		語り手　*katarite*　narrator, storyteller	57

	68	**KŌ, [AN], i(ku), yu(ku)** – go **GYŌ** – line (of text) **okona(u)** – do, perform, carry out	
行	3i3.1	一行　*ikkō*　party, retinue	2
	彳 二 丨	*ichigyō*　a line (of text)	
	/29　4　2	行間　*gyōkan*　space between lines (of text)	43
	行	行き先　*ikisaki, yukisaki*　destination	50

	69	**RAI, ku(ru), kita(ru)** – come **kita(su)** – bring about	
来	0a7.6	来年　*rainen*　next year	45
	米 一	来月　*raigetsu*　next month	17
	62　1	来日　*rainichi*　come to Japan	5
	来 耒	本来　*honrai*　originally, primarily; properly, rightfully	25
		以来　*irai*　(ever) since	46

	70	**HŌ** – direction; side **kata** – person; method; side	
方	4h0.1	一方　*ippō*　one side; on the other hand; only	2
	方	四方　*shihō*　north, south, east, west; all directions	6
	/48	八方　*happō*　all directions, all sides	10
	方	方言　*hōgen*　dialect	66
		目方　*mekata*　weight	55

東	**71** 0a8.9 ⋯ 木 日 41 42 東	**TŌ, higashi** – east

71

TŌ, higashi – east

東方	tōhō	eastward, the east	70
中東	Chūtō	Middle East	28
東大	Tōdai	Tokyo University (short for *Tōkyō Daigaku*)	26
東アジア	Higashi-Ajia	East Asia	
東ヨーロッパ	Higashi-Yōroppa	East Europe	

72   0a6.20   口 一 丨   24 14 2   西

SEI – west; (short for) Spain **SAI, nishi** – west

西方	seihō	westward, the west	70
東西	tōzai	east and west	71
西風	seifū, nishikaze	westerly wind	29
西日	nishibi	the afternoon sun	5
西ヨーロッパ	Nishi-Yōroppa	Western Europe	

73   0a5.5   匕 一 丨   13 1 2   北

HOKU, kita – north

北方	hoppō	northward, the north	70
北風	hokufū, kitakaze	wind from the north	29
東北	Tōhoku	(region in northern Honshū)	71
北東	hokutō	northeast	71
北北東	hokuhokutō	north-northeast	71

74   2k7.1   十 冂 儿   /12 20 16   南

NAN, [NA], minami – south

西南	seinan	southwest	72
東南アジア	Tōnan-Ajia	Southeast Asia	71
南北	nanboku	south and north, north-south	73
南アルプス	Minami-Arupusu	Southern (Japan) Alps	
南口	minamiguchi	southern entrance/exit	54

75   0a5.20   工 十   38 12   左

SA, hidari – left

左方	sahō	left side	70
左手	hidarite	left hand; (on) the left	57
左足	hidariashi	left foot/leg	58
左目	hidarime	left eye	55
左上	hidariue	upper left	32

76   3d2.15   口 十   /24 12   右

U, YŪ, migi – right

右方	uhō	right side	70
左右	sayū	left and right; control	75
右手	migite	right hand; (on) the right	57
右から左へ	migi kara hidari e	from right to left; quickly	75
右と言えば左	migi to ieba hidari	contrarian	66, 75

77   3n3.3   ⺌ 彐   /35 39   当 當

TŌ, a(teru), a(taru) – hit, be on target

本当	hontō	truth; really	25
当時	tōji	at present; at that time	42
当分	tōbun	for now, for a while	38
手当て	teate	allowance, compensation; medical treatment	57
一人当たり	hitoriatari	per person, per capita	2, 1

石	**78** 5a0.1 □ 石 /53 石	**SEKI, [SHAKU], ishi** – stone **[KOKU]** – (unit of volume, about 180 liters)
		石けん *sekken* soap
		木石 *bokuseki* trees and stones; inanimate objects ... 22
		小石 *koishi* small stone, pebble ... 27
		石切り *ishikiri* stonecutting, quarrying ... 39

物	**79** 4g4.2 ⊞ 牛 犭 /47 27 物	**BUTSU, MOTSU, mono** – object, thing
		人物 *jinbutsu* person, personage ... 1
		生物 *seibutsu* living beings, life ... 44
		見物 *kenbutsu* sightseeing ... 63
		物語 *monogatari* tale, story ... 67
		本物 *honmono* genuine, the real thing ... 25

事	**80** 0a8.15 ⋯ 口 ヨ 十 24 39 12 事 亊	**JI, [ZU], koto** – thing, affair
		人事 *jinji* human/personnel affairs ... 1
		火事 *kaji* a fire ... 20
		事前/後 *jizen/go* before/after the fact ... 47, 48
		大事 *daiji* great thing, important ... 26
		出来事 *dekigoto* event, occurrence ... 53, 69

夕	**81** 0a3.14 □ 夕 30 夕	**SEKI, yū** – evening
		一夕 *isseki* one evening ... 2
		夕方 *yūgata* evening ... 70
		夕日 *yūhi* evening/setting sun ... 5
		夕月 *yūzuki* evening moon ... 17
		七夕 *tanabata* Star Festival (July 7) ... 9

名	**82** 3d3.12 ▣ 口 夕 /24 30 名	**MEI, MYŌ, na** – name; reputation
		人名 *jinmei* name of a person ... 1
		名人 *meijin* master, expert, virtuoso ... 1
		名物 *meibutsu* noted product (of a locality) ... 79
		大名 *daimyō* (Japanese) feudal lord ... 26
		名前 *namae* a name ... 47

外	**83** 2m3.1 ⊞ 卜 夕 /13 30 外	**GAI, GE, soto** – outside **hoka** – other **hazu(reru/su)** – slip off, miss
		外（国）人 *gai(koku)jin* foreigner ... 40, 1
		外来語 *gairaigo* word of foreign origin, loanword ... 69, 67
		外出 *gaishutsu* go out ... 53
		以外 *igai* besides, except (for) ... 46

内	**84** 0a4.23 ⋯ イ 冂 3 20 内	**NAI, [DAI], uchi** – inside
		国内 *kokunai* domestic, internal ... 40
		体内 *tainai* inside the body ... 61
		内外 *naigai* inner and outer; domestic and foreign ... 83
		年内に *nennai ni* before the year is out ... 45
		一年以内に *ichinen inai ni* within a year ... 2, 45, 46

死	**85** 0a6.6 ⊞ 夕 亠 一 30 13 1 死	**SHI** – death **shi(nu)** – die	
		死体 *shitai* dead body, corpse	61
		死人 *shinin* dead person, the dead	1
		死後 *shigo* after death	48
		水死 *suishi* drowning	21
		死語 *shigo* dead language; passé word	67

部	**86** 2d8.15 ⊞ 阝 立 口 /7 54 24 部	**BU** – part, section; copy (of a publication)	
		一部 *ichibu* a part; a copy (of a publication)	2
		部分 *bubun* a part	38
		大部分 *daibubun* greater part, most	26, 38
		本部 *honbu* headquarters	25
		北部 *hokubu* the north (of a country)	73

倍	**87** 2a8.14 ⊞ 亻 立 口 /3 54 24 倍	**BAI** – double, times, -fold	
		一倍 *ichibai* as much again	2
		二倍 *nibai* double, twice as much	3
		三倍 *sanbai* 3 times as much, threefold	4
		三倍以上 *sanbai ijō* at least 3 times as much	4, 46, 32
		倍にする *bai ni suru* double	

半	**88** 0a5.24 ⋯ 十 儿 一 12 16 1 半	**HAN, naka(ba)** – half	
		半分 *hanbun* half	38
		半年 *hantoshi* half a year, 6 months	45
		三時半 *sanjihan* half past three, 3:30	4, 42
		前半 *zenhan, zenpan* first half	47
		大半 *taihan* greater part, majority	26

全	**89** 2a4.16 ⊞ 亻 王 /3 46 全	**ZEN, matta(ku)** – all, whole, entirely **sube(te)** – all	
		全部 *zenbu* all	86
		全国 *zenkoku* the whole country	40
		全体 *zentai* the whole, (in) all	61
		全身 *zenshin* the entire body	59
		万全 *banzen* perfect, absolutely sure	16

回	**90** 3s3.1 ▢ 口 /24 回 囘	**KAI, [E]** – times, repetitions **mawa(su)** – send around, rotate **mawa(ru)** – go around, revolve	
		十回 *jikkai* 10 times	12
		今/前回 *kon/zenkai* this/last time	51, 47
		言い回し *iimawashi* expression, turn of phrase	66
		上回る *uwamawaru* be more than, exceed	32

周	**91** 2r6.1 ⋯ 月 口 43 24 周	**SHŪ, mawa(ri)** – lap; circumference; surroundings	
		一周 *isshū* one lap, one revolution	2
		半周 *hanshū* semicircle, halfway around	88
		円周 *enshū* circumference	13
		百周年 *hyakushūnen* 100th anniversary	14, 45

	92	**SHŪ** – week	
週	2q8.7 ▢	二週間 *nishūkan* two weeks	3, 43
	辶 月 日	先週 *senshū* last week	50
	/19 43 24	今週 *konshū* this week	51
		来週 *raishū* next week	69
	週	週日 *shūjitsu* weekday	5

	93	**MU, BU** – not, (prefix) un-, without, -less **na(i)** – not be	
無	4d8.8 ▢	無名 *mumei* anonymous; unknown	82
	火 艹 亠	無口 *mukuchi* taciturn, laconic	54
	/44 32 15	無言 *mugon* silent, mute	66
		無休 *mukyū* no holidays, always open (shop)	60
	無	無事 *buji* safe and sound	80

	94	**FU, BU** – (prefix) not, un-	
不	0a4.2 ⋯	不足 *fusoku* insufficiency, shortage	58
	一 丨 丶	不十分 *fujūbun* not enough, inadequate	12, 38
	14 2 2	行方不明 *yukue fumei* whereabouts unknown,	68, 70, 18
		不当 *futō* improper, unjust ⌐missing	77
	不	不死身 *fujimi* invulnerable	85, 59

	95	**CHŌ** – long; chief, head **naga(i)** – long	
長	0a8.2 ▤	部長 *buchō* department head, director	86
	礻 十 二	身長 *shinchō* person's height	59
	57 13 4	長時間 *chōjikan* long time, many hours	42, 43
		長年 *naganen* many years, long years	45
	長	長い間 *nagai aida* for a long time	43

	96	**HATSU, HOTSU** – emit, start from, depart	
発	0a9.5 ▤	出発 *shuppatsu* departure, start out	53
	火 艹 一	発明 *hatsumei* invention	18
	44 32 1	発見 *hakken* discovery	63
		発行 *hakkō* publish, issue	68
	発 發	発足 *hossoku, hassoku* start, inauguration	58

	97	**SHIN, kokoro** – heart, mind, core	
心	4k0.1 ▢	中心 *chūshin* center, midpoint	28
	心	内心 *naishin* one's inmost heart	84
	/51	本心 *honshin* one's real mind; real intention	25
		一心に *isshin ni* with singlehearted devotion, fervently	2
	心	心身 *shinshin* body and mind/spirit	59

	98	**SEI** – sex; nature (of) **SHŌ** – temperament, propensity	
性	4k5.4 ▥	中性 *chūsei* neuter gender; neutral (in chemistry)	28
	心 土 亠	人生 *jinsei* human nature; humanity	1, 44
	/51 22 15	性行 *seikō* character and conduct	68
		性分 *shōbun* nature, temperament	38
	性	本性 *honshō, honsei* true nature/character	25

99

思

5f4.4	⊟
甲 心 /58 51	
思	

SHI, omo(u) – think, believe

思い出	omoide	memories	53
思い出す	omoidasu	remember	53
思い切って	omoikitte	resolutely, daringly	39
思いやり	omoiyari	consideration, sympathy, compassion	
思い上がった	omoiagatta	conceited, cocky	32

100

力

2g0.1	□
力 /8	
力	

RYOKU, RIKI, chikara – force, power

体力	tairyoku	physical strength	61
水力	suiryoku	water power, hydraulic power	21
風力	fūryoku	force of the wind; wind power	29
全力	zenryoku	all one's power, utmost efforts	89
無力	muryoku	powerless, helpless	93

101

男

5f2.2	□
甲 力 /58 8	
男	

DAN, NAN, otoko – man, human male

男性	dansei	man; masculine gender	98
長男	chōnan	eldest son	95
男の人	otoko no hito	man	1
山男	yamaotoko	mountain dweller; mountaineer	34
大男	ōtoko	giant, tall man	26

102

女

3e0.1	□
女 /25	
女	

JO, NYO, [NYŌ], onna – woman **me** – feminine

女性	josei	woman; feminine gender	98
長女	chōjo	eldest daughter	95
男女	danjo	men and women	101
女の人	onna no hito	woman	1
女心	onnagokoro	a woman's heart	97

103

子

2c0.1	□
子 /6	
子	

SHI, SU, ko – child

男子	danshi	boy, man	101
男の子	otokonoko	boy	101
女子	joshi	girl, woman	102
女の子	onnanoko	girl	102
分子	bunshi	molecule; numerator (of a fraction)	38

104

好

3e2.1	⊞
女 子 /25 6	
好	

KŌ, kono(mu), su(ku) – like

好物	kōbutsu	favorite food	79
好人物	kōjinbutsu	good-natured person	1, 79
物好き	monozuki	idle curiosity	79
大好き	daisuki	like very much	26
好き好き	sukizuki	matter of individual preference	

105

安

3m3.1	⊟
宀 女 /33 25	
安	

AN – peace, peacefulness **yasu(i)** – cheap

安心	anshin	feel relieved/reassured	97
安全	anzen	safety	89
不安	fuan	unease, anxiety, fear	94
目安	meyasu	standard, yardstick	55
安物	yasumono	cheap goods, low-quality merchandise	79

案

106		**AN** – plan, proposal			
3m7.6		案内	*annai*	guidance, information	84
宀 木 女		案外	*angai*	contrary to expectations	83
/33 41 25		名案	*meian*	good idea	82
		思案	*shian*	consideration, reflection	99
案		案出	*anshutsu*	contrive, devise	53

用

107		**YŌ** – business, usage **mochi(iru)** – use			
2r3.1	…	用事	*yōji*	business affair; errand	80
月 丨		用語	*yōgo*	(technical) term, vocabulary	67
43 2		無用	*muyō*	useless; unnecessary	93
		男子用	*danshiyō*	for men, men's	101, 103
用		用水	*yōsui*	city/tap water	21

電

108		**DEN** – electricity			
8d5.2		電力	*denryoku*	electrical power/energy	100
雨 日 丨		電子	*denshi*	electron	103
/74 42 2		電子レンジ	*denshi renji*	microwave oven	103
		発電	*hatsuden*	generation of electricity	96
電		風力発電	*fūyoku hatsuden*	wind power generation	29, 100, 96

学

109		**GAKU** – science, study **mana(bu)** – learn			
3n4.2		大学	*daigaku*	university, college	26
⺍ 冖 子		学部	*gakubu*	academic department; faculty	86
/35 20 6		入学	*nyūgaku*	entry/admission into a school	52
		学生	*gakusei*	student	44
学 學		言語学	*gengogaku*	linguistics	66, 67

字

110		**JI** – character, letter **aza** – village section			
3m2.1		国字	*kokuji*	national/Japanese script	40
宀 子		ローマ字	*rōmaji*	roman letters	
/33 6		当て字	*ateji*	kanji used phonetically/for meaning	77
		字体	*jitai*	form of a character, typeface, font	61
字		十字	*jūji*	a cross	12

文

111		**BUN, MON** – literature, text, sentence **fumi** – letter, note			
2j2.4		文字	*moji, monji*	letter, character	110
亠 乂		文学	*bungaku*	literature	109
/11 12		本文	*honbun*	text, wording	25
		文語	*bungo*	the written language	67
文		文明	*bunmei*	civilization	18

母

112		**BO, haha** – mother			
0a5.36	…	母子	*boshi*	mother and child	103
母 丶		生母	*seibo*	one's biological mother	44
25 2		母国語	*bokokugo*	one's mother tongue	40, 67
		母方	*hahakata*	maternal, on the mother's side	70
母		お母さん	*okāsan*	mother	

	113	**FU, chichi** – father
	2o2.3	父母 *fubo, chichihaha* father and mother — 112
		父子 *fushi* father and child/son — 103
	/16 12	父方 *chichikata* paternal, on the father's side — 70
	父	父上 *chichiue* father — 32
		お父さん *otōsan* father

	114	**KŌ** – intersection; coming and going **ma(jiru), ma(zaru)** – (intr.) mix
	2j4.3	**maji(eru), ma(zeru)** – (tr.) mix **maji(waru), ka(u)** – associate (with)
	/11 16 12	**ka(wasu)** – exchange (greetings)
	交	国交 *kokkō* diplomatic relations — 40
		外交 *gaikō* foreign policy, diplomacy — 83
		性交 *seikō* sexual intercourse — 98

	115	**KŌ** – school; (printing) proof
	4a6.24	学校 *gakkō* school — 109
		小学校 *shōgakkō* elementary school — 27, 109
	/41 11 16	中学校 *chūgakkō* junior high school — 28, 109
	校	母校 *bokō* alma mater — 112
		校長 *kōchō* principal, headmaster — 95

	116	**MAI** – every, each
	0a6.25	毎年 *mainen, maitoshi* every year, annual — 45
		毎月 *maigetsu, maitsuki* every month, monthly — 17
	25 15 2	毎週 *maishū* every week, weekly — 92
	毎	毎日 *mainichi* every day, daily — 5
		毎時 *maiji* every hour, hourly, per hour — 42

	117	**KAI, umi** – sea, ocean
	3a6.20	大海 *taikai* an ocean — 26
		海上 *kaijō* ocean, seagoing, marine — 32
	/21 25 15	海外 *kaigai* overseas, abroad — 83
	海	内海 *uchiumi, naikai* inland sea — 84
		日本海 *Nihonkai* Sea of Japan — 5, 25

	118	**CHI, JI** – earth, land
	3b3.1	土地 *tochi* land, soil — 24
		地下 *chika* underground, subterranean — 31
	/22 12 2	地方 *chihō* region, area — 70
	地	地名 *chimei* place name ⌐birthplace 82
		生地 *kiji* ffabric; inherent nature; dough *seichi* one's — 44

	119	**CHI, ike** – pond
	3a3.4	用水池 *yōsuichi* water reservoir — 107, 21
		電池 *denchi* battery — 108
	/21 12 2	池田 *Ikeda* (surname) — 35
	池	小池 *Koike* (surname) — 27

他 120

他

TA, hoka – other, another

2a3.4

イ 十 丨
/3 12 2

他人	tanin	another person; stranger	1
他国	takoku	another/foreign country	40
他方	tahō	the other side/party/direction	70
自他	jita	oneself and others	62
その他	sono ta	and so forth	

立 121

立

RITSU, [RYŪ], ta(tsu) – stand (up) **ta(teru)** – set up, raise

5b0.1

立
/54

国立	kokuritsu	national, state-supported	40
自立	jiritsu	independent, self-supporting	62
中立	chūritsu	neutral, neutrality	28
目立つ	medatsu	be conspicuous, stick out	55
立ち上がる	tachiagaru	stand up	32

位 122

位

I, kurai – rank, position

2a5.1

イ 立
/3 54

地位	chii	position, rank	118
学位	gakui	academic degree	109
上位	jōi	higher rank	32
本位	hon'i	monetary standard; basis, principle	25
位取り	kuraidori	position (before/after decimal point)	65

法 123

法

HŌ, HA', HO' – law

3a5.20

氵 土 ム
/21 22 17

国法	kokuhō	laws of the country	40
立法	rippō	enactment of legislation	121
法案	hōan	bill, legislative proposal	106
文法	bunpō	grammar	111
方法	hōhō	method	70

和 124

和

WA, [O] – peace, harmony; (short for) Japanese **yawa(rageru/ragu), nago(mu)** – soften, calm down **nago(yaka)** – mild, gentle, congenial

5d3.1

禾 口
/56 24

和文	wabun	Japanese script	111
和風	wafū	Japanese style	29
不和	fuwa	disharmony, discord, enmity	94
大和	Yamato	(old) Japan	26

私 125

私

SHI, watakushi, watashi – I; private

5d2.2

禾 ム
/56 17

私事	shiji	personal affairs	80
私物	shibutsu	private property	79
私用	shiyō	private use	107
私立	shiritsu	private, privately supported	121
私自身	watakushi jishin	personally, as for me	62, 59

公 126

公

KŌ, ōyake – public, official

2o2.2

ソ ム
/16 17

公安	kōan	public peace/security	105
公法	kōhō	public law	123
公立	kōritsu	public	121
公海	kōkai	international waters	117
公言	kōgen	public declaration, avowal	66

林	**127** 4a4.1 木 /41 林	**RIN, hayashi** – woods, forest 山林　*sanrin*　mountains and forests; mountain forest　　34 (山)林学　*(san)ringaku*　forestry　　34, 109 林立　*rinritsu*　stand close together in large numbers　　121 林　*Hayashi*　(surname) 小林　*Kobayashi*　(surname)　　27
森	**128** 4a8.39 木 /41 森	**SHIN, mori** – woods, forest 森林　*shinrin*　woods, forest　　127 大森　*Ōmori*　(area of Tōkyō)　　26 森　*Mori*　(surname)
竹	**129** 6f0.1 ⺮ /66 竹	**CHIKU, take** – bamboo 竹林　*chikurin, takebayashi*　bamboo grove/thicket　　127 竹刀　*shinai*　bamboo sword (for *kendō*)　　37 竹の子　*takenoko*　bamboo shoots　　103 竹のつえ　*take no tsue*　bamboo cane 竹やぶ　*takeyabu*　bamboo thicket
筆	**130** 6f6.1 ⺮　十 /66 39 12 筆	**HITSU, fude** – writing brush 万年筆　*mannenhitsu*　fountain pen　　16, 45 自筆　*jihitsu*　one's own handwriting; autograph　　62 筆名　*hitsumei*　pen name, pseudonym　　82 文筆　*bunpitsu*　literary work, writing　　111 筆先　*fudesaki*　tip of the writing brush　　50
書	**131** 4c6.6 日　土　⺕ /42 22 39 書	**SHO, ka(ku)** – write 書物　*shomotsu*　book　　79 文書　*bunsho, monjo*　(in) writing, document　　111 書名　*shomei*　book title　　82 前書き　*maegaki*　foreword, preface　　47 書き取り　*kakitori*　dictation　　65
意	**132** 5b8.2 立　日　心 /54 42 51 意	**I** – will, heart, mind, thought; meaning, sense 意見　*iken*　opinion　　63 用意　*yōi*　preparations, readiness　　107 好意　*kōi*　goodwill, good wishes, kindness　　104 意外　*igai*　unexpected, surprising　　83 不意　*fui*　sudden, unexpected　　94
車	**133** 7c0.1 車 /69 車	**SHA, kuruma** – vehicle; wheel 電車　*densha*　electric train　　108 人力車　*jinrikisha*　rickshaw　　1, 100 発車　*hassha*　departure　　96 下車　*gesha*　get off (a train)　　31 水車　*suisha*　waterwheel　　21

気
汽
原
元
光
工
空

134		**KI, KE** – spirit, soul, mood		
0a6.8		人気	*ninki* popularity	1
一 十 一		気分	*kibun* feeling, mood	38
15 12 1		本気	*honki* seriousness, (in) earnest	25
気 氣		気体	*kitai* a gas	61
		電気	*denki* electricity	108

135		**KI** – steam	
3a4.16		汽車 *kisha* train	133
氵 一 一			
/21 15 1			
汽			

136		**GEN** – original, fundamental **hara** – plain, field, wilderness		
2p8.1		原点	*genten* starting point	169
厂 日 小		原案	*gen'an* the original plan/proposal	106
/18 42 35		原文	*genbun* the text, the original	111
原		原子	*genshi* atom	103
		原子力	*genshiryoku* atomic energy, nuclear power	103, 100

137		**GEN** – origin; (Chinese monetary unit) **GAN** – origin **moto** – origin; (as prefix) former, ex-		
0a4.5		元日	*ganjitsu* New Year's Day	5
二 儿		元金	*gankin* principal (vs. interest), principal amount	23
4 16		元気	*genki* healthy, peppy	134
元		地元	*jimoto* local	118

138		**KŌ, hikari** – light **hika(ru)** – shine		
3n3.2		日光	*nikkō* sunlight, sunshine	5
丷 儿 一		月光	*gekkō* moonlight	17
/35 16 1		光年	*kōnen* light-year	45
光		発光	*hakkō* luminosity, emit light	96
		電光	*denkō* electric light; lightning	108

139		**KŌ, KU** – artisan, manufacturing, construction		
0a3.6		工事	*kōji* construction	80
工		大工	*daiku* carpenter	26
38		女工	*jokō* woman factory-worker	102
工		工学	*kōgaku* engineering	109
		人工	*jinkō* man-made, artificial	1

140		**KŪ, sora** – sky; empty **a(keru/ku)** – make/be unoccupied **kara** – empty		
3m5.12		空気	*kūki* air	134
宀 工 儿		(時間と)空間	*(jikan to) kūkan* (time and) space	42, 43, 43
/33 38 16		空車	*kūsha* empty car, For Hire (taxi)	133
空		空手	*karate* karate	57
		大空	*ōzora* sky, firmament	26

天	**141** 0a4.21 ... 大 一 34　1 天	**TEN, ame, [ama]** – heaven 天気　*tenki*　weather　　134 天文学　*tenmongaku*　astronomy　　111, 109 天国　*tengoku*　paradise　　40 天性　*tensei*　nature, natural constitution　　98 天の川　*amanogawa*　Milky Way　　33
里	**142** 0a7.9 ... 日 土 42　22 里	**RI** – village; (old unit of length, about 2.9 km) **sato** – village, one's parents' home 千里　*senri*　1000 ri; a great distance　　15 海里　*kairi*　nautical mile　　117 里子　*satogo*　foster child　　103 里心　*satogokoro*　homesickness　　97
理	**143** 4f7.1 王 日 土 /46　42　22 理	**RI** – reason, logic, principle 地理（学）　*chiri(gaku)*　geography　　118, 109 心理学　*shinrigaku*　psychology　　97, 109 理学部　*rigakubu*　department of science　　109, 86 無理　*muri*　unreasonable; impossible; (by) force　　93 理事　*riji*　director　　80
少	**144** 3n1.1 ... ソ 丨 /35　2 少	**SHŌ, suko(shi)** – a little, a few **suku(nai)** – little, few 少年　*shōnen*　boy　　45 少年法　*shōnenhō*　the Juvenile Law　　45, 123 少女　*shōjo*　girl　　102 少々　*shōshō*　a little 少しずつ　*sukoshizutsu*　little by little, a little at a time
省	**145** 5c4.7 ... 日 小 丨 /55　35　2 省	**SEI, kaeri(miru)** – reflect upon, give heed to **SHŌ** – (government) ministry; province (in China); save **habu(ku)** – omit, cut down on 自省　*jisei*　reflection, introspection　　62 内省　*naisei*　Introspection　　84 人事不省　*jinjifusei*　unconsciousness, fainting　　1, 80, 94 省エネ（ルギー）　*shō-ene(rugī)*　energy saving
相	**146** 4a5.3 木 日 /41　55 相	**SŌ** – aspect, phase **SHŌ** – (government) minister **ai-** – together, fellow, each other 相当　*sōtō*　suitable, appropriate　　77 法相　*hōshō*　Minister of Justice　　123 外相　*gaishō*　foreign minister　　83 相手　*aite*　the other party, partner, opponent　　57
想	**147** 4k9.18 心 日 木 /51　55　41 想	**SŌ, [SO]** – idea, thought 思想　*shisō*　idea, thought　　99 回想　*kaisō*　retrospection, reminiscense　　90 理想　*risō*　an ideal　　143 空想　*kūsō*　fantasy, daydream　　140 めい想　*meisō*　meditation

148

2o7.2 目	
⺀ 月 ⼀	
/16 55 14	
首	

SHU, kubi – neck, head

首相	shushō	prime minister	146
元首	genshu	sovereign, ruler	137
首位	shui	leading position, top spot	122
部首	bushu	radical of a kanji	86
手首	tekubi	wrist	57

149

2q9.14 囗	
⻌ 月 儿	
/19 55 16	
道	

DŌ, [TŌ], michi – road, way, path; dao/tao

国道	kokudō	national highway	40
水道	suidō	water conduits, running water	21
北海道	Hokkaidō	Hokkaidō	73, 117
書道	shodō	calligraphy	131
回り道	mawarimichi	a detour	90

150

2q7.18 囗	
⻌ 月 ⼀	
/19 43 1	
通	

TSŪ, [TSU], tō(ru) – go through, pass **tō(su)** – let through
kayo(u) – commute

交通	kōtsū	traffic, transportation	114
文通	buntsū	correspondence, letter-exchange	111
通学	tsūgaku	attend school	109
見通し	mitōshi	prospects, outlook	63

151

7d6.5 田	
⻊ 夂 口	
/70 49 24	
路	

RO, -ji – street, way

道路	dōro	street, road	149
十字路	jūjiro	intersection, crossroads	12, 110
水路	suiro	waterway, aqueduct	21
海路	kairo	sea route	117
通路	tsūro	passageway, walkway, aisle	150

152

4m0.1 □	
戸	
/40	
戸	

KO, to – door

戸外で	kogai de	outdoors, in the open air	83
下戸	geko	nondrinker, teetotaler	31
戸口	toguchi	doorway	54
木戸	kido	gate, entrance; castle gate	22
雨戸	amado	storm door, shutter	30

153

4m4.3 ⊞	
戸 斤	
/40 50	
所	

SHO, tokoro – place

案内所	annaijo	inquiry office, information desk	106, 84
名所	meisho	noted place, sights (to see)	82
所長	shochō	director, head manager	95
長所	chōsho	strong point, merit, advantage	95
原子力発電所	genshiryoku hatsudensho	nuclear power plant	

154

3b9.6 田	
土 日 犭	
/22 42 27	
場 塲	

JŌ, ba – place

工場	kōjō, kōba	factory, plant	139
出場	shutsujō	stage appearance; participation	53
場所	basho	place, location	153
立場	tachiba	standpoint, point of view	121
相場	sōba	market price	146

主	**155** 4f1.1 王 丶 /46　2 主	**SHU, [SU]** – main; master, lord **nushi** – owner, master **omo** – main, principal	
		主人　shujin　husband, head of household	1
		主人公　shujinkō　hero, main character	1, 126
		自主　jishu　independence, autonomy	62
		主語　shugo　subject (in grammar)	67
		地主　jinushi　landowner, landlord	118

住	**156** 2a5.19 亻 王 丶 /3　46　2 住	**JŪ, su(mu), su(mau)** – live, dwell, reside	
		住所　jūsho　an address	153
		住人　jūnin　inhabitant, resident	1
		安住　anjū　peaceful living	105
		住まい　sumai　residence, where one lives, address	
		住み心地　sumigokochi　comfortableness, livability	97, 118

信	**157** 2a7.1 亻 言 /3　67 信	**SHIN** – faith, trust, belief	
		信用　shin'yō　trust	107
		不信　fushin　bad faith, insincerity; distrust	94
		自信　jishin　(self-)confidence	62
		所信　shoshin　one's conviction, opinion	153
		通信　tsūshin　communication, correspondence, dispatch	150

会	**158** 2a4.19 亻 二 ム /3　4　17 会 會	**KAI** – meeting, association **E, a(u)** – meet	
		国会　kokkai　parliament, diet, congress	40
		大会　taikai　mass meeting; sports meet, tournament	26
		学会　gakkai　learned/academic society	109
		会見　kaiken　interview, news conference	63
		出会う　deau　happen to meet, run into	53

合	**159** 2a4.18 亻 口 一 /3　24　1 合	**GŌ, GA', [KA'], a(u)** – fit **a(waseru), a(wasu)** – put together	
		合意　gōi　mutual consent, agreement	132
		場合　baai, bawai　(in this) case	154
		（お）見合い　(o)miai　marriage interview	63
		間に合う　maniau　be in time (for); will do/suffice	43
		見合わせる　miawaseru　look at each other; postpone	63

答	**160** 6f6.12 竹 口 亻 /66　24　3 答	**TŌ, kota(e)** – an answer **kota(eru)** – answer	
		回答　kaitō　an answer, reply	90
		口答　kōtō　oral answer	54
		筆答　hittō　written answer	130
		名答　meitō　correct answer	82
		答案　tōan　examination paper	106

門	**161** 8e0.1 門 /75 門	**MON, kado** – gate	
		入門（書）　nyūmon(sho)　introduction, primer	52, 131
		部門　bumon　group, category, branch	86
		名門　meimon　distinguished/illustrious family	82
		門下生　monkasei　(someone's) pupil	31, 44
		門口　kadoguchi　front door, entrance	54

問	**162** 8e3.1　□ 門 口 /75　24 問	**MON, to(i), [ton]** – question, problem **to(u)** – ask, inquire 問答　*mondō*　questions and answers, dialogue　160 学問　*gakumon*　learning, science　109 問い合わせ　*toiawase*　inquiry　159 問いただす　*toitadasu*　inquire, question
員	**163** 3d7.10　□ 口 貝 /24　68 員	**IN** – member 会員　*kaiin*　member (of a society)　158 海員　*kaiin*　seaman, sailor　117 工員　*kōin*　factory worker　139 人員　*jin'in*　staff, personnel　1 全員　*zen'in*　all members, entire staff　89
者	**164** 4c4.13　… 日 土 丨 /42　22　2 者	**SHA, mono** – person 学者　*gakusha*　scholar　109 日本学者　*Nihongakusha*　Japanologist　5, 25, 109 筆者　*hissha*　writer, author　130 信者　*shinja*　believer, the faithful　157 後者　*kōsha*　the latter　48
家	**165** 3m7.1　□ 宀 犭 ヽ /33　27　10 家	**KA, KE, ie, ya** – house, home, family 家事　*kaji*　family affairs; household chores　80 家内　*kanai*　(one's own) wife　84 国家　*kokka*　state, nation　40 家来　*kerai*　retainer, vassal　69 家主　*yanushi*　landlord, house owner　155
室	**166** 3m6.4　目 宀 土 ム /33　22　17 室	**SHITSU** – a room **muro** – greenhouse, cellar 和室　*washitsu*　Japanese-style room　124 私室　*shishitsu*　private room　125 室内　*shitsunai*　in a room, indoor　84 分室　*bunshitsu*　isolated room; annex　38 室長　*shitsuchō*　senior roommate; section chief　95
屋	**167** 3r6.3　□ 尸 土 ム /40　22　17 屋	**OKU** – house **ya** – roof; house; shop, dealer 家屋　*kaoku*　house, building　165 屋上　*okujō*　roof, rooftop　32 部屋　*heya*　a room　86 小屋　*koya*　cottage, hut, shack　27 八百屋　*yaoya*　vegetable shop, greengrocer　10, 14
店	**168** 3q5.4　□ 广 口 卜 /18　24　13 店	**TEN, mise** – shop, store 書店　*shoten*　bookstore　131 本店　*honten*　head office, main shop　25 店員　*ten'in*　store employee, clerk　163 店先　*misesaki*　storefront　50 出店　*demise*　branch store　53

点	**169** 2m7.2 ⼘ ⽕ ⼞ /13 44 24 点 點	**TEN** – point

出発点	*shuppatsuten*	starting point	53, 96
原点	*genten*	starting point; origin (of coordinates)	136
合点	*gaten, gatten*	understanding; consent	159
点字	*tenji*	Braille	110
点火	*tenka*	ignite	20

局	**170** 3r4.4 ⼫ ⼞ ⼀ /40 24 1 局	**KYOKU** – bureau, office

当局	*tōkyoku*	the authorities, responsible officials	77
局長	*kyokuchō*	director of a bureau; postmaster	95
局員	*kyokuin*	staff member of a bureau	163
局外者	*kyokugaisha*	outsider, onlooker	83, 164
時局	*jikyoku*	the situation	42

居	**171** 3r5.3 ⼫ ⼞ ⼗ /40 24 12 居	**KYO, i(ru)** – be (present), exist

住居	*jūkyo*	dwelling, residence	156
居住地	*kyojūchi*	place of residence	156, 118
居間	*ima*	living room	43
長居	*nagai*	stay (too) long	95
居合わせる	*iawaseru*	(happen to) be present	159

古	**172** 2k3.1 ⼗ ⼞ /12 24 古	**KO, furu(i)** – old **furu(su)** – wear out

古風	*kofū*	old customs; antiquated	29
古語	*kogo*	archaic word; old adage	67
古文	*kobun*	classical literature, ancient classics	111
古今東西	*kokon-tōzai*	all ages and countries	51, 71, 72
古本	*furuhon*	secondhand/used book	25

故	**173** 4i5.2 ⼂ ⼞ ⼗ /49 24 12 故	**KO** – deceased **yue** – reason, cause, circumstances

故人	*kojin*	the deceased	1
故事	*koji*	historical event	80
事故	*jiko*	accident	80
故国	*kokoku*	one's homeland, native country	40
故意	*koi*	intention, purpose	132

新	**174** 5b8.3 ⽴ ⽊ ⽄ /54 41 50 新	**SHIN, atara(shii), ara(ta), nii-** – new

新聞	*shinbun*	newspaper	64
古新聞	*furushinbun*	old newspapers	172, 64
新年	*shinnen*	the New Year	45
新人	*shinjin*	newcomer, new face	1
一新	*isshin*	renovation, reform	2

親	**175** 5b11.1 ⽴ ⾙ ⽊ /54 68 41 親	**SHIN** – intimacy; parent **oya** – parent **shita(shii)** – intimate, close (friend) **shita(shimu)** – get to know better

親切	*shinsetsu*	kind, friendly	39
親日	*shin-Nichi*	pro-Japanese	5
母親	*hahaoya*	mother	112
親子	*oyako*	parent and child	103

質	**176** 7b8.7 貝 斤 /68 50 質 质	**SHITSU** – quality, nature **SHICHI, [CHI]** – hostage, pawn

質問　shitsumon　a question　162
性質　seishitsu　nature, property　98
物質　busshitsu　matter, material, substance　79
本質　honshitsu　essence, substance　25
人質　hitojichi　hostage　1

民	**177** 0a5.23 尸 十 40　12 民	**MIN, tami** – people, nation

国民　kokumin　people, nation, citizen　40
人民　jinmin　the people, citizens　1
(原)住民　(gen)jūmin　(aboriginal) native of a place　136, 156
民間　minkan　private (not public)　43
民意　min'i　will of the people　132

宅	**178** 3m3.4 宀 十 丿 /33　12　2 宅	**TAKU** – house, home, residence

住宅　jūtaku　house, residence　156
自宅　jitaku　one's own home, private residence　62
私宅　shitaku　one's private residence　125
宅地　takuchi　land for housing, residential site　118
家宅　kataku　house, the premises　165

宿	**179** 3m8.3 宀 日 亻 /33　42　3 宿	**SHUKU, yado** – lodging, inn **yado(ru)** – take shelter; be pregnant **yado(su)** – give shelter, conceive (a child)

下宿　geshuku　room and board; boardinghouse　31
合宿　gasshuku　lodging together　159
宿屋　yadoya　inn　167
民宿　minshuku　tourist home, bed-and-breakfast　177

紙	**180** 6a4.4 糸 厂 十 /61　18　12 紙 昏	**SHI, kami** – paper

和紙　washi　Japanese paper　124
日本紙　Nihonshi　Japanese paper　5, 25
新聞紙　shinbunshi　newspaper; newsprint　174, 64
質問用紙　shitsumon yōshi　questionnaire　176, 162, 107
手紙　tegami　letter　57

市	**181** 2j3.1 亠 巾 /11　26 市	**SHI** – city, town, market **ichi** – market

市長　shichō　mayor　95
市会　shikai　municipal assembly, city council　158
市立　shiritsu　municipal　121
市民　shimin　citizen, townspeople　177
市場　ichiba, shijō　marketplace, market　154

町	**182** 5f2.1 田 丁 /58　14 町 甼	**CHŌ, machi** – town, quarter, street

町民　chōmin　townsman, townsfolk　177
町人　chōnin　merchant; townsfolk　1
町内　chōnai　neighborhood　84
下町　shitamachi　(low-lying) downtown area　31
室町　Muromachi　(historical period, 1392–1573)　166

区 区 區	**183** 2t2.1 匸 十 /20 12	**KU** – ward, municipal administrative district

地区 *chiku* district, area, zone — 118
区間 *kukan* section, interval — 43
区切る *kugiru* partition; punctuate — 39
区分 *kubun* division, partition; classification — 38
北区 *Kita-ku* Kita Ward (Tōkyō) — 73

丁 丁	**184** 0a2.4 一 14	**CHŌ** – city block-size area; two-page leaf of paper; even number, (counter for dishes of food) **TEI** – D, No. 4 (in a series), adult; T shape

一丁目 *itchōme* city block No. 1 (in addresses) — 2, 55
丁年 *teinen* (age of) majority, adulthood — 45
丁字路 *teijiro* T-shaped street, street intersection — 110, 151

番 番	**185** 5f7.4 田 米 丨 /58 62 2	**BAN** – keeping watch; number; order

一番 *ichiban* the first; number one, most — 2
二番目 *nibanme* the second, number 2 — 3, 55
番地 *banchi* lot/house number — 118
局番 *kyokuban* exchange (part of a phone number) — 170
交番 *kōban* police box — 114

街 街	**186** 3i9.2 彳 土 二 /29 22 4	**GAI, [KAI], machi** – street

街路 *gairo* street — 151
街道 *kaidō* street, highway — 149
市街 *shigai* the streets (of a city); town — 181
名店街 *meitengai* arcade of well-known stores — 82, 168
地下街 *chikagai* underground shopping mall — 118, 31

術 術	**187** 3i8.2 彳 木 二 /29 41 4	**JUTSU** – art, technique, means, conjury

手術 *shujutsu* (surgical) operation — 57
手術室 *shujutsushitsu* operating room — 57, 166
学術 *gakujutsu* science, learning — 109
学術用語 *gakujutsu yōgo* technical term — 109, 107, 67

都 都	**188** 2d8.13 阝 日 土 /7 42 22	**TO, TSU, miyako** – capital (city)

（大)都市 *(dai)toshi* (major/large) city — 26, 181
都会 *tokai* city — 158
首都 *shuto* capital (city) — 148
都内 *tonai* in (the city of) Tōkyō — 84
都合 *tsugō* circumstances, reasons — 159

京 京 京	**189** 2j6.3 亠 口 小 /11 24 35	**KYŌ, KEI** – the capital

東京（都) *Tōkyō(-to)* (City of) Tōkyō — 71, 188
京都（市) *Kyōto(-shi)* (City of) Kyōto — 188, 181
上京 *jōkyō* go/come to Tōkyō — 32
北京 *Pekin* Peking, Beijing — 73
南京 *Nankin* Nanking — 74

高	**190** 2j8.6　目 亠 口 冂 /11　24　20 高	**KŌ, taka(i)** – high; expensive **taka** – amount, quantity **taka(maru)** – rise **taka(meru)** – raise
		高原　　kōgen　　plateau, heights, tableland　　　　　136 上高地　Kamikōchi　(scenic valley in Japanese Alps)　32, 118 高校　　kōkō　senior high school (short for kōtō gakkō)　115 名高い　nadakai　renowned, famous　　　　　　　82

村	**191** 4a3.11　□□ 木 寸 /41　37 村 邨	**SON, mura** – village
		市町村　shichōson　cities, towns, and villages　　181, 182 村会　　sonkai　village assembly　　　　　　　158 村長　　sonchō　village mayor　　　　　　　　95 村民　　sonmin　villager　　　　　　　　　177 村人　　murabito　villager　　　　　　　　　1

付	**192** 2a3.6　□□ 亻 寸 /3　37 付	**FU, tsu(ku)** – be attached, belong (to) **tsu(keru)** – attach, apply (cf. No. 1843)
		交付　　kōfu　deliver, hand over　　　　　　　114 日付け　hizuke　date (of a letter)　　　　　　　5 気付く　kizuku　(take) notice　　　　　　　134 付き物　tsukimono　what (something) entails, adjunct　79

郡	**193** 2d7.12　□□ 阝 ヨ 口 /7　39　24 郡	**GUN** – county, district
		郡部　　gunbu　rural district　　　　　　　　86 新田郡　Nitta-gun　Nitta District (Gunma Prefecture)　174, 35

県	**194** 3n6.3　… ⺍ 目 丨 /35　55　2 県 縣	**KEN** – prefecture, province
		郡県　　gunken　districts/counties and prefectures　193 県立　　kenritsu　prefectural, provincial　　　　121 県道　　kendō　prefectural highway　　　　　149 県会　　kenkai　prefectural assembly　　　　　158 山口県　Yamaguchi-ken　Yamaguchi Prefecture　34, 54

州	**195** 2f4.1　⠀ 丬 /16 州	**SHŪ** – state, province **su** – sandbank, shoals
		本州　　Honshū　(largest of the 4 main islands of Japan)　25 九州　　Kyūshū　(one of the 4 main islands of Japan)　11 カリフォルニア州　Kariforunia-shū　(State of) California 五大州　godaishū　the 5 continents (Asia, Africa, Europe,　7, 26 中州　　nakasu　sandbank in a river　⌊America, and Australia)　28

共	**196** 3k3.3　目 卄 儿 一 /32　16　1 共	**KYŌ** – together; (short for) communism **tomo** – together **-tomo** – including
		共学　　kyōgaku　coeducation　　　　　　　　109 共通　　kyōtsū　(in) common (with)　　　　　150 公共　　kōkyō　the public, community　　　　　126 共和国　kyōwakoku　republic　　　　　　　124, 40

	197	**KYŌ, [KU]** – offer **sona(eru)** – make an offering, dedicate
供	2a6.13	**tomo** – attendant, companion

供出　kyōshutsu　delivery　53
自供　jikyō　confession, admission　62
供物　kumotsu　votive offering　79
子供　kodomo　child　103

	198	**DŌ, ona(ji)** – same
同	2r4.2	

同時に　dōji ni　at the same time, simultaneously　42
共同　kyōdō　joint, communal, cooperative　196
合同　gōdō　combination, merger, joint　159
同意　dōi　agreement, consent　132
同居　dōkyo　live in the same house, live together　171

	199	**KŌ, mu(kau)** – face (toward), proceed (to) **mu(keru)** – (tr.) turn
向	3d3.10	**mu(ku)** – (intr.) turn **mu(kō)** – opposite side

方向　hōkō　direction　70
向上　kōjō　elevation, betterment　32
意向　ikō　intention, inclination　132
外人向け　gaijinmuke　for foreigners　83, 1

	200	**RYŌ** – both, (obsolete Japanese coin)
両	0a6.11	

両親　ryōshin　parents　175
両方　ryōhō　both　70
両手　ryōte　both hands　57
両立　ryōritsu　coexist, be compatible (with)　121
車両　sharyō　car, vehicle　133

	201	**MAN** – full; (short for) Manchuria **mi(chiru)** – become full
満	3a9.25	**mi(tasu)** – fill, fulfill

満足　manzoku　satisfaction　58
不満　fuman　dissatisfaction, discontent　94
満員　man'in　full to capacity　163
満点　manten　perfect score　169

	202	**HEI, BYŌ, tai(ra), hira** – flat, level
平	2k3.4	

平行　heikō　parallel　68
平和　heiwa　peace　124
不平　fuhei　discontent, complaint　94
平方メートル　heihōmētoru　square meter　70
平家　Heike　Heike (historic clan)　hiraya　1-story house　165

	203	**JITSU** – truth, actuality **mi** – fruit, nut **mino(ru)** – bear fruit
実	3m5.4	

事実　jijitsu　fact　80
口実　kōjitsu　pretext, excuse　54
実行　jikkō　put into practice, carry out, realize　68
実力　jitsuryoku　actual ability, competence　100
実用　jitsuyō　practical use　107

204

色

2n4.1
ク 尸 ｜
/15 40 2
色

SHOKU, SHIKI, iro – color; erotic passion

原色	genshoku	primary color	136
好色	kōshoku	sensuality, lust, eroticism	104
色紙	shikishi	(type of calligraphy paper)	180
	irogami	colored paper	
金色	kin'iro, kinshoku, konjiki	gold color	23

205

白

4c1.3
日 ｜
/42 2
白

HAKU, BYAKU, shiro(i), shiro, [shira] – white

白紙	hakushi	white/blank paper	180
白書	hakusho	a white paper (on), report	131
白人	hakujin	a white, Caucasian	1
自白	jihaku	confession, admission	62
空白	kūhaku	a blank; vacuum	140

206

黒

4d7.2
火 日 土
/44 42 22
黒

KOKU, kuro(i), kuro – black

黒人	kokujin	a black, Negro	1
黒白	kuroshiro	black and/or white; right and wrong	205
黒字	kuroji	(in the) black, black figures	110
黒子	kuroko	black-clad kabuki stagehand	103
黒海	Kokkai	the Black Sea	117

207

赤

3b4.10
土 儿
/22 16
赤

SEKI, [SHAKU], aka(i), aka – red **aka(ramu)** – become red, blush
aka(rameru) – make red, blush

赤十字	Sekijūji	Red Cross	12, 110
赤道	sekidō	equator	149
赤字	akaji	deficit, red figures, (in the) red	110
赤ちゃん	akachan	baby	

208

青

4b4.10
月 土 一
/43 22 1
青

SEI, [SHŌ], ao(i), ao – blue, green; unripe

青年	seinen	young man/people	45
青少年	seishōnen	young people, youth	144, 45
青空	aozora	blue sky	140
青空市場	aozora ichiba	open-air market	140, 181, 154
青物	aomono	green vegetables	79

209

情

4k8.9
心 月 土
/51 43 22
情

JŌ, [SEI], nasa(ke) – emotion, sympathy

人情	ninjō	human feelings, humanity	1
同情	dōjō	sympathy	198
無情	mujō	heartlessness, callousness	93
事情	jijō	circumstances, situation	80
実情	jitsujō	actual situation, the facts	203

210

的

4c4.12
日 ク ｜
/42 15 2
的

TEKI – (attributive suffix); target **mato** – target

目的	mokuteki	purpose, aim, goal	55
一時的	ichijiteki	temporary	2, 42
民主的	minshuteki	democratic	177, 155
理想的	risōteki	ideal	143, 147
自発的	jihatsuteki	voluntary, spontaneous	62, 96

211

約

6a3.7

糸 宀 丶
/61 15 2

約

YAKU – approximately; promise

公約	*kōyaku* public commitment	126
口約	*kōyaku* verbal promise	54
約三キロ	*yaku san kiro* approximately 3 km/kg	4
約半分	*yaku hanbun* approximately half	88, 38
先約	*sen'yaku* previous engagement	50

212

弓

3h0.1

弓
/28

弓

KYŪ, yumi – bow (for archery/violin)

弓術	*kyūjutsu* (Japanese) archery	187
弓道	*kyūdō* (Japanese) archery	149

213

矢

0a5.19

大 宀
34 15

矢

SHI, ya – arrow

弓矢	*yumiya* bow and arrow	212

214

知

3d5.14

口 大 宀
/24 34 15

知

CHI, shi(ru) – know

通知	*tsūchi* a notification, communication	150
周知	*shūchi* common knowledge, generally known	91
知事	*chiji* governor (of a prefecture)	80
知人	*chijin* an acquaintance	1
知り合い	*shiriai* an acquaintance	159

215

短

3d9.27

口 大 宀
/24 34 15

短

TAN, mijika(i) – short

長短	*chōtan* (relative) length; good and bad points	95
短刀	*tantō* short sword, dagger	37
短気	*tanki* short temper, touchiness, hastiness	134
短所	*tansho* defect, shortcoming	153
短大	*tandai* junior college (short for *tanki daigaku*)	26

216

引

3h1.1

弓 丨
/28 2

引

IN, hi(ku) – pull, attract **hi(keru)** – be ended; make cheaper

引力	*inryoku* attraction, gravitation	100
引用	*in'yō* quotation, citation	107
引き出し	*hikidashi* drawer	53
取り引き	*torihiki* transaction, trade	65
引き上げ	*hikiage* raise, increase	32

217

強

3h8.3

弓 虫 ム
/28 64 17

強

KYŌ, GŌ, tsuyo(i) – strong **tsuyo(maru)** – become strong(er)
tsuyo(meru) – make strong(er), strengthen **shi(iru)** – force

強力	*kyōryoku* strength, power	100
強国	*kyōkoku* strong country, great power	40
強情	*gōjō* stubbornness, obstinacy	209
強引に	*gōin ni* by force	216

弱	**218** 3h7.2 弓 冫 /28 5 弱	**JAKU, yowa(i)** – weak(er) **yowa(ru), yowa(maru)** – become weak(er) **yowa(meru)** – make weak(er), weaken

強弱　　*kyōjaku*　strengths and weaknesses, strength　217
弱点　　*jakuten*　a weakness, weak point　169
弱体　　*jakutai*　weak　61
弱気　　*yowaki*　faintheartedness; bearishness　134

独	**219** 3g6.1 犭 虫 /27 64 独　獨	**DOKU** – alone; (short for) Germany **hito(ri)** – alone

独立　　*dokuritsu*　independence　121
独身　　*dokushin*　unmarried, single　59
独学　　*dokugaku*　study on one's own, self-instruction　109
日独　　*Nichi-Doku*　Japan and Germany, Japanese-German　5
和独　　*Wa-Doku*　Japanese-German (dictionary)　124

医	**220** 2t5.2 匚 大 ㄷ /20 34 15 医　醫	**I** – medicine, healing

医学　　*igaku*　medicine　109
医学部　　*igakubu*　medical department/school　109, 86
医学用語　　*igaku yōgo*　medical term　109, 107, 67
医者　　*isha*　physician, doctor　164
女医　　*joi*　woman physician, lady doctor　102

族	**221** 4h7.3 方 大 ㄷ /48 34 15 族	**ZOKU** – family, tribe

家族　　*kazoku*　family　165
親族　　*shinzoku*　relative, kin　175
一族　　*ichizoku*　one's whole family, kin　2
部族　　*buzoku*　tribe　86
民族学　　*minzokugaku*　ethnology　177, 109

旅	**222** 4h6.4 方 ㇐ 亻 /48 15 3 旅	**RYO, tabi** – trip, travel

旅行　　*ryokō*　trip, travel　68
旅行者　　*ryokōsha*　traveler, tourist　68, 164
旅先　　*tabisaki*　destination　50
旅立つ　　*tabidatsu*　start on a journey　121

肉	**223** 2a4.20 亻 冂 /3 20 肉	**NIKU** – meat, flesh; personal-seal inkpad

肉屋　　*nikuya*　butcher (shop)　167
肉体　　*nikutai*　the body, the flesh　61
肉親　　*nikushin*　blood relationship/relative　175
肉付きのよい　　*nikuzuki no yoi*　well-fleshed, plump　192
肉筆　　*nikuhitsu*　one's own handwriting; autograph　130

米	**224** 6b0.1 米 /62 米	**BEI** – rice; (short for) America **MAI, kome** – rice

白米　　*hakumai*　polished rice　205
新米　　*shinmai*　new rice; novice　174
外米　　*gaimai*　imported rice　83
日米　　*Nichi-Bei*　Japan and America, Japanese-U.S.　5
南米　　*Nanbei*　South America　74

225	**SŪ, [SU], kazu** – number **kazo(eru)** – count	
4i9.1	数字	*sūji* digit, numeral, figures	110
攵 米 女 /49 62 25	数学	*sūgaku* mathematics	109
	人数	*ninzū* number of people	1
数 數	無数	*musū* countless, innumerable	93
	手数	*tesū* trouble, bother	57

226	**RUI, tagu(i)** – kind, type, genus	
9a9.1	親類	*shinrui* relative, kin	175
頁 米 六 /76 62 34	人類	*jinrui* mankind	1
	書類	*shorui* papers, documents	131
類	分類	*bunrui* classification	38
	類語	*ruigo* synonym	67

227	**JŪ, CHŌ, omo(i)** – heavy **kasa(naru)** – lie on top of one another **kasa(neru)** – pile on top of one another **-e** – -fold, -ply	
0a9.18	体重	*taijū* body weight	61
車 一 丨 69 1 2	重力	*jūryoku* gravity, gravitation	100
	重大	*jūdai* weighty, grave, important	26
重	二重	*nijū, futae* double, twofold	3

228	**SHU** – kind, type; species **tane** – seed; cause	
5d9.1	種類	*shurui* kind, type, sort	226
禾 車 一 /56 69 1	一種	*isshu* kind, sort	2
	人種	*jinshu* a human race	1
種	種子	*shushi* seed, pit	103
	不安の種	*fuan no tane* cause of unease	94, 105

229	**TA, ō(i)** – much, many, numerous	
0a6.5	多少	*tashō* much or little, many or few; some	144
夕 30	多数	*tasū* large number (of); majority	225
	大多数	*daitasū* the overwhelming majority	26, 225
多 彡	多元的	*tagenteki* pluralistic	137, 210
	数多く	*kazuōku* many, great number (of)	225

230	**HIN** – refinement; article **shina** – goods; quality	
3d6.15	上品	*jōhin* refined, elegant, graceful	32
口 /24	下品	*gehin* unrefined, gross, vulgar	31
	品質	*hinshitsu* quality	176
品	部品	*buhin* (spare/machine) parts	86
	品物	*shinamono* merchandise	79

231	**DŌ** – motion **ugo(ku)** – (intr.) move **ugo(kasu)** – (tr.) move	
2g9.1	自動車	*jidōsha* automobile, car	62, 133
力 車 丨 /8 69 2	動物	*dōbutsu* animal	79
	動力	*dōryoku* (motive) power	100
動	行動	*kōdō* action	68
	動員	*dōin* mobilize	163

	232	**DŌ, hatara(ku)** – work
	2a11.1 ⽥	実働時間　*jitsudō jikan*　actual working hours　203, 42, 43
	イ 車 力	働き　*hataraki*　work; functioning; ability
	/3　69　8	働き口　*hatarakiguchi*　job, position　54
	働 仂	働き者　*hatarakimono*　hard worker　164
		働き手　*hatarakite*　breadwinner　57

	233	**RŌ** – labor, toil
	3n4.3 ⽬	労働　*rōdō*　work, labor　232
	⺌ ⼍ 力	労働者　*rōdōsha*　worker, laborer　232, 164
	/35　20　8	労働時間　*rōdō jikan*　working hours　232, 42, 43
	労 勞	労力　*rōryoku*　trouble, effort; labor　100
		心労　*shinrō*　worry, concern　97

	234	**KYŌ** – cooperation
	2k6.1 ⽥	協力　*kyōryoku*　cooperation　100
	⼗ 力	協力者　*kyōryokusha*　collaborator, coworker　100, 164
	/12　8	協同　*kyōdō*　cooperation, collaboration, partnership　198
	協	協会　*kyōkai*　society, association 「Society 158
		日米協会　*Nichi-Bei Kyōkai*　the America-Japan　5, 224, 158

	235	**MU, tsuto(meru)** – work, serve **tsuto(maru)** – be fit/competent for
	4i7.6 ⽥	事務所　*jimusho*　office　80, 153
	夂 ⼄ 力	公務員　*kōmuin*　government employee　126, 163
	/49　14　8	国務　*kokumu*　affairs of state　40
	務	外務省　*Gaimushō*　Ministry of Foreign Affairs　83, 145

	236	**YA, no** – field, plain
	0a11.5 ⽥	野生　*yasei*　wild (animal/plant)　44
	⽇ ⼟ ⼀	平野　*heiya*　a plain　202
	42　22　14	*Hirano*　(surname)
	野 埜	分野　*bun'ya*　field (of endeavor)　38
		野原　*nohara*　field, plain　136

	237	**KATSU** – life, activity
	3a6.16 ⽥	生活　*seikatsu*　life　44
	⺡ ⼝ ⼂	活発　*kappatsu*　active, lively　96
	/21　24　12	活動　*katsudō*　activity　231
	活	活用　*katsuyō*　practical use; conjugate, inflect　107
		活字　*katsuji*　printing/movable type　110

	238	**WA, hanashi** – conversation, story **hana(su)** – speak
	7a6.8 ⽥	会話　*kaiwa*　conversation　158
	⾔ ⼝ ⼂	電話　*denwa*　telephone　108
	/67　24　12	立ち話　*tachibanashi*　chat while standing　121
	話	話し手　*hanashite*　speaker　57
		話し合う　*hanashiau*　talk over　159

売	**239** 3p4.3 目 士 冂 儿 /22 20 16 売 賣	**BAI, u(ru)** – sell **u(reru)** – be sold

売店　*baiten*　stand, newsstand, kiosk　168
売り子　*uriko*　store salesclerk　103
売り手　*urite*　seller　57
売り切れ　*urikire*　sold out　39
小売り　*kouri*　retailing, retail　27

貝	**240** 7b0.1 □ 貝 /68 貝	**kai** – shellfish

貝類　*kairui*　shellfish (plural)　226
ほら貝　*horagai*　trumpet shell, conch
貝ボタン　*kaibotan*　shell button

買	**241** 5g7.2 罒 貝 /55 68 買	**BAI, ka(u)** – buy

売買　*baibai*　buying and selling, trade, dealing　239
買い物　*kaimono*　shopping, purchase　79
買い手　*kaite*　buyer　57
買い主　*kainushi*　buyer　155
買い入れる　*kaiireru*　purchase, stock up on　52

糸	**242** 6a0.1 □ 糸 /61 糸 絲	**SHI, ito** – thread

一糸まとわぬ　*isshi matowanu*　stark naked　2
糸口　*itoguchi*　end of a thread; beginning; clue　54
糸車　*itoguruma*　spinning wheel　133
糸目　*itome*　a fine thread　55

続	**243** 6a7.5 田 糸 土 冂 /61 22 20 続 續	**ZOKU, tsuzu(ku)** – (intr.) continue **tsuzu(keru)** – (tr.) continue

続出　*zokushutsu*　appear one after another　53
続行　*zokkō*　continuation　68
相続　*sozoku*　succession; inheritance　146
手続き　*tetsuzuki*　procedures, formalities　57
引き続いて　*hikitsuzuite*　continuously, uninterruptedly　216

読	**244** 7a7.9 田 言 土 冂 /67 22 20 読 讀	**DOKU, TOKU, [TŌ], yo(mu)** – read

読者　*dokusha*　reader　164
読書　*dokusho*　reading　131
読本　*tokuhon*　reader, book of readings　25
読み物　*yomimono*　reading matter　79
読み方　*yomikata*　reading, pronunciation (of a word)　70

教	**245** 4i6.1 □ 攵 土 子 /49 22 6 教	**KYŌ, oshi(eru)** – teach **oso(waru)** – be taught, learn

教室　*kyōshitsu*　classroom　166
教員　*kyōin*　teacher, instructor; teaching staff　163
教会　*kyōkai*　church　158
回教　*kaikyō*　Islam, Mohammedanism　90
教え方　*oshiekata*　teaching method　70

育	**246**	**IKU, soda(tsu)** – grow up **soda(teru), haguku(mu)** – raise
	2j6.4 ▤	教育　kyōiku　education　245
	亠 月 厶	体育　taiiku　physical education　61
	/11 43 17	発育　hatsuiku　growth, development　96
	育 毓	生育　seiiku　growth, development　44
		育ての親　sodate no oya　foster/adoptive parent　175

流	**247**	**RYŪ** – a current, style, school (of thought) **[RU], naga(reru)** – flow **naga(su)** – pour
	3a7.10 ⊞	流通　ryūtsū　circulation, distribution, ventilation　150
	氵 亠 厶	海流　kairyū　ocean current　117
	/21 11 17	流行　ryūkō　fashion, fad, popularity　68
	流	一流　ichiryū　first class　2

早	**248**	**SŌ, [SA'], haya(i)** – early, fast **haya(maru)** – be hasty **haya(meru)** – hasten
	4c2.1 ▤	早々　sōsō　early, immediately
	日 十	早目に　hayame ni　a little early (leaving leeway)　55
	/42 12	早耳　hayamimi　quick-eared, in the know　56
	早	手早い　tebayai　quick, nimble, agile　57

草	**249**	**SŌ, kusa** – grass, plants
	3k6.13 ▤	草原　sōgen　grassy plain, grasslands　136
	艹 日 十	草木　sōmoku, kusaki　plants and trees, vegetation　22
	/32 42 12	草本　sōhon　herb　25
	草	草書　sōsho　(cursive script form of kanji)　131
		草案　sōan　(rough) draft　106

芝	**250**	**shiba** – lawn, grass
	3k2.1 ▤	芝生　shibafu　lawn　44
	艹 一 丨	芝草　shibakusa　lawn　249
	/32 1 2	人工芝　jinkō shiba　artificial turf　1, 139
	芝	芝居　shibai　stage play, theater　171
		芝居小屋　shibai-goya　playhouse, theater　171, 27, 167

茶	**251**	**CHA, SA** – tea
	3k6.19 ▤	茶色　chairo　brown　204
	艹 木 亻	茶畑　chabatake　tea plantation　36
	/32 41 3	茶室　chashitsu　tea-ceremony room　166
	茶	茶の間　cha no ma　living room　43
		茶道　chadō, sadō　tea ceremony　149

世	**252**	**SEI, SE, yo** – world, era
	0a5.37 …	二世　nisei　second generation　3
	艹 一 丨	中世　chūsei　Middle Ages　28
	32 1 2	世間　seken　the world, public, people　43
	世 丗	出世　shusse　success in life, getting ahead　53
		世話　sewa　taking care of, looking after　238

	253	**YŌ, ha** – leaf, foliage
	3k9.21	葉書　*hagaki*　postcard　131
	艹　木　一	青葉　*aoba*　green foliage　208
	/32　41　1	言葉　*kotoba*　word; language　66
		木の葉　*ko no ha*　tree leaves, foliage　22
	葉	千葉県　*Chiba-ken*　Chiba Prefecture (east of Tōkyō)　15, 194

	254	**KA, KE, ba(keru)** – turn oneself (into) **ba(kasu)** – bewitch
	2a2.6	文化　*bunka*　culture　111
	亻　匕	化学　*kagaku*　chemistry　109
	/3　13	強化　*kyōka*　strengthening　217
		合理化　*gōrika*　rationalization, streamlining　159, 143
	化	化け物　*bakemono*　spook, ghost, monster　79

	255	**KA, hana** – flower, blossom
	3k4.7	草花　*kusabana*　flower, flowering plant　249
	艹　亻　匕	生け花　*ikebana*　flower arranging　44
	/32　3　13	花屋　*hanaya*　flower shop, florist　167
		花見　*hanami*　viewing cherry blossoms　63
	花	花火　*hanabi*　fireworks　20

	256	**DAI** – generation; age; price **TAI, ka(waru)** – represent
	2a3.3	**ka(eru)** – replace **yo** – generation **shiro** – price; substitute; margin
	亻　戈	時代　*jidai*　era, period　42
	/3　52	古代　*kodai*　ancient times, antiquity　172
		世代　*sedai*　generation　252
	代	代理　*dairi*　representation; agent　143

	257	**HEN, ka(waru)** – (intr.) change **ka(eru)** – (tr.) change
	2j7.3	変化　*henka*　change, alteration　254
	亠　夂　几	変動　*hendō*　change, fluctuation　231
	/11　49　16	変種　*henshu*　variety, strain　228
		変人　*henjin*　an eccentric　1
	変　變	不変　*fuhen*　immutability, constancy　94

	258	**REN, koi** – (romantic) love **ko(u)** – be in love **koi(shii)** – dear, fond, long for
	2j8.2	
	亠　心　几	恋人　*koibito*　boyfriend, girlfriend, lover　1
	/11　51　16	恋文　*koibumi*　love letter　111
		恋心　*koigokoro*　(awakening of) love　97
	恋　戀	道ならぬ恋　*michi naranu koi*　forbidden love　149

	259	**AI** – love
	4i10.1	恋愛　*ren'ai*　love　258
	夂　心　小	愛情　*aijō*　love　209
	/49　51　35	愛国心　*aikokushin*　patriotic sentiment, patriotism　40, 97
		愛読　*aidoku*　like to read　244
	愛	愛想　*aisō*　amiability, sociability　147

受	**260**	**JU, u(keru)** – receive, take (an exam) **u(karu)** – pass (an exam)	
	2h6.2	受理　*juri*　acceptance	143
	又 小 冂	受動　*judō*　passive	231
	/9 35 20	受け身　*ukemi*　passivity; passive (in grammar)	59
		受け取る　*uketoru*　receive, accept, take	65
	受	受(け)付(け)　*uketsuke*　receptionist, reception desk	192

成	**261**	**SEI, [JŌ], na(ru)** – become, consist (of) **na(su)** – do, form	
	4n2.1	成長　*seichō*　growth	95
	戈 ノ	成年　*seinen*　(age of) majority, adulthood	45
	/52 15	成立　*seiritsu*　establishment, founding	121
		平成　*Heisei*　Heisei (Japanese era, 1989 –)	202
	成	成り行き　*nariyuki*　course (of events), development	68

感	**262**	**KAN** – feeling, sensation	
	4k9.21	五感　*gokan*　the five senses	7
	心 戈 口	感心　*kanshin*　admire	97
	/51 52 24	感想　*kansō*　one's thoughts, impressions	147
		感情　*kanjō*　feelings, emotion	209
	感	感受性　*kanjusei*　sensibility, sensitivity	260, 98

最	**263**	**SAI, motto(mo)** – highest, most	
	4c8.10	最後　*saigo*　end; last	48
	日 耳 又	最新　*saishin*　newest, latest	174
	/42 65 9	最大　*saidai*　maximum, greatest, largest	26
		最高　*saikō*　maximum, highest, best	190
	最	最上　*saijō*　best, highest	32

友	**264**	**YŪ, tomo** – friend	
	2h2.3	友人　*yūjin*　friend	1
	又 十	学友　*gakuyū*　fellow student, classmate; alumnus	109
	/9 12	親友　*shin'yū*　close friend	175
		友好　*yūkō*　friendship	104
	友	友情　*yūjō*　friendliness, friendship	209

有	**265**	**YŪ, U, a(ru)** – be, exist, have	
	4b2.3	国有　*kokuyū*　state-owned	40
	月 十	私有　*shiyū*　privately-owned	125
	/43 12	所有　*shoyū*　possession, ownership	153
		有名　*yūmei*　famous	82
	有	有力　*yūryoku*　influential, powerful	100

号	**266**	**GŌ** – number; pseudonym	
	3d2.10	番号　*bangō*　(identification) number	185
	口 丂	三号室　*sangōshitsu*　Room No. 3	4, 166
	/24 14	年号　*nengō*　name/year of a reign era	45
		信号　*shingō*　signal	157
	号 號	号外　*gōgai*　an extra (edition of a newspaper)	83

別	**267** 2f5.3 刂 口 宀 /16 24 15 別	**BETSU** – different, separate, another, special **waka(reru)** – diverge, part, bid farewell
		別人 *betsujin* different person 1
		別居 *bekkyo* (legal) separation; live separately 171
		区別 *kubetsu* difference, distinction 183
		分別 *funbetsu* discretion, good judgment 38

在	**268** 3b3.8 土 一 丨 /22 12 2 在	**ZAI** – outskirts, country; be located **a(ru)** – be, exist
		所在地 *shozaichi* (prefectural) capital; (county) seat; 153, 118
		在日 *zainichi* (stationed) in Japan ⌐location 5
		在外 *zaigai* overseas, abroad 83
		不在 *fuzai* absence 94

存	**269** 2c3.1 子 一 丨 /6 12 2 存	**SON, ZON** – exist; know, believe
		存在 *sonzai* existence 268
		生存 *seizon* existence, life 44
		存続 *sonzoku* continuance, duration 243
		共存 *kyōson* coexistence 196
		存分に *zonbun ni* as much as one likes, freely 38

麦	**270** 4i4.2 夂 土 一 /49 22 1 麦 麥	**BAKU, mugi** – wheat, barley, rye, oats
		小麦 *komugi* wheat 27
		大麦 *ōmugi* barley 26
		麦畑 *mugibatake* wheat field 36
		麦わら *mugiwara* (wheat) straw
		麦茶 *mugicha* wheat tea, barley water 251

素	**271** 6a4.12 糸 土 一 /61 22 1 素	**SO** – element, beginning **SU** – naked, uncovered, simple
		素質 *soshitsu* nature, makeup 176
		質素 *shisso* simple, plain 176
		元素 *genso* chemical element 137
		水素 *suiso* hydrogen 21
		素人 *shirōto* amateur, layman 1

表	**272** 0a8.6 衤 二 57 4 表	**HYŌ** – table, chart; surface; expression **omote** – surface, obverse **arawa(reru)** – be expressed **arawa(su)** – express
		時間表 *jikanhyō* timetable, schedule 42, 43
		代表的 *daihyōteki* representative, typical 256, 210
		表情 *hyōjō* facial expression 209
		発表 *happyō* announcement, publication 96

裏	**273** 2j11.2 亠 衤 日 /11 57 42 裏 裡	**RI, ura** – reverse side, back, rear
		表裏 *hyōri* inside and outside; double-dealing 272
		裏口 *uraguchi* back door, rear entrance 54
		裏道 *uramichi* back street; secret path 149
		裏付け *urazuke* backing, support; corroboration 192
		裏切る *uragiru* betray, double-cross 39

面

正

頭

顔

産

業

犬

274		
3s6.1	日	
口 一 儿		
/24 14 16		
面		

MEN – face, mask, surface, aspect **omote, omo, tsura** – face

方面	hōmen	direction, side	70
表面	hyōmen	surface, exterior	272
面会	menkai	interview, meeting	158
面目	menmoku, menboku	face, honor, dignity	55

275		
2m3.3	...	
一 一 丨		
38 1 2		
正		

SEI, SHŌ, tada(shii) – correct, just **tada(su)** – correct
masa (ni) – just, exactly, certainly

校正	kōsei	proofreading	115
不正	fusei	injustice	94
正面	shōmen	front, front side	274
正月	shōgatsu	January; New Year	17

276		
9a7.6	田	
頁 口 儿		
/76 24 16		
頭		

TŌ, [TO], ZU, atama, kashira – head, leader, top

後頭（部）	kōtō(bu)	back of the head	48, 86
出頭	shuttō	appearance, attendance, presence	53
先頭	sentō	(in the) front, lead	50
口頭	kōtō	oral, verbal	54
頭上	zujō	overhead	32

277		
9a9.3	田	
頁 立 彡		
/76 54 31		
顔 顔		

GAN, kao – face

顔面	ganmen	face	274
顔色	kaoiro	complexion; a look	204
素顔	sugao	face without makeup	271
新顔	shingao	stranger; newcomer	174
知らん顔	shirankao	pretend not to notice, ignore	214

278		
5b6.4	日	
立 土 厂		
/54 22 15		
産		

SAN – childbirth; production; property **u(mu)** – give birth/rise to
u(mareru) – be born **ubu** – birth; infant

出産	shussan	childbirth, delivery	53
生産	seisan	production	44
産物	sanbutsu	product	79
不動産	fudōsan	immovable property, real estate	94, 231

279		
0a13.3	日	
丷 王 一		
/16 46 1		
業		

GYŌ – occupation, business, undertaking **GŌ** – karma **waza** – act,
deed, work, art

工業	kōgyō	industry	139
産業	sangyō	industry	278
事業	jigyō	undertaking, enterprise	80
実業家	jitsugyōka	businessman, industrialist	203, 165

280		
3g0.1	□	
犭		
/27		
犬		

KEN, inu – dog

番犬	banken	watchdog	185
愛犬	aiken	pet/favorite dog	259
野犬	yaken	stray dog	236
小犬	koinu	puppy	27
犬小屋	inugoya	doghouse	27, 167

牛	**281** 4g0.1 ☐ 牛 /47 牛	**GYŪ, ushi** – cow, bull, cattle	
		牛肉 *gyūniku* beef	223
		野牛 *yagyū* buffalo, bison	236
		水牛 *suigyū* water buffalo	21
		子牛 *koushi* calf	103
		牛小屋 *ushigoya* cowshed, barn	27, 167

特	**282** 4g6.1 ☐ 牛 土 寸 /47 22 37 特	**TOKU** – special	
		特別 *tokubetsu* special	267
		特色 *tokushoku* distinguishing characteristic	204
		特有 *tokuyū* characteristic, peculiar (to)	265
		独特 *dokutoku* peculiar, original, unique	219
		特長 *tokuchō* strong point, forte	95

馬	**283** 10a0.1 ☐ 馬 /78 馬	**BA, uma, [ma]** – horse	
		馬車 *basha* horse-drawn carriage	133
		馬力 *bariki* horsepower	100
		馬術 *bajutsu* horseback riding, dressage	187
		竹馬 *takeuma, chikuba* stilts	129
		馬小屋 *umagoya* a stable	27, 167

駅	**284** 10a4.4 ☐ 馬 尸 丶 /78 40 2 駅 驛	**EKI** – (train) station	
		東京駅 *Tōkyō-eki* Tōkyō Station	71, 189
		当駅 *tōeki* this station	77
		駅前 *ekimae* (in) front of/opposite the station	47
		駅長 *ekichō* stationmaster	95
		駅員 *ekiin* station employee	163

鳥	**285** 11b0.1 ☐ 鳥 /80 鳥	**CHŌ, tori** – bird	
		白鳥 *hakuchō* swan	205
		野鳥 *yachō* wild bird	236
		花鳥 *kachō* flowers and birds	255
		一石二鳥 *isseki-nichō* killing 2 birds with 1 stone	2, 78, 3
		鳥居 *torii* torii, Shintō shrine archway	171

島	**286** 3o7.9 屮 尸 一 /36 40 1 島 嶋	**TŌ, shima** – island	
		半島 *hantō* peninsula	88
		島民 *tōmin* islander	177
		無人島 *mujintō* uninhabited island	93, 1
		島国 *shimaguni* island country	40
		島々 *shimajima* (many) islands	

毛	**287** 0a4.33 … 十 一 丨 12 1 2 毛	**MŌ, ke** – hair, fur, feather, down	
		原毛 *genmō* raw wool	136
		毛筆 *mōhitsu* brush (for writing/painting)	130
		体毛 *taimō* body hair	61
		不毛 *fumō* barren, unproductive	94
		毛糸 *keito* wool yarn, knitting wool	242

羊	**288** 2o4.1 ⊟ 丷 王 /16 46 羊	**YŌ, hitsuji** – sheep

羊毛　　yōmō　　wool　　　　　　　　　　　　287
羊肉　　yōniku　　mutton　　　　　　　　　　223
小/子羊　kohitsuji　lamb　　　　　　　　　　27, 103

洋	**289** 3a6.19 ⊞ 氵 王 儿 /21 46 16 洋	**YŌ** – ocean; foreign, Western

大洋　　taiyō　　ocean　　　　　　　　　　　26
東洋　　tōyō　　the East, Orient　　　　　　71
西洋　　seiyō　　the West, Occident　　　　72
大西洋　Taiseiyō　Atlantic Ocean　　　　26, 72
洋書　　yōsho　　foreign/Western book　　131

魚	**290** 11a0.1 ☐ 魚 /79 魚	**GYO, sakana, uo** – fish

魚類　　gyorui　　a variety of fish　　　　　226
金魚　　kingyo　　goldfish　　　　　　　　23
魚肉　　gyoniku　　fish (meat)　　　　　　223
魚市場　uoichiba　fish market　　　　181, 154
魚屋　　sakanaya　fish shop/dealer　　　　167

義	**291** 2o11.3 ⊟ 丷 王 戈 /16 46 52 義	**GI** – justice, honor; meaning; in-law; artificial

民主主義　minshu shugi　democracy　　177, 155, 155
義務　　gimu　　obligation, duty　　　　　235
義理　　giri　　duty, debt of gratitude　　143
同義語　dōgigo　synonym　　　　　　198, 67
類義語　ruigigo　word of similar meaning, synonym　226, 67

議	**292** 7a13.4 ⊞ 言 王 戈 /67 46 52 議	**GI** – deliberation; proposal

会議　　kaigi　　conference, meeting　　　158
協議　　kyōgi　　council, conference　　　234
議会　　gikai　　parliament, diet, congress　158
議員　　giin　　M.P., dietman, congressman　163
不思議　fushigi　marvel, wonder, mystery　94, 99

論	**293** 7a8.13 ⊞ 言 艹 亻 /67 32 3 論	**RON** – discussion; argument, thesis, dissertation

論理　　ronri　　logic　　　　　　　　　　143
理論　　riron　　theory　　　　　　　　　143
世論　　yoron, seron　public opinion　　　252
論議　　rongi　　discussion, argument　　292
論文　　ronbun　thesis, essay　　　　　　111

王	**294** 4f0.1 ☐ 王 /46 王	**Ō** – king

王国　　ōkoku　　kingdom　　　　　　　　40
国王　　kokuō　king　　　　　　　　　　40
女王　　joō　　queen　　　　　　　　　102
王子　　ōji　　prince　　　　　　　　　103
法王　　hōō　　pope　　　　　　　　　123

	295	**GYOKU, tama** – gem, jewel; sphere, ball	
玉	4f0.2 … 王 丶 /46 2 玉	玉石 *gyokuseki* wheat and chaff, good and bad 玉子 *tamago* egg (cf. No. 1058) 水玉 *mizutama* drop of water 目玉 *medama* eyeball 十円玉 *jūendama* 10-yen piece/coin	78 103 21 55 12, 13
宝	296 3m5.2 宀 王 丶 /33 46 2 宝 寶	**HŌ, takara** – treasure 宝石 *hōseki* precious stone, gem 宝玉 *hōgyoku* precious stone, gem 国宝 *kokuhō* national treasure 家宝 *kahō* family heirloom 宝物 *hōmotsu, takaramono* treasure, prized possession	 78 295 40 165 79
皇	297 4f5.9 王 日 丨 /46 42 2 皇	**KŌ, Ō** – emperor 天皇 *tennō* emperor 皇女 *kōjo* imperial princess 皇居 *kōkyo* imperial palace 皇室 *kōshitsu* imperial household 皇位 *kōi* imperial throne	 141 102 171 166 122
現	298 4f7.3 王 貝 /46 68 現	**GEN** – present *arawa(reru)* – appear *arawa(su)* – show 現代 *gendai* contemporary, modern 現在 *genzai* current, present; present tense 現金 *genkin* cash 表現 *hyōgen* an expression 実現 *jitsugen* realize, attain; come true	 256 268 23 272 203
線	299 6a9.7 糸 白 氵 /61 42 21 線	**SEN** – line; track; route; wire, cable 光線 *kōsen* light, light ray 内線 *naisen* (telephone) extension 無線 *musen* wireless, radio 二番線 *nibansen* Track No. 2 地平線 *chiheisen* horizon	 138 84 93 3, 185 118, 202
単	300 3n6.2 ⑫ 日 十 /35 42 12 単 單	**TAN** – single, simple; mono- 単語 *tango* word 単位 *tan'i* unit, denomination 単一 *tan'itsu* single, simple, individual 単数 *tansū* singular (in grammar) 単独 *tandoku* independent, single-handed	 67 122 2 225 219
戦	301 4n9.2 戈 日 小 /52 42 35 戦 戰	**SEN, ikusa** – war, battle *tataka(u)* – wage war, fight 内戦 *naisen* civil war 交戦 *kōsen* war, warfare 合戦 *kassen* battle; contest 休戦 *kyūsen* truce, cease-fire 戦後 *sengo* postwar	 84 114 159 60 48

302

争

2n4.2
ノ フ ヨ ｜
/15 39 2

争 爭

SŌ, araso(u) – dispute, argue, contend for

戦争	sensō	war	301
争議	sōgi	dispute, strife	292
論争	ronsō	dispute, controversy	293
争点	sōten	point of contention, issue	169
言い争う	iiarasou	quarrel, argue	66

303

急

2n7.2
ノ 心 ヨ
/15 51 39

急

KYŪ – urgent, sudden **iso(gu)** – be in a hurry

急行	kyūkō	rush, hurry, hasten; express (train, bus)	68
特急	tokkyū	limited express (train); (at) super speed	282
急変	kyūhen	sudden change	257
急用	kyūyō	urgent business	107
急性	kyūsei	acute	98

304

悪

4k7.17
心 エ 口
/51 38 24

悪 惡

AKU, O, waru(i) – bad, evil

悪化	akka	change for the worse	254
悪性	akusei	malignant, vicious	98
悪事	akuji	evil deed	80
最悪	saiaku	the worst, at worst	263
悪口	akkō, warukuchi	abusive language, speaking ill of	54

305

末

0a5.26
木 一
41 1

末

MATSU, BATSU, sue – end

週末	shūmatsu	weekend	92
月末	getsumatsu	end of the month	17
年末	nenmatsu	year's end	45
末代	matsudai	all ages to come, eternity	256
末っ子	suekko	youngest child	103

306

未

0a5.27
木 一
41 1

未

MI – not yet

未来	mirai	future	69
未知	michi	unknown	214
前代未聞	zendai mimon	unprecedented	47, 256, 64
未満	miman	less than, under	201
未明	mimei	early dawn, before daybreak	18

307

味

3d5.3
口 木 一
/24 41 1

味

MI, aji – taste **aji(wau)** – taste, relish, appreciate

意味	imi	meaning, significance, sense	132
正味	shōmi	net (amount/weight/price)	275
不気味	bukimi	uncanny, eerie, ominous	94, 134
地味	jimi	plain, subdued, undemonstrative	118
三味線	shamisen	samisen (3-stringed instrument)	4, 299

308

社

4e3.1
ネ 土
/45 22

社

SHA – Shinto shrine; company; firm **yashiro** – Shinto shrine

社会	shakai	society, social	158
会社	kaisha	company, firm	158
本社	honsha	our company; head office	25
社長	shachō	company president	95
社員	shain	employee, staff member	163

申	**309** 0a5.39 … 日 丨 42　2 申	**SHIN, mō(su)** – say, be named	
		答申　tōshin　report, findings	160
		上申　jōshin　report (to a superior)	32
		内申　naishin　unofficial/confidential report	84
		申し入れ　mōshiire　offer, proposal, notice	52
		申し合わせ　mōshiawase　an understanding	159

神	**310** 4e5.1 ▯ ネ 日 丨 /45　42　2 神	**SHIN, JIN, kami, [kan], [kō]** – god, God	
		神道　shintō　Shintoism	149
		神社　jinja　Shinto shrine	308
		神話　shinwa　myth, mythology	238
		神父　shinpu　(Catholic) priest, Father	113
		神風　kamikaze　divine wind; kamikaze	29

失	**311** 0a5.28 … 大 ノ 34　15 失	**SHITSU, ushina(u)** – lose	
		失業　shitsugyō　unemployment	279
		失意　shitsui　disappointment, despair	132
		失神　shisshin　faint, lose consciousness	310
		失恋　shitsuren　unrequited love	258
		見失う　miushinau　lose sight of	63

鉄	**312** 8a5.6 金 大 ノ /72　34　15 鉄｜鐵	**TETSU** – iron	
		鉄道　tetsudō　railroad	149
		地下鉄　chikatetsu　subway	118, 31
		私鉄　shitetsu　private railway	125
		鉄かぶと　tetsukabuto　steel helmet	

銀	**313** 8a6.3 ▯ 金 食 /72　/71 銀	**GIN** – silver	
		銀行　ginkō　bank	68
		日銀　Nichigin　the Bank of Japan	5
		銀色　gin'iro　silver color	204
		水銀　suigin　mercury	21
		銀メダル　ginmedaru　silver medal	

根	**314** 4a6.5 木 食 /41　77 根	**KON** – root; perseverance **ne** – root, base, origin	
		大根　daikon　daikon, Japanese radish	26
		根本的　konponteki　fundamental; radical	25, 210
		根気　konki　patience, perseverance	134
		屋根　yane　roof	167
		根強い　nezuyoi　deep-rooted, firmly established	217

夫	**315** 0a4.31 … 大 一 34　1 夫	**FU, [FŪ], otto** – husband	
		夫人　fujin　wife, Mrs.	1
		人夫　ninpu　laborer	1
		水夫　suifu　sailor, seaman	21
		工夫　kōfu　laborer	139
		kufū　contrivance	

婦	**316**	**FU** – woman, wife		
	3e8.6 田	夫婦	*fūfu*	husband and wife, married couple	315
	女 ヨ 巾 /25 39 26	主婦	*shufu*	housewife	155
		婦人	*fujin*	lady, woman	1
	婦	婦女(子)	*fujo(shi)*	woman	102, 103
		婦長	*fuchō*	head nurse	95

帰	**317**	**KI, kae(ru)** – return **kae(su)** – let return, dismiss		
	2f8.8 田	帰国	*kikoku*	return to one's country	40
	リ ヨ 巾 /16 39 26	帰宅	*kitaku*	return/come/get home	178
		帰路	*kiro*	the way home	151
	帰 歸	帰化	*kika*	become naturalized	254
		日帰り	*higaeri*	go and return in a day	5

支	**318**	**SHI** – branch; support **sasa(eru)** – support		
	2k2.1	支出	*shishutsu*	expenditure, disbursement	53
	十 又 /12 9	支社	*shisha*	branch (office)	308
		支店	*shiten*	branch office/store	168
	支	支部	*shibu*	branch, local chapter	86
		支流	*shiryū*	tributary (of a river)	247

料	**319**	**RYŌ** – materials; fee		
	6b4.4	料理	*ryōri*	cooking, cuisine; dish, food	143
	米 十 丶 /62 12 2	原料	*genryō*	raw materials	136
		料金	*ryōkin*	fee, charge, fare	23
	料	手数料	*tesūryō*	fee; commission	57, 225
		有/無料	*yū/muryō*	pay, toll, charging a fee / free	265, 93

科	**320**	**KA** – academic course, department, faculty		
	5d4.3	科学	*kagaku*	science	109
	禾 十 丶 /56 12 2	理科	*rika*	natural sciences (department)	143
		外科	*geka*	surgery	83
	科	産婦人科医	*sanfujinkai*	gynecologist	278, 316, 1, 220
		教科書	*kyōkasho*	textbook, schoolbook	245, 131

良	**321**	**RYŌ, yo(i)** – good		
	0a7.3	良好	*ryōkō*	good, favorable, satisfactory	104
	食 77	良質	*ryōshitsu*	good quality	176
		最良	*sairyō*	best	263
	良	不良	*furyō*	bad, unsatisfactory; delinquency	94
		良心	*ryōshin*	conscience	97

食	**322**	**SHOKU, [JIKI]** – food, eating **ta(beru), ku(u), ku(rau)** – eat		
	8b0.1	食事	*shokuji*	meal, dinner	80
	食 /77	食料品	*shokuryōhin*	food, foodstuffs	319, 230
		和/洋食	*wa/yōshoku*	Japanese/Western food	124, 289
	食	夕食	*yūshoku*	evening meal, supper	81
		食べ物	*tabemono*	food	79

	323	**IN, no(mu)** – drink	
飲	8b4.1	飲食 *inshoku* food and drink, eating and drinking	322
	食 夂	飲料 *inryō* drink, beverage	319
	/77 49	飲料水 *inryōsui* drinking water	319, 21
	飲 飲	飲み水 *nomimizu* drinking water	21
		飲み物 *nomimono* (something to) drink, beverage	79

	324	**HAN, [HON]** – anti- **[TAN]** – (unit of land/cloth measurement)	
反	2p2.2	**so(ru)** – (intr.) warp, bend back **so(rasu)** – (tr.) warp, bend back	
	厂 又	反発 *hanpatsu* repulsion, repellence; opposition	96
	/18 9	反日 *han-Nichi* anti-Japanese	5
	反	反面 *hanmen* the other side	274
		反省 *hansei* reflection, introspection; reconsideration	145

	325	**HAN, meshi** – cooked rice; meal, food	
飯	8b4.5	ご飯 *gohan* cooked rice; meal, food	
	食 厂 又	赤飯 *sekihan* (festive) rice boiled with red beans	207
	/77 18 9	夕飯 *yūhan, yūmeshi* evening meal, supper, dinner	81
	飯	麦飯 *mugimeshi* boiled barley and rice	270
		飯田 *Iida* (surname)	35

	326	**KAN** – government, authorities	
官	3m5.6	半官半民 *hankan-hanmin* semigovernmental	88, 88, 177
	宀 尸 冂	国務長官 *kokumu chōkan* secretary of state	40, 235, 95
	/33 40 20	外交官 *gaikōkan* diplomat	83, 114
	官	高官 *kōkan* high government official/ office	190
		神官 *shinkan* Shintō priest	310

	327	**KAN, yakata** – (large) building, hall	
館	8b8.3	旅館 *ryokan* Japanese-style inn	222
	食 宀 尸	水族館 *suizokukan* aquarium	21, 221
	/77 33 40	会館 *kaikan* (assembly) hall	158
	館 舘	本館 *honkan* main building	25
		別館 *bekkan* annex, extension	267

	328	**KAN** – pipe, wind instrument; control **kuda** – pipe, tube	
管	6f8.12	管内 *kannai* (area of) jurisdiction	84
	竹 宀 尸	管理 *kanri* administration, supervision	143
	/66 33 40	水道管 *suidōkan* water pipe/conduit	21, 149
	管	気管 *kikan* wind pipe, trachea	134
		鉄管 *tekkan* iron tube/pipe	312

	329	**RI** – advantage, (loan) interest **ki(ku)** – take effect, work	
利	5d2.1	有利 *yūri* profitable, advantageous	265
	禾 刂	利子 *rishi* interest (on a loan)	103
	/56 16	利用 *riyō* make use of	107
	利	利口 *rikō* smart, clever, bright	54
		左利き *hidarikiki* left-hander	75

便	**330** 2a7.5 ⬚ 亻 日 一 /3 42 14 便	**BEN** – convenience; excrement **BIN** – opportunity; mail **tayo(ri)** – news, tidings

	便利	benri	convenient, handy	329
	不便	fuben	inconvenient	94
	便所	benjo	toilet	153
	別便	betsubin	separate mail	267

使	**331** 2a6.2 ⬚ 亻 口 十 /3 24 12 使	**SHI** – use; messenger **tsuka(u)** – use

	大使	taishi	ambassador	26
	公使	kōshi	minister, envoy	126
	天使	tenshi	angel	141
	使用法	shiyōhō	how to use, directions for use	107, 123
	使い方	tsukaikata	how to use, way to handle	70

史	**332** 0a5.38 ⋯ 口 十 24 12 史	**SHI** – history, chronicles

	日本史	Nihon shi	Japanese history	5, 25
	中世史	chūsei shi	medieval history	28, 252
	文学史	bungaku shi	history of literature	111, 109
	史実	shijitsu	historical fact	203
	女史	joshi	(honorific) Madame, Miss, Mrs.	102

仕	**333** 2a3.2 ⬚ 亻 士 /3 22 仕	**SHI, [JI], tsuka(eru)** – serve

	仕事	shigoto	work, job	80
	仕立て屋	shitateya	tailor; dressmaker	121, 167
	仕方	shikata	way, method, means	70
	仕手	shite	protagonist, leading role (in Noh)	57
	仕上げる	shiageru	finish up, complete	32

任	**334** 2a4.9 ⬚ 亻 王 /3 46 任	**NIN** – duty, responsibility; office **maka(seru/su)** – entrust (to)

	主任	shunin	person in charge, manager, head	155
	信任	shinnin	confidence, trust	157
	後任	kōnin	successsor	48
	任務	ninmu	duty, office, mission	235
	任意	nin'i	optional, voluntary	132

権	**335** 4a11.18 ⬚ 木 催 冖 /41 73 15 権 權	**KEN, [GON]** – authority, power, right

	権利	kenri	a right	329
	人権	jinken	human rights	1
	特権	tokken	special right, privilege	282
	主権	shuken	sovereignty	155
	三権分立	sanken bunritsu	seperation of powers	4, 38, 121

極	**336** 4a8.11 ⬚ 木 口 一 /41 24 14 極	**KYOKU** – end, pole **GOKU** – very, extremely **kiwa(mi)** – height, end **kiwa(meru)** – carry to its end **kiwa(maru)** – reach its end

	極東	kyokutō	the Far East	71
	北/南極	hok/nankyoku	north/south pole	73, 74
	見極める	mikiwameru	see through, discern	63

337

句

3d2.13
日 ⼇
/24 15

句

KU – phrase, sentence, verse

語句	*goku*	words and phrases	67
成句	*seiku*	set phrase, idiom	261
文句	*monku*	words, expression; objection	111
句読点	*kutōten*	punctuation mark	244, 169
引用句	*in'yōku*	quotation	216, 107

338

旬

4c2.5
日 ⼇
/42 15

旬

JUN – 10-day period **SHUN** – the season (for vegetables/oysters)

上旬	*jōjun*	first 10 days of a month (1st to 10th)	32
中旬	*chūjun*	second 10 days of a month (11th to 20th)	28
下旬	*gejun*	last third of a month (21st to end)	31

339

図

3s4.3
口 ⼗ 丶
/24 12 2

図 圖

ZU – drawing, diagram, plan **TO, haka(ru)** – plan

地図	*chizu*	map	118
図表	*zuhyō*	chart, table, graph	272
合図	*aizu*	signal, sign, gesture	159
意図	*ito*	intention	132
図書館	*toshokan*	library	131, 327

340

計

7a2.1
言 ⼗
/67 12

計

KEI – measuring, plan, total **haka(ru)** – measure, compute **haka(rau)** – arrange, manage, see to

時計	*tokei*	clock, watch	42
会計	*kaikei*	accounting; paying a bill	158
合計	*gōkei*	total	159
家計	*kakei*	household finances	165

341

針

8a2.3
金 ⼗
/72 12

針

SHIN, hari – needle

方針	*hōshin*	course, line, policy	70
針路	*shinro*	course (of a ship)	151
長/分針	*chō/funshin*	minute hand	95, 38
短針	*tanshin*	hour hand	215
針金	*harigane*	wire	23

342

調

7a8.16
言 月 口
/67 43 24

調

CHŌ, shira(beru) – investigate, check **totono(eru)** – prepare, arrange, put in order **totono(u)** – be prepared, arranged

協調	*kyōchō*	cooperation, harmony	234
好調	*kōchō*	good, favorable	104
調子	*chōshi*	tone; mood; condition	103
取り調べ	*torishirabe*	investigation, questioning	65

343

画

0a8.7
日 ⼀ 冂
42 14 20

画 畫

GA – picture **KAKU** – stroke (in writing kanji)

画家	*gaka*	painter	165
日本/洋画	*Nihon/yōga*	J./Western-style painting	5, 25, 289
画用紙	*gayōshi*	drawing paper	107, 180
画面	*gamen*	(TV/computer/movie) screen	274
計画	*keikaku*	plan, project	340

演	**344**	***EN*** – performance, play, presentation	
	3a11.13 ⊞	上演 *jōen* performance, dramatic presentation	32
	氵日 宀	公演 *kōen* public performance	126
	/21 42 33	独演 *dokuen* solo performance	219
		出演 *shutsuen* appearance, performance	53
	演	演出 *enshutsu* production, staging (of a play)	53

絵	**345**	***KAI, E*** – picture	
	6a6.8 ⊞	絵画 *kaiga* pictures, paintings, drawings	343
	糸 亻 二	絵葉書 *ehagaki* picture postcard	253, 131
	/61 3 4	絵本 *ehon* picture book	25
		口絵 *kuchie* frontispiece	54
	絵 繪	大和絵 *Yamato-e* ancient Japanese-style painting	26, 124

給	**346**	***KYŪ*** – supply; salary	
	6a6.7 ⊞	給料 *kyūryō* pay, wages, salary	319
	糸 口 亻	月給 *gekkyū* monthly salary	17
	/61 24 3	支給 *shikyū* supply, provisioning, allowance	318
		供給 *kyōkyū* supply	197
	給	給水 *kyūsui* water supply	21

音	**347**	***ON, IN, oto, ne*** – sound	
	5b4.3 ⊟	発音 *hatsuon* pronunciation	96
	立 日	表音文字 *hyōon moji* phonetic symbol	272, 111, 110
	/54 42	母音 *boin* vowel	112
		本音 *honne* one's true intention	25
	音	足音 *ashioto* sound of footsteps	58

暗	**348**	***AN, kura(i)*** – dark, dim	
	4c9.2 ⊞	暗黒 *ankoku* darkness	206
	日 立	暗号 *angō* (secret) code, cipher	266
	/42 54	明暗 *meian* light and darkness, shading	18
		暗がり *kuragari* darkness	
	暗		

闇	**349**	***yami*** – darkness; black market	
	8e9.5 ▢	暗闇 *kurayami* darkness	348
	門 立 日	夕闇 *yūyami* dusk, twilight	81
	/75 54 42	闇雲に *yamikumo ni* at random, haphazardly	646
		闇市 *yamiichi* black market	181
	闇	闇取引 *yamitorihiki* black-market dealings, illegal 「transaction	65, 216

韻	**350**	***IN*** – rhyme; sound; elegant	
	7b12.2 ⊞	音韻学 *on'ingaku* phonology	347, 109
	貝 立 日	韻文 *inbun* verse, poetry	111
	/68 54 42	韻語 *ingo* rhyming words	67
		頭韻 *tōin* alliteration	276
	韻 韵		

351

損

3c10.12

扌 貝 口
/23 68 24

損

SON – loss, damage **soko(nau), soko(neru)** – harm, injure
-soko(nau) – fail to, err in

損失	sonshitsu	loss	311
大損	ōzon	great loss	26
見損なう	misokonau	miss (seeing); misjudge	63
読み損なう	yomisokonau	misread	244

352

央

0a5.33

大 冂
34 20

央

Ō – center, middle

中央	chūō	center	28
中央口	chūōguchi	main/middle exit	28, 54
中央部	chūōbu	central part, middle	28, 86
中央線	Chūō-sen	the Chūō (train) Line	28, 299
中央区	Chūō-ku	Chūō Ward (Tōkyō)	28, 183

353

映

4c5.1

日 大 冂
/42 34 20

映 暎

EI, utsu(su) – reflect, project **utsu(ru)** – be reflected/projected
ha(eru) – shine, be brilliant

映画	eiga	movie	343
反映	han'ei	reflection	324
上映	jōei	showing, screening (of a movie)	32
夕映え	yūbae	the glow of sunset	81

354

英

3k5.5

艹 大 冂
/32 34 20

英

EI – brilliant, talented, gifted; (short for) England

英気	eiki	energetic spirit, enthusiasm	134
石英	sekiei	quartz	78
英語	Eigo	the English language	67
和英	Wa-Ei	Japanese-English	124
英会話	Ei-kaiwa	English conversation	158, 238

355

題

9a9.7

頁 日 宀
/76 42 14

題

DAI – topic, theme, title

問題	mondai	problem, question	162
議題	gidai	topic for discussion, agenda	292
話題	wadai	topic	238
表題	hyōdai	title, caption	272
宿題	shukudai	homework	179

356

定

3m5.8

宀 疋 亻
/33 14 3

定

TEI, JŌ, sada(meru) – determine, decide **sada(maru)** – be
determined/decided **sada(ka)** – certain, definite

安定	antei	stability, equilibrium	105
協定	kyōtei	agreement, pact	234
定食	teishoku	meal of fixed menu, complete meal	322
未定	mitei	undecided, unsettled, not yet fixed	306

357

決

3a4.6

氵 大 一
/21 34 1

決 決

KETSU, ki(meru) – decide **ki(maru)** – be decided

決定	kettei	decision, determination	356
決心	kesshin	determination, resolution	97
決意	ketsui	determination, resolution	132
議決	giketsu	decision (of a committee)	292
未決	miketsu	pending	306

注	**358**	***CHŪ*** – note, comment ***soso(gu)*** – pour, flow	
	3a5.16	注意 *chūi* attention, caution, warning	132
	氵 王 丶	注目 *chūmoku* attention, notice	55
	/21 46 2	注文 *chūmon* order, commission	111
	注	発注 *hatchū* ordering	96
		注入 *chūnyū* injection; pour into, infuse	52

楽	**359**	***GAKU*** – music ***RAKU*** – pleasure ***tano(shimu)*** – enjoy ***tano(shii)*** – fun, enjoyable, pleasant	
	4a9.29	音楽 *ongaku* music	347
	木 日 冫	文楽 *bunraku* Japanese puppet theater	111
	/41 42 5	楽天家 *rakutenka* optimist	141, 165
	楽 樂	安楽死 *anrakushi* euthanasia	105, 85

薬	**360**	***YAKU, kusuri*** – medicine	
	3k13.15	薬学 *yakugaku* pharmacy	109
	艹 木 日	薬品 *yakuhin* medicine, drugs	230
	/32 41 42	薬味 *yakumi* spices	307
	薬 藥	薬局 *yakkyoku* pharmacy	170
		薬屋 *kusuriya* drugstore, pharmacy	167

作	**361**	***SAKU, SA, tsuku(ru)*** – make	
	2a5.10	作家 *sakka* writer	165
	亻 亠 卜	作品 *sakuhin* literary work	230
	/3 15 13	作戦 *sakusen* military operation, tactics	301
	作	作り話 *tsukuribanashi* made-up story, fabrication	238
		手作り *tezukuri* handmade	57

昨	**362**	***SAKU*** – past; yesterday	
	4c5.3	昨年 *sakunen* last year	45
	日 亠 卜	昨日 *sakujitsu, kinō* yesterday	5
	/42 15 13	一昨日 *issakujitsu* day before yesterday	2, 5
	昨	一昨年 *issakunen* year before last	2, 45
		昨今 *sakkon* these days, recent	51

段	**363**	***DAN*** – step, stairs, rank; column	
	2s7.2	一段 *ichidan* step; single-stage	2
	几 又 厂	石段 *ishidan* stone stairway	78
	/20 9 18	段々畑 *dandanbatake* terraced fields	36
	段	手段 *shudan* means, measure	57
		段取り *dandori* program, plan, arrangements, setup	65

由	**364**	***YU, YŪ, [YUI], yoshi*** – reason, cause, significance	
	0a5.35	由来 *yurai* origin, derivation	69
	日 丨	理由 *riyū* reason, grounds	143
	42 2	自由 *jiyū* freedom	62
	由	不自由 *fujiyū* disabled, impaired; want, privation	94, 62
		事由 *jiyū* reason, cause	80

油

365
3a5.6
氵 日 丨
/21 42 2
油

YU, abura – oil

石油	sekiyu	oil, petroleum	78
原油	gen'yu	crude oil	136
油田	yuden	oil field	35
給油所	kyūyusho, kyūyujo	filling/gas station	346, 153
油絵	aburae	oil painting	345

対

366
2j5.5
亠 寸 十
/11 37 12
対 對

TAI – against **TSUI** – pair

反対	hantai	opposite; opposition	324
対立	tairitsu	confrontation	121
対決	taiketsu	showdown	357
対面	taimen	interview, meeting	274
対話	taiwa	conversation, dialog; interactive	238

曲

367
0a6.27
日 儿
42 16
曲

KYOKU – curve; melody, musical composition **ma(geru)** – bend, distort **ma(garu)** – (intr.) bend, turn

作曲	sakkyoku	musical composition	361
名曲	meikyoku	famous/well-known melody	82
曲線	kyokusen	a curve	299
曲がり道	magarimichi	winding street	149

典

368
2o6.5
ソ 八 冂
/16 32 20
典

TEN – law code, rule; ceremony

古典	koten	classical literature, the classics	172
百科事典	hyakka jiten	encyclopedia	14, 320, 80
法典	hōten	code of laws	123
出典	shutten	literary source, authority	53
特典	tokuten	special favor, privilege	282

興

369
2o14.2
ソ 口 厂
/16 24 18
興

KŌ, KYŌ – interest, entertainment, prosperity **oko(ru)** – flourish, prosper **oko(su)** – revive, retrieve

興行	kōgyō	entertainment, industry; performance	68
興業	kōgyō	industrial enterprise	279
興味	kyōmi	interest	307
興信所	kōshinjo	private inquiry/detective agency	157, 153

農

370
2p11.1
厂 衤 日
/18 57 42
農

NŌ – agriculture

農業	nōgyō	agriculture	279
農村	nōson	farm village	191
農民	nōmin	farmer, peasant	177
農家	nōka	farmhouse, farm household; farmer	165
農産物	nōsanbutsu	agricultural product	278, 79

己

371
0a3.12
弓
28
己

KO, KI, onore – self

自己	jiko	self-	62
自己中心	jiko chūshin	egocentric	62, 28, 97
利己	riko	selfishness, egoism	329
利己的	rikoteki	selfish, self-centered	329, 210
知己	chiki	acquaintance	214

372

記

7a3.5
言 弓
/67 28

記

KI, shiru(su) – write/note down

記者	kisha	newspaperman, journalist	164
記事	kiji	article, report	80
日記	nikki	diary	5
暗記	anki	memorize	348
記号	kigō	mark, symbol	266

373

紀

6a3.5
糸 弓
/61 28

紀

KI – narrative, history

紀元	kigen	era (of year reckoning)	137
紀元前／後	kigenzen/go	B.C./A.D.	137, 47, 48
世紀	seiki	century	252
紀行（文）	kikō(bun)	account of a journey	68, 111
風紀	fūki	discipline, public morals	29

374

起

3b7.11
土 弓 ⼘
/22 28 13

起

KI – awakening, rise, beginning **o(kiru)** – get/wake/be up
o(koru) – occur **o(kosu)** – give rise to; wake (someone) up

起原	kigen	origin, beginning	136
起点	kiten	starting point	169
早起き	hayaoki	get up early	248
起き上がる	okiagaru	get up, pick oneself up	32

375

得

3i8.4
彳 日 寸
/29 42 37

得

TOKU – profit, advantage **e(ru), u(ru)** – gain, acquire

損得	sontoku	profit and loss	351
所得	shotoku	income	153
得点	tokuten	one's score, points made	169
得意	tokui	prosperity; pride; one's strong point	132
心得る	kokoroeru	know, understand	97

376

役

3i4.2
彳 冂 又
/29 20 9

役

YAKU – service, use, office; post **EKI** – battle; service

役所	yakusho	government office/bureau	153
役人	yakunin	public official	1
役員	yakuin	(company) officer, director	163
役者	yakusha	player, actor	164
使役	shieki	employment, service	331

377

船

6c5.4
舟 口 几
/63 24 16

船 舩

SEN, fune, [funa] – ship

船長	senchō	captain	95
船員	sen'in	crewman, seaman, sailor	163
船室	senshitsu	cabin	166
汽船	kisen	steamship, steamer	135
船旅	funatabi	sea voyage	222

378

度

3q6.1
广 廿 又
/18 32 9

度

DO, [TAKU], [TO] – degree, measure, limit; times **tabi** – times

一度	ichido	once; 1 degree (temperature; angle)	2
今度	kondo	this time; soon; next time	51
年度	nendo	business/fiscal year	45
高度成長	kōdo seichō	high growth	190, 261, 95
支度	shitaku	preparations	318

渡	**379**	**TO, wata(ru)** – cross **wata(su)** – hand over	
	3a9.35	渡来 *torai* introduction (into)	69
	氵 艹 厂	渡し船 *watashibune* ferryboat	377
	/21 32 18	渡り鳥 *wataridori* migratory bird	285
		見渡す *miwatasu* look out over	63
	渡	手渡す *tewatasu* hand deliver, hand over	57

席	**380**	**SEKI** – seat, place	
	3q7.4	出席 *shusseki* attendance	53
	广 艹 巾	満席 *manseki* full, fully occupied	201
	/18 32 26	議席 *giseki* seat (in parliament)	292
		主席 *shuseki* top seat, head, chief	155
	席	席上 *sekijō* (at) the meeting; (on) the occasion	32

病	**381**	**BYŌ, [HEI], ya(mu)** – fall ill, suffer from **yamai** – illness	
	5i5.3	病気 *byōki* sickness, disease	134
	疒 一 冂	重病 *jūbyō* serious illness	227
	/60 14 20	急病 *kyūbyō* sudden illness	303
		性病 *seibyō* venereal disease, sexually transmitted disease	98
	病	病人 *byōnin* sick person	1

憶	**382**	**OKU** – remember, think	
	4k13.5	記憶 *kioku* memory, recollection	372
	心 立 日	憶病 *okubyō* cowardice, timidity	381
	/51 54 42		
	憶		

億	**383**	**OKU** – 100 million	
	2a13.6	一億 *ichioku* 100 million	2
	亻 立 日	億万長者 *okuman chōja* multimillionaire	16, 95, 164
	/3 54 42	数億年 *sūokunen* hundreds of millions of years	225, 45
	億		

欠	**384**	**KETSU, ka(ku)** – lack **ka(keru)** – be lacking	
	4j0.1	欠点 *ketten* defect, flaw	169
	欠	出欠 *shukketsu* attendance (and/or absence)	53
	/49	欠席 *kesseki* absence, nonattendance	380
		欠員 *ketsuin* vacant position, opening	163
	欠 缺	欠損 *kesson* deficit, loss	351

次	**385**	**JI, SHI, tsugi** – next **tsu(gu)** – come/rank next	
	2b4.1	次官 *jikan* vice-minister	326
	冫 欠	次男 *jinan* second-oldest son	101
	/5 49	二次 *niji* second, secondary	3
		目次 *mokuji* table of contents	55
	次	相次ぐ *aitsugu* follow/happen one after another	146

	386	**SHOKU** – employment, job, occupation, office
職	6e12.1 田 耳 日 戈 /65 42 52 職	職業 *shokugyō* occupation, profession 279 職場 *shokuba* place of work, jobsite 154 職員 *shokuin* personnel, staff, staff member 163 現職 *genshoku* one's present post 298 無職 *mushoku* unemployed 93
能	387 4b6.15 田 月 厶 ヒ /43 17 13 能	**NŌ** – ability, function; Noh play 能力 *nōryoku* capacity, talent 100 本能 *honnō* instinct 25 能筆 *nōhitsu* calligraphy, skilled penmanship 130 能楽 *nōgaku* Noh play 359 能面 *nōmen* Noh mask 274
態	388 4k10.14 田 心 月 厶 /51 43 17 態	**TAI** – condition, appearance 態度 *taido* attitude 378 生態 *seitai* mode of life, ecology 44 変態 *hentai* metamorphosis; abnormality 257 事態 *jitai* situation, state of affairs 80 実態 *jittai* actual conditions/situation 203
熊	389 4d10.6 田 月 火 厶 /43 44 17 熊	**kuma** – bear 北極熊 *hokkyokuguma* polar bear 73, 336 熊手 *kumade* rake 57 大熊座 *ōkuma-za* Great Bear, Ursa Major 26, 800 小熊座 *koguma-za* Little Bear, Ursa Minor 27, 800 熊本県 *Kumamoto-ken* Kumamoto Prefecture 25, 194
可	390 3d2.12 ⋯ 口 一 /24 14 可	**KA** – possible, -able 可能(性) *kanō(sei)* possibility 387, 98 不可能 *fukanō* impossible 94, 387 不可欠 *fukaketsu* indispensable, essential 94, 384 不可分 *fukabun* indivisible 94, 38 可決 *kaketsu* approval (of a proposed law) 357
河	391 3a5.30 田 氵 口 一 /21 24 14 河	**KA, kawa** – river 河川 *kasen* rivers 33 河口 *kakō, kawaguchi* mouth of a river 54 大河 *taiga, ōkawa* large river 26 銀河 *ginga* the Milky Way 313 河原 *kawara* dry riverbed 136
何	392 2a5.21 田 亻 口 一 /3 24 14 何	**KA, nani, [nan]** – what, which, how many 何事 *nanigoto* what, whatever 80 何曜日 *nan'yōbi* what day of the week 19, 5 何日 *nannichi* how many days; what day of the month 5 何時 *nanji* what time 42 何時間 *nanjikan* how many hours 42, 43

荷	**393** 3k7.10 艹 口 亻 /32 24 3 荷	***KA, ni*** – load, cargo, baggage 在荷 *zaika* stock, inventory 268 入荷 *nyūka* fresh supply/arrival of goods 52 出荷 *shukka* shipment, shipping 53 (手)荷物 *(te)nimotsu* (hand) baggage, luggage 57, 79 重荷 *omoni* heavy burden 227
苛	**394** 3k5.30 艹 口 亠 /32 24 14 苛	***KA*** – harsh 苛性 *kasei* caustic 98
歌	**395** 4j10.2 欠 口 亠 /49 24 14 歌 謌	***KA, uta*** – poem, song ***uta(u)*** – sing 歌手 *kashu* singer 57 国歌 *kokka* national anthem 40 和歌 *waka* 31-syllable Japanese poem 124 短歌 *tanka* (synonym for waka) 215 流行歌 *ryūkōka* popular song 247, 68
唄	**396** 3d7.1 口 貝 /24 68 唄	***uta*** – song 小唄 *kouta* ditty, ballad 27 長唄 *nagauta* song accompanied on the samisen 95 地唄 *jiuta* ballad, folk song 118 はやり唄 *hayariuta* pop song
予	**397** 0a4.12 亠 一 丶 14 1 2 予 豫	***YO*** – in advance, previously 予約 *yoyaku* subscription, reservation, booking 211 予定 *yotei* plan; expectation 356 予想 *yosō* expectation, supposition 147 予知 *yochi* foresee, predict 214 予言 *yogen* prophecy, prediction 66
預	**398** 9a4.5 頁 亠 一 /76 14 1 預	***YO, azu(keru)*** – entrust for safekeeping ***azu(karu)*** – receive for safekeeping 預金 *yokin* deposit, bank account 23 預かり所 *azukarisho/jo* depository, warehouse 153 手荷物一時預かり(所) *tenimotsu ichiji azukari(sho/jo)* (place for) temporary handbaggage storage 57, 393, 79, 2, 42, 153
形	**399** 3j4.1 彡 艹 一 /31 32 1 形	***KEI, GYŌ, katachi, kata*** – form, shape 円形 *enkei* round/circular shape 13 正方形 *seihōkei* square 275, 70 無形 *mukei* formless, immaterial, intangible 93 人形 *ningyō* doll, puppet 1 手形 *tegata* (bank) bill, note, draft 57

開	**400**	**KAI** – opening, development **a(ku)** – (intr.) open **a(keru)** – (tr.) open **hira(keru)** – become developed **hira(ku)** – (tr. or intr.) open
	8e4.6	
	門 艹 一 /75 32 1	公開 kōkai open to the public 126
		開会 kaikai opening of a meeting 158
	開	未開 mikai uncivilized, backward, savage 306
		開発 kaihatsu development 96

閉	**401**	**HEI, shi(meru), to(jiru), to(zasu)** – close, shut **shi(maru)** – become closed
	8e3.3	
	門 艹 丨 /75 12 2	開閉 kaihei opening and closing 400
		閉会 heikai closing, adjournment 158
	閉 閉	閉店 heiten store closing 168
		閉口 heikō be dumbfounded 54

関	**402**	**KAN, seki** – barrier **kaka(waru)** – be related (to), have to do (with)
	8e6.7	関門 kanmon gateway, barrier 161
	門 大 儿 /75 34 16	関心 kanshin interest 97
		関東（地方） Kantō (chihō) (region including Tōkyō) 71, 118, 70
	関 關	関西（地方） Kansai (chihō) (region including Ōsaka 72, 118, 70
		関所 sekisho barrier station, checkpoint ⌊and Kyōto) 153

税	**403**	**ZEI** – tax
	5d7.4	税金 zeikin tax 23
	禾 日 儿 /56 24 16	所得税 shotokuzei income tax 153, 375
		関税 kanzei customs, duty, tariff 402
	税	税関 zeikan customs, customshouse 402
		無税 muzei tax-free, duty-free 93

説	**404**	**SETSU** – opinion, theory **ZEI, to(ku)** – explain, persuade
	7a7.12	説明 setsumei explanation 18
	言 日 儿 /67 24 16	社説 shasetsu an editorial 308
		小説 shōsetsu novel, story 27
	説	演説 enzetsu a speech 344
		説教 sekkyō sermon 245

美	**405**	**BI, utsuku(shii)** – beautiful
	2o7.4	美術館 bijutsukan art museum/gallery 187, 327
	丷 王 大 /16 46 34	美学 bigaku esthetics 109
		美人 bijin beautiful woman 1
	美	美化 bika beautification 254
		美点 biten beauty, merit, good point 169

養	**406**	**YŌ, yashina(u)** – rear, adopt; support; recuperate
	2o13.1	養育 yōiku upbringing, nurture 246
	丷 食 王 /16 77 46	養成 yōsei training, cultivation 261
		教養 kyōyō culture, education 245
	養	養子 yōshi adopted child 103
		休養 kyūyō rest, recreation; recuperation 60

様	**407** 4a10.25 木 王 儿 /41 46 16 様 樣	**YŌ** – way, manner; similarity; condition **sama** – condition **-sama** – Mr./Mrs./Miss ... 様子　*yōsu*　situation, aspect, appearance　103 同様　*dōyō*　same; diversity, variety　198 神様　*kamisama*　God　310 田中明様　*Tanaka Akira sama*　Mr. Akira Tanaka　35, 28, 18
第	**408** 6f5.5 竹 弓 丨 /66 28 2 第	**DAI** – (prefix for ordinals); degree 第一　*dai-ichi*　No. 1; first, best, main　2 第三者　*daisansha*　third person/party　4, 164 次第　*shidai*　sequence; circumstances; as soon as　385 毎月第二土曜日　*maitsuki dai-ni doyōbi*　second 　　　　Saturday of every month　116, 17, 3, 24, 19, 5
弟	**409** 2o5.1 丷 弓 丨 /16 28 2 弟	**TEI, [DAI], [DE], otōto** – younger brother 義弟　*gitei*　younger brother-in-law　291 子弟　*shitei*　sons, children　103 弟子　*deshi*　pupil, apprentice, disciple　103 門弟　*montei*　pupil, follower　161 弟分　*otōtobun*　like a younger brother　38
兄	**410** 3d2.9 口 儿 /24 16 兄	**KEI, [KYŌ], ani** – elder brother 兄弟　*kyōdai*　brothers, brothers and sisters　409 父兄　*fukei*　parents and brothers; guardians　113 義兄　*gikei*　elder brother-in-law　291 実兄　*jikkei*　one's brother by blood　203 兄さん　*niisan*　elder brother
姉	**411** 3e5.8 女 巾 亠 /25 26 11 姉	**SHI, ane** – elder sister 義姉　*gishi*　elder sister-in-law　291 姉さん　*nēsan*　elder sister; young lady
妹	**412** 3e5.4 女 木 一 /25 41 1 妹	**MAI, imōto** – younger sister 姉妹　*shimai*　sisters　411 姉妹都市　*shimai toshi*　sister cities　411, 188, 181 弟妹　*teimai*　younger brothers and sisters　409 義妹　*gimai*　younger sister-in-law　291
昧	**413** 4c5.2 日 木 一 /42 41 1 昧	**MAI** – dark, unenlightened, ignorant 三昧　*sanmai, zanmai*　concentration, absorption　4

	414	**AI** – dark; not clear	
	4c13.1	曖昧 *aimai* vague, ambiguous, equivocal	413
	日 忝 女 /42 51 49		
	曖		

	415	**SHI** – teacher; army	
	3f7.2	教師 *kyōshi* teacher, instructor	245
	巾 尸 冂 /26 40 20	医師 *ishi* physician	220
		法師 *hōshi* Buddhist priest	123
	師	山師 *yamashi* speculator; adventurer; charlatan	34
		師弟 *shitei* master and pupil	409

	416	**DŌ, warabe** – child	
	5b7.3	学童 *gakudō* schoolchild	109
	立 日 土 /54 42 22	童話 *dōwa* nursery story, fairy tale	238
		童顔 *dōgan* childlike/boyish face	277
	童	童心 *dōshin* child's mind/feelings	97
		神童 *shindō* child prodigy	310

	417	**RYŌ** – quantity **haka(ru)** – (tr.) measure, weigh	
	4c8.9	大 / 小量 *tai/shōryō* large/small quantity	26, 27
	日 土 一 /42 22 1	雨量 *uryō* (amount of) rainfall	30
		大量生産 *tairyō seisan* mass production	26, 44, 278
	量	分量 *bunryō* quantity, amount; dosage	38
		重量 *jūryō* weight	227

	418	**SHŌ** – trade, merchant; quotient (in math) **akina(u)** – deal (in), trade	
	2j9.7	商人 *shōnin* merchant, dealer	1
	亠 日 儿 /11 24 16	商品 *shōhin* goods, merchandise	230
		商業 *shōgyō* commerce, business	279
	商	商売 *shōbai* trade, business; one's trade	239
		商工 *shōkō* commerce and industry	139

	419	**KA, su(giru)** – pass, exceed; too much **su(gosu)** – spend (time) **ayama(tsu)** – err **ayama(chi)** – error	
	2q9.18	過度 *kado* excessive, too much	378
	辶 日 冂 /19 24 20	通過 *tsūka* passage, transit	150
		過半数 *kahansū* majority, more than half	88, 225
	過	食べ過ぎる *tabesugiru* eat too much, overeat	322

	420	**KYO, KO, sa(ru)** – leave, move away; pass, elapse	
	3b2.2	去年 *kyonen* last year	45
	土 厶 /22 17	死去 *shikyo* death	85
		去来 *kyorai* coming and going	69
	去	過去 *kako* past	419
		立ち去る *tachisaru* leave, go away	121

	421	**TEKI** – fit, be suitable	
	2q11.3	適当 *tekitō* suitable, appropriate	77
	/19 24 11	適度 *tekido* to a proper degree, moderate	378
		適切 *tekisetsu* pertinent, appropriate	39
		適用 *tekiyō* application (of a rule)	107
	適	適合 *tekigō* conformity, compatibility	159

	422	**TEKI, kataki** – enemy, opponent, competitor	
	4i11.2	宿敵 *shukuteki* old/hereditary enemy	179
	/49 24 11	強敵 *kyōteki* powerful foe, formidable rival	217
		敵意 *tekii* enmity, hostility	132
		敵対 *tekitai* hostility, antagonism	366
	敵	不敵 *futeki* fearless, daring	94

	423	**TEI, hodo** – degree, extent	
	5d7.2	程度 *teido* degree, extent, grade	378
	/56 46 24	過程 *katei* a process	419
		工程 *kōtei* progress of the work; manufacturing process	139
		日程 *nittei* schedule for the day	5
	程	音程 *ontei* musical interval, step	347

	424	**SO, kumi** – group, crew, class, gang **ku(mu)** – put together	
	6a5.7	組成 *sosei* composition, makeup	261
	/61 43 1	番組 *bangumi* (TV) program	185
		労働組合 *rōdō kumiai* labor union	233, 232, 159
		組み立て *kumitate* construction; assembling	121
	組	組み合わせる *kumiawaseru* combine, fit together	159

	425	**YŌ** – main point, necessity **i(ru)** – need, be necessary **kaname** – pivot; main point	
	3e6.11	重要 *jūyō* important	227
	/25 24 14	主要 *shuyō* principal, major	155
		要素 *yōso* element, factor	271
	要	要約 *yōyaku* summary	211

	426	**GU** – tool, equipment, gear	
	5c3.1	具体的 *gutaiteki* concrete, specific	61, 210
	/55 16 1	道具 *dōgu* tool, implement	149
		家具 *kagu* furniture	165
		金具 *kanagu* metal fitting	23
	具 愚	不具 *fugu* deformity, crippled	94

	427	**KA, atai** – price, value	
	2a6.3	物価 *bukka* prices (of commodities)	79
	/3 24 14	米価 *beika* price of rice	224
		単価 *tanka* unit price	300
		定価 *teika* fixed/list price	356
	価 價	現金正価 *genkin seika* cash price	298, 23, 275

真	**428**	**SHIN** – truth, genuineness, reality **ma** – true, pure, exactly
	2k8.1 目	真実 *shinjitsu* the truth, a fact — 203
	十 目 儿	真理 *shinri* truth — 143
	/12 55 16	真相 *shinsō* the truth/facts, the real situation — 146
		真空 *shinkū* vacuum — 140
	真 眞	真っ暗 *makkura* pitch dark — 348

直	**429**	**CHOKU, JIKI** – honest, frank, direct **nao(su)** – fix, correct **nao(ru)** – be fixed, corrected **tada(chi ni)** – immediately
	2k6.2 目	直線 *chokusen* straight line — 299
	十 目 丨	直前／後 *chokuzen/go* immediately before/after — 47, 48
	/12 55 2	正直 *shōjiki* honest, upright — 275
	直	書き直す *kakinaosu* write over again, rewrite — 131

植	**430**	**SHOKU, u(eru)** – plant **u(waru)** – be planted
	4a8.32 田	植物 *shokubutsu* a plant — 79
	木 目 十	動植物 *dōshokubutsu* animals and plants — 231, 79
	/41 55 12	植民地 *shokuminchi* colony — 177, 118
		植木 *ueki* garden/potted plant — 22
	植	田植え *taue* rice planting — 35

値	**431**	**CHI, ne, atai** – value, price
	2a8.30	価値 *kachi* value — 427
	亻 目 十	値うち *neuchi* value; public estimation
	/3 55 12	値段 *nedan* price — 363
		値上げ *neage* price increase — 32
	値	値切る *negiru* haggle over the price, bargain — 39

置	**432**	**CHI, o(ku)** – put, set, leave behind, leave as is
	5g8.8 目	位置 *ichi* position, location — 122
	罒 十 丨	置き物 *okimono* ornament; figurehead — 79
	/55 12 2	物置き *monooki* storeroom, shed — 79
		前置き *maeoki* introductory remarks, preface — 47
	置	一日置き *ichinichioki* every other day — 2, 5

制	**433**	**SEI** – system; regulations
	2f6.1	制度 *seido* system — 378
	刂 牛 冂	税制 *zeisei* system of taxation — 403
	/16 47 20	新制 *shinsei* new order, reorganization — 174
		強制 *kyōsei* compulsion, force — 217
	制	管制 *kansei* control — 328

製	**434**	**SEI** – produce, manufacture, make
	5e8.9 目	製作 *seisaku* a work, production — 361
	衤 牛 冂	製品 *seihin* product — 230
	/57 47 20	製鉄 *seitetsu* iron manufacturing — 312
		木製 *mokusei* wooden, made of wood — 22
	製	日本製 *nihonsei* Japanese-made, Made in Japan — 5, 25

走	**435**	***SŌ, hashi(ru)* – run**	
	3b4.9 ⊟	走路 *sōro* (race) track, course	151
	土 ⼘ イ	走行時間 *sōkō jikan* travel time	68, 42, 43
	/22 13 3	走り回る *hashirimawaru* run around	90
	走 辵	走り書き *hashirigaki* flowing/hasty handwriting	131
		口走る *kuchibashiru* babble, blurt out	54

徒	**436**	***TO* – on foot; companions; vain, useless**	
	3i7.1 ⊞	生徒 *seito* pupil, student	44
	イ 土	教徒 *kyōto* believer, adherent	245
	/29 22 13	使徒 *shito* apostle	331
	徒	徒手 *toshu* empty-handed; penniless	57
		徒労 *torō* vain effort	233

歩	**437**	***HO, BU, [FU], aru(ku), ayu(mu)* – walk**	
	3n5.3 ⊟	歩道 *hodō* footpath	149
	⺌ ⼘ 亠	歩行者 *hokōsha* pedestrian	68, 164
	/35 13 11	一歩 *ippo* a step	2
	歩	歩調 *hochō* pace, step	342
		歩合 *buai* rate, percentage; commission	159

渉	**438**	***SHŌ* – go across, go through; have to do with**	
	3a8.20 ⊞	交渉 *kōshō* negotiations	114
	氵 ⼩ 亠		
	/21 35 13		
	渉		

転	**439**	***TEN, koro(bu), koro(garu), koro(geru)* – roll over, fall down**	
	7c4.3	***koro(gasu)* – roll, knock down**	
	車 二 ム	自転車 *jitensha* bicycle	62, 133
	/69 4 17	回転 *kaiten* rotation, revolution	90
	転 轉	空転 *kūten* idling (of an engine)	140
		転任 *tennin* transfer of assignments/personnel	334

伝	**440**	***DEN, tsuta(eru)* – transmit, impart *tsuta(waru)* – be transmitted,**	
	2a4.14 ⊞	**imparted *tsuta(u)* – go along**	
	イ 二 ム	伝記 *denki* biography	372
	/3 4 17	伝説 *densetsu* legend, folklore	404
	伝 傳	伝道 *dendō* evangelism, missionary work	149
		手伝い *tetsudai* help, helper	57

芸	**441**	***GEI* – art, craft**	
	3k4.12 ▤	芸者 *geisha* geisha	164
	⼗⼗ 二 ム	芸術 *geijutsu* art	187
	/32 4 17	文芸 *bungei* literary art, literature	111
	芸 藝	演芸 *engei* performance, entertainment	344
		民芸 *mingei* folkcraft	177

442

SHŪ, atsu(maru), tsudo(u) – (intr.) gather **atsu(meru)** – (tr.) gather

8c4.2			
隹 木			
/73 41			

集金	shūkin	bill collecting	23
集中	shūchū	concentration	28
全集	zenshū	the complete works	89
特集	tokushū	special edition	282
万葉集	Man'yōshū	(Japan's oldest anthology of poems)	16, 253

443

SHIN, susu(mu) – advance, progress **susu(meru)** – advance, promote

2q8.1	
辶 隹	
/19 73	

進歩	shinpo	progress, improvement	437
進行	shinkō	progress, onward movement	68
進学	shingaku	entrance to a higher school	109
前進	zenshin	advance, forward movement	47
先進国	senshinkoku	developed/advanced country	50, 40

444

GUN – army, troops; war

2i7.1	
冖 車	
/20 69	

軍人	gunjin	soldier, military man	1
軍事	gunji	military affairs, military	80
海軍	kaigun	navy	117
敵軍	tekigun	enemy army/troops	422
軍国主義	gunkoku shugi	militarism	40, 155, 291

445

UN – fate, luck **hako(bu)** – carry, transport

2q9.10	
辶 車 冂	
/19 69 20	

運転手	untenshu	driver, chauffeur	439, 57
(労働)運動	(rōdō) undō	(labor) movement	233, 232, 231
運動不足	undō-busoku	lack of exercise	231, 94, 58
運河	unga	canal	391
不運	fuun	misfortune	94

446

REN – group; accompaniment **tsu(reru)** – take (someone) along
tsura(naru) – stand in a row **tsura(neru)** – link, put in a row

2q7.2	
辶 車	
/19 69	

連続	renzoku	series, continuity	243
連合	rengō	combination, league, coalition	159
国連	Kokuren	UN, United Nations	40
家族連れ	kazokuzure	with the family	165, 221

447

SŌ, oku(ru) – send

2q6.9	
辶 大 儿	
/19 34 16	

運送	unsō	transport, shipment	445
回送	kaisō	forwarding	90
送金	sōkin	remittance	23
送別会	sōbetsukai	going-away/farewell party	267, 158
見送る	miokuru	see (someone) off; escort	63

448

HEN, kae(su) – (tr.) return **kae(ru)** – (intr.) return

2q4.5	
辶 厂 又	
/19 18 9	

返事	henji	reply	80
返信	henshin	reply (letter, email)	157
見返す	mikaesu	look back; triumph over (an old enemy)	63
読み返す	yomikaesu	reread	244
送り返す	okurikaesu	send back	447

坂	**449**	**HAN, saka** – slope, hill	
	3b4.7	急な坂　*kyū na saka*　steep slope/hill	303
	土 厂 又	坂道　*sakamichi*　road on a slope	149
	/22　18　9	上り坂　*noborizaka*　ascent; on the rise	32
	坂	下り坂　*kudarizaka*　descent; decline	31
		赤坂　*Akasaka*　(area of Tōkyō)	207

阪	**450**	**HAN** – slope; embankment	
	2d4.4	大阪　*Ōsaka*　Ōsaka	26
	阝 厂 又	京阪　*Kei-Han*　Kyōto-Ōsaka (area)	189
	/7　18　9	阪神　*Han-Shin*　Ōsaka-Kōbe (area)	310
	阪	京阪神　*Kei-Han-Shin*　Kyōto-Ōsaka-Kōbe (area)	189, 310

逆	**451**	**GYAKU** – reverse, inverse, opposite; treason **saka** – reverse, inverse **saka(rau)** – be contrary (to)	
	2q6.8	逆転　*gyakuten*　reversal	439
	辶 兀 丷	逆説　*gyakusetsu*　paradox	404
	/19　16　14	反逆　*hangyaku*　treason	324
	逆	逆立つ　*sakadatsu*　stand on end	121

近	**452**	**KIN, chika(i)** – near, close	
	2q4.3	近所　*kinjo*　vicinity, neighborhood	153
	辶 斤	付近　*fukIn*　vicinity, environs	192
	/19　50	最近　*saikin*　recent; most recent, latest	263
	近	近代　*kindai*　modern times, modern	256
		近道　*chikamichi*　shortcut, shorter way	149

遠	**453**	**EN, [ON], tō(i)** – far, distant	
	2q10.4	遠方　*enpō*　great distance, (in) the distance	70
	辶 衤 土	遠近法　*enkinhō*　(law of) perspective	452, 123
	/19　57　22	遠足　*ensoku*　excursion, outing	58
	遠	遠心力　*enshinryoku*　centrifugal force	97, 100
		遠回し　*tōmawashi*　indirect, roundabout	90

園	**454**	**EN, sono** – garden	
	3s10.1	公園　*kōen*　(public) park	126
	口 衤 土	動物園　*dōbutsuen*　zoo	231, 79
	/24　57　22	植物園　*shokubutsuen*　botanical garden	430, 79
	園 薗	学園　*gakuen*　educational institution, academy	109
		楽園　*rakuen*　paradise	359

達	**455**	**TATSU** – reach, arrive at	
	2q9.8	上達　*jōtatsu*　progress; proficiency	32
	辶 王 土	発達　*hattatsu*　development	96
	/19　46　22	達成　*tassei*　achieve, attain	261
	達 達	達人　*tatsujin*　expert, master	1
		友達　*tomodachi*　friend	264

期	**456** 4b8.11 田 月 艹 二 /43 32 4 期 碁	**KI, [GO]** – time, period, term

期間　kikan　period of time, term　　43
定期　teiki　fixed period　　356
過渡期　katoki　transition period　　419, 379
学期　gakki　semester, trimester, school term　　109
短期大学　tanki daigaku　junior college　　215, 26, 109

基	**457** 3b8.12 日 土 艹 二 /22 32 4 基	**KI, moto, motoi** – basis, foundation, origin

基本　kihon　basics, fundamentals; standard　　25
基金　kikin　fund, endowment　　23
基地　kichi　(military) base　　118
基石　kiseki　foundation stone, cornerstone　　78
基調　kichō　keynote　　342

持	**458** 3c6.8 田 扌 土 寸 /23 22 37 持	**JI, mo(tsu)** – have, possess, hold, maintain

支持　shiji　support　　318
持続　jizoku　continuance, maintenance　　243
持ち主　mochinushi　owner, possessor　　155
金持ち　kanemochi　rich person　　23
気持ち　kimochi　mood, feeling　　134

待	**459** 3i6.4 田 彳 土 寸 /29 22 37 待	**TAI, ma(tsu)** – wait for

期待　kitai　expectation, anticipation　　456
特待　tokutai　special treatment, distinction　　282
待ち合い室　machiaishitsu　waiting room　　159, 166
待ち合わせる　machiawaseru　wait for (as previously　　159
待ちぼうけ　machibōke　getting stood up　⌐arranged)

介	**460** 2a2.9 … 亻 几 /3 16 介	**KAI** – shellfish (cf. No. 240); be in between, mediate

介入　kainyū　intervention　　52
介在　kaizai　lie/stand/come between　　268
魚介　gyokai　fish and shellfish, marine products　　290
一介の　ikkai no　mere, only　　2

界	**461** 5f4.7 日 甲 亻 几 /58 3 16 界 畍	**KAI** – world; boundary

世界　sekai　world　　252
世界史　sekaishi　world history　　252, 332
学界　gakkai　academic world　　109
外界　gaikai　external world, outside　　83
下界　gekai　this world, the earth below　　31

招	**462** 3c5.22 田 扌 口 力 /23 24 8 招	**SHŌ, mane(ku)** – beckon to, invite, cause

招待　shōtai　invitation　　459
手招き　temaneki　beckoning　　57

紹	**463** 6a5.10 田 糸 ⼝ 力 /61 24 8 紹	**SHŌ** – introduce, help

紹介 *shōkai* introduction, presentation — 460
自己紹介 *jiko shōkai* introduce oneself — 62, 371, 460

寒	**464** 3m9.3 目 宀 艹 土 /33 32 22 寒	**KAN** – cold; midwinter ***samu(i)*** – cold

寒気 *kanki* the cold — 134
寒中 *kanchū* the cold season — 28
極寒 *gokkan* severe cold — 336
寒村 *kanson* poor/lonely village — 191
寒空 *samuzora* wintry sky, cold weather — 140

塞	**465** 3m10.2 目 宀 艹 土 33 32 22 塞	**SAI, SOKU, fusa(gu)** – stop/plug up, block ***fusa(garu)*** – be closed/blocked

閉塞 *heisoku* blockade; obstruction — 401
要塞 *yōsai* fortress, stronghold — 425

終	**466** 6a5.9 田 糸 夂 丶 /61 49 2 終	**SHŪ, o(waru)** – come to an end ***o(eru)*** – bring to an end

最終 *saishū* last — 263
終戦 *shūsen* end of the war — 301
終点 *shūten* end of the line, last stop, terminus — 169
終身 *shūshin* for life, lifelong — 59
終日 *shūjitsu* all day long — 5

冬	**467** 4i2.1 目 夂 丶 /49 2 冬	**TŌ, fuyu** – winter

立冬 *rittō* first day of winter — 121
真冬 *mafuyu* midwinter, dead of winter — 428
冬向き *fuyumuki* for winter — 199
冬物 *fuyumono* winter clothing — 79
冬空 *fuyuzora* winter sky — 140

春	**468** 4c5.13 ⋯ Ⅱ 大 二 /42 34 4 春	**SHUN, haru** – spring

春分（の日）*shunbun (no hi)* vernal equinox — 38, 5
立春 *risshun* beginning of spring — 121
青春 *seishun* springtime of life, youth — 208
売春 *baishun* prostitution — 239
春画 *shunga* obscene picture, pornography — 343

夏	**469** 4i7.5 目 夂 日 一 /49 55 14 夏	**KA, [GE], natsu** – summer

夏期 *kaki* the summer period — 456
立夏 *rikka* beginning of summer — 121
真夏 *manatsu* midsummer, height of summer — 428
夏物 *natsumono* summer clothing — 79
夏休み *natsuyasumi* summer vacation — 60

秋	**470** 5d4.1 ⊡ 禾 火 /56 44 秋 穐	**SHŪ, aki** – fall, autumn	
		春夏秋冬　*shunkashūtō*　all the year round	468, 469, 467
		春秋　*shunjū*　spring and autumn; years, age	468
		秋分（の日）　*shūbun (no hi)*　autumnal equinox	38, 5
		秋気　*shūki*　the autumn air	134
		秋風　*akikaze*　autumn breeze	29

即	**471** 2e5.1 ⊡ 卩 食 /7 77 即	**SOKU** – on the spot, immediate	
		即時　*sokuji*　instantly, immediately, on the spot	42
		即日　*sokujitsu*　on the same day	5
		即金　*sokkin*　cash; payment in cash	23
		即席　*sokuseki*　extemporaneous, impromptu	380
		即興　*sokkyō*　improvised, ad-lib	369

節	**472** 6f7.3 ⊟ ⺮ 食 阝 /66 77 7 節	**SETSU, [SECHI]** – season; occasion; section; paragraph; verse **fushi** – joint; knuckle; melody; point	
		時節　*jisetsu*　time of the year; the times	42
		調節　*chōsetsu*　adjustment, regulation	342
		使節　*shisetsu*　envoy, mission	331
		節約　*setsuyaku*　economizing, thrift	211

季	**473** 5d2.3 ⊟ 禾 子 /56 6 季	**KI** – season	
		季節　*kisetsu*　season, time of the year	472
		四季　*shiki*　the four seasons	6
		季節風　*kisetsufū*　seasonal wind, monsoon	472, 29
		季節外れ　*kisetsuhazure*　out of season	472, 83
		季語　*kigo*　word indicating the season (in haiku)	67

委	**474** 5d3.2 ⊟ 禾 女 /56 25 委	**I, yuda(neru)** – entrust (to)	
		委任　*inin*　trust, mandate, authorization	334
		委員　*iin*　committee member	163
		委員会　*iinkai*　committee	163, 158

湖	**475** 3a9.8 ⊞ 氵 月 口 /21 43 24 湖	**KO, mizuumi** – lake	
		湖水　*kosui*　lake	21
		火口湖　*kakōko*　crater lake	20, 54
		湖面　*komen*　surface of a lake	274
		山中湖　*Yamanaka-ko*　(lake near Mt. Fuji)	34, 28
		十和田湖　*Towada-ko*　(lake in Tōhoku)	12, 124, 35

潮	**476** 3a12.1 ⊞ 氵 日 月 /21 42 43 潮	**CHŌ, shio** – tide; salt water; opportunity	
		満潮　*manchō*　high tide	201
		潮流　*chōryū*　tidal current; trend of the times	247
		風潮　*fūchō*　tide; tendency, trend	29
		潮時　*shiodoki*　favorable tide; opportunity	42
		黒潮　*Kuroshio*　Japan Current	206

	477	**CHŌ** – morning; dynasty **asa** – morning
朝	4b8.12 ⊞	
	月 日 十	
	/43 42 12	
	朝	

朝食　chōshoku　breakfast — 322
平安朝　Heianchō　Heian period (794–1185) — 202, 105
朝日　asahi　morning/rising sun — 5
毎朝　maiasa　every morning — 116
今朝　kesa, konchō　this morning — 51

	478	**CHŪ, hiru** – daytime, noon
昼	4c5.15 ⊞	
	日 尸 一	
	/42 40 1	
	昼 畫	

昼食　chūshoku　lunch — 322
白昼に　hakuchū ni　in broad daylight — 205
昼飯　hirumeshi　lunch — 325
昼間　hiruma　daytime — 43
昼休み　hiruyasumi　lunch break, noon recess — 60

	479	**YA, yoru, yo** – night
夜	2j6.1 ⊞	
	亠 夕 亻	
	/11 30 3	
	夜	

昼夜　chūya　day and night — 478
今夜　kon'ya　tonight — 51
夜行　yakō　traveling by night; night train — 68
夜学　yagaku　evening class — 109
夜明け　yoake　dawn, daybreak — 18

	480	**EKI** – liquid, fluid
液	3a8.29 ⊞	
	氵 夕 亠	
	/21 30 11	
	液	

液体　ekitai　liquid, fluid — 61
液化　ekika　liquefaction — 254

	481	**KAKU** – angle, corner **kado** – corner, angle **tsuno** – horn, antlers
角	2n5.1 ⊟	
	勹 月 丨	
	/15 43 2	
	角	

角度　kakudo　degrees of an angle, angle — 378
三角（形）　sankaku(kei)　triangle — 4, 399
直角　chokkaku　right angle — 429
街角　machikado　street corner — 186

	482	**KAI, GE, to(ku)** – untie, solve **to(keru)** – come loose, be solved
解	4g9.1 ⊞	**to(kasu)** – comb
	牛 月 勹	
	/47 43 15	
	解 解	

理解　rikai　understanding — 143
解説　kaisetsu　explanation, commentary — 404
解決　kaiketsu　solution, settlement — 357
和解　wakai　compromise — 124

	483	**KIKU** – chrysanthemum
菊	3k8.30 ⊟	
	艹 米 勹	
	/32 62 15	
	菊	

白菊　shiragiku　white chrysanthemum — 205
菊の花　kiku no hana　chrysanthemum — 255
菊の節句　Kiku no Sekku　Chrysanthemum Festival — 472, 337
菊人形　kikuningyō　chrysanthemum doll — 1, 399
菊地　Kikuchi　(surname) — 118

	484	**Ō, oku** – interior
奥	6b6.9	奥義　ōgi, okugi　secrets, hidden mysteries　291
	米 大 門	奥行き　okuyuki　depth (vs. height & width)　68
	/62　34　20	山奥　yamaoku　deep in the mountains　34
	奥 奥	奥付け　okuzuke　colophon　192
		奥さん　okusan　wife; ma'am

	485	**SHI, to(maru)** – come to a stop **to(meru)** – bring to a stop
止	2m2.2 …	終止　shūshi　termination　466
	上 广	中止　chyūshi　discontinue, suspend, cancel　28
	/13　11	通行止め　tsūkōdome　Road Closed, No Thoroughfare　150, 68
	止	口止め料　kuchidomeryō　hush money　54, 319
		足止め　ashidome　keep indoors, confinement　58

	486	**SHI, ha** – tooth
歯	6b6.11	門/犬歯　mon/kenshi　incisor/canine　161, 280
	米 上 广	義歯　gishi　false teeth, dentures　291
	/62　13　11	歯科医　shikai　dentist　320, 220
	歯 齒	歯医者　haisha　dentist　220, 164
		歯車　haguruma　toothed wheel, gear　133

	487	**SAI** – year, years old **[SEI]** – year
歳	4n9.5	満四歳　man'yonsai　4 (full) years old　201, 6
	戈 小 上	20歳　hatachi　20 years old
	/52　35　13	万歳　banzai　Hurrah! Long live … !　16
	歳	歳月　saigetsu　time, years　⌐expenditure　17
		歳入歳出　sainyū saishutsu　yearly revenue and　52, 53

	488	**SEKI** – relatives, kin
戚	4n7.2	親戚　shinseki　a relative　175
	戈 小 上	
	/52　35　13	
	戚	

	489	**REKI** – continuation, passage of time; successive
歴	2p12.4	歴史　rekishi　history　332
	厂 木 广	学歴　gakureki　school career, academic background　109
	/18　41　13	前歴　zenreki　personal history, background　47
	歴	歴任　rekinin　successive holding of various posts　334

	490	**KI, kuwada(teru)** – plan, undertake, attempt
企	2a4.17 …	企業　kigyō　enterprise, undertaking　279
	亻 上 广	企画　kikaku　planning, plan　343
	/3　13　11	企図　kito　plan, project, scheme　339
	企	中小企業　chūshō kigyō　small- and medium-size
		enterprises　28, 27, 279

491

禁

4e8.3

礻 木
/45 41

禁

KIN – prohibition

禁止	*kinshi*	prohibition	485
立ち入り禁止	*tachiiri kinshi*	Keep Out	121, 52, 485
禁制	*kinsei*	prohibition, ban	433
禁物	*kinmotsu*	forbidden things, taboo	79
発禁	*hakkin*	prohibition of sale	96

492

政

4i5.1

攵 工 一
/49 38 1

政

SEI, [SHŌ], matsurigoto – government, rule

政局	*seikyoku*	political situation	170
行政	*gyōsei*	administration	68
内政	*naisei*	domestic politics, internal affairs	84
市政	*shisei*	municipal government	181
家政	*kasei*	management of a household, housekeeping	165

493

証

7a5.5

言 工 一
/67 38 1

証 證

SHŌ – proof, evidence, certificate

証明	*shōmei*	proof, testimony, corroboration	18
証書	*shōsho*	deed, bond, in writing	131
証人	*shōnin*	witness	1
証言	*shōgen*	testimony	66
内証	*naisho, naishō*	secret	84

494

結

6a6.5

糸 土 口
/61 22 24

結

KETSU, musu(bu) – tie, bind; conclude (a contract); bear (fruit)
yu(waeru) – tie **yu(u)** – do up (one's hair)

結論	*ketsuron*	conclusion	293
結成	*kessei*	formation, organization	261
結合	*ketsugō*	union, combination	159
終結	*shūketsu*	conclusion, termination	466

495

接

3c8.10

扌 立 女
/23 54 25

接

SETSU – touch, contact **tsu(gu)** – join together

直接	*chokusetsu*	direct	429
間接	*kansetsu*	indirect	43
面接	*mensetsu*	interview	274
接続	*setsuzoku*	connecting, joining	243
接待	*settai*	reception, welcome; serving, offering	459

496

果

0a8.8

日 木
42 41

果

KA – fruit, result **ha(tasu)** – carry out, complete **ha(teru)** – come to an end **ha(te)** – end; limit; result

結果	*kekka*	result	494
成果	*seika*	result	261
果実	*kajitsu*	fruit	203
果物	*kudamono*	fruit	79

497

課

7a8.2

言 日 木
/67 42 41

課

KA – lesson; section

第一課	*dai-ikka*	Lesson 1	408, 2
課目	*kamoku*	subject (in school)	55
課程	*katei*	course, curriculum	423
課長	*kachō*	section chief	95
人事課	*jinjika*	personnel section	1, 80

保	**498** 2a7.11 亻 木 口 /3　41　24 保	**HO, tamo(tsu)** – keep, preserve, maintain

保証　　　*hoshō*　guarantee, warranty　　　　　　　　　　　493
保証人　　*hoshōnin*　guarantor, sponsor　　　　　　　　493, 1
保存　　　*hozon*　preservation　　　　　　　　　　　　269
保育所　　*hoikusho, hoikujo*　daycare nursery　　　　　246, 153
保養所　　*hoyōsho, hoyōjo*　sanatorium, rest home　　　406, 153

守	**499** 3m3.2 宀 寸 /33　37 守	**SHU, [SU], mamo(ru)** – protect; obey, abide by **mori** – babysitter; (lighthouse) keeper

保守的　　*hoshuteki*　conservative　　　　　　　　　　498, 210
子守　　　*komori*　baby-sitting; baby-sitter, nursemaid; lullaby　103
見守る　　*mimamoru*　keep watch over; stare at　　　　63
お守り　　*omamori*　charm, amulet

団	**500** 3s3.3　口 口 寸 /24　37 団　團	**DAN, [TON]** – group

団体（旅行）　*dantai (ryokō)*　group (tour)　　　　　61, 222, 68
集団　　　*shūdan*　group, mass　　　　　　　　　　　442
団地　　　*danchi*　public housing development/complex　118
団結　　　*danketsu*　unity, solidarity　　　　　　　　494
師団　　　*shidan*　(army) division　　　　　　　　　　415

台	**501** 3d2.11 口 ム /24　17 台　臺	**DAI, TAI** – stand, pedestal; platform, plateau

台所　　　*daidokoro*　kitchen　　　　　　　　　　　　153
天文台　　*tenmondai*　observatory　　　　　　　　　141, 111
高台　　　*takadai*　high ground, a height　　　　　　190
台本　　　*daihon*　script, screenplay, libretto　　　　25
台風　　　*taifū*　typhoon　　　　　　　　　　　　　　29

治	**502** 3a5.28 氵 口 ム /21　24　17 治	**JI, CHI** – peace; government; healing **osa(meru)** – govern; suppress **osa(maru)** – be at peace, quelled **nao(su)** – (tr.) heal **nao(ru)** – (intr.) heal

政治　　　*seiji*　politics　　　　　　　　　　　　　　492
自治　　　*jichi*　self-government, autonomy　　　　　62
明治時代　*Meiji jidai*　Meiji era (1868–1912)　　　18, 42, 256

始	**503** 3e5.9 女 口 ム /25　24　17 始	**SHI, haji(maru)** – (intr.) start, begin **haji(meru)** – (tr.) start, begin

始末　　　*shimatsu*　circumstances; management, disposal　305
始終　　　*shijū*　from first to last, all the while　　　466
開始　　　*kaishi*　the first (train) departure; beginning, opening　400
原始的　　*genshiteki*　primitive, original　　　　　136, 210

党	**504** 3n7.2 丷 口 儿 /35　24　16 党　黨	**TŌ** – party, faction

政党　　　*seitō*　political party　　　　　　　　　　　492
野党　　　*yatō*　party out of power, opposition　　　236
党員 / 首　*tōin/shu*　party member/leader　　　　　163, 148
徒党　　　*totō*　confederates, clique, conspiracy　　436
社会党　　*Shakaitō*　Socialist Party　　　　　　　308, 158

堂	**505** 3n8.4 丷 口 土 /35 24 22 堂	**DŌ** – temple; hall

食堂　*shokudō*　dining hall, restaurant　　322
能楽堂　*nōgakudō*　Noh theater　　387, 359
公会堂　*kōkaidō*　public hall, community center　　126, 158
本堂　*hondō*　main temple building　　25
国会議事堂　*kokkai gijidō*　Diet Building　　40, 158, 292, 80

常	**506** 3n8.3 丷 口 巾 /35 24 26 常	**JŌ, tsune** – normal, usual, continual **toko-** – ever-, always

日常生活　*nichijō seikatsu*　everyday life　　5, 44, 237
正常　*seijō*　normal　　275
通常　*tsūjō*　ordinary, usual　　150
常務　*jōmu*　regular business, routine duties　　235
常任委員　*jōnin iin*　member of a standing ┌committee　　334, 474, 163

非	**507** 0a8.1 二 卜 一 4 13 1 非	**HI** – mistake; (prefix) non-, un-

非常口　*hijōguchi*　emergency exit　　506, 54
非常事態　*hijō jitai*　state of emergency　　506, 80, 388
非公開　*hikōkai*　not open to the public, private　　126, 400
非人間的　*hiningenteki*　inhuman, impersonal　　1, 43, 210
非合法　*higōhō*　illegal　　159, 123

掌	**508** 3n9.4 丷 口 扌 /35 24 23 掌	**SHŌ** – palm of the hand; administer

合掌　*gasshō*　clasp one's hands (in prayer)　　159
掌中　*shōchū*　pocket (edition), in the hand　　28
掌中の玉　*shōchū no tama*　apple of one's eye　　28, 295
車掌　*shashō*　(train) conductor　　133

賞	**509** 3n12.1 丷 貝 口 /35 68 24 賞	**SHŌ** – prize; praise

文学賞　*bungaku-shō*　prize for literature　　111, 109
ノーベル賞　*Nōberu-shō*　Nobel Prize
賞品　*shōhin*　a prize　　230
賞金　*shōkin*　cash prize, prize money　　23
受賞者　*jushōsha*　prizewinner　　260, 164

束	**510** 0a7.8 木 口 41 24 束	**SOKU, taba** – bundle, sheaf

一束　*issoku, hitotaba*　a bundle　　2
約束　*yakusoku*　promise, appointment　　211
結束　*kessoku*　unity, union, bond　　494
花束　*hanataba*　bouquet　　255
束ねる　*tabaneru*　tie in a bundle; control

速	**511** 2q7.4 辶 木 口 /19 41 24 速	**SOKU, haya(i), sumi(yaka)** – fast, speedy **haya(meru)** – hasten, expedite **haya(maru)** – speed up, gather speed

速力、速度　*sokuryoku, sokudo*　speed, velocity　　100, 378
高速道路　*kōsoku dōro*　expressway, freeway　　190, 149, 151
速達　*sokutatsu*　special/express delivery　　455
速記　*sokki*　shorthand, stenography　　372

512

4i12.3

攵 木 二
/49 41 38

整

SEI, totono(eru) – put in order; prepare **totono(u)** – be put in order, prepared

整理	seiri	arrangement, adjustment	143
調整	chōsei	adjustment, modulation	342
整形外科	seikei geka	plastic surgery	399, 83, 320
整数	seisū	integer	225

513

3q5.2

广 寸 イ
/18 37 3

府

FU – storehouse; government office; capital city

政府	seifu	government	492
無政府	museifu	anarchy	93, 492
首府	shufu	the capital	148
京都府	Kyōto-fu	Kyōto Prefecture	189, 188
都道府県	to-dō-fu-ken	the Japanese prefectures	188, 149, 194

514

6f5.12

⺮ 寸 イ
/66 37 3

符

FU – sign, mark

切符	kippu	ticket	39
切符売り場	kippu uriba	ticket office/window	39, 239, 154
音符	onpu	diacritical mark; musical note	347
符号	fugō	mark, symbol	266
符合	fugō	coincidence, agreement, correspondence	159

515

2f6.10

火 丨 力
44 2 8

券 劵

KEN – ticket, certificate

入場券	nyūjōken	admission ticket	52, 154
旅券	ryoken	passport	222
回数券	kaisūken	coupon ticket	90, 225
定期券	teikiken	commutation ticket, (train) pass	356, 456
(有価)証券	(yūka) shōken	securities	265, 427, 493

516

0a9.11

丷 火 弓
2o 44 28

巻 卷

KAN, maki – roll, reel, volume **ma(ku)** – roll, wind

上／中／下巻	jō/chū/gekan	first/middle/last volume	32, 28, 31
第一巻	dai-ikkan	Volume 1	408, 2
絵巻(物)	emaki(mono)	picture scroll	345, 79
葉巻	hamaki	cigar	253
取り巻く	torimaku	surround, encircle	65

517

3s9.1

口 火 弓
/24 44 28

圏 圈

KEN – circle, range, sphere

ドイツ語圏	Doitsugo-ken	the German-speaking region	67
極地圏	kyokuchiken	polar region	336, 118
北／南極圏	hok/nankyokuken	Arctic/Antarctic Circle	73, 74, 336
首都圏	shutoken	the capital region	148, 188
圏内／外	kennai/gai	within/outside the range (of)	84, 83

518

4b8.4

月 火 二
/43 44 4

勝

SHŌ, ka(tsu) – win **masa(ru)** – be superior (to)

勝利	shōri	victory	329
勝(利)者	shō(ri)sha	victor, winner	329, 164
決勝	kesshō	decision (of a competition)	357
連勝	renshō	series of victories, winning streak	446
勝ち通す	kachitōsu	win successive victories	150

	519	**FU, ma(keru)** – be defeated, lose; give a discount **ma(kasu)** – beat, defeat **o(u)** – carry, bear, owe
負	2n7.1	
	ク 貝 /15 68	勝負　*shōbu*　victory or defeat; game, match　518
		自負　*jifu*　conceit, self-importance　62
	負	負けん気　*makenki*　unyielding/competitive spirit　134
		負け犬　*makeinu*　loser　280

	520	**HAI** – a defeat **yabu(reru)** – be defeated
敗	7b4.1	敗北　*haiboku*　defeat　73
	貝 攵 /68 49	勝敗　*shōhai*　victory or defeat, outcome　518
		失敗　*shippai*　failure, blunder　311
	敗	敗戦　*haisen*　lost battle, defeat　301
		敗者　*haisha*　the defeated, loser　164

	521	**HŌ, hana(tsu)** – set free, release; fire (a gun); emit **hana(su)** – set free, release **hana(reru)** – get free of **hō(ru)** – throw; leave as is
放	4h4.1	解放　*kaihō*　liberation, emancipation　482
	方 攵 /48 49	放送　*hōsō*　(radio/TV) broadcasting　447
	放	放火　*hōka*　arson　20

	522	**BŌ, fuse(gu)** – defend/protect from, prevent
防	2d4.1	防止　*bōshi*　prevention, keeping in check　485
	阝 方 /7 48	予防　*yobō*　prevention, precaution　397
		国防　*kokubō*　national defense　40
	防	防火　*bōka*　fire prevention/fighting　20
		防水　*bōsui*　waterproof, watertight　21

	523	**KAI, arata(meru)** – alter, renew, reform **arata(maru)** – be altered, renewed, corrected
改	4i3.1	改正　*kaisei*　improvement; revision　275
	攵 弓 /49 28	改良　*kairyō*　improvement, reform　321
		改新　*kaishin*　renovation, reformation　174
	改	改名　*kaimei*　changing one's name　82

	524	**HAI, kuba(ru)** – distribute, pass out
配	7e3.2	心配　*shinpai*　worry, concern　97
	酉 弓 /71 28	支配　*shihai*　management, administration, rule　318
		配達　*haitatsu*　deliver　455
	配	配置　*haichi*　arrangement, placement　432
		気配　*kehai*　sign, indication　134

	525	**SAN, su(i)** – acid, sour
酸	7e7.2	酸味　*sanmi*　acidity, sourness　307
	酉 攵 厶 /71 49 17	酸性　*sansei*　acidity　98
		酸化　*sanka*　oxidation　254
	酸	酸素　*sanso*　oxygen　271
		酸っぱい　*suppai*　sour, tart

	526	**SHU, sake, [saka]** – saké, rice wine, liquor	
	3a7.1 □	日本酒　*Nihon-shu*　saké, Japanese rice wine	5, 25
	氵 酉	ぶどう酒　*budōshu*　(grape) wine	
	/21　71	禁酒　*kinshu*　abstinence from drink; temperance	491
	酒	酒屋　*sakaya*　wine dealer, liquor store	167
		酒場　*sakaba*　bar, saloon, tavern	154

	527	**GAI** – injury, harm, damage	
	3m7.4	公害　*kōgai*　pollution	126
	宀 土 口	水害　*suigai*　flood damage, flooding	21
	/33　22　24	損害　*songai*　injury, loss	351
	害	利害　*rigai*　advantages and disadvantages	329
		有害　*yūgai*　harmful, noxious, injurious	265

	528	**KATSU, wa(ru)** – divide, separate, split **wa(reru)** – break, crack/split apart **wari** – proportion; profit; 10 percent **sa(ku)** – cut up, separate; spare (time)	
	2f10.1	分割　*bunkatsu*　division, partitioning	38
	リ 宀 土	割合　*wariai*　rate, proportion; percentage	159
	/16　33　22	割引　*waribiki*　discount	216
	割		

	529	**HITSU, kanara(zu)** – surely, (be) sure (to), without fail	
	0a5.16 …	必要　*hitsuyō*　necessary, requisite	425
	心 丶	必死　*hisshi*　certain death; desperation	85
	51　2	必読　*hitsudoku*　required reading	244
	必	必勝　*hisshō*　sure victory	518
		必ずしも…ない　*kanarazu shimo … nai*　not necessarily	

	530	**KEN** – law, constiltution	
	3m13.2	憲法　*kenpō*　constitution	123
	宀 目 心	改憲　*kaiken*　constitutional revision	523
	/33　55　51	憲政　*kensei*　constitutional government	492
	憲	立憲　*rikken*　constitutional	121
		官憲　*kanken*　the (government) authorities	326

	531	**DOKU** – poison	
	0a8.14	毒薬　*dokuyaku*　poison	360
	土 母 一	有毒　*yūdoku*　poisonous	265
	22　25　1	中毒　*chūdoku*　poisoning	28
	毒	毒草　*dokusō*　poisonous plant	249
		気の毒　*kinodoku*　pitiable, regrettable, unfortunate	134

	532	**JŌ, no(ru)** – get in/on, ride, take (a train); be fooled **no(seru)** – let ride, take aboard; deceive, trick, take in	
	0a9.19 …	乗用車　*jōyōsha*　passenger car	107, 133
	木 卄 一	乗車券　*jōshaken*　(passenger) ticket	133, 515
	41　32　1	乗組員　*norikumiin*　(ship's) crew	424, 163
	乗 乘	乗っ取る　*nottoru*　take over, commandeer, hijack	65

郵	**533** 2d8.12 □ 阝 艹 土 /7 32 22 郵	**YŪ** – mail

郵便局　*yūbinkyoku*　post office　　　　　　　　　「postman 330, 170
郵便配達（人）　*yūbin haitatsu(nin)*　mailman,　330, 524, 455, 1
郵便料金　*yūbin ryōkin*　postage　　　　　　　330, 319, 23
郵税　*yūzei*　postage　　　　　　　　　　　　　403
郵送料　*yūsōryō*　postage　　　　　　　　　447, 319

式	**534** 4n3.2 □ 弋 工 /52 38 式	**SHIKI** – ceremony, rite; style, form; method; formula

正式　*seishiki*　prescribed form, formal　　　　　　　275
公式　*kōshiki*　formula (in mathematics); formal, official　126
様式　*yōshiki*　mode, style　　　　　　　　　　　　407
方式　*hōshiki*　formula, mode; method, system　　　　70
新式　*shinshiki*　new type　　　　　　　　　　　　174

試	**535** 7a6.18 □ 言 弋 工 /67 52 38 試	**SHI, kokoro(miru), tame(su)** – give it a try, try out, attempt

試合　*shiai*　game, match　　　　　　　　　　　159
試作　*shisaku*　trial manufacture/cultivation　　　361
試食　*shishoku*　sample, taste　　　　　　　　　322
試運転　*shiunten*　trial run　　　　　　　　445, 439
試金石　*shikinseki*　touchstone, test　　　　　23, 78

器	**536** 3d12.13 … 口 大 /24 34 器 器	**KI, utsuwa** – container, apparatus; capacity, ability

楽器　*gakki*　musical instrument　　　　　　　　359
器楽　*kigaku*　instrumental music　　　　　　　359
器具　*kigu*　utensil, appliance, tool, apparatus　426
食器　*shokki*　eating utensils　　　　　　　　　322
（不 / 無）器用　*(bu)kiyō*　(not) dexterous　　94, 93, 107

機	**537** 4a12.1 □ 木 弋 厶 /41 52 17 機	**KI** – machine; opportunity **hata** – loom

機関　*kikan*　engine; machinery, organ, medium　　　402
制動機　*seidōki*　a brake　　　　　　　　　433, 231
起重機　*kijūki*　crane　　　　　　　　　　374, 227
機能　*kinō*　a function　　　　　　　　　　　387
機会　*kikai*　opportunity, occasion, chance　　　158

械	**538** 4a7.22 □ 木 弋 艹 /41 52 32 械	**KAI** – fetters; machine

器械　*kikai*　instrument, apparatus, appliance　　536
機械　*kikai*　machine, machinery　　　　　　　537
機械化　*kikaika*　mechanization　　　　　　537, 254
機械文明　*kikai bunmei*　technological civilization　537, 111, 18

飛	**539** 0a9.4 … 匕 十 一 10 12 1 飛	**HI, to(bu)** – fly **to(basu)** – let fly, skip over, omit

飛行　*hikō*　flight, aviation　　　　　　　　　　68
飛行機　*hikōki*　airplane　　　　　　　　　68, 537
飛行場　*hikōjō*　airport　　　　　　　　　68, 154
飛び石　*tobiishi*　stepping-stones　　　　　　　78
飛び火　*tobihi*　flying sparks, leaping flames　　　20

検	**540** 4a8.28 ⊞ 木 口 亻 /41 24 3 検 檢	**KEN** – investigation, inspection	
		検事 *kenji* public procurator/prosecutor	80
		検定 *kentei* official approval, inspection	356
		検証 *kenshō* verification, inspection	493
		検死 *kenshi* coroner's inquest, autopsy	85
		点検 *tenken* inspection, examination	169

験	**541** 10a8.4 ⊞ 馬 口 亻 /78 24 3 験 驗	**KEN** – effect; testing *[GEN]* – beneficial effect	
		実験 *jikken* experiment	203
		試験 *shiken* examination, test	535
		入学試験 *nyūgaku shiken* entrance exam	52, 109, 535
		体験 *taiken* experience	61
		受験 *juken* take a test/exam	260

険	**542** 2d8.8 ⊞ 阝 口 亻 /7 24 3 険 險	**KEN, kewa(shii)** – steep, inaccessible; stern, harsh	
		保険 *hoken* insurance	498
		険悪 *ken'aku* dangerous, threatening	304
		険路 *kenro* steep path	151
		険しい道 *kewashii michi* steep/treacherous road	149
		険しい顔つき *kewashii kaotsuki* stern/fierce look	277

危	**543** 2n4.3 ⊟ ク 厂 阝 /15 18 7 危	**KI, abu(nai), aya(ui)** – dangerous **aya(bumu)** – fear	
		危険 *kiken* danger	542
		危険物 *kikenbutsu* hazardous articles	542, 79
		危機 *kiki* crisis, critical moment	537
		危急 *kikyū* emergency, crisis	303
		危害 *kigai* injury, harm	527

探	**544** 3c8.16 ⊞ 扌 木 冂 /23 41 20 探	**TAN, sagu(ru)** – search/grope for **saga(su)** – look for	
		探検 *tanken* exploration, expedition	540
		探知 *tanchi* detection	214
		探り出す *saguridasu* spy/sniff out (a secret)	53
		探し回る *sagashimawaru* look/search around for	90
		家探し *iesagashi* house hunting	165

深	**545** 3a8.21 ⊞ 氵 木 冂 /21 41 20 深	**SHIN, fuka(i)** – deep **fuka(meru)** – make deeper, intensify **fuka(maru)** – become deeper, intensify	
		深度 *shindo* depth, deepness	378
		深夜 *shin'ya* dead of night, late at night	479
		情け深い *nasakebukai* compassionate, merciful	209
		興味深い *kyōmibukai* very interesting	369, 307

緑	**546** 6a8.15 ⊞ 糸 彐 氵 /61 39 21 緑	**RYOKU, [ROKU], midori** – green	
		緑地 *ryokuchi* green tract of land	118
		新緑 *shinryoku* fresh verdure/greenery	174
		葉緑素 *yōryokuso* chlorophyll	253, 271
		緑青 *rokushō* verdigris, green/copper rust	208
		緑色 *midoriiro* green, green-colored	204

錄	**547** 8a8.16 ⊞ 釒 彐 氵 /72 39 21 録	**ROKU** – record	
		記録 *kiroku* record, document(ary)	372
		録音 *rokuon* (audio) recording	347
		録画 *rokuga* (video) recording	343
		目録 *mokuroku* catalog, inventory, list	55
		付録 *furoku* supplement, appendix, addendum	192

与	**548** 0a3.23 ⋯ 十 一 12 1 与 興	**YO** – give; participate in **ata(eru)** – give, grant	
		与党 *yotō* party in power, government	504
		与野党 *yoyatō* government and opposition parties	236, 504
		給与 *kyūyo* allowance, wage	346
		付与 *fuyo* give, grant, confer	192
		賞与 *shōyo* bonus, reward	509

写	**549** 2i3.1 冖 十 一 /20 12 1 写 寫	**SHA, utsu(su)** – copy down, copy, duplicate; depict; photograph **utsu(ru)** – be taken, turn out (photo)	
		写真 *shashin* photograph	428
		映写機 *eishaki* projector	353, 537
		写生 *shasei* sketch, painting from nature	44
		写実的 *shajitsuteki* realistic, graphic	203, 210

考	**550** 2k4.4 ⋯ 土 22 考 攷	**KŌ, kanga(eru)** – think, consider	
		思考 *shikō* thinking, thought	99
		考案 *kōan* conception, idea, design	106
		考証 *kōshō* historical research	493
		考古学 *kōkogaku* archaeology	172, 109
		考え方 *kangaekata* way of thinking, viewpoint	70

孝	**551** 2k4.3 ⋯ 土 子 一 22 6 1 孝	**KŌ** – filial piety	
		(親)孝行 *(oya)kōkō* filial piety, obedience to parents	175, 68
		孝養 *kōyō* discharge of filial duties	406
		(親)不孝 *(oya)fukō* undutifulness to one's parents	175, 94

老	**552** 2k4.5 ⋯ 土 22 老	**RŌ** – old age **o(iru), fu(keru)** – grow old	
		老人 *rōjin* old man/woman/people	1
		長老 *chōrō* an elder	95
		老夫婦 *rōfūfu* old married couple	315, 316
		海老 *ebi* shrimp, prawn	117
		老子 *Rōshi* Laozi, Lao-tzu	103

若	**553** 3k5.12 ⊟ 艹 ⼝ 十 /32 24 12 若	**JAKU, [NYAKU], waka(i)** – young **mo(shikuwa)** – or	
		老若 *rōnyaku, rōjaku* young and old, youth and age	552
		若者 *wakamono* young man/people	164
		若手 *wakate* young man, a younger member	57
		若人 *wakōdo* young man, a youth	1
		若死に *wakajini* die young	85

	554	**KU** – pain, suffering(s) **kuru(shimu)** – suffer **kuru(shimeru)** – torment **kuru(shii)** – painful **niga(i)** – bitter **niga(ru)** – scowl

苦 3k5.24

苦労　kurō　trouble, hardship, adversity　233
苦心　kushin　pains, efforts　97
病苦　byōku　the pain of illness　381
重苦しい　omokurushii　oppressed, gloomy, ponderous　227

	555	**YU** – send, transport

輸 7c9.5

輸入　yunyū　import　52
輸出　yushutsu　export　53
輸送　yusō　transport　447
運輸　un'yu　transport, conveyance　445
空輸　kūyu　air transport, shipment by air　140

	556	**KEI, karu(i), karo(yaka)** – light

軽 7c5.3

軽工業　keikōgyō　light industry　139, 279
軽食　keishoku　light meal　322
軽音楽　keiongaku　light music　347, 359
手軽　tegaru　easy, simple, informal　57
気軽　kigaru　lighthearted, cheerful, feel free (to)　134

	557	**KEI** – longitude; sutra; passage of time **KYŌ** – sutra **he(ru)** – pass, elapse

経 6a5.11

経験　keiken　experience　541
経歴　keireki　one's life history, career　489
経理　keiri　accounting　143
神経　shinkei　a nerve　310

	558	**SAI, su(mu)** – come to an end; be paid; suffice **su(masu)** – finish, settle; pay; make do, manage

済 3a8.30

経済　keizai　economy, economics　557
返済　hensai　payment, repayment　448
決済　kessai　settlement of accounts　357
使用済み　shiyōzumi　used up　331, 107

	559	**ZAI** – medicine, preparation

剤 2f8.6

薬剤　yakuzai　medicine, drug　360
薬剤師　yakuzaishi　pharmacist, druggist　360, 415
調剤　chōzai　compounding/preparation of medicines　342
下剤　gezai　laxative　31
解毒剤　gedokuzai　antidote　482, 531

	560	**SAI** – ability, talent; (as suffix) years old

才 0a3.27

天才　tensai　a genius　141
才子　saishi　talented person　103
才能　sainō　talent, ability　387
多才　tasai　many-talented　229
十八才　jūhassai　18 years old　12, 10

	561	**ZAI** – wood, material; talent	
	4a3.7	材料 *zairyō* materials, ingredients	319
	木 十 丨	取材 *shuzai* data collection, news gathering	65
	/41 12 2	教材 *kyōzai* teaching materials	245
	材 杙	題材 *daizai* subject matter, theme	355
		材木 *zaimoku* wood, lumber	22

	562	**ZAI, [SAI]** – money, wealth, property	
	7b3.1	財産 *zaisan* estate, assets, property	278
	貝 十 丨	財政 *zaisei* finances, financial affairs	492
	/68 12 2	財界 *zaikai* financial world, business circles	461
	財 賊	財務省 *Zaimushō* Ministry of Finance; (U.S.) Treasury	235, 145
		文化財 *bunkazai* cultural asset ⌐Department	111, 254

	563	**IN** – cause **yo(ru)** – depend (on), be limited (to)	
	3s3.2 □	原因 *gen'in* cause	136
	口 大	主因 *shuin* primary/main cause	155
	/24 34	死因 *shiin* cause of death	85
	因	要因 *yōin* important factor, chief cause	425
		因果 *inga* cause and effect	496

	564	**ON** – kindness, goodness, favor; gratitude	
	4k6.23 ⊟	恩給 *onkyū* pension	346
	心 口 大	恩賞 *onshō* a reward	509
	/51 24 34	恩人 *onjin* benefactor; patron	1
	恩	恩返し *ongaeshi* repayment of a favor	448
		恩知らず *onshirazu* ingratitude; ingrate	214

	565	**KAN** – Han (Chinese dynasty); China; man, fellow	
	3a10.17 ⊞	漢字 *kanji* kanji, Chinese character	110
	氵 艹 口	漢文 *kanbun* Chinese writing; Chinese classics	111
	/21 32 24	漢時代 *Kan jidai* Han dynasty/period	42, 256
	漢	好/悪漢 *kō/akkan* nice fellow/scoundrel, villain	104, 304
		門外漢 *mongaikan* outsider, layman	161, 83

	566	**NAN, muzuka(shii), kata(i)** – difficult	
	8c10.2 □	難題 *nandai* difficult problem/question	355
	隹 艹 口	難病 *nanbyō* incurable disease	381
	/73 32 24	難民 *nanmin* refugees	177
	難	海難 *kainan* disaster at sea, shipwreck	117
		非難 *hinan* adverse criticism	507

	567	**KON, koma(ru)** – be distressed, be troubled	
	3s4.1 □	困難 *konnan* difficulty, trouble	566
	口 木	困苦 *konku* hardships, adversity	554
	/24 41	困り切る *komarikiru* be in a bad fix, at a loss	39
	困	困り果てる *komarihateru* be greatly troubled, nonplussed	496

	568	**KIN** – service, work **[GON]** – Buddhist religious services
勤	2g10.1 田	**tsuto(meru)** – be employed **tsuto(maru)** – be fit for

勤労	kinrō	work, labor	233
勤務	kinmu	service, being on duty/at work	235
通勤	tsūkin	going to work, commuting	150
勤め先	tsutomesaki	place of work, employer	50

	569	**TEI** – resist
抵	3c5.18	

抵当	teitō	mortgage, hypothec	77
大抵	taitei	generally, for the most part, usually	26

	570	**TEI, hiku(i)** – low **hiku(meru)** – make lower **hiku(maru)** – become lower
低	2a5.15	

最低	saitei	lowest, minimum	263
低所得	teishotoku	low income	153, 375
低成長	teiseichō	low growth	261, 95
低能	teinō	weak intellect, mental deficiency	387

	571	**TEI, soko** – bottom
底	3q5.3	

根底	kontei	base, foundation	314
海底	kaitei	bottom of the sea, ocean floor	117
河底	katei	bottom of a river, riverbed	391
底力	sokojikara	latent energy/power	100
底値	sokone	rock-bottom price	431

	572	**TEI** – mansion, residence
邸	2d5.10	

公邸	kōtei	official residence	126
官邸	kantei	official residence	326
私邸	shitei	one's private residence	125
邸宅	teitaku	residence, mansion	178
邸内	teinai	the grounds, the premises	84

	573	**JŌ** – article, clause; line, stripe
条	4i4.1	

条約	jōyaku	treaty	211
条文	jōbun	the text, provisions	111
第一条	dai-ichijō	Article 1 (in a law/contract/treaty)	408, 2
条理	jōri	logic, reason	143
信条	shinjō	a belief, article of faith	157

	574	**KEI, chigi(ru)** – pledge, vow, promise
契	2f7.6	

契約	keiyaku	contract, agreement	211
契機	keiki	opportunity, chance	537

575 氏

| 575 | 0a4.25 ... | 厂 十 | 18 12 | 氏 |

SHI – clan, family; surname; (as suffix) Mr. **uji** – clan, lineage

氏名	shimei	(full) name	82
同氏	dōshi	the said person, he	198
両氏	ryōshi	both (gentlemen)	200
氏神	ujigami	tutelary deity, genius loci	310
セ氏	seshi	Celsius, centigrade	

576 婚

| 576 | 3e8.4 | 女 日 厂 | /25 42 18 | 婚 |

KON – marriage

結婚	kekkon	marriage	494
結婚式	kekkonshiki	marriage ceremony, wedding	494, 534
婚約	kon'yaku	engagement	211
未婚	mikon	unmarried	306
新婚旅行	shinkon ryokō	honeymoon	174, 222, 68

577 級

| 577 | 6a3.2 | 糸 力 丶 | /61 8 2 | 級 |

KYŪ – rank, class

進級	shinkyū	(school/military) promotion	443
高級	kōkyū	high rank; high class, de luxe	190
上級	jōkyū	upper grade, senior	32
学級	gakkyū	class in school	109
同級生	dōkyūsei	classmate	198, 44

578 等

| 578 | 6f6.9 | ⺮ 上 寸 | /66 22 37 | 等 |

TŌ – class, grade; equality; etc. **hito(shii)** – equal

等級	tōkyū	class, grade, rank	577
一等	ittō	first class	2
平等	byōdō	equality	202
同等	dōtō	equality, same rank	198
高等学校	kōtō gakkō	senior high school	190, 109, 115

579 詩

| 579 | 7a6.5 | 言 士 寸 | /67 22 37 | 詩 |

SHI – poetry, poem

詩人	shijin	poet	1
詩歌	shiika, shika	poetry	395
詩情	shijō	poetic sentiment	209
詩集	shishū	collection of poems	442
漢詩	kanshi	Chinese poem/poetry	565

580 侍

| 580 | 2a6.11 | 亻 士 寸 | /3 22 37 | 侍 |

JI, samurai – samurai

侍者	jisha	attendant, valet, page	164
侍女	jijo	lady-in-waiting, lady's attendant	102
侍医	jii	court physician	220
侍気質	samurai katagi	the samurai spirit	134, 176
七人の侍	Shichinin no samurai	The Seven Samurai	9, 1

581 士

| 581 | 3p0.1 | 士 | /22 | 士 |

SHI – samurai; man; scholar

同士	dōshi	fellow, companion	198
力士	rikishi	sumo wrestler	100
代議士	daigishi	dietman, congressman, M.P.	256, 292
学士	gakushi	university graduate	109
税理士	zeirishi	(licensed) tax accountant	403, 143

582 3p4.1 志 心 /22 51 志	**SHI, kokorozashi** – will, intention, aim **kokoroza(su)** – intend, aim at, have in view

意志　ishi　will　132
志向　shikō　intention, inclination　199
同志　dōshi　like-minded (person)　198
有志　yūshi　voluntary; those interested　265

583 7a7.8 言 心 土 /67 51 22 誌	**SHI** – write down; chronicle; magazine

誌上　shijō　in a magazine　32
誌面　shimen　page of a magazine　274
日誌　nisshi　diary　5
書誌　shoshi　bibliography　131
地誌　chishi　a topography, geographical description　118

584 8c6.2 隹 木 十 /73 41 12 雑 雜	**ZATSU, ZŌ** – miscellany, a mix

雑誌　zasshi　magazine　583
雑音　zatsuon　noise, static　347
雑感　zakkan　miscellaneous thoughts/impressions　262
雑草　zassō　weeds　249
雑木林　zōkibayashi　thicket of assorted trees　22, 127

585 4a6.35 木 十 冂 /41 12 20 殺	**SATSU, [SETSU], koro(su)** – kill **[SAI]** – lessen

自殺　jisatsu　suicide　62
暗殺　ansatsu　assassination　348
毒殺　dokusatsu　killing by poison　531
殺人　satsujin　a murder　1
人殺し　hitogoroshi　murder; murderer　1

586 7a4.7 言 冂 又 /67 20 9 設	**SETSU, mō(keru)** – establish, set up, prepare

設立　setsuritsu　establishment, founding　121
設定　settei　establishment, creation, setting　356
新設　shinsetsu　newly established/organized　174
私設　shisetsu　private　125
設置　setchi　establishment, founding, institution　432

587 2a6.26 亻 口 阝 /3 24 7 命	**MEI** – command, fate, life **MYŌ, inochi** – life

生命（保険）　seimei (hoken)　life (insurance)　44, 498, 542
運命　unmei　fate　445
使命　shimei　mission, errand　331
短命　tanmei　a short life　215
任命　ninmei　appointment, nomination　334

588 2a6.24 亻 心 一 /3 51 1 念	**NEN** – thought, idea; desire; concern, attention

記念日　kinenbi　memorial day, anniversary　372, 5
記念切手　kinen kitte　commemorative stamp　372, 39, 57
理念　rinen　idea, doctrine, ideology　143
信念　shinnen　belief, faith, conviction　157
念入り　nen'iri　careful, scrupulous, thorough　52

源	**589** 3a10.25 氵 日 小 /21 42 35 源	**GEN, minamoto** – source, origin

起源　*kigen*　origin　374
根源　*kongen*　origin　314
財源　*zaigen*　source of revenue　562
源平　*Gen-Pei*　Genji and Heike clans　202
源氏物語　*Genji Monogatari*　(The Tale of Genji)　575, 79, 67

願	**590** 9a10.2 頁 日 小 /76 42 35 願	**GAN, nega(u)** – petition, request, desire

大願　*taigan*　great ambition, earnest wish　26
念願　*nengan*　one's heart's desire　588
出願　*shutsugan*　application　53
願書　*gansho*　written request, application　131
志願　*shigan*　application, volunteering, desire　582

払	**591** 3c2.2 扌 厶 /23 17 払 拂	**FUTSU, hara(u)** – pay; sweep away

払底　*futtei*　shortage, scarcity　571
支払い　*shiharai*　payment　318
前払い　*maebarai*　payment in advance　47
現金払い　*genkinbarai*　cash payment　298, 23
分割払い　*bunkatsubarai*　payment in installments　38, 528

仏	**592** 2a2.5 亻 厶 /3 17 仏 佛	**BUTSU, hotoke** – Buddha *[FUTSU]* – (short for) France

仏教　*bukkyō*　Buddhism　245
大仏　*daibutsu*　great statue of Buddha　26
石仏　*sekibutsu, ishibotoke*　stone image of Buddha　78
念仏　*nenbutsu*　Buddhist prayer　588
日仏　*Nichi-Futsu*　Japanese-French　5

干	**593** 2k1.1 干 14 干	**KAN, hi(ru)** – get dry **ho(su)** – dry; drink up

(潮の)干満　*(shio no) kanman*　tide, ebb and flow　476, 201
干潮　*kanchō*　ebb/low tide　476
干渉　*kanshō*　interfere, meddle　438
若干　*jakkan*　some, a number of　553
物干し　*monohoshi*　frame for drying clothes　79

刊	**594** 2f3.1 刂 干 一 /16 14 1 刊	**KAN** – publish

週刊（誌）　*shūkan(shi)*　weekly magazine　92, 583
日刊（紙）　*nikkan(shi)*　daily newspaper　5, 180
夕刊　*yūkan*　evening newspaper/edition　81
新刊　*shinkan*　new publication　174
未刊行　*mikankō*　unpublished　306, 68

岸	**595** 3o5.11 山 厂 屮 /36 18 14 岸	**GAN, kishi** – bank, shore, coast

西岸　*seigan*　west bank/coast　72
対岸　*taigan*　opposite shore　366
海岸　*kaigan*　seashore, coast　117
河岸　*kawagishi, kagan*　riverbank　391
川岸　*kawagishi*　riverbank　33

皆	**596**	***KAI, mina*** – all	
	4c5.14 ⊞	皆済 *kaisai* payment in full	558
	日 ⼅ 丨	皆勤 *kaikin* perfect attendance (at work/school)	568
	/42 13 2	皆無 *kaimu* nothing/none at all	93
		皆目 *kaimoku* utterly; (not) at all	55
	皆	皆さん *minasan* everybody; Ladies and Gentlemen	

階	**597**	***KAI*** – stair, story, level	
	2d9.6 ⊞	三階 *sangai, sankai* third floor	4
	⻖ 日 ⼅	階段 *kaidan* stairs, stairway	363
	/7 42 13	段階 *dankai* stage, phase	363
		階級 *kaikyū* social class	577
	階	音階 *onkai* musical scale	347

楷	**598**	***KAI*** – rule, model	
	4a9.18	楷書 *kaisho* noncursive (kanji), printed style	131
	木 ⺫ ⼅		
	/41 42 13		
	楷		

陛	**599**	***HEI*** – steps (of the throne)	
	2d7.6	天皇陛下 *tennō heika* H.M. the Emperor	141, 297, 31
	⻖ 土 ⼅	国王陛下 *kokuō heika* H.M. the King	40, 294, 31
	/7 22 13	女王陛下 *joō heika* H.M. the Queen	102, 294, 31
		両陛下 *ryōheika* Their Majesties the Emperor and	
	陛	Empress	200, 31

羽	**600**	***U, ha, hane*** – feather; wing	
	2b4.5 ☐	羽毛 *umō* feather, plumage	287
	彐	白羽 *shiraha* white feather	205
	39	羽音 *haoto* flapping of wings	347
		一羽 *ichiwa* 1 bird/rabbit	2
	羽	羽田 *Haneda* (airport in Tōkyō)	35

習	**601**	***SHŪ, nara(u)*** – learn	
	4c7.11	学習 *gakushū* learning, study	109
	日 彐 丨	独習 *dokushū* learn on one's own, teach oneself	219
	/42 39 2	予習 *yoshū* preparation of lessons	397
		常習 *jōshū* custom; habit	506
	習	習字 *shūji* penmanship, calligraphy	110

翌	**602**	***YOKU*** – the next, following	
	5b6.6 ⊞	翌朝 *yokuasa, yokuchō* the next morning	477
	立 彐	翌日 *yokujitsu* the next/following day	5
	/54 39	翌翌日 *yokuyokujitsu* two days later/thereafter	5
		翌年 *yokunen* the following year	45
	翌	翌週 *yokushū* the following week, the week thereafter	92

603

談

7a8.7

言 火
/67 44

談

DAN – conversation

会談	kaidan	a conversation, conference	158
対談	taidan	face-to-face talk, conversation	366
談話	danwa	conversation	238
相談	sōdan	consultation	146
下相談	shitasōdan	preliminary negotiations	31, 146

604

訳

7a4.8

言 尸 丶
/67 40 2

訳 譯

YAKU – translation **wake** – reason; meaning; circumstances

通訳	tsūyaku	interpreting; interpreter	150
英訳	eiyaku	a translation into English	354
全訳	zen'yaku	a complete translation	89
訳者	yakusha	translator	164
言い訳	iiwake	apology; excuse	66

605

釈

6b5.5

米 尸 丨
/62 40 2

釈 釋

SHAKU – explanation, interpretation; release

解釈	kaishaku	comments, annotation	482
注釈	chūshaku	interpretation, construal	358
釈明	shakumei	explanation, vindication	18
釈放	shakuhō	release, discharge	521
保釈	hoshaku	bail	498

606

翻

6b12.3

米 田 彐
/62 58 39

翻 飜

HON – (tr.) turn over, translate **hirugae(su)** – change (one's opinion), wave (a flag) **hirugae(ru)** – (intr.) turn over; wave

翻訳	hon'yaku	translation, translate	604
翻案	hon'an	an adaptation	106
翻意	hon'i	change one's mind	132

607

橋

4a12.8

木 大 口
/41 34 24

橋

KYŌ, hashi – bridge

歩道橋	hodōkyō	pedestrian bridge	437, 149
鉄橋	tekkyō	iron bridge; railway bridge	312
石橋	ishibashi	stone bridge	78
つり橋	tsuribashi	suspension bridge	
日本橋	Nihonbashi	(area of Tōkyō)	5, 25

608

柱

4a5.12

木 王 丶
/41 46 2

柱

CHŪ, hashira – pillar, column, pole

支柱	shichū	prop, support, strut	318
電柱	denchū	utility/electric pole	108
水銀柱	suiginchū	column of mercury	21, 313
円柱	enchū	column, cylinder	13
大黒柱	daikokubashira	central pillar, mainstay	26, 206

609

駐

10a5.2

馬 王 丶
/78 46 2

駐

CHŪ – stop; reside

駐車場	chūshajō	parking lot	133, 154
駐在	chūzai	stay, residence	268
駐日	chūnichi	resident/stationed in Japan	5
進駐	shinchū	stationing, occupation	443

専

博

授

確

観

覚

視

610

0a9.16 ☐

日 寸 十
42　37　12

専　專

SEN, moppa(ra) – entirely, exclusively

専門家	senmonka	specialist, expert	161, 165
専任	sennin	exclusive duty, full-time	334
専制	sensei	absolutism, despotism	433
専売	senbai	monopoly	239
専用 (駐車場)	sen'yō (chūshajō)	private (parking lot)	107

611

2k10.1 ☐

十 日 寸
/12　42　37

博　愽

HAKU, [BAKU] – extensive, broad; many

博物館	hakubutsukan	museum	79, 327
博学	hakugaku	broad knowledge, erudition	109
博士	hakase, hakushi	doctor	581
博愛	hakuai	philantrophy	259
万博	banpaku	international exhibition	16

612

3c8.15 ☐

扌 小 冂
/23　35　20

授

JU, sazu(keru) – grant; teach **sazu(karu)** – be granted/taught

授業	jugyō	teaching, instruction	279
教授	kyōju	instruction; professor	245
授受	juju	giving and receiving; transfer	260
授与	juyo	confer, award	548
授賞	jushō	awarding a prize	509

613

5a10.3 ☐

石 隹 冂
/53　73　20

確

KAKU, tashi(ka) – certain **tashi(kameru)** – make sure of, verify

確立	kakuritsu	establishment, settlement	121
確定	kakutei	decision, settlement	356
確実	kakujitsu	certain, reliable	203
確信	kakushin	firm belief, conviction	157
正確	seikaku	accurate, precise, correct	275

614

5c13.7 ☐

隹 貝 ⺅
73　68　15

観　觀

KAN – appearance, view

観光	kankō	sight-seeing, tourism	138
外観	gaikan	(external) appearance	83
主観的	shukanteki	subjective	155, 210
楽観的	rakkanteki	optimistic	359, 210
観念	kannen	idea; sense (of duty/justice)	588

615

3n9.3 ☐

⺍ 貝 冂
/35　68　20

覚　覺

KAKU, obo(eru) – remember, bear in mind; learn; feel
sa(meru), sa(masu) – (intr./tr.) awake, wake up

感覚	kankaku	sense, sensation, feeling	262
直覚	chokkaku	intuition, insight	429
見覚え	mioboe	recognition, knowing by sight	63
目覚まし (時計)	mezamashi(dokei)	alarm clock	55, 42, 340

616

4e7.1 ☐

ネ 貝
/45　68

視

SHI – seeing, regarding as

視力	shiryoku	visual acuity, eyesight	100
近視	kinshi	nearsightedness, shortsightedness	452
重視	jūshi	attach importance to, stress	227
無視	mushi	ignore, disregard	93
視界	shikai	field of vision	461

617

規

5c6.9
貝 大 一
68 34 1

規

KI – standard, measure

規定	*kitei*	stipulations, provisions, regulations	356
定規	*jōgi*	ruler, square; standard, norm	356
正規	*seiki*	regular, normal, formal, legal	275
新規	*shinki*	new	174
法規	*hōki*	laws and regulations	123

618

則

7b2.1
貝 刂
/68 16

則

SOKU – rule, law

規則	*kisoku*	rule, regulation	617
原則	*gensoku*	general rule, principle	136
法則	*hōsoku*	a law	123
変則	*hensoku*	irregularity, anomaly	257
会則	*kaisoku*	rules of an association	158

619

側

2a9.4
亻 貝 刂
/3 68 16

側

SOKU, gawa, kawa – side

側面	*sokumen*	side, flank	274
側近者	*sokkinsha*	one's close associates	452, 164
左側	*hidarigawa*	left side	75
反対側	*hantaigawa*	opposite side	324, 366
日本側	*Nihongawa*	the Japanese (side)	5, 25

620

測

3a9.4
氵 貝 刂
/21 68 16

測

SOKU, haka(ru) – measure

測量	*sokuryō*	measurment, surveying	417
測定	*sokutei*	measuring	356
観測	*kansoku*	observation	614
目測	*mokusoku*	measurement by eye, estimation	55
予測	*yosoku*	estimate, forecast	397

621

列

2f4.4
刂 夕 一
/16 30 1

列

RETSU – row

列車	*ressha*	train	133
列島	*rettō*	chain of islands, archipelago	286
列国	*rekkoku*	world powers, nations	40
行列	*gyōretsu*	queue; procession; matrix	68
後列	*kōretsu*	back row	48

622

例

2a6.7
亻 夕 刂
/3 30 16

例

REI – example; custom, precedent **tato(eru)** – compare

例外	*reigai*	exception	83
特例	*tokurei*	special case, exception	282
先例	*senrei*	previous example, precedent	50
例年	*reinen*	normal year; every year	45
条例	*jōrei*	regulations, ordinance	573

623

完

3m4.6
宀 二 儿
/33 4 16

完

KAN – completion

完結	*kanketsu*	completion	494
完全	*kanzen*	complete, perfect	89
完成	*kansei*	completion, accomplishment	261
未完成	*mikansei*	incomplete, unfinished	306, 261
完敗	*kanpai*	complete defeat	520

624

院

2d7.9
阝宀二
/7 33 4

院

IN – institution; house (of a legislature), parliament

病院	byōin	hospital	381
入院	nyūin	admission to a hospital	52
大学院	daigakuin	graduate school	26, 109
寺院	jiin	temple	41
両院	ryōin	both houses (of the Diet/ Congress/Parliament)	200

625

示

4e0.1
礻
/45

示

JI, SHI, shime(su) – show

公示	kōji	public announcement	126
明示	meiji	clear statement	18
教示	kyōji	instruction, teaching	245
暗示	anji	hint, suggestion	348
示談	jidan	out-of-court settlement	603

626

宗

3m5.1
宀礻
/33 45

宗

SHŪ – religion, sect **SŌ** – head, leader

宗教	shūkyō	religion	245
宗門	shūmon	sect	161
宗徒	shūto	adherent, believer	436
改宗	kaishū	conversion, become a convert	523
宗家	sōke	the head family	165

627

祭

4e6.3
礻夕又
/45 30 9

祭

SAI, matsu(ru) – deify, worship **matsu(ri)** – festival

祭日	saijitsu	holiday; festival day	5
百年祭	hyakunensai	centennial	14, 45
文化祭	bunkasai	cultural festival	111, 254
秋祭り	akimatsuri	autumn festival	470
後の祭り	ato no matsuri	Too late!	48

628

際

2d11.1
阝礻夕
/7 45 30

際

SAI – time, occasion **kiwa** – side, brink, edge

国際	kokusai	international	40
交際	kōsai	association, company, acquaintance	114
実際	jissai	truth, reality, actual practice	203
水際	mizugiwa	water's edge, shore	21
際立つ	kiwadatsu	be conspicuous, stand out	121

629

察

3m11.6
宀礻夕
/33 45 30

察

SATSU – surmise, judge, understand, sympathize

観察	kansatsu	observation	614
検察	kensatsu	criminal investigation, prosecution	540
視察	shisatsu	inspection, observation	616
考察	kōsatsu	consideration, examination	550
明察	meisatsu	discernment, keen insight	18

630

礼

4e1.1
礻丨
/45 2

礼 禮

REI, RAI – courtesy; salutation; gratitude, remuneration

祭礼	sairei	religious festival	627
礼式	reishiki	etiquette	534
失礼	shitsurei	rudeness	311
非礼	hirei	impoliteness	507
無礼	burei	rudeness, impertinence, affront	93

祈	**631** 4e4.3 ネ 斤 /45 50 祈	**KI, ino(ru)** – pray	
		祈念 *kinen* a prayer	588
		祈願 *kigan* a prayer	590
		祈とう（書） *kitō(sho)* prayer (book)	131
		祈り *inori* a prayer	
		主の祈り *shu no inori* the Lord's Prayer	155

祖	**632** 4e5.4 ネ 月 一 /45 43 1 祖	**SO** – ancestor	
		祖先 *sosen* ancestor, forefather	50
		祖母／父 *sobo/fu* grandmother/father	112, 113
		祖国 *sokoku* one's homeland/fatherland	40
		元祖 *ganso* originator, founder, inventor	137
		宗祖 *shūso* founder of a sect	626

助	**633** 2g5.1 力 月 | /8 43 2 助	**JO, tasu(keru)** – help, rescue **tasu(karu)** – be helped, rescued **suke** – assistance	
		助力 *joryoku* help, assistance	100
		助言 *jogen* advice	66
		助手 *joshu* helper, assistant	57
		助け合う *tasukeau* help each other	159

査	**634** 4a5.32 木 月 一 /41 43 1 査	**SA** – investigate	
		調査 *chōsa* investigation, inquiry, observation	342
		検査 *kensa* inspection, examination	540
		査問 *samon* inquiry, hearing	162
		査察 *sasatsu* inspection, observation	629
		査定 *satei* assessment	356

宣	**635** 3m6.2 宀 日 · /33 42 1 宣	**SEN** – announce	
		宣言 *sengen* declaration, manifesto ⌈independence	66
		独立宣言 *dokuritsu sengen* declaration of	219, 121, 66
		宣伝 *senden* propaganda; advertising, publicity	440
		宣戦 *sensen* declaration of war	301
		宣教師 *senkyōshi* a missionary	245, 415

状	**636** 2b5.1 冫 犭 | /5 27 2 状	**JŌ** – condition, circumstances; form; letter	
		状態 *jōtai* circumstances, situation	388
		現状 *genjō* present situation	298
		白状 *hakujō* confession	205
		礼状 *reijō* letter of thanks	630
		招待状 *shōtaijō* written invitation	462, 459

将	**637** 2b8.3 冫 小 寸 /5 35 37 将 將	**SHŌ** – commander, general; soon	
		将来 *shōrai* future	69
		将軍 *shōgun* shogun, general	444
		大将 *taishō* general, leader	26
		将校 *shōkō* officer	115
		主将 *shushō* (team) captain	155

	638	**TEI** – present, submit **sa(geru)** – carry (in the hand)	
提	3c9.4 ⊞	提案 teian proposition, proposal	106
	扌 𠃌 宀	提供 teikyō offer	197
	/23 42 14	提議 teigi proposal, suggestion	292
		提出 teishutsu presentation, filing	53
	提	前提 zentei premise	47

	639	**TAI, TA** – big **futo(i)** – fat **futo(ru)** – get fat	
太	0a4.18 ⋯	太平洋 Taiheiyō Pacific Ocean	202, 289
	大 丶	皇太子 kōtaishi crown prince	297, 103
	34 2	太古 taiko ancient times, antiquity	172
		太字 futoji thick character, boldface	110
	太	太刀 tachi (long) sword	37

	640	**YŌ** – yang principle; active; positive; sun	
陽	2d9.5 ⊞	太陽 taiyō sun	639
	阝 日 彡	陽光 yōkō sunshine, sunlight	138
	/7 42 27	陽気 yōki season, weather; cheerfulness, gaiety	134
		陽性 yōsei positive	98
	陽	陽子 yōshi proton	103

	641	**YŌ, a(geru)** – raise; fry **a(garu)** – rise	
揚	3c9.5 ⊞	高揚 kōyō uplift, surge	190
	扌 日 彡	揚水車 yōsuisha scoop wheel	21, 133
	/23 42 27	意気揚々 iki-yōyō triumphantly, exultantly	132, 134
		荷揚げ niage unloading, discharge, landing	393
	揚	引き揚げ hikiage withdrawal, evacuation	216

	642	**TŌ, yu** – hot water	
湯	3a9.23 ⊞	湯治 tōji hot-spring cure	502
	氵 日 彡	湯元 yumoto source of a hot spring	137
	/21 42 27	湯船 yubune bathtub	377
		茶の湯 cha no yu tea ceremony	251
	湯	湯上がり yuagari just after a bath	32

	643	**SHŌ, kizu** – wound, injury **ita(mu)** – hurt **ita(meru)** – injure	
傷	2a11.10 ⊞	負傷 fushō wound, injury	519
	亻 日 彡	傷害 shōgai injury, damage	527
	/3 42 27	重 / 軽傷 jū/keishō severe/minor injuries	227, 556
		死傷者 shishōsha the killed and injured, casualties	85, 164
	傷		

	644	**ON, atata(kai), atata(ka)** – warm **atata(meru)** – (tr.) warm up **atata(maru)** – (intr.) warm up	
温	3a9.21 ⊞	温度 ondo temperature ⌐temperature	378
	氵 皿 日	気 / 水 / 体温 ki/sui/tai-on air/water/body	134, 21, 61
	/21 59 42	温室 onshitsu hothouse, greenhouse	166
	温	温和 onwa mild, gentle	124

暖	**645** 4c9.4 田 日 小 二 /42 35 4 暖	**DAN, atata(kai), atata(ka)** – warm **atata(meru)** – (tr.) warm up **atata(maru)** – (intr.) warm up 寒暖計　kandankei　thermometer　464, 340 温暖　ondan　warm　644 暖流　danryū　warm ocean current　247 暖冬　dantō　warm/mild winter　467
雲	**646** 8d4.1 目 雨 二 ム /74 4 17 雲	**UN, kumo** – cloud 風雲　fūun　wind and clouds; situation　29 暗雲　an'un　dark clouds　348 雨雲　amagumo　rain cloud　30 入道雲　nyūdōgumo　cumulonimbus, thunderhead　52, 149 出雲大社　Izumo Taisha　Izumo Shrine (Shimane Pref.)　53, 26, 308
曇	**647** 4c12.1 目 日 雲 二 /42 74 4 曇	**DON, kumo(ru)** – cloud up, get cloudy 曇天　donten　cloudy/overcast sky　141 曇りがち　kumorigachi　mostly cloudy 曇りガラス　kumori garasu　ground/frosted/matte glass 花曇り　hanagumori　cloudy weather in cherry-blossom season 　255
暑	**648** 4c8.5 … 日 土 ｜ /42 22 2 暑	**SHO, atsu(i)** – hot (weather) 寒暑　kansho　cold and heat　464 暑気　shoki　the heat　134 暑中　shochū　middle of summer　28 大暑　taisho　Midsummer Day (about July 24)　26 暑苦しい　atsukurushii　oppressively hot, sultry　554
厚	**649** 2p6.1 匚 厂 日 子 /18 42 6 厚	**KŌ, atsu(i)** – thick; kind, cordial 厚意　kōi　kind intentions, kindness　132 厚顔　kōgan　impudence, effrontery　277 厚生労働省　Kōsei-rōdō-shō　Ministry of Health, Labour 　and Welfare　44, 233, 232, 145 厚紙　atsugami　thick paper, cardboard　180
宴	**650** 3m7.3 目 宀 日 女 /33 42 25 宴	**EN** – feast, banquet 宴会　enkai　dinner party, banquet　158 宴席　enseki　(one's seat in) a banquet hall　380 酒宴　shuen　feast, drinking bout　526 きょう宴　kyōen　banquet, feast, dinner
客	**651** 3m6.3 目 宀 夊 口 /33 49 24 客	**KYAKU, KAKU** – guest, customer 客間/室　kyakuma/shitsu　guest room　43, 166 客船　kyakusen　passenger ship　377 乗客　jōkyaku　passenger　532 旅客　ryokaku　passenger, traveler　222 客観的　kyakkanteki　objective　614, 210

	652 4i3.3 … 夂 口 /49 24 各	**KAKU, onoono** – each, every, various	
		各地 *kakuchi* every area; various places	118
		各国 *kakkoku* all/various countries	40
		各種 *kakushu* every kind, various types	228
		各人 *kakujin* each person, everyone	1
		各自 *kakuji* each person, everyone	62

	653 4a6.17 □ 木 夂 口 /41 49 24 格	**KAKU, [KŌ]** – status, rank; standard, rule; case (in grammar)	
		人格 *jinkaku* personality, character	1
		性格 *seikaku* character, personality	98
		価格 *kakaku* price; value	427
		合格 *gōkaku* pass (an exam)	159
		格子 *kōshi* lattice, bars, grating, grille	103

	654 0a3.28 … 十 丶 12 2 丸	**GAN** – ball **maru(i)** – round **maru(meru)** – make round, form into a ball **-maru** – (suffix for names of ships)	
		丸薬 *gan'yaku* pill	360
		丸太小屋 *marutagoya* log cabin	639, 27, 167
		日本丸 *Nihon-maru* the ship Nihon	5, 25
		日の丸 *Hi no Maru* (Japanese) Rising-Sun Flag	5

	655 4d11.4 田 火 土 儿 /44 22 16 熱	**NETSU** – heat, fever **atsu(i)** – hot (object)	
		熱病 *netsubyō* fever	381
		高熱 *kōnetsu* high fever	190
		熱湯 *nettō* boiling water	642
		情熱 *jōnetsu* passion	209
		熱心 *nesshin* enthusiasm, zeal	97

	656 2g11.6 田 力 土 儿 /8 22 16 勢	**SEI, ikio(i)** – force, energy, vigor; trend	
		勢力 *seiryoku* influence, force	100
		国勢 *kokusei* state/condition of a country	40
		情勢 *jōsei* the situation	209
		大勢 *taisei* general situation/trend	26
		ōzei many people, large crowd	

	657 2d8.4 田 阝 土 儿 /7 22 16 陸	**RIKU** – land	
		大陸 *tairiku* continent, mainland	26
		陸上 *rikujō* land, ground	32
		上陸 *jōriku* landing, going ashore	32
		陸路 *rikuro* land route	151
		陸軍 *rikugun* army	444

	658 5c8.6 田 目 土 儿 /55 22 16 睦	**BOKU** – getting along well together, harmonious, friendly, intimate	
		親睦 *shinboku* friendship	175
		親睦会 *shinbokukai* social get-together	175, 158
		和睦 *waboku* rapprochement, reconciliation, peace	124

	659	**SEN** – money; 1/100 yen **zeni** – money	
錢	8a6.1 ▢	金銭 *kinsen* money	23
	釒 戈 二	口銭 *kōsen* commission, percentage	54
	/72 52 4	悪銭 *akusen* ill-gotten money	304
	銭 錢	銭湯 *sentō* public bath	642
		小銭 *kozeni* small change	27

	660	**SEN, asa(i)** – shallow	
浅	3a6.4 ▢	浅海 *senkai* shallow sea	117
	氵 戈 二	浅見 *senken* superficial view	63
	/21 52 4	浅学 *sengaku* superficial knowledge	109
	浅 淺	浅黒い *asaguroi* dark-colored, swarthy	206
		遠浅 *tōasa* shoaling beach	453

	661	**ZAN, noko(ru)** – remain **noko(su)** – leave behind	
残	0a10.11 ▢	残念 *zannen* regret, disappointment; too bad	588
	戈 夕 二	残業 *zangyō* overtime	279
	52 30 4	残高 *zandaka* balance, remainder	190
	残 殘	残り物 *nokorimono* leftovers	79
		生き残る *ikinokoru* survive	44

	662	**ZEN, NEN** – as, like	
然	4d8.10 ▢	全然 *zenzen* (not) at all; completely	89
	火 夕 犭	当然 *tōzen* naturally, (as a matter) of course	77
	/44 30 27	必然 *hitsuzen* inevitability, necessity	529
	然	自然 *shizen* nature	62
		天然 *tennen* natural	141

	663	**NEN, mo(eru)** – (intr.) burn **mo(yasu), mo(su)** – (tr.) burn	
燃	4d12.2 ▢	燃料 *nenryō* fuel	319
	火 夕 犭	不燃性 *funensei* nonflammable, fireproof	94, 98
	/44 30 27	可燃性 *kanensei* flammable, combustible 「engine	390, 98
	燃	内燃機関 *nainen kikan* internal-combustion	84, 537, 402
		燃え上がる *moeagaru* blaze up, burst into flames	32

	664	**KOKU, tani** – valley	
谷	2o5.3 …	谷間 *tanima* valley	43
	火 口	谷底 *tanisoko* bottom of a ravine/gorge	571
	44 24	谷川 *tanigawa* mountain stream	33
	谷	長谷川 *Hasegawa* (surname)	95, 33
		四谷 *Yotsuya* (area of Tōkyō)	6

	665	**YŌ** – form, appearance; content	
容	3m7.8 ▢	美容院 *biyōin* beauty parlor, hairdresser's	405, 624
	宀 火 口	形容 *keiyō* form; metaphor	399
	/33 44 24	内容 *naiyō* content	84
	容	容器 *yōki* container	536
		容量 *yōryō* capacity, volume	417

	666	**SEKI** – responsibility; censure **se(meru)** – condemn, censure; torture
責	7b4.4	責任　　sekinin　responsibility　334
	/68　22　1	重責　　jūseki　heavy responsibility　227
	責	責務　　sekimu　duty, obligation　235
		自責　　jiseki　self-reproach, pangs of conscience　62
		引責　　inseki　assume responsibility　216

	667	**SEKI** – accumulation; product (in math); size, volume **tsu(moru)** – be piled up, accumulate **tsu(mu)** – heap up, load
積	5d11.5	面積　　menseki　(surface) area　274
	/56　68　22	積極的　sekkyokuteki　positive, active　336, 210
	積	見積(書)　mitsumori(sho)　(written) estimate　63, 131
		積み重ねる　tsumikasaneru　stack up one on another　227

	668	**CHAKU, [JAKU]** – arrival; clothing **ki(ru), tsu(keru)** – put on, wear **ki(seru)** – dress (someone) **tsu(ku)** – arrive
着	2o10.1	着陸　　chakuriku　(airplane) landing　657
	/16　55　46	決着　　ketchaku　conclusion, settlement, decision　357
	着	着物　　kimono　kimono; clothing　79
		下着　　shitagi　underwear　31

	669	**SA** – difference **sa(su)** – hold (an umbrella), wear (a sword), offer (a cup of saké)
差	2o8.4	時差　　jisa　time difference/lag　42
	/16　46　38	差別　　sabetsu　discrimination　267
	差	交差点　kōsaten　intersection　114, 169
		差し支え　sashitsukae　impediment; objection　318

	670	**SEI, [SHŌ]** – spirit; energy, vitality
精	6b8.1	精力　　seiryoku　energy, vigor, vitality　100
	/62　43　22	精神　　seishin　mind, spirit　310
	精	精液　　seieki　semen, sperm　480
		精進　　shōjin　diligence, devotion; purification　443
		不精　　bushō　sloth, laziness, indolence　94

	671	**SEI, [SHŌ], kiyo(i)** – pure, clean, clear **kiyo(meru)** – purify, cleanse **kiyo(maru)** – be purified, cleansed
清	3a8.18	清酒　　seishu　refined saké　526
	/21　43　22	清書　　seisho　fair/clean copy　131
	清	清水　　seisui, shimizu　pure/clean water　21
		清水寺　Kiyomizu-dera　(temple in Kyōto)　21, 41

	672	**SEI, SHIN, ko(u)** – ask for **u(keru)** – receive
請	7a8.8	請願　　seigan　petition, application　590
	/67　43　22	要請　　yōsei　demand, requirement, request　425
	請	申請　　shinsei　application, petition　309
		強請　　kyōsei　importunate demand; extortion　217
		下請け　shitauke　subcontract　31

晴	**673** 4c8.2 ⊞ 日 月 士 /42 43 22 晴	**SEI** – clear **ha(reru)** – (intr.) clear up **ha(rasu)** – (tr.) clear up
		晴天　　seiten　clear sky, fine weather　　141 晴曇　　seidon　changeable, fair to cloudy　　647 秋晴れ　akibare　clear autumn weather　　470 見晴らし　miharashi　view, vista　　63 気晴らし　kibarashi　pastime, diversion　　134

静	**674** 4b10.9 ⊞ 月 士 /43 22 39 静 靜	**SEI, [JŌ], shizu, shizu(ka)** – quiet, peaceful, still **shizu(meru)** – make peaceful **shizu(maru)** – become peaceful
		静物　　seibutsu　still life　　79 静止　　seishi　stillness, rest, stationary　　485 安静　　ansei　rest, quiet, repose　　105 平静　　heisei　calm, serenity　　202

浄	**675** 3a6.18 ⊞ 氵 彐 ㇒ /21 39 15 浄 淨	**JŌ** – pure
		清浄　　seijō　purity, cleanliness　　671 浄化　　jōka　purification　　254 不浄　　fujō　dirtiness, impurity　　94 浄土宗　Jōdoshū　the Jōdo sect (of Buddhism)　　24, 626

破	**676** 5a5.1 ▢ 石 丿 又 /53 18 9 破	**HA, yabu(ru)** – tear, break **yabu(reru)** – get torn/broken
		破産　　hasan　bankruptcy　　278 破局　　hakyoku　catastrophe, ruin　　170 破約　　hayaku　breach of contract/promise　　211 破れ目　yabureme　a tear, split　　55 見破る　miyaburu　see through　　63

波	**677** 3a5.9 ▢ 氵 厂 又 /21 18 9 波	**HA, nami** – wave
		波止場　hatoba　wharf, pier　　485, 154 電波　　denpa　electric/radio wave　　108 短波　　tanpa　shortwave　　215 波長　　hachō　wavelength　　95 波乗り　naminori　surfing　　532

律	**678** 3i6.1 ▢ 彳 彐 十 /29 39 12 律	**RITSU, [RICHI]** – law, regulation
		法律　　hōritsu　law　　123 規律　　kiritsu　order, discipline, regulations　　617 不文律　fubunritsu　unwritten law　　94, 111 韻律　　inritsu　rhythm, meter　　350 自律神経　jiritsu shinkei　autonomic nerve　　62, 310, 557

津	**679** 3a6.1 ▢ 氵 彐 十 /21 39 12 津	**SHIN, tsu** – harbor; ferry
		津波　　tsunami　tsunami, "tidal" wave　　677 興味津々　kyōmi-shinshin　very interesting　　369, 307 津軽半島　Tsugaru hantō　Tsugaru Peninsula　　556, 88, 286

港	**680** 3a9.13 □ 氵 艹 弓 /21 32 28 港	**KŌ, minato** – harbor, port 空港　kūkō　airport　140 商 / 軍港　shō/gunkō　trading/naval port　418, 444 内港　naikō　inner harbor　84 港内　kōnai　in the harbor　84 港町　minatomachi　port city　182
湾	**681** 3a9.15 □ 氵 弓 亠 /21 28 11 湾 灣	**WAN** – bay 東京湾　Tōkyō-wan　Tōkyō Bay　71, 189 湾曲　wankyoku　curvature, bend　367 港湾　kōwan　harbor　680 港湾労働者　kōwan rōdōsha　port laborer,　680, 233, 232, 164 台湾　Taiwan　Taiwan, Formosa　└longshoreman　501
妻	**682** 3e5.10 □ 女 彐 十 /25 39 12 妻	**SAI, tsuma** – wife 夫妻　fusai　husband and wife, Mr. and Mrs.　315 妻子　saishi　wife and child/children, family　103 後妻　gosai　second wife　48 良妻　ryōsai　good wife　321 老妻　rōsai　one's aged wife　552
凄	**683** 2b8.4 □ 氵 彐 女 75 39 25 凄	**SEI** – awful, tremendous, terrible 凄惨　seisan　ghastly, gruesome, lurid　1843 凄絶　seizetsu　ghastly, gruesome　755
亡	**684** 2j1.1 □ 亠 丨 /11 2 亡	**BŌ, [MŌ]** – die **na(i)** – dead, deceased 死亡者　shibōsha　the dead　85, 164 亡父　bōfu　one's late father　113 亡夫　bōfu　one's late husband　315 未亡人　mibōjin　widow　306, 1 亡命　bōmei　fleeing one's country, going into exile　587
望	**685** 4f7.6 □ 王 夕 亠 /46 30 11 望	**BŌ, MŌ, nozo(mu)** – desire, wish, hope for 志望　shibō　wish, aspiration　582 宿望　shukubō　long-cherished desire　179 要望　yōbō　demand, wish　425 失望　shitsubō　despair, disappointment　311 大望　taimō　great desire, ambition　26
聖	**686** 4f9.9 □ 王 耳 口 /46 65 24 聖	**SEI** – holy 聖人　seijin　sage, holy man　1 神聖　shinsei　sacredness, sanctity　310 聖書　Seisho　the Bible　131 聖堂　seidō　Confucian temple; church　505 聖母　Seibo　the Holy Mother, the Blessed Mary　112

巾	**687** 3f0.1 ☐ 巾 /26 巾	**KIN** – a cloth, rag, towel 雑巾　*zōkin*　wiping cloth, mopping rag　　584 頭巾　*zukin*　hood, kerchief　　276 赤頭巾　*akazukin*　red hood　　207, 276 赤頭巾（ちゃん）　*Akazukin(-chan)*　Little Red Riding　207, 276 巾着　*kinchaku*　moneybag, purse　└Hood　668
布	**688** 3f2.1 ☐ 巾 ⼗ /26 12 布	**FU** – spread; cloth **nuno** – a cloth 財布　*saifu*　purse, wallet　　562 布巾　*fukin*　dish towel, dishcloth　　687 毛布　*mōfu*　a blanket　　287 分布　*bunpu*　distribution, range　　38 公布　*kōfu*　official announcement, promulgation　126
希	**689** 3f4.1 ⋯ 巾 ⼗ /26 12 希	**KI** – hope, desire; rarity, scarcity 希望　*kibō*　wish, hope　　685 希少　*kishō*　scarce, rare　　144 希少価値　*kishō kachi*　scarcity value　　144, 427, 431 メーカー希望価格　*mēkā kibō kakaku*　manufacturer's 　　suggested price, list price　　685, 427, 653
衣	**690** 5e0.1 ☐ 衤 /57 衣	**I, koromo** – garment, clothes 衣類　*irui*　clothing　　226 黒衣　*kokui*　black clothes　　206 法衣　*hōi*　priestly robes, vestment　　123 衣食住　*ishokujū*　food, clothing, and shelter　322, 156 羽衣　*hagoromo*　robe of feathers　　600
依	**691** 2a6.1 ☐ 亻 衤 /3 57 依	**I, [E]** – depend on, be due to; request 依存（度）　*izon(do)*　(extent of) dependence　269, 378 依然として　*izen toshite*　as ever, as before　662 帰依　*kie*　faith, devotion; conversion　　317
初	**692** 5e2.1 ☐ 衤 力 /57 8 初	**SHO** – first; beginning **haji(me)** – beginning **haji(mete)** – for the first time **hatsu-, ui-** – first **-so(meru)** – begin to 最初　*saisho*　beginning, first　　263 初歩　*shoho*　rudiments, ABCs　　437 初演　*shoen*　first performance, premiere　344 初恋　*hatsukoi*　one's first love　　258
織	**693** 6a12.6 ☐☐ 糸 戈 日 /61 52 42 織	**SHOKU, SHIKI, o(ru)** – weave 織機　*shokki*　loom　　537 組織　*soshiki*　organization, structure; tissue　424 織物　*orimono*　cloth, fabric, textiles　　79 毛織（物）　*keori(mono)*　woolen fabric　287, 79 羽織　*haori*　haori, Japanese half-coat　600

694		SHIKI – know; discriminate			
7a12.6	意識	ishiki	consciousness		132
言 戈 日	知識	chishiki	knowledge		214
/67 52 42	常識	jōshiki	common sense/knowledge		506
識	学識	gakushiki	learning		109
	識別	shikibetsu	discrimination, recognition		267

695		HEN – compile, edit a(mu) – knit, crochet			
6a9.13	編集	henshū	editing		442
糸 尸 艹	短編小説	tanpen shōsetsu	short novel, story	215, 27, 404
/61 40 32	編成	hensei	organizing, formation		261
編	編み物	amimono	knitting; knitted goods		79
	手編み	teami	knitting by hand		57

696		FUKU – clothes, dress; obey, serve; dose			
4b4.6	衣服	ifuku	clothing		690
月 阝 又	洋/和服	yō/wafuku	Western/Japanese clothing	289, 124
/43 7 9	心服	shinpuku	admiration and devotion		97
服	着服	chakufuku	embezzlement, misappropriation		668
	服役	fukueki	penal servitude; military service		376

697		KŌ, saiwa(i), shiawa(se), sachi – happiness, good fortune			
3b5.9	幸運	kōun	good fortune, luck		445
立 十 一	不幸	fukō	unhappiness, misfortune		94
54 12 1					
幸					

698		HŌ – news, report; remuneration muku(iru) – reward, requite			
3b9.16	情報	jōhō	information		209
立 十 阝	報道機関	hōdō kikan	news media, the press	149, 537, 402
54 12 7	天気予報	tenki yohō	weather forecast	141, 134, 397
報	報知	hōchi	information, news, intelligence		214
	急報	kyūhō	telegram		303

699		SHITSU, SHŪ – carry out, execute to(ru) – take, grasp			
3b8.15	執行	shikkō	execution, performance		68
立 十 一	執権	shikken	regent		335
54 12 1	執心	shūshin	devotion, attachment, infatuation		97
執	執着	shūjaku, shūchaku	attachment to; tenacity		668
	執念	shūnen	tenacity of purpose; vindictiveness		588

700		JUKU – ripe; mature u(reru) – ripen, come to maturity			
4d10.5	円熟	enjuku	maturity, mellowness		13
火 日 亠	成熟	seijuku	ripeness, maturity		261
/44 24 11	未熟	mijuku	unripe, immature, green		306
熟	半熟	hanjuku	half-cooked, soft-boiled (egg)		88
	熟語	jukugo	compound word; phrase		67

701	**JI** – word; resignation **ya(meru)** – quit, resign	
5b8.4 田	辞書／典　*jisho/ten*　dictionary	131, 368
立 口 十	（お）世辞　*(o)seji*　compliment, flattery	252
/54 24 12	式辞　*shikiji*　address, oration	534
辞 辭	辞職　*jishoku*　resignation	386
	辞表　*jihyō*　(letter of) resignation	272

702	**RAN** – disorder; riot, rebellion **mida(reru)** – be in disorder, be confused/disorganized **mida(su)** – put in disorder/confusion	
3d4.21 田	反乱　*hanran*　rebellion, insurgency, insurrection	324
口 十 丨	内乱　*nairan*　internal strife, civil war; disorder, confusion	84
/24 12 2	乱筆　*ranpitsu*　hasty writing, scrawl	130
乱 亂		

703	**KOKU, tsu(geru)** – tell, announce, inform	
3d4.18 ☰	報告　*hōkoku*　report	698
口 土 丨	通告　*tsūkoku*　notice, notification	150
/24 22 2	申告　*shinkoku*　report, declaration, (tax) return	309
告	告発　*kokuhatsu*　prosecution, indictment, accusation	96
	告白　*kokuhaku*　confession, avowal, profession	205

704	**ZŌ, tsuku(ru)** – produce, build	
2q7.11 ▯	製造　*seizō*　manufacture, production	434
辶 口 土	造船　*zōsen*　shipbuilding	377
/19 24 22	木造　*mokuzō*　made of wood, wooden	22
造	人造　*jinzō*　man-made, artificial	1
	手造り　*tezukuri*　handmade	57

705	**SEN, ara(u)** – wash	
3a6.12 ⊞	洗剤　*senzai*　detergent	559
氵 土 儿	洗面器　*senmenki*　wash basin	274, 536
/21 22 16	洗面所　*senmenjo*　washroom, lavatory	274, 153
洗	（お）手洗い　*(o)tearai*　washroom, lavatory	57
	洗い立てる　*araitateru*　inquire into, rake up, ferret out	121

706	**O, kitana(i), kega(rawashii)** – dirty **yogo(reru), kega(reru)** – become dirty **yogo(su), kega(su)** – make dirty	
3a3.5 ▯	汚職　*oshoku*　corruption, bribery	386
氵 二 一	汚物　*obutsu*　dirt, filth; sewage	79
/21 14 1	汚点　*oten*　blot, blotch, blemish, tarnish	169
汚	汚名　*omei*　stigma, stain on one's name, dishonor	82

707	**KŌ, hiro(i)** – broad, wide **hiro(geru)** – extend, enlarge **hiro(garu)** – spread, expand **hiro(meru)** – broaden, propagate **hiro(maru)** – spread, be propagated	
3q2.1 ▯	広告　*kōkoku*　advertisement	703
广 厶	広大　*kōdai*　vast, extensive, huge	26
/18 17	広場　*hiroba*　plaza, public square	154
広 廣		

708	**SAI** – narrow, small, fine **hoso(i)** – thin, narrow, slender
6a5.1	**hoso(ru)** – get thinner **koma(kai), koma(ka)** – small, detailed

糸 田 /61 58 細		
委細	isai	details, particulars	474
細説	saisetsu	detailed explanation	404
細工	saiku	work, workmanship; artifice, trick	139
細長い	hosonagai	long and thin, lean and lanky	95

709	**SHŌ, matsu** – pine
4a4.16	

木 儿 ム /41 16 17 松 杦		
松原	matsubara	pine grove	136
松林	matsubayashi	pine woods	127
松葉	matsuba	pine needle	253
門松	kadomatsu	pine decoration for New Year's	161
松島	Matsushima	(scenic coastal area near Sendai)	286

710	**SŌ** – general, overall
6a8.20	

糸 心 儿 /61 51 16 総 總		
総会	sōkai	general meeting, plenary session	158
総合	sōgō	synthesis, comprehensive	159
総計	sōkei	(sum) total ⌈product	340
国内総生産	kokunai sōseisan	gross domestic	40, 177, 44, 278
総理	sōri	prime minister	143

711	**SŌ, mado** – window
3m8.7	

宀 心 儿 /33 51 16 窓 窗		
同窓生	dōsōsei	fellow graduate (of the same school),	198, 44
車窓	shasō	car window ⌈former classmate, alumnus	133
窓口	madoguchi	(ticket) window	54
二重窓	nijūmado	double window	3, 227
窓際の席	madogiwa no seki	seat next to the window	628, 380

712	**GYO, RYŌ** – fishing
3a11.1	

氵 魚 /21 79 漁		
漁業	gyogyō	fishery, fishing industry	279
漁船	gyosen	fishing boat/vessel	377
漁場	gyojō	fishing ground/banks	154
漁村	gyoson	fishing village	191
漁師	ryōshi	fisherman	415

713	**GEI, kujira** – whale
11a8.9	

魚 口 小 /79 24 35 鯨		
鯨肉	geiniku	whale meat	223
鯨油	geiyu	whale oil	365
鯨飲	geiin	drink like a fish, guzzle	323
白鯨	Hakugei	(Moby Dick, or The White Whale – Melville)	205

714	**SEN, aza(yaka)** – fresh, vivid, clear, brilliant
11a6.7	

魚 王 儿 /79 46 16 鮮		
新鮮	shinsen	fresh	174
鮮明	senmei	clear, distinct	18
鮮度	sendo	(degree of) freshness	378
鮮魚	sengyo	fresh fish	290
朝鮮	Chōsen	Korea	477

715

遲

2q9.17 ⽊

辶 ⺩ 尸
/19 46 40

遅 遅

CHI, oso(i) – late, tardy; slow **oku(reru)** – be late (for); be slow (clock)
oku(rasu) – defer; put back (a clock)

遅配	chihai	delay in apportioning/delivery	524
遅着	chichaku	late arrival	668
乗り遅れる	noriokureru	be too late to catch, miss (a bus/train)	532

716

導

5c9.3 ⽬

目 寸 辶
/55 37 19

導

DŌ, michibi(ku) – lead, guide

主導	shudō	leadership, guidance	155
先導	sendō	guidance, leadership	50
導入	dōnyū	introduction	52
導火線	dōkasen	fuse; cause, occasion	20, 299
半導体	handōtai	semiconductor	88, 61

717

尊

2o10.3 ⾣

酉 寸 儿
71 37 16

尊

SON, tatto(bu), tōto(bu) – value, esteem, respect
tatto(i), tōto(i) – valuable, precious, noble, august

尊重	sonchō	value, respect, pay high regard to	227
自尊(心)	jison(shin)	self-respect, pride	62, 97
尊大	sondai	haughtiness, arrogance	26
本尊	honzon	Buddha; idol; he himself, she herself	25

718

敬

4i8.4 ⽥

攵 艹 ⼝
/49 32 24

敬

KEI, uyama(u) – respect, revere

尊敬	sonkei	respect, deference	717
敬意	keii	respect, homage	132
敬老	keirō	respect for the aged	552
敬遠	keien	keep at a respectful distance	453
敬語	keigo	an honorific, term of respect	67

719

警

7a12.7 ⽥

言 攵 艹
/67 49 32

警

KEI – admonish, warn

警察	keisatsu	police	629
警官	keikan	policeman	326
警視	keishi	police superintendent	616
警告	keikoku	warning, admonition	703
警報	keihō	warning (signal), alarm	698

720

卸

2e7.1 ⽥

⼧ ⼂ ⼗
/7 15 12

卸

oro(su) – sell wholesale **oroshi** – wholesaling

卸商	oroshishō	wholesaler	418
卸値	oroshine	wholesale price	431
卸し売り物価	oroshiuri bukka	wholesale prices	239, 79, 427

721

御

3i9.1 ⽥

彳 阝 ⼧
/29 7 15

御

GYO, GO, on- – (honorific prefix)

制御	seigyo	control, governing, suppression	433
御飯	gohan	boiled rice; meal	325
御用の方	goyō no kata	customer, inquirer	107, 70
御所	gosho	imperial palace	153
御中	onchū	Dear sirs:, Gentlemen:, Messrs.	28

加	**722** 2g3.1 ⊞ 力 口 /8 24 加口	**KA** – add, append; (short for) Canada, California **kuwa(eru)** – join, take part (in) **kuwa(waru)** – increase; join in

加入　*kanyū*　joining　52
加工　*kakō*　processing　139
倍加　*baika*　doubling　87
付加価値税　*fukakachi-zei*　value-added tax　192, 427, 431, 403

参 参	**723** 3j5.1 ⊟ 彡 大 ム /31 34 17 参 參	**SAN** – three (in documents), go, come, visit **mai(ru)** – go, come, visit, visit a temple/shrine

参加　*sanka*　participation　722
参列　*sanretsu*　attendance, presence　621
参考書　*sankōsho*　reference book/work　550, 131
参議院　*Sangiin*　(Japanese) House of Councilors　292, 624

弁	**724** 0a5.30 ⊟ 艹 ム 32 17 弁 辯	**BEN** – speech, dialect; discrimination; petal; valve

弁当　*bentō*　box/sack lunch　77
駅弁　*ekiben*　box lunch sold at a train station　284
答弁　*tōben*　reply, answer　160
弁解　*benkai*　explanation, justification, excuse　482
関西弁　*Kansai-ben*　Kansai dialect/accent　402, 72

増	**725** 3b11.3 ⊞ 土 田 日 /22 58 42 増	**ZŌ, ma(su), fu(eru)** – increase, rise **fu(yasu)** – increase, raise

増加　*zōka*　increase, rise, growth　722
増産　*zōsan*　increase in production　278
増税　*zōzei*　tax increase　403
増進　*zōshin*　increase, furtherance, improvement　443

富	**726** 3m9.5 ⊞ 宀 田 口 /33 58 24 富 冨	**FU, [FŪ]** – wealth **tomi** – wealth; lottery ticket **to(mu)** – be/become rich

国富　*kokufu*　national wealth　40
富強　*fukyō*　wealth and power (of a nation)　217
富力　*furyoku*　wealth, resources　100
富者　*fusha*　rich person, the wealthy　164
富士山　*Fuji-san*　Mount Fuji　581, 34

副	**727** 2f9.2 ⊟ 刂 田 口 /16 58 24 副	**FUKU** – assistant, accompany, supplement

副社長　*fukushachō*　company vice-president　308, 95
副業　*fukugyō*　side business, sideline　279
副産物　*fukusanbutsu*　by-product　278, 79
副作用　*fukusayō*　side effects　361, 107
副題　*fukudai*　subtitle, subheading　355

減	**728** 3a9.37 ⊞ 氵 戈 口 /21 52 24 減	**GEN, he(ru)** – decrease, diminish **he(rasu)** – decrease, shorten

増減　*zōgen*　increase and/or decrease　725
加減　*kagen*　addition and subtraction; state of health　722
減少　*genshō*　decrease, reduction　144
半減　*hangen*　reduction by half　88
減法　*genpō*　subtraction (in math)　123

益	**729** 2o8.5 丷 皿 一 /16 59 1 益	**EKI, [YAKU]** – profit, use, advantage	
		利益 *rieki* profit, advantage	329
		公益 *kōeki* the public good	126
		有益 *yūeki* useful, beneficial, profitable	265
		無益 *mueki* useless, in vain	93
		益鳥 *ekichō* beneficial bird	285

盟	**730** 5h8.1 皿 日 月 /59 42 43 盟	**MEI** – oath, alliance	
		連盟 *renmei* league, federation	446
		同盟 *dōmei* alliance, confederation	198
		加盟 *kamei* joining, affiliation	722
		盟主 *meishu* the leader, leading power	155
		盟約 *meiyaku* pledge, pact; alliance	211

誠	**731** 7a6.3 言 戈 一 /67 52 1 誠	**SEI, makoto** – truth, reality, sincerity, fidelity	
		誠実 *seijitsu* sincere, faithful, truthful	203
		誠意 *seii* sincerity, good faith	132
		誠心誠意 *seishin-seii* sincerely, wholeheartedly	97, 132
		誠に *makoto ni* truly, indeed; sincerely; very	

盛	**732** 5h6.1 皿 戈 一 /59 52 1 盛	**SEI, [JŌ], saka(n)** – prosperous, energetic **saka(ru)** – flourish, prosper **mo(ru)** – serve (food), heap up	
		盛大 *seidai* thriving, grand, magnificent	26
		全盛 *zensei* height of prosperity, zenith, heyday	89
		最盛期 *saiseiki* golden age, zenith	263, 456
		花盛り *hanazakari* in full bloom, at its best	255

城	**733** 3b6.1 土 戈 一 /22 52 1 城	**JŌ, shiro** – castle	
		城下町 *jōkamachi* castle town	31, 182
		城主 *jōshu* feudal lord of a castle	155
		開城 *kaijō* surrender of a fortress, capitulation	400
		城門 *jōmon* castle gate	161
		古城 *kojō* old castle	172

宮	**734** 3m7.5 宀 口 丨 /33 24 2 宮	**KYŪ, GŪ, [KU], miya** – shrine; palace; prince	
		宮城 *kyūjō* imperial palace	733
		神宮 *jingū* Shintō shrine	310
		御宮参り *omiyamairi* taking one's baby to a shrine	721, 723
		宮城県 *Miyagi-ken* Miyagi Prefecture	733, 194
		子宮 *shikyū* uterus, womb	103

営	**735** 3n9.2 丷 口 冂 /35 24 20 営	**EI** – run (a business); build; camp, barracks **itona(mu)** – conduct (business), perform; build	
		経営 *keiei* management, administration	557
		運営 *un'ei* operation, management, running	445
		営業 *eigyō* (running a) business	279
		営利 *eiri* profit, profit-making	329

栄	**736** 3n6.1 ⺍ 木 冂 /35 41 20 栄 榮	**El, ha(e)** – glory, honor, splendor **ha(eru)** – shine, be brilliant **saka(eru)** – thrive, prosper

栄養	eiyō	nutrition	406
光栄	kōei	honor, glory	138
栄光	eikō	glory	138
見栄え	mibae	outward appearance	63

求	**737** 2b5.5 [...] 氵 一 丨 21 1 2 求	**KYŪ, moto(meru)** – seek, want, request, demand

請求	seikyū	a claim, demand	672
要求	yōkyū	demand	425
求職	kyūshoku	seeking employment, job hunting	386
求人	kyūjin	job offer, Help Wanted	1
探求	tankyū	research, investigation	544

救	**738** 4i7.1 ▢ 攵 氵 一 /49 21 1 救	**KYŪ, suku(u)** – rescue, aid

救急	kyūkyū	first aid	303
救助	kyūjo	rescue, relief	633
救済	kyūsai	relief, aid, redemption, salvation	558
救命ボート	kyūmei bōto	lifeboat	587
救世軍	Kyūseigun	Salvation Army	252, 444

球	**739** 4f7.2 ▢ 王 氵 一 /46 21 1 球	**KYŪ, tama** – ball, sphere

野球	yakyū	baseball	236
球場	kyūjō	baseball stadium, ballpark	154
(軽)気球	(kei)kikyū	(hot-air/helium) balloon	556, 134
地球	chikyū	the earth, globe	118
北半球	kita-hankyū	Northern Hemisphere	73, 88

儀	**740** 2a13.4 亻 王 戈 /3 46 52 儀	**GI** – rule; ceremony; affair, matter

礼儀	reigi	politeness, courtesy, propriety	630
礼儀正しい	reigitadashii	courteous, decorous	630, 275
儀式	gishiki	ceremony, formality, ritual	534
儀典長	gitenchō	chief of protocol	368, 95
地球儀	chikyūgi	a globe	118, 739

犠	**741** 4g13.1 ▢ 牛 王 戈 /47 46 52 犠 犧	**GI** – sacrifice

牲	**742** 4g5.1 ▢ 牛 土 亠 /47 22 15 牲	**SEI** – sacrifice

犠牲	gisei	sacrifice	741
犠牲者	giseisha	victim	741, 164

743

星

4c5.7

日 土 宀
/42 22 15

星

SEI, [SHŌ], hoshi – star

火星	kasei	Mars	20
明星	myōjō	morning star, Venus	18
すい星	suisei	comet	
流れ星	nagareboshi	shooting star, meteor	247
星空	hoshizora	starry sky	140

744

牧

4g4.1

牛 攵
/47 49

牧

BOKU, maki – pasture

牧場	bokujō, makiba	pasture, meadow	154
牧草地	bokusōchi	pasture, grassland, meadowland	249, 118
放牧	hōboku	pasturage, grazing	521
牧羊者	bokuyōsha	sheep raiser, shepherd	288, 164
牧師	bokushi	pastor, minister	415

745

件

2a4.4

亻 牛
/3 47

件

KEN – matter, affair, case

事件	jiken	incident, affair, case	80
条件	jōken	condition, terms, stipulation	573
要件	yōken	important matter; condition, requisite	425
用件	yōken	(item of) business	107
案件	anken	matter, case, item	106

746

免

2n6.1

ク 口 儿
/15 24 16

免

MEN, manuka(reru) – escape, avoid, be exempt from

御免	gomen	pardon; declining, refusal	721
免責	menseki	exemption from responsibility	666
免税	menzei	tax exemption	403
免状	menjō	diploma; license	636
免職	menshoku	dismissal from one's job/ office	386

747

逸

2q8.6

辶 口 宀
/19 24 15

逸

ITSU – idleness; diverge, deviate from

逸話	itsuwa	anecdote	238
逸品	ippin	superb article, masterpiece	230
放逸	hōitsu	self-indulgence, licentiousness	521
独逸	Doitsu	Germany	219

748

勉

2n8.1

ク 口 儿
/15 24 16

勉

BEN – effort, hard work

勉強	benkyō	studying; diligence; sell cheap	217
勉強家	benkyōka	diligent student; hard worker	217, 165
勉学	bengaku	study, pursuit of one's studies	109
勤勉	kinben	industriousness, diligence, hard work	568

749

晩

4c8.3

日 口 宀
/42 24 15

晩

BAN – evening, night

今晩	konban	this evening, tonight	51
毎晩	maiban	every evening	116
一晩	hitoban	a night, all night	2
朝晩	asaban	mornings and evenings, day and night	477
晩年	bannen	latter part of one's life	45

許	**750** 7a4.3 言 亠 十 /67 15 12 許	**KYO, yuru(su)** – permit, allow

免許 *menkyo* permission, license — 746
許可 *kyoka* permission, approval, authorization — 390
許容 *kyoyō* permission, tolerance — 665
特許 *tokkyo* special permission; patent — 282
特許法 *tokkyo-hō* patent law — 282, 123

認	**751** 7a7.10 言 心 力 /67 51 8 認	**NIN, mito(meru)** – perceive; recognize; approve of

認可 *ninka* approval — 390
認定 *nintei* approval, acknowledgment — 356
確認 *kakunin* confirmation, certification — 613
公認 *kōnin* official recognition/sanction — 126
認識 *ninshiki* cognition, recognition, perception — 694

象	**752** 2n10.1 ク 口 豸 /15 24 27 象	**SHŌ** – image, shape **ZŌ** – elephant

具象的 *gushōteki* concrete, embodied — 426, 210
現象 *genshō* phenomenon — 298
対象 *taishō* object, subject, target — 366
気象 *kishō* weather; disposition, temperament — 134
気象学 *kishōgaku* meteorology — 134, 109

像	**753** 2a12.8 亻 口 豸 /3 24 27 像	**ZŌ** – statue, image

仏像 *butsuzō* statue/image of Buddha — 592
画像 *gazō* portait, picture, image — 343
自画像 *jigazō* self-portrait — 62, 343
受像機 *juzōki* television set — 260, 537
想像 *sōzō* imagination — 147

株	**754** 4a6.3 木 ケ /41 15 株	**kabu** – share, stock; stump

株式会社 *kabushiki-gaisha* Co., Ltd. — 534, 158, 308
株券 *kabuken* share, stock certificate — 515
株主 *kabunushi* stockholder ⌐shareholders — 155
株主総会 *kabunushi sōkai* general meeting of — 155, 710, 158
切り株 *kirikabu* (tree) stump, (grain) stubble — 39

絶	**755** 6a6.11 糸 尸 ケ /61 40 15 絶	**ZETSU, ta(eru)** – die out, end **ta(tsu)** – cut off, interrupt; eradicate **ta(yasu)** – kill off, let die out

絶対 *zettai* absolute — 366
絶大 *zetsudai* greatest, immense — 26
絶望 *zetsubō* despair — 685
中絶 *chūzetsu* termination; abortion — 28

練	**756** 6a8.2 糸 木 日 /61 41 42 練	**REN, ne(ru)** – knead; train; polish up

練習 *renshū* practice, exercise — 601
教練 *kyōren* (military) drill — 245
試練 *shiren* trial, test, ordeal — 535
熟練 *jukuren* practiced skill, expertness, mastery — 700
洗練 *senren* polish, refine — 705

	757	**TAI, ka(eru)** – replace **ka(waru)** – be replaced	
替	4c8.12 田	代替 *daitai, daigae* substitution	256
	日 六 一	両替 *ryōgae* exchanging/changing money	200
	/42 34 1	着替える *kigaeru, kikaeru* change clothes	668
		切り替え *kirikae* renewal, changeover	39
	替	取り替え *torikae* exchange, swap, replacement	65

	758	**SAN** – praise, agreement	
賛	7b8.6 田	賛成 *sansei* agreement, approbation	261
	貝 六 一	賛助 *sanjo* support, backing	633
	/68 34 1	協賛 *kyōsan* approval, consent, support	234
		賞賛 *shōsan* praise, admiration	509
	賛 贊	賛美 *sanbi* praise, glorification	405

	759	**SEI, [SHŌ], koe, [kowa-]** – voice	
声	3p4.4 田	声明 *seimei* declaration, statement, proclamation	18
	声 尸	名声 *meisei* fame, reputation	82
	/22 40 2	音声学 *onseigaku* phonetics	347, 109
		声変わり *koegawari* change/cracking of voice	257
	声 聲	声色 *kowairo* imitated/assumed voice	204

	760	**SAN** – calculate	
算	6f8.7 目	計算 *keisan* calculation, computation	340
	竹 目 廾	公算 *kōsan* probability, likelihood	126
	/66 55 32	予算 *yosan* an estimate; budget	397
		清算 *seisan* exact calculation; (fare) adjustment	670
	算	暗算 *anzan* mental arithmetic/ calculation	348

	761	**TAI, ka(su)** – rent out, lend	
貸	7b5.9 田	貸与 *taiyo* lend, loan	548
	貝 弋 イ	貸し家 *kashiya* house for rent, rented house	165
	/68 52 3	貸しボート *kashibōto* boat for rent, rented boat	
		貸し出す *kashidasu* lend/hire out	53
	貸	貸し切り *kashikiri* reservations, booking	39

	762	**HI** – expenses, cost **tsui(yasu)** – spend **tsui(eru)** – be wasted	
費	7b5.4 田	経費 *keihi* expenses, cost	557
	貝 弓 儿	費用 *hiyō* expense, cost	107
	/68 28 16	生活費 *seikatsuhi* living expenses, cost of living; heating	
		and lighting expenses	44, 237
	費	旅費 *ryohi* traveling expenses	222

	763	**SHI** – resources, capital, funds	
資	7b6.7 田	資源 *shigen* resources	589
	貝 攵 冫	資本（主義）*shihon(shugi)* capital(ism)	25, 155, 291
	/68 49 5	資金 *shikin* funds	23
		物資 *busshi* goods, (raw) materials	79
	資	資格 *shikaku* qualification, competence	653

賃	764	**CHIN** – rent, wages; fare, fee	
	7b6.6	賃金　chingin　wages, pay	23
	貝 王 亻	賃上げ　chin'age　raise in wages	32
	/68　46　3	運賃　unchin　passenger fare; shipping charges	445
	賃	電車賃　denshachin　train fare	108, 133
		家賃　yachin　rent	165

貨	765	**KA** – freight; goods, property	
	7b4.5	貨物　kamotsu　freight	79
	貝 亻 卜	百貨店　hyakkaten　department store	14, 168
	/68　3　13	通貨　tsūka　currency	150
	貨	外貨　gaika　foreign goods/currency	83
		銀貨　ginka　silver coin	313

貧	766	**HIN, BIN, mazu(shii)** – poor	
	2o9.5	貧富　hinpu　poverty and wealth, the rich and poor	726
	貝 儿 力	貧困　hinkon　poverty, need	567
	/68　16　8	貧弱　hinjaku　poor, meager, scanty	218
	貧	貧相　hinsō　poor-looking, seedy	146
		清貧　seihin　honest poverty	671

乏	767	**BŌ, tobo(shii)** – scanty, meager, scarce	
	0a3.11	貧乏　binbō　poor	766
	一 丨	欠乏　ketsubō　shortage, deficiency	384
	1　2		
	乏		

架	768	**KA, ka(keru)** – hang, build (bridge) **ka(karu)** – hang, be built	
	4a5.36	架設　kasetsu　construction, laying	586
	木 口 力	架橋　kakyō　bridge building	607
	/41　24　8	書架　shoka　bookshelf	131
	架	十字架像　jūjikazō　crucifix	12, 110, 753
		架空　kakū　overhead, aerial; fanciful	140

賀	769	**GA** – congratulations, felicitations	
	7b5.10	賀状　gajō　greeting card	636
	貝 口 力	年賀　nenga　New Year's greetings	45
	/68　24　8	年賀状　nengajō　New Year's card	45, 636
	賀	賀正　gashō　New Year's greetings	275
		志賀高原　Shiga Kōgen　Shiga Plateau	582, 190, 136

収	770	**SHŪ, osa(meru)** – obtain, collect **osa(maru)** – be obtained, end	
	2h2.2	収支　shūshi　income and expenditures	318
	又 丨	収入　shūnyū　income, receipts, revenue, earnings	52
	/9　2	収益　shūeki　earnings, proceeds, profit	729
	収　收	収容　shūyō　admission, accommodation	665

納	**771** 6a4.5 糸 亻 冂 /61 3 20 納	**NŌ, [TŌ], [NA], [NA'], [NAN], osa(meru)** – pay; supply; accept, store **osa(maru)** – be paid (in), supplied 納税　*nōzei*　payment of taxes　403 出納　*suitō*　receipts and disbursements　53 納得　*nattoku*　accept, become persuaded/convinced　375 納屋　*naya*　(storage) shed　167
易	**772** 4c4.9 日 勿 /42 27 易	**EKI** – divination **I, yasa(shii)** – easy 易者　*ekisha*　fortune-teller　164 不易　*fueki*　immutability, unchangeableness　94 交易　*kōeki*　trade, commerce, barter　114 容易　*yōi*　easy, simple　665 難易(度)　*nan'i(do)*　(degree of) difficulty　566, 378
貿	**773** 7b5.8 貝 厂 力 /68 18 8 貿	**BŌ** – exchange, trade 貿易　*bōeki*　foreign trade, trade　772 自由貿易　*jiyū bōeki*　free trade　62, 364, 772 貿易会社　*bōeki-gaisha*　trading firm/company　772, 158, 308 貿易収支　*bōeki shūshi*　balance of trade　772, 770, 318 日米貿易　*Nichi-Bei bōeki*　Japan-U.S. trade　5, 224, 772
留	**774** 5f5.4 畊 厂 力 /58 18 8 留 畄	**RYŪ, [RU], to(meru)** – fasten down, hold, keep (in) **to(maru)** – stay, settle 留学　*ryugaku*　study abroad　109 留守　*rusu*　absence from home　499 書留　*kakitome*　registered mail　131 局留(め)　*kyokudome*　general delivery　170
貯	**775** 7b5.1 貝 宀 丁 /68 33 14 貯	**CHO** – storage 貯金　*chokin*　savings, deposit　23 貯水池　*chosuichi*　reservoir　21, 119
餌	**776** 8b6.2 食 耳 /77 65 餌	**JI, e, esa** – feed, food; bait 食餌　*shokuji*　diet, food　322 餌食　*ejiki*　food, bait, prey　322
庁	**777** 3q2.2 广 丁 /18 14 庁 廳	**CHŌ** – government office, agency 官庁　*kanchō*　government office, agency　326 県庁　*kenchō*　prefectural office　194 気象庁　*Kishōchō*　Meteorological Agency　134, 752 警視庁　*Keishichō*　Metropolitan Police Department　719, 616 教皇庁　*Kyōkōchō*　the Vatican　245, 297

昔	**778** 3k5.28 目 艹 日 一 /32 42 1 昔	**SEKI, [SHAKU], mukashi** – antiquity, long ago
		今昔 *konjaku* past and present 51 大昔 *ōmukashi* remote antiquity, time immemorial 26 昔々 *mukashi-mukashi* Once upon a time ... 昔話 *mukashi-banashi* old tale, legend 238 昔の事 *mukashi no koto* thing of the past 80

惜	**779** 4k8.11 田 忄 日 艹 /51 42 32 惜	**SEKI, o(shii)** – regrettable; precious; wasteful **o(shimu)** – regret; value; begrudge; be sparing of
		惜敗 *sekihai* narrow defeat (after a hard-fought contest); be loath to part 520 口惜しい *kuchioshii* regrettable, vexing 54 負け惜しみ *makeoshimi* unwillingness to admit defeat 519

借	**780** 2a8.22 田 亻 日 艹 /3 42 32 借	**SHAKU, ka(riru)** – borrow, rent
		借金 *shakkin* debt 23 借財 *shakuzai* debt 562 貸借 *taishaku* debits and credits 761 転借 *tenshaku* subleasing 439 賃借/借り *chinshaku/gari* lease 764, 764

散	**781** 4i8.1 田 夂 月 艹 /49 43 32 散	**SAN** – scatter, disperse **chi(rakasu)** – scatter, strew **chi(rakaru)** – lie scattered, be in disorder **chi(rasu)** – (tr.) scatter **chi(ru)** – (intr.) scatter
		解散 *kaisan* breakup, dissolution, disbanding 482 散文 *sanbun* prose 111 散歩 *sanpo* walk, stroll 437

備	**782** 2a10.4 田 亻 月 艹 /3 43 32 備	**BI, sona(eru)** – furnish, provide (for) **sona(waru)** – possess
		設備 *setsubi* equipment, facilities 586 整備 *seibi* maintenance, servicing 512 軍備 *gunbi* military preparations, armaments 444 予備費 *yobihi* reserves, reserve funds 397, 762 備考 *bikō* explanatory notes, remarks 550

順	**783** 9a3.2 田 頁 儿 丨 /76 16 2 順	**JUN** – order, sequence
		順番 *junban* order, one's turn 185 順位 *jun'i* ranking, standing 122 語順 *gojun* word order 67 五十音順 *gojū-on jun* in order of the kana syllabary 7, 12, 347 順調 *junchō* favorable, smooth, without a hitch 342

序	**784** 3q4.4 囗 广 マ 一 /18 14 1 序	**JO** – beginning; preface; order; precedence
		順序 *junjo* order, method, procedure 783 序説 *josetsu* introduction, preface 404 序論 *joron* introduction, preface 293 序文 *jobun* preface, foreword, introduction 111 序曲 *jokyoku* overture, prelude 367

	785	**KUN** – Japanese reading of a kanji; teaching, precept	
	7a3.6	訓育 *kun'iku* education, discipline	246
	言 儿 丨	教訓 *kyōkun* teaching, precept, moral	245
	/67 16 2	訓練 *kunren* training	756
		訓読み *kun-yomi* kun reading (of a kanji)	244, 244
	訓	音訓 *on-kun* Chinese and Japanese readings	347

	786	**JUN, tate** – shield	
	5c4.8	後ろ盾 *ushirodate* support, backing; supporter, backer	48
	目 厂 十		
	/55 18 12		
	盾		

	787	**MU, hoko** – halberd	
	0a5.6	矛盾 *mujun* contradiction	786
	予 一 丨	矛先 *hokosaki* point of a spear; aim of an attack	50
	14 1 2		
	矛		

	788	**JŪ, NYŪ, yawa(rakai), yawa(raka)** – soft	
	4a5.34	柔道 *jūdō* judo	149
	木 マ 一	柔術 *jūjutsu* jujitsu	187
	/41 14 1	柔弱 *nyūjaku* weakness, enervation	218
		柔和 *nyūwa* gentle, mild(-mannered)	124
	柔	物柔らか *mono-yawaraka* mild(-mannered), quiet, gentle	79

	789	**HEN, ata(ri), -be** – vicinity	
	2q2.1	近辺 *kinpen* neighborhood, vicinity	452
	辶 力	周辺 *shūhen* periphery, environs	91
	/19 8	辺地 *henchi* remote place, out-of-the-way place	118
		多辺形 *tahenkei* polygon	229, 399
	辺 邊	海辺 *umibe* beach, seashore	117

	790	**ko(mu)** – be crowded, congested **ko(meru)** – include, count in; load (a gun); concentrate	
	2q2.3	巻き込む *makikomu* entangle, involve, implicate	516
	辶 イ	払い込む *haraikomu* pay in	591
	/19 3	申し込み *mōshikomi* proposal, offer, application	309
	込	見込み *mikomi* prospects, outlook	63

	791	**JUN, megu(ru)** – go around	
	2q3.3	巡回 *junkai* tour, patrol, one's rounds	90
	辶 巛	巡視 *junshi* tour of inspection, round of visits	616
	/19 2	巡査 *junsa* policeman, cop	634
		巡礼 *junrei* pilgrimage; pilgrim	630
	巡	巡業 *jungyō* tour (of a troupe/team)	279

準	**792** 2k11.1 ⊞ 十 隹 氵 /12 73 21 準	**JUN** – semi-, quasi-; level; correspond (to)	
		水準　*suijun*　water level; level, standard	21
		基準　*kijun*　standard, criterion	457
		規準　*kijun*　criterion, standard, norm	617
		準備　*junbi*　preparation	782
		準決勝　*junkesshō*　semifinal game/round	357, 518

染	**793** 4a5.35 ⊞ 木 氵 十 /41 21 12 染	**SEN, so(maru)** – dye, color **so(meru)** – be dyed, imbued **shi(miru)** – soak into; be infected; smart; hurt **shi(mi)** – stain, blot, smudge	
		(大気)汚染　*(taiki) osen*　(air) pollution	26, 134, 706
		伝染病　*densenbyō*　contagious disease	440, 381
		感染　*kansen*　infection	262

黄	**794** 3k8.16 ⊟ ⺿ 日 一 /32 42 14 黄	**KŌ, Ō, ki, [ko]** – yellow	
		黄葉　*kōyō*　yellow (autumn) leaves	253
		黄熱(病)　*(k)ōnetsu(byō)*　yellow fever	655, 381
		黄金　*ōgon, kogane*　gold	23
		黄色　*kiiro*　yellow	204
		黄身　*kimi*　egg yolk	59

横	**795** 4a11.13 ⊞ 木 日 ⺿ /41 42 32 横	**Ō, yoko** – side; horizontal direction	
		専横　*sen'ō*　arbitrariness, tyranny	610
		横道　*yokomichi*　side street; side issue, digression	149
		横切る　*yokogiru*　cross, traverse	39
		横顔　*yokogao*　profile	277
		横目　*yokome*　side glance; amorous glance	55

再	**796** 0a6.26 ⋯ 土 冂 一 22 20 1 再	**SAI, [SA], futata(bi)** – once more, again, twice	
		再会　*saikai*　meeting again, reunion	158
		再開　*saikai*　reopening	400
		再編成　*saihensei*　reorganization	695, 261
		再婚　*saikon*　second marriage, remarriage	576
		再来週　*saraishū*　week after next	69, 92

講	**797** 7a10.3 ⊞ 言 ⺿ 土 /67 32 22 講	**KŌ** – lecture; study	
		講義　*kōgi*　lecture	291
		講演　*kōen*　lecture, address	344
		講師　*kōshi*　lecturer, instructor	415
		講堂　*kōdō*　lecture hall	505
		講和　*kōwa*　(make) peace	124

兵	**798** 2o5.6 ⊟ 丷 斤 一 /16 50 1 兵	**HEI, HYŌ** – soldier; warfare	
		兵器　*heiki*　weapon	536
		兵士　*heishi*　soldier	581
		歩兵　*hohei*　infantry; infantryman, foot soldier	437
		志願兵　*shiganhei*　a volunteer (soldier)	582, 590
		兵役　*heieki*　military service, conscription	376

799 — HIN, hama – beach
3a7.7

海浜　kaihin　seashore, beach　117
京浜　Kei-Hin　Tōkyō–Yokohama　189
横浜　Yokohama　(port city near Tōkyō)　795
浜辺　hamabe　beach, seashore　789
浜田　Hamada　(surname)　35

800 — ZA – seat; theater; constellation　suwa(ru) – sit down
3q7.2

座席　zaseki　seat　380
座談会　zadankai　round-table discussion, symposium　603, 158
(通信)講座　(tsūshin) kōza　(correspondence)　150, 157, 797
口座　kōza　(savings) account　course　54
銀座　Ginza　(area of Tōkyō)　313

801 — SOTSU – soldier, private; end
2j6.2

卒業　sotsugyō　graduation　examination　279
卒業試験　sotsugyō shiken　graduation　279, 535, 541
卒業証書　sotsugyō shōsho　diploma　279, 493, 131
卒中　sotchū　cerebral stroke, apoplexy　28
兵卒　heisotsu　a private, common soldier　798

802 — SOTSU – lead; light, easy; sudden　RITSU – rate, proportion
hiki(iru) – lead, command
2j9.1

率直　sotchoku　straightforward, frank　429
軽率　keisotsu　rash, hasty, heedless　556
能率　nōritsu　efficiency　387
成長率　seichōritsu　rate of growth　261, 95

803 — KETSU, chi – blood
5h1.1

血液　ketsueki　blood　480
血管　kekkan　blood vessel　328
(内)出血　(nai)shukketsu　(internal) hemorrhage　84, 53
止血剤　shiketsuzai　a hemostatic, styptic (agent)　485, 559
流血　ryūketsu　bloodshed　247

804 — SAN, kasa – umbrella
2a10.7

傘下　sanka　affiliated　31
日傘　higasa　parasol　5
雨傘　amagasa　umbrella　30
傘立て　kasatate　umbrella stand　121
こうもり傘　kōmorigasa　umbrella, parasol

805 — SHA – house, hut, quarters
2a6.23

校舎　kōsha　schoolhouse, school building　115
兵舎　heisha　barracks　798
国民宿舎　kokumin shukusha　government-sponsored hostels　40, 177, 179
田舎　inaka　the country, rural areas　35

	806	**SHŪ, [SHU]** – multitude, populace
衆	5h7.1	公衆（電話）　*kōshū (denwa)*　public (telephone)　126, 108, 238
	皿 衤 丨	大衆文学　*taishū bungaku*　popular literature　26, 111, 109
	/59　57　2	民衆　*minshū*　the people, masses　177
	衆	衆議院　*Shūgiin*　the House of Representatives　292, 624
		アメリカ合衆国　*Amerika Gasshūkoku*　U.S.A.　159, 40

	807	**KUN** – (suffix for male personal names); ruler ***kimi*** – you (in masculine speech); ruler
君	3d4.23	田中君　*Tanaka-kun*　(Mr.) Tanaka　35, 28
	口 ヨ 丨	君主　*kunshu*　monarch, sovereign　155
	/24　39　2	立憲君主政（国）　*rikken kunshusei (koku)*　constitutional
	君	monarchy　121, 530, 155, 492, 40

	808	**GUN, mu(re), [mura]** – group, herd ***mu(reru)*** – crowd, flock
群	3d10.14	群衆　*gunshū*　crowd of people　806
	口 王 ヨ	群集　*gunshū*　crowd of people　442
	/24　46　39	群像　*gunzō*　group of people (in an artwork)　753
	群 羣	魚群　*gyogun*　school of fish　290
		群島　*guntō*　group of islands, archipelago　286

	809	**TAI** – party, squad, unit
隊	2d9.7	軍隊　*guntai*　troops, army, the military　444
	阝 犭 儿	部隊　*butai*　military unit, squad　86
	/7　27　16	兵隊　*heitai*　soldier; troops　798
	隊	探検隊　*tankentai*　expedition, expeditionary group　544, 540
		楽隊　*gakutai*　(musical) band　359

	810	**TON, buta** – pig
豚	4b7.2	養豚　*yōton*　pig raising　406
	月 犭 ヒ	豚カツ　*tonkatsu*　pork cutlet
	/43　27　10	豚肉　*butaniku*　pork　223
	豚	豚小屋　*butagoya*　pigsty, pigpen　27, 167

	811	**GEKI** – drama, play
劇	2f13.2	劇場　*gekijō*　theater, playhouse　154
	刂 犭 厂	演劇　*engeki*　drama, theatrical performance　344
	/16　27　18	歌劇　*kageki*　opera　395
	劇	劇的　*gekiteki*　dramatic　210
		劇薬　*gekiyaku*　powerful medicine; virulent poison　360

	812	**HI** – comparison; (short for) Philippines ***kura(beru)*** – compare
比	2m3.5	比率　*hiritsu*　ratio　802
	匕	比例　*hirei*　proportion　622
	/13	対比　*taihi*　contrast, contradistinction　366
	比	比重　*hijū*　specific gravity　227
		見比べる　*mikuraberu*　compare　63

	813	**KON, ma(zeru)** – mix **ma(zaru/jiru)** – be mixed **ko(mu)** – be crowded/full/packed
混	3a8.14 ⊞	混乱 *konran* confusion, disorder, chaos ... 702
	氵日 匕 /21 42 13	混雑 *konzatsu* confusion, congestion ... 584
	混	混合 *kongō* mixture ... 159
		混ぜ物 *mazemono* adulteration ... 79

	814	**SEN, era(bu)** – choose, select
選	2q12.3 ▢	当選 *tōsen* be elected ... 77
	辶 弓 艹 /19 28 32	改選 *kaisen* reelection ... 523
	選	精選 *seisen* careful selection ... 670
		予選 *yosen* preliminary match; primary election ... 397
		選手 *senshu* (sports) player ... 57

	815	**KYO** – all, whole; arrest, capture; name, give, cite **a(geru)** – name, give, enumerate; arrest, apprehend **a(garu)** – be apprehended; be found, recovered
挙	3n7.1 ☰	選挙 *senkyo* election ... 814
	丷 扌 儿 /35 23 16	挙党 *kyotō* the whole party ... 504
	挙 擧	列挙 *rekkyo* enumerate, list ... 621

	816	**YO, homa(re)** – glory, honor
誉	3n10.1 ☰	栄誉 *eiyo* honor, glory ... 736
	丷 言 儿 /35 67 16	名誉 *meiyo* honor ... 82
	誉 譽	名誉職 *meiyoshoku* honorary post ... 82, 386
		名誉市民 *meiyo shimin* honorary citizen ... 82, 181, 177
		名誉教授 *meiyo kyōju* professor emeritus ... 82, 245, 612

	817	**KEN, kobushi** – fist
拳	3c6.18 ...	拳闘 *kentō* boxing ... 1612
	扌 火 二 /23 44 4	少林寺拳法 *Shōrinji kenpō* Shorinji Kempo, Shaolin kungfu ... 144, 127, 41, 123
	拳	じゃん拳 *janken* rock-paper-scissors (hand game)

	818	**HŌ, ho(meru)** – praise
褒	2j13.1 ☰	褒賞 *hōshō* prize ... 509
	亠 衤 林 /11 57 41	褒美 *hōbi* reward ... 405
	褒 襃	過褒 *kahō* excessive/undeserved praise ... 419
		褒め上げる *homeageru* praise very highly, extol ... 32
		褒め立てる *hometateru* admire, praise highly ... 121

	819	**HŌ, tsutsu(mu)** – wrap up
包	0a5.9 ...	包容力 *hōyōryoku* capacity; tolerance, catholicity ... 665, 100
	弓 ケ 28 15	包丁 *hōchō* kitchen knife ... 184
	包	小包み *kozutsumi* parcel ... 27
		紙包み *kamizutsumi* parcel wrapped in paper ... 180
		包み紙 *tsutsumigami* wrapping paper, wrapper ... 180

820

均

3b4.8

土 宀 冫
/22 15   5

均

KIN – equal, even

平均	heikin	average	202
均一	kin'itsu	uniform	2
均等	kintō	equality, uniformity, parity	578
均質	kinshitsu	homogeneous	176
均分	kinbun	divide equally	38

821

蜂

6d7.6

虫 夂 十
/64 49   12

蜂

HŌ, hachi – bee

養蜂	yōhō	beekeeping	406
蜂起	hōki	revolt, uprising	374
蜂の巣	hachi no su	beehive, honeycomb	1640
虻蜂取らず	abu-hachi torazu	attempting two things simultaniously, accomplishing neither	65

822

密

3m8.5

宀 心 山
/33 51   36

密

MITSU – close, dense, crowded; minute, fine; secret

（人口）密度	(jinkō) mitsudo	(population) density	1, 54, 378
密接	missetsu	close, intimate	495
精密	seimitsu	minute, accurate, precision	670
機密	kimitsu	a secret	537
密輸	mitsuyu	smuggling	555

823

蜜

3m11.7

宀 虫 心
/33 64   51

蜜

MITSU – honey

蜂蜜	hachimitsu	honey	821
蜜蜂	mitsubachi	honeybee	821
蜜月	mitsugetsu	honeymoon	17

824

秘

5d5.6

禾 心 丨
/56 51   2

秘　祕

HI, hi(meru) – conceal, keep secret

秘密	himitsu	a secret	822
極秘	gokuhi	strict secrecy, top secret	336
秘書	hisho	secretary	131
神秘	shinpi	mystery	310
便秘	benpi	constipation	330

825

邦

2d4.7

阝 十 二
/7 12   4

邦

HŌ – country; Japan

（在米）邦人	(zaibei) hōjin	Japanese (living in America)	268, 224
邦字新聞	hōji shinbun	Japanese-lang. newspaper	110, 174, 64
連邦	renpō	federation, federal	446
連邦政府	renpō seifu	federal government	446, 492, 513
連邦首相	renpō shushō	Federal Chancellor	446, 148, 146

826

那

2d4.6

阝 力 二
/7 8   4

那

NA – what, which

| 支那 | Shina | China (since WWII regarded as derogatory) | 318 |
| 南支那海 | Minami-Shina-kai | the South China Sea (since WWII usually written 南シナ海) | 74, 318, 117 |

827	**SATSU, SETSU** – temple

2f6.8 木 41
刹

名刹	*meisatsu*	famous temple	82
刹那	*setsuna*	moment, instant	826
一刹那	*issetsuna*	an instant, a moment	2, 826

828	**RIN, tonari** – next door, adjoining **tona(ru)** – be neighboring

2d13.1 阝米夕 /7 62 30
隣 鄰

隣国	*ringoku*	neighboring country/province	40
隣席	*rinseki*	next seat, seat next to one	380
隣接	*rinsetsu*	border on, be contiguous, adjoin	495
隣人	*rinjin*	a neighbor	1
隣り合う	*tonariau*	adjoin/be next door to each other	159

829	**BU, ma(u)** – dance, flutter about **mai** – dance

0a15.1 艹夕一 32 30 15
舞

舞台	*butai*	the stage	501
舞楽	*bugaku*	old Japanese court-dance music	359
仕舞	*shimai*	end, conclusion	333
舞い上がる	*maiagaru*	fly up, soar	32
(お)見舞い	*(o)mimai*	visit, inquiry (after someone's health)	63

830	**MU, yume** – dream

3k10.14 艹目夕 /32 55 30
夢 梦

夢想	*musō*	dream, vision, fancy	147
悪夢	*akumu*	bad dream, nightmare	304
夢中	*muchū*	rapture; absorption, intentness; frantic	28
夢を見る	*yume o miru*	(have a) dream	63
夢にも	*yume nimo*	(not) even in a dream	

831	**SŌ, hōmu(ru)** – bury, inter

3k9.15 艹夕卜 /32 30 13
葬

葬儀/式	*sōgi/shiki*	funeral	740, 534
火葬	*kasō*	cremation	20
葬列	*sōretsu*	funeral procession	621
副葬品	*fukusōhin*	burial accessories	727, 230
改葬	*kaisō*	reburial, reinterment	523

832	**BI, hana** – nose

5f9.3 甲目艹 /58 55 32
鼻

鼻先	*hanasaki*	tip of the nose	50
鼻血	*hanaji*	nosebleed, bloody nose	803
鼻薬	*hanagusuri*	a bribe	360
耳鼻科	*jibika*	ENT clinic/department	56, 320
鼻音	*bion*	nasal sound	347

833	**I** – be different; violation **chiga(u)** – be different; be mistaken **chiga(eru)** – alter; violate

2q10.5 辶口艹 /19 24 12
違

相違	*sōi*	difference, disparity	146
違反	*ihan*	violation	324
違法	*ihō*	illegal	123
間違い	*machigai*	mistake, error; accident, mishap	43

834

衛

3i13.3
彳 口 十
/29 24 12

衛 衞

EI – defend, protect

防衛	*bōei*	defense	522
自衛隊	*Jieitai*	(Japanese) Self-Defense Forces	62, 809
前衛	*zen'ei*	advance guard; avant-garde	47
衛生	*eisei*	hygiene, sanitation	44
衛星	*eisei*	satellite	743

835

効

2g6.2
力 亠 儿
/8 11 16

効 効

KŌ, ki(ku) – be effective

効力	*kōryoku*	effectiveness, effect, validity	100
効果	*kōka*	effect, effectiveness	496
有効	*yūkō*	validity, effectiveness	265
無効	*mukō*	invalidity, ineffectiveness	93
時効	*jikō*	prescription (in statute of limitations)	42

836

郊

2d6.8
阝 亠 儿
/7 11 16

郊

KŌ – suburbs, rural areas

近郊	*kinkō*	suburbs, outskirts	452
郊外	*kōgai*	suburbs, outskirts	83

837

功

2g3.2
力 工
/8 38

功

KŌ, [KU] – merits, success

成功	*seikō*	success	261
功労	*kōrō*	meritorious service	233
功業	*kōgyō*	achievement, exploit	279
功名	*kōmyō*	great achievement, glorious deed	82
年功	*nenkō*	long service/experience	45

838

攻

4i3.2
攵 工
/49 38

攻

KŌ, se(meru) – attack

攻勢	*kōsei*	the offensive	656
攻防	*kōbō*	offense and defense	522
攻守	*kōshu*	offense and defense	499
攻城	*kōjō*	siege	733
専攻	*senkō*	one's major (study)	610

839

紅

6a3.6
糸 工
/61 38

紅

KŌ, [KU], kurenai – deep red **beni** – rouge, lipstick

紅葉	*kōyō, momiji*	red (autumn) leaves; maple tree	253
紅茶	*kōcha*	black tea	251
紅白	*kōhaku*	red and white	205
真紅	*shinku*	crimson, scarlet	428
口紅	*kuchibeni*	lipstick	54

840

江

3a3.8
氵 工
/21 38

江

KŌ, e – inlet, bay

江湖	*kōko*	the public, world	475
入り江	*irie*	inlet, small bay	52
江ノ島	*Enoshima*	(island near Kamakura)	286
江戸	*Edo*	(old name for Tōkyō)	152
江戸っ子	*Edokko*	true Tokyoite	152, 103

841

嚴

3n14.1

⍾ 耳 攵
/35 65 49

厳 嚴

GEN, [GON], kibi(shii) – severe, strict, rigorous, intense
ogoso(ka) – solemn, grave, stately

厳重	genjū	strict, stringent, rigid	227
厳格	genkaku	strict, stern, severe	653
厳禁	genkin	strict prohibition	491
尊厳	songen	dignity	717

842

航

6c4.2

舟 宀 冂
/63 11 20

航

KŌ – navigation, sailing

航空便	kōkūbin	airmail	140, 330
航空券	kōkūken	flight/airplane ticket	140, 515
航路	kōro	sea route, course	151
航海	kōkai	sea voyage/navigation	117
巡航	junkō	a cruise	791

843

抗

3c4.15

扌 宀 冂
/23 11 20

抗

KŌ – resist

対抗	taikō	opposition, confrontation	366
抵抗	teikō	resistance	569
反抗	hankō	resistance, opposition	324
抗議	kōgi	protest	292
抗争	kōsō	contention, dispute	302

844

庫

3q7.1

广 車
/18 69

庫

KO, [KU] – storehouse

車庫	shako	garage	133
金庫	kinko	a safe	23
国庫	kokko	the (National) Treasury	40
文庫本	bunkobon	small cheap paperback	111, 25
在庫品	zaikohin	goods in stock, inventory	268, 230

845

床

3q4.1

广 木
/18 41

床 牀

SHŌ, toko – bed; floor **yuka** – floor

起床	kishō	rise, get up (from bed)	374
病床	byōshō	sickbed	381
万年床	mannendoko	futon left spread out during daytime	16, 45
床屋	tokoya	barber; barbershop	167
床の間	tokonoma	alcove in Japanese-style room	43

846

応

3q4.2

广 心
/18 51

応 應

Ō – reply, respond; comply with, fulfill, satisfy **kota(eru)** – respond

反応	hannō	reaction	324
順応	junnō	adaption, adjustment	783
相応	sōō	correspond, be suitable	146
応用	ōyō	(practical) application	107
応接間	ōsetsuma	reception room	495, 43

847

充

2j4.5

亠 厶 儿
/11 17 16

充

JŪ – fill **a(teru)** – allot, allocate, apply (to)

充分	jūbun	enough, sufficient	38
充満	jūman	fullness, abundance	201
充足	jūsoku	sufficiency	58
充実	jūjitsu	repletion, perfection	203
充血した目	jūketsu shita me	bloodshot eyes	803, 55

848

銃

JŪ – gun

8a6.9
釒 宀 厶
/72 11 17

銃

銃器	jūki	firearm	536
小銃	shōjū	rifle	27
拳銃	kenjū	pistol, handgun	817
機関銃	kikanjū	machine gun	537, 402
銃殺	jūsatsu	shoot dead	585

849

統

TŌ, su(beru) – govern, control

6a6.10
糹 宀 厶
/61 11 17

統

統制	tōsei	control, regulation	433
統治	tōchi, tōji	reign, rule	502
統一	tōitsu	unity, unification	2
統計	tōkei	statistics	340
伝統	dentō	tradition	440

850

令

REI – order, command; good; (honorific prefix)

2a3.9
亻 一 丨
/3 1 2

令

命令	meirei	an order	587
号令	gōrei	an order, command	266
訓令	kunrei	instructions, directive	785
政令	seirei	cabinet order, government ordinance	492
発令	hatsurei	official announcement	96

851

冷

REI, tsume(tai) – cold **hi(yasu), sa(masu)** – chill, cool
hi(eru), sa(meru) – become cold **hi(ya)** – cold water; cold saké
hi(yakasu) – poke fun at, tease; browse

2b5.3
冫 亻 一
/5 3 1

冷

冷水	reisui	cold water	21
冷戦	reisen	cold war	301
冷静	reisei	calm, cool, dispassionate	674

852

齢

REI – age

6b11.5
米 止 囗
/62 13 20

齢 齡

年齢	nenrei	age	45
学齢	gakurei	(of) school age	109
老齢	rōrei	old age	552
高齢者	kōreisha	elderly person	190, 164
高齢化社会	kōreika shakai	aging society	190, 254, 308, 158

853

領

RYŌ – govern, rule

9a5.2
頁 亻 一
/76 3 1

領

領土/地	ryōdo/chi	territory	24, 118
大統領	daitōryō	president (of a country)	26, 849
領事	ryōji	consul	80
領収書/証	ryōshūsho/shō	receipt	770, 131, 493
横領	ōryō	usurpation, embezzlement	795

854

臣

SHIN, JIN – retainer, subject

2t4.3
匚 丨
/20 2

臣

大臣	daijin	(government) minister	26
総理大臣	sōri daijin	prime minister	710, 143, 26
臣民	shinmin	subject	177
臣下	shinka	subject, retainer	31
君臣	kunshin	sovereign and subject, ruler and ruled	807

855 臨

2t15.1

匚 卩 一
/20 24 15

臨

RIN – look out over; go to, be present; rule, subjugate
nozo(mu) – face, confront; attend, be present

臨時	rinji	temporary, provisional, extraordinary	42
臨床	rinshō	clinical	845
臨終	rinjū	one's last moments/deathbed	466
臨席	rinseki	attendance, presence	380

856 閣

8e6.3

門 夂 卩
/75 49 24

閣

KAKU – tower; palace; the cabinet

内閣	naikaku	the cabinet	84
閣議	kakugi	meeting of the cabinet	292
組閣	sokaku	formation of a cabinet	424
閣下	kakka	Your/His Excellency	31
金閣寺	Kinkakuji	Temple of the Golden Pavilion	23, 41

857 額

9a9.6

頁 夂 宀
/76 49 33

額

GAKU – amount; framed picture **hitai** – forehead

金額	kingaku	amount of money	23
額面	gakumen	face value, par	274
総額	sōgaku	total amount, sum total	710
差額	sagaku	the difference, balance	669
半額	hangaku	half the amount/price	88

858 落

3k9.13

艹 夂 氵
/32 49 21

落

RAKU, o(chiru) – fall **o(tosu)** – drop, lose

転落	tenraku	a fall	439
落第	rakudai	failure in an examination	408
部落	buraku	village, settlement	86
落語	rakugo	Japanese comic storytelling	67
落ち着いた	ochitsuita	calm, composed	668

859 絡

6a6.6

糸 夂 卩
/61 49 24

絡

RAKU, kara(mu), kara(maru) – get entangled **kara(meru)** – bind, tie up

連絡	renraku	contact, liaison, communication	446
連絡駅	renraku-eki	connecting station, junction	446, 284
絡み付く	karamitsuku	coil around, cling to	192
絡み合う	karamiau	intertwine	159

860 略

5f6.4

田 夂 卩
/58 49 24

略 畧

RYAKU – abbreviation, omission

省略	shōryaku	omission, abridgment, abbreviation	145
略語	ryakugo	abbreviation	67
略歴	ryakureki	brief personal history	489
計略	keiryaku	plan, stratagem, scheme	340
戦略	senryaku	strategy	301

861 司

3d2.14

口 一
/24 1

司

SHI – administer, conduct

司法	shihō	administration of justice, judicial	123
司令	shirei	commandant, commanding officer	850
司会者	shikaisha	emcee, chairman	158, 164
司書	shisho	librarian	131
上司	jōshi	one's superior (officer)	32

詞	**862** 7a5.15 ▢ 言 丨 一 /67 24 1 詞	**SHI** – words	
		品詞 *hinshi* part of speech	230
		名詞 *meishi* noun	82
		(他)動詞 *(ta)dōshi* (transitive) verb	120, 231
		歌詞 *kashi* lyrics, words to a song	395
		賀詞 *gashi* congratulations, greetings	769

肖	**863** 3n4.1 ▢ ⺌ 月 /35 43 肖	**SHŌ** – resemble	
		肖像画 *shōzōga* portrait	753, 343
		不肖 *fushō* unlike/unworthy of one's father; (humble) I	94

消	**864** 3a7.16 ▢ 氵 月 小 /21 43 35 消	**SHŌ, ke(su)** – extinguish; erase **ki(eru)** – go out, disappear	
		消防(車) *shōbō(sha)* fire fighting (engine)	522, 133
		消火器 *shōkaki* fire extinguisher	20, 536
		消費者 *shōhisha* consumer	762, 164
		消化 *shōka* digestion	254
		消極的 *shōkyokuteki* negative, passive	336, 210

退	**865** 2q6.3 ▢ 辶 食 /19 77 退	**TAI, shirizo(ku)** – retreat **shirizo(keru)** – drive away, repel	
		退職 *taishoku* retirement, resignation	386
		退院 *taiin* leave/be discharged from the hospital	624
		退学 *taigaku* leave/drop out of school	109
		引退 *intai* retire (from public life)	216

限	**866** 2d6.1 ▢ 阝 食 /7 77 限	**GEN, kagi(ru)** – limit	
		無限 *mugen* unlimited, infinite	93
		制限 *seigen* restriction, limitation	433
		限度 *gendo* a limit	378
		期限 *kigen* term, time limit, deadline	456
		権限 *kengen* authority, competence, jurisdiction	335

眼	**867** 5c6.1 ▢ 目 食 /55 77 眼	**GAN, [GEN], manako** – eye	
		両眼 *ryōgan* both eyes	200
		近眼 *kingan* nearsightedness, shortsightedness	452
		眼科医 *gankai* eye doctor, ophthalmologist	320, 220
		眼識 *ganshiki* discernment, insight	694
		千里眼 *senrigan* clairvoyance, clairvoyant	15, 142

眠	**868** 5c5.2 ▢ 目 尸 亠 /55 40 12 眠	**MIN, nemu(ru)** – sleep **nemu(i)** – tired, sleepy	
		不眠 *fumin* sleeplessness, insomnia	94
		安眠 *anmin* a quiet/sound sleep	105
		冬眠 *tōmin* hibernation	467
		居眠り *inemuri* a doze, falling asleep in one's seat	171
		眠り薬 *nemurigusuri* sleeping drug/pills	360

	869	**KYŌ** – circumstances, situation	
	3a5.21	状況、情況 *jōkyō* conditions, situation	636, 209
	氵 口 儿	現況 *genkyō* present situation	298
	/21 24 16	実況 *jikkyō* actual state of affairs	203
		市況 *shikyō* market conditions, the market	181
	況 況	不況 *fukyō* recession, economic slump	94

	870	**SHUKU, [SHŪ], iwa(u)** – celebrate, congratulate	
	4e5.5	祝辞 *shukuji* (speech of) congratulations	701
	ネ 日 儿	祝賀 *shukuga* celebration; congratulations	769
	/45 24 16	祝日 *shukujitsu* festival day, holiday	5
		祝儀 *shūgi* (wedding) celebration; gift	740
	祝	祝い事 *iwaigoto* auspicious/festive occasion	80

	871	**KYŌ, KEI, kiso(u)** — compete, vie for **se(ru)** — compete, vie, bid for	
	5b15.1	競争 *kyōsō* competition	302
	立 口 儿	競走 *kyōsō* race	435
	/54 24 16	競売 *kyōbai* auction	239
		競馬 *keiba* horse racing	283
	競 競		

	872	**KEI** – view, scene	
	4c8.8	景色 *keshiki* scenery	204
	日 口 小	風景 *fūkei* scenery	29
	/42 24 35	景勝（地） *keishō(chi)* (place of) picturesque scenery	518, 118
		景気 *keiki* business conditions	134
	景	不景気 *fukeiki* hard times, recession	94, 134

	873	**EI, kage** – light; shadow, silhouette; figure; trace	
	3j12.1	影像 *eizō* image; shadow	753
	彡 日 口	人影 *hitokage, jin'ei* silhouette; human figure	1
	/31 42 24	影法師 *kagebōshi* person's shadow	123, 415
		影絵 *kagee* shadow picture, silhouette	345
	影	面影 *omokage* face, traces, vestiges	274

	874	**KYŌ** – village, native place **GŌ** – rural area, country	
	2d8.14	故郷 *kokyō* one's hometown, native place	173
	阝 食 厶	郷里 *kyōri* one's hometown, native place	142
	/7 77 17	郷土 *kyōdo* one's hometown	24
		望郷の念 *bōkyō no nen* homesickness, nostalgia	685, 588
	郷	近郷 *kingō* neighboring districts	452

	875	**KYŌ, hibi(ku)** – sound, resound, be echoed; affect	
	4c15.3	影響 *eikyō* effect, influence	873
	日 食 立	反響 *hankyō* echo, response	324
	/42 77 54	音響 *onkyō* sound	347
		交響曲 *kōkyōkyoku* symphony	114, 367
	響	響き渡る *hibikiwataru* resound, reverberate	379

	876	**SHŌ** – chapter; badge, mark	
	5b6.3	文章 *bunshō* composition, writing	111
	/54 42 12	第三章 *dai-sanshō* Chapter 3	408, 4
		第三楽章 *dai-san gakushō* third movement	408, 4, 359
	章	憲章 *kenshō* charter, constitution	530
		記章 *kishō* medal, badge	372

	877	**SHŌ, sawa(ru)** – hinder, interfere with, harm, hurt	
	2d11.2	保障 *hoshō* guarantee, security	498
	/7 54 42	支障 *shishō* hindrance, impediment	318
		障害 *shōgai* obstacle, impediment	527
	障	故障 *koshō* trouble, breakdown, out of order	173
		障子 *shōji* Japanese sliding paper door	103

	878	**CHO, arawa(su)** – write, publish ***ichijiru(shii)*** – marked, striking, remarkable, conspicuous	
	3k8.4	著者 *chosha* author	164
	/32 42 22	著書 *chosho* a (literary) work	131
		名著 *meicho* a famous/great work	82
	著	著名 *chomei* prominent, well-known	82

	879	**SHO** – government office, station	
	5g8.1	税務署 *zeimusho* tax office	403, 235
	/55 42 22	消防署 *shōbōsho* fire station, firehouse	864, 522
		警察署 *keisatsusho* police station	719, 629
	署	部署 *busho* one's post/place of duty	86
		署名 *shomei* signature, autograph	82

	880	**SHO** – all, various	
	7a8.3	諸国 *shokoku* all/various countries	40
	/67 42 22	諸島 *shotō* islands	286
		諸説 *shosetsu* various views/accounts	404
	諸	諸事 *shoji* various matters/affairs	80
		諸君 *shokun* (Ladies and) Gentlemen!	807

	881	**SHO, [CHO]** – beginning ***o*** – cord, strap, thong	
	6a8.3	緒戦 *shosen, chosen* beginning of war	301
	/61 42 22	緒論 *shoron, choron* introduction	293
		由緒 *yuisho* history; pedigree, lineage	364
	緒	情緒 *jōcho, jōsho* emotion, feeling	209
		鼻緒 *hanao* clog thong, geta strap	832

	882	**KYŌ, kagami** – mirror	
	8a11.6	鏡台 *kyōdai* dressing table	501
	/72 54 42	三面鏡 *sanmenkyō* a dresser with three mirrors	4, 274
		望遠鏡 *bōenkyō* telescope	685, 453
	鏡	手鏡 *tekagami* hand mirror	57
		眼鏡 *megane, gankyō* eyeglasses	867

	883	**KYŌ, [KEI], sakai** – boundary	
境	3b11.1 ⊞	国境 *kokkyō* border	40
	土 立 日	境界 *kyōkai* boundary, border	461
	/22 54 42	苦境 *kukyō* distress, difficulties	554
	境	境内 *keidai* precincts, grounds	84
		境目 *sakaime* borderline; crisis	55

	884	**KAN** – ring; surround	
環	4f13.1 ⊞	環境 *kankyō* environment	883
	王 罒 衣	環境省 *Kankyōshō* Ministry of the Environnment	883, 145
	/46 55 57	環状 *kanjō* ring-shaped	636
	環	環状線 *kanjōsen* loop (line)	636, 299
		一環 *ikkan* a link, part	2

	885	**KAN** – return	
還	2q13.4 ⊡	返還 *henkan* return, restoration; repayment	448
	辶 罒 衣	帰還 *kikan* return home, repatriation	317
	/19 55 57	送還 *sōkan* sending home, repatriation	447
	還	還元 *kangen* restoration; reduction	137

	886	**IN** – yin principle; negative, hidden; shadow, secret **kage** – shadow, back **kage(ru)** – get dark/clouded	
陰	2d8.7 ⊞	陰陽 *in'yo* yin and yang, positive and negative	640
	阝 亻 厶	陰性 *insei* negative; dormant, latent	98
	/7 3 17	陰気 *inki* gloomy, dismal, melancholy	134
	陰	日陰 *hikage* shade from the sun	5

	887	**IN, kaku(reru)** – (intr.) hide **kaku(su)** – (tr.) hide	
隠	2d11.3 ⊞	隠語 *ingo* secret language; argot, jargon	67
	阝 心 ヨ	隠者 *inja* hermit	164
	/7 51 39	隠居 *inkyo* retirement from active life	171
	隠 隱	隠し芸 *kakushigei* parlor trick; hidden talent	441

	888	**ON, oda(yaka)** – calm, quiet, mild, peaceful, moderate	
穏	5d11.4 ⊞	穏和 *onwa* mild, gentle, genial	124
	禾 心 ヨ	平穏 *heion* calmness, quiet, serenity	202
	/56 51 39	平穏無事 *heion-buji* peace and quiet	202, 93, 80
	穏 穩	穏当 *ontō* proper, appropriate; gentle	77
		穏便 *onbin* gentle, quiet, amicable	330

	889	**SHI, eda** – branch	
枝	4a4.18 ⊞	枝葉 *shiyō, edaha* branches and leaves; digression	253
	木 十 又	大枝 *ōeda* bough, limb	26
	/41 12 9	小枝 *koeda* twig	27
	枝	枝切り *edakiri* lopping off/pruning of branches	39
		枝接ぎ *edatsugi* grafting	495

伎	**890**	***KI*** – skill; performer	
	2a4.13 田	歌舞伎 *kabuki* kabuki	395, 829
	亻 艹 又	歌舞伎役者 *kabuki yakusha* kabuki actor	395, 829, 376, 164
	/3 12 9		
	伎		

技	**891**	***GI, waza*** – technique; ability; feat	
	3c4.16 田	技術 *gijutsu* technique, technology	187
	扌 艹 又	技師 *gishi* engineer	415
	/23 12 9	技能 *ginō* technical skill, ability	387
	技	演技 *engi* acting, performance	344
		競技 *kyōgi* match, contest, competition	871

岐	**892**	***KI*** – forked road	
	3o4.1 田	分岐 *bunki* divergence, branching	38
	屮 艹 又	分岐点 *bunkiten* point of divergence, junction	38, 169
	/36 12 9	岐路 *kiro* fork in the road, crossroads	151
	岐		

虫	**893**	***CHŪ, mushi*** – bug, insect	
	6d0.1 □	益/害虫 *eki/gaichū* beneficial/harmful insect	729, 527
	虫	殺虫剤 *satchūzai* insecticide	585, 559
	/64	毛虫 *kemushi* hairy caterpillar	287
	虫 蟲	油虫 *aburamushi* cockroach; hanger-on, parasite	365
		虫歯 *mushiba* decayed tooth, cavity	486

触	**894**	***SHOKU, sawa(ru)*** – touch, feel ***fu(reru)*** – touch (upon); announce	
	6d7.10 田	触覚 *shokkaku* sense of touch	615
	虫 月 𠂉	接触 *sesshoku* touch, contact	495
	/64 43 15	感触 *kanshoku* the touch, feel	262
	触 觸	触角 *shokkaku* feeler, antenna, tentacle	481
		抵触 *teishoku* conflict	569

騒	**895**	***SŌ, sawa(gu)*** – make a noise/fuss	
	10a8.5 田	騒音 *sōon* noise	347
	馬 虫 又	騒動 *sōdō* disturbance, riot	231
	/78 64 9	騒然 *sōzen* noisy, tumultuous	662
	騒 騷	大騒ぎ *ōsawagi* clamor, uproar, hullabaloo	26
		騒ぎ立てる *sawagitateru* raise a great fuss/furor	121

戒	**896**	***KAI, imashi(meru)*** – admonish, warn	
	4n3.1 □	警戒 *keikai* caution, precaution, warning	719
	戈 艹	訓戒 *kunkai* admonition, warning	785
	/52 32	厳戒 *genkai* strict watch/guard	841
	戒	戒律 *kairitsu* (Buddhist) precepts	678
		十戒 *jikkai* the Ten Commandments	12

幾	**897** 4n8.4 戈 厶 イ /52 17 3 幾	**KI, iku** – how much/many; some

幾何学　*kikagaku*　geometry　392, 109
幾日　*ikunichi*　how many days; what day of the month　5
幾分　*ikubun*　some, a portion, more or less　38
幾つ　*ikutsu*　how much/many/old
幾ら　*ikura*　how much/long/expensive

畿	**898** 5f10.3 田 戈 厶 /58 52 17 畿	**KI** – capital; capital region

近畿地方　*Kinki chihō*　the Kinki Region (around the ancient
　　capitals of Nara and Kyōto)　452, 118, 70
畿内　*Kinai*　(the five home provinces of Japan: Yamato,
Yamashiro, Kawachi, Settsu, and Izumi)　84

倹	**899** 2a8.27 イ 口 亠 /3 24 14 倹 儉	**KEN** – thrifty, simple, modest

倹約　*ken'yaku*　thriftiness, economy　211
節倹　*sekken*　frugality, economy　472
勤倹　*kinken*　diligence and thrift　568

剣	**900** 2f8.5 刂 口 イ /16 24 3 剣 劍	**KEN, tsurugi** – sword

剣道　*kendō*　kendo, Japanese fencing　149
刀剣　*tōken*　swords　37
短剣　*tanken*　short sword, dagger　215
剣劇　*kengeki*　swordplay/samurai drama　811
真剣　*shinken*　serious, earnest　428

策	**901** 6f6.2 ⺮ 木 冂 /66 41 20 策	**SAKU** – plan, means, measure, policy

政策　*seisaku*　policy　492
対策　*taisaku*　measure, countermeasure　366
具体策　*gutaisaku*　specific measure　426, 61
策略　*sakuryaku*　stratagem, scheme, tactic　860
術策　*jussaku*　artifice, stratagem, intrigue　187

刺	**902** 2f6.2 刂 木 冂 /16 41 20 刺	**SHI, sa(su)** – pierce **sa(saru)** – stick, get stuck in

名刺　*meishi*　name/business card　82
風刺　*fūshi*　satire　29
刺し殺す　*sashikorosu*　stab to death　585
刺し傷　*sashikizu*　a stab; (insect) bite　643
刺身　*sashimi*　sashimi, sliced raw fish　59

犯	**903** 3g2.1 犭 阝 /27 7 犯	**HAN** – crime **oka(su)** – commit (a crime); violate, defy

犯人　*hannin*　criminal, culprit　1
犯行　*hankō*　crime　68
現行犯で　*genkōhan de*　in the act, red-handed　298, 68
共犯　*kyōhan*　complicity　196
防犯　*bōhan*　crime prevention/fighting　522

狂	**904** 3g4.2 □ 犭 王 /27 46 狂	**KYŌ** – mad, crazy; mania **kuru(u)** – go crazy; get out of order **kuru(oshii)** – be nearly mad (with worry/grief)
		狂言　　*kyōgen*　play, drama; Noh farce　　　　　　　66
		発狂　　*hakkyō*　insanity, madness　　　　　　　　　96
		狂気　　*kyōki*　insanity, madness　　　　　　　　　134
		狂乱　　*kyōran*　frenzy, madness　　　　　　　　　702

獄	**905** 3g11.1 □ 犭 言 /27 67 獄	**GOKU** – prison
		地獄　　　*jigoku*　hell　　　　　　　　　　　　　　　118
		受験地獄　*juken jigoku*　the ordeal of examinations　260, 541, 118
		獄舎　　　*gokusha*　prison, jail (building)　　　　　805
		出獄　　　*shutsugoku*　release from prison　　　　　53
		獄死　　　*gokushi*　die in prison　　　　　　　　　　85

罪	**906** 5g8.4 ⊞ 罒 一 ｜ /55 4 13 罪	**ZAI, tsumi** – crime, sin, guilt
		犯罪　　*hanzai*　crime　　　　　　　　　　　　　　903
		罪人　　*zainin*　criminal　　　　　　　　　　　　　1
		tsumibito　sinner　　　　　　　　　　　　　1
		有罪　　*yūzai*　guilty　　　　　　　　　　　　　　265
		罪業　　*zaigō*　sin　　　　　　　　　　　　　　　279

罰	**907** 5g9.1 ⊞ 罒 言 儿 /55 67 16 罰 罸	**BATSU** – punishment, penalty **BACHI** – (divine) punishment
		罰金　　　*bakkin*　a fine　　　　　　　　　　　　　23
		体罰　　　*taibatsu*　corporal punishment　　　　　61
		厳罰　　　*genbatsu*　severe punishment　　　　　841
		天罰　　　*tenbatsu*　punishment from God/heaven　141
		罰当たり　*bachiatari*　damned, cursed　　　　　　77

刑	**908** 2f4.2 □ 刂 艹 一 /16 32 1 刑	**KEI** – penalty, punishment, sentence
		刑事　　*keiji*　criminal case; (police) detective　　80
		刑法　　*keihō*　criminal law, the Criminal Code　123
		刑罰　　*keibatsu*　punishment, penalty　　　　　907
		死刑　　*shikei*　capital punishment　　　　　　　85
		刑務所　*keimusho*　prison　　　　　　　　　235, 153

型	**909** 3b6.11 ⊞ 土 艹 儿 /22 32 16 型	**KEI, kata** – model, form
		類型的　　　*ruikeiteki*　stereotyped; typical　　226, 210
		原型　　　　*genkei*　prototype, model　　　　　　136
		紙型　　　　*kamigata, shikei*　papier-mâché mold　180
		血液型　　　*ketsuekigata*　blood type　　　　803, 480
		大型トラック　*ōgata torakku*　large truck　　　　　　26

補	**910** 5e7.1 □□ 衤 月 十 /57 43 12 補	**HO, ogina(u)** – supply, make up for, compensate for
		補給　　　　*hokyū*　supply, replenishment　　　　346
		補正　　　　*hosei*　revision, compensation　　　　275
		補助　　　　*hojo*　assistance, supplement, subsidy　633
		補充　　　　*hojū*　supplement, replacement　　　847
		補習教育　　*hoshū kyōiku*　continuing education　601, 245, 246

捕	**911** 3c7.3 扌 月 十 /23 43 12 捕	**HO, to(ru), to(raeru), tsuka(maeru)** – catch, grasp **to(rawareru), tsuka(maru)** – be caught, hold on to

捕鯨　*hogei*　whaling　713
捕鯨船　*hogeisen*　whaling ship　713, 377
だ捕　*daho*　capture, seize
生け捕り　*ikedori*　capturing alive　44

逮	**912** 2q8.2 辶 氵 ヨ /19 21 39 逮	**TAI** – chase

逮捕　*taiho*　arrest　911
逮捕状　*taihojō*　arrest warrant　911, 636
逮夜　*taiya*　eve of the anniversary of a death　479

建	**913** 2q6.2 辶 ヨ 十 /19 39 12 建	**KEN, [KON], ta(teru)** – build　**ta(tsu)** – be built

建設　*kensetsu*　construction　586
建立　*konryū*　erection, building　121
建物　*tatemono*　a building　79
二階建て　*nikaidate*　two-story　3, 597
建て前　*tatemae*　erection of the framework; principle　47

健	**914** 2a8.34 亻 ヨ 辶 /3 39 19 健	**KEN, suko(yaka)** – healthy

保健　*hoken*　preservation of health, hygiene　498
穏健　*onken*　moderate, sound　888
強健　*kyōken*　robust health, strong physique　217
健在　*kenzai*　healthy, sound　268
健勝　*kenshō*　healthy　518

鍵	**915** 8a8.18 釒 ヨ 辶 /72 39 19 鍵	**KEN, kagi** – key

合鍵　*aikagi*　duplicate key; passkeys　159
鍵束　*kagitaba*　bunch of keys　510

康	**916** 3q8.1 广 氵 ヨ /18 21 39 康	**KŌ** – peace, composure

健康　*kenkō*　health　914
不健康　*fukenkō*　not healthy, unhealthful　94, 914
小康　*shōkō*　lull, brief respite　27

究	**917** 3m4.5 宀 儿 十 /33 16 12 究	**KYŪ, kiwa(meru)** – investigate thoroughly/exhaustively

究明　*kyūmei*　study, investigation, inquiry　18
探究　*tankyū*　research, investigation　544
学究　*gakkyū*　scholar, student　109
究極　*kyūkyoku*　final, ultimate　336
論究　*ronkyū*　discuss thoroughly　293

	918	**KEN, to(gu)** – whet, hone, sharpen; polish, wash (rice)	
研	5a4.1 石 艹 一 /53 32 1 研	研究 *kenkyū* research 研究所 *kenkyūjo* research institute 研学 *kengaku* study	917 917, 153 109

	919	**KYŪ** – extreme, distress **kiwa(maru)** – reach an extreme; come to an end **kiwa(meru)** – carry to extremes; bring to an end	
窮	3m12.4 穴 月 弓 /33 43 28 窮	窮極目的 *kyūkyoku mokuteki* ultimate goal 窮地／境 *kyūchi/kyō* predicament 窮乏 *kyūbō* poverty 困窮 *konkyū* poverty	336, 55, 210 118, 883 767 567

	920	**TOTSU, tsu(ku)** – thrust, poke, strike	
突	3m5.11 穴 大 儿 /33 34 16 突	突然 *totsuzen* suddenly 突破 *toppa* break through, overcome 突入 *totsunyū* rush in, storm 羽根突き *hanetsuki* Japanese badminton 突き当たる *tsukiataru* run/bump into; reach the end	662 676 52 600, 314 77

	921	**KETSU, ana** – hole, cave	
穴	3m2.2 穴 儿 /33 16 穴	穴居人 *kekkyojin* caveman 落とし穴 *otoshiana* pitfall, trap 穴あけ器 *ana akeki* punch, perforator 鍵穴 *kagiana* keyhole 穴子 *anago* conger eel	171, 1 858 536 915 103

	922	**SHA, i(ru)** – shoot	
射	0a10.8 月 寸 丨 43 37 2 射	発射 *hassha* fire, launch 射殺 *shasatsu* shoot dead 注射 *chūsha* injection, shot 放射能 *hōshanō* radioactivity 反射 *hansha* reflection; reflex	96 585 358 521, 387 324

	923	**SHA** – gratitude; apology **ayama(ru)** – apologize	
謝	7a10.1 言 月 寸 /67 43 37 謝	感謝 *kansha* gratitude 謝礼 *sharei* remuneration, honorarium 月謝 *gessha* monthly tuition 謝罪 *shazai* apology 代謝 *taisha* metabolism	262 630 17 906 256

	924	**SHI** – utmost **ita(ru)** – arrive, lead to	
至	3b3.6 土 ム 一 /22 17 1 至	必至 *hisshi* inevitable 至急 *shikyū* urgency, urgent 夏至 *geshi* summer solstice 至る所 *itaru tokoro* everywhere 至東京 *itaru Tōkyō* To Tōkyō (at the edge of a map)	529 303 469 153 71, 189

925

致

4i6.2

夊 士 厶
/49 22 17

致

CHI – bring about **ita(su)** – do (deferential, used like *suru*)

一致	*itchi*	agreement, consistency	2
合致	*gatchi*	agreement, consistency	159
致命傷	*chimeishō*	fatal wound	587, 643
致死量	*chishiryō*	lethal dose	85, 417
風致	*fūchi*	scenic beauty; taste, elegance	29

926

到

2f6.4

刂 士 厶
/16 22 17

到

TŌ – arrive, reach

到着	*tōchaku*	arrival	668
到来	*tōrai*	arrival, advent	69
到達	*tōtatsu*	reach, attain	455
殺到	*sattō*	rush, stampede	585
周到	*shūtō*	meticulous	91

927

倒

2a8.5

亻 士 儿
/3 22 16

倒

TŌ, tao(reru) – fall over, collapse **tao(su)** – knock down, topple, defeat

卒倒	*sottō*	faint	801
倒産	*tōsan*	bankruptcy	278
倒閣	*tōkaku*	overthrowing the cabinet	856
共倒れ	*tomodaore*	mutual destruction, common ruin	196

928

誤

7a7.2

言 口 儿
/67 24 16

誤

GO – mistake, mis- **ayama(ru)** – err, make a mistake

誤解	*gokai*	misunderstanding	482
誤報	*gohō*	erroneous report/information	698
誤算	*gosan*	miscalculation	760
誤植	*goshoku*	a misprint	430
読み誤る	*yomiayamaru*	misread	244

929

互

0a4.15

一 一
14 1

互

GO, taga(i) – mutual, reciprocal, each other

相互	*sōgo*	mutual	146
交互	*kōgo*	mutual; alternating	114
互助	*gojo*	mutual aid	633
互選	*gosen*	mutual election	814
互い違いに	*tagaichigai ni*	alternately	833

930

系

6a1.1

糸 丨
/61 2

系

KEI – system; lineage, group

体系	*taikei*	system	61
系統	*keitō*	system; lineage, descent	849
日系	*nikkei*	of Japanese descent	5
直系	*chokkei*	direct descent	429
系図	*keizu*	genealogy, family tree	339

931

係

2a7.8

亻 糸 丨
/3 61 2

係

KEI, kaka(ru) – have to do with **kakari** – person in charge

関係	*kankei*	relation, relationship, connection	402
関係者	*kankeisha*	interested party, those concerned	402, 164
無関係	*mukankei*	unrelated, irrelevant	93, 402
係争	*keisō*	dispute, contention	302
係長	*kakarichō*	chief clerk	95

932

孫

2c7.1 ▢
子 糸 |
/6 61 2

孫

SON, mago – grandchild

子孫	shison	descendant	103
皇孫	kōson	imperial grandchild/descendant	297
天孫	tenson	of divine descent	141

933

懸

4k16.2 ▢
心 糸 目
/51 61 55

懸

KEN, [KE], ka(karu) – hang **ka(keru)** – offer, give

一生懸命	isshōkenmei	utmost effort, all one's might	2, 44, 587
懸案	ken'an	unsettled problem	106
懸賞	kenshō	offer of a prize	509
懸念	kenen	fear, apprehension	588
命懸け	inochigake	risking one's life	587

934

派

3a6.21 ▢
氵 厂 乀
/21 18 10

派

HA – group, faction, sect, school (of thought)

宗派	shūha	sect	626
党派	tōha	party, faction	504
左／右派	sa/uha	the left/right wing	75, 76
派出所	hashutsujo	branch office; police box	53, 153
特派員	tokuhain	correspondent	282, 163

935

脈

4b6.8
月 厂 乀
/43 18 10

脈 脉

MYAKU – pulse, vein, blood vessel

動脈	dōmyaku	artery	231
静脈	jōmyaku	vein	674
山脈	sanmyaku	mountain range	34
文脈	bunmyaku	context	111
脈略	myakuraku	logical connection, coherence	860

936

貫

7b4.3
貝 女 |
/68 25 2

貫

KAN – pierce; carry out; (old monetary unit; unit of weight, about 3.75 kg) **tsuranu(ku)** – pierce; carry out

一貫	ikkan	consistency, coherence, integrated	2
貫通	kantsū	pass through, pierce	150
貫流	kanryū	flow through	247
貫き通す	tsuranukitōsu	carry out (one's will)	150

937

慣

4k11.9 ▢
心 貝 女
/51 68 25

慣

KAN, na(reru) – get used to **na(rasu)** – accustom to; tame

習慣	shūkan	custom, practice	601
慣習	kanshū	custom, practice	601
慣例	kanrei	custom, convention	622
慣用句	kan'yōku	idiom, common expression	107, 337
見慣れる	minareru	get used to seeing	63

938

複

5e9.3 ▢
衤 日 夊
/57 42 49

複

FUKU – double, multiple, composite; again

複雑	fukuzatsu	complicated	584
複合	fukugō	composition, compound, complex	159
重複	chōfuku, jūfuku	duplication, overlapping	227
複製	fukusei	reproduction, duplicate, facsimile	434
複数	fukusū	plural	225

	939	**FUKU** – return; be restored	
	3i9.4 ⊞	復習 fukushū review	601
	彳 日 夂	反復 hanpuku repetition	324
	/29 42 49	復活 fukkatsu revival	237
	復	復興 fukkō reconstruction, revival	369
		回復 kaifuku recovery, recuperation	90

	940	**Ō** – go	
	3i5.6 ⊞	往復 ōfuku round trip	939
	彳 王 丶	往来 ōrai comings and goings, traffic; street, way	69
	/29 46 2	立ち往生 tachiōjō standstill, getting stalled	121, 44
	往 徃	右往左往 uō-saō rush about in confusion	76, 75
		往年 ōnen the past, formerly	45

	941	**EN, kemuri** – smoke **kemu(ru)** – smoke, smolder **kemu(i)** – smoky	
	4d9.3 ⊞	禁煙 kin'en No Smoking	491
	火 口 土	煙突 entotsu chimney	920
	/44 24 22	発煙 hatsuen emitting smoke, fuming	96
	煙 烟	黒煙 kokuen black smoke	206

	942	**SHŌ, ya(keru)** – (intr.) burn; be roasted, broiled, baked **ya(ku)** – (tr.) burn, roast, broil, bake	
	4d8.4 ⊞	全焼 zenshō be totally destroyed by fire	89
	火 艹 土	焼(き)鳥 yakitori grilled chicken	285
	/44 32 12	日焼け hiyake sunburn, suntan	5
	焼 燒	夕焼け yūyake glow of sunset	81

	943	**SEN** – move, change; climb	
	2q12.1 ⊡	変遷 hensen undergo changes	257
	辶 口 弓	左遷 sasen demotion	75
	/19 24 28	遷都 sento transfer of the capital	188
	遷		

	944	**HYŌ** – slip of paper, ballot, vote	
	4e6.2 ⊟	一票 ippyō a vote	2
	礻 口 一	得票 tokuhyō votes obtained	375
	/45 24 14	反対票 hantaihyō no vote, adverse vote	324, 366
	票	開票 kaihyō vote counting	400
		伝票 denpyō slip of paper	440

	945	**HYŌ** – sign, mark	
	4a11.8 ⊞	目標 mokuhyō goal, purpose	55
	木 礻 口	標語 hyōgo slogan, motto	67
	/41 45 24	標準語 hyōjungo the standard language	792, 67
	標	標本 hyōhon specimen, sample	25
		商標 shōhyō trademark	418

漂	**946** 3a11.9 ⊞ 氵 ネ 口 /21 45 24 漂	**HYŌ, tadayo(u)** – drift about, float 漂流　*hyōryū*　drift, be adrift　247 漂着　*hyōchaku*　drift ashore　668 漂白剤　*hyōhakuzai*　bleach　205, 559 漂々　*hyōhyō*　light, buoyant
奈	**947** 4e3.3 ⋯ ネ 大 /45 34 奈	**NA** – what?, how? 奈落　*naraku*　hell, hades; theater basement　858 奈良　*Nara*　(capital of Nara Prefecture)　321 神奈川県　*Kanagawa-ken*　Kanagawa Prefecture　310, 33, 194
鳴	**948** 3d11.1 ⊡ 口 鳥 /24 80 鳴	**MEI, na(ku)** – (animals) cry, sing, howl **na(ru)** – (intr.) sound, ring **na(rasu)** – (tr.) sound, ring 共鳴　*kyōmei*　resonance; sympathy　196 鳴動　*meidō*　rumble　231 鳴き声　*nakigoe*　cry, call, chirping (of animals)　759 海鳴り　*uminari*　rumbling/noise of the sea　117
鶏	**949** 11b8.4 ⊞ 鳥 小 大 /80 35 34 鶏 鷄	**KEI, niwatori** – chicken, hen, rooster 鶏肉　*keiniku*　chicken, fowl　223 養鶏　*yōkei*　poultry raising　406 鶏舎　*keisha*　chicken coop, henhouse　805 鶏鳴　*keimei*　cockcrow　948 鶏頭　*keitō*　cockscomb (flower)　276
鶴	**950** 11b10.1 ⊡ 鳥 隹 門 /80 73 20 鶴	**tsuru** – crane, stork 千羽鶴　*senbazuru*　(string of) many origami cranes (a symbol 　for good health); many-cranes design　15, 600 鶴の一声　*tsuru no hitokoe*　the voice of authority　2, 759
咲	**951** 3d6.12 ⊞ 口 大 儿 /24 34 16 咲	**sa(ku)** – bloom 咲き出す　*sakidasu*　begin to bloom　53 咲き乱れる　*sakimidareru*　bloom in profusion　702 遅咲き　*osozaki*　blooming late　715 狂い咲き　*kuruizaki*　flowering out of season　904 返り咲き　*kaerizaki*　second bloom; comeback　448
桜	**952** 4a6.15 ⊞ 木 女 小 /41 25 35 桜 櫻	**Ō, sakura** – cherry tree 桜花　*ōka*　cherry blossoms　255 八重桜　*yaezakura*　double-petal cherry blossoms　10, 227 桜んぼ　*sakuranbo*　cherry 桜色　*sakurairo*　pink, cerise　204 桜肉　*sakuraniku*　horsemeat　223

953	**SHI, sugata** – form, figure, shape, appearance, posture	
3e6.10	姿勢　shisei　posture, stance	656
女 夊 冫	容姿　yōshi　face and figure, appearance	665
/25　49　5	姿態　shitai　figure, pose	388
	姿見　sugatami　full-length mirror	63
	後ろ姿　ushiro-sugata　view (of someone) from behind	48

954	**SHI** – as one pleases, self-indulgent, arbitrary	
4k6.22	恣意　shii　arbitrariness, selfishness	132
心 夊 冫	恣意的　shiiteki　arbitrary, selfish	132, 210
/51　49　5	放恣　hōshi　self-indulgent, licentious	521
	専恣　senshi　self-indulgent, wanton, arbitrary	610

955	**ibara** – brier	
3k6.11	茨城県　Ibaraki-ken　Ibaraki Prefecture	733, 194
艹 夊 冫		
/32　49　5		

956	**DA** – peace, contentment	
3e4.9	妥協　dakyō　compromise	234
女 小 丨	妥結　daketsu　compromise, agreement	494
/25　35　2	妥当　datō　proper, appropriate, adequate	77
	妥協案　dakyōan　compromise plan	234, 106

957	**SAI** – general's baton; dice; take; coloring; appearance; fief	
4a4.24	采配　saihai　baton of command	524
木 小 丨		
/41　35　2		

958	**SAI, na** – vegetable; rape, mustard plant	
3k8.25	野菜　yasai　vegetable	236
艹 木 小	菜園　saien　vegetable garden	454
/32　41　35	菜食　saishoku　vegetarian/herbivorous diet	322
	山菜　sansai　edible wild plant	34
	菜種　natane　rapeseed, coleseed, colza	228

959	**SAI, irodo(ru)** – color	
3j8.1	色彩　shikisai　color, coloration	204
彡 木 小	彩色　saishiki　coloring, coloration	204
/31　41　35	多彩　tasai　colorful	229
	光彩　kōsai　luster, brilliancy	138
	水彩画　suisaiga　a watercolor painting	21, 343

	960	**SAI, to(ru)** – take (on), accept, employ; collect	
採	3c8.14	採用 saiyō adopt; employ	107
	扌 木 小	採決 saiketsu voting	357
	/23 41 35	採集 saishū collecting (plants/butterflies)	442
		採録 sairoku record (in a book)	547
	採	採算 saisan a profit	760

	961	**SHŪ, [JU], tsu(ku)** – take (a seat), engage (in an occupation)	
就	3d9.21	**tsu(keru)** – employ	
	口 小 尢	就職 shūshoku find employment	386
	/24 35 27	就任 shūnin assumption of office	334
		就業時間 shūgyō jikan working hours	279, 42, 43
	就	成就 jōju accomplish, attain	261

	962	**SHŪ, ke(ru)** – kick	
蹴	7d12.2	蹴球 shūkyū football	739
	昆 口 小	一蹴 isshū a kick	2
	/70 24 35	一蹴する isshū suru kick; reject flatly, brush off; beat easily,	
		give a drubbing	2
	蹴	蹴飛ばす ketobasu kick away/out; reject	539

	963	**BOTSU** – sink, go down	
没	3a4.15	没落 botsuraku downfall, ruin	858
	氵 冂 又	没入 botsunyū become immersed (in)	52
	/21 20 9	出没 shutsubotsu appear and disappear, frequent	53
		没収 bosshū confiscation, forfeiture	770
	没 没	没交渉 bokkōshō unrelated, independent	114, 438

	964	**CHIN, shizu(mu)** – (intr.) sink **shizu(meru)** – (tr.) sink	
沈	3a4.9	沈没 chinbotsu sinking	963
	氵 冂 丨	沈下 chinka sinking, subsidence, settling	31
	/21 20 2	沈静 chinsei stillness, stagnation	674
		沈着 chinchaku composed, calm	668
	沈	沈思 chinshi meditation, contemplation	99

	965	**makura** – pillow	
枕	4a4.8	水枕 mizumakura water-filled pillow	21
	木 冂 丨	枕木 makuragi railroad tie	22
	/41 20 2		
	枕		

	966	**DEKI, obo(reru)** – drown; indulge (in)	
溺	3a10.1	溺死 dekishi drowning	85
	氵 弓 冫	溺愛 dekiai dote upon	259
	/21 28 5	耽溺 tandeki addiction, dissipation	
	溺		

	967	**SEN** – dive, hide **mogu(ru)** – dive; crawl into **hiso(mu)** – lurk, lie hidden
潜	3a12.6	潜水　sensui　dive, submerge　　21 潜水夫　sensuifu　diver　　21, 315 潜在　senzai　hidden, latent, potential　　268 潜入　sennyū　infiltrate (into)　　52

	968	**FU, u(kabu)** – float, rise to the surface, appear **u(kaberu)** – set afloat; show **u(ku)** – float, rise to the surface **u(kareru)** – feel buoyant, be in high spirits
浮	3a6.11	思い浮ぶ　omoiukabu　come to mind, occur to　　99 浮かぬ顔　ukanu kao　dejected look　　277 浮世絵　ukiyoe　Japanese woodblock print　　252, 345

	969	**NYŪ, chichi, chi** – mother's milk; breast
乳	3n4.4	牛乳　gyūnyū　(cow's) milk　　281 母乳　bonyū　mother's milk　　112 乳飲み子　chinomigo　suckling infant　　323, 103 乳首　chikubi, chichikubi　nipple　　148 乳母車　ubaguruma　baby carriage　　112, 133

	970	**KŌ** – hole; Confucius
孔	2c1.1	気孔　kikō　pore　　134 通気 / 空気孔　tsūki/kūkikō　air hole　　150, 134, 140, 134 鼻孔　bikō　nostril　　832 多孔　takō　porous　　229 孔子　Kōshi　Confucius　　103

	971	**RYŌ** – finish, complete; understand
了	2c0.3	終了　shūryō　end, completion, expiration　　466 完了　kanryō　completion; perfect tense　　623 （任期）満了　(ninki) manryō　expiration (of a term　334, 456, 201 校了　kōryō　final proofreading　⌊of office)　115 了解　ryōkai　understand, comprehend; Roger!　　482

	972	**SHŌ, uketamawa(ru)** – hear, be told
承	0a7.7	承知　shōchi　consent; be aware of　　214 承認　shōnin　approval　　751 承服　shōfuku　consent, acceptance　　696 了承　ryōshō　acknowledgment　　971 伝承　denshō　hand down (from generation to generation)　　440

	973	**JŌ** – steam **mu(su)** – steam, be sultry **mu(rasu)** – steam **mu(reru)** – be steamed; get hot and stuffy
蒸	3k9.19	（水）蒸気　(sui)jōki　(water) vapor, steam　　21, 134 蒸発　jōhatsu　evaporate; disappear　　96 蒸し暑い　mushiatsui　hot and humid, sultry　　648 蒸し返す　mushikaesu　reheat; repeat, rehash　　448

候	**974** 2a8.10 ▯▯▯ 亻 大 ⺀ /3 34 15 候	**KŌ** – season; weather **sōrō** – (classical verb suffix) 天候　tenkō　weather　　　　　　　　　　141 気候　kikō　climate　　　　　　　　　　　134 測候所　sokkōjo　meteorological station　620, 153 候補者　kōhosha　candidate　　　　　910, 164 居候　isōrō　hanger-on, parasite　　　　　171
修	**975** 2a8.11 ▯▯▯ 亻 夊 彡 /3 49 31 修	**SHŪ, [SHU], osa(meru)** – study; master **osa(maru)** – govern oneself 修理　shūri　repair　　　　　　　　　　143 修正　shūsei　revise, correct, retouch　　　275 修業　shūgyō　pursuit/completion of one's studies　279 必修科目　hisshū kamoku　required subject　529, 320, 55 修行　shugyō　training, study　　　　　　68
隆	**976** 2d8.6 阝 夊 土 /7 49 22 隆	**RYŪ** – prosperity; high 隆盛　ryūsei　prosperity　　　　　　　　732 興隆　kōryū　rise, prosperity, flourishing　369 隆起　ryūki　protuberance, rise, elevation　374 隆々　ryūryū　prosperous, thriving; muscular 法隆寺　Hōryūji　(temple in Nara)　　　123, 41
降	**977** 2d7.7 ▯ 阝 夊 十 /7 49 12 降	**KŌ, o(riru)** – go down, descend, get off (a bus) **o(rosu)** – let off (a passenger), dismiss **fu(ru)** – fall (rain/snow) 降雨量　kōuryō　(amount of) rainfall　　30, 417 降下　kōka　descent, fall, landing　　　　31 以降　ikō　since, from ... on　　　　　　46 飛び降りる　tobioriru　jump down (from)　539
霜	**978** 8d9.2 雨 日 木 /74 55 41 霜	**SŌ, shimo** – frost 霜害　sōgai　frost damage　　　　　　　527 霜柱　shimobashira　ice/frost columns　　608 霜解け　shimodoke　thawing　　　　　　482 霜焼け　shimoyake　frostbite　　　　　　942 霜降り　shimofuri　marbled (meat), salt-and-pepper pattern　977
雪	**979** 8d3.2 雨 ヨ /74 39 雪	**SETSU, yuki** – snow 残雪　zansetsu　lingering snow　　　　　661 初雪　hatsuyuki　first snow of the year/winter　692 雪空　yukizora　snowy sky　　　　　　　140 雪景色　yukigeshiki　snowy landscape　　872, 204 雪国　yukiguni　snowy region, snow country　40
霧	**980** 8d11.1 ▯ 雨 夊 力 /74 49 8 霧	**MU, kiri** – fog 五里霧中　gori-muchū　in a fog, mystified　7, 142, 28 霧雨　kirisame　misty rain, drizzle　　　30 朝霧　asagiri　morning mist/fog　　　　477 夕霧　yūgiri　evening mist/fog　　　　　81 黒い霧　kuroi kiri　dark machinations　　206

	981	**RO, [RŌ]** – open, public **tsuyu** – dew	
	8d13.1	露天で *roten de* outdoors, in the open air	141
		露店 *roten* street stall, booth	168
	/74 70 49	露出 *roshutsu* (indecent/film) exposure	53
		露見 *roken* discovery, detection, exposure	63
	露	朝露 *asatsuyu* morning dew	477

	982	**RAI** – thunder; mine, torpedo **kaminari** – thunder	
	8d5.1	雷鳴 *raimei* thunder	948
		落雷 *rakurai* thunderbolt, bolt of lightning	858
	/74 58	雷雨 *raiu* thunderstorm	30
		地雷 *jirai* (land) mine	118
	雷	魚雷 *gyorai* torpedo	290

	983	**SHIN, furu(eru), furu(u)** – tremble, shake	
	8d7.3	地震 *jishin* earthquake	118
		震動 *shindō* tremor, vibration	231
	/74 57 18	震度5 *shindo go* magnitude 5	378
		震央／源 *shin'ō, shingen* epicenter	352, 589
	震	身震い *miburui* shiver, tremble, shudder	59

	984	**SHIN, fu(ruu)** – swing, wield; flourish **fu(ru)** – wave, shake **fu(reru)** – swing, lean toward	
	3c7.14	振興 *shinkō* advancement, promotion	369
		振動 *shindō* swing, oscillation, vibration	231
	/23 57 18	振り替え *furikae* transfer	757
	振	振り返る *furikaeru* turn one's head, look back	448

	985	**NIN** – conception, pregnancy	
	3e4.3	妊婦 *ninpu* pregnant woman	316
		妊婦服 *ninpufuku* maternity dress	316, 696
	/25 46	不妊 *funin* sterile, infertile	94
	妊 姙	妊産婦 *ninsanpu* expectant and nursing mothers	278, 316

	986	**SHIN** – pregnancy	
	3e7.10	妊娠 *ninshin* pregnancy	985
	/25 57 18	妊娠中絶 *ninshin chūzetsu* abortion	985, 28, 755
	娠		

	987	**NŌ, ko(i)** – dark, thick, heavy, strong (coffee)	
	3a13.7	濃度 *nōdo* (degree of) concentration	378
		濃厚 *nōkō* thickness, richness, strength	649
	/21 57 42	濃霧 *nōmu* dense fog	980
	濃		

豆	**988**	**TŌ, [ZU], mame** – bean, pea; (prefix) miniature	
	3d4.22 目	大豆　*daizu*　soybean	26
	口 儿 一	小豆　*azuki*　adzuki bean	27
	/24 16 1	枝豆　*edamame*　green soybean	889
	豆	コーヒー豆　*kōhīmame*　coffee bean	
		豆本　*mamehon*　miniature book, pocket edition	25

豊	**989**	**HŌ, yuta(ka)** – abundant, rich	
	3d10.15	豊富　*hōfu*　abundance, wealth	726
	口 日 儿	豊作　*hōsaku*　good harvest	361
	/24 42 16	豊漁　*hōryō*　good catch (of fish)	712
	豊 豐	豊年　*hōnen*　fruitful year	45
		豊満　*hōman*　plump, voluptuous, buxom	201

艶	**990**	**EN, tsuya** – gloss, luster; charm, romance, love	
	3d16.3 田	**ade(yaka)** – charming, fascinating	
	日	艶美　*enbi*　voluptuous charm, bewitching beauty	405
	42	艶事　*tsuyagoto*　love affair, romance	80
	艶	艶消し　*tsuyakeshi*　non-glossy, frosted (glass);	
		disappointment, disillusionment	864

登	**991**	**TŌ, TO, nobo(ru)** – climb	
	3d9.26 目	登山　*tozan*　mountain climbing	34
	口 火 儿	登場　*tōjō*　stage entrance; appearance	154
	/24 44 16	登記　*tōki*　registration	372
	登	登録　*tōroku*　registration	547
		登用　*tōyō*　appointment; promotion	107

廃	**992**	**HAI** – abolish, abandon, discontinue; decay; scrapped	
	3q9.3 匚	**suta(reru), suta(ru)** – become outmoded; decay	
	广 火 艹	廃止　*haishi*　abolition, abrogation	485
	/18 44 32	廃業　*haigyō*　going out of business	279
	廃 廢	退廃　*taihai*　degeneracy, decadence	865
		廃人　*haijin*　cripple, invalid	1

棄	**993**	**KI** – abandon, throw out, give up	
	2j11.5 目	廃棄物　*haikibutsu*　waste (matter)	992, 79
	亠 木 艹	放棄　*hōki*　give up, renounce, waive	521
	/11 41 32	棄権　*kiken*　abstention, nonvoting; renunciation	335
	棄 弃	自棄　*jiki*　self-abandonment	62
		破棄　*haki*　destruction; annulment, revocation	676

帯	**994**	**TAI** – belt, zone **obi** – belt, sash **o(biru)** – wear; be entrusted (with)	
	3f7.1 目	包帯　*hōtai*　bandage	819
	巾 艹 冂	地帯　*chitai*　zone, area, region, belt	118
	/26 32 20	熱帯　*nettai*　the tropics	655
	帯 帶	所帯　*shotai*　household	153

滞	**995** 3a10.14 ⊞ 氵 艹 巾 /21 32 26 滞 滞	**TAI** – stay, stopping over **todokō(ru)** – be left undone; fall into arrears, be overdue, be left unpaid 滞在　taizai　stay, sojourn　268 遅滞　chitai　delay, procrastination　715 滞納　tainō　delinquency (in payment)　771 沈滞　chintai　stagnation, inactivity　964
純	**996** 6a4.3 糸 亠 冂 /61 12 20 純	**JUN** – pure 純毛　junmō　pure/100 percent wool　287 純益　jun'eki　net profit　729 純文学　junbungaku　pure literature, belles lettres　111, 109 純日本風　jun Nihon-fū　classical Japanese style　5, 25, 29 単純　tanjun　simple　300
鈍	**997** 8a4.2 金 亠 冂 /72 12 20 鈍	**DON, nibu(i)** – dull, thick, slow-witted, sluggish, blunt, dim **nibu(ru)** – become dull/blunt, weaken 鈍感　donkan　obtuse, thick, insensitive　262 鈍重　donjū　dull-witted, phlegmatic, stolid　227 鈍角　donkaku　obtuse angle　481 鈍器　donki　blunt object (used as a weapon)　536
迷	**998** 2q6.1 ⊡ 辶 米 /19 62 迷	**MEI, mayo(u)** – be perplexed, vacillate; get lost; go astray 迷宮 / 路　meikyū/ro　maze/labyrinth　734, 151 迷信　meishin　superstition　157 迷彩　meisai　camouflage　959 低迷　teimei　be low, in a slump (market prices)　570 迷子　maigo　lost child　103
謎	**999** 7a9.20 ⊡ 言 米 辶 /67 62 19 謎	**nazo** – riddle, puzzle, enigma; hint, suggestion 字謎　jinazo　kanji puzzle (inferring a kanji from a cryptic description of its parts)　110
述	**1000** 2q5.3 辶 木 丶 /19 41 2 述	**JUTSU, no(beru)** – state, mention, refer to, explain 供述　kyōjutsu　testimony, deposition　197 記述　kijutsu　description　372 上述　jōjutsu　above-mentioned　32 口述　kōjutsu　oral statement; dictation　54 著述家　chojutsuka　writer, author　878, 165
惑	**1001** 4k8.16 ⊟ 心 戈 口 /51 52 24 惑	**WAKU, mado(u)** – go astray, be misguided, be tempted 迷惑　meiwaku　trouble, inconvenience　998 当惑　tōwaku　puzzlement, confusion　77 思惑　omowaku　opinion, intention, expectation　99 惑星　wakusei　planet　743 戸惑い　tomadoi　become disoriented/flurried　152

	1002	**IKI** – region, area	
域	3b8.3 ⊞ 土 戈 口 /22 52 24 域	地域 *chiiki* region, area, zone 区域 *kuiki* boundary, zone, district 領域 *ryōiki* territory, domain 流域 *ryūiki* (river) basin, valley 聖域 *seiiki* sacred ground	118 183 853 247 686
償	**1003** 2a15.4 ⊞ 亻 貝 小 /3 68 35 償	**SHŌ, tsuguna(u)** – make up for, compensate, indemnify, atone for 補償 *hoshō* compensation, indemnification 弁償 *benshō* compensation, reimbursement 報償 *hōshō* compensation, remuneration 代償 *daishō* compensation, idemnification 無償 *mushō* free of charge, gratis	910 724 698 256 93
固	**1004** 3s5.2 ▣ 口 十 /24 12 固	**KO, kata(i)** – hard **kata(maru)** – (intr.) harden **kata(meru)** – (tr.) harden 固体 *kotai* a solid 固有 *koyū* own, peculiar, characteristic 固定 *kotei* fixed; hold fast to, persist in, insist on 強固 *kyōko* firm, solid, strong	61 265 356 217
個	**1005** 2a8.36 ⊞ 亻 口 十 /3 24 12 個 个	**KO** – individual, (counter for various objects) 個人 *kojin* an individual 個体 *kotai* an individual 個性 *kosei* individuality 個別的 *kobetsuteki* individual, separate 一個 *ikko* one piece	1 61 98 267, 210 2
錮	**1006** 8a8.21 ⊞ 金 口 十 /72 24 12 錮	**KO** – tie, bind 禁錮（罰） *kinko(batsu)* imprisonment	491, 907
枯	**1007** 4a5.26 ⊞ 木 口 十 /41 24 12 枯	**KO, ka(reru)** – wither **ka(rasu)** – blight, let wither 枯死 *koshi* wither away, die 栄枯 *eiko* ups and downs, vicissitudes 枯れ木 *kareki* dead/withered tree 枯れ葉 *kareha* dead/withered leaf 木枯らし *kogarashi* cold winter wind	85 736 22 253 22
皮	**1008** 2h3.1 ⋯ 又 厂 /9 18 皮	**HI, kawa** – skin, hide, leather, pelt, bark, rind 皮肉 *hiniku* irony 皮相 *hisō* superficiality, shallowness 毛皮 *kegawa* fur 皮細工 *kawazaiku* leatherwork 皮切り *kawakiri* beginning, start	223 146 287 708, 139 39

1009

被

5e5.3
衤 厂 又
/57 18 9
被

HI, kōmu(ru) – incur, suffer, receive

被害者	*higaisha*	victim	527, 164
被告（人）	*hikoku(nin)*	defendant	703, 1
被選挙資格	*hisenkyo shikaku*	eligibility for election	
			814, 815, 763, 653
被服	*hifuku*	covering, coating	696

1010

彼

3i5.2
彳 厂 又
/29 18 9
彼

HI – he, that **kare** – he **[kano]** – that

彼岸	*higan*	equinoctal week; the other shore	595
彼ら	*karera*	they	
彼氏	*kareshi*	he; boyfriend, lover	575
彼女	*kanojo*	she; girlfriend, lover	102

1011

称

5d5.8
禾 小 亠
/56 35 15
称 稱

SHŌ – name, title

名称	*meishō*	name, designation	82
愛称	*aishō*	term of endearment, pet name	259
尊称	*sonshō*	honorific title	717
称号	*shōgō*	title, degree	266
相／対称	*sō/taishō*	symmetry	146, 366

1012

弥

3h5.2
弓 小 亠
/28 35 15
弥

ya – all the more, increasingly

弥次馬	*yajiuma*	bystanders, spectators, crowd of onlookers	
			236, 385, 283
弥生	*yayoi*	third lunar month; spring	44
弥生時代	*Yayoi jidai*	Yayoi period (200 B.C.–250 A.D.)	42, 256
阿弥陀	*Amida*	Amida Buddha	

1013

飾

8b5.3
食 巾 亠
/77 26 15
飾 餙

SHOKU, kaza(ru) – decorate, adorn

修飾	*shūshoku*	embellishment; modify (in grammar)	975
飾り付け	*kazaritsuke*	decoration	192
飾り気	*kazarike*	affectation, love of display	134
首飾り	*kubikazari*	necklace, choker	148
着飾る	*kikazaru*	dress up	668

1014

郎

2d6.5
阝 食
/7 77
郎

RŌ – man, husband; (suffix for male given names)

新郎新婦	*shinrō-shinpu*	bride and groom	174, 174, 316
郎党	*rōtō*	vassals, retainers	504
野郎	*yarō*	guy	236
太郎	*Tarō*	(male given name)	639
二郎、次郎	*Jirō*	(male given name)	3, 385

1015

廊

3q8.4
广 食 阝
/18 77 7
廊

RŌ – corridor, hall

廊下	*rōka*	corridor, hall	31
回廊	*kairō*	corridor, gallery	90
画廊	*garō*	picture gallery	343

	1016	**KŌ** – A, No. 1 (in a series); shell, tortoise shell **KAN** – high-pitched
甲	0a5.34 ... 日 丨 42 2 甲	甲種　*kōshu*　Grade A, first class　228 甲鉄　*kōtetsu*　armor, armor plating　312 甲高い　*kandakai*　high-pitched, shrill　190 生き甲斐　*ikigai*　something worth living for　44

	1017	**OTSU** – B, No. 2 (in a series), the latter; duplicate; bass (voice); strange; stylish; fine
乙	0a1.5 一 1 乙	甲乙　*kō-otsu*　A and B; discrimination, gradation　1016 乙女　*otome*　virgin, maiden　102 乙な味　*otsu na aji*　delicate flavor　307

	1018	**HEI** – C, No. 3 (in a series)
丙	0a5.21 ... 一 冂 丶 14 20 2 丙	甲乙丙　*kō-otsu-hei*　A, B, C; Nos. 1, 2, 3　1016, 1017 丙午　*hinoeuma*　(year in the Chinese 60-year cycle)　49

	1019	**HEI, gara** – pattern, design; build; character **e** – handle
柄	4a5.9 ☐ 木 一 冂 /41 14 20 柄	横柄　*ōhei*　arrogance; one's person　795 人柄　*hitogara*　character, personality　1 事柄　*kotogara*　matters, affairs　80 間柄　*aidagara*　relation, relationship　43

	1020	**ko(u)** – ask (for), beg
乞	0a3.4 ... 𠂉 一 15 1 乞	乞食　*kojiki*　beggar　322

	1021	**Ō, o(su)** – push **o(saeru)** – restrain, hold in check, suppress
押	3c5.5 ☐ 扌 日 丨 /23 42 2 押	押収　*ōshū*　confiscation　770 押韻　*ōin*　rhyme　350 押し入れ　*oshiire*　closet, wall-cupboard　52 後押し　*atooshi*　push, support, back　48 押し付ける　*oshitsukeru*　press against; force (upon)　192

	1022	**CHŪ** – pull, extract
抽	3c5.7 ☐ 扌 日 丨 /23 42 2 抽	抽出　*chūshutsu*　extraction, sampling　53 抽象　*chūshō*　abstraction　752 抽象的　*chūshōteki*　abstract　752, 210 抽せん　*chūsen*　drawing, lottery 抽せん券　*chūsenken*　lottery/raffle ticket　515

軸	**1023** 　 7c5.1 　 車 日 丨 　 /69 42 2 　 軸	**JIKU** – axis, axle, shaft; (picture) scroll

車軸　*shajiku*　axle　　　　　　　　　　　　133
地軸　*chijiku*　earth's axis　　　　　　　　118
自転軸　*jitenjiku*　axis of rotation　　　　62, 439

袖	**1024** 　 5e5.1 　 礻 日 丨 　 /57 42 2 　 袖	**SHŪ, sode** – sleeve

領袖　*ryōshū*　leader, boss　　　　　　　　853
半袖　*hansode*　short sleeves　　　　　　　88
長袖　*nagasode*　long sleeves　　　　　　　95
袖口　*sodeguchi*　edge of a sleeve, cuff　　54

裾	**1025** 　 5e8.8 　 礻 尸 口 　 /57 40 24 　 裾	**suso** – hem, skirt, cuff; foot (of a mountain)

山裾　*yamasuso*　foot of a mountain　　　　34
裾野　*susono*　foot of a mountain　　　　　236

捜	**1026** 　 3c7.5 　 扌 日 又 　 /23 42 9 　 捜 捜	**SŌ, saga(su)** – look/search for

捜査　*sōsa*　investigation　　　　　┌premises　634
家宅捜査　*kataku sōsa*　search of the house/　165, 178, 634
捜査本部　*sōsa honbu*　investigation headquarters　634, 25, 86
捜し回る　*sagashimawaru*　search around for　　90
捜し当てる　*sagashiateru*　find out, discover, locate　77

宇	**1027** 　 3m3.3 　 宀 日 一 　 /33 14 1 　 宇	**U** – roof, house; sky

宇内　*udai*　the whole world　　　　　　　84
気宇広大　*kiu-kōdai*　magnanimous　　　134, 707, 26
宇都宮　*Utsunomiya*　(capital of Tochigi Prefecture)　188, 734

宙	**1028** 　 3m5.5 　 宀 日 丨 　 /33 42 2 　 宙	**CHŪ** – midair, space, heaven

宇宙　*uchū*　space, the universe　　　　　1027
宇宙旅行　*uchū ryokō*　space flight　　1027, 222, 68
宇宙飛行士　*uchū hikōshi*　astronaut　1027, 539, 68, 581
大宇宙　*daiuchū*　macrocosm, the universe　26, 1027
宙返り　*chūgaeri*　somersault　　　　　　448

届	**1029** 　 3r5.1 　 尸 日 丨 　 /40 42 2 　 届 届	**todo(ku)** – reach, arrive **todo(keru)** – report, notify; send, deliver

欠席届け　*kessekitodoke*　report of absence (school)　384, 380
欠勤届け　*kekkintodoke*　report of absence (work)　384, 568
無届け　*mutodoke*　(absence) without notice　　93
届け先　*todokesaki*　where to report; receiver's address　50

択	**1030** 3c4.21 ⊞ 扌 尸 ヽ /23 40 2 択 擇	**TAKU** – selection, choice

選択　*sentaku*　selection, choice　814
選択科目　*sentaku kamoku*　an elective (subject)　814, 320, 55
採択　*saitaku*　adoption, selection　960
二者択一　*nisha-takuitsu*　either-or alternative　3, 164, 2

沢	**1031** 3a4.18 氵 尸 ヽ /21 40 2 沢 澤	**TAKU, sawa** – swamp, marsh; blessing

光沢　*kōtaku*　luster, gloss　138
贅沢　*zeitaku*　luxury, extravagance
毛沢東　*Mō Takutō*　Mao Zedong, Mao Tse-tung　287, 71
金沢　*Kanazawa*　(capital of Ishikawa Prefecture)　23

召	**1032** 2f3.3 ⊟ 口 24 召	**SHŌ** – (honorific) summon **me(su)** – (honorific) summon; eat, drink; wear, put on; take (a bath/bus); buy

召集　*shōshū*　convene (the Diet)　442
応召　*ōshō*　be drafted, called up　846
召し上がる　*meshiagaru*　eat, drink, have (polite)　32
お召し物　*omeshimono*　clothes, item of clothing (polite)　79

沼	**1033** 3a5.24 ⊞ 氵 口 力 /21 24 8 沼	**SHŌ, numa** – swamp, marsh

沼沢　*shōtaku*　marsh, swamp, bog　1031
湖沼　*koshō*　lakes and marshes　475
沼地　*numachi*　marshland, swampland　118
沼田　*numata*　marshy rice field　35
沼津　*Numazu*　(city, Shizuoka Prefecture)　679

昭	**1034** 4c5.4 ⊞ 日 口 力 /42 24 8 昭	**SHŌ** – bright, clear

昭和　*Shōwa*　(Japanese era, 1926–1989)　124
昭和６３年　*Shōwa rokujūsan-nen*　1988　124, 45
昭和年間　*Shōwa nenkan*　the Shōwa era　124, 45, 43
昭和元年　*Shōwa gannen*　first year of the Shōwa era (1926)
124, 137, 45

照	**1035** 4d9.12 ⊞ 火 日 口 /44 42 24 照	**SHŌ, te(ru)** – shine **te(rasu)** – shine on; compare (with) **te(reru)** – feel embarrassed

照明　*shōmei*　illumination, lighting　18
対照　*taishō*　contrast　366
参照　*sanshō*　reference　723
天照大神　*Amaterasu Ōmikami*　the Sun Goddess　141, 26, 310

焦	**1036** 8c4.3 ⊟ 隹 火 /73 44 焦	**SHŌ** – fire, impatience, yearning **ko(gasu)** – scorch, singe, pine for **ko(geru)** – get scorched **ko(gareru)** – yearn for **ase(ru)** – be in a hurry, hasty, impatient

焦点　*shōten*　focal point, focus　169
焦熱地獄　*shōnetsu jigoku*　an inferno　655, 118, 905
黒焦げ　*kurokoge*　charred, burned　206

	1037	**CHŌ** – super-, ultra-; be above **ko(su)** – go beyond, exceed
	3b9.18 ⋯	**ko(eru)** – go beyond, exceed

超過	chōka	excess	419
超音速	chōonsoku	supersonic speed	347, 511
超大国	chōtaikoku	a superpower	26, 40
超満員	chōman'in	crowded beyond capacity	201, 163

	1038	**ETSU, ko(su)** – cross, go over, exceed; (short for) Vietnam
	4n8.2 ⋯	**ko(eru)** – cross, go over; clear, surmount

超越	chōetsu	transcendence; overstepping one's authority	1037
越境	ekkyō	jumping the border	883
引っ越す	hikkosu	move, change residences	216
勝ち越し	kachikoshi	a net win, being ahead	518

	1039	**SHU, omomuki** – purport, gist; taste; elegance; appearance
	6e9.1 ⋯	

趣味	shumi	interest, liking, taste; hobby	307
趣向	shukō	plan, idea	199
趣意	shui	purport, meaning; aim, object	132
情趣	jōshu	mood; artistic effect	209
野趣	yashu	rural life and beauty, rusticity	236

	1040	**YŪ, [YU], aso(bu)** – play, enjoy oneself, be idle
	2q8.3 ▢	

遊歩道	yūhodō	promenade, mall, boardwalk	437, 149
周遊（券）	shūyū(ken)	excursion (ticket)	91, 515
遊説	yūzei	speaking tour, political campaigning	404
遊休	yūkyū	idle, unused	60
遊び相手	asobiaite	playmate	146, 57

	1041	**SHI, SE, hodoko(su)** – give, bestow; carry out, perform, conduct
	4h5.1 ▢	

施設	shisetsu	facilities, institution	586
施行	shikō	enforce; put in operation	68
施政	shisei	administration, governing	492
実施	jisshi	carry into effect, enforce, implement	203

	1042	**SEN** – go around, revolve, rotate
	4h7.2 ▢	

旋回	senkai	turning, revolving, circling	90
周旋	shūsen	good offices, mediation	91
旋律	senritsu	melody	678
旋風	senpū	whirlwind, cyclone, tornado	29
斡旋	assen	good offices, mediation	

	1043	**KI, hata** – flag, banner
	4h10.1 ▢	

国旗	kokki	flag (of a country)	40
校旗	kōki	school banner/flag	115
半旗	hanki	flag at half-mast	88
星条旗	seijōki	the Stars & Stripes (U. S. flag)	743, 573
旗色	hatairo	the tide of war; things, the situation	204

1044

吏

0a6.22 …
日 十 乀
24 12 2
吏

RI – an official

官吏	kanri	an official	326
吏員	riin	an official	163
能吏	nōri	capable official	387
吏党	ritō	party of officials	504

1045

更

0a7.12 …
日 一 乀
42 14 2
更

KŌ, sara – anew, again, furthermore **fu(kasu)** – stay up till late (at night) **fu(keru)** – grow late

変更	henkō	alteration, change, modification	257
更衣室	kōishitsu	clothes-changing room	690, 166
更年期	kōnenki	menopause	45, 456
更生	kōsei	rebirth, rehabilitation	44

1046

硬

5a7.1 ⊞
石 日 一
/53 42 14
硬

KŌ, kata(i) – hard, firm

硬質	kōshitsu	hard, rigid	176
硬度	kōdo	(degree of) hardness	378
硬化	kōka	hardening	254
硬貨	kōka	coin; hard currency	765
強硬	kyōkō	firm, unyielding	217

1047

梗

4a7.1 ⊞
木 日 一
/41 42 14
梗

KŌ – block, close off

梗塞	kōsoku	myocardial infarction	465
桔梗	kikyō	Chinese bellflower, balloonflower	
桔梗色	kikyōiro	dark violet	204

1048

構

4a10.10 ⊞
木 艹 土
/41 32 22
構

KŌ, kama(eru) – build, set up; assume a posture/position **kama(u)** – mind, care about; meddle in; look after

機構	kikō	mechanism, structure, organization	537
構成	kōsei	composition, makeup	261
構想	kōsō	conception, plan	147
心構え	kokorogamae	mental attitude, readiness	97

1049

購

7b10.3 ⊞
貝 艹 土
/68 32 22
購

KŌ – buy, purchase

購入	kōnyū	purchase	52
購入者	kōnyūsha	purchaser, buyer	52, 164
購買	kōbai	purchase	241
購読	kōdoku	subscription	244
購読料	kōdokuryō	subscription price/fee	244, 319

1050

溝

3a10.9 ⊞
氵 艹 土
/21 32 22
溝

KŌ, mizo – ditch, gutter, groove

下水溝	gesuikō	drainage ditch, sewage pipe	31, 21
海溝	kaikō	an ocean deep, sea trench	117
日本海溝	Nihon/Nippon Kaikō	Japan Deep/Trench	5, 25, 117

1051

譲

7a13.1

言 衤 艹
/67 57 32

譲 讓

JŌ, yuzu(ru) – transfer, assign; yield, concede

譲歩	*jōho*	concession, compromise	437
割譲	*katsujō*	cede (territory)	528
互譲	*gojō*	mutual concession	929
譲り渡す	*yuzuriwatasu*	turn over, transfer	379
親譲り	*oyayuzuri*	inheritance from a parent	175

1052

暴

4c11.2

日 艹 氵
/42 32 21

暴

BŌ, aba(reru) – act violently, rage, rampage, run amuck
[BAKU], aba(ku) – disclose, expose, bring to light

暴力団	*bōryokudan*	gangster syndicate	100, 500
暴風	*bōfū*	high winds, windstorm	29
乱暴	*ranbō*	violence, roughness	702
暴露	*bakuro*	expose, bring to light	981

1053

爆

4d15.2

火 日 艹
/44 42 32

爆

BAKU – explode

爆発	*bakuhatsu*	explosion	96
爆発的	*bakuhatsuteki*	explosive	96, 210
原爆	*genbaku*	atomic bomb	136
被爆者	*hibakusha*	bombing victim	1009, 164
爆薬	*bakuyaku*	explosives	360

1054

撃

3c11.7

扌 車 冂
/23 69 20

撃

GEKI, u(tsu) – attack; fire, shoot

攻撃	*kōgeki*	attack	838
反撃	*hangeki*	counterattack	324
爆撃	*bakugeki*	bombing raid	1053
撃沈	*gekichin*	(attack and) sink	964
目撃者	*mokugekisha*	eyewitness	55, 164

1055

股

4b4.8

月 冂 又
/43 20 9

股

KO, mata – thigh; crotch

股関節	*kokansetsu*	hip joint	402, 472
内股	*uchimata*	inner thigh	84
二股	*futamata*	bifurcation, fork; (have/play it) two ways; fence-sitting	3

1056

激

3a13.1

氵 日 方
/21 42 48

激

GEKI, hage(shii) – violent, fierce, strong, intense

過激派	*kagekiha*	radicals, extremist faction	419, 934
感激	*kangeki*	deep emotion/gratitude	262
激情	*gekijō*	violent emotion, passion	209
激動	*gekidō*	violent shaking; excitement, stir	231
激流	*gekiryū*	swift current	247

1057

討

7a3.3

言 寸
/67 37

討

TŌ, u(tsu) – attack, defeat

検討	*kentō*	examination, investigation, study	540
討論	*tōron*	debate, discussion	293
討議	*tōgi*	discussion, deliberation, debate	292
討ち死に	*uchijini*	fall in battle	85
討ち取る	*uchitoru*	capture; kill	65

1058

訂

7a2.3
言 一
/67 14
訂

TEI – correcting

訂正	*teisei*	correction, revision	275
校訂	*kōtei*	revision	115
改訂	*kaitei*	revision	523
増訂	*zōtei*	revised and enlarged (edition)	725

1059

打

3c2.3
扌 一
/23 14
打

DA, u(tsu) – hit, strike

打開	*dakai*	a break, development, new turn	400
打算的	*dasanteki*	calculating, selfish, mercenary	760, 210
打楽器	*dagakki*	percussion instrument	359, 536
打ち合わせ	*uchiawase*	previous arrangement	159
打ち消し	*uchikeshi*	denial; negation	864

1060

投

3c4.18
扌 冂 又
/23 20 9
投

TŌ, na(geru) – throw

投票	*tōhyō*	vote	944
投書	*tōsho*	letter to the editor, contribution	131
投資	*tōshi*	investment	763
投機	*tōki*	speculation	537
投影	*tōei*	projection	873

1061

欧 歐

4j4.2
欠 冂 ㆒
/49 20 12
欧 歐

Ō – Europe

欧州	*Ōshū*	Europe	195
西欧	*Seiō*	Western Europe	72
欧米	*Ō-Bei*	Europe and America/the U. S.	224
欧州連合	*Ōshū Rengō*	the European Union	195, 446, 159
北欧諸国	*hokuō shokoku*	Scandinavian countries	73, 880, 40

1062

枢 樞

4a4.22
木 冂 ㆒
/41 20 12
枢 樞

SŪ – pivot

枢軸	*sūjiku*	pivot, axis, center	1023
中枢	*chūsū*	center	28
枢要	*sūyō*	important	425
枢密	*sūmitsu*	state secret	822

1063

断 斷

6b5.6
米 斤 丨
/62 50 2
断 斷

DAN – decision, judgment **kotowa(ru)** – decline, refuse; give warning; prohibit **ta(tsu)** – cut off

決断	*ketsudan*	(prompt) decision, resolution	357
油断	*yudan*	inattention, negligence	365
横断	*ōdan*	crossing	795
断念	*dannen*	abandonment, giving up	588

1064

継 繼

6a7.8
糸 米 丨
/61 62 2
継 繼

KEI, tsu(gu) – follow, succeed to, inherit

後継	*kōkei*	succession	48
継承	*keishō*	succession, inheritance	972
継続	*keizoku*	continuance	243
中継	*chūkei*	(radio/TV) relay, hookup	28
受け継ぐ	*uketsugu*	inherit, succeed to	260

判	**1065** 2f5.2 □ 刂 十 一 /16 12 1 判	**HAN** – stamp, seal **BAN** – (paper) size

判断（力）　*handan(ryoku)*　judgment　　1063, 100
判決　*hanketsu*　a decision, ruling　　357
判事　*hanji*　a judge　　80
公判　*kōhan*　(public) trial　　126
判明　*hanmei*　become clear, be ascertained　　18

伴	**1066** 2a5.4 □ 亻 十 儿 /3 12 16 伴	**HAN, BAN, tomona(u)** – go with, accompany; entail, be accompanied by, be associated with

同伴　*dōhan*　keep (someone) company　　198
相伴う　*aitomonau*　accompany　　146

評	**1067** 7a5.3 □ 言 一 儿 /67 14 16 評	**HYŌ** – criticism, comment

評論　*hyōron*　criticism, critique, commentary　　293
論評　*ronpyō*　criticism, comment, review　　293
評価　*hyōka*　appraisal　　427
評判　*hyōban*　fame, popularity; rumor, gossip　　1065
書評　*shohyō*　book review　　131

批	**1068** 3c4.13 ▥ 扌 ⺊ /23 13 批	**HI** – critique

批判　*hihan*　critique　　1065
批判的　*hihanteki*　critical　　1065, 210
批評　*hihyō*　critique, criticism, review　　1067
批評眼　*hihyōgan*　critical eye　　1067, 867
文芸批評　*bungei hihyō*　literary criticism　　111, 441, 1067

諧	**1069** 7a9.11 □ 言 日 ⺊ /67 42 13 諧	**KAI** – order, harmony

諧謔　*kaigyaku*　jest, humor
諧謔的　*kaigyakuteki*　humorous, witty　　210

弐	**1070** 4n3.3 ⋯ 戈 二 丨 /52 4 2 弐 貳	**NI** – two (in documents)

弐万円　*niman'en*　20,000 yen　　16, 13

武	**1071** 4n5.3 ⋯ 戈 ⺊ 一 /52 13 1 武	**BU, MU** – military

武器　*buki*　weapon, arms　　536
武力　*buryoku*　military force　　100
武道　*budō*　military arts　　149
武士　*bushi*　samurai, warrior　　581
武者　*musha*　warrior　　164

1072

拭

3c6.17

扌 戈 工
/23 52 38

拭

SHOKU, fu(ku), nugu(u) – wipe

払拭	fusshoku	sweep away, wipe out	591
拭浄	shokujō	clean, wipe	675
拭き込む	fukikomu	shine up, polish, wipe thoroughly	790
拭き掃除	fukisōji	cleaning (a house)	1128, 1112

1073

憂

4i12.1

夂 月 心
/49 43 51

憂

YŪ, ure(eru) – grieve, be distressed, be anxious **ure(i), ure(e)** – grief, distress, anxiety **u(i)** – unhappy, gloomy

物憂い	monoui	languid, weary, listless	79
憂き目	ukime	grief, misery, hardship	55
憂い顔	ureigao	sorrowful face, troubled look	277
憂さ晴らし	usabarashi	diversion, distraction	673

1074

優

2a15.1

亻 月 心
/3 43 51

優

YŪ – superior; gentle; actor **sugu(reru)** – excel **yasa(shii)** – gentle, tender, kindhearted

優勢	yūsei	predominance, superiority	656
優勝	yūshō	victory, championship	518
優先	yūsen	priority	50
女優	joyū	actress	102

1075

悲

4k8.18

心 二 卜
/51 4 13

悲

HI, kana(shii) – sad **kana(shimu)** – be sad, lament, regret

悲劇	higeki	tragedy	811
悲恋	hiren	disappointed love	258
悲鳴	himei	shriek, scream	948
悲観	hikan	pessimism	614

1076

俳

2a8.8

亻 二 卜
/3 4 13

俳

HAI – actor

俳優	haiyū	actor	1074
俳句	haiku	haiku, 17-syllable Japanese poem	337
俳諧	haikai	joke; haikai, haiku	1069
俳人	haijin	haiku poet	1

1077

排

3c8.8

扌 二 卜
/23 4 13

排

HAI – exclude; reject, expel

排気ガス	haikigasu	exhaust gas/fumes	134
排液	haieki	drainage (in surgery)	480
排撃	haigeki	reject, denounce	1054
排日	hai-Nichi	anti-Japanese	5
排他的	haitateki	exclusive, cliquish	120, 210

1078

輩

7c8.7

車 二 卜
/69 4 13

輩

HAI – fellow, colleague, companion

先輩	senpai	one's senior (at school/ work)	50
後輩	kōhai	one's junior, younger people	48
年輩	nenpai	age, elderliness	45
同年輩の人	dōnenpai no hito	someone of the same age	198, 45, 1
輩出	haishutsu	appear one after another	53

徳	**1079** 3i11.3 田 彳 日 心 /29 55 51 徳 悳	**TOKU** – virtue	
		道徳 *dōtoku* marality, morals	149
		公徳 *kōtoku* public morality	126
		人徳 *jintoku, nintoku* one's natural virtue	1
		不徳 *futoku* lack of virtue, vice, immorality	94
		徳川 *Tokugawa* (historical surname)	33

聴	**1080** 6e11.3 田 耳 日 心 /65 55 51 聴 聽	**CHŌ, ki(ku)** – hear, listen	
		聴取 *chōshu* listening	65
		聴衆 *chōshū* audience	806
		聴講 *chōkō* attendance at a lecture	797
		公聴会 *kōchōkai* public hearing	126, 158
		聴覚 *chōkaku* sense of hearing	615

旨	**1081** 4c2.2 日 日 匕 /42 13 旨	**SHI, mune** – purport, content, gist; instructions	
		趣旨 *shushi* purport, content, gist	1039
		要旨 *yōshi* gist, essential points	425
		本旨 *honshi* main purpose, true aim	25
		論旨 *ronshi* point/drift of an argument	293

指	**1082** 3c6.15 田 扌 日 匕 /23 42 13 指	**SHI** – finger; point to, direct **yubi** – finger **sa(su)** – point to	
		指導 *shidō* guidance, leadership	716
		指令 *shirei* order, instruction	850
		指名 *shimei* nomination, designation	82
		指定席 *shiteiseki* reserved seat	356, 380
		人さし指 *hitosashiyubi* index finger, forefinger	1

脂	**1083** 4b6.7 田 月 日 匕 /43 42 13 脂	**SHI, abura** – (animal) fat	
		油脂 *yushi* oils and fats	365
		脂身 *aburami* fat (of meat)	59
		脂っ濃い *aburakkoi* greasy, rich (foods)	987

稽	**1084** 5d11.3 田 禾 日 尤 /56 42 27 稽	**KEI** – practice, train	
		稽古 *keiko* practice, training, drill, rehearsal	172
		下稽古 *shitageiko* rehearsal, run-through	31, 172

詣	**1085** 7a6.13 田 言 日 匕 /67 42 13 詣	**KEI, mō(deru)** – visit (a shrine, a temple; a famous place, an event)	
		造詣 *zōkei* scholarship, attainments	704
		参詣 *sankei* temple/shrine visit; pilgrimage	723
		初詣 *hatsumōde* first shrine/temple visit in the new year	692

	1086	**IN** – seal, stamp; (short for) India **shirushi** – sign, mark	
印	2e4.1 ⬚	印象 *inshō* impression	752
	卩 厂 二	調印 *chōin* signing, signature	342
	/7 18 4	印税 *inzei* a royalty (on a book)	403
	印	印紙 *inshi* revenue stamp	180
		矢印 *yajirushi* (direction) arrow	213

	1087	**SATSU, su(ru)** – print	
刷	2f6.9 ⬚	印刷 *insatsu* printing	1086
	刂 尸 巾	印刷物 *insatsubutsu* printed matter	1086, 79
	/16 40 26	増刷 *zōsatsu* additional printing, reprinting	725
	刷	刷新 *sasshin* reform	174
		刷り直す *surinaosu* reprint to correct mistakes	429

	1088	**HEN** – part **kata-** – one (of two)	
片	2j2.5 ⋯	破片 *hahen* broken piece, fragment, splinter	676
	亠 一 丨	断片 *danpen* fragment, piece, snippet	1063
	/11 1 2	木片 *mokuhen* block/chip of wood, wood shavings	22
	片	片目 *katame* one eye	55
		片道 *katamichi* one way, each way	149

	1089	**HAN** – printing block/plate; printing; edition	
版	2j6.8 ⬚	出版社 *shuppansha* publishing house	53, 308
	亠 厂 又	版権 *hanken* copyright	335
	/11 18 9	初版 *shohan* first edition	692
	版	改訂版 *kaiteiban* revised edition	523, 1058
		版画 *hanga* print, woodblock print	343

	1090	**HAN, BAN, ita** – board, plank	
板	4a4.21 ⬚	甲板 *kanpan, kōhan* deck (of a ship)	1016
	木 厂 又	合板 *gōban, gōhan* plywood	159
	/41 18 9	黒板 *kokuban* blackboard	206
	板	床板 *yukaita* floorboard	845
		表示板 *hyōjiban* display panel	272, 625

	1091	**HAN** – sell	
販	7b4.2 ⬚	販売 *hanbai* sales, selling	239
	貝 厂 又	販売値段 *hanbai nedan* selling price	239, 431, 363
	/68 18 9	自動販売機 *jidō hanbaiki* vending machine	62, 231, 239, 537
	販	市販 *shihan* marketing; commercially available	181
		販路 *hanro* market (for goods), outlet	151

	1092	**KA, [KE], kari** – temporary, provisional, tentative, supposing	
仮	2a4.15 ⬚	仮説 *kasetsu* hypothesis, supposition	404
	亻 厂 又	仮定 *katei* supposition, assumption, hypothesis	356
	/3 18 9	仮面 *kamen* a mask	274
	仮 假	仮名 *kamei* fictitious name *kana* kana (hiragana,	82
		仮病 *kebyō* pretended illness, malingering ⌊katakana)	381

寛	**1093** 3m10.3 □ 宀 貝 艹 /33 68 32 寛	**KAN** – leniency, generosity 寛大　*kandai*　magnanimity, tolerance, leniency　　26 寛容　*kan'yō*　magnanimity, generosity, forbearance　665 寛厚　*kankō*　generous, large-hearted　649 寛厳　*kangen*　severity and leniency　841
勧	**1094** 2g11.1 力 隹 宀 /8 73 15 勧 勸	**KAN, susu(meru)** – recommend, offer, advise, encourage 勧告　*kankoku*　recommendation, advice　703 勧業　*kangyō*　encouragement of industry　279 勧進　*kanjin*　soliciting religious contributions　443
歓	**1095** 4j11.1 □ 欠 隹 宀 /49 73 15 歓 歡	**KAN** – joy, pleasure 歓待　*kantai*　hospitality　459 歓談　*kandan*　pleasant chat　603 歓声　*kansei*　shout of joy, cheer　759 歓楽街　*kanrakugai*　amusement center　359, 186 歓心を買う　*kanshin o kau*　curry favor　97, 241
偉	**1096** 2a10.5 □ 亻 口 十 /3 24 12 偉	**I, era(i)** – great, eminent, extraordinary, excellent 偉大　*idai*　great, mighty, grand　26 偉人　*ijin*　great man　1 偉才　*isai*　man of extraordinary talent　560 偉業　*igyō*　great achievement　279 偉観　*ikan*　a spectacular sight　614
緯	**1097** 6a10.7 □ 糸 口 十 /61 24 12 緯	**I** – woof (horizontal thread in weaving); latitude 緯度　*ido*　latitude　378 緯線　*isen*　a parallel (of latitude)　299 北緯　*hokui*　north latitude　73 南緯　*nan'i*　south latitude　74 経緯　*keii*　longitude and latitude; the details　557
迎	**1098** 2q4.4 □ 辶 厂 阝 /19 18 7 迎	**GEI, muka(eru)** – go to meet, receive, invite, send for 歓迎　*kangei*　welcome　1095 迎合　*geigō*　flattery　159 送迎　*sōgei*　welcome and sendoff　447 出迎え　*demukae*　meeting (someone) on arrival, reception　53 迎え撃つ　*mukaeutsu*　fight to repulse (an attack)　1054
仰	**1099** 2a4.10 □ 亻 厂 阝 /3 18 7 仰	**GYŌ, [KŌ], ao(gu)** – look up at; look up to, respect, ask for, rely (on) **ō(se)** – what you say, (your/his) wish 仰視　*gyōshi*　look up (at)　616 仰天　*gyōten*　be astonished, frightened　141 信仰　*shinkō*　faith, religious conviction　157 仰向け　*aomuke*　facing upward, on one's back, supine　199

抑	**1100** 3c4.12 ▥ 扌 厂 阝 /23 18 7 抑	**YOKU, osa(eru)** – hold down/in check, suppress, control 抑制　*yokusei*　control, restrain, suppress　433 抑留　*yokuryū*　dentention, internment　774 抑止　*yokushi*　deter, stave off　485 抑揚　*yokuyō*　rising and falling of tones, intonation　641
挨	**1101** 3c7.12 ▤ 扌 大 厶 /23 34 17 挨	**AI** – push open
拶	**1102** 3c6.13 ▤ 扌 夕 丨 /23 30 2 拶	**SATSU** – be imminent 挨拶　*aisatsu*　greeting, salutation, courtesy call; address, message　1101
卵	**1103** 2e5.2 ▢ 卩 厂 丨 /7 18 2 卵	**RAN, tamago** – egg 鶏卵　*keiran*　(hen's) egg　949 産卵　*sanran*　egg-laying, spawning　278 卵黄　*ran'ō*　yolk　794 卵管　*rankan*　Fallopian tube, oviduct　328 卵形　*tamagogata, rankei*　egg-shaped, oval　399
索	**1104** 2k8.2 ▢ 十 糸 冂 /12 61 20 索	**SAKU** – rope, cord; search for 索引　*sakuin*　an index　216 捜索　*sōsaku*　search　⌐premises　1026 家宅捜索　*kataku sōsaku*　search of the house/　165, 178, 1026 探索　*tansaku*　search, inquiry, investigation　544 思索　*shisaku*　thinking, speculation, contemplation　99
累	**1105** 5f6.5 ▤ 田 糸 /58 61 累	**RUI** – accumulate, pile up 累加／増　*ruika/zō*　acceleration, successive　722, 725 累積　*ruiseki*　accumulation, cumulative　⌐increase　667 累計　*ruikei*　(sum) total　340 係累　*keirui*　family encumbrances, dependents　931 累進　*ruishin*　successive/progressive promotions　443
異	**1106** 5f6.7 ▤ 田 艹 儿 /58 32 16 異	**I, koto** – uncommon, strange; difference 異常　*ijō*　unusual, abnormal　506 異質　*ishitsu*　heterogeneity　176 異国　*ikoku*　foreign country　40 異議　*igi*　objection　292 異教　*ikyō*　heathenism, paganism, heresy　245

翼	**1107** 2o15.2 �121 �131 �231 /16 58 32 翼	**YOKU, tsubasa** – wing 左翼　*sayoku*　the left wing, leftist　　75 右翼　*uyoku*　the right wing, rightist　　76 両翼　*ryōyoku*　both wings　　200 比翼の鳥　*hiyoku no tori*　happily married couple　　812, 285
戴	**1108** 5f12.2 田 戈 艹 /58 52 32 戴	**TAI** – receive 戴冠式　*taikanshiki*　coronation (ceremony)　　1723, 534
余	**1109** 2a5.24 亻 木 一 /3 41 1 余 餘	**YO, ama(ru)** – be left over, in excess **ama(su)** – leave over 二十余年　*nijūyonen*　more than 20 years　　3, 12, 45 余命　*yomei*　the rest of one's life　　587 余計　*yokei*　too much, unwanted, uncalled-for　　340 余地　*yochi*　room, margin　　118 余震　*yoshin*　aftershock　　983
暇	**1110** 4c9.1 日 尸 二 /42 40 4 暇	**KA, hima** – free time, leisure 休暇　*kyūka*　holiday, vacation, time off　　60 余暇　*yoka*　leisure, spare time　　1109 暇つぶし　*himatsubushi*　a waste of time, killing time 暇取る　*himadoru*　take a long time, be delayed　　65 暇な時　*hima na toki*　leisure time, when one is free　　42
隙	**1111** 2d10.4 阝 日 小 /7 42 35 隙	**GEKI, suki** – crevice, crack, opening 空隙　*kūgeki*　gap, opening　　140 間隙　*kangeki*　gap, opening, crevice　　43 隙間　*sukima*　crevice, opening, gap, space　　43
除	**1112** 2d7.10 阝 木 亻 /7 41 3 除	**JO, [JI]** – exclude; division (in math) **nozo(ku)** – exclude; remove 解除　*kaijo*　cancellation　　482 除名　*jomei*　remove (someone's) name, expel　　82 除外　*jogai*　except, exclude　　83 免除　*menjo*　exemption　　746 取り除く　*torinozoku*　remove, rid　　65
徐	**1113** 3i7.2 彳 木 亻 /29 41 3 徐	**JO** – slowly 徐々に　*jojo ni*　slowly, gradually 徐行　*jokō*　go/drive slowly　　68 徐歩　*joho*　walk slowly, saunter, mosey　　437

叙	**1114** 2h7.1 □ 又 木 亻 /9 41 3 叙 敍	**JO** – narrate, describe
		叙述　*jojutsu*　description, narration　1000 叙景　*jokei*　description of scenery　872 叙情詩　*jojōshi*　lyric poem/poetry　209, 579 叙事詩　*jojishi*　epic poem/poetry　80, 579 自叙伝　*jijoden*　autobiography　62, 440

剰	**1115** 2f9.1 □ 刂 木 艹 /16 41 32 剰 剰	**JŌ** – surplus
		剰余（金）　*jōyo(kin)*　a surplus　1109, 23 （出生）過剰　*(shussei) kajō*　surplus, excess (of births)　53, 44, 419 余剰　*yojō*　surplus　1109 剰員　*jōin*　superfluous personnel, overstaffing　163

斜	**1116** 2a9.21 □ 亻 木 艹 /3 41 12 斜	**SHA, nana(me)** – slanting, diagonal, oblique
		斜面　*shamen*　a slope, slant, incline　274 斜線　*shasen*　slanting line, slash [/]　299 斜辺　*shahen*　oblique side, hypotenuse　789 斜陽　*shayō*　setting sun　640 斜視　*shashi*　squint　616

垂	**1117** 0a8.12 … 土 艹 一 22 32 1 垂	**SUI, ta(reru)** – (intr.) hang down, dangle, drip **ta(rasu)** – (tr.) hang down, dangle, drip
		垂直　*suichoku*　perpendicular, vertical　429 垂線　*suisen*　a perpendicular (line)　299 虫垂　*chūsui*　the appendix　893 雨垂れ　*amadare*　raindrops　30

睡	**1118** 5c8.2 □ 目 土 艹 /55 22 32 睡	**SUI** – sleep
		睡眠　*suimin*　sleep　868 睡眠不足　*suimin-busoku*　lack of sleep　868, 94, 58 午睡　*gosui*　nap, siesta　49 熟睡　*jukusui*　sound/deep sleep　700 昏睡（状態）　*konsui (jōtai)*　coma　636, 388

唾	**1119** 3d8.2 □ 口 土 艹 /24 22 32 唾	**DA, tsuba** – saliva
		唾液　*daeki*　saliva　480 唾棄　*daki*　detest, abhor　993

途	**1120** 2q7.16 □ 辶 木 亻 /19 41 3 途	**TO** – way, road
		途中　*tochū*　on the way, midway　28 前途　*zento*　one's future, prospects　47 途絶える　*todaeru*　come to a stop　755 帰途　*kito*　one's way home　┌country　317 （開発）途上国　*(kaihatsu) tojōkoku*　developing　400, 96, 32, 40

1121

塗

3b10.10 田
土 木 氵
/22 41 21

塗

TO, nu(ru) – paint

塗料	*toryō* paints, paint and varnish	319
塗布	*tofu* apply (salve)	688
塗り物	*nurimono* lacquerware	79
塗り立て	*nuritate* freshly painted	121
塗り替える	*nurikaeru* repaint, put on a new coating	757

1122

華

3k7.1
卄 十 一
/32 12 14

華

KA, [KE], hana – flower, florid, showy, brilliant

華道	*kadō* (Japanese) flower arranging	149
華美	*kabi* splendor, pomp, gorgeousness	405
中華料理	*chūka ryōri* Chinese food/cooking	28, 319, 143
中華人民共和国	*Chūka jinmin kyōwakoku* People's	
	Republic of China	28, 1, 177, 196, 124, 40

1123

革

3k6.2
卄 口 一
/32 24 14

革

KAKU – reform **kawa** – leather

革命	*kakumei* revolution	587
革新	*kakushin* reform	174
改革	*kaikaku* reform, reorganization	523
変革	*henkaku* reform, innovation, revolutionize	257
皮革	*hikaku* leather	1008

1124

靴

3k10.34 田
卄 口 亻
/32 24 3

靴

KA, kutsu – shoe

製靴	*seika* shoemaking	434
革靴	*kawagutsu* leather shoes	1123
靴下	*kutsushita* socks, stockings	31
靴屋	*kutsuya* shoe store	167
靴一足	*kutsu issoku* one pair of shoes	2, 58

1125

侵

2a7.15
亻 彐 冖
/3 39 20

侵

SHIN, oka(su) – invade, violate, infringe on, damage

侵略	*shinryaku* aggression, invasion	860
侵入	*shinnyū* invasion, raid, trespass	52
侵害	*shingai* infringement	527
不可侵条約	*fukashin jōyaku* nonaggression	94, 390, 573, 211
侵食	*shinshoku* erosion, weathering ⌐pact	322

1126

浸

3a7.17 田
氵 彐 冖
/21 39 20

浸

SHIN, hita(ru) – be soaked, steeped **hita(su)** – dip, immerse

浸水	*shinsui* inundation, submersion	21
浸出	*shinshutsu* exuding, oozing out, percolation	53
浸食	*shinshoku* erosion, corrosion	322
水浸し	*mizubitashi* submersion, inundation	21

1127

寝

3m10.1 …
宀 彐 氵
/33 39 5

寝 寝

SHIN, ne(ru) – go to bed, sleep **ne(kasu)** – put to bed

寝室	*shinshitsu* bedroom	166
寝台	*shindai* bed	501
寝具（類）	*shingu(rui)* bedclothes, bedding	426, 226
昼寝	*hirune* nap, siesta	478
寝苦しい	*negurushii* unable to sleep well	554

掃	**1128** 3c8.22 ⊞ 扌 ヨ 巾 /23 39 26 掃	**SŌ, ha(ku)** – sweep （大）掃除　(ō)sōji　(general) housecleaning　　26, 1112 清掃夫　seisōfu　street sweeper, cleaning man　671, 315 掃除婦　sōjifu　cleaning lady　　1112, 316 掃討　sōtō　sweeping, clearing, mopping up　1057 一掃　issō　sweep away, eradicate, stamp out　　2
兼	**1129** 2o8.1 ⊟ ソ ヨ 一 /16 39 14 兼	**KEN** – combine, double as **ka(neru)** – combine, double as; (as suffix) cannot 兼業　kengyō　a side business　　279 兼任　kennin　hold 2 posts (simultaneously)　334 待ち兼ねる　machikaneru　cannot wait　459 気兼ね　kigane　feel constraint, be afraid of giving trouble　134
鎌	**1130** 8a10.8 釒 ヨ 儿 /72 39 16 鎌	**kama** – sickle 鎌をかける　kama o kakeru　trick someone (into confessing), 　　ask a leading question
釜	**1131** 2o8.7 … 王 46 釜	**kama** – kettle, cooking pot 茶釜　chagama　teakettle　　251 電気釜　denkigama　electric rice-cooker　108, 134 釜飯　kamameshi　rice dish served in a small pot　325
尋	**1132** 3d9.29 ⊟ 口 ヨ 工 /24 39 38 尋	**JIN, tazu(neru)** – search for; ask, inquire 尋問　jinmon　questioning, interrogation　162 尋常　jinjō　normal, ordinary　506 尋ね人　tazunebito　person being sought, missing person　1
租	**1133** 5d5.7 ⊞ 禾 月 一 /56 43 1 租	**SO** – crop tax, tribute 租税　sozei　taxes　　403 地租　chiso　land tax　118 租借　soshaku　lease (land)　780 租借地　soshakuchi　leased territory　780, 118
粗	**1134** 6b5.2 ⊞ 米 月 一 /62 43 1 粗	**SO, ara(i)** – coarse, rough 粗末　somatsu　coarse, plain, crude, rough, rude　305 粗暴　sobō　wild, rough, rude, violent　1052 粗野　soya　rustic, loutish, vulgar, ill-bred　236 粗悪　soaku　coarse, crude, base, inferior　304 粗食　soshoku　coarse food, plain diet　322

1135

阻

2d5.1 ☐
阝 月 一
/7 43 1
阻

SO, haba(mu) – obstruct, prevent, impede

阻止	soshi obstruct, impede	485
阻害	sogai check, impediment, hindrance	527
険阻	kenso steep, precipitous, rugged	542

1136

狙

3g5.3 ☐
犭 月 一
/27 43 1
狙

SO, nera(u) – aim at

狙撃、狙い撃ち	sogeki, neraiuchi shooting, sharpshooting; sniping	1054
狙撃兵／手	sogekihei/shu sharpshooter	1054, 798, 57
狙撃者	sogekisha sniper	1054, 164
付け狙う	tsukenerau prowl after, stalk	192

1137

宜

3m5.7 ☐
宀 月 一
/33 43 1
宜

GI – good, all right

便宜	bengi convenience, expediency	330
便宜上	bengijō for convenience/expediency	330, 32
時宜	jigi right time/opportunity	42
適宜	tekigi suitable, appropriate, fitting	421

1138

畳

5f7.3 ☐
甲 月 冂
/58 43 20
畳 疊

JŌ, tatami – tatami, straw floor-mat **tata(mu)** – fold up

四畳半	yojōhan 4 1/2-mat room	6, 88
畳表	tatami-omote woven covering of a tatami	272
畳替え	tatamigae replace old tatami with new ones	757
畳屋	tatamiya tatami maker/store	167

1139

援

3c9.7 ☐
扌 小 又
/23 35 9
援

EN – help, assistance

援助	enjo assistance, aid	633
応援	ōen aid, support, backing, cheering	846
後援	kōen support, backing	48
声援	seien shout of encouragement, cheers, rooting	759
援軍	engun reinforcements	444

1140

緩

6a9.8 ☐
糸 小 又
/61 35 9
緩

KAN, yuru(mu) – become loose, abate, slacken **yuru(meru)** – loosen, relieve, relax, slacken **yuru(i)** – loose, generous, lax, gentle (slope), slow **yuru(yaka)** – loose, slack, magnanimous, gentle, easy, slow

緩和	kanwa relieve, ease, lighten	124
緩急	kankyū fast and slow speed; emergency	303

1141

筋

6f6.4 ☐
⺮ 月 力
/66 43 8
筋

KIN, suji – muscle, tendon; blood vessel; line, reason, logic, plot (of a story), coherence, source (of information)

筋肉	kinniku muscle	223
筋道	sujimichi reason, logic, coherence	149
筋違い	sujichigai, sujikai a cramp; illogical; wrong	833
筋書き	sujigaki synopsis, outline, plan	131

箱	**1142** 6f9.4 ⊞ ⺮ 目 木 /66 55 41 箱	***hako*** – box	
		本箱　*honbako*　bookcase	25
		貯金箱　*chokinbako*　savings box, (piggy) bank	775, 23
		重箱　*jūbako*　nested boxes	227
		豚箱　*butabako*　police lockup, jail, hoosegow	810
		箱根　*Hakone*　(resort area near Mt. Fuji)	314

範	**1143** 6f9.3 ⊞ ⺮ 車 阝 /66 69 7 範	***HAN*** – example, model, pattern; limit	
		範例　*hanrei*　example	622
		師範　*shihan*　teacher, master	415
		規範　*kihan*　norm, criterion	617
		広範　*kōhan*　extensive, wide, far-reaching	707

丹	**1144** 0a4.34 … 冂 一 ＼ 20 1 2 丹	***TAN*** – red, red lead	
		丹念　*tannen*　application, diligence	588
		丹誠　*tansei*　sincerity; efforts, diligence	731
		丹精　*tansei*　exertion, diligence, painstaking care	670
		丹前　*tanzen*　man's padded kimono	47

舟	**1145** 6c0.1 □ 舟 /63 舟	***SHŪ, fune, [funa]*** – boat	
		小舟　*kobune*　boat, skiff	27
		舟遊び　*funaasobi*　boating	1040
		舟歌　*funauta*　sailor's song, chantey	395

舶	**1146** 6c5.2 ⊞ 舟 日 丨 /63 42 2 舶	***HAKU*** – ship	
		船舶　*senpaku*　ship, vessel; shipping	377
		舶来　*hakurai*　imported	69
		舶来品　*hakuraihin*　imported article/goods	69, 230

般	**1147** 6c4.3 ⊞ 舟 冂 又 /63 20 9 般	***HAN*** – carry; all, general	
		一般的　*ippanteki*　general	2, 210
		一般化　*ippanka*　generalization, popularization	2, 254
		全般　*zenpan*　the whole	89
		全般的　*zenpanteki*　general, overall	89, 210
		先般　*senpan*　recently, some time ago	50

皿	**1148** 5h0.1 □ 皿 /59 皿	***sara*** – plate, dish, saucer	
		皿洗い　*saraarai*　washing dishes	705
		サラダ一皿　*sarada hitosara*　1 plate of salad	2
		大皿　*ōzara*　large dish, platter	26
		小皿　*kozara*　small plate	27
		受け皿　*ukezara*　saucer	260

盤	**1149** 5h10.2 皿 舟 舟 /59 63 20 盤	**BAN** – (chess/go) board, tray, platter, basin

基盤 *kiban* basis, foundation — 457
円盤 *enban* disk; discus — 13
水盤 *suiban* basin — 21
終盤戦 *shūbansen* end game — 466, 301
鍵盤 *kenban* keyboard — 915

盆	**1150** 2o7.6 皿 儿 力 /59 16 8 盆	**BON** – Buddhist Festival of the Dead; tray

盆地 *bonchi* basin, valley — 118
盆景 *bonkei* miniature landscape on a tray — 872
（お）盆 *(O)Bon* the Bon Festival
   (o)bon tray

盗	**1151** 5h6.2 皿 欠 冫 /59 49 5 盗 盗	**TŌ, nusu(mu)** – steal

強盗 *gōtō* burglar, robber — 217
盗難（保険） *tōnan (hoken)* theft (insurance) — 566, 498, 542
盗用 *tōyō* embezzlement; surreptitious use — 107
盗作 *tōsaku* plagiarism — 361
盗品 *tōhin* stolen goods, loot — 230

塩	**1152** 3b10.4 土 皿 口 /22 59 24 塩 鹽	**EN, shio** – salt

食塩 *shokuen* table salt — 322
塩分 *enbun* salt content, salinity — 38
塩酸 *ensan* hydrochloric acid — 525
塩水 *shiomizu, ensui* salt water, brine — 21
塩入れ *shioire* saltshaker — 52

凡	**1153** 2s1.1 几 丶 /20 2 凡	**BON, [HAN]** – common, ordinary

凡人 *bonjin* ordinary person, man of mediocre ability — 1
平凡 *heibon* commonplace, mediocre — 202
凡才 *bonsai* common ability, mediocre talent — 560
凡例 *hanrei* explanatory notes; legend (on a map/diagram) — 622

帆	**1154** 3f3.1 巾 几 丶 /26 20 2 帆	**HAN, ho** – sail

出帆 *shuppan* sailing, departure — 53
帆走 *hansō* sailing — 435
帆船 *hansen, hobune* sailing ship, sailboat — 377
帆柱 *hobashira* mast — 608

汎	**1155** 3a3.11 氵 几 丨 /21 20 2 汎	**HAN** – overflowing, pan-

汎用 *han'yō* all-purpose, general purpose — 107
汎論 *hanron* outline, summary — 293
汎太平洋 *han-Taiheiyō* Pan-Pacific — 639, 202, 289

冒	**1156** 4c5.6 日 /42 55 冒 冒	**BŌ, oka(su)** – risk, brave, defy, dare, desecrate 冒険　bōken　adventure　542 冒険小説　bōken shōsetsu　adventure novel　542, 27, 404 冒頭　bōtō　beginning, opening (paragraph)　276 感冒　kanbō　a cold　262 冒瀆　bōtoku　blasphemy, sacrilege, defilement
帽	**1157** 3f9.1 巾 日 日 /26 55 42 帽	**BŌ** – cap, hat, headgear 帽子　bōshi　hat, cap　103 宇宙帽　uchūbō　space helmet　1027, 1028 赤帽　akabō　redcap, luggage porter　207 無帽　mubō　hatless, bareheaded　93 帽章　bōshō　badge on a cap　876
張	**1158** 3h8.1 弓 ネ 二 /28 57 4 張	**CHŌ, ha(ru)** – stretch, spread 主張　shuchō　insistence, assertion, contention　155 出張　shutchō　business trip　53 出張所　shutchōjo　branch office, agency　53, 153 引っ張る　hipparu　pull, tug at　216 見張る　miharu　keep watch, be on the lookout　63
帳	**1159** 3f8.2 巾 ネ 二 /26 57 4 帳	**CHŌ** – notebook; register; curtain 手帳　techō　(pocket) notebook　57 電話帳　denwachō　telephone book/directory　108, 238 (貯金)通帳　(chokin) tsūchō　bankbook, passbook　775, 23, 150 帳面　chōmen　notebook, account book　274 帳消し　chōkeshi　cancellation, writing off (debts)　864
伸	**1160** 2a5.3 イ 日 l /3 42 2 伸	**SHIN, no(biru)** – (intr.) stretch, extend; grow **no(basu)** – (intr.) stretch, extend **no(beru)** – (tr.) stretch out, extend 伸張　shinchō　extend, expand　1158 二伸　nishin　postscript, P. S.　3 伸び伸び　nobinobi　at ease, relieved, refreshed
紳	**1161** 6a5.2 糸 日 l /61 42 2 紳	**SHIN** – gentleman 紳士　shinshi　gentleman　581 紳士用　shinshiyō　men's, for men　581, 107 紳士服　shinshifuku　men's clothing　581, 696 紳士協定　shinshi kyōtei　gentleman's agreement　581, 234, 356
縮	**1162** 6a11.9 糸 日 宀 /61 42 33 縮	**SHUKU, chiji(maru/mu)** – shrink, contract **chiji(meru)** – shorten, condense **chiji(reru)** – become curly **chiji(rasu)** – make curly 伸縮　shinshuku　expansion and contraction, flexibility　1160 短縮　tanshuku　shortening, reduction　215 縮図　shukuzu　reduced/scaled-down drawing　339 軍縮　gunshuku　arms reduction　444

1163

廷

2q4.2

辶 王
/19 46

廷

TEI – imperial court, government office

宮廷	*kyūtei*	imperial court	734
法廷	*hōtei*	(law) court	123
開廷	*kaitei*	holding (law) court	400
出廷	*shuttei*	appearance in court	53
廷臣	*teishin*	court official, courtier	854

1164

庭

3q6.3

广 王 辶
/18 46 19

庭

TEI, niwa – garden

家庭	*katei*	home, family	165
校庭	*kōtei*	schoolyard, school grounds	115
庭球	*teikyū*	tennis	739
庭園	*teien*	garden	454
前庭	*maeniwa, zentei*	front garden	47

1165

拡

3c5.25

扌 厂 ム
/23 18 17

拡 擴

KAKU – extend, expand

拡大	*kakudai*	magnification, expansion	26
拡大鏡	*kakudaikyō*	magnifiying glass	26, 882
拡張	*kakuchō*	extension, expansion	1158
拡散	*kakusan*	diffusion, scattering, proliferation	781
拡声器	*kakuseiki*	loudspeaker	759, 536

1166

征

3i5.3

彳 エ 一
/29 38 1

征

SEI – conquer

征服	*seifuku*	conquer, subjugate	696
征服者	*seifukusha*	conqueror	696, 164
出征	*shussei*	going to the front, taking the field	53
遠征	*ensei*	(military) expedition; playing tour	453
長征	*chōsei*	the Long March (in China)	95

1167

延

2q5.4

辶 丿 丶
/19 13 11

延

EN, no(basu/beru) – lengthen, prolong, postpone **no(biru)** – be postponed, delayed, prolonged

延長	*enchō*	extension	95
延期	*enki*	postponement, extension	456
遅延	*chien*	delay, being behind time	715
引き延ばす	*hikinobasu*	draw out, prolong, enlarge	216

1168

誕

7a7.15

言 辶 ㇏
/67 19 13

誕

TAN – birth

誕生	*tanjō*	birth	44
誕生日	*tanjōbi*	birthday	44, 5
誕生祝い	*tanjōiwai*	birthday celebration	44, 870
生誕（百年）	*seitan (hyakunen)*	(centenary of someone's) birth	
			44, 14, 45

1169

績

6a11.8

糸 貝 土
/61 68 22

績

SEKI – achievements; spinning

成績	*seiseki*	performance, results	261
成績表	*seisekihyō*	list of grades, report card	261, 272
業績	*gyōseki*	work, achievements; business performance	279
功績	*kōseki*	meritorious service	837
実績	*jisseki*	record of performance, actual results	203

債	**1170** 2a11.11 亻 貝 土 /3　68　22 債	**SAI** – debt, loan 負債　*fusai*　debt, liabilities　　　　　　　　　　519 国債　*kokusai*　national debt, public loan　　　　40 債券　*saiken*　bond, debenture　　　　　　　515 債権（者）　*saiken(sha)*　credit(or)　　　335, 164 債務（者）　*saimu(sha)*　debt(or)　　　　235, 164
后	**1171** 3d3.11 ロ 厂 一 /24　18　1 后	**KŌ** – empress 皇后　*kōgō*　empress　　　　　　　　　　　　297 皇后陛下　*kōgō-heika*　Her Majesty the Empress　297, 599, 31 皇太后　*kōtaigō, kōtaikō*　the empress dowager　297, 639
稿	**1172** 5d10.5 禾 口 亠 /56　24　11 稿　稾	**KŌ** – manuscript, draft 原稿（用紙）　*genkō (yōshi)*　manuscript (paper)　136, 107, 180 草稿　*sōkō*　rough draft, notes　　　　　　249 投稿　*tōkō*　contribution (to a periodical)　1060 稿料　*kōryō*　fee for a manuscript/ article/artwork　319
移	**1173** 5d6.1 禾 夕 /56　30 移	**I, utsu(ru)** – move (one's residence), change; be catching **utsu(su)** – move (one's residence/ office), transfer; infect 移動　*idō*　moving, migration　　　　　　　231 移転　*iten*　move, change of address　　　439 移（住）民　*i(jū)min*　emigrant, immigrant　156, 177 移植　*ishoku*　transplant　　　　　　　　　430
崩	**1174** 3o8.7 山 月 /36　43 崩	**HŌ** – collapse; (of an emperor) die **kuzu(reru)** – fall to pieces, collapse **kuzu(su)** – demolish; change, break (a large bill); write (cursive simplified kanji) 崩御　*hōgyo*　death of the emperor　　　721 山崩れ　*yamakuzure*　landslide　　　　　34 荷崩れ　*nikuzure*　a load falling off (a truck)　393
裁	**1175** 5e6.9 衤 戈 十 /57　52　12 裁	**SAI** – pass judgment; cut out (cloth/leather) **saba(ku)** – pass judgment **ta(tsu)** – cut out (cloth/leather) 裁判　*saiban*　trial, hearing　　　　　　1065 裁決　*saiketsu*　decision, ruling　　　　357 独裁　*dokusai*　dictatorship　　　　　　219 洋裁　*yōsai*　(Western-style) dressmaking　289
載	**1176** 7c6.5 車 戈 十 /69　52　12 載	**SAI** – print; load **no(ru)** – be recorded, appear (in print); be placed (on), be loaded **no(seru)** – place on top of, load (luggage), publish, run (an ad) 満載　*mansai*　fully loaded　　　　　　　201 記載　*kisai*　statement, mention　　　　372 連載　*rensai*　a serial　　　　　　　　　446

栽	**1177** 4n6.1 … 戈 木 十 /52 41 12 栽	**SAI** – planting

盆栽　*bonsai*　a bonsai, potted dwarf tree　　　　　1150

俗	**1178** 2a7.17 亻火口 /3 44 24 俗	**ZOKU** – customs, manners; the world, laity; vulgar

俗語	*zokugo*	colloquial language	67
俗名	*zokumyō*	secular name	82
民俗	*minzoku*	folk	177
風俗	*fūzoku*	manners, customs; public morals	29
通俗文学	*tsūzoku bungaku*	popular literature	150, 111, 109

欲	**1179** 4j7.1 欠火口 /49 44 24 欲 慾	**YOKU** – covetousness, desire **hos(suru), ho(shii)** – desire, want

食欲	*shokuyoku*	appetite	322
性欲	*seiyoku*	sexual desire, sex drive	98
欲望	*yokubō*	desire, appetite, craving	685
無欲	*muyoku*	free from avarice, unselfish	93

浴	**1180** 3a7.18 氵火口 /21 44 24 浴	**YOKU, a(biru)** – be bathed in **a(biseru)** – pour over, shower

入浴	*nyūyoku*	bathing, (hot) bath	52
浴室	*yokushitsu*	bathroom	166
海水浴場	*kaisuiyokujō*	(swimming) beach	117, 21, 154
日光浴	*nikkōyoku*	sunbathing	5, 138
浴衣	*yukata*	cotton kimono for summer	690

展	**1181** 3r7.2 尸 衤 艹 /40 57 32 展	**TEN** – expand

展示（会）	*tenji(kai)*	show, exhibition	625, 158
展望台	*tenbōdai*	observation platform	685, 501
親展	*shinten*	confidential	175
進展	*shinten*	development, evolution ┌country	443
発展途上国	*hatten tojōkoku*	developing	96, 1120, 32, 40

殿	**1182** 3r10.1 尸 艹 儿 /40 32 16 殿	**DEN, TEN** – hall, palace; mister **tono** – lord **-dono** – Mr.

宮殿	*kyūden*	palace	734
御殿	*goten*	palace	721
殿下	*denka*	His/Your Highness	31
湯殿	*yudono*	bathroom	642

縁	**1183** 6a9.10 糸 彐 豸 /61 39 27 縁	**EN** – relation, connection; marriage; fate; veranda **fuchi** – edge, brink, rim, border

絶縁	*zetsuen*	(electrical) insulation; break off relations	755
因縁	*innen*	causality, connection, fate	563
縁側	*engawa*	veranda, porch, balcony	619
額縁	*gakubuchi*	(picture) frame	857

1184

墜

3b11.7 □

土 犭 阝
/22 27 7

墜

TSUI – fall

墜落	*tsuiraku*	fall, (airplane) crash	858
墜死	*tsuishi*	fatal fall, fall to one's death	85
撃墜	*gekitsui*	shoot down (a plane)	1054
失墜	*shittsui*	loss, fall	311

1185

遂

2q9.13 □

辶 犭 儿
/19 27 16

遂

SUI, to(geru) – accomplish, attain, carry through

遂行	*suikō*	accomplish, execute, perform	68
完遂	*kansui*	successful execution, completion	623
(殺人)未遂	*(satsujin) misui*	attempted (murder)	585, 1, 306
(自殺)未遂	*(jisatsu) misui*	attempted (suicide)	62, 585, 306
やり遂げる	*yaritogeru*	go through with, carry out	

1186

逐

2q7.6 □

辶 犭 厶
/19 27 10

逐

CHIKU – one by one; drive away

放逐	*hōchiku*	expulsion, banishment	521
逐語訳	*chikugoyaku*	word-for-word/literal translation	67, 604
逐次	*chikuji*	one after another, one by one	385
逐一	*chikuichi*	one by one, in detail	2
逐電	*chikuden*	abscond, make a getaway	108

1187

懇

4k13.12 □

心 犭 食
/51 27 77

懇

KON, nengo(ro) – intimacy, friendship

懇談会	*kondankai*	get-together, friendly discussion	603, 158
懇親会	*konshinkai*	social gathering	175, 158
懇意	*kon'i*	intimacy, friendship	132
懇切	*konsetsu*	cordial; exhaustive, detailed	39
懇願	*kongan*	entreaty, earnest appeal	590

1188

墾

3b13.6 □

土 食 犭
/22 77 27

墾

KON – opening up farmland, cultivation

開墾	*kaikon*	clearing, reclamation (of land)	400
開墾地	*kaikonchi*	developed/cultivated land	400, 118

1189

処

4i2.2 □

夂 几
/49 20

処 處

SHO – deal with, treat; sentence, condemn; behave, act

処分	*shobun*	disposal, disposition; punishment	38
処置	*shochi*	disposition, measures, steps	432
処理	*shori*	treat, manage, deal with	143
対処	*taisho*	cope with, tackle	366
処女	*shojo*	virgin	102

1190

拠

3c5.26 □

扌 夂 几
/23 49 20

拠 據

KYO, KO – be due to, based on

根拠	*konkyo*	basis, grounds	314
拠点	*kyoten*	(military) position, base	169
準拠	*junkyo*	be based on, conform to	792
論拠	*ronkyo*	grounds/basis of an argument	293
証拠	*shōko*	evidence	493

1191	***ZEN, yo(i)* – good**	
2o10.2	善悪　*zen'aku*　good and evil; quality (whether good or bad)	304
゛王リ	善良　*zenryō*　good, honest, virtuous	321
/16 46 24	善意　*zen'i*　good intentions; favorable sense	132
善 譱	親善　*shinzen*　friendship	175
	改善　*kaizen*　improvement, betterment	523

1192	***ZEN, tsukuro(u)* – repair, mend**	
6a12.2	修繕　*shūzen*　repair	975
糸王リ	営繕　*eizen*　building and repairing	735
/61 46 24		
繕		

1193	***ZEN* – (low Japanese) dining table; filled ricebowl; (counter for pairs of chopsticks)**	
4b12.2	食膳　*shokuzen*　dining table	322
月王リ	一膳　*ichizen*　a bowl (of rice); a pair (of chopsticks)	2
/43 46 24	お膳立て　*ozendate*　arrangement, preparations	121
膳		

1194	***KICHI, KITSU* – good luck**	
3p3.1	吉報　*kippō*　good news, glad tidings	698
士リ	吉日　*kichinichi*　lucky day	5
/22 24	不吉　*fukitsu*　ill omen, portentous	94
吉	石部金吉　*Ishibe Kinkichi*　man of strict morals	78, 86, 23
	吉田　*Yoshida*　(surname)	35

1195	***KITSU* – packed *tsu(meru)* – cram, stuff; shorten *tsu(maru)* – be stopped up, be jammed; shrink; be cornered *tsu(mu)* – be pressed/packed in**	
7a6.7	詰問　*kitsumon*　cross-examination, tough questioning	162
言士リ	詰め込む　*tsumekomu*　cram, stuff	790
/67 22 24	気詰まり　*kizumari*　embarrassment, awkwardness	134
詰		

1196	***KI, yoroko(bu)* – be glad**	
3p9.1	喜劇　*kigeki*　a comedy	811
吉リ儿	歓喜　*kanki*　joy, delight	1095
/22 24 16	狂喜　*kyōki*　wild joy, exultation	904
喜	一喜一憂　*ikki-ichiyū*　alternation of joy and sorrow	2, 2, 1073
	大喜び　*ōyorokobi*　great joy	26

1197	***JU* – tree, bush**	
4a12.3	樹木　*jumoku*　tree	22
木土リ	果樹　*kaju*　fruit tree	496
/41 22 24	樹皮　*juhi*　bark (of a tree)	1008
樹	樹脂　*jushi*　resin	1083
	樹立　*juritsu*　establish, found	121

1198

膨

4b12.1

月 土 口
/43 22 24

膨

BŌ, fuku(reru), fuku(ramu) – swell, bulge, rise (dough), expand; sulk, pout

膨大	*bōdai*	swelling; large, enormous	26
膨張	*bōchō*	swelling, expansion	1158
膨れっ面	*fukurettsura*	sullen/sulky look	274
下膨れ	*shimobukure*	full-cheeked, round-faced	31

1199

肢

4b4.7

月 十 又
/43 12 9

肢

SHI – limbs

肢体	*shitai*	limbs; body and limbs	61
下肢	*kashi*	lower limbs, legs	31
上肢	*jōshi*	upper limbs, arms	32
四肢	*shishi*	the limbs, members	6

1200

鼓

3p10.2

壴 口 儿
/22 24 16

鼓 皷

KO, tsuzumi – hand drum

太鼓	*taiko*	drum	639
鼓手	*koshu*	drummer	57
鼓動	*kodō*	(heart) beat	231
鼓舞	*kobu*	encouragement, inspiration	829

1201

髪

3j11.3

髟 十 又
/31 12 9

髪 髮

HATSU, kami – hair (on the head)

散髪	*sanpatsu*	haircut, hairdressing	781
洗髪	*senpatsu*	hair washing, a shampoo	705
間一髪	*kan'ippatsu*	by a hairsbreadth	43, 2
金髪	*kinpatsu*	blond	23
白髪	*hakuhatsu, shiraga*	white/gray hair	205

1202

彫

3j8.2

彡 土 口
/31 22 24

彫

CHŌ, ho(ru) – carve, engrave, chisel, sculpt

彫像	*chōzō*	carved statue	753
彫金	*chōkin*	chasing, metal carving	23
木彫	*mokuchō*	wood carving	22
木彫り	*kibori*	wood carving	22
浮き彫り	*ukibori*	relief	968

1203

劣

3n3.4

丷 力 丨
/35 8 2

劣

RETSU, oto(ru) – be inferior to

劣等	*rettō*	inferiority	578
劣等感	*rettōkan*	inferiority complex	578, 262
劣性	*ressei*	inferior; recessive (gene)	98
劣勢	*ressei*	numerical inferiority	656
優劣	*yūretsu*	superiority or inferiority, relative merit	1074

1204

砂

5a4.3

石 小 丨
/53 35 2

砂

SA, SHA, suna – sand

砂利	*jari*	gravel	329
土砂降り	*doshaburi*	pouring rain, downpour	24, 977
土砂崩れ	*doshakuzure*	washout, landslide	24, 1174
砂浜	*sunahama*	sandy beach	799
砂時計	*sunadokei*	hourglass	42, 340

	1205	**SA** – sand
沙	3a4.13 ⬚	
	氵 小 ｜ /21 35 2	
	沙	

	1206	**TA** – sort, select (the good)
汰	3a4.8 ⬚	沙汰 *sata* news, notice; instructions; case, matter 1205
	氵 大 ｜ /21 34 2	ご/御無沙汰 *gobusata* neglect to visit/write 721, 93, 1205
	汰	音沙汰 *otosata* news, tidings 347, 1205
		淘汰 *tōta* sort out; reduce (personnal); (natural/artificial) selection

	1207	**BYŌ** – second (of time/arc)
秒	5d4.2 ⬚	秒針 *byōshin* second hand (of a clock) 341
	禾 小 ｜ /56 35 2	数秒 *sūbyō* several seconds 225
	秒	1分20秒 *ippun nijūbyō* 1 minute 20 seconds 38
		秒読み *byōyomi* countdown 244
		秒速5メートル *byōsoku gomētoru* 5 meters per second 511

	1208	**SHŌ** – selection, summary, excerpt
抄	3c4.11 ⬚	抄録 *shōroku* excerpt, abstract, summary 547
	扌 小 ｜ /23 35 2	抄本 *shōhon* extract, abridged transcript 25
	抄	抄訳 *shōyaku* abridged translation 604
		詩抄 *shishō* a selection of poems 579

	1209	**MYŌ** – strange, odd; a mystery; adroitness, knack
妙	3e4.5 ⬚	奥妙 *ōmyō* secret, mystery 484
	女 小 ｜ /25 35 2	妙案 *myōan* good idea, ingenious plan 106
	妙	妙技 *myōgi* extraordinary skill 891
		妙手 *myōshu* expert, master, virtuoso 57
		絶妙 *zetsumyō* miraculous, superb, exquisite 755

	1210	**HAI** – cup; (counter for cupfuls) **sakazuki** – winecup (for saké)
杯盃	4a4.11 ⬚	一杯 *ippai* a glass (of); a drink; full 2
	木 一 ｜ /41 14 2	祝杯 *shukuhai* a toast 870
		銀杯 *ginpai* silver cup 313
		デ杯（戦） *Dehai(sen)* Davis Cup (tournament) 301

	1211	**MAI** – sheet; (counter for thin, flat objects)
枚	4a4.4 ⬚	紙一枚 *kami ichimai* 1 sheet of paper 180, 2
	木 攵 /41 49	何枚 *nanmai* how many (sheets/plates/stamps) 392
	枚	枚挙 *maikyo* enumerate, count, list 815
		枚数 *maisū* number of sheets 225
		大枚 *taimai* a big sum (of money) 26

札	**1212** 4a1.1 木 丨 /41　2 札	**SATSU** – paper money, slip of paper **fuda** – chit, card, label 千円札　sen'ensatsu　1,000-yen bill/note　　　　　　15, 13 札束　satsutaba　bundle/roll of bills　　　　　　　　510 改札口　kaisatsuguchi　wicket, ticket gate　　　　523, 54 標/表札　hyōsatsu　nameplate　　　　　　　945, 272 入札　nyūsatsu　a bid, tender　　　　　　　　　　52
冊	**1213** 0a5.42 艹 冂 32　20 冊 冊	**SATSU** – book; (counter for books) **SAKU** – book 十二冊　jūnisatsu　12 books/volumes　　　　　　12, 3 別冊　bessatsu　separate volume　　　　　　　　267 分冊　bunsatsu　individual/separate volumes　　　38 冊子　sasshi　booklet, brochure, pamphlet　　　103 短冊　tanzaku　strip of fancy paper (for a poem)　215
偏	**1214** 2a9.16 亻 尸 艹 /3　40　32 偏	**HEN, katayo(ru)** – lean, incline, be one-sided, partial 不偏(不党)　fuhen(-futō)　nonpartisan　　94, 94, 504 偏向　henkō　propensity, leaning, deviation　　　199 偏見　henken　biased view, prejudice　　　　　　63 偏食　henshoku　unbalanced diet　　　　　　　322 偏差　hensa　deviation, deflection, declination　669
遍	**1215** 2q9.16 辶 尸 艹 /19　40　32 遍	**HEN** – far, widespread, general 遍歴　henreki　travel, pilgrimage　　　　　　　489 遍路　henro　pilgrim　　　　　　　　　　　　151 一遍　ippen　once, one time　　　　　　　　　　2
瓦	**1216** 0a5.11 丆 一 丨 14　1　2 瓦	**GA, kawara** – tile 瓦解　gakai　collapse, fall to pieces　　　　　　482 瓦礫　gareki　rubble; rubbish 煉瓦　renga　brick 瓦屋　kawaraya　tilemaker; tiler; tile-roofed house　167 瓦版　kawaraban　tile block print　　　　　　　1089
瓶	**1217** 2o9.6 丷 艹 一 /16　32　1 瓶	**BIN** – bottle 花瓶　kabin　vase　　　　　　　　　　　　　255 瓶詰　binzume　bottled, in a glass jar　　　　　1195 ビール瓶　bīrubin　beer bottle 鉄瓶　tetsubin　iron kettle　　　　　　　　　312 空き瓶　akibin　empty bottle　　　　　　　　140
併	**1218** 2a6.17 亻 艹 儿 /3　32　16 併	**HEI** – simultaneously, together **awa(seru)** – put together, unite, 合併　gappei　merger　　　　　　　　⌐combine　159 併合　heigō　annexation, amalgamation, merger　159 併用　heiyō　use jointly/in combination　　　　107 併発　heihatsu　(medical) complications　　　　96 併記　heiki　write side by side/on the same page　372

	1219	**HEI, mochi** – rice cake
餅	8b6.4 食 /77 餅	焼き餅 *yakimochi* toasted rice cake; jealousy 942 柏餅 *kashiwa-mochi* rice cake wrapped in an oak leaf (served at Boy's Festival on May 5)

	1220	**RIN** – principle, code
倫	2a8.28 亻 艹 冂 /3 32 20 倫	倫理 *rinri* ethics, morals 143 倫理学 *rinrigaku* ethics, moral philosophy 143, 109 人倫 *jinrin* humanity, morality 1 不倫 *furin* immoral, illicit 94 絶倫 *zetsurin* peerless, unsurpassed 755

	1221	**RIN** – wheel, ring, circle; (counter for flowers) **wa** – ring, circle, hoop,
輪	7c8.4 車 艹 亻 /69 32 3 輪	車輪 *sharin* wheel ⌐loop 133 輪番 *rinban* taking turns, in rotation 185 五輪（大会） *Gorin (Taikai)* the Olympic Games 7, 26, 158 競輪 *keirin* bicycle race 871 指輪 *yubiwa* (finger) ring 1082

	1222	**HEI, nara(bu)** – be lined up, be in a row **nara(beru)** – arrange, put side by side **nara(bi ni)** – and **nami** – ordinary, average
並	2o6.1 丷 エ 丨 /16 38 2 並 竝	並行 *heikō* parallel 68 並列 *heiretsu* stand in a row; parataxis 621 並木 *namiki* row of trees, roadside trees 22 平年並み *heinennami* as in an average/normal year 202, 45

	1223	**FU** – general, universal
普	2o10.5 丷 日 エ /16 42 38 普	普通 *futsū* usual, ordinary 150 普（通）選（挙） *fu(tsū) sen(kyo)* general elections 150, 814, 815 普遍的 *fuhenteki* universal, ubiquitous 1215, 210 普請 *fushin* building, construction 672 普段 *fudan* usual, ordinary, everyday 363

	1224	**FU** – (sheet) music, notes, staff, score; a genealogy; record
譜	7a12.2 言 日 エ /67 42 38 譜	楽譜 *gakufu* (written) notes, the score 359 譜面 *fumen* sheet music, score 274 暗譜 *anpu* learning the notes by heart 348 年譜 *nenpu* chronological record 45 系譜 *keifu* genealogical chart, family tree 930

	1225	**REI, RYŌ, tama** – soul, spirit
霊	8d7.2 雨 エ 儿 /74 38 16 霊 靈	霊肉 *reiniku* body and soul/spirit 223 亡霊 *bōrei* soul/spirit of a dead person 684 聖霊 *seirei* the Holy Spirit 686 霊園 *reien* cemetery park ⌐man 454 万物の霊長 *banbutsu no reichō* crown of creation, 16, 79, 95

湿	**1226** 3a9.22 氵日 儿 /21 42 16 湿 濕	**SHITSU, shime(ru)** – become damp **shime(su)** – moisten 湿気　*shikke, shikki*　moisture, humidity　　134 湿度　*shitsudo*　humidity　　378 湿地　*shitchi*　damp ground, bog　　118 湿布　*shippu*　wet compress, poultice　　688
顕	**1227** 9a9.5 頁 日 儿 /76 42 16 顕 顯	**KEN** – clear, plain, obvious 露顕　*roken*　dicovery, disclosure, exposure　　981 顕著　*kencho*　notable, striking, marked　　878 顕花植物　*kenka shokubutsu*　flowering plant　　255, 430, 79
貴	**1228** 7b5.7 貝 口 亠 /68 24 11 貴	**KI** – valuable, noble; esteemed, your **tatto(i), tōto(i)** – valuable, noble **tatto(bu), tōto(bu)** – value, esteem, respect 貴重　*kichō*　valuable, precious　　227 貴重品　*kichōhin*　valuables　　227, 230 貴族　*kizoku*　nobleman, the nobility　　221 富貴　*fūki, fukki*　riches and honors, wealth and rank　　726
潰	**1229** 3a12.14 氵貝 口 /21 68 24 潰	**KAI** – destruction **tsubu(su)** – crush, wreck; kill (time) **tsubu(reru)** – be crushed, be destroyed; collapse 崩潰　*hōkai*　collapse, disintegration　　1174 噛み潰す　*kamitsubusu*　chew up
遺	**1230** 2q12.4 辶 貝 口 /19 68 24 遺	**I, [YUI]** – leave behind, bequeath 遺伝　*iden*　heredity　　440 遺体　*itai*　corpse, the remains　　61 遺産　*isan*　an inheritance, estate　　278 遺族　*izoku*　family of the deceased, survivors　　221 遺言　*yuigon*　will, last wishes　　66
遣	**1231** 2q10.2 辶 口 尸 /19 24 40 遣	**KEN** – send **tsuka(wasu)** – send, give **tsuka(u)** – use 派遣　*haken*　dispatch, send (a person)　　934 小遣い（銭）　*kozukai(sen)*　pocket money　　27, 659 気遣い　*kizukai*　worry, apprehension　　134 心遣い　*kokorozukai*　solicitude, consideration　　97
追	**1232** 2q6.4 辶 尸 冂 /19 40 20 追	**TSUI, o(u)** – drive away, pursue 追放　*tsuihō*　banishment, purge　　521 追求　*tsuikyū*　pursue, follow up　　737 追加　*tsuika*　addition, supplement　　722 追い風　*oikaze*　favorable/tail wind　　29 追い越す　*oikosu*　overtake, pass　　1038

1233

迫

2q5.5
辶 日 丨
/19 42 2

迫

HAKU, sema(ru) – press (someone) for, urge, approach, draw near

切迫	seppaku dr, draw near, press, be imminent	39
迫力	hakuryoku force, power, impressiveness	100
迫害	hakugai persecution	527
窮迫	kyūhaku straitened circumstances, poverty	919

1234

伯

2a5.7
亻 日 丨
/3 42 2

伯

HAKU – elder sibling of a parent; count, earl; (short for) Brazil

画伯	gahaku great artist, master painter	343
伯母	oba aunt (elder sister of parent)	112
伯父	oji uncle (elder brother of parent)	113

1235

泊

3a5.15
氵 日 丨
/21 42 2

泊

HAKU – anchoring; lodge **to(maru)** – (intr.) put up (for the night), lodge **to(meru)** – (tr.) put up (for the night), lodge

宿泊	shukuhaku lodging	179
一泊	ippaku overnight stay	2
漂泊	hyōhaku wander, drift	946
泊り客	tomarikyaku house guest; (hotel) guest	651

1236

拍

3c5.14
扌 日 丨
/23 42 2

拍

HAKU, HYŌ – beat (in music)

拍手	hakushu handclapping, applause	57
拍車	hakusha a spur	133
拍子	hyōshi time, tempo; chance, the moment	103
拍子木	hyōshigi wooden clappers	103, 22
脈拍	myakuhaku pulse	935

1237

帝

2j7.1
亠 巾 儿
/11 26 16

帝

TEI – emperor

帝国	teikoku empire	40
帝国主義	teikoku shugi imperialism	40, 155, 291
帝政	teisei imperial rule	492
皇帝	kōtei emperor	297
カール大帝	Kāru Taitei Charlemagne	26

1238

諦

7a9.16
言 巾 亠
/67 26 11

諦

TEI, akira(meru) – give up, abandon

諦観	teikan clear vision; resign oneself to	614
要諦	yōtei secret, key, special knowledge	425
成功の要諦	seikō no yōtei secret of success, key to success	261, 837, 425

1239

締

6a9.11
糸 巾 亠
/61 26 11

締

TEI, shi(meru) – tie, tighten **shi(maru)** – be shut, tighten

条約の締結	jōyaku no teiketsu conclusion of a treaty	573, 211, 494
取り締まり	torishimari control, supervision	65
締め切り	shimekiri closing (date), deadline; tighten, stiffen	39
締め出す	shimedasu shut/lock out	53

訪	**1240** 7a4.1 ▢ 言 方 /67 48 訪	**HŌ, tazu(neru), otozu(reru)** – visit
		訪問 *hōmon* visit 162
		来訪 *raihō* visit 69
		訪日 *hōnichi* visit to Japan 5
		訪客 *hōkyaku* visitor, guest 651
		探訪 *tanbō* inquiries, inquiring into 544

妨	**1241** 3e4.1 ▢ 女 方 /25 48 妨	**BŌ, samata(geru)** – prevent, obstruct, hamper
		妨害 *bōgai* obstruction, disturbance, interference 527

傍	**1242** 2a10.6 ▢ 亻 方 宀 /3 48 11 傍	**BŌ, katawa(ra)** – side
		傍観 *bōkan* look on, remain a spectator 614
		傍聴 *bōchō* hearing, attendance 1080
		傍系 *bōkei* collateral (descendant) 930
		傍証 *bōshō* supporting evidence, corroboration 493
		傍受 *bōju* intercept, monitor (a radio message) 260

亭	**1243** 2j7.5 ▤ 宀 口 冂 /11 24 20 亭	**TEI** – restaurant, pavilion, arbor
		亭主 *teishu* host; innkeeper; husband 155
		料亭 *ryōtei* (Japanese) restaurant 319

停	**1244** 2a9.14 ▢ 亻 口 宀 /3 24 11 停	**TEI** – stop
		停止 *teishi* suspension, stopping 485
		停滞 *teitai* stagnation, accumulation 995
		調停 *chōtei* mediation, arbitration 342
		停留所 *teiryūjo* (bus/streetcar) stop 774, 153
		各駅停車 *kakueki teisha* a local (train) 652, 284, 133

轄	**1245** 7c10.1 ▢ 車 宀 士 /69 33 22 轄	**KATSU** – a wedge; control, administration
		管轄 *kankatsu* jurisdiction, competence 328
		管轄官庁 *kankatsu kanchō* the proper 328, 326, 777
		所轄 *shokatsu* jurisdiction ⌐authorities 153
		統轄 *tōkatsu* supervision, general control 849
		直轄 *chokkatsu* direct control/jurisdiction 429

軒	**1246** 7c3.1 ▢ 車 干 一 /69 14 1 軒	**KEN** – house; (counter for buildings) **noki** – eaves
		一軒 *ikken* 1 house 2
		軒数 *kensū* number of houses 225
		軒並 *nokinami* row of houses 1222
		軒先 *nokisaki* edge of the eaves; front of the house 50

汗	**1247** 3a3.6 ▦ 氵 一 一 /21 14 1 汗	**KAN, ase** – sweat

発汗　*hakkan*　perspire, sweat　96
冷汗　*reikan, hiyaase*　a cold sweat　851
汗顔　*kangan*　sweating from shame　277

幹	**1248** 4c9.8 ⋯ 日 十 亻 /42 12 3 幹	**KAN** – main part **miki** – (tree) trunk

幹部　*kanbu*　key officers, executives, management　86
幹事長　*kanjichō*　executive secretary, secretary-general　80, 95
根幹　*konkan*　basis, root, nucleus　314
語幹　*gokan*　stem of a word　67
新幹線　*Shinkansen*　New Trunk Line, bullet train　174, 299

乾	**1249** 4c7.14 ▦ 日 十 乁 /42 12 15 乾	**KAN** – dry **kawa(ku)** – become dry, dry up **kawa(kasu)** – dry (out), parch

乾季　*kanki*　the dry season　473
乾電池　*kandenchi*　dry cell, battery　108, 119
乾物　*kanbutsu*　dry provisions, groceries　79
乾杯　*kanpai*　a toast; Cheers!　1210

韓	**1250** 4c14.3 ▦ 日 日 十 /42 24 12 韓	**KAN** – Korea

韓国　*Kankoku*　South Korea　40
日韓　*Nik-Kan*　Japan and South Korea　5
在韓　*zai-Kan*　resident/stationed in South Korea　268

綿	**1251** 6a8.8 ▦ 糸 日 巾 /61 42 26 綿 緜	**MEN, wata** – cotton

木綿　*momen*　cotton　22
綿布　*menpu*　cotton (cloth)　688
綿織物　*men'orimono*　cotton fabrics, cotton goods　693, 79
海綿　*kaimen*　a sponge　117
綿密　*menmitsu*　minute, close, meticulous　822

錦	**1252** 8a8.6 ▦ 釒 日 巾 /72 42 26 錦	**KIN, nishiki** – brocade

錦絵　*nishikie*　colored woodblock print　345
錦の御旗　*nishiki no mihata*　the imperial standard　721, 1043

泉	**1253** 3a5.33 ▤ 氵 日 丨 /21 42 2 泉 湶	**SEN, izumi** – spring, fountainhead, fountain

温泉　*onsen*　hot spring, spa　644
冷泉　*reisen*　cold mineral spring　851
泉水　*sensui*　garden pond, fountain　21
源泉　*gensen*　fountainhead, source　589
平泉　*Hiraizumi*　(town in Tōhoku)　202

| 腺 | **1254**
4b9.6
月 日 氵
/43 42 21
腺 | **SEN** – gland

甲状腺　*kōjōsen*　thyroid gland　　　　　　　　1016, 636
乳腺　*nyūsen*　mammary gland　　　　　　　　　969
前立腺　*zenritsusen*　prostate gland　　　　　　47, 121 |

| 井 | **1255**
0a4.46　…
艹 一
32 1
井 | **SEI, [SHŌ], i** – a well

井泉　*seisen*　a well　　　　　　　　　　　　　1253
油井　*yusei*　oil well　　　　　　　　　　　　　365
天井　*tenjō*　ceiling　　　　　　　　　　　　　141
井戸　*ido*　a well　　　　　　　　　　　　　　152
軽井沢　*Karuizawa*　(summer resort town NW of ⌜Tōkyō)　556, 1031 |

| 丼 | **1256**
0a5.40　…
艹 一 丨
32 1 2
丼 | **donburi, don** – bowl

天丼　*tendon*　bowl of rice and tempura　　　141
丼勘定　*donburi-kanjō*　slipshod accounting, rough estimate
　　　　　　　　　　　　　　　　　　　　　1601, 356 |

| 囲 | **1257**
3s4.2　▢
口 艹 一
/24 32 1
囲 圍 | **I, kako(mu/u)** – surround, enclose, lay siege to

範囲　*han'i*　extent, scope, range　　　　　　1143
周囲　*shūi*　circumference, surroundings　　　　91
包囲　*hōi*　encirclement, siege　　　　　　　　819
取り囲む　*torikakomu*　surround, enclose; besiege　65 |

| 囚 | **1258**
3s2.1　▢
口 亻
/24 3
囚 | **SHŪ** – arrest, imprison, prisoner

囚人　*shūjin*　prisoner, convict　　　　　　　　1
未決囚　*miketsushū*　unconvicted prisoner　　306, 357
死刑囚　*shikeishū*　criminal sentenced to death　85, 908
女囚　*joshū*　female prisoner　　　　　　　　102
免囚　*menshū*　released prisoner, ex-convict　　746 |

| 耕 | **1259**
0a10.13　…
耒 艹 二
41 32 4
耕 畊 | **KŌ, tagaya(su)** – plow, till, cultivate

耕地　*kōchi*　arable land, cultivated land　　　118
耕作　*kōsaku*　cultivation, farming　　　　　　361
耕作物　*kōsakubutsu*　farm products　　　　361, 79
農耕　*nōkō*　agriculture, farming　　　　　　370
水耕（法）　*suikō(hō)*　hydroponics　　　　　21, 123 |

| 耗 | **1260**
0a10.12　…
耒 二 十
41 4 12
耗 | **MŌ, [KŌ]** – decrease

消耗　*shōmō*　consumption, wear and tear　　　864
消耗品　*shōmōhin*　supplies, expendables　　864, 230
消耗戦　*shōmōsen*　war of attrition　　　　864, 301
損耗　*sonmō*　wear and tear, loss　　　　　　351
減耗　*genmō, genkō*　decrease, shrinkage　　　728 |

籍	**1261** 6f14.1 ⅶ 木 日 /66 41 42 籍	**SEKI** – (family) register

戸籍　　*koseki*　census registration　　　　　　　152
本籍　　*honseki*　one's domicile, legal residence　25
除籍　　*joseki*　removal from the register　　　1112
国籍　　*kokuseki*　nationality　　　　　　　　　40
書籍　　*shoseki*　books　　　　　　　　　　　131

錯	**1262** 8a8.10 釒 日 ⅶ /72 42 32 錯	**SAKU** – mix, be in disorder

錯覚　　*sakkaku*　illusion　　　　　　　　　　615
錯誤　　*sakugo*　error　　　　　　　　　　　　928
錯乱　　*sakuran*　distraction, derangement　　702
交錯　　*kōsaku*　mixture; intricacy　　　　　　114
倒錯　　*tōsaku*　perversion　　　　　　　　　927

措	**1263** 3c8.20 扌 日 ⅶ /23 42 32 措	**SO** – give up, discontinue, set aside

措置　　　　*sochi*　measures, steps　　　　　　　　432
報復措置　　*hōfuku sochi*　retaliatory measures　698, 939, 432

拝	**1264** 3c5.3 扌 王 一 /23 46 1 拝 拜	**HAI, oga(mu)** – pray, venerate

参拝　　　*sanpai*　visit (a shrine/grave)　　　　　　　723
礼拝　　　*reihai*　worship, (church) services　　　　　630
拝見　　　*haiken*　see, have a look at　　　　　　　　63
拝借　　　*haishaku*　borrow　　　　　　　　　　　　780
拝み倒す　*ogamitaosu*　entreat (someone) into consent　927

欄	**1265** 4a16.4 木 門 日 /41 75 42 欄	**RAN** – (newspaper) column; railing

家庭欄　*kateiran*　home-life section　　　　　　165, 1164
投書欄　*tōshoran*　letters-to-the-editor column　1060, 131
欄外　　*rangai*　margin (of a page)　　　　　　　　　83
空欄　　*kūran*　blank column/space　　　　　　　　140
欄干　　*rankan*　railing, banister　　　　　　　　　593

潤	**1266** 3a12.20 氵 門 王 /21 75 46 潤	**JUN** – damp, wet; enrich **uruo(su)** – moisten, wet, water; profit, enrich **uruo(u)** – become wet; profit, become rich **uru(mu)** – become wet/blurred/turbid/clouded

浸潤　　　*shinjun*　permeation, infiltration　　　　1126
利潤　　　*rijun*　profits　　　　　　　　　　　　　329
潤飾 / 色　*junshoku*　embellishment　　　　　1013, 204

涼	**1267** 3a8.31 氵 口 小 /21 24 35 涼 涼	**RYŌ, suzu(shii)** – cool, refreshing **suzu(mu)** – cool off, enjoy the evening cool

清涼飲料　*seiryō inryō*　carbonated beverage　671, 323, 319
涼味　　　*ryōmi*　the cool, coolness　　　　　　　307
涼風　　　*ryōfū, suzukaze*　cool breeze　　　　　　29
夕涼み　　*yūsuzumi*　the evening cool　　　　　　　81

1268 2b8.2 冫木日 /5 41 42 凍	**TŌ, kō(ru)** – freeze **kogo(eru)** – become frozen/numb

冷凍器	reitōki	refrigerator, freezer	851, 536
凍結	tōketsu	freeze (assets)	494
凍傷	tōshō	frostbite	643
凍死	tōshi	freeze to death	85
凍え死に	kogoejini	freeze to death	85

1269 3a1.2 冫丶 /21 2 氷 冰	**HYŌ, kōri, hi** – ice

氷山	hyōzan	iceberg	34
氷河	hyōga	glacier	391
流氷	ryūhyō	floating ice, ice floe	247
氷点（下）	hyōten(ka)	(below) the freezing point	169, 31
氷結	hyōketsu	freeze (over)	494

1270 3a1.1 冫丶 /21 2 永	**EI, naga(i)** – long (time)

永住	eijū	permanent residence	156
永遠	eien	eternity	453
永眠	eimin	eternal sleep, death	868
永続	eizoku	permanence, perpetuity	243
永田町	Nagatachō	(area of Tōkyō)	35, 182

1271 3a5.14 氵丶 /21 2 泳	**EI, oyo(gu)** – swim

水泳	suiei	swimming	21
競泳	kyōei	swimming race	871
泳法	eihō	swimming style/stroke	123
遠泳	en'ei	long-distance swim	453
平泳ぎ	hiraoyogi	the breaststroke	202

1272 7a5.14 言氵丶 /67 21 2 詠 咏	**EI** – poem; recite, sing **yo(mu)** – compose, write (a poem)

詠歌	eika	composition of a poem; (Buddhist) chant	395
詠草	eisō	draft of a poem	249

1273 0a3.7 𠂉丶 15 2 久	**KYŪ, [KU], hisa(shii)** – long (time)

永久	eikyū	permanence, perpetuity, eternity	1270
長久	chōkyū	long continuance, eternity	95
持久	jikyū	endurance, persistence	458
久遠	kuon	eternity	453
久し振り	hisashiburi	(after) a long time	984

1274 2f6.7 刂亠厶 /16 11 17 刻	**KOKU** – time; carve **kiza(mu)** – cut fine, chop up, carve, engrave

彫刻	chōkoku	sculpture	1202
深刻	shinkoku	grave, serious	545
時刻	jikoku	time	42
一刻	ikkoku	moment; stubborn	2
夕刻	yūkoku	evening	81

	1275	**KAKU** – core, nucleus	
核	4a6.22	核心　kakushin　core, kernel	97
	木 宀 厶	原子核　genshikaku　(atomic) nucleus	136, 103
	/41　11　17	核燃料　kakunenryō　nuclear fuel	663, 319
	核	核兵器　kakuheiki　nuclear weapons	798, 536
		結核　kekkaku　tuberculosis	494

	1276	**GAI** – (prefix) the said; vast	
該	7a6.10	当該官庁　tōgai kanchō　relevant authorities	77, 326, 777
	言 宀 厶	当該人物　tōgai jinbutsu　the said person	77, 1, 79
	/67　11　17	該当　gaitō　pertain (to), come/fall under	77
	該	該博な知識　gaihaku na chishiki　profound/vast learning	
			611, 214, 694

	1277	**SHIN, mi(ru)** – diagnose, examine	
診	7a5.9	診察　shinsatsu　medical examination	629
	言 彡 亻	検診　kenshin　medical examination	540
	/67　31　3	診断　shindan　diagnosis	1063
	診	打診　dashin　percussion, tapping; sound out	1059
		往診　ōshin　doctor's visit to a patient, house call	940

	1278	**CHIN, mezura(shii)** – rare, unusual	
珍	4f5.6	珍品　chinpin　a rarity, curiosity	230
	王 彡 亻	珍談　chindan　amusing story, anecdote	603
	/46　31　3	珍味　chinmi　a delicacy	307
	珍 珎	珍重　chinchō　value highly, prize	227
		珍客　chinkyaku　least-expected/welcome visitor	651

	1279	**KYŪ** – old, former	
旧	4c1.1	旧式　kyūshiki　old-type, old-fashioned	534
	日 丨	復旧　fukkyū　recovery, restoration	939
	/42　2	新旧　shinkyū　old and new	174
	旧 舊	旧悪　kyūaku　one's past misdeed	304
		旧約（聖書）　Kyūyaku (Seisho)　Old Testament	211, 686, 131

	1280	**JI, [NI]** – small child, infant	
児	4c3.3	児童　jidō　child, juvenile	416
	日 儿 丨	育児園　ikujien　daycare nursery	246, 454
	/42　16　2	産児制限　sanji seigen　birth control	278, 433, 866
	児 兒	乳児　nyūji　(nursing) baby, infant	969
		小児科医　shōnikai　pediatrician	27, 320, 220

	1281	**KAN, ochii(ru)** – fall, get, run (into), fall, be reduced **otoshii(reru)** – ensnare, entice, capture	
陥	2d7.11	欠陥　kekkan　defect, shortcoming	384
	阝 臼 宀	陥落　kanraku　fall, capitulation	858
	/7　42　15	陥没　kanbotsu　depression, subsidence, cave-in	963
	陥 陷	陥穽　kansei　pitfall, trap, plot	

1282
惠

4k6.16
心 日 十
/51 42 12

惠 惠

KEI, E, megu(mu) – bestow a favor; bless

天恵	tenkei	gift of nature, natural advantage	141
恩恵	onkei	benefit, favor	564
互恵	gokei	mutual benefit, reciprocity	929
知恵	chie	wisdom, sense, brains, intelligence	214
知恵者	chiesha	wise/resourceful man	214, 164

1283
稲

5d9.2
禾 日 小
/56 42 35

稲 稲

TŌ, ine, [ina-] – rice plant

水稲	suitō	paddy rice	21
稲作	inasaku	rice crop	361
稲荷	Inari	god of harvests, fox deity	393
早稲	wase	(early-ripening variety of rice)	248
早稲田	Waseda	(area of Tōkyō)	248, 35

1284
穂

5d10.2
禾 日 心
/56 42 51

穂 穂

SUI, ho – ear, head (of grain)

稲穂	inaho	ear of rice	1283
穂先	hosaki	tip of an ear/spear/knife/brush	50
穂波	honami	waves of grain	677

1285
菌

3k8.32
艹 禾 囗
/32 56 24

菌

KIN – fungus, germ, bacteria

細菌	saikin	bacteria	708
保菌者	hokinsha	(germ) carrier	498, 164
殺菌	sakkin	sterilization	585
無菌	mukin	germ-free, sterilized	93
抗菌性	kōkinsei	antibacterial	843, 98

1286
蓋

3k10.15
艹 皿 土
/32 59 22

蓋

GAI, futa – cover, lid

蓋然性	gaizensei	probability	662, 98
目蓋	mabuta	eyelid	55

1287
畜

2j8.7
亠 田 厶
/11 58 17

畜

CHIKU – animal raising; domestic animals

家畜	kachiku	domestic animal, livestock	165
畜産	chikusan	stock raising	278
牧畜業	bokuchikugyō	stock farming, cattle	744, 279
畜舎	chikusha	cattle shed, barn	805
畜生	chikushō	beast, brute; Dammit!	44

1288
蓄

3k10.16
艹 田 亠
/32 58 11

蓄

CHIKU, takuwa(eru) – store, save, put aside

貯蓄	chochiku	savings, saving	775
備蓄	bichiku	saving for emergencies, storing	782
蓄積	chikuseki	accumulation	667
蓄電池	chikudenchi	storage battery	108, 119

	1289	**GEN** – dark, mystery	
玄	2j3.2 ⊟ 亠 厶 丨 /11 17 2 玄	玄関 *genkan* entranceway 玄関番 *genkanban* doorkeeper, doorman, porter 玄米 *genmai* unpolished/brown rice 玄人 *kurōto* expert, professional, specialist	402 402, 185 224 1

	1290	**GEN, tsuru** – bowstring, string	
弦	3h5.1 ⊞ 弓 亠 厶 /28 11 17 弦	弦楽器 *gengakki* string instrument, the strings 管弦楽（団） *kangengaku(dan)* orchestra 正弦曲線 *seigen kyokusen* sine curve 上弦 *jōgen* first quarter (of the moon) 下弦 *kagen* last quarter (of the moon)	359, 536 328, 359, 500 275, 367, 299 32 31

	1291	**GEN, maboroshi** – illusion, phantom, vision	
幻	0a4.6 ☐ 厶 一 丨 17 1 2 幻	幻覚 *genkaku* hallucination 幻影 *gen'ei* vision, phantom, illusion 幻想 *gensō* fantasy, illusion 夢幻 *mugen* dreams and phantasms	615 873 147 830

	1292	**YŪ** – quiet, deep	
幽	3o6.6 ⋯ 凵 厶 丨 /36 17 2 幽	幽玄 *yūgen* the profound, occult 幽霊 *yūrei* ghost 幽閉 *yūhei* confinement, imprisonment 幽谷 *yūkoku* deep ravine, narrow valley 幽門 *yūmon* pylorus	1289 1225 401 664 161

	1293	**YŌ, osana(i)** – very young, infantile, childish	
幼	2g3.3 ☐ 力 厶 丨 /8 17 2 幼	幼児 *yōji* baby, small child, tot 幼少 *yōshō* infancy, childhood 幼虫 *yōchū* larva 幼子 *osanago* little child 幼心 *osanagokoro* child's mind/heart	1280 144 893 103 97

	1294	**CHI** – child	
稚	5d8.1 ☐ 禾 隹 /56 73 稚 稺	幼稚園 *yōchien* kindergarten 稚気 *chiki* childlike state of mind 稚児 *chigo* child; child in a Buddhist procession	1293, 454 134 1280

	1295	**I** – tie, rope	
維	6a8.1 ☐ 糸 隹 /61 73 維	維持 *iji* maintenance, support 維持費 *ijihi* upkeep expenses 明治維新 *Meiji Ishin* Meiji Restoration	458 458, 762 18, 502, 174

	1296	**JUN** – semi-, quasi-; permit	
准	2b8.1	批准 *hijun* ratify	1068
	冫 隹 /5 73 准		

	1297	**SUI, o(su)** – infer, deduce, recommend, propose	
推	3c8.1	推定 *suitei* presumption, inference	356
	扌 隹 /23 73 推	推論 *suiron* reasoning, inference	293
		推理 *suiri* reasoning, inference	143
		類推 *ruisui* (inference by) analogy	226
		推進 *suishin* propulsion, drive	443

	1298	**YUI, [I]** – solely, only, merely	
唯	3d8.1	唯物論 *yuibutsuron* materialism	79, 293
	口 隹 /24 73 唯	唯心論 *yuishinron* spiritualism, idealism	97, 293
		唯理論 *yuiriron* rationalism	143, 293
		唯美主義 *yuibi shugi* estheticism	405, 155, 291
		唯一 *yuiitsu* the only, sole	2

	1299	**SHŌ, wara(u)** – laugh **e(mu)** – smile	
笑	6f4.1	苦笑 *kushō* wry smile, forced laugh	554
	竹 大 丨 /66 34 2 笑	冷笑 *reishō* scornful laugh, sneer	851
		談笑 *danshō* friendly talk, chat	603
		大笑い *ōwarai* loud laughter, hearty laugh	26
		笑顔 *egao* smiling face	277

	1300	**KYŪ, na(ku)** – cry	
泣	3a5.1	感泣 *kankyū* be moved to tears	262
	氵 立 /21 54 泣	号泣 *gōkyū* wailing, lamentation	266
		泣き声 *nakigoe* tearful voice, sob, whimper	759
		泣き虫 *nakimushi* crybaby ⌈tears	893
		泣き落とす *nakiotosu* obtain (someone's) consent by	858

	1301	**RA** – drag; (short for) Latin	
拉	3c5.2	拉致 *rachi* take (someone) away	925
	扌 立 /23 54 拉	拉致被害者 *rachi higaisha* abductee	925, 1009, 527, 164

	1302	**MEN** – noodles	
麺	4i13.3	拉麺 *rāmen* ramen, Chinese noodles in soup	1301
	夂 土 口 /49 22 24 麺	素麺 *sōmen* vermicelli, thin noodles	271

1303

房

4m4.2 戸
戸 方
/40 48
房

BŌ – a room; tassel **fusa** – tassel, tuft, cluster

暖房	danbō	heating	645
独房	dokubō	solitary (prison) cell	219
官房長（官）	kanbōchō(kan)	chief secretary	326, 95, 326
文房具	bunbōgu	stationery	111, 426
女房	nyōbō	(one's own) wife	102

1304

戻

4m3.1 戸
戸 大
/40 34
戻

REI – rebel; perverse **modo(ru)** – go/come back, return
modo(su) – give/send back, return, restore; throw up, vomit

取り戻す	torimodosu	take back, regain, recoup	65
払い戻す	haraimodosu	pay back, refund	591
立ち戻る	tachimodoru	return to	121
逆戻り	gyakumodori	going backward, retrogression	451

1305

涙

3a7.21 氵
氵 尸 大
/21 40 34
涙 泪

RUI, namida – teardrop

感涙	kanrui	tears of strong emotion	262
血涙	ketsurui	tears of blood, bitter tears	803
空涙	soranamida	false/crocodile tears	140
涙声	namidagoe	tearful voice	759
涙ぐましい	namidagumashii	touching, moving	

1306

喫

3d9.7 ⋯
口 士 大
/24 22 34
喫

KITSU – eat, drink, smoke

喫茶店	kissaten	teahouse, café	251, 168
喫煙	kitsuen	smoking	941
満喫	mankitsu	eat/drink one's fill, enjoy fully	201
喫する	kissuru	eat, drink, smoke	

1307

潔

3a12.10 氵
氵 糸 士
/21 61 22
潔

KETSU – pure **isagiyo(i)** – brave, manly, righteous, pure

清潔	seiketsu	clean, neat	671
純潔	junketsu	pure, chaste	996
潔白	keppaku	pure, upright, of integrity	205
高潔	kōketsu	noble, lofty, high-minded	190
不潔	fuketsu	impure, unclean, filthy	94

1308

息

4k6.17 心
心 目 丨
/51 55 2
息

SOKU – son; breath **iki** – breath

休息	kyūsoku	a rest, breather	60
消息	shōsoku	news, information	864
利息	risoku	interest (on a loan)	329
息切れ	ikigire	shortness of breath	39
息子	musuko	son	103

1309

憩

4k12.10 心
心 目 口
/51 55 24
憩 憩

KEI, iko(i) – rest **iko(u)** – rest

休憩	kyūkei	rest, recess	60
休憩所	kyūkeijo	resting place, lobby	60, 153
休憩時間	kyūkei jikan	rest period, recess	60, 42, 43
小憩	shōkei	brief recess, a break	27

1310

臭

5c4.3 ⊟
日 大 |
/55 34 2

臭

SHŪ – smell **kusa(i)** – foul-smelling, smelling of

臭気	shūki	offensive odor, stink	134
悪臭	akushū	bad odor, stench	304
俗臭	zokushū	low taste, vulgarity	1178
古臭い	furukusai	old, outdated; trite, hackneyed	172
カビ臭い	kabikusai	musty, moldy	

1311

嗅

3d10.3 ⊟
口 日 犭
/24 55 27

嗅

KYŪ, ka(gu) – smell, sniff

嗅覚	kyūkaku	sense of smell	615
嗅神経	kyūshinkei	olfactory nerve	310, 557
嗅ぎ回る	kagimawaru	sniff around (looking for)	90
嗅ぎ付ける	kagitsukeru	scent, smell out, detect	192

1312

腐

3q11.3
广 寸 亻
/18 37 3

腐

FU, kusa(ru), kusa(reru) – rot, go bad, spoil, turn sour
kusa(rasu) – spoil, rot, putrefy, corrode

豆腐	tōfu	tofu, bean curd	988
腐食	fushoku	corrosion	322
腐敗	fuhai	decomposition, decay; corruption	520
腐心	fushin	take pains, be intent on	97

1313

嘆

3d10.8
口 艹 大
/24 32 34

嘆

TAN – grief, lamentation; praise, admiration **nage(ku)** – grieve, lament **nage(kawashii)** – deplorable, regrettable

感嘆	kantan	admiration, exclamation	262
嘆願	tangan	entreaty, petition	590
嘆息	tansoku	sigh; lament	1308
悲嘆	hitan	grief, sorrow, lamentation	1075

1314

謹

7a10.6 ⊞
言 艹 口
/67 32 24

謹

KIN – be respectful **tsutsushi(mu)** – respect

謹聴	kinchō	listen attentively	1080
謹賀新年	kinga shinnen	Happy New Year.	769, 174, 45
謹言	kingen	Sincerely/Respectfully yours	66
謹んで	tsutsushinde	respectfully, humbly	

1315

僅

2a10.10 ⊞
亻 艹 口
/3 32 24

僅

KIN, wazu(ka) – few, little; narrow, less (than)

僅差	kinsa	slight difference, narrow margin	669
僅少	kinshō	few, little	144

1316

否

3d4.20 ⊟
口 一 |
/24 14 2

否

HI – no, negative **ina** – no, nay

否定	hitei	denial, negation	356
否認	hinin	denial, repudiation, disavow	751
否決	hiketsu	rejection, voting down	357
賛否	sanpi	approval or disapproval, yes or no	758
安否	anpi	how (someone) is getting on	105

含	**1317** 2a5.25 目 亻 口 一 /3 24 1 含	**GAN** – contain, include **fuku(mu)** – hold in one's mouth; bear in mind; contain, include **fuku(meru)** – include; give instructions 含蓄　*ganchiku*　significance, implication　　　1288 包含　*hōgan*　include, cover, imply　　　819 含有　*gan'yū*　contain　　　265
吟	**1318** 3d4.8 田 口 亻 一 /24 3 1 吟	**GIN** – sing, chant, recite 独吟　*dokugin*　(vocal) solo　　　219 詩吟　*shigin*　recitation of Chinese poems　　　579 吟詠　*gin'ei*　sing, recite; compose a poem　　　1272 吟味　*ginmi*　close inquiry, scrutiny　　　307
琴	**1319** 4f8.11 田 王 亻 一 /46 3 1 琴	**KIN, koto** – koto, Japanese zither 心の琴線　*kokoro no kinsen*　heartstrings　　　97, 299 木琴　*mokkin*　xylophone　　　22 風琴　*fūkin*　organ, harmonium　　　29 手風琴　*tefūkin*　accordion, concertina　　　57, 29 竪琴　*tategoto*　harp, lyre
爪	**1320** 0a4.9 囗 广 丨 18 2 爪	**tsume, tsuma** – nail, claw, talon; plectrum 爪切り　*tsumekiri*　nail clippers　　　39 爪先　*tsumasaki*　tip of the toe, tiptoe　　　50 爪弾く　*tsumabiku*　pluck (a samisen) with one's fingers　　　1641 爪弾き　*tsumahajiki*　flick of the finger, fillip; ostracize, shun, 　　　give the cold shoulder　　　1641
叫	**1321** 3d3.4 田 口 十 丨 /24 12 2 叫	**KYŌ, sake(bu)** – shout, cry out 絶叫　*zekkyō*　scream, exclamation　　　755 叫び声　*sakebigoe*　a shout, cry, scream　　　759
吐	**1322** 3d3.1 田 口 土 /24 22 吐	**TO, ha(ku)** – spew, vomit, throw up; express, give vent to 吐血　*toketsu*　vomit blood　　　803 吐息　*toiki*　a sigh　　　1308 吐露　*toro*　express, voice, speak out　　　981 吐き気　*hakike*　nausea　　　134 吐き出す　*hakidasu*　vomit, disgorge, spew out　　　53
叱	**1323** 3d2.2 田 口 十 /24 12 叱	**SHITSU, shika(ru)** – scold, reprimand 叱責　*shisseki*　reproach, reprimand　　　666 叱咤　*shitta*　scold; spur on 叱りつける/付ける　*shikaritsukeru*　scold/rebuke severely　192 叱り飛ばす　*shikaritobasu*　blow up at, bawl out　　　539

1324

呪

3d5.11

口 儿
/24 16

呪

JU – spell, curse, incantation **noro(u)** – curse

呪文	jumon	spell, curse, magic formula	111
呪術	jujutsu	incantation, sorcery, magic	187
呪物	jubutsu	fetish	79

1325

呼

3d5.4

口 十 儿
/24 12 16

呼

KO, yo(bu) – call, send for, invite, name

点呼	tenko	roll call	169
呼応	koō	act in concert	846
呼び声	yobigoe	a call, cry, shout	759
呼び出す	yobidasu	call out/up/forth, summon	53
呼び戻す	yobimodosu	call back, recall	1304

1326

吹

3d4.3

口 攵
/24 49

吹

SUI, fu(ku) – blow

鼓吹	kosui	inspire, instill	1200
吹雪	fubuki	snowstorm	979
吹き出し	fukidashi	blowoff, bleeder (valve); speech balloon	53
吹き飛ばす	fukitobasu	be blown away	539
吹き出物	fukidemono	skin rash, spots, pimple	53, 79

1327

吸

3d3.5

口 力 丨
/24 8 2

吸

KYŪ, su(u) – suck in, inhale, smoke

呼吸	kokyū	breathing	1325
吸入	kyūnyū	inhale	52
吸引	kyūin	absorb (by suction)	216
吸収	kyūshū	absorb	770
吸い取り紙	suitorigami	blotting paper	65, 180

1328

及

0a3.24

力 丨
8 2

及

KYŪ, oyo(bu) – reach, amount to, extend to, match, equal
oyo(bosu) – exert **oyo(bi)** – and, as well as

普及	fukyū	spread, come into wide use	1223
及第点	kyūdaiten	passing mark/grade	408, 169
言及	genkyū	refer to, mention	66
言い及ぶ	iioyobu	refer to, touch upon	66

1329

扱

3c3.5

扌 力 丨
/23 8 2

扱

atsuka(u) – handle, treat, deal with

取り扱う	toriatsukau	treat, deal with, handle	65
取り扱い方	toriatsukaikata	how to handle	65, 70
取(り)扱(い)注意	toriatsukai chūi	Handle with Care	65, 358, 132
客扱い	kyakuatsukai	hospitality, service to customers	651

1330

柵

4a5.4

木 艹 冂
/41 32 20

柵

SAKU – fence, lattice

| 鉄柵 | tessaku | iron railing/fence | 312 |
| 城柵 | jōsaku | castle palisade/stockade | 733 |

	1331	**ZETSU, shita** – tongue
舌	3d3.9 口 十 丨 /24 12 2 舌	舌戦 *zessen* verbal warfare, war of words 301 弁舌 *benzetsu* eloquence, tongue, speech 724 毒舌 *dokuzetsu* venomous tongue, malicious remarks 531 二枚舌 *nimaijita* forked tongue, duplicity 3, 1211 舌打ち *shitauchi* clicking one's tongue, tsk, tch 1059

	1332	**KATSU** – tie together, fasten
括	3c6.12 扌 口 十 /23 24 12 括	一括 *ikkatsu* lump together, summarize 2 総括 *sōkatsu* generalization, summarization 710 包括的 *hōkatsuteki* comprehensive, general, sweeping 819, 210

	1333	**KEN, kinu** – silk
絹	6a7.3 糸 月 口 /61 43 24 絹	人絹 *jinken* artificial silk, rayon 1 絹布 *kenpu* silk fabric, silk 688 絹糸 *kenshi, kinuito* silk thread 242 絹織物 *kinuorimono* silk fabrics 693, 79 絹針 *kinubari* needle for silk 341

	1334	**KŌ** – agree to, consent
肯	4b4.11 月 丄 亠 /43 13 11 肯	肯定 *kōtei* affirmation, affirmative 356 首肯 *shukō* assent, consent 148

	1335	**KYŌ, obiya(kasu), odo(kasu), odo(su)** – threaten
脅	2g8.2 力 月 /8 43 脅	脅迫 *kyōhaku* threat, intimidation 1233 脅迫状 *kyōhakujō* threatening letter 1233, 636 脅し文句 *odoshimonku* threatening words 111, 337

	1336	**waki** – side, flank; supporting role
脇	4b6.3 月 力 /43 08 脇	脇役 *wakiyaku* supporting role 376 脇腹 *wakibara* one's side, flank; illegitimate child 1345 脇目 *wakime* looking aside; onlooker's eyes 55 脇目も振らず *wakime mo furazu* without looking aside, 55, 984 脇見 *wakimi* look aside/away ⌐wholehartedly 63

	1337	**KEN, kata** – shoulder
肩	4m4.1 戸 月 /40 43 肩	肩章 *kenshō* epaulet, shoulder pips 876 比肩 *hiken* rank (with), be comparable (to) 812 肩書き *katagaki* one's title, degree 131 肩身が広い *katami ga hiroi* feel proud 59, 707 肩代わり *katagawari* take-over, transfer (of business) 256

	1338	**HAI, se** – back, height **sei** – height, stature **somu(ku)** – act contrary (to) **somu(keru)** – avert, turn away
	4b5.15	背景 *haikei* background — 872
背	月 ⼾ 一 /43 13 1	背信 *haishin* breach of faith, betrayal, infidelity — 157
	背	背中 *senaka* the back — 28
		背広 *sebiro* business suit — 707

	1339	**SEKI** – spine
	4b6.13	脊柱 *sekichū* spinal cord — 608
脊	月 亻 二 /43 03 4	
	脊	

	1340	**KOTSU, hone** – bone
	4b6.14	骨格 *kokkaku* skeleton, framework — 653
骨	月 冂 一 /43 20 1	頭骨 *tōkotsu* skull — 276
	骨	骨子 *kosshi* essential part, main points — 103
		鉄骨 *tekkotsu* steel frame — 312
		骨惜しみ *honeoshimi* avoid effort, spare oneself — 779

	1341	**KATSU, KOTSU, sube(ru)** – slide, glide, slip **name(raka)** – smooth
	3a10.6	滑走路 *kassōro* runway — 435, 151
滑	氵 月 冂 /21 43 20	滑稽 *kokkei* comic, funny; joke — 1084
	滑	円滑 *enkatsu* smooth, harmonious, amicable — 13
		滑り台 *suberidai* (playground) slide — 501

	1342	**I** – stomach
	5f4.3	胃病 *ibyō* stomach disorder/trouble — 381
胃	田 月 /58 43	胃酸 *isan* stomach acid — 525
	胃	胃癌 *igan* stomach cancer
		胃下垂 *ikasui* gastric ptosis — 31, 1117
		胃弱 *ijaku* weak digestion, indigestion, dyspepsia — 218

	1343	**FU** – the skin
	2m13.1	皮膚 *hifu* the skin — 1008
膚	田 月 厂 58 43 18	皮膚病 *hifubyō* skin disease — 1008, 381
	膚	皮膚移植 *hifu ishoku* skin graft/transplant — 1008, 1173, 430
		完膚なきまで *kanpu-naki made* thoroughly, completely — 623

	1344	**CHŌ** – intestines, entrails
	4b9.8	胃腸 *ichō* stomach and intestines — 1342
腸	月 日 彡 /43 42 27	大腸 *daichō* large intestine, colon — 26
	腸 腸	腸閉塞 *chōheisoku* intestinal obstruction, ileus — 401, 465
		断腸の思い *danchō no omoi* heartrending grief — 1063, 99

1345

腹

腹

4b9.4 田
月 日 攵
/43 42 49

FUKU, hara – belly, heart, mind

切腹	*seppuku*	disembowelment, harakiri	39
立腹	*rippuku*	anger, offense	121
空腹	*kūfuku*	empty belly, hunger	140
脇腹	*wakibara*	one's side, flank; illegitimate child	1336
太っ腹	*futoppara*	magnanimous; bold, daring	639

1346

肝

肝

4b3.2 田
月 一 一
/43 14 1

KAN – liver; important **kimo** – liver; heart, spirit, courage

肝硬変	*kankōhen*	cirrhosis of the liver	1046, 257
肝油	*kan'yu*	cod-liver oil	365
肝要	*kan'yō*	important, vital	425
肝心	*kanjin*	main, vital, essential	97
肝っ玉	*kimottama*	pluck, courage, grit	295

1347

胆

胆 膽

4b5.6 田
月 日 一
/43 42 1

TAN – gallbladder; courage

胆石	*tanseki*	gallstone	78
大胆	*daitan*	bold, daring	26
胆力	*tanryoku*	courage, mettle	100
落胆	*rakutan*	discouragement, disappointment	858

1348

担

担 擔

3c5.20 田
扌 日 一
/23 42 1

TAN – carry, bear **katsu(gu)** – shoulder, put on, lift; choose (someone); trick (someone); be superstitious **nina(u)** – carry on the shoulder, bear, take on

担当	*tantō*	being in charge, overseeing	77
負担	*futan*	burden, load, liability	519
担保	*tanpo*	a security, guarantee	498

1349

恒

恒 恆

4k6.5 田
心 日 一
/51 42 1

KŌ – always, constant, fixed

恒久	*kōkyū*	permanence, perpetuity	1273
恒星	*kōsei*	fixed star, sidereal	743
恒心	*kōshin*	constancy, steadfastness	97
恒例	*kōrei*	established practice, custom	622
恒常	*kōjō*	constancy	506

1350

垣

垣

3b6.5 田
土 日 一
/22 42 1

kaki – fence, hedge

石垣	*ishigaki*	stone wall	78
竹垣	*takegaki*	bamboo fence	129
生け垣	*ikegaki*	hedge	44
垣根	*kakine*	fence, hedge	314
垣間見る	*kaimamiru*	peek in, get a glimpse	43, 63

1351

肺

肺

4b5.9 田
月 巾 亠
/43 26 11

HAI – lung

肺病	*haibyō*	lung/pulmonary disease	381
肺結核	*haikekkaku*	pulmonary tuberculosis	494, 1275
肺癌	*haigan*	lung cancer	
肺活量	*haikatsuryō*	lung capacity	237, 417
肺肝	*haikan*	lungs and liver; one's innermost heart	1346

脑	**1352** 4b7.7 ⊞ 月 小 冂 /43 35 20 脑 腦	**NŌ** – brain	
		頭脳 *zunō* brains, intelligence	276
		脳下垂体 *nōka suitai* pituitary gland	31, 1117, 61
		脳卒中 *nōsotchū* stroke, cerebral apoplexy	801, 28
		洗脳 *sennō* brainwashing	705
		首脳会談 *shunō kaidan* summit conference	148, 158, 603

悩	**1353** 4k7.11 ⊞ 忄 小 冂 /51 35 20 悩 惱	**NŌ, naya(mu)** – be troubled, be distressed, suffer **naya(masu)** – afflict, beset, worry	
		苦悩 *kunō* affliction, distress, agony	554
		悩殺 *nōsatsu* enchant, captivate	585
		伸び悩む *nobinayamu* continue stagnant, level off	1160
		恋の悩み *koi no nayami* the torments of love	258

凶	**1354** 0a4.19 ⋯ 冂 十 20 12 凶	**KYŌ** – evil, misfortune	
		凶作 *kyōsaku* bad harvest	361
		凶行 *kyōkō* violence, crime, murder	68
		凶悪 *kyōaku* heinous, brutal	304
		凶器 *kyōki* murder/lethal weapon	536
		吉凶 *kikkyō* good or ill luck, fortune	1194

離	**1355** 8c10.3 ⊞ 隹 亠 冂 /73 11 20 離	**RI, hana(reru)** – leave, separate **hana(su)** – separate, keep apart	
		分離 *bunri* separation, secession, segregation	38
		離婚 *rikon* divorce	576
		離反 *rihan* estrangement, alienation, breakaway	324
		離陸 *ririku* (airplane) takeoff	657
		切り離す *kirihanasu* cut off, sever	39

刈	**1356** 2f2.1 ⊞ 刂 亠 /16 12 刈	**ka(ru)** – mow, clip, cut (hair)	
		刈り入れ *kariire* harvest, reaping	52
		稲刈り *inekari* rice reaping/harvesting	1283
		刈り取る *karitoru* mow, cut down	65
		刈り込む *karikomu* cut, trim, prune	790
		芝刈り機 *shibakariki* lawn mower	250, 537

胸	**1357** 4b6.9 ⊞ 月 勹 冂 /43 15 20 胸	**KYŌ, mune, [muna]** – breast, chest	
		胸像 *kyōzō* (sculptured) bust	753
		胸部 *kyōbu* the chest	86
		胸囲 *kyōi* girth/circumference of the chest	1257
		胸中 *kyōchū* one's bosom, heart, feelings	28
		度胸 *dokyō* courage, daring, nerve	378

胞	**1358** 4b5.5 ⊞ 月 弓 勹 /43 28 15 胞	**HŌ** – sac, sheath; placenta, afterbirth	
		細胞 *saibō* cell	708
		単細胞 *tansaibō* one cell, single cell	300, 708
		脳細胞 *nōsaibō* brain cell	1352, 708
		胞子 *hōshi* spore	103
		同胞 *dōhō* brethren, countrymen	198

1359

抱

3c5.15 □
扌 弓 宀
/23 28 15
抱

HŌ, da(ku) – hug, hold in one's arms, embrace **ida(ku)** – embrace; harbor (feelings) **kaka(eru)** – carry in one's arms; have (dependents); employ, hire

包括	hōkatsu	inclusive, comprehensive	819, 1332
介抱	kaihō	nursing, care	460
抱き合う	dakiau	embrace each other	159

1360

蔵

3k12.17 □
艹 戈 厂
/32 52 20
蔵 藏

ZŌ, kura – storehouse, warehouse, repository

冷蔵庫	reizōko	refrigerator	851, 844
蔵書	zōsho	collection of books, one's library	131
貯蔵	chozō	storage	775
地蔵	Jizō	(a Buddhist guardian deity of children)	118
武蔵	Musashi	(ancient kuni)	1071

1361

臓

4b15.2 □
月 戈 艹
/43 52 32
臓 臟

ZŌ – internal organs

内臓	naizō	internal organs, viscera	84
臓器	zōki	internal organs, viscera	536
心臓	shinzō	the heart	97
肺臓	haizō	the lungs	1351
肝臓	kanzō	the liver	1346

1362

賢

7b9.2 □
貝 冂 又
/68 20 9
賢

KEN, kashiko(i) – wise, intelligent

賢明	kenmei	wise, intelligent	18
先賢	senken	wise men of old, ancient sages	50
賢人	kenjin	wise man, sage, the wise	1
賢母	kenbo	wise mother	112
悪賢い	warugashikoi	sly, wily, cunning	304

1363

堅

3b9.13 □
土 丨丨 又
/22 20 9
堅

KEN, kata(i) – firm, hard, solid

堅実	kenjitsu	solid, sound, reliable	203
堅固	kengo	strong, solid, steadfast	1004
中堅	chūken	mainstay, backbone, nucleus	28
堅持	kenji	hold fast to, adhere to	458
手堅い	tegatai	firm, solid, dependable	57

1364

緊

6a9.17 □
糸 冂 又
/61 20 9
緊

KIN – hard, tight

緊張	kinchō	tension	1158
緊迫	kinpaku	tension	1233
緊急	kinkyū	emergency	303
緊縮	kinshuku	contraction; austerity	1162
緊密	kinmitsu	close, tight	822

1365

腎

4b9.11 □
月 冂 又
/43 20 9
腎

JIN – kidney

腎臓	jinzō	kidney	1361
腎石、腎結石	jinseki, jinkesseki	kidney stone	78, 494, 78
肝腎	kanjin	main, vital, essential	1346
肝腎要な点	kanjin-kaname na ten	an essential/a crucial point	1346, 425, 169

1366 覧
5c12.7
貝 門 ⼍
68 20 15
覧 覽

RAN – see, look at

展/博覧会	ten/hakurankai	an exhibition	1181, 611, 158
遊覧船	yūransen	excursion ship, pleasure boat	1040, 377
観覧	kanran	viewing, inspection	614
一覧表	ichiranhyō	table, list	2, 272
回覧	kairan	read-and-pass-on circulation	90

1367 繁
6a10.13
糸 攵 女
/61 49 25
繁

HAN – fullness, luxury, frequency

繁栄	han'ei	prosperity	736
繁盛	hanjō	prosperity; success	732
繁華街	hankagai	thriving shopping area	1122, 186

1368 巨
2t2.2
匸
/20
巨

KYO – large, gigantic

巨大	kyodai	huge, gigantic, enormous	26
巨人	kyojin	giant	1
巨漢	kyokan	very large man, big fellow	565
巨星	kyosei	giant star; great/prominent man	743
巨万	kyoman	millions, immense amount	16

1369 距
7d5.8
𧾷 匸
/70 20
距

KYO – distance

距離	kyori	distance	1355
短/近距離	tan/kinkyori	short distance	215, 452, 1355
長/遠距離	chō/enkyori	long distance	95, 453, 1355
中距離競走	chūkyori kyōsō	medium-distance race	28, 1355, 871, 435

1370 拒
3c5.29
扌 匸
/23 20
拒

KYO, koba(mu) – refuse, decline

拒否	kyohi	denial, refusal; rejection, veto	1316
拒否権	kyohiken	right of veto	1316, 335
拒絶	kyozetsu	refusal, rejection, repudiation	755

1371 胎
4b5.10
月 口 厶
/43 24 17
胎

TAI – womb, uterus; fetus

胎盤	taiban	placenta, afterbirth	1149
母胎	botai	mother's womb/uterus	112
受胎	jutai	conception	260
胎児	taiji	embryo, fetus	1280
胎動	taidō	fetal movement, quickening	231

1372 怠
4k5.21
心 口 厶
/51 24 17
怠

TAI, nama(keru) – be idle, be lazy, neglect **okota(ru)** – neglect, be remiss in, default on

怠業	taigyō	work stoppage, slowdown strike	279
倦怠	kentai	fatigue, weariness	
怠け者	namakemono	idler, lazybones	164

腰	**1373**	**YŌ, koshi** – pelvic region, loins, hips, small of back	
	4b9.3	腰部　*yōbu*　pelvic region, waist, hips, loins	86
	月 口 女	腰布　*koshinuno*　loincloth	688
	/43 24 25	弱腰　*yowagoshi*　without backbone, faint-hearted	218
		物腰　*monogoshi*　one's manner, demeanor	79
	腰	本腰　*hongoshi*　serious, in earnest	25

宛	**1374**	**a(teru)** – address (a letter)	
	3m5.9	宛名　*atena*　address, addressee	82
	宀 夕 阝	宛先　*atesaki*　address	50
	/33 30 7	名宛人　*naatenin*　addressee	82, 1
	宛		

怨	**1375**	**EN, ON** – bear a grudge, resent, reproach	
	4k5.20	怨恨　*enkon*　grudge, malice, hatred	1879
	心 夕 阝	怨念　*onnen*　grudge, enmity	588
	/51 30 7		
	怨		

腕	**1376**	**WAN, ude** – arm; ability, talent, skill	
	4b8.6	手腕　*shuwan*　ability, capability, skill	57
	月 宀 夕	腕力　*wanryoku*　physical strength	100
	/43 33 30	腕前　*udemae*　ability, skill	47
		腕輪　*udewa*　bracelet	1221
	腕	腕時計　*udedokei*　wristwatch	42, 340

肘	**1377**	**hiji** – elbow	
	4b3.3	肘掛け　*hijikake*　arm (of a chair)	1559
	月 寸	肘掛け椅子　*hijikake-isu*　armchair	1559, 2048, 103
	/43 37	肘鉄　*hijitetsu*　rebuff, rejection	312
		肘鉄砲　*hijideppō*　rebuff, rejection	312, 1894
	肘		

臆	**1378**	**OKU** – timidity; conjecture	
	4b13.3	臆病　*okubyō*　cowardly, timid	381
	月 立 日	臆測　*okusoku*　speculation, conjecture	620
	/43 54 42		
	臆		

胴	**1379**	**DŌ** – torso, trunk	
	4b6.10	胴体　*dōtai*　the body, torso; fuselage	61
	月 口 冂	胴回り　*dōmawari*　one's girth	90
	/43 24 20	胴上げ/揚げ　*dōage*　hoist (someone) shoulder-high	32, 641
	胴		

1380

洞

3a6.25 ⃞
氵 冂 冂
/21 24 20

洞

DŌ – penetrate; cave **hora** – cave

洞察	*dōsatsu*	insight, discernment	629
空洞	*kūdō*	cave, cavity	140
洞穴	*dōketsu, horaana*	cave	921

1381

我

0a7.10 ⋯
戈 艹 丨
52 12 2

我

GA, ware, wa – I, self, my, our

自我	*jiga*	self, ego	62
我利	*gari*	one's own interests, self-interest	329
無我	*muga*	self-effacement, selflessness	93
我勝ち	*waregachi*	each striving to be first	518
我が国	*wagakuni*	our country	40

1382

餓

8b7.1 ⃞
食 戈 艹
/77 52 12

餓

GA – starve

| 餓死 | *gashi* | starve to death | 85 |

1383

飢

8b2.1 ⃞
食 冂
/77 20

飢

KI, u(eru) – starve

飢餓	*kiga*	hunger, starvation	1382
飢饉	*kikin*	famine	
飢え死に	*uejini*	starve to death	85

1384

机

4a2.4 ⃞
木 冂
/41 20

机

KI, tsukue – desk

机上	*kijō*	desk-top, academic, theoretical	32
机上の空論	*kijō no kūron*	mere academic theorizing	
			32, 140, 293
事務机	*jimuzukue*	office desk	80, 235
書き物机	*kakimono-zukue*	writing desk	131, 79

1385

肌

4b2.2 ⃞
月 冂
/43 20

肌

hada – the skin; type, character

肌色	*hadairo*	flesh-colored	204
地肌	*jihada*	one's skin; surface of the ground	118
肌着	*hadagi*	underwear	668
肌触り	*hadazawari*	the touch, feel	894
肌寒い	*hadasamui, hadazamui*	chilly	464

1386

倉

2a8.37 ⋯
食 口
77 24

倉

SŌ, kura – storehouse, warehouse, depository

倉庫	*sōko*	warehouse	844
倉荷	*kurani*	warehouse goods	393
鎌倉	*Kamakura*	(town, Kanagawa Prefecture)	1130

	1387	**SŌ, tsuku(ru)** – create	
創	2f10.3 ⊞	創造　　sōzō　creation	704
	リ 食 ㅂ	創作　　sōsaku　(literary) creation	361
	/16　77　24	創立　　sōritsu　establishment, founding	121
	創	独創　　dokusō　originality, creativity	219
		創価学会　Sōka Gakkai　(Buddhist sect)	427, 109, 158

	1388	**FUN, furu(u)** – be enlivened, rouse up	
奮	5f11.2 ⊟	興奮　　kōfun　excitement	369
	田 隹 大	奮発　　funpatsu　exertion, strenuous effort; splurge	96
	/58　73　34	奮起　　funki　rouse oneself (to action), be inspired	374
	奮	奮って　furutte　energetically, willingly	

	1389	**DATSU, uba(u)** – snatch away, take by force; captivate	
奪	8c6.4 ⊟	争奪（戦）sōdatsu(sen)　a competition, struggle	302, 301
	隹 寸 大	略奪　　ryakudatsu　plunder, pillage, despoliation	860
	/73　37　34	強奪　　gōdatsu　seizure, robbery	217
	奪	奪回 / 還　dakkai/kkan　recapture, retaking	90, 885
		奪い合う　ubaiau　scramble, struggle (for)	159

	1390	**SEKI** – (counter for ships); one (of a pair)	
隻	8c2.1 ⊟	三隻　　sanseki　three ships	4
	隹 又	数隻（の船）sūseki (no fune)　several (ships)	225, 377
	/73　9	隻眼　　sekigan　one-eyed	867
	隻	一隻眼　issekigan　discerning eye	2, 867
		隻手　　sekishu　one-armed	57

	1391	**GO** – defend, protect	
護	7a13.3 ⊞	弁護士　bengoshi　lawyer, attorney	724, 581
	言 隹 艹	保護　　hogo　protection, preservation	498
	/67　73　32	援護　　engo　support, backing, protection	1139
	護	介護保険　kaigo hoken　nursing-care insurance	460, 498, 542
		護符　　gofu　amulet, talisman	514

	1392	**KAKU, e(ru)** – obtain, acquire, gain	
獲	3g13.1 ⊞	獲得　　kakutoku　acquire, gain, win	375
	犭 隹 艹	捕獲　　hokaku　catch; capture, seizure	911
	/27　73　32	漁獲　　gyokaku　fishing, a catch of fish	712
	獲	乱獲　　rankaku　excessive fishing/hunting	702
		獲物　　emono　game, a catch, trophy	79

	1393	**KAKU** – harvest	
穫	5d13.4 ⊞	収穫　　shūkaku　harvest, harvesting	770
	禾 隹 艹	収穫高　shūkakudaka　the yield, crop	770, 190
	/56　73　32	収穫期　shūkakuki　harvest time	770, 456
	穫		

串	**1394** 0a7.13 ⋯ 口 丨 24　2 串	**kushi** – spit, skewer 串刺し　*kushizashi*　skewering　902 玉串　*tamagushi*　branch of a sacred tree (in Shintō)　295
患	**1395** 4k7.18 心 口 丨 /51　24　2 患	**KAN, wazura(u)** – be ill, suffer (from) 患者　*kanja*　a patient　164 急患　*kyūkan*　person suddenly taken ill　303 患部　*kanbu*　affected/diseased part　86 長患い　*nagawazurai*　long illness　95
呂	**1396** 3d4.16 口 丨 /24　2 呂	**RO** – tone 語呂　*goro*　the sound, euphony　67 語呂合わせ　*goroawase*　play on words, pun　67, 159 (お)風呂　*(o)furo*　bath; bathtub　⌐wrapper　29 風呂敷　*furoshiki*　(square of) cloth for wrapping, cloth　29, 1544 伊呂波　*iroha*　iroha (Japanese syllabary); ABC's, basics　677
侶	**1397** 2a7.13 亻 口 丨 /3　24　2 侶	**RYO** – companion, follower 伴侶　*hanryo*　companion　1066 人生の伴侶　*jinsei no hanryo*　life partner, one's spouse 1, 44, 1066
看	**1398** 5c4.4 目 扌 /55　23 看	**KAN** – see, watch; look after, care for 看護婦　*kangofu*　nurse　1391, 316 看病　*kanbyō*　tending the sick, nursing　381 看守　*kanshu*　(prison) guard　499 看破　*kanpa*　see through, detect　676 看板　*kanban*　sign, signboard　1090
催	**1399** 2a11.12 亻 催 山 /3　73　36 催	**SAI, moyō(su)** – hold, sponsor; feel 開催　*kaisai*　hold (a meeting)　400 主催　*shusai*　sponsor, promote　155 催眠　*saimin*　hypnosis　868 催涙ガス　*sairuigasu*　tear gas　1305 催し物　*moyōshimono*　(program of) entertainments　79
症	**1400** 5i5.4 疒 亠 一 /60　38　1 症	**SHŌ** – illness, symptoms 病症　*byōshō*　nature of a disease　381 症状、症候　*shōjō, shōkō*　symptom　636, 974 不眠症　*fuminshō*　insomnia　94, 868 敗血症　*haiketsushō*　blood poisoning, sepsis　520, 803 自閉症　*jiheishō*　autism　62, 401

	1401	**EKI, [YAKU]** – epidemic	
	5i4.2	疫病　ekibyō　epidemic, plague	381
	疒 冂 又	悪疫　akueki　plague, pestilence, epidemic	304
	/60　20　9	防疫　bōeki　prevention of epidemics	522
	疫	検疫　ken'eki　quarantine	540
		免疫　men'eki　immunity	746

	1402	**TSŪ** – pain; penetrating **ita(mu)** – feel painful, hurt **ita(meru)** – hurt, cause pain **ita(i)** – painful	
	5i7.7	苦痛　kutsū　pain	554
	疒 月 一	頭痛　zutsū　headache	276
	/60　43　1	痛飲　tsūin　drink heavily, carouse	323
	痛	痛手　itade　severe wound; hard blow	57

	1403	**HI, tsuka(reru)** – get tired, become exhausted	
	5i5.2	疲労　hirō　fatigue, weariness	233
	疒 厂 又	気疲れ　kizukare　mental fatigue/exhaustion	134
	/60　18　9	疲れ果てる　tsukarehateru　be completely exhausted	496
	疲	お疲れ様　otsukaresama　Thank you (for your tiring work).	407

	1404	**RYŌ** – heal, cure, treat medically	
	5i12.3	治療　chiryō　medical treatment, therapy	502
	疒 火 日	医療　iryō　medical treatment	220
	/60　44　42	診療　shinryō　diagnosis and treatment	1277
	療	施療　seryō　free medical treatment	1041
		療養所　ryōyōsho, ryōyōjo　sanatorium, nursing home	406, 153

	1405	**RYŌ** – hostel, dormitory	
	3m12.2	学生寮　gakuseiryō　dormitory	109, 44
	宀 火 日	社員寮　shainryō　company dormitory	308, 163
	/33　44　42	独身寮　dokushinryô　dormitory for bachelors	219, 59
	寮	寮生　ryōsei　student living in a dormitory	44

	1406	**RYŌ** – an official; companion	
	2a12.4	官僚　kanryō　bureaucrat	326
	亻 火 日	官僚主義　kanryō shugi　bureaucratism,	326, 155, 291
	/3　44　42	閣僚　kakuryō　cabinet member/minister ⌊bureaucracy	856
	僚	同僚　dōryō　colleague, coworker	198
		僚友　ryōyū　fellow worker, colleague	264

	1407	**RYŌ** – clear	
	5c12.4	明瞭　meiryō　clear, distinct, obvious	18
	日 火 小	不明瞭　fumeiryō　unclear, indistinct	94, 18
	/42　44　35	一目瞭然　ichimoku ryōzen　clear at a glance, obvious	2, 55, 662
	瞭		

1408

丈

0a3.26 ...

十 丶
12　2

丈

JŌ – (unit of length, about 3 m); high, strong *take* – height, length

丈夫	*jōbu* strong and healthy; strong, durable	315
偉丈夫	*ijōfu* great man	1096, 315
気丈	*kijō* stout-hearted, courageous	134
八丈島	*Hachijō-jima* (island south of Tōkyō)	10, 286
背丈	*setake* one's height	1338

1409

壮

2b4.2 ⫿

冫 土 丨
/5　22　2

壮 壯

SŌ – manly, strong, in one's prime

壮大	*sōdai* magnificent, grand, imposing	26
強壮	*kyōsō* strong, robust, husky	217
壮健	*sōken* healthy, hale and hearty	914
悲壮	*hisō* tragic, touching, pathetic	1075
壮年	*sōnen* prime of manhood/life	45

1410

荘

3k6.12 ⊞

艹 土 冫
/32　22　5

荘 莊

SŌ – villa, inn; solemn

別荘	*bessō* country house, cottage, villa	267
山荘	*sansō* mountain villa	34
荘重	*sōchō* solemn, sublime, impressive	227
荘厳	*sōgon* sublime, grand, majestic	841

1411

装

5e6.8 ⊞

衤 土 冫
/57　22　5

装 裝

SŌ, SHŌ, yosō(u) – wear, feign, pretend, disguise oneself as

服装	*fukusō* style of dress, attire	696
変装	*hensō* disguise	257
装置	*sōchi* device, apparatus, equipment	432
装飾	*sōshoku* ornament, decoration	1013
武装	*busō* arms, armament	1071

1412

袋

5e5.11 ⊞

衤 戈 亻
/57　52　3

袋

TAI, fukuro – sack, bag

手袋	*tebukuro* glove	57
足袋	*tabi* Japanese socks (worn with kimono)	58
紙袋	*kamibukuro* paper sack/bag	180
袋小路	*fukurokōji* blind alley, cul-de-sac	27, 151
胃袋	*ibukuro* stomach	1342

1413

裂

5e6.7 ⊞

衤 夕 儿
/57　30　16

裂

RETSU, sa(keru) – (intr.) split, tear, rip *sa(ku)* – (tr.) split, tear, rip

分裂	*bunretsu* breakup, dissolution, division	38
破裂	*haretsu* burst, rupture, explode	676
決裂	*ketsuretsu* (negotiations) break down	357
裂け目	*sakeme* a rip, split, crack, fissure	55

1414

烈

4d6.3 ⊞

火 夕 儿
/44　30　16

烈

RETSU – violent, intense

烈震	*resshin* violent earthquake	983
熱烈	*netsuretsu* ardent, fervent, vehement	655
壮烈	*sōretsu* heroic, brave	1409
強烈	*kyōretsu* intense, severe	217
痛烈	*tsūretsu* severe, fierce, bitter	1402

1415

奨

3n10.4 ⊟

⺌ 寸 大
/35 37 34

奨 獎

SHŌ – urge, encourage

奨学金	shōgakukin	a scholarship	109, 23
奨学生	shōgakusei	student on a scholarship	109, 44
勧奨	kanshō	encouragement, promotion	1094
推奨	suishō	recommendation, commendation	1297

1416

灯

4d2.1 ⊞

火 一
/44 14

灯 燈

TŌ, hi – a light, lamp

電灯	dentō	electric light/lamp	108
灯火	tōka	a light, lamplight	20
街灯	gaitō	streetlight	186
船灯	sentō	ship light	377
灯台	tōdai	lighthouse	501

1417

澄

3a12.11 ⊟

氵 火 口
/21 44 24

澄 澂

CHŌ, su(mu) – become clear, clear **su(masu)** – make clear, perk (one's ears), look prim/unconcerned/nonchalant

清澄	seichō	clear, limpid, lucid, serene	671
澄み切る	sumikiru	become perfectly clear	39
澄み渡る	sumiwataru	be crystal clear	379
澄まし顔	sumashigao	unconcerned look	277

1418

災

4d3.3

火 丨
/44 2

災

SAI, wazawa(i) – misfortune, disaster

災難	sainan	mishap, accident, calamity	566
災害	saigai	disaster, accident	527
火災	kasai	fire, blaze, conflagration	20
天災	tensai	natural disaster/calamity	141
震災	shinsai	earthquake disaster	983

1419

炎

4d4.4

火
/44

炎

EN, honō – flame

火炎瓶	kaenbin	firebomb, Molotov cocktail	20, 1217
炎症	enshō	inflammation	1400
肺炎	haien	pneumonia	1351
脳炎	nōen	brain inflammation, encephalitis	1352
中耳炎	chūjien	inflammation of the middle ear	28, 56

1420

淡

3a8.15 ⊞

氵 火
/21 44

淡

TAN, awa(i) – light, faint, pale, transitory

濃淡	nōtan	light and shade, shading	987
淡彩	tansai	light coloring	959
冷淡	reitan	indifferent, apathetic	851
淡水	tansui	fresh water	21
淡雪	awayuki	light snow	979

1421

滅

3a10.26 ⊟

氵 戈 火
/21 52 44

滅

METSU, horo(biru) – fall to ruin, perish, die out **horo(bosu)** – ruin, destroy, overthrow, annihilate

破滅	hametsu	ruin, downfall, collapse	676
滅亡	metsubō	downfall, destruction	684
消滅	shōmetsu	extinction, disappearance	864
幻滅	genmetsu	disillusionment	1291

1422

威

4n5.2
戈 女 一
/52 25 1

威

I – authority, dignity, majesty; threat

権威	ken'i	authority	335
威勢	isei	power, influence; high spirits	656
威厳	igen	dignity, stateliness	841
威信	ishin	prestige, dignity	157
脅威	kyōi	menace, threat, danger	1335

1423

励

2g5.4
力 厂 一
/8 18 14

励 勵

REI – encouragement, diligence **hage(mu)** – be diligent
hage(masu) – encourage, urge on

奨励	shōrei	encouragement, promotion	1415
激励	gekirei	urging, encouragement	1056
精励	seirei	diligence, industriousness	670
励行	reikō	strict enforcement	68

1424

厄

2p2.3
厂 阝
/18 7

厄

YAKU – misfortune, disaster

厄介	yakkai	troublesome, burdensome; help, care	460
厄介者	yakkaimono	a dependent; burden	460, 164
厄日	yakubi	unlucky day; critical day	5
厄年	yakudoshi	unlucky year; critical age	45
厄払い	yakubarai/harai	exorcism	591

1425

圧

2p3.1
厂 土
/18 22

圧 壓

ATSU – pressure

圧力	atsuryoku	pressure	100
圧迫	appaku	pressure, oppression	1233
気圧	kiatsu	atmospheric pressure	134
抑圧	yokuatsu	restraint, suppression	1100
圧倒的	attōteki	overwhelming	927, 210

1426

灰

2p4.1
厂 火
/18 44

灰

KAI, hai – ash

灰燼	kaijin	ashes	
石灰	sekkai	(chemical) lime	78
灰皿	haizara	ashtray	1148
火山灰	kazanbai	volcanic ash	20, 34
灰色	haiiro	gray	204

1427

炭

3o6.5
屮 火 厂
/36 44 18

炭

TAN – coal **sumi** – charcoal

石炭	sekitan	coal	78
木炭	mokutan	charcoal	22
採炭	saitan	coal mining	960
炭素	tanso	carbon	271
炭酸	tansan	carbonic acid	525

1428

岩

3o5.10
屮 石
/36 53

岩

GAN, iwa – rock

岩石	ganseki	rock	78
火成岩	kaseigan	igneous rock	20, 261
岩塩	gan'en	rock salt	1152
岩屋	iwaya	cave, cavern	167
岩登り	iwanobori	rock climbing	991

1429

沖

3a4.5 □
氵口丨
/21 24 2
沖 沖

CHŪ, oki – open sea, offing

沖積世、沖積期　*chūsekisei, chūsekiki*　the alluvial epoch
667, 252, 667, 456
沖合　*iokiai*　open sea, offshore　159

1430

仲

2a4.7 □
亻口丨
/3 24 2
仲

CHŪ, naka – relationship, terms

仲裁　*chūsai*　arbitration　1175
仲介　*chūkai*　mediation　460
伯仲　*hakuchū*　be nearly equal, evenly matched　1234
仲良く　*nakayoku*　on good terms, like good friends　321
仲人　*nakōdo*　go-between, matchmaker　1

1431

忠

4k4.6 □
心口丨
/51 24 2
忠

CHŪ – loyalty, faithfulness

忠実　*chūjitsu*　faithful, devoted, loyal　203
忠義　*chūgi*　loyalty　291
忠誠　*chūsei*　loyalty, allegiance　731
忠告　*chūkoku*　advice, admonition　703
忠臣蔵　*Chūshingura*　(the 47 Rōnin story)　854, 1360

1432

縫

6a9.15 □
糸夊辶
/61 49 19
縫

HŌ, nu(u) – sew

裁縫　*saihō*　sewing　1175
縫合　*hōgō*　a suture, stitch　159
天衣無縫　*ten'i-muhō*　of flawless beauty, perfect　141, 690, 93
縫い目　*nuime*　seam, stitch　55
仮縫い　*karinui*　temporary sewing, basting, fitting　1092

1433

峰

3o7.6 □
山夊十
/36 49 12
峰 峯

HŌ, mine – peak, summit

連峰　*renpō*　mountain range　446
高峰　*kōhō*　lofty peak　190
霊峰　*reihō*　sacred mountain　1225

1434

峠

3o6.3 □
山上下
/36 13 14
峠

tōge – mountain pass; crisis, height

峠道　*tōgemichi*　road through a mountain pass　149
峠を越す　*tōge o kosu*　cross a pass　1038
十国峠　*Jikkoku Tōge*　(pass in Hakone)　12, 40

1435

峡

3o6.1 □
山大儿
/36 34 16
峡 峽

KYŌ – gorge, ravine

山峡　*sankyō*　(mountain) gorge　34
峡谷　*kyōkoku*　gorge, ravine, canyon　664
海峡　*kaikyō*　strait, channel, narrows　117
峡湾　*kyōwan*　fjord　681

	1436	**KYŌ, sema(i)** – narrow, small (in area) **seba(maru)** – (intr.) narrow, contract **seba(meru)** – (tr.) narrow, contract
狭	3g6.2 □	狭量　*kyōryō*　narrow-minded　　417
	犭 大 儿	偏狭　*henkyō*　narrow-minded, parochial　⌐pectoris 1214
	/27 34 16	狭心症　*kyōshinshō*　stricture of the heart, angina　97, 1400
	狭 狹	狭苦しい　*semakurushii*　cramped　　554

	1437	**KYŌ, hasa(mu)** – put between, interpose **hasa(maru)** – get between, get caught/ hemmed/sandwiched between
挟	3c6.1 □	挟撃　*kyōgeki*　pincer attack　　1054
	扌 大 亻	挟み撃ち　*hasamiuchi*　pincer attack　　1054
	/23 34 3	挟み込む　*hasamikomu*　put between, insert　　790
	挟 挾	挟み上げる　*hasamiageru*　pick up (with chopsticks)　32

	1438	**KEN, [KON]** – present, offer
献	3g9.6 □	献金　*kenkin*　gift of money, contribution　　23
	犭 十 冂	献血　*kenketsu*　blood donation　　803
	/27 12 20	献上　*kenjō*　presentation　　32
	献 獻	文献　*bunken*　the literature, documentary records　111
		献立　*kondate*　menu; arrangements, plan, program　121

	1439	**FUKU, fu(su)** – bend down, lie down/prostrate **fu(seru)** – cast down (one's eyes); turn over, cover, put over, conceal
伏	2a4.1 □	降伏　*kōfuku*　surrender, capitulation　　977
	亻 犭	伏兵　*fukuhei*　an ambush　　798
	/3 27	潜伏　*senpuku*　hide; be dormant, latent　　967
	伏	伏線　*fukusen*　foreshadowing　　299

	1440	**oka** – hill
岡	2r6.2 □	静岡　*Shizuoka*　(city, Okayama-ken)　　674
	冂 ㎜ 儿	盛岡　*Morioka*　(city, Morioka-ken)　　732
	/20 36 16	岡山　*Okayama*　(city, Okayama-ken)　　34
	岡	長岡　*Nagaoka*　(city; family name)　　95
		岡本　*Okamoto*　(family name)　　25

	1441	**KYŪ, oka** – hill
丘	0a5.12 ⊟	砂丘　*sakyū*　sand dune　　1204
	斤 一	
	50 1	
	丘	

	1442	**GAKU, take** – mountain, peak
岳	3o5.12 ⊟	山岳　*sangaku*　mountains　　34
	㎜ 斤 一	山岳部　*sangakubu*　mountaineering club　　34, 86
	/36 50 1	岳父　*gakufu*　father of one's wife　　113
	岳 嶽	谷川岳　*Tanigawa-dake*　(mountain about 150 km north of Tōkyō)　　664, 33

匠	**1443** 2t4.2 匚 斤 /20 50 匠	**SHŌ** – artisan, workman; idea, design

巨匠　　kyoshō　　(great) master　　1368
名匠　　meishō　　master craftsman　　82
師匠　　shishō　　master, teacher　　415
宗匠　　sōshō　　master, teacher　　626
意匠　　ishō　　a design　　132

奇	**1444** 3d5.17 口 大 一 /24 34 14 奇 啇	**KI** – strange, curious

好奇心　　kōkishin　　curiosity　　104, 97
奇妙　　kimyō　　strange, curious, odd　　1209
奇術　　kijutsu　　conjuring, sleight of hand　　187
奇病　　kibyō　　strange disease　　381
奇数　　kisū　　odd number　　225

寄	**1445** 3m8.8 宀 大 口 /33 34 24 寄	**KI** – depend on; give **yo(ru)** – approach, draw near, meet, drop in **yo(seru)** – bring near, push aside, gather together, send

寄付　　kifu　　contribution, donation　　192
寄宿舎　　kishukusha　　dormitory　　179, 805
寄生　　kisei　　parasitism　　44
立ち寄る　　tachiyoru　　drop in, stop (at)　　121

埼	**1446** 3b8.8 土 大 口 /22 34 24 埼	**sai** – cape, promontory

埼玉県　　Saitama-ken　　Saitama Prefecture　　295, 194

崎	**1447** 3o8.3 山 大 口 /36 34 24 崎 嵜	**saki** – cape, promontory, headland, point (of land)

長崎　　Nagasaki　　(city on western coast of Kyūshū)　　95
宮崎　　Miyazaki　　(city on southern coast of Kyūshū)　　734

阜	**1448** 2k6.3 十 尸 门 /12 40 20 阜	**FU** – hill, mound

埠頭　　futō　　wharf　　276
岐阜県　　Gifu-ken　　Gifu Prefecture　　892, 194

岬	**1449** 3o5.4 山 日 丨 /36 42 2 岬	**misaki** – promontory, headland, point (of land)

宗谷岬　　Sōya-misaki　　(northern tip of Hokkaidō)　　626, 664
知床岬　　Shiretoko-misaki　　(eastern tip of Hokkaidō)　　214, 845
潮岬　　Shio-no-misaki　　(southern tip of Kii Peninsula)　　476
足ずり岬　　Ashizuri-misaki　　(southern tip of Shikoku)　　58

1450

曽

2o9.3 ⊞

田 日 儿
58 42 16

曽

SŌ, ZO – once, formerly, before

曽孫	sōson	great-grandchild	932
曽祖父	sōsofu	great-grandfather	632, 113
曽祖母	sōsobo	great-grandmother	632, 112
曽祖父母	sōsofubo	great-grandparents	632, 113, 112
未曽有	mizou	unprecedented, unheard-of	306, 265

1451

贈

7b11.2

貝 田 日
/68 58 42

贈

ZŌ, [SŌ], oku(ru) – give, present, bestow

贈与（証書）	zōyo (shōsho)	gift (certificate)	548, 493, 131
寄贈	kizō, kisō	presentation, donation, contribution	1445
贈答	zōtō	exchange of gifts	160
贈り物	okurimono	gift, present	79
贈り主	okurinushi	sender (of a gift)	155

1452

憎

4k11.7

心 田 日
/51 58 42

憎

ZŌ, niku(mu) – hate **niku(i), niku(rashii)** – hateful, horrible, repulsive **niku(shimi)** – hatred, animosity

愛憎	aizō	love and hate; partiality	259
憎悪	zōo	hatred	304
憎まれっ子	nikumarekko	bad/naughty boy	103
憎まれ口	nikumareguchi	offensive/malicious remarks	54

1453

僧

2a11.7

亻 田 日
/3 58 42

僧

SŌ – Buddhist priest/monk

僧侶	sōryo	(Buddhist) priest, monk, bonze	1397
僧正	sōjō	Buddhist high priest, bishop	275
高僧	kōsō	high/exemplary priest	190
小僧	kozō	young priest; apprentice; boy	27
僧院	sōin	temple; monastery	624

1454

層

3r11.2

尸 田 日
/40 58 42

層

SŌ – layer, level

上層	jōsō	upper layer/classes/floors	32
多層	tasō	multilayer	229
層雲	sōun	stratus (cloud)	646
読者層	dokushasō	class/level of readers	244, 164
階層	kaisō	social stratum, class	597

1455

悦

4k7.15 ⊞

心 日 儿
/51 24 16

悦

ETSU – joy

喜悦	kietsu	joy, delight	1196
悦楽	etsuraku	joy, pleasure, gaiety	359
法悦	hōetsu	religious exultation; ecstasy	123
満悦	man'etsu	delighted, very satisfied	201
悦に入る	etsu ni iru	be pleased (with)	52

1456

閲

8e7.2 ▢

門 日 儿
/75 24 16

閲

ETSU – inspection, review

閲覧	etsuran	perusal, inspection, reading	1366
閲覧室	etsuranshitsu	reading room	1366, 166
校閲	kōetsu	revision (of a manuscript)	115
検閲	ken'etsu	censorship	540
閲歴	etsureki	one's career/personal history	489

脱	**1457** 4b7.8 月 日 儿 /43 24 16 脱	**DATSU** – omit, escape **nu(gu)** – take off (clothes) **nu(geru)** – come off, slip off (footwear/clothing)
		脱衣所 *datsuisho, datsuijo* changing/dressing room 690, 153
		脱線 *dassen* derailment; digression 299
		離脱 *ridatsu* secession, breakaway 1355
		脱税 *datsuzei* tax evasion 403

鋭	**1458** 8a7.12 金 日 儿 /72 24 16 鋭	**EI, surudo(i)** – sharp
		鋭利 *eiri* sharp 329
		鋭気 *eiki* spirit, mettle, energy 134
		精鋭 *seiei* elite, choice 670
		新鋭 *shin'ei* fresh, new 174
		鋭角 *eikaku* acute angle 481

克	**1459** 2k5.1 十 日 儿 /12 24 16 克	**KOKU** – conquer
		克服 *kokufuku* conquest, subjugation 696
		克己 *kokki* self-denial, self-control 371
		克明 *kokumei* faithful, conscientious 18

忙	**1460** 4k3.2 忄 亠 丨 /51 11 2 忙	**BŌ, isoga(shii)** – busy, be very occupied
		多忙 *tabō* busy, hectic 229
		繁忙 *hanbō* (very) busy 1367
		忙殺される *bōsatsu sareru* be busily occupied 585

忘	**1461** 2j5.4 亠 心 丨 /11 51 2 忘	**BŌ, wasu(reru)** – forget
		健忘（症） *kenbō(shō)* forgetfulness 914, 1400
		忘恩 *bōon* ingratitude 564
		忘年会 *bōnenkai* year-end party 45, 158
		忘れ物 *wasuremono* article left behind 79
		度/胴忘れ *do/dōwasure* forget for the moment 378, 1379

盲	**1462** 2j6.6 亠 目 丨 /11 55 2 盲	**MŌ** – blind
		盲人 *mōjin* blind person, the blind 1
		盲目 *mōmoku* blindness 55
		色盲 *shikimō* color blindness 204
		文盲 *monmō* illiteracy 111
		盲腸 *mōchō* caecum, appendix 1344

妄	**1463** 2j4.6 亠 女 丨 /11 25 2 妄	**MŌ, BŌ** – incoherent, reckless, false
		迷妄 *meimō* illusion, fallacy 998
		妄想 *mōsō* wild fancy, foolish fantasy, delusion 147
		妄信 *mōshin, bōshin* blind belief, overcredulity 157
		被害妄想 *higai mōsō* delusions of persecution, paranoia 1009, 527, 147

荒	**1464** 3k6.18 ▤ 艹 亠 儿 /32 11 16 荒	**KŌ, ara(i)** – rough, wild, violent **a(reru)** – get rough/stormy, run wild, go to ruin **a(rasu)** – devastate, lay waste

荒廃　　kōhai　　desolation, devastation　　　　　　　992
荒野　　kōya, areno　　wilderness, wasteland　　　　　236
荒れ狂う　　arekuruu　　rage, run amuck　　　　　　904
荒仕事　　arashigoto　　heavy work, hard labor　　333, 80

慌	**1465** 4k9.10 心 艹 亠 /51 32 11 慌	**KŌ, awa(teru)** – get flustered, be in a flurry, panic **awa(tadashii)** – bustling, flurried, confused

大慌て　　ōawate　　great haste　　　　　　　　　　　26
慌て者　　awatemono　　absentminded person, scatterbrain　164

福	**1466** 4e9.1 礻 田 口 /45 58 24 福	**FUKU** – fortune, blessing, wealth, welfare

幸福　　kōfuku　　happiness　　　　　　　　　　　　697
祝福　　shukufuku　　blessing　　　　　　　　　　　870
福音　　fukuin　　the Gospel; good news　　　　　　347
福引き　　fukubiki　　lottery, raffle　　　　　　　　216
七福神　　Shichifukujin　　the Seven Gods of Good Fortune　9, 310

幅	**1467** 3f9.2 ▦ 巾 田 口 /26 58 24 幅	**FUKU, haba** – width, breadth, range; influence

振幅　　shinpuku　　amplitude　　　　　　　　　　984
大幅　　ōhaba　　broad; large, wholesale, substantial　26
幅の広い　　haba no hiroi　　wide, broad　　　　707
横幅　　yokohaba　　breadth, width　　　　　　　795
幅が利く　　haba ga kiku　　be influential　　　329

班	**1468** 4f6.3 ▥ 王 儿 /46 16 班	**HAN** – squad, group

首班　　shuhan　　head, chief　　　　　　　　　　148
班長　　hanchō　　squad/group leader　　　　　　95
救護班　　kyūgohan　　relief squad　　　　738, 1391
班点　　hanten　　spot, speckle, dot　　　　　169

斑	**1469** 4f8.3 ▥ 王 亠 艹 /46 11 12 斑	**HAN** – spot

斑点　　hanten　　spot, speck　　　　　　　　　169
斑紋　　hanmon　　spot, speckle　　　　　　　1547

藩	**1470** 3k15.4 ▤ 艹 米 田 /32 62 58 藩	**HAN** – feudal clan/lord

藩主　　hanshu　　lord of a feudal clan　　　　　155
藩学　　hangaku　　samurai school for clan children　109
廃藩置県　　haihan-chiken　　abolition of clans and establishment
　　　　　　　of prefectures (in 1871)　　　　992, 432, 194

	1471	**SHIN** – hearing, investigation, trial
審	3m12.1	審査 *shinsa* examination, investigation — 634
	宀 米 田	審議 *shingi* deliberation, consideration — 292
	/33 62 58	審問 *shinmon* trial, hearing, inquiry — 162
		不審 *fushin* doubt, suspicion — 94
	審	審判 *shinpan* decision, judgment, refereeing — 1065

	1472	**RYO** – thought, consideration
慮	2m13.2	考慮 *kōryo* consideration, reflection — 550
	田 心 厂	遠慮 *enryo* reserve, restraint, hesitation — 453
	58 51 18	配慮 *hairyo* consideration, solicitude — 524
		憂慮 *yūryo* apprehension, concern — 1073
	慮	焦慮 *shōryo* impatience; worry — 1036

	1473	**RYO** – captive
虜	2m11.2	捕虜 *horyo* prisoner of war — 911
	厂 田 十	捕虜収容所 *horyo shūyōjo* POW camp — 911, 770, 665, 153
	18 58 12	
	虜	

	1474	**YŪ** – brave, courageous **isa(mu)** – be in high spirits
勇	2g7.3	勇気 *yūki* courage — 134
	力 田 一	武勇 *buyū* bravery, valor — 1071
	/8 58 1	勇士 *yūshi* brave warrior, hero — 581
		勇退 *yūtai* retire voluntarily ⌈going too far 865
	勇	勇み足 *isamiashi* (lose a sumo match by) overstepping; 58

	1475	**YŪ, wa(ku)** – well up, gush out; grow
湧	3a9.31	湧出 *yūshutsu* gush forth/out, well/bubble up — 53
	氵 田 力	湧き水 *wakimizu* sprlng water — 21
	/21 58 8	
	湧	

	1476	**YŪ** – male, brave; great **osu, o** – male
雄	8c4.1	英雄 *eiyū* hero — 354
	隹 十 厶	雄弁 *yūben* eloquence — 724
	/73 12 17	雄大 *yūdai* grand, magnificent — 26
		雄鳥 *ondori* rooster, male bird — 285
	雄	両雄 *ryōyū* two great men (rivals) — 200

	1477	**SHI, mesu, me** – female
雌	8c6.1	雌伏 *shifuku* remain in obscurity, lie low — 1439
	隹 ⺊ 丨	雌雄 *shiyū* male and female; victory or defeat — 1476
	/73 13 2	雌犬 *mesuinu* a bitch — 280
		雌牛 *meushi* (female) cow — 281
	雌	雌花 *mebana* female flower — 255

紫	**1478** **SHI, murasaki** – purple, violet
6a6.15	紫外線　*shigaisen*　ultraviolet rays　　83, 299
糸 `├` `│`	紫煙　*shien*　tobacco smoke, blue cigarette smoke　941
/61　13　2	紫雲　*shiun*　auspicious purple clouds　　646
紫	山紫水明　*sanshi-suimei*　beautiful scenery　34, 21, 18
	紫色　*murasakiiro*　purple　　204

祉	**1479** **SHI** – happiness
4e4.1	福祉　*fukushi*　welfare, well-being　　1466
ネ `├` `亠`	福祉国家　*fukushi kokka*　welfare state　1466, 40, 165
/45　13　11	社会福祉　*shakai fukushi*　social/public welfare　308, 158, 1466
祉	

裕	**1480** **YŪ** – surplus
5e7.3	余裕　*yoyū*　room, margin, leeway; composure　1109
ネ `火` `口`	富裕　*fuyū*　wealth, affluence　　726
/57　44　24	裕福　*yūfuku*　wealth, affluence　　1466
裕	余裕しゃくしゃく　*yoyū-shakushaku*　calm and composed　1109

溶	**1481** **YŌ, to(keru)** – (intr.) melt, dissolve **to(kasu), to(ku)** – (tr.) melt, dissolve
3a10.15	溶解　*yōkai*　(intr.) melt, dissolve　　482
氵 `火` `宀`	溶岩　*yōgan*　lava　　1428
/21　44　33	溶液　*yōeki*　solution　　480
溶	水溶性　*suiyōsei*　water-soluble　　21, 98

析	**1482** **SEKI** – divide, take apart, analyze
4a4.12	分析　*bunseki*　analysis　　38
木 斤	分析化学　*bunseki kagaku*　analytical chemistry　38, 254, 109
/41　50	市場分析　*shijō bunseki*　market analysis　181, 154, 38
析	精神分析学　*seishin-bunseki-gaku*　psychoanalysis　670, 310, 38, 109

折	**1483** **SETSU** – break; fold; turn (left/right) **o(ru)** – (tr.) fold; break; bend **o(reru)** – (intr.) break; be folded; yield, compromise; turn (left/right) **ori** – occasion, opportunity
3c4.7	右折禁止　*usetsu kinshi*　No Right Turn　76, 491, 485
扌 斤	曲折　*kyokusetsu*　twists and turns, complications　367
/23　50	折り紙　*origami*　paper folding; paper for origami　180
折	

誓	**1484** **SEI, chika(u)** – swear, pledge, vow
7a7.17	誓約　*seiyaku*　oath, vow, pledge　　211
言 斤 扌	宣誓　*sensei*　oath　　635
/67　50　23	祈誓　*kisei*　oath, vow　　631
誓	誓文　*seimon*　written oath　　111

1485	**SEI, yu(ku), i(ku)** – die, pass away	
2q7.8 ⬜	逝去　seikyo　death	420
辶 斤 扌	急逝　kyūsei　sudden/untimely death	303
/19　50　23		
逝		

1486	**TETSU** – wisdom	
3d7.13 ⬛	哲学　tetsugaku　philosophy	109
口 斤 扌	哲学者　tetsugakusha　philosopher	109, 164
/24　50　23	賢哲　kentetsu　wise man, sage	1362
	先哲　sentetsu　wise man of the past, sage of old	50
哲	哲人　tetsujin　wise man, philosopher	1

1487	**KEI** – open; say	
3d8.17 ⬛	啓発　keihatsu　enlightenment, edification	96
口 攵 尸	啓示　keiji　revelation	625
/24　49　40	天啓　tenkei　divine revelation	141
	拝啓　haikei　Dear Sir:	1264
啓	啓蒙　keimō　enlightenment, instruction	

1488	**ZAN** – (for) a while	
4c11.3 ⬜	暫時　zanji　(for) a short time	42
日 車 斤	暫定　zantei　tentative, provisional	356
/42　69　50		
暫		

1489	**ZEN** – gradually, gradual advance	
3a11.2 ⬛	漸次　zenji　gradually, step by step	385
氵 車 斤	漸進　zenshin　gradual progress	443
/21　69　50	漸増　zenzō　increase gradually	725
	漸減　zengen　decrease gradually, taper off	728
漸		

1490	**SEKI** – repel, reject	
0a5.18 ⬜	排斥　haiseki　rejection, exclusion, boycott	1077
斤 丶	排斥運動　haiseki undō　agitation for expulsion/exclusion	
50　2		1077, 445, 231
斥		

1491	**SO, utta(eru)** – sue, complain of, appeal (to)	
7a5.2 ⬛	起訴　kiso　prosecution, indictment	374
言 斤 丶	提訴　teiso　bring before (the court), file (suit)	638
/67　50　2	告訴　kokuso　complaint, accusation, charges	703
	敗訴　haiso　losing a suit/case	520
訴	勝訴　shōso　winning a suit/case	518

1492

訟

7a4.6

言 儿 厶
/67 16 17

訟

SHŌ – accuse

訴訟	soshō	lawsuit, litigation	1491
刑事訴訟	keiji soshō	criminal suit	908, 80, 1491
民事訴訟	minji soshō	civil suit	177, 80, 1491
離婚訴訟	rikon soshō	suit for divorce	1355, 576, 1491
訴訟費用	soshō hiyō	costs of litigation	1491, 762, 107

1493

陣

2d7.1

阝 車
/7 69

陣

JIN – battle array; camp; brief time, sudden

陣営	jin'ei	camp, encampment	735
陣地	jinchi	(military) position	118
陣容	jin'yō	battle array, lineup	665
退陣	taijin	decampment, withdrawal	865
陣痛	jintsū	labor (pains)	1402

1494

陳

2d8.2

阝 木 日
/7 41 42

陳

CHIN – state, explain; show; old

陳列	chinretsu	display, exhibit	621
陳情	chinjō	petition, appeal	209
陳述	chinjutsu	statement, declaration	1000
陳謝	chinsha	apology	⌐regeneration 923
新陳代謝	shinchin taisha	metabolism;	174, 256, 923

1495

棟

4a8.3

木 日
/41 42

棟

TŌ – building; ridge of a roof **mune, [muna]** – ridge of a roof; (counter for buildings)

上棟式	jōtōshiki	roof-laying ceremony	32, 534
病棟	byōtō	(hospital) ward	381
別棟	betsumune	separate building	267
棟上げ式	muneageshiki	roof-laying ceremony	32, 534

1496

壊

3b13.3

土 衤 日
/22 57 55

壊 壞

KAI – break **kowa(reru)** – get broken, break **kowa(su)** – break, tear down, destroy, damage

壊滅	kaimetsu	destruction, annihilation	1421
破壊	hakai	destruction, wrecking	676
崩壊	hōkai	collapse, breakdown, cave-in	1174
壊血病	kaiketsubyō	scurvy	803, 381

1497

懐

4k13.9

心 日 衤
/51 55 57

懐 懷

KAI – pocket; nostalgia **natsu(kashii)** – dear, fond, longed-for **natsu(kashimu)** – yearn for **natsu(ku)** – take kindly (to) **natsu(keru)** – win over, tame **futokoro** – breast (pocket)

| 懐中電灯 | kaichū dentō | flashlight | 28, 108, 1416 |
| 述懐 | jukkai | (relating) one's thoughts and reminiscences | 1000 |

1498

快

4k4.2

心 大 一
/51 34 1

快

KAI, kokoroyo(i) – pleasant, delightful

快適	kaiteki	comfortable, pleasant, agreeable	421
快活	kaikatsu	cheerful, lighthearted	237
全快	zenkai	complete recovery (from illness)	89
快晴	kaisei	fine weather, clear skies	673
快速	kaisoku	high-speed; express (train)	511

1499

慢

4k11.8 田
心　日　日
/51　55　42
慢

MAN – lazy; boasting

我慢	gaman	exercise patience, tolerate	1381
自慢	jiman	pride, boasting, vanity	62
怠慢	taiman	negligence, dereliction	1372
緩慢	kanman	slow, sluggish	1140
慢性	mansei	chronic	98

1500

漫

3a11.11 田
氵　日　日
/21　55　42
漫

MAN – aimless, random, involuntarily

漫画	manga	cartoon, comic book/strip	343
漫談	mandan	chat, idle talk	603
散漫	sanman	vague, loose, desultory	781
漫然	manzen	random, rambling, discursive	662
漫才	manzai	comic (stage) dialogue	560

1501

寧

3m11.8 目
宀　日　心
/33　55　51
寧

NEI – peaceful, quiet; rather, preferably

丁寧	teinei	polite; careful, meticulous	184
安寧	annei	public peace/order	105

1502

刃

0a3.22 ⋯
力　丶
8　2
刃　刃

JIN, ha – blade, edge

白刃	hakujin	naked blade, drawn sword	205
刃先	hasaki	edge (of a blade)	50
刃物	hamono	edged tool, cutlery	79
諸刃の剣	moroha no tsurugi	double-edged sword	880, 900

1503

忍

4k3.3 目
心　力　丶
/51　8　2
忍

NIN, shino(bu) – bear, endure; lie hidden; avoid (being seen)
shino(baseru) – hide, conceal

忍苦	ninku	endurance, stoicism	554
残忍	zannin	brutal, ruthless	661
忍者	ninja	(feudal) professional spy/assassin	164
忍び足	shinobiashi	stealthy steps	58

1504

耐

2r7.1 田
冂　寸　丂
/20　37　14
耐

TAI, ta(eru) – endure, bear, withstand; be fit, competent

忍耐	nintai	perseverance, patience	1503
耐熱	tainetsu	heatproof, heat-resistant	655
耐火	taika	fireproof, fire-resistant	20
耐久	taikyū	endurance; durability	1273
耐乏生活	taibō seikatsu	austerity	767, 44, 237

1505

需

8d6.1 目
雨　丅　冂
/74　14　20
需

JU – request, need, demand

需要(供給)	juyō (kyōkyū)	demand (and supply)	425, 197, 346
需給	jukyū	supply and demand	346
特需	tokuju	special procurement (in wartime)	282
軍需品	gunjuhin	military supplies, materiel	444, 230
必需品	hitsujuhin	necessary articles, necessities	529, 230

	1506	**JU** – Confucianism; Confucian scholar
儒	2a14.1	儒教　jukyō　Confucianism　245
	イ 需 一	儒学　jugaku　Confucianism　109
	/3　74　14	儒学者　jugakusha　Confucian scholar　109, 164
	儒	儒家　juka　Confucian scholar, Confucianist　165

	1507	**TAN** – end, tip; correct **hashi** – end, edge **hata** – side, edge, nearby **ha** – edge
端	5b9.2	極端　kyokutan　extreme, ultra-　336
	立 山 一	異端　itan　heresy, heathenism　1106
	/54　36　14	道端　michibata　roadside, wayside　149
	端	端折る　hashoru　tuck up; cut short, abridge　1483

	1508	**BI** – minute, slight
微	3i10.1	微妙　bimyō　delicate, subtle　1209
	彳 攵 山	微笑　bishō　smile　1299
	/29　49　36	微熱　binetsu　a slight fever　655
	微	微生物　biseibutsu　microorganism, microbe　44, 79
		顕微鏡　kenbikyō　microscope　1227, 882

	1509	**CHŌ** – collect; demand; sign, symptom
徴	3i11.2	徴候　chōkō　sign, indication, symptom　974
	彳 王 攵	象徴　shōchō　symbol　752
	/29　46　49	特徴　tokuchō　distinctive feature　282
	徴	徴税　chōzei　tax collection　403
		徴兵　chōhei　conscription, military service; draftee　798

	1510	**CHŌ, ko(rasu), ko(rashimeru)** – chastise, punish, discipline **ko(riru)** – learn by experience, be taught a lesson, be sick of
懲	4k14.3	懲罰　chōbatsu　disciplinary measure, punishment　907
	心 王 攵	懲役　chōeki　penal servitude, imprisonment　376
	/51　46　49	勧善懲悪　kanzen-chōaku　good over evil, poetic justice
	懲	1094, 1191, 304

	1511	**TETSU** – pierce, go through
徹	3i12.2	徹底的　tetteiteki　thorough　571, 210
	彳 月 攵	貫徹　kantetsu　carry through, accomplish　936
	/29　43　49	徹夜　tetsuya　stay up all night　479
	徹	冷徹　reitetsu　coolheaded, levelheaded　851

	1512	**TETSU** – withdraw, remove
撤	3c12.3	撤回　tekkai　withdraw, retract, rescind　90
	扌 月 攵	撤去　tekkyo　withdraw, evacuate, remove　420
	/23　43　49	撤退　tettai　withdraw, pull out, retreat　865
	撤	撤兵　teppei　withdraw troops, disengage　798
		撤廃　teppai　abolish, do away with, repeal　992

1513
崇

308.9 ⊟
出 礻 宀
/36 45 33
崇

SŪ – respect, revere; lofty, sublime

崇拝	sūhai	worship, adoration	1264
祖先崇拝	sosen sūhai	ancestor worship	632, 50, 1264
崇敬	sūkei	veneration, reverence	718
崇高	sūkō	lofty, sublime, noble	190

1514
模

4a10.16 ⊞
木 日 艹
/41 42 32
模 糢

MO, BO – copy, imitate; model

模様	moyō	pattern, design; appearance; situation	407
模範	mohan	model, exemplar	1143
模型	mokei	(scale) model; a mold	909
模造	mozō	imitation	704
規模	kibo	scale, scope	617

1515
膜

4b10.6 ⊞
月 日 艹
/43 42 32
膜

MAKU – membrane

角膜	kakumaku	cornea	481
鼓膜	komaku	eardrum	1200
処女膜	shojomaku	hymen	1189, 102
腹膜炎	fukumakuen	peritonitis	1345, 1419
結膜炎	ketsumakuen	conjunctivitis, pinkeye	494, 1419

1516
漠

3a10.18 ⊞
氵 日 艹
/21 42 32
漠

BAKU – vague, obscure; desert; wide

砂漠、沙漠	sabaku	desert	1204, 1205
広漠	kōbaku	vast, boundless	707
漠然	bakuzen	vague, hazy, nebulous	662

1517
暮

3k11.14 ⊟
艹 日 六
/32 42 34
暮

BO, ku(reru) – grow dark, come to an end **ku(rasu)** – live

歳暮	seibo	end of the year; year-end gift	487
野暮	yabo	uncouth, rustic, boorish	236
夕暮れ	yūgure	evening, twilight	81
一人暮らし	hitorigurashi	living alone	2, 1

1518
墓

3k10.18 ⊟
艹 日 土
/32 42 22
墓

BO, haka – a grave

墓地	bochi	cemetery	118
墓標	bohyō	grave marker/post	945
墓石	boseki	gravestone	78
墓穴	boketsu	grave (pit)	921
墓参り	hakamairi	visit to a grave	723

1519
募

3k9.23 ⊟
艹 日 六
/32 42 34
募

BO – appeal for, invite, raise **tsuno(ru)** – appeal for, invite, raise, grow

募集	boshū	recruiting, solicitation	intense 442
応募	ōbo	apply for, enlist, enroll	846
応募者	ōbosha	applicant, entrant	846, 164
募金	bokin	fund raising	23
公募	kōbo	offer for public subscription	126

1520

慕

3k11.12
艹 日 心
/32 42 51

慕

BO, shita(u) – yearn for, love dearly, idolize

慕情	bojō	longing, love, affection	209
思慕	shibo	longing (for), deep attachment (to)	99
敬慕	keibo	love and respect	718
恋慕	renbo	love, affection	258
追慕	tsuibo	cherish (someone's) memory, sigh for	1232

1521

幕

3k10.19
艹 日 巾
/32 42 26

幕

MAKU – (stage) curtain; act (of a play) **BAKU** – shogunate

開幕	kaimaku	commencement of a performance	400
序幕	jomaku	opening act, prelude	784
除幕	jomaku	unveiling	1112
内幕	uchimaku, naimaku	behind-the-scenes story	84
幕府	Bakufu	Japan's feudal government, shogunate	513

1522

冥

2i8.2
冂 日 亠
/20 42 11

冥

MEI, MYŌ – realm of the dead; dark

冥土	meido	hades, realm of the dead	24
冥利	myōri	divine favor, providence, luck	329
冥加	myōga	divine protection	722

1523

添

3a8.22
氵 心 大
/21 51 34

添

TEN, so(eru) – add (to), append **so(u)** – accompany

添加物	tenkabutsu	an additive	722
添付	tenpu	attach, append	192
添乗員	tenjōin	tour conductor	532, 163
力添え	chikarazoe	help, assistance	100
付き添い	tsukisoi	attending (someone), escorting	192

1524

恭

3k7.16
艹 心 儿
/32 51 16

恭

KYŌ, uyauya(shii) – respectful, reverent, deferential

恭順	kyōjun	fealty, allegiance	783
恭敬	kyōkei	reverence, respect	718
恭賀新年	kyōga shinnen	Best wishes for a happy New Year.	
			769, 174, 45

1525

洪

3a6.14
氵 艹 儿
/21 32 16

洪

KŌ – flood, inundation; vast

| 洪水 | kōzui | flood, inundation, deluge | 21 |
| 洪積層 | kōsekisō | diluvium, diluvial formation | 667, 1454 |

1526

呉

2o5.7
丶 口 一
/16 24 1

呉

GO – Wu (dynasty of ancient China; Chinese surname)

呉服	gofuku	drapery, dry goods	696
呉服屋	gofukuya	draper's shop, dry-goods dealer	696, 167
呉音	go-on	the Wu reading (an on reading of a kanji)	564
呉越	Go-Etsu	Wu and Yue/Yüeh (rival states of China)	1038
呉越同舟	Go-Etsu dōshū	enemies in the same boat	198, 1145

	1527	**GO** – pleasure, enjoyment
娯	3e7.3	娯楽　*goraku*　amusement, enterainment　　　359 娯楽番組　*goraku bangumi*　entertainment program 359, 185, 424
	女 口 儿 /25　24　16	
	娯	

	1528	**GO, sato(ru)** – perceive, understand, realize, be enlightened
悟	4k7.5	覚悟　*kakugo*　readiness, preparedness, resoluteness　　615 悟り　*satori*　comprehension, understanding; spiritual awakening
	心 口 一 /51　24　14	
	悟	

	1529	**KŌ** – item, clause, paragraph
項	9a3.1	事項　*jikō*　matters, facts; items, particulars　　　80 事項索引　*jikō sakuin*　subject index　　80, 1104, 216 要項　*yōkō*　essential points, gist　　　425 条項　*jōkō*　provision, clause　　　573 項目　*kōmoku*　heading, item　　　55
	頁 工 /76　38	
	項	

	1530	**CHŌ, itadaki** – summit, top **itada(ku)** – be capped with; receive
頂	9a2.1	頂上　*chōjō*　summit, peak, top; climax　　　32 山頂　*sanchō*　summit, mountain top　　　34 頂点　*chōten*　zenith, peak, climax　　　169 絶頂　*zetchō*　peak, height, climax　please (give me)　755 頂戴　*chōdai*　accept, receive; eat and drink, have, enjoy;　1530
	頁 一 /76　14	
	頂	

	1531	**SU** – should, ought, necessary
須	3j9.1	必須　*hissu*　indispensable, essential, compulsory　　529 必須科目　*hissu kamoku*　required subject, compulsory course 必須アイテム　*hissu aitemu*　a must-have item　　529 那須　*Nasu*　(town, Tochigi Pref., center of resort area)　826 恵比須　*Ebisu*　Ebisu (one of the 7 gods of fortune)　1282, 812
	彡 頁 /31　76	
	須	

	1532	**koro** – time, when, about
頃	9a2.2	今頃　*imagoro*　at about this time　　　51 先頃　*sakigoro*　recently, the other day　　　50 近頃　*chikagoro*　recently, nowadays　　　452 頃合い　*koroai*　suitable time; propriety; moderation　159
	頁 匕 /76　13	
	頃	

	1533	**KEI, katamu(ku/keru)** – (intr./tr.) lean, incline, tilt
傾	2a11.3	傾向　*keikō*　tendency, trend; inclination　　　199 傾斜　*keisha*　inclination, slant, slope　　　1116 左傾　*sakei*　leftward leanings, radicalization　　75 傾聴　*keichō*　listen　　　1080 傾倒　*keitō*　devote oneself (to), be absorbed (in)　927
	亻 頁 匕 /3　76　13	
	傾	

浦	**1534** 3a7.2 氵月 十 /21 43 12 浦	**ura** – bay, inlet, seashore 浦波　*uranami*　wave breaking on the beach, breaker　677 津々浦々　*tsutsu-uraura*　throughout the land, the entire country 三浦半島　*Miura hanto*　Miura peninsula (south of Kamakura)　4, 88, 286 浦島太郎　*Urashima Tarō*　(character in a folktale)　286, 639, 1014
哺	**1535** 3d7.4 口 月 十 /24 43 12 哺	**HO** – suckle 哺乳類　*honyūrui*　mammal　969, 226 哺育　*hoiku*　suckle, nurse　246
舗	**1536** 3b12.4 土 月 口 /22 43 24 舖 舗	**HO** – shop, store; pavement 店舗　*tenpo*　shop, store　168 老舗　*shinise, rōho*　long-established store　552 舗装　*hosō*　pave　1411 舗（装）道（路）　*ho(sō) dō(ro)*　paved road/street　1411, 149, 151
捨	**1537** 3c8.26 扌 亼 口 /23 22 24 捨	**SHA, su(teru)** – throw away, abandon, forsake 取捨　*shusha*　adoption or rejection, selection　65 投げ捨てる　*nagesuteru*　throw away　1060 捨て子　*sutego*　abandoned child, foundling　103 見捨てる　*misuteru*　abandon, desert, forsake　63 切り捨てる　*kirisuteru*　cut down; discard, omit　39
拾	**1538** 3c6.14 扌 口 亻 /23 24 3 拾	**SHŪ, hiro(u)** – pick up, find　**JŪ** – ten (in documents) 拾得物　*shūtokubutsu*　an acquisition　375, 79 収拾　*shūshū*　get under control, deal with　770 拾い物　*hiroimono*　something found lying on the ground, a find　79 （金）拾万円　*(kin) jūman en*　(amount of) 100,000 yen　23, 16, 13
滴	**1539** 3a11.14 氵 口 亠 /21 24 11 滴	**TEKI, shizuku** – a drop　**shitata(ru)** – drip, trickle 水滴　*suiteki*　drop of water　21 雨滴　*uteki*　raindrop　30 滴下　*tekika*　drip, trickle down　31 点滴　*tenteki*　falling drop of water, (intravenous) drip　169
摘	**1540** 3c11.5 扌 口 亠 /23 24 11 摘	**TEKI, tsu(mu)** – pick, pluck, nip 摘発　*tekihatsu*　exposure, disclosure　96 摘出　*tekishutsu*　pluck out, extract; expose　53 指摘　*shiteki*　point out　1082 摘要　*tekiyō*　summary, synopsis　425 茶摘み　*chatsumi*　tea picking　251

縛	**1541** 6a10.3 ⊞ 糸 日 寸 /61 42 37 縛	**BAKU, shiba(ru)** – tie up, bind
		束縛　*sokubaku*　restraint, constraint, shackles　510
		捕縛　*hobaku*　capture, apprehension, arrest　911
		呪縛　*jubaku*　a spell　1324
		金縛り　*kanashibari*　be bound; be tied down with money　23
		縛り首　*shibarikubi*　(execution by) hanging　148

薄	**1542** 3k13.11 ⊞ 艹 日 氵 /32 42 21 薄	**HAKU, usu(i)** – thin (paper), weak (tea), light (color) **usu(maru), usu(ragu), usu(reru)** – thin out, fade **usu(meru)** – dilute
		浅薄　*senpaku*　shallow, superficial　660
		薄情　*hakujō*　unfeeling, heartless, coldhearted　209
		薄弱　*hakujaku*　feebleness　218
		薄明　*hakumei*　twilight　18

簿	**1543** 6f13.4 ⊞ ⺮ 日 氵 /66 42 21 簿	**BO** – record book, ledger, register, list
		簿記　*boki*　bookkeeping　372
		帳簿　*chōbo*　account book, ledger　1159
		家計簿　*kakeibo*　housekeeping account book　165, 340
		名簿　*meibo*　list of names, roster　82
		会員名簿　*kaiin meibo*　list of members　158, 163, 82

敷	**1544** 4i11.1 ⊞ 攵 日 攵 /49 42 49 敷	**FU, shi(ku)** – spread, lay, put down
		敷設　*fusetsu*　laying, construction　586
		屋敷　*yashiki*　mansion; residential lot　167
		座敷　*zashiki*　a room, reception room　800
		敷金　*shikikin*　a deposit, security　23
		敷布　*shikifu*　(bed) sheet　688

絞	**1545** 6a6.9 ⊞ 糸 亠 儿 /61 11 16 絞	**KŌ, shi(meru)** – strangle, wring **shi(maru)** – be wrung out, pressed together **shibo(ru)** – wring, squeeze, press, milk
		絞殺　*kōsatsu*　strangle to death; hang　585
		絞首刑　*kōshukei*　(execution by) hanging　148, 908
		お絞り　*oshibori*　wet towel (provided in restaurants)

較	**1546** 7c6.3 ⊞ 車 亠 儿 /69 11 16 較	**KAKU** – compare
		比較　*hikaku*　comparison　812
		比較的　*hikakuteki*　comparatively, relatively　812, 210
		比較級　*hikakukyū*　the comparative (of an adjective)　812, 577
		比較文学　*hikaku bungaku*　comparative literature　812, 111, 109

紋	**1547** 6a4.9 ⊞ 糸 亠 十 /61 11 12 紋	**MON** – (family) crest; (textile) pattern
		紋章　*monshō*　crest, coat of arms　「crest　876
		菊の御紋　*kiku no gomon*　imperial chrysanthemum　483, 721
		紋切り形 / 型　*monkirigata*　conventional pattern　39, 399, 909
		指紋　*shimon*　a fingerprint　1082
		波紋　*hamon*　a ripple　677

	1548	**GA, GE, kiba** – tooth, fang, canine tooth, tusk	
牙	0a4.28 ⋯	歯牙 *shiga* teeth	486
	⼀⼆⼁	象牙 *zōge* ivory	752
	14 11 2	象牙海岸 *Zōge Kaigan* Ivory Coast	752, 117, 595
	牙	毒牙 *dokuga* poison fang; perfidy, nasty trick	531
		牙をむく *kiba o muku* bare one's fangs, snarl (at)	

	1549	**GA, me** – a sprout, bud	
芽	3k5.9	発芽 *hatsuga* germinate, sprout, bud	96
	艹⼅⼆	麦芽 *bakuga* malt	270
	/32 14 11	新芽 *shinme* new bud, sprout, shoot	174
	芽	芽生え *mebae* bud, sprout, seedling	44
		木の芽 *ki no me* leaf bud; Japanese pepper bud	22

	1550	**GA** – elegance, gracefulness	
雅	8c5.1 ▢	優雅 *yūga* elegance, grace, refinement	1074
	隹⼅⼆	風雅 *fūga* elegance, refinement, (good) taste	29
	/73 14 11	雅趣 *gashu* elegance, tastefulness, artistry	1039
	雅	雅楽 *gagaku* ancient Japanese court music	359

	1551	**JA** – evil, wrong	
邪	2d5.8	邪推 *jasui* groundless suspicion, mistrust	1297
	⻖⼅⼆	邪道 *jadō* evil course, vice; heresy	149
	/7 14 11	邪教 *jakyō* heretical religion, heathenism	245
	邪	邪宗 *jashū* heretical sect, heathenism	626
		風邪 *kaze* a cold	29

	1552	**KI, sude (ni)** – already, previously	
既	0a10.5	既成(の)事実 *kisei (no) jijitsu* accomplished fact	261, 80, 203
	食⼅⼆	既製服 *kiseifuku* ready-made clothes	434, 696
	77 14 11	既婚 *kikon* married	576
	既	既報 *kihō* previous report	698
		既往症 *kiōshō* previous illness; medical history	940, 1400

	1553	**GAI** – general, approximate	
概	4a10.2 ▢	概算 *gaisan* rough estimate	760
	木食⼅	概略 *gairyaku* outline, summary	860
	/41 77 14	概括 *gaikatsu* summary, generalization	1332
	概	概況 *gaikyō* general situation, outlook	869
		概念 *gainen* concept	588

	1554	**GAI** – regret, lament, deplore	
慨	4k10.3	慨嘆 *gaitan* regret, lament, deplore	1313
	忄食⼅	感慨 *kangai* deep emotion	262
	/51 77 14	感慨無量 *kangai-muryō* filled with deep emotion	262, 93, 417
	慨		

	1555	**GAI** – shore; end, limit
涯	3a8.33 ⊞	生涯　*shōgai*　a life, one's lifetime　　44
	氵 土 厂	生涯学習　*shōgai gakushū*　lifelong learning　44, 109, 601
	/21　22　18	生涯教育　*shōgai kyōiku*　lifelong education　44, 245, 246
	涯	一生涯　*isshōgai*　one's (whole) life (long)　2, 44
		天涯　*tengai*　horizon; a distant land　141

	1556	**GAI, gake** – cliff
崖	3o8.11	断崖　*dangai*　cliff, precipice　1063
	山 土 厂	崖っぷち　*gakeppuchi*　edge of a cliff; critical situation
	/36　22　18	
	崖	

	1557	**KA** – good, beautiful
佳	2a6.10 ⊞	佳人　*kajin*　beautiful woman, a beauty　1
	亻 土	佳作　*kasaku*　a fine piece of work　361
	/3　22	風光絶佳　*fūkō-zekka*　scenic beauty　29, 138, 755
	佳	佳境　*kakyō*　interesting part, climax (of a story)　883

	1558	**FŪ** – seal **HŌ** – fief
封	3b6.13 ⊞	同封　*dōfū*　enclose (with a letter)　198
	土 寸	封入　*fūnyū*　enclose (with a letter)　52
	/22　37	封書　*fūsho*　sealed letter/document　131
	封	開封　*kaifū*　open (a letter)　400
		封建制度　*hōken seido*　the feudal system　913, 433, 378

	1559	**ka(karu)** – hang; cost, take **ka(keru)** – hang up, put on top of; spend; multiply **kakari** – expenses; tax; relation, connection
掛	3c8.6 ⊞	腰掛け　*koshikake*　seat, bench; stepping-stone　1373
	扌 土 卜	掛け布団　*kakebuton*　quilt, bedspread　688, 500
	/23　22　13	掛け軸　*kakejiku*　hanging scroll　1023
	掛	心掛け　*kokorogake*　intention; attitude; attention　97

	1560	**FU, omomu(ku)** – go, proceed; become
赴	3b6.14 ...	赴任　*funin*　proceed to one's new post　334
	土 卜 亻	赴任地　*funinchi*　one's post/place of appointment　334, 118
	/22　13　3	赴任先　*funinsaki*　one's post/place of appointment　334, 50
	赴	

	1561	**FU** – report of death, obituary
訃	7a2.2 ⊞	訃報　*fuhō*　news of someone's death　698
	言 卜	訃告　*fukoku*　obituary, death notice　703
	/67　13	
	訃	

	1562	**BOKU** – simple, plain	
朴	4a2.3 ☐	素朴 *soboku* simple, unsophisticated	271
	木 /41 13	質朴 *shitsuboku* simplehearted, unsophisticated	176
	朴	朴直 *bokuchoku* simple and honest, ingenuous	429
		純朴 *junboku* simple and honest	996

	1563	**MO, shige(ru)** – grow thick/rank/luxuriantly	
茂	3k5.7 ☐	繁茂 *hanmo* luxuriant growth	1367
	艹 戈 /32 52 2	生い茂る *oishigeru* grow luxuriantly	44
	茂 楙		

	1564	**BETSU, sagesu(mu)** – despise, scorn	
蔑	3k11.11☐	軽蔑 *keibetsu* contempt, scorn, disdain	556
	艹 目 戈 /32 55 52	蔑視 *besshi* look down on, regard with contempt	616
	蔑		

	1565	**BYŌ, nae, [nawa]** – seedling, sapling	
苗	3k5.2 ☐	苗木 *naegi* sapling, seedling, young tree	22
	艹 /32 58	苗床 *naedoko* nursery, seedbed	845
		苗代 *nawashiro* bed for rice seedlings	256
	苗	苗字 *myōji* family name, surname	110

	1566	**BYŌ, ega(ku), ka(ku)** – draw, paint, sketch, depict, portray	
描	3c8.21 ☐	描写 *byōsha* depiction, portrayal, description	549
	扌 田 艹 /23 58 32	心理描写 *shinri byōsha* psychological description	97, 143, 549
		素描 *sobyō* rough sketch	271
	描	絵描き *ekaki* painter, artist	345

	1567	**BYŌ, neko** – cat	
猫	3g8.5 ☐	愛猫 *aibyō* pet/favorite cat	259
	犭 田 艹 /27 58 32	野良猫 *noraneko* stray cat	236, 321
		山猫争議 *yamaneko sōgi* wildcat strike	34, 302, 292
	猫	猫撫声 *nekonadegoe* coaxing voice ⌐in stores	759
		招き猫 *manekineko* porcelain cat beckoning customers	462

	1568	**TEKI, fue** – flute, whistle	
笛	6f5.6 ☐	警笛 *keiteki* alarm whistle; (automobile) horn	719
	⺮ 目 丨 /66 42 2	汽笛 *kiteki* steam whistle	135
		霧笛 *muteki* foghorn	980
	笛	口笛 *kuchibue* (give a) whistle	54
		角笛 *tsunobue* bugle; huntsman's horn	481

	1569	**TŌ, tsutsu** – pipe, tube	
筒	6f6.15 ⺮ 卩 冂 /66 24 20 筒	封筒 *fūtō* envelope	1558
		水筒 *suitō* canteen, flask	21
		円筒（形） *entō(kei)* cylinder	13, 399
		気筒 *kizutsu* (engine) cylinder	134
		竹筒 *takezutsu* bamboo tube	129

	1570	**KA** – (single) object, (counter for inanimate objects)	
箇	6f8.15 ⺮ 卩 十 /66 24 12 箇 ケ	箇所 *kasho* place, part, passage (in a book)	153
		箇条 *kajō* article, provision, item	573
		箇条書き *kajōgaki* an itemization	573, 131
		一箇年 *ikkanen* one year	2, 45

	1571	**KEI, kukI** – stalk, stem	
茎	3k5.23 艹 土 又 /32 22 9 茎 莖	地下茎 *chikakei* underground stem, rhizome	118, 31
		球茎 *kyūkei* (tulip) bulb	739
		陰茎 *inkei* penis	886
		歯茎 *haguki* gums	486

	1572	**KEI** – path; diameter	
径	3i5.5 彳 土 又 /29 22 9 径 徑	直径 *chokkei* diameter	429
		半径 *hankei* radius	88
		口径 *kōkei* caliber	54
		径路 *keiro* course, route, process	151
		直情径行 *chokujō keikō* straightforwardness	429, 209, 68

	1573	**KAI, aya(shii)** – dubious; suspicious-looking; strange, mysterious; poor, clumsy **aya(shimu)** – doubt, be skeptical/surprised, marvel at	
怪	4k5.11 忄 土 又 /51 22 9 怪 恠	怪奇 *kaiki* mysterious, grotesque, eerie	1444
		怪談 *kaidan* ghost story	603
		怪我 *kega* injury, wound	1381
		怪し気 *ayashige* suspicious, questionable, shady	134

	1574	**SEI** – in order, equal	
斉	2j6.5 亠 十 儿 /11 12 16 斉 齊	一斉に *issei ni* all at one, all together	2
		均斉 *kinsei* symmetry, good balance	820

	1575	**SAI** – religious purification; a room	
斎	2j9.6 亠 小 十 /11 35 12 斎 齋	書斎 *shosai* a study, library	131
		斎戒 *saikai* purification	896
		斎戒沐浴 *saikai mokuyoku* ablution, purification	896, 1180

循	**1576** 3i9.6 ⬚ 彳 日 厂 /29 55 18 循	**JUN** – follow; circulate 循環　*junkan*　circulation　　　　　　　　　　884 血液循環　*ketsueki junkan*　blood circulation　803, 480, 884 悪循環　*akujunkan*　vicious circle　　　　　304, 884
孤	**1577** 2c6.2 ⬚ 子 厂 ム /6 18 17 孤	**KO** – lone, alone 孤独　*kodoku*　solitary, lonely　　　　　　　219 孤立　*koritsu*　isolation　　　　　　　　　121 孤島　*kotō*　solitary/desert island　　　　　286 孤客　*kokaku*　solitary traveler　　　　　　651 孤児（院）　*koji(in)*　orphan(age)　　　　1280, 624
弧	**1578** 3h6.2 ⬚ 弓 厂 ム /28 18 17 弧	**KO** – arc 弧状　*kojō*　arc-shaped　　　　　　　　　636 円弧　*enko*　circular arc　　　　　　　　　13 括弧　*kakko*　parentheses ( )　　　　　　1332
従	**1579** 3i7.3 ⬚ 彳 几 一 /29 16 14 従 從	**JŪ, [JU], [SHŌ], shitaga(u)** – obey, comply with, follow **shitaga(eru)** – be attended by; conquer 服従　*fukujū*　obedience, submission　　　　696 盲従　*mōjū*　blind obedience　　　　　　　1462 従来　*jūrai*　up to now, usual, conventional　69 従業員　*jūgyōin*　employee　　　　　　279, 163
縦	**1580** 6a10.2 ⬚ 糸 彳 几 /61 29 16 縦 縱	**JŪ, tate** – lengthwise; height, length; vertical 縦線　*jūsen*　vertical line　　　　　　　　299 放縦　*hōjū*　self-indulgent, dissolute, licentious　521 縦横　*jūō, tateyoko*　length and breadth　　795 縦断　*jūdan*　vertical section; traverse, travel across　1063
為	**1581** 4d5.8 … 灬 十 一 /44 12 1 為 爲	**I** – do 為政者　*iseisha*　statesman, administrator　492, 164 人為的　*jin'iteki*　artificial　　　　　　　1, 210 行為　*kōi*　act, deed; behavior, conduct　　68 無為　*mui*　idleness, inaction　　　　　　93 為替　*kawase*　money order; (foreign) exchange　757
偽	**1582** 2a9.2 ⬚ 亻 灬 十 /3 44 12 偽 僞	**GI** – falsify, deceive, lie **itsuwa(ru)** – lie, misrepresent; feign; deceive **nise** – fake, counterfeit 偽造　*gizō*　forgery　　　　　　　　　　704 偽証　*gishō*　perjury　　　　　　　　　　493 真偽　*shingi*　true or false; truth　　　　428 偽物　*nisemono*　fake, imitation, counterfeit　79

	1583	**JI, ni(ru)** – be similar (to), be like, resemble	
似	2a5.11	類似 *ruiji* resemblance, similarity	226
	イ 丨	相似 *sōji* resemblance, similarity	146
	/3 2	似顔 *nigao* likeness, portrait	277
		空似 *sorani* accidental resemblance	140
	似	似合う *niau* be becoming, suit, go well (with)	159

	1584	**SHIN, kara(i)** – hot, spicy, salty; hard, trying	
辛	5b2.2	辛苦 *shinku* hardships, labor, trouble	554
	立 十	辛酸 *shinsan* hardships, privations	525
	/54 12	辛勝 *shinshō* win after a hard fight	518
		辛抱 *shinbō* patience, perseverance	1359
	辛	辛味 *karami* pungent taste, spiciness	307

	1585	**RATSU** – bitter, severe	
辣	5b9.6	辛辣 *shinratsu* bitter, biting, harsh	1584
	立 木 日	辣腕 *ratsuwan* astute, sharp	1376
	/54 41 24	悪辣 *akuratsu* unscrupulous, wily	304
	辣		

	1586	**SAI** – manage, rule	
宰	3m7.2	主宰 *shusai* superintendence, presiding over	155
	宀 立 十	主宰者 *shusaisha* president, chairman, leader	155, 164
	/33 54 12	宰相 *saishō* prime minister, premier	146
	宰		

	1587	**HEKI, kabe** – wall	
壁	3b13.7	障壁 *shōheki* fence, wall, barrier, obstacle	877
	土 立 尸	防壁 *bōheki* protective wall, bulwark	522
	/22 54 40	岩壁 *ganpeki* rock wall/face	1428
		壁画 *hekiga* fresco, mural	343
	壁	壁紙 *kabegami* wallpaper	180

	1588	**HEKI** – pierced jewel-disk, jewel; splendid	
璧	4f13.2	完璧 *kanpeki* perfect, flawless	623
	王 立 尸	双璧 *sōheki* two great masters, the two greatest	
	/46 54 40	authorities	1701
	璧		

	1589	**HEKI, kuse** – personal habit, quirk, propensity	
癖	5i13.2	性癖 *seiheki* disposition, proclivity	98
	疒 立 尸	悪癖 *akuheki* bad habit	304
	/60 54 40	潔癖 *keppeki* love of cleanliness, fastidiousness	1307
		盗癖 *tōheki* kleptomania	1151
	癖	口癖 *kuchiguse* habit of saying, favorite phrase	54

1590 避 2q13.3 辶 立 尸 /19 54 40 避	**HI, sa(keru)** – avoid 回避 *kaihi* evasion, avoidance ... 90 不可避 *fukahi* unavoidable ... 94, 390 避難 *hinan* refuge, evacuation ... 566 避妊 *hinin* contraception ... 985 避雷針 *hiraishin* lightning rod ... 982, 341
1591 甘 0a5.32 艹 二 32 4 甘	**KAN, ama(i)** – sweet; insufficiently salted; indulgent; over-optimistic **ama(eru)** – coax, wheedle, act spoiled, presume upon (another's) love **ama(yakasu)** – be indulgent 甘味料 *kanmiryō* sweetener ... 307, 319 甘美 *kanbi* sweet, dulcet ... 405 甘言 *kangen* honeyed words, flattery ... 66
1592 紺 6a5.5 糸 艹 二 /61 32 4 紺	**KON** – dark/navy blue 紺色 *kon'iro* dark/navy blue ... 204 濃紺 *nōkon* deep/dark/navy blue ... 987 紺屋 *kon'ya, kōya* dyer, dyer's shop ... 167
1593 某 4a5.33 木 艹 二 /41 32 4 某	**BŌ** – a certain 某所 *bōsho* a certain place ... 153 某氏 *bōshi* a certain person ... 575 某国 *bōkoku* a certain country ... 40 某日 *bōjitsu* a certain day, one day ... 5 何某 *nanibō* a certain person ... 392
1594 謀 7a9.8 言 木 艹 /67 41 32 謀	**BŌ, [MU], haka(ru)** – plan (secretly), devise; deceive 陰謀 *inbō* plot, intrigue, conspiracy ... 886 共謀 *kyōbō* conspiracy, collusion ... 196 主謀者 *shubōsha* ringleader, mastermind ... 155, 164 謀略 *bōryaku* strategem, scheme ... 860 参謀 *sanbō* (general) staff ... 723
1595 媒 3e9.2 女 木 艹 /25 41 32 媒	**BAI** – go-between 触媒 *shokubai* catalyst ... 894 触媒作用 *shokubai sayō* catalytic action ... 894, 361, 107 媒介 *baikai* mediation; matchmaking ... 460 媒介物 *baikaibutsu* a medium; carrier (of a disease) ... 460, 79 霊媒 *reibai* (spiritualistic) medium ... 1225
1596 搾 3c10.9 扌 宀 儿 /23 33 16 搾	**SAKU, shibo(ru)** – squeeze, press, extract, milk 圧搾 *assaku* pressure, compression ... 1425 圧搾器 *assakuki* press, compressor ... 1425, 536 搾乳 *sakunyū* milk (a cow) ... 969 搾取 *sakushu* exploitation ... 65 搾り取る *shiboritoru* press out, extract ... 65

詐	**1597** 7a5.6 ▯ 言 ノー ト /67 15 13 詐	**SA** – lie, deceive	
		詐称　*sashō*　misrepresent oneself	1011
		詐取　*sashu*　fraud, swindle	65

欺	**1598** 4j8.1 ▯ 欠 艹 二 /49 32 4 欺	**GI, azamu(ku)** – deceive, dupe	
		詐欺　*sagi*　fraud	1597
		詐欺師　*sagishi*　swindler	1597, 415

匹	**1599** 2t2.3 ▯ 匚 儿 /20 16 匹	**HITSU** – same kind, comparable; a man **hiki** – (counter for animals); (unit of cloth length, about 21.2 m)	
		匹敵　*hitteki*　be a match (for), comparable (to)	422
		匹夫　*hippu*　man; man of humble position	315
		犬一匹　*inu ippiki*　one dog	280, 2

甚	**1600** 0a9.10 ▯ 艹 二 一 32 4 14 甚	**JIN, hanaha(da/dashii)** – very much, extreme, intense	
		甚大　*jindai*　very great, immense, serious, heavy	26
		激甚　*gekijin*　intense, violent, severe	1056
		幸甚　*kōjin*　very glad, much obliged	697
		甚六　*jinroku*　simpleton, blockhead	8

勘	**1601** 2g9.3 ▯ 力 ＂ 二 /8 32 4 勘	**KAN** – perception, intuition, sixth sense	
		勘定　*kanjō*　counting, accounts, bill	356
		割り勘　*warikan*　splitting the bill equally, Dutch treat	528
		勘弁　*kanben*　pardon, forgive, overlook	724
		勘違い　*kanchigai*　misunderstanding, mistaken idea	833
		勘当　*kandō*　disown, disinherit	77

朱	**1602** 0a6.13 ▯ 木 ノ 41 15 朱	**SHU** – scarlet	
		朱色　*shuiro*　scarlet, cinnabar, vermilion	204
		朱印　*shuin*　red seal	1086
		朱肉　*shuniku*　red ink pad	223
		朱筆を加える　*shuhitsu o kuwaeru*　correct, retouch	130, 722

珠	**1603** 4f6.2 ▯ 王 木 ノ /46 41 15 珠	**SHU** – pearl	
		真珠　*shinju*　pearl	428
		珠玉　*shugyoku*　jewel, gem	295
		珠算　*shuzan*　calculation on the abacus	760
		数珠　*juzu*　rosary	225
		真珠湾　*Shinju-wan*　Pearl Harbor	428, 681

殊	**1604** 0a10.7 木 夕 ﾆ 41 30 15 殊	**SHU, koto (ni)** – especially, in particular 特殊　*tokushu*　special, unique　　282 特殊性　*tokushusei*　special characteristics, peculiarity　282, 98 殊勝　*shushō*　admirable, praiseworthy　518 殊の外　*koto no hoka*　exceedingly, exceptionally　83
瑠	**1605** 4f10.3 王 田 厂 /46 58 18 瑠	**RU** – lapis lazuli; light-blue
璃	**1606** 4f10.5 王 亠 冂 /46 11 20 璃	**RI** – lapis lazuli 瑠璃　*ruri*　lapis lazuli　1605 浄瑠璃　*jōruri*　(type of ballad-drama)　675, 1605
殖	**1607** 5c7.4 目 夕 十 /55 30 12 殖	**SHOKU, fu(eru)** – grow in number, increase **fu(yasu)** – increase 増殖　*zōshoku*　increase, multiply, proliferate　725 生殖　*seishoku*　reproduction, procreation　44 繁殖　*hanshoku*　breeding, reproduction　1367 養殖　*yōshoku*　raising, culture, cultivation　406
迭	**1608** 2q5.2 辶 大 ﾆ /19 34 15 迭	**TETSU** – alternate 更迭　*kōtetsu*　change (in personnel), reshuffle　1045
秩	**1609** 5d5.2 禾 大 ﾆ /56 34 15 秩	**CHITSU** – order, sequence 秩序　*chitsujo*　order, system, regularity　784 安寧秩序　*annei-chitsujo*　peace and order　105, 1501, 784 無秩序　*muchitsujo*　disorder, chaos, confusion　93, 784 秩父　*Chichibu*　(resort area NW of Tōkyō)　113
伐	**1610** 2a4.5 亻 戈 /3 52 伐	**BATSU** – attack; cut down 征伐　*seibatsu*　conquest, subjugation　1166 討伐　*tōbatsu*　subjugation, suppression　1057 殺伐　*satsubatsu*　bloody, savage, warlike, fierce　585 伐採　*bassai*　timber felling, lumbering　960 乱伐　*ranbatsu*　reckless deforestation, overcutting　702

閥	1611 8e6.2 門 戈 亻 /75 52 3 閥	**BATSU** – clique, clan, faction	
		派閥　*habatsu*　clique, faction	934
		財閥　*zaibatsu*　financial combine	562
		軍閥　*gunbatsu*　military clique, the militarists	444
		藩閥　*hanbatsu*　clan, clique, faction	1470
		門閥　*monbatsu*　lineage; distinguished family	161

闘	1612 8e10.2 門 口 寸 /75 24 37 鬪 鬭	**TŌ, tataka(u)** – fight, struggle	
		闘争　*tōsō*　struggle, conflict; strike	302
		戦闘　*sentō*　battle, combat	301
		奮闘　*funtō*　hard fighting, strenuous efforts	1388
		春闘　*shuntō*　spring (labor) offensive	468
		格闘　*kakutō*　hand-to-hand fighting, scuffle	653

頼	1613 9a7.1 頁 木 口 /76 41 24 頼	**RAI, tano(mu)** – ask for, request, entrust (to) **tano(moshii)** – reliable, dependable, promising **tayo(ru)** – rely, depend (on)	
		依頼　*irai*　request; entrust (to); reliance	691
		信頼　*shinrai*　reliance, trust, confidence	157
		頼み込む　*tanomikomu*　earnestly request	790

瀬	1614 3a16.3 氵 頁 木 /21 76 41 瀬	**se** – shallows, rapids	
		浅瀬　*asase*　shoal, shallows, sandbank; ford	660
		早瀬　*hayase*　swift current, rapids	248
		瀬戸際　*setogiwa*　crucial moment, crisis, brink (of war)	152, 628
		瀬戸物　*setomono*　porcelain, china, earthenware	152, 79
		瀬戸内海　*Seto Naikai*　Seto Inland Sea	152, 84, 117

疎	1615 0a11.4 木 口 卜 41 24 13 疎 疎	**SO** – distance **uto(mu)** – shun, neglect, treat coldly **uto(i)** – distant, estranged, know little (of)	
		疎遠　*soen*　estrangement, alienation	453
		疎開　*sokai*　evacuation, removal	400
		空疎　*kūso*　empty, unsubstantial　⌐understanding	140
		(意志の)疎通　*(ishi no) sotsū*　mutual	132, 582, 150

礎	1616 5a13.2 石 木 一 /53 41 14 礎	**SO, ishizue** – cornerstone, foundation (stone)	
		基礎　*kiso*　foundation, basis	457
		基礎工事　*kiso kōji*　foundation work, groundwork	457, 139, 80
		基礎知識　*kiso chishiki*　elementary knowledge	457, 214, 694
		礎石　*soseki*　foundation (stone)	78
		定礎式　*teisoshiki*　laying of the cornerstone	356, 534

疑	1617 2m12.1 匕 矢 乛 /13 34 15 疑	**GI, utaga(u)** – doubt, distrust, be suspicious of	
		疑問　*gimon*　question, doubt, problem	162
		疑惑　*giwaku*　suspicion, distrust, misgivings	1001
		疑獄　*gigoku*　scandal	905
		容疑者　*yōgisha*　a suspect　⌐(session)	665, 164
		質疑応答　*shitsugi-ōtō*　question and answer	176, 846, 160

301

擬	**1618** 3c14.2 ▥ 扌 大 ト /23 34 13 擬	**GI** – imitate 擬人　*gijin*　personification　　　　　　　　　　1 擬音　*gion*　an imitated sound; sound effects　　347 模擬　*mogi*　imitation, simulated　　　　　　　1514 模擬試験　*mogi shiken*　mock/trial examination　1514, 535, 541
凝	**1619** 2b14.1 ▥ 冫 大 ト /5 34 13 凝	**GYŌ, ko(ru)** – get stiff; be engrossed (in); be fastidious, elaborate (about) **ko(rasu)** – concentrate, strain 凝固　*gyōko*　solidification, coagulation, freezing　　1004 凝結　*gyōketsu*　coagulation, curdling, condensation　494 凝視　*gyōshi*　stare at, watch intently　　　　　　616 凝り性　*korishō*　fastidiousness, perfectionism　　　98
擦	**1620** 3c14.5 ▦ 扌 ネ 宀 /23 45 33 擦	**SATSU** – rub **su(ru)** – rub, file **su(reru)** – rub, chafe, become worn; lose one's simplicity 擦過傷　*sakkashō*　an abrasion, scratch　　　　　419, 643 靴擦れ　*kutsuzure*　shoe sore　　　　　　　　　　1124 擦れ違う　*surechigau*　pass by each other　　　　833
撮	**1621** 3c12.13 ▦ 扌 耳 日 /23 65 42 撮	**SATSU** – pick up; summarize **to(ru)** – take (a picture) 撮影　*satsuei*　photography, filming　　　　　　　873 撮影所　*satsueijo*　movie studio　　　　　　　873, 153 夜間撮影　*yakan satsuei*　night photography　479, 43, 873 戸/野外撮影　*ko/ya-gai satsuei*　outdoor photography, 　　　　outdoor shooting　　　　　　152, 236, 83, 873
卑	**1622** 5f4.8 ▤ 田 十 丨 /58 12 2 卑	**HI, iya(shii)** – humble, lowly, base, ignoble, vulgar **iya(shimeru/shimu)** – despise, look down on 卑俗　*hizoku*　vulgar, coarse　　　　　　　　　1178 卑劣漢　*hiretsukan*　mean bastard, low-down skunk　1203, 565 卑語　*higo*　vulgar word/expression　⌈over women　67 男尊女卑　*danson-johi*　predominance of men　101, 717, 102
碑	**1623** 5a9.2 ▥ 石 田 十 /53 58 12 碑	**HI** – tombstone, monument 記念碑　*kinenhi*　monument, memorial　　　　　372, 588 墓碑　*bohi*　tombstone, gravestone　　　　　　　1518 石碑　*sekihi*　tombstone, (stone) monument　　　78 碑文　*hibun*　epitaph, inscription　　　　　　　111
鬼	**1624** 5f5.6 ▤ 田 儿 ム /58 16 17 鬼	**KI** – demon, devil; spirits of the dead **oni** – demon, devil 鬼神　*kijin, kishin, onigami*　fierce god; departed soul　310 餓鬼　*gaki*　hungry ghost; little brat　　　　　　1382 鬼才　*kisai*　genius, man of remarkable talent　　560 鬼ごっこ　*onigokko*　tag; blindman's buff

塊	**1625** 3b10.2 土 田 儿 /22 58 16 塊	**KAI, katamari** – lump, clod, clump

土塊　　dokai　　clod of dirt　　　　　　　　　　　24
金塊　　kinkai　　gold nugget/bar　　　　　　　　　23
肉塊　　nikkai　　piece of meat　　　　　　　　　223
塊根　　kaikon　　tuberous root　　　　　　　　　314
塊状　　kaijō　　massive　　　　　　　　　　　　636

魂	**1626** 5f9.2 田 二 厶 /58 4 17 魂	**KON, tamashii** – soul, spirit

霊魂　　reikon　　the soul　　　　　　　　　　　1225
商魂　　shōkon　　commercial spirit, salesmanship　418
魂胆　　kontan　　soul; ulterior motive　　　　　1347
負けじ魂　　makeji-damashii　　unyielding spirit　519
大和魂　　Yamato-damashii　　the Japanese spirit　26, 124

魅	**1627** 5f10.1 田 木 儿 /58 41 16 魅	**MI** – charm, enchant, fascinate

魅力　　miryoku　　charm, appeal, fascination　　　100
魅力的　　miryokuteki　　fascinating, captivating　100, 210
魅了　　miryō　　charm, captivate, hold spellbound　971
魅惑　　miwaku　　fascination, charm, lure　　　1001

醜	**1628** 7e10.1 酉 田 儿 /71 58 16 醜	**SHŪ, miniku(i)** – ugly; indecent

醜聞　　shūbun　　scandal　　　　　　　　　　　64
醜悪　　shūaku　　ugly, abominable, scandalous　　304
醜態　　shūtai　　unseemly sight; disgraceful behavior　388
醜女　　shūjo, shikome　　ugly woman　　　　　102
美醜　　bishū　　beauty or ugliness; appearance　405

魔	**1629** 3q18.2 广 田 木 /18 58 41 魔	**MA** – demon, devil, evil spirit

悪魔　　akuma　　devil　　　　　　　　　　　　304
魔術　　majutsu　　black magic, sorcery, witchcraft　187
魔法　　mahō　　magic　　　　　　　　　　　　123
魔法瓶　　mahōbin　　thermos bottle　　　　123, 1217
邪魔　　jama　　encumbrance, interruption, disturbance　1551

麻	**1630** 3q8.3 广 木 /18 41 麻	**MA, asa** – flax, hemp

大麻　　taima, ōasa　　hemp, marijuana　　　　　26
麻薬　　mayaku　　narcotics, drugs　　　　　　360
麻痺　　mahi　　paralysis
小児麻痺　　shōni mahi　　infantile paralysis, polio　27, 1280
麻糸　　asaito　　hempen yarn, linen thread　　242

摩	**1631** 3q12.6 广 木 扌 /18 41 23 摩	**MA** – rub, rub off, scrape

摩擦　　masatsu　　friction　　　　　　　　　1620
冷水摩擦　　reisui masatsu　　rubdown with a wet towel
　　　　　　　　　　　　　　　　　　　　　851, 21, 1620
按摩　　anma　　massage; masseur, masseuse

1632

磨

3q13.3

广 石 木
/18 53 41

磨

MA, miga(ku) – polish, brush

研磨	kenma	grind, polish; study hard	918
磨滅	mametsu	wear, abrasion	1421
達磨	Daruma	Bodhidharma; Dharma doll (legless)	455
歯磨き	hamigaki	brushing one's teeth; toothpaste	486
磨き上げる	migakiageru	polish up	32

1633

閑

8e4.2

門 木
/75 41

閑

KAN – leisure; quiet; neglect

閑静	kansei	quiet, peaceful	674
森閑	shinkan	stillness, quiet	128
安閑	ankan	idleness	105
閑散	kansan	leisure; (market) inactivity	781
農閑期	nōkanki	the slack season for farming	370, 456

1634

簡

6f12.5

⺮ 門 日
/66 75 42

簡

KAN – simple, brief

簡単	kantan	simple, brief	300
簡略	kanryaku	simple, concise	860
簡潔	kanketsu	concise	1307
簡素	kanso	plain and simple	271
書簡	shokan	letter, correspondence	131

1635

暦

2p12.3

厂 木 日
/18 41 42

暦

REKI, koyomi – calendar

西暦	seireki	the Western calendar, A.D.	72
旧暦	kyūreki	the old (lunar) calendar	1279
太陽暦	taiyōreki	the solar calendar	639, 640
還暦	kanreki	one's 60th birthday	885
花暦	hanagoyomi	floral calendar	255

1636

菓

3k8.2

⺾ 日 木
/32 42 41

菓

KA – cake; fruit

（お）菓子	(o)kashi	candy, confections, pastry	103
菓子屋	kashiya	candy store, confectionery shop	103, 167
和菓子	wagashi	Japanese-style confection	124, 103
茶菓	chaka, saka	tea and cake, refreshments	251
水菓子	mizugashi	fruit	21, 103

1637

彙

2i11.1

冂 日 木
/20 42 41

彙

I – classify and compile

| 語彙 | goi | vocabulary | 67 |

1638

裸

5e8.1

⻭ 日 木
/57 42 41

裸

RA, hadaka – naked

裸婦	rafu	nude woman	316
裸体画	rataiga	nude picture	61, 343
赤裸々	sekirara	naked; frank, outspoken	207
裸馬	hadakauma	unsaddled horse	body 283
裸一貫	hadaka-ikkan	with no property but one's own	2, 936

1639

襟

KIN, eri – neck; collar, lapel

5e13.2

衤 木 ネ
/57 41 45

襟

胸襟	*kyōkin*	bosom, heart	1357
開襟シャツ	*kaikin shatsu*	open-necked shirt	400
襟巻き	*erimaki*	muffler, scarf	516
襟首	*erikubi*	nape, back/scruff of the neck	148
襟元	*erimoto*	the neck	137

1640

巣

SŌ, su – nest

3n8.1

⺌ 日 木
/35 42 41

巣

卵巣	*ransō*	ovary	⌐inflammation	1103
炎症病巣	*enshō byōsō*	focus of an	1419, 1400, 381
巣立ち	*sudachi*	leave the nest, become independent	121
古巣	*furusu*	old nest, one's old haunt	172
空き巣狙い	*akisunerai*	burglar; burglary (of an empty house)	

1641

弾

DAN – bullet, shell; bounce; play (a string instrument) **tama** – bullet **hazu(mu)** – bounce; be stimulated; fork out, splurge on **hi(ku)** – play (a string instrument)

3h9.3

弓 日 小
/28 42 35

弾 彈

爆弾	*bakudan*	a bomb	1053
弾丸	*dangan*	projectile, bullet, shell	654
弾力(性)	*danryoku(sei)*	elasticity; flexibility	100, 98

1642

禅

ZEN – Zen Buddhism

4e9.2

衤 日 小
/45 42 35

禅 禪

禅宗	*Zenshū*	the Zen sect	626
座禅	*zazen*	religious meditation (done while sitting)	800
禅僧	*zensō*	Zen priest	1453
禅寺	*zendera*	Zen temple	⌐dialogue 41
禅問答	*zen mondō*	Zen dialogue; incomprehensible	162, 160

1643

奉

HŌ, [BU] – offer, present; revere; serve **tatematsu(ru)** – offer, present; revere

0a8.13

大 二 十
34 4 12

奉

奉納	*hōnō*	dedication, offering	⌐revere 771
奉献	*hōken*	dedication, consecration	1438
信奉	*shinpō*	belief, faith	157
奉仕	*hōshi*	attendance; service	333
奉公	*hōkō*	public duty; domestic service	126

1644

俸

HŌ – salary

2a8.18

イ 大 二
/3 34 4

俸

俸給	*hōkyū*	salary, pay	346
年俸	*nenpō*	annual salary	45
号俸	*gōhō*	pay level, salary class	266
減俸	*genpō*	salary reduction, pay cut	⌐allowance 728
年功加俸	*nenkō kahō*	long-service pension/	45, 837, 722

1645

棒

BŌ – stick, pole

4a8.20

木 大 二
/41 34 4

棒

鉄棒	*tetsubō*	iron bar; the horizontal bar (in gymnastics)	312
心棒	*shinbō*	axle, shaft	97
棒立ち	*bōdachi*	standing bolt upright	121
相棒	*aibō*	pal; accomplice	146
棒暗記	*bōanki*	indiscriminate memorization	348, 372

1646

奏

0a9.17 [...]
大 二 一
34 4 1
奏

SŌ – play (a musical instrument); report (to a superior); take effect
kana(deru) – play (a musical instrument)

演奏会	ensōkai	concert, recital	344, 158
独奏	dokusō	a solo (performance)	219
二重奏	nijūsō	duet	3, 227
伴奏	bansō	accompaniment	1066

1647

泰

3a5.34
氵 大 二
/21 34 4
泰

TAI – calm, peace; (short for) Thailand

泰然自若	taizen-jijaku	imperturbability	662, 62, 553
安泰	antai	tranquility; security	105
泰平	taihei	peace, tranquility	202
泰西	taisei	Occident, the West	72
泰西名画	taisei meiga	famous Western painting	72, 82, 343

1648

漆

3a11.10 [田]
氵 木 亻
/21 41 3
漆

SHITSU, urushi – lacquer

漆器	shikki	lacquerware	536
漆黒	shikkoku	jet-black, pitch-black	206
乾漆像	kanshitsuzō	dry-lacquered image (of Buddha)	1249, 753
漆くい	shikkui	mortar, plaster	
漆塗り	urushinuri	lacquered, japanned	1121

1649

慈

2o11.1 [目]
丷 心 厶
/16 51 17
慈

JI, itsuku(shimu) – love, be affectionate to; pity

慈善	jizen	charity, philanthropy	1191
慈悲	jihi	mercy, benevolence, pity	1075
慈恵	jikei	charity	1282
慈愛	jiai	affection, kindness, love	259
慈雨	jiu	beneficial/welcome rain	30

1650

磁

5a9.6 [田]
石 儿 厶
/53 16 17
磁

JI – magnetism; porcelain

磁気	jiki	magnetism, magnetic	134
磁石	jishaku	magnet	78
電磁石	denjishaku	electromagnet	108, 78
磁場	jiba, jijō	magnetic field	154
磁器	jiki	porcelain	536

1651

滋

3a9.27
氵 儿 厶
/21 16 17
滋

JI – luxuriant, rich

滋養	jiyō	nourishment, nutrition	406
滋養分	jiyōbun	nutritious element, nutriment	406, 38
滋賀県	Shiga-ken	Shiga Prefecture	769, 194

1652

寿

0a7.15 [...]
寸 十 二
37 12 4
寿 壽

JU – longevity; congratulations **kotobuki** – congratulations; longevity

寿命	jumyō	lifespan, life	587
長寿	chōju	long life, lonevity	95
喜寿	kiju	one's 77th birthday	1196
寿司	sushi	sushi	861

1653

鋳

8a7.2	⊞
釒 寸 十	
/72 37 12	

鋳 鑄

CHŪ, i(ru) – cast (metal)

鋳造	chūzō	casting; minting, coinage	704
鋳鉄	chūtetsu	cast iron	312
改鋳	kaichū	recoinage; recasting	523
鋳型	igata	a mold, cast	909
鋳物	imono	an article of cast metal, a casting	79

1654

銘

8a6.4	⊞
釒 口 夕	
/72 24 30	

銘

MEI – inscription, signature, name; precept, motto

銘記	meiki	bear in mind	372
感銘	kanmei	deep impression	262
銘柄	meigara	a brand (name)	1019
座右銘	zayūmei	motto	800, 76
碑銘	himei	inscription; epitaph	1623

1655

雇

4m8.1	
戸 隹	
/40 73	

雇

KO, yato(u) – employ, hire; charter

終身雇用	shūshin koyō	lifetime employment	466, 59, 107
解雇	kaiko	dismiss, fire	482
雇い人	yatoinin	employee; servant	1
雇い主	yatoinushi	employer	155

1656

顧

9a12.2	
頁 隹 厂	
/76 73 40	

顧

KO, kaeri(miru) – look back; take into consideration

回顧	kaiko	recollection, retrospect	90
回顧録	kaikoroku	reminiscences, memoirs	90, 547
顧慮	koryo	regard, consideration	1472
顧問	komon	adviser	162
顧客	kokaku, kokyaku	customer	651

1657

扇

4m6.1	
戸 彐	
/40 39	

扇

SEN, ōgi – fan, folding fan

扇子	sensu	folding fan	103
扇風機	senpūki	electric fan	29, 537
扇形	senkei, ōgigata	fan shape, sector, segment	399
扇動	sendō	incitement, instigation, agitation	231
舞扇	maiōgi	dancer's fan	829

1658

扉

4m8.2	▢
戸 ⼗ 二	
/40 13 4	

扉

HI, tobira – door; title page

| 開扉 | kaihi | opening of the door | 400 |
| 門扉 | monpi | the doors of a gate | 161 |

1659

促

2a7.3	⊞
亻 ⾜	
/3 70	

促

SOKU, unaga(su) – urge, prompt, spur on

促進	sokushin	promotion, acceleration	443
催促	saisoku	press, urge, demand	1399
促成	sokusei	artificially accelerate, force (growth)	261

1660

捉

3c7.1
扌 罒
/23 70
捉

SOKU, tora(eru) – catch, capture

捕捉	*hosoku*	catch, capture, seize	911
択捉島	*Etorofu-tō*	Etorofu/Iturup Island (largest of the Kuril islands)	1030, 286

1661

踊

7d7.2
⻊ 月 一
/70 43 1
踊 踴

YŌ, odo(ru) – dance **odo(ri)** – a dance, dancing

舞踊	*buyō*	a dance, dancing	829
盆踊り	*Bon odori*	Bon Festival dance	1150
踊り子	*odoriko*	dancer, dancing girl	103
踊り狂う	*odorikuruu*	dance ecstatically	904
踊り場	*odoriba*	dance hall/floor; (stairway) landing	154

1662

踏

7d8.3
⻊ 日 氵
/70 42 21
踏 蹈

TŌ, fu(mu) – step on **fu(maeru)** – stand on, be based on

舞踏会	*butōkai*	ball, dance party	829, 158
雑踏	*zattō*	hustle and bustle, (traffic) congestion	584
踏査	*tōsa*	survey, field investigation	634
踏切	*fumikiri*	railroad crossing	39
足踏み	*ashibumi*	step, stamp, mark time	58

1663

躍

7d14.2
⻊ 隹 ⺕
/70 73 39
躍

YAKU, odo(ru) – jump, leap, hop

飛躍	*hiyaku*	a leap; activity; rapid progress	539
活躍	*katsuyaku*	active, action	237
暗躍	*an'yaku*	behind-the-scenes maneuvering	348
躍進	*yakushin*	advance by leaps and bounds	443
躍動	*yakudō*	lively motion	231

1664

濯

3a14.5
氵 隹 ⺕
/21 73 39
濯

TAKU – wash, rinse

洗濯	*sentaku*	washing, the wash, laundry	705
洗濯機	*sentakuki*	washing machine, washer	705, 537
洗濯物	*sentakumono*	the wash, laundry	705, 79

1665

兆

2b4.4
⼃ 儿 ⼂
/5 16 10
兆

CHŌ – sign, indication; trillion **kiza(shi)** – sign, symptoms
kiza(su) – show signs, sprout, germinate

兆候	*chōkō*	sign, indication	974
前兆	*zenchō*	omen, portent, foreshadowing	47
吉兆	*kitchō*	good omen/sign	1194
億兆	*okuchō*	the multitude, the people	383

1666

跳

7d6.3
⻊ 氵 儿
/70 5 16
跳

CHŌ, to(bu), ha(neru) – leap, spring up, jump, bounce

跳躍	*chōyaku*	spring, jump, leap	1663
跳び上がる	*tobiagaru*	jump up	32
跳ね上がる	*haneagaru*	jump up	32
走り高跳び	*hashiri-takatobi*	the (running) high jump	435, 190
飛び跳ねる	*tobihaneru*	jump up and down	539

挑	**1667** 3c6.5 ▦ 扌 冫 儿 /23 5 16 挑	**CHŌ, ido(mu)** – challenge	
		挑戦 *chōsen* challenge	301
		挑戦者 *chōsensha* challenger	301, 164
		挑発 *chōhatsu* arouse, excite, provoke	96
		挑発的 *chōhatsuteki* provocative, suggestive	96, 210

眺	**1668** 5c6.2 ▦ 目 冫 儿 /55 5 16 眺	**CHŌ, naga(meru)** – look at, watch, gaze at	
		眺望 *chōbō* a view (from a window)	685

逃	**1669** 2q6.5 ▢ 辶 冫 儿 /19 5 16 逃 逃	**TŌ, ni(geru)** – run away, escape, flee **noga(reru)** – escape **ni(gasu), noga(su)** – let go, set free, let escape	
		逃走 *tōsō* escape, flight	435
		逃亡 *tōbō* escape, flight, desertion	684
		逃げ出す *nigedasu* break into a run, run off/ away	53
		見逃す *minogasu* overlook	63

桃	**1670** 4a6.10 ▦ 木 冫 儿 /41 5 16 桃	**TŌ, momo** – peach	
		桃色 *momoiro* pink	204
		桃の節句 *Momo no Sekku* Doll Festival (March 3)	472, 337
		桃山時代 *Momoyama jidai* Momoyama period (1583–1602)	
		⌐earth	34, 42, 256
		桃源郷／境 *Tōgenkyō* Shangri-la, paradise on	589, 874, 883

践	**1671** 7d6.1 ▢ 𧾷 戈 丨 /70 52 2 践 踐	**SEN** – step, step up; realize, put into practice	
		実践 *jissen* practice	203
		実践的 *jissenteki* practical	203, 210
		実践理性批判 *Jissen Risei Hihan* (Critique of Practical	
		Reason – Kant)	203, 143, 98, 1068, 1065

箋	**1672** 6f8.9 ▢ ⺮ 戈 /66 52 箋	**SEN** – paper, label	
		付箋 *fusen* tag, label	192
		便箋 *binsen* stationery, notepaper	330
		処方箋 *shohōsen* (medical) prescription; formula (to mend	
		something)	1189, 70

跡	**1673** 7d6.7 ▢ 𧾷 亠 儿 /70 11 16 跡	**SEKI, ato** – mark, traces, vestiges, remains, ruins	
		遺跡 *iseki* remains, ruins, relics	1230
		史跡 *shiseki* historic site/relics	332
		足跡 *ashiato, sokuseki* footprint	58
		傷跡 *kizuato* a scar	643
		跡継ぎ *atotsugi* successor, heir	1064

1674

踪

7d8.4
⻊ 礻 宀
/70 45 33
踪

SŌ – footprint, traces

| 踪跡 | *sōseki* | one's tracks/whereabouts | 1673 |
| 失踪 | *shissō* | disappear, be missing | 311 |

1675

赦

4i7.3
攵 土 儿
/49 22 16
赦

SHA – forgive

大赦	*taisha*	(general) amnesty	26
恩赦	*onsha*	an amnesty, general pardon	564
赦免	*shamen*	pardon, clemency	746
特赦	*tokusha*	an amnesty	282
容赦	*yōsha*	pardon, forgiveness, mercy	665

1676

纖

6a11.1
糸 戈 十
/61 52 12
繊 纖

SEN – fine, slender

繊維	*sen'i*	fiber, textiles	1295
繊維工業	*sen'i kōgyō*	textile industry	1295, 139, 279
合成繊維	*gōsei sen'i*	synthetic fiber	159, 261, 1295
化繊	*kasen*	synthetic fiber	254
繊細	*sensai*	delicate, fine, subtle	708

1677

虎

2m6.3
厂 十 儿
18 12 16
虎

KO, tora – tiger

虎穴	*koketsu*	tiger's den; dangerous situation	921
虎視眈々と	*koshitantan to*	with hostile vigilance, waiting one's chance to pounce	616
虎の子	*tora no ko*	tiger cub; one's treasure	103
虎の巻	*tora no maki*	pony, answer book; (trade) secrets	516

1678

虚

2m9.1
厂 十 儿
18 12 16
虚

KYO, [KO] – empty

虚無主義	*kyomu shugi*	nihilism	93, 155, 291
虚栄（心）	*kyoei(shin)*	vanity	736, 97
虚弱	*kyojaku*	weak, feeble, frail	218
虚偽	*kyogi*	false, untrue	1582
虚空	*kokū*	empty space, the air	140

1679

戯

4n11.1
戈 厂 十
/52 18 12
戯 戲

GI, tawamu(reru) – play, sport, jest, flirt

遊戯	*yūgi*	amusement	1040
戯曲	*gikyoku*	drama, play	367
前戯	*zengi*	(sexual) foreplay	47
戯画	*giga*	a caricature	343
悪戯	*akugi, itazura*	mischief, prank; lewdness	304

1680

虐

2m7.3
厂 十 冂
18 12 20
虐

GYAKU, shiita(geru) – oppress, tyrannize

虐待	*gyakutai*	treat cruelly, mistreat	459
暴虐	*bōgyaku*	tyrannical, cruel	1052
虐殺	*gyakusatsu*	massacre, slaughter, butchery	585
残虐	*zangyaku*	cruel, brutal, inhuman	661
自虐的	*jigyakuteki*	self-tormenting, masochistic	62, 210

1681

龔

5e16.2 田
衤 立 月
/57 54 43
襲

SHŪ, oso(u) – attack, assail; succeed to, inherit

来襲	raishū	attack, assault, invasion	69
空襲	kūshū	air raid	140
夜襲	yashū	night attack	479
世襲	seshū	hereditary	252
因襲	inshū	long-established custom, convention	563

1682

祥

4e6.1 田
衤 王 几
/45 46 16
祥

SHŌ – happiness, good omen

不祥事	fushōji	scandal	94, 80
発祥	hasshō	origin	96
発祥地	hasshōchi	birthplace, cradle	96, 118
吉祥	kisshō	good omen	1194
吉祥天	Kichijōten, Kisshōten	(Buddhist goddess)	1194, 141

1683

詳

7a6.12 田
言 王 几
/67 46 16
詳

SHŌ, kuwa(shii) – detailed, full; familiar with (something)

詳細	shōsai	details, particulars	708
不詳	fushō	unknown, unidentified	94
未詳	mishō	unknown, unidentified	306
詳報	shōhō	full/detailed report	698
詳述	shōjutsu	detailed explanation, full account	1000

1684

黙

4d11.5 田
火 日 土
/44 42 22
黙 默

MOKU, dama(ru) – become silent, say nothing

沈黙	chinmoku	silence	964
黙認	mokunin	tacit approval	751
黙殺	mokusatsu	take no notice of, ignore	585
黙秘権	mokuhiken	right against self-incrimination	824, 335

1685

猛

3g7.4 田
犭 皿 子
/27 59 6
猛

MŌ – strong, fierce

猛烈	mōretsu	fierce, violent, strong	1414
猛打	mōda	hard hit, heavy blow	1059
猛暑	mōsho	fierce heat	648
猛犬	mōken	vicious dog	280
猛者	mosa	man of courage, stalwart veteran	164

1686

猟

3g8.6 田
犭 小 冂
/27 35 20
猟 獵

RYŌ – hunting

猟師	ryōshi	hunter	415
猟人	kariudo, karyūdo, ryōjin	hunter	1
猟犬	ryōken	hunting dog	280
猟銃	ryōjū	hunting gun, shotgun	848
渉猟	shōryō	read extensively, search for far and wide	438

1687

狩

3g6.5 田
犭 宀 寸
/27 33 37
狩

SHU, ka(ri) – hunting **ka(ru)** – hunt

狩猟（期）	shuryō(ki)	hunting (season)	1686, 456
狩り小屋	karigoya	hunting cabin	27, 167
狩人	karyūdo	hunter	1
潮干狩り	shiohigari	shell gathering (at low tide)	476, 593
みかん狩り	mikangari	picking satsuma oranges	

1688

獣 獣

3g12.3
犭 田 小
/27 58 35

JŪ, kemono – animal, beast

野獣	yajū	wild animal	236
猛獣	mōjū	vicious animal, ferocious beast	1685
怪獣	kaijū	monster	1573
鳥獣保護区域	chōjū hogo kuiki		285, 498, 1391, 183, 1002
獣医	jūi	veterinarian ⌐wildlife sanctuary	220

1689

猶

3g9.5
犭 酉 儿
/27 71 16

YŪ – delay; still, still more

猶予	yūyo	postponement, deferment	397
猶予なく	yūyonaku	without delay, promptly	397
執行猶予	shikkō yūyo	suspended sentence, probation	
			699, 68, 397

1690

猿

3g10.3
犭 衤 土
/27 57 22

EN, saru – monkey

野猿	yaen	wild monkey	236
類人猿	ruijin'en	anthropoid ape	226, 1
猿知恵	sarujie	shallow cleverness	214, 1282
犬猿の仲	ken'en no naka	hating each other, like cats and dogs	280, 1430

1691

桁

4a6.8
木 彳 二
/41 29 4

keta – beam, girder; digit, place (in numbers)

橋桁	hashigeta	bridge girder	607
桁はずれ	ketahazure	extraordinary	
桁違い	ketachigai	off/differing by an order of magnitude	833
一桁	hitoketa	single digit	2
二桁	futaketa	two digits, double-digit	3

1692

衡

3i13.1
彳 田 大
/29 58 34

KŌ – scales, weigh

均衡	kinkō	balance, equilibrium	820
平衡	heikō	balance, equilibrium	202
平衡感覚	heikō kankaku	sense of equilibrium	202, 262, 615
度量衡	doryōkō	weights and measures	378, 417

1693

換

3c9.15
扌 大 ㇗
/23 34 15

KAN, ka(eru) – substitute **ka(waru)** – be replaced

交換	kōkan	exchange, substitution	114
変換	henkan	change, conversion	257
換算(率)	kansan(ritsu)	conversion, exchange (rate)	760, 802
互換性	gokansei	compatibility, interchangeability	929, 98
乗り換え	norikae	transfer, change (of trains)	532

1694

喚

3d9.19
口 大 ㇗
/24 34 15

KAN – call

召喚	shōkan	summons, subpoena	1032
(証人)喚問	(shōnin) kanmon	summons (of a	493, 1, 162
喚起	kanki	evoke, awaken, call forth ⌐witness)	374
叫喚	kyōkan	shout, outcry, scream	1321
阿鼻叫喚	abikyōkan	(2 of Buddhism's 8 hells)	832, 1321

融	**1695** 6d10.5 ⊞ 虫 口 冂 /64 24 20 融	**YŪ** – dissolve, melt

融合　　yūgō　fusion　　　　　　　　　　　　　159
融通　　yūzū　accomodation, loan; versatility　　150
金融　　kin'yū　money, finance　　　　　　　　　23
金融機関　kin'yū kikan　financial institution　　23, 537, 402
融資　　yūshi　financing, loan　　　　　　　　　763

隔	**1696** 2d10.2 ⊞ 阝 口 冂 /7 24 20 隔	**KAKU** – every other, alternate; distance **heda(teru)** – separate, inter- pose, estrange **heda(taru)** – be distant, apart; become estranged

間隔　　kankaku　space, spacing, interval　　　　43
隔離　　kakuri　isolation, quarantine　　　　　　1355
遠隔　　enkaku　distant, remote, outlying　　　　453
横隔膜　ōkakumaku　the diaphragm　　　　　795, 1515

呈	**1697** 3d4.14 ⊟ 口 王 /24 46 呈	**TEI** – offer, present, exhibit

進呈　　shintei　give, present　　　　　　　　　443
贈呈　　zōtei　present, donate　　　　　　　　　1451
献呈本　kenteibon　presentation copy　　　　1438, 25
謹呈　　kintei　With the compliments of the author　1314
露呈　　rotei　exposure, disclosure　　　　　　　981

是	**1698** 4c5.9 ⊟ 日 一 亻 /42 14 3 是	**ZE** – right, correct, just

是非　　zehi　right and wrong; by all means　　　507
是正　　zesei　correct, rectify　　　　　　　　　275
是認　　zenin　approval, sanction　　　　　　　751
是々非々　zeze-hihi　being fair and unbiased　　507

堤	**1699** 3b9.7 ⊞ 土 日 一 /22 42 14 堤	**TEI, tsutsumi** – bank, embankment, dike

堤防　　teibō　embankment, dike, levee　　　　　522
防波堤　bōhatei　breakwater　　　　　　　522, 677

又	**1700** 2h0.1 ☐ 又 /9 又	**mata** – again, also, moreover

又聞き　matagiki　hearsay, secondhand information　64
又貸し　matagashi　sublease　　　　　　　　　761
又々　　matamata　once again
又は　　matawa　or, either … or …

双	**1701** 2h2.1 ☐ 又 /9 双　雙	**SŌ, futa** – pair, both

双方　　sōhō　both parties/sides　　　　　　　　70
双生児　sōseiji　twins　　　　　　　　　44, 1280
双眼鏡　sōgankyō　binoculars　　　　　　867, 882
双肩　　sōken　one's shoulders　　　　　　　　1337
双子　　futago　twins　　　　　　　　　　　　103

努	**1702** 2g5.6 力 女 又 /8 25 9 努	**DO, tsuto(meru)** – exert oneself, make efforts, strive 努力　*doryoku*　effort, endeavor　　　　100 努力家　*doryokuka*　hard worker　　　100, 165
怒	**1703** 4k5.19 心 女 又 /51 25 9 怒	**DO, oko(ru), ika(ru)** – become angry 怒気　*doki*　(fit of) anger　　　　134 激怒　*gekido*　wild rage, wrath, fury　　　1056 怒髪天を突く　*dohatsu ten o tsuku*　be infuriated　1201, 141, 920 怒号　*dogō*　angry roar　　　266 喜怒　*kido*　joy and anger, emotion　　　1196
悠	**1704** 4k7.20 心 女 イ /51 49 3 悠	**YŪ** – distant; leisure 悠然　*yūzen*　calm, perfect composure　　　662 悠長　*yūchō*　leisurely, slow, easygoing　　　95 悠々　*yūyū*　calm, composed, leisurely 悠揚　*yūyō*　composed, calm, serene　　　641 悠久　*yūkyū*　eternity, perpetuity　　　1273
愉	**1705** 4k9.13 心 月 イ /51 43 3 愉	**YU** – joy, pleasure 愉快　*yukai*　pleasant, merry, cheerful　　　1498 不愉快　*fuyukai*　unpleasant, disagreeable　94, 1498 愉楽　*yuraku*　pleasure, joy　　　359
諭	**1706** 7a9.13 言 月 イ /67 43 3 諭	**YU, sato(su)** – admonish, remonstrate, warn, counsel 教諭　*kyōyu*　teacher, instructor　　　245 説諭　*setsuyu*　admonition, reproof, caution　　　404 諭旨　*yushi*　official suggestion (to a subordinate)　　　1081
癒	**1707** 5i13.3 疒 月 心 /60 43 51 癒 癒	**YU** – heal, cure **ie(ru)** – be healed, recover **iya(su)** – heal, cure 癒着　*yuchaku*　heal up, adhere, knit together　　　668 治癒　*chiyu*　healing, cure, recovery　　　502 平癒　*heiyu*　recovery　　　202
愁	**1708** 4k9.16 心 禾 火 /51 56 44 愁	**SHŪ, ure(i)** – grief, sorrow, distress, anxiety, cares **ure(eru)** – grieve, be distressed, fear, be apprehensive 郷愁　*kyōshū*　homesickness, nostalgia　　　874 旅愁　*ryoshū*　loneliness on a journey　　　222 憂愁　*yūshū*　melancholy, grief, gloom　　　1073 ご愁傷様　*goshūshō-sama*　My heartfelt sympathy.　643, 407

1709

恐

4k6.19
心 エ 冂
/51 38 20

恐

KYŌ, oso(reru) – fear, be afraid of **oso(roshii)** – terrible, frightful, awful

恐縮	*kyōshuku* be very grateful; be sorry	1162
恐慌	*kyōkō* panic	1465
恐妻家	*kyōsaika* henpecked husband	682, 165
空恐ろしい	*soraosoroshii* have a vague fear	140

1710

築

6f10.5
⺮ 木 エ
/66 41 38

築

CHIKU, kizu(ku) – build, erect

建築	*kenchiku* architecture, construction	913
建築家	*kenchikuka* architect	913, 165
新築	*shinchiku* new construction	174
改築	*kaichiku* rebuilding, reconstruction	523
築山	*tsukiyama* mound, artificial hill	34

1711

鉱

8a5.15
金 厂 ム
/72 18 17

鉱 鑛

KŌ – ore

鉱石	*kōseki* ore, mineral, crystal	78
鉱物	*kōbutsu* mineral	79
鉄鉱	*tekkō* iron ore	312
鉱山	*kōzan* a mine	34
鉱業	*kōgyō* mining	279

1712

銅

8a6.12
金 口 冂
/72 24 20

銅

DŌ – copper

銅山	*dōzan* copper mine	34
銅版画	*dōhanga* copper print	1089, 343
銅像	*dōzō* bronze statue	753
青銅	*seidō* bronze	208
銅メダル	*dōmedaru* bronze medal	

1713

鉛

8a5.14
金 口 儿
/72 24 16

鉛

EN, namari – lead

鉛筆	*enpitsu* pencil	130
黒鉛	*kokuen* graphite	206
鉛版	*enban* stereotype, printing plate	1089
鉛毒	*endoku* lead poisoning	531
鉛色	*namariiro* lead color/gray	204

1714

沿

3a5.23
氵 口 儿
/21 24 16

沿

EN, so(u) – stand along (a street), run parallel (to)

沿岸	*engan* coast, shore	595
沿海	*enkai* coastal waters, coast	117
沿線	*ensen* along the (train) line	299
沿革	*enkaku* history, development	1123
川沿い	*kawazoi* along the river	33

1715

鋼

8a8.20
金 岡 冂
/72 36 20

鋼

KŌ, hagane – steel

鋼鉄	*kōtetsu* steel	312
特殊鋼	*tokushukō* special steel	282, 1604
鋼板	*kōhan, kōban* steel plate	1090
製鋼所	*seikōjo* steel plant	434, 153
製鋼業	*seikōgyō* steel industry	434, 279

綱	**1716** 6a8.23 糸 巾 冂 /61 36 20 綱	**KŌ, tsuna** – rope, cord

綱領　*kōryō*　plan, program, platform　853
綱紀　*kōki*　official discipline, public order　373
手綱　*tazuna*　bridle, reins　57
綱渡り　*tsunawatari*　tightrope walking　379
横綱　*yokozuna*　sumo grand champion　795

剛	**1717** 2f8.7 刂 巾 冂 /16 36 20 剛	**GŌ** – strong, hard, rigid

外柔内剛　*gaijū-naigō*　gentle-looking but sturdy　83, 788, 84
剛健　*gōken*　strong and sturdy, virile　914
剛勇　*gōyū*　valor, bravery　1474
金剛石　*kongōseki*　diamond　23, 78

削	**1718** 2f7.4 刂 月 小 /16 43 35 削	**SAKU, kezu(ru)** – whittle down, sharpen (a pencil); delete; curtail

削除　*sakujo*　deletion, elimination　1112
削減　*sakugen*　reduction, cutback　728
添削　*tensaku*　correction (of a composition)　1523
鉛筆削り　*enpitsu-kezuri*　pencil sharpener　1713, 130

剥	**1719** 2f8.4 彐 氵 儿 39 21 16 剥	**HAKU** – come/peel off; deprive off **ha(geru)** – come/peel off; fade, discolor **ha(gareru)** – come/peel off **ha(gu)** – tear/peel/strip off; deprive of **ha(gasu)** – tear/peel/strip off

剥奪　*hakudatsu*　deprive/divest of　1389
剥製　*hakusei*　stuffing, stuffed/mounted specimen　434

網	**1720** 6a8.25 糸 亠 冂 /61 38 20 網	**MŌ, ami** – net

漁網　*gyomō*　fishing net　712
交通網　*kōtsūmō*　traffic network　114, 150
支店網　*shitenmō*　network of branch offices　318, 168
金網　*kanaami*　wire mesh/netting, chain-link (fence)　23
網袋　*amibukuro*　net (shopping) bag　1412

坑	**1721** 3b4.6 土 亠 冂 /22 11 20 坑	**KŌ** – pit, hole

炭坑　*tankō*　coalpit, coal mine　1427
坑夫　*kōfu*　coal miner　315
坑道　*kōdō*　(mine) shaft, level, gallery　149
坑内事故　*kōnai jiko*　mine accident　84, 80, 173
廃坑　*haikō*　abandoned mine　992

冗	**1722** 2i2.1 冖 一 /20 冗	**JŌ** – redundant, superfluous

冗談　*jōdan*　a joke　603
冗語　*jōgo*　redundancy　67
冗員　*jōin*　superfluous member/personnel　163
冗長　*jōchō*　redundant, verbose　95
冗漫　*jōman*　wordy, verbose, rambling　1500

1723	**KAN, kanmuri** – crown	
2i7.2	王冠	ōkan	(royal) crown; bottle cap	294
	金冠	kinkan	gold crown	23
/20 37 4	栄冠	eikan	crown (of victory), laurels	736
	弱冠	jakkan	20 years of age; youth	218
冠	草冠	kusa-kanmuri	the radical 艹	249

1724	**A** – rank next, come after, sub-; (short for) Asia	
0a7.14	亜熱帯	anettai	subtropical zones, subtropics	655, 994
	亜鉛	aen	zinc	1713
38 24 2	亜麻	ama	flax	1630
	亜流	aryū	follower, epigone	247
亜 亞	東亜	Tōa	East Asia	71

1725	**I** – officer	
4e6.4	尉官	ikan	officer below the rank of major	326
	大尉	taii	captain	26
/45 40 37	中尉	chūi	lieutenant	28
	少尉	shōi	second lieutenant	144
尉	准尉	jun'i	warrant officer	1296

1726	**I, nagusa(meru)** – comfort, console, cheer up, amuse, divert	
4k11.13	**nagusa(mu)** – be diverted, banter, make a plaything of	
	慰問	imon	consolation, sympathy	162
/51 45 40	慰安	ian	comfort, recreation, amusement	105
	慰霊祭	ireisai	a memorial service	1225, 627
慰	慰謝料	isharyō	consolation money, solatium	923, 319

1727	**JIN, [NI]** – virtue, benevolence, humanity, charity	
2a2.8	仁義	jingi	humanity and justice	291
	仁愛	jin'ai	benevolence, charity, philanthropy	259
/3 4	仁術	jinjutsu	benevolent act; the healing art	187
	仁徳	jintoku	benevolence, goodness	1079
仁	仁王(門)	Niō(mon)	Deva (gate)	294, 161

1728	**NI, ama** – nun	
3r2.2	尼僧	nisō	nun	1453
	尼寺	amadera	convent	41
/40 13				
尼				

1729	**DEI, doro** – mud	
3a5.29	泥炭	deitan	peat	1427
	雲泥の差	undei no sa	enormous difference	646, 669
/21 40 13	泥沼	doronuma	bog, quagmire	1033
泥	泥棒	dorobō	thief, robber, burglar, burglary	1645

匂	**1730** 0a4.7 勹 宀 15　13 匂	**nio(u)** – be fragrant 匂わす　*niowasu*　give out a scent; hint, suggest 匂い袋　*nioibukuro*　sachet, scent bag　　　　　1412
渇	**1731** 3a8.13 氵 日 宀 /21　42　15 渇	**KATSU, kawa(ku)** – be thirsty 飢渇　*kikatsu*　hunger and thirst　　　　　1383 渇望　*katsubō*　craving, longing, thirst　　　685 枯渇　*kokatsu*　run dry, become depleted　　1007 渇水　*kassui*　water shortage　　　　　　21 渇きを覚える　*kawaki o oboeru*　feel thirsty　　615
褐	**1732** 5e8.7 礻 日 宀 /57　42　15 褐	**KATSU** – brown 褐色　*kasshoku*　brown　　　　　　　204 茶褐色　*chakasshoku*　brown, chestnut brown　251, 204 赤褐色　*sekkasshoku*　reddish brown　　　207, 204 黒褐色　*kokkasshoku*　dark/blackish brown　206, 204
掲	**1733** 3c8.13 扌 日 宀 /23　42　15 掲	**KEI, kaka(geru)** – put up (a sign), hoist (a flag); publish, print 掲揚　*keiyō*　hoist, raise, fly (a flag)　　　641 掲示　*keiji*　notice, bulletin　　　　　　625 掲示板　*keijiban*　bulletin board　　　625, 1090 掲載　*keisai*　publish, print, carry, mention　1176 前掲　*zenkei*　shown above, aforementioned　　47
勾	**1734** 0a4.8 勹 厶 15　17 勾	**KŌ** – be bent, slope; capture 勾配　*kōbai*　slope, incline, gradient　　　524 勾留　*kōryū*　detention, custody　　　　774 勾留状　*kōryūjō*　warrant of detention pending trial　774, 636
濁	**1735** 3a13.8 氵 虫 日 /21　64　55 濁	**DAKU, nigo(ru)** – become muddy, turbid; be voiced; be vague **nigo(su)** – make turbid 混濁　*kondaku*　turbidity, muddiness　　　813 清濁　*seidaku*　purity and impurity, good and evil　671 濁流　*dakuryū*　muddy river, turbid waters　247 濁音　*dakuon*　voiced sound; cardiac dullness　347
潟	**1736** 3a12.9 氵 火 臼 /21　44　39 潟	**kata** – beach, lagoon, inlet 干潟　*higata*　dry beach, beach at ebb tide　593 新潟県　*Niigata-ken*　Niigata Prefecture　174, 194

1737

巧

0a5.7 □
亠一
38 14
巧

KŌ, taku(mi) – skill, dexterity, ingenuity

技巧	gikō	art, craftsmanship, technical skill	891
巧妙	kōmyō	skilled, clever, ingenious	1209
巧者	kōsha	skilled, adroit, clever	164
精巧	seikō	elaborate, exquisite, sophisticated	670
老巧	rōkō	experienced, seasoned, veteran	552

1738

朽

4a2.6 □
木 一
/41 14
朽

KYŪ, ku(chiru) – rot, decay

不朽	fukyū	immortal, undying ⌐masterpiece	94
不朽の名作	fukyū no meisaku	immortal	94, 82, 361
腐朽	fukyū	deteriorate, rot away, molder	1312
老朽	rōkyū	senescence, advanced age	552
朽ち葉	kuchiba	decayed/dead leaves	253

1739

誇

7a6.9 □
言 大 二
/67 34 4
誇

KO, hoko(ru) – boast of, be proud of

誇張	kochō	exaggeration, overstatement	1158
誇大	kodai	exaggeration, overstatement	26
誇大妄想（狂）	kodai mōsō(kyō)	delusions of	26, 1463, 147, 904
誇示	koji	display, flaunt ⌐grandeur, megalomania	625
勝ち誇る	kachihokoru	exult in one's triumph	518

1740

麗

3q16.5 □
广 門 ⼀
/18 20 13
麗

REI, uruwa(shii) – beautiful, pretty

美麗	birei	beautiful, pretty	405
華麗	karei	glory, splendor, magnificence	1122
麗人	reijin	beautiful woman	1
端麗	tanrei	grace, elegance, beauty ⌐flourishes	1507
美辞麗句	biji-reiku	speech full of rhetorical	405, 701, 337

1741

薦

3k13.25 □
艹 火 广
/32 44 18
薦

SEN, susu(meru) – recommend

推薦	suisen	recommendation	1297
推薦状	suisenjō	letter of recommendation	1297, 636
他薦	tasen	recommendation (by another)	120
自薦	jisen	self-recommendation	62

1742

慶

3q12.8 □
广 心 夊
/18 51 49
慶

KEI – rejoice, be happy over; congratulate

慶賀	keiga	congratulation	769
慶祝	keishuku	congratulation; celebration	870
慶事	keiji	happy event, matter for congratulation	80
慶応	Keiō	(Japanese era, 1865–68) ⌐China	846
国慶節	Kokkeisetsu	Anniversary of Founding of P.R.	40, 472

1743

覇

4b15.4 □
月 日 艹
/43 24 32
覇

HA – supremacy, domination, hegemony

覇権	haken	hegemony	335
制覇	seiha	conquest, domination; championship	433
連覇	renpa	successive championships	446
覇気	haki	ambition, aspirations	134
那覇	Naha	(capital of Okinawa Prefecture)	826

	1744	***FUKU*** – cover; overturn; repeat ***ō(u)*** – cover, conceal ***kutsugae(ru)*** – be overturned ***kutsugae(su)*** – overturn, overthrow
覆	4c14.6 日 攵 冂 /42 49 24 覆	覆面 *fukumen* mask 274 転覆 *tenpuku* overturn, topple 439 覆水盆に返らず *fukusui bon ni kaerazu* What's done is done. 21, 1150, 448

	1745	***RI*** – footwear; take steps, do ***ha(ku)*** – put on, wear (shoes/socks)
履	3r12.1 尸 日 攵 /40 42 49 履	履歴書 *rirekisho* curriculum vitae 489, 131 履行 *rikō* perform, fulfill, implement 68 草履 *zōri* (toe-strap) sandals 249 履き物 *hakimono* footwear 79 履き古し *hakifurushi* worn-out shoes/socks 172

	1746	***TAKU*** – entrust (to)
託	7a3.1 言 十 丨 /67 12 2 託	委託 *itaku* trust, charge, commission 474 信託 *shintaku* trust 157 託児所 *takujisho* day nursery 1280, 153 託宣 *takusen* oracle, revelation from God 635 結託 *kettaku* conspiracy, collusion 494

	1747	***dare*** – who
誰	7a8.1 言 隹 /67 73 誰	誰か *dare ka* someone, somebody 誰も、誰でも *dare mo, dare demo* everybody, everyone 誰も...ない *dare mo ... nai* nobody, no one

	1748	***TSUI*** – vertebra, backbone
椎	4a8.1 木 隹 /41 73 椎	脊椎 *sekitsui* vertebra; spinal column, spine 1339 脊椎動物 *sekitsui dōbutsu* vertebrates 1339, 231, 79 腰椎 *yōtsui* lumbar vertebra 1373 頸椎 *keitsui* the cervical vertebrae 椎茸 *shiitake* shiitake mushroom

	1749	***TAI*** – pile, heap
堆	3b8.1 土 隹 /22 73 堆	堆積 *taiseki* accumulation, pile, heap 667 堆積岩 *taisekigan* sedimentary/stratified rock 667, 1428 堆積物 *taisekibutsu* sediment, deposits 667, 79

	1750	***ZOKU*** – belong (to)
属	3r9.1 尸 虫 冂 /40 64 20 属 屬	所属 *shozoku* belong, be assigned (to) 153 付属 *fuzoku* attached, affiliated, incidental 192 金属 *kinzoku* metal 23 専属 *senzoku* belong exclusively (to) 610 従属 *jūzoku* subordination, dependence 1579

嘱 1751

SHOKU – request, entrust, commission

3d12.11
口 虫 尸
/24 64 40
嘱 囑

嘱託	shokutaku	part-time worker	1746
委嘱	ishoku	commission, charge, request	474
嘱望	shokubō	expect much of	685

偶 1752

GŪ – chance, accidental; (married) couple; even number; doll

2a9.1
亻 日 厶
/3 42 17
偶

偶然	gūzen	chance, accident	662
偶発	gūhatsu	chance occurrence	96
偶像	gūzō	image, statue, idol	753
配偶者	haigūsha	spouse	524, 164
偶数	gūsū	even number	225

隅 1753

GŪ, sumi – corner, nook

2d9.1
阝 日 厶
/7 42 17
隅

一隅	ichigū	corner, nook	2
片隅	katasumi	corner, nook	1088
四隅	yosumi	the 4 corners	6
隅々	sumizumi	every nook and cranny, all over	
隅田川	Sumida-gawa	Sumida River	35, 33

遇 1754

GŪ – treat, deal with, entertain; receive, meet

2q9.1
辶 日 厶
/19 42 17
遇

待遇	taigū	treatment; service; pay	459
優遇	yūgū	cordial reception, hospitality	1074
冷遇	reigū	cold reception, inhospitality	851
境遇	kyōgū	one's circumstances	883
奇遇	kigū	chance meeting	1444

愚 1755

GU, oro(ka) – foolish, stupid

4k9.15
心 日 厶
/51 42 17
愚

愚劣	guretsu	stupidity, foolishness, nonsense	1203
愚鈍	gudon	stupid, dim-witted	997
愚問	gumon	stupid question	162
愚連隊	gurentai	gang of hoodlums	446, 809

遭 1756

SŌ, a(u) – meet, see, come across, encounter

2q11.2
辶 日 艹
/19 42 32
遭

遭難	sōnan	disaster, accident, mishap	566
遭難者	sōnansha	victim	566, 164
遭難信号	sōnan shingō	distress signal, SOS	566, 157, 266
遭遇	sōgū	encounter	1754
災難に遭う	sainan ni au	meet with disaster	1418, 566

槽 1757

SŌ – tub, tank, vat

4a11.7
木 日 艹
/41 42 32
槽

水槽	suisō	water tank, cistern	21
浴槽	yokusō	bathtub	1180

晶	**1758**	**SHŌ** – clear; crystal	
	4c8.6 ⊞	結晶 *kesshō* crystal, crystallization	494
	日 /42	愛の結晶 *ai no kesshō* fruit of love, child	259, 494
	晶	晶化 *shōka* crystallization	254
		水晶 *suishō* (rock) crystal, quartz	21
		紫水晶 *murasaki suishō* amethyst	1478, 21

唱	**1759**	**SHŌ** – chant, sing; advocate **tona(eru)** – cry; advocate, espouse	
	3d8.9	合唱（団） *gasshō(dan)* chorus	159, 500
	口 日 /24 42	独唱 *dokushō* vocal solo	219
	唱	唱歌 *shōka* singing	395
		主/首唱 *shushō* advocacy, promotion	155, 148
		提唱 *teishō* advocate	638

謡	**1760**	**YŌ** – song **utai** – Noh chanting **uta(u)** – sing	
	7a9.9 ⊞	民謡 *min'yō* folk song	177
	言 小 屮 /67 35 36	童謡 *dōyō* children's song	416
	謡 謡	歌謡 *kayō* song	395
		歌謡曲 *kayōkyoku* popular song	395, 367
		謡曲 *yōkyoku* Noh song	367

揺	**1761**	**YŌ, yu(reru), yu(ragu), yu(rugu)** – shake, sway, vibrate, roll, pitch, joggle **yu(ru/suru/suburu/saburu)** – shake, rock, joggle	
	3c9.8	動揺 *dōyō* shaking; unrest, tumult	231
	扌 小 屮 /23 35 36	揺(す)り起こす *yu(su)riokosu* awaken by shaking	374
	揺 揺	揺り返し *yurikaeshi* aftershock	448

缶	**1762**	**KAN** – can	
	2k4.6 ⋯	缶詰 *kanzume* canned goods	1195
	屮 ← 一 36 15 1	製缶工場 *seikan kōjō* cannery, canning factory	434, 139, 154
	缶 罐	缶切り *kankiri* can opener	39
		空き缶 *akikan* empty can	140

陶	**1763**	**TŌ** – porcelain, pottery	
	2d8.11 ⊞	陶器 *tōki* china, ceramics, pottery	536
	阝 屮 ← /7 36 15	陶磁器 *tōjiki* ceramics, china and porcelain	1650, 536
	陶	陶芸 *tōgei* ceramic art	441
		陶工 *tōkō* potter	139

鬱	**1764**	**UTSU** – melancholy, gloom	
	4a25.1 ⊡	鬱陶しい *uttōshii* glooming, depressing	1763
	木 屮 彡 /41 36 31	憂鬱 *yūutsu* melancholy, dejection, gloom	1073
	鬱	気鬱 *kiutsu* gloom, melancholy, depression	134

	1765	**SŌ, sa(su)** – insert	
挿	3c7.2	挿入　　sōnyū　insertion	52
	扌 日 十	挿話　　sōwa　episode, little story	238
	/23 42 12	挿し木　sashiki　a cutting	22
	挿 挿	挿し絵　sashie　an illustration	345

	1766	**KI** – command; brandish, wield; scatter	
揮	3c9.14	指揮　　shiki　command, direct, conduct	1082
	扌 車 冂	指揮者　shikisha　(orchestra) conductor	1082, 164
	/23 69 20	指揮官　shikikan　commander	1082, 326
	揮	発揮　　hakki　exhibit, display, manifest	96
		揮発　　kihatsu　volatilization	96

	1767	**KI, kagaya(ku)** – shine, gleam, sparkle, be brilliant	
輝	7c8.8	光輝　　kōki　brilliance, brightness; glory	138
	車 小 儿	輝度　　kido　(degree of) brightness, luminance	378
	/69 35 16	光り輝く　hikarikagayaku　shine, beam, glisten	138
	輝	輝かしい　kagayakashii　bright, brilliant	

	1768	**ku(ru)** – reel, wind, spin (thread); turn (pages); consult (a reference book), look up; count	
繰	6a13.3	繰り返す　kurikaesu　repeat	448
	糸 木 口	繰り言　kurigoto　same old story, complaint	66
	/61 41 24	繰り延べ　kurinobe　postponement, deferment	1167
	繰	繰り上げる　kuriageru　advance, move up (a date)	32

	1769	**SŌ, ayatsu(ru)** – manipulate, operate **misao** – chastity, constancy, fidelity, honor	
操	3c13.3	操縦　　soju　control, operate, manipulate	1580
	扌 木 口	(遠隔)操作　(enkaku) sōsa　(remote) control	453, 1696, 361
	/23 41 24	体操　　taisō　gymnastics, exercises	61
	操	節操　　sessō　fidelity, integrity; chastity	472

	1770	**SŌ** – dry	
燥	4d13.6	乾燥　　kansō　dry (up/out)	1249
	火 木 口	乾燥機　kansōki　(clothes) dryer	1249, 537
	/44 41 24	無味乾燥　mumi-kansō　dry, uninteresting	93, 307, 1249
	燥	焦燥　　shōsō　impatience, nervous restlessness	1036

	1771	**SŌ, mo** – water plant	
藻	3k16.8	藻類　　sōrui　water plants	226
	艹 木 氵	海藻　　kaisō　saltwater plant, seaweed	117
	/32 41 21	藻草　　mogusa　water plant	249
	藻		

暁	**1772** 4c8.1 □ 日 土 儿 /42 22 16 暁 暁	**GYŌ, akatsuki** – dawn, daybreak	
		暁天 gyōten dawn, daybreak	141
		暁星 gyōsei morning stars; Venus	743
		今暁 kongyō early this morning	51
		通暁 tsūgyō thorough knowledge, mastery	150
		暁には akatsuki niwa in the event, in case (of)	

奔	**1773** 2k6.5 … く 大 十 /10 34 22 奔	**HON** – run	
		奔走 honsō running about, efforts	435
		奔放 honpō wild, extravagant, uninhibited	521
		狂奔 kyōhon rush madly about	904
		奔馬 honba galloping/runaway horse	283
		出奔 shuppon abscond; elope	53

噴	**1774** 3d12.8 □ 口 貝 土 /24 68 22 噴	**FUN, fu(ku)** – emit, spout, spew forth	
		噴火 funka (volcanic) eruption	20
		噴火山 funkazan erupting/active volcano	20, 34
		噴出 funshutsu eruption, gushing, spouting	53
		噴水 funsui jet of water; fountain	21
		噴霧器 funmuki sprayer, vaporizer, atomizer	980, 536

憤	**1775** 4k12.6 □ 心 貝 土 /51 68 22 憤	**FUN, ikidō(ru)** – resent, be enraged, be indignant	
		憤慨 fungai indignation, resentment	1554
		公憤 kōfun public/righteous indignation	126
		義憤 gifun righteous indignation	291
		憤然と funzen to indignantly	662
		発憤 happun be stimulated, roused	96

墳	**1776** 3b12.1 □ 土 貝 土 /22 68 22 墳	**FUN** – burial mound, tomb	
		墳墓 funbo grave, tomb	1518
		古墳 kofun ancient burial mound, old tomb	172
		前方後円墳 zenpō-kōen fun ancient burial mound (square at the head and rounded at the foot)	47, 70, 48, 13

監	**1777** 5h10.1 □ 皿 冂 亠 /59 20 15 監	**KAN** – keep watch over	
		監視 kanshi monitoring, supervision, surveillance	616
		監査 kansa inspection; auditing	634
		総監 sōkan inspector/superintendent general	710
		監禁 kankin imprison, confine	491
		監獄 kangoku prison	905

鑑	**1778** 8a15.2 □ 金 皿 冂 /72 59 20 鑑	**KAN** – model, pattern, example; mirror **kanga(miru)** – take into consideration	
		鑑定 kantei appraisal, expert opinion	356
		鑑賞 kanshō admiration, enjoyment	509
		鑑別 kanbetsu discrimination, differentiation	267
		年鑑 nenkan yearbook, almanac	45
		印鑑 inkan one's seal, seal impression	1086

1779

艦

6c15.2

舟 皿 冂
/63 59 20

艦

KAN – warship

軍艦	*gunkan*	warship	444
戦艦	*senkan*	battleship	301
航空母艦	*kōkū bokan*	aircraft carrier	842, 140, 112
潜水艦	*sensuikan*	submarine	967, 21
艦隊	*kantai*	fleet, squadron	809

1780

艇

6c6.2

舟 王 辶
/63 46 19

艇

TEI – small boat

艦艇	*kantei*	naval vessels	1779
舟艇	*shūtei*	boat, craft	1145
巡視艇	*junshitei*	patrol boat	791, 616
艇庫	*teiko*	boathouse	844
艇身	*teishin*	a boat length	59

1781

舷

6c5.5

舟 亠 厶
/63 11 17

舷

GEN – ship's side, gunwale

| 左舷 | *sagen* | port (not starboard) | 75 |
| 右舷 | *ugen* | starboard | 76 |

1782

叔

2h6.1

又 小 卜
/9 35 13

叔

SHUKU – younger sibling of a parent

| 叔母 | *oba, shukubo* | aunt | 112 |
| 叔父 | *oji, shukufu* | uncle | 113 |

1783

淑

3a8.5

氵 小 又
/21 35 9

淑

SHUKU – graceful, virtuous, pure

淑女	*shukujo*	lady, gentlewoman	102
淑徳	*shukutoku*	feminine virtues	1079
私淑	*shishuku*	look up to as one's model	125

1784

寂

3m8.2

宀 小 又
/33 35 9

寂

JAKU – lonely, quiet; nirvana **[SEKI], sabi(shii)** – lonely
sabi(reru) – decline in prosperity **sabi** – elegant simplicity

静寂	*seijaku*	stillness, silence	674
閑寂	*kanjaku*	quietness, tranquility	1633
寂然	*sekizen, jakunen*	lonesome, desolate	662

1785

督

5c8.9

目 小 又
/55 35 9

督

TOKU – supervise, superintend, lead, command

監督	*kantoku*	supervision, direction; (movie) director	1777
督励	*tokurei*	encourage, urge	1423
督促	*tokusoku*	urge, press, dun	1659
総督	*sōtoku*	governor-general	165, 146, 243 710
家督相続	*katoku sōzoku*	succession to a house, heirship	

1786	**GŌ** – strength, power; splendor, magnificence; (short for) Australia
2j12.3 ▤	豪華　　gōka　　splendor, gorgeousness, pomp　　　　　　1122
宀 犭 口	豪壮　　gōsō　　magnificent, grand　　　　　　　　　　　1409
/11　27　24	富豪　　fugō　　man of great wealth, multimillionaire　　726
豪	豪族　　gōzoku　　powerful/influential family　　　　　　221
	豪雨　　gōu　　heavy rainfall, torrential downpour　　　　30

1787	**KYŌ** – enjoy; receive
2j5.1 ▤	享楽　　kyōraku　　enjoyment　　　　　　　　　　　　　359
宀 口 子	享楽主義　kyōraku shugi　epicureanism, hedonism　359, 155, 291
/11　24　6	享受　　kyōju　　enjoy, have, be given　　　　　　　　　260
享	享有　　kyōyū　　enjoyment, possession　　　　　　　　265
	享年７５歳　kyōnen nanajūgo-sai　dead at the age of 75　45, 487

1788	**KAKU** – enclosure, quarters
2d7.14 ⊞	輪郭　　rinkaku　　contours, outline　　　　　　　　　1221
阝 口 宀	外郭　　gaikaku　　outer wall (of a castle); perimeter　　83
/7　24　11	外郭団体　gaikaku dantai　auxiliary organization　83, 500, 61
郭	城郭　　jōkaku　　castle, fortress; castle walls　　　　733
	郭公　　kakkō　　(Japanese) cuckoo　　　　　　　　　126

1789	**JUKU** – private school
3b10.7 ⊞	私塾　　shijuku　　private class at a teacher's home　　125
土 口 宀	学習塾　gakushūjuku　(private) cram school　　　　109, 601
/22　24　11	塾生　　jukusei　　student of a juku　　　　　　　　　　44
塾	

1790	**AI** – sorrow **awa(re)** – sorrowful, piteous **awa(remu)** – pity, feel compassion
2j7.4 ▤	哀愁　　aishū　　sadness, sorrow, grief　　　　　　　1708
宀 衤 口	悲哀　　hiai　　sorrow, grief, misery　　　　　　　　1075
/11　57　24	哀願　　aigan　　plead, implore, beg　　　⌐emotions　　590
哀	喜怒哀楽　kido-airaku　joy and pathos,　1196, 1703, 359

1791	**SUI, otoro(eru)** – grow weak, decline, wane
2j8.1 ▤	老衰　　rōsui　　feebleness of old age, senility　　　552
宀 衤 口	衰弱　　suijaku　　weakening, debility　　　　　　　218
/11　57　24	衰微　　suibi　　decline, wane　　　　　　　　　　1508
衰	衰亡　　suibō　　decline and fall, ruin, downfall　　684
	盛衰　　seisui　　rise and fall, vicissitudes　　　　　732

1792	**CHŪ** – heart, mind, inside
0a9.9 ▤	衷心　　chūshin　　one's inmost heart/feelings　　　97
衤 口 十	衷情　　chūjō　　one's inmost feelings　　　　　　　209
57　24　12	苦衷　　kuchū　　anguish, predicament　　　　　　　554
衷	折衷　　setchū　　compromise, cross, blending　⌐styles　1483
	和洋折衷　wa-yō setchū　blending of Japanese and Western

	1793	**SŌ, mo** – mourning	
喪	3b9.20 ⊟	喪失 sōshitsu loss	311
	禾 日 艹	喪服 mofuku mourning clothes	696
	57 24 12	喪章 moshō mourning badge/band	876
		喪主 moshu chief mourner	155
	喪	喪中 mochū period of mourning	28

	1794	**TAKU** – table, desk; excel	
卓	2m6.2	食卓 shokutaku dining table	322
	卜 日 十	卓球 takkyū table tennis, ping-pong	739
	/13 42 12	電卓 dentaku (desk-top) calculator	108
		卓上 takujō table-top, desk-top	32
	卓	卓越 takuetsu be superior, excel, surpass	1038

	1795	**TŌ, ita(mu)** – grieve over, mourn, lament	
悼	4k8.13 ⊞	追悼 tsuitō mourning	1232
	忄 日 卜	追悼会 tsuitōkai memorial services	1232, 158
	/51 42 13	追悼式 tsuitōshiki memorial services	1232, 534
		哀悼 aitō condolence, mourning, grief	1790
	悼	悼辞 tōji message of condolence, funeral address	701

	1796	**TEI** – chastity, constancy, righteousness	
貞	2m7.1 ⊟	貞淑 teishuku chastity, feminine modesty	1783
	卜 貝	貞節 teisetsu fidelity, chastity	472
	/13 68	貞操 teisō chastity, female honor, virginity	1769
		貞潔 teiketsu chaste and pure	1307
	貞	不貞 futei unchastity, infidelity	94

	1797	**KŌ, [KYŌ], kao(ri), ka** – fragrance, aroma **kao(ru)** – smell good/ sweet	
香	5d4.5	香気 kōki fragrance, aroma, sweet smell	134
	禾 日	香料 kōryō spices; perfume	319
	/56 42	線香 senkō stick of incense	299
	香	色香 iroka color and scent; (feminine) beauty	204

	1798	**SHŪ, hii(deru)** – excel, surpass	
秀	5d2.4	優秀 yūshū excellent, superior	1074
	禾 力	秀逸 shūitsu superb, masterly	747
	/56 8	秀麗 shūrei graceful, beautiful, handsome	1740
		秀才 shūsai talented man, bright boy/girl	560
	秀	閨秀作家 keishū sakka woman writer	343, 165

	1799	**YŪ, saso(u)** – invite, induce, lure, entice	
誘	7a7.4 ⊞	誘惑 yūwaku temptation, seduction	1001
	言 禾 力	勧誘 kan'yū invitation, canvassing, solicitation	1094
	/67 56 8	誘因 yūin enticement, inducement	563
		誘発 yūhatsu induce, give rise to	96
	誘	誘い水 sasoimizu pump priming; (economic) stimulus	21

1800

透

2q7.10

辶 禾 力
/19 56 8

透

TŌ – transparent **su(ku)** – be transparent; leave a gap **su(keru)** – be transparent **su(kasu)** – look through; leave a space

透明	tōmei	transparent	18
透視	tōshi	seeing through; fluoroscopy; clairvoyance	616
浸透	shintō	permeation, osmosis, infiltration	1126
透き通る	sukitōru	be transparent	150

1801

携

3c10.4

扌 隹 力
/23 73 8

携 攜

KEI, tazusa(eru) – carry (in one's hand); have with one **tazusa(waru)** – participate (in)

携帯	keitai	carrying, bringing with; portable	994
必携	hikkei	handbook, manual; indispensable	529
提携	teikei	cooperation, tie-up	638
連携	renkei	cooperation, league, concert	446

1802

謙

7a10.10

言 ヨ 儿
/67 39 16

謙

KEN – modesty, humility

謙虚	kenkyo	modest, humble	1678
謙譲	kenjō	modest, humble	1051
謙譲の美徳	kenjō no bitoku	the virtue of modesty	1051, 405, 1079
恭謙	kyōken	modesty, humility, deference	1524

1803

嫌

3e10.7

女 ヨ 儿
/25 39 16

嫌

KEN, [GEN], kira(u) – dislike, hate **iya** – disagreeable

嫌悪	ken'o	hatred, dislike, loathing	304
嫌疑	kengi	suspicion	1617
機嫌	kigen	mood, humor	537
大嫌い	daikirai	hate, strong aversion	26
毛嫌い	kegirai	antipathy, prejudice	287

1804

廉

3q10.1

广 ヨ 儿
/18 39 16

廉

REN – pure; honest; low price

清廉	seiren	integrity, uprightness	671
清廉潔白	seiren-keppaku	spotless integrity	671, 1307, 205
廉売	renbai	bargain sale	239
廉価	renka	low price	427

1805

恥

6e4.2

耳 心
/65 51

恥 耻

CHI, haji – shame, disgrace **ha(jiru)** – feel shame **ha(jirau)** – be shy **ha(zukashii)** – shy, ashamed

無恥	muchi	shameless, brazen	93
破廉恥	harenchi	shameless, disgraceful	676, 1804
恥知らず	hajishirazu	shameless person	214

1806

羞

2o9.4

𦍌 儿 十
46 16 12

羞

SHŪ – feel ashamed

| 羞恥心 | shūchishin | sense of shame | 1805, 97 |
| 含羞 | ganshū | shyness, coyness, diffidence | 1317 |

1807

敢

4i8.5

攵 耳 一
/49 65 14

敢

KAN – daring, bold

勇敢	yūkan	brave, daring, courageous	1474
果敢	kakan	resolute, determined, bold, daring	496
敢然	kanzen	bold, fearless	662
敢闘	kantō	fight courageously	1612
敢行	kankō	take decisive action, dare; carry out	68

1808

摂

3c10.6

扌 耳 冫
/23 65 5

摂 攝

SETSU – act in place of; take

摂取	sesshu	take in, ingest	65
摂生	sessei	taking care of one's health	44
摂政	sesshō	regency; regent	492
摂理	setsuri	providence	143
摂氏２０度	sesshi nijūdo	20 degrees Celsius	575, 378

1809

渋

3a8.19

氵 ⺊ 亠
/21 13 11

渋 澁

JŪ, shibu(i) – astringent; puckery; glum; quiet and tasteful
shibu – astringent juice (of unripe persimmons) **shibu(ru)** – hesitate, be reluctant

渋滞	jūtai	impeded flow, congestion, traffic jam, delay	995
渋面	jūmen, shibutsura	sour face, scowl	274
渋味	shibumi	puckery taste; severe elegance	307

1810

塁

5f7.2

畐 土 冫
/58 22 5

塁 壘

RUI – parapet, rampart; base (in baseball)

堅塁	kenrui	fortress, stronghold	1363
敵塁	tekirui	enemy's fortress/position	422
塁審	ruishin	base umpire	1471
本塁打	honruida	home run	25, 1059
満塁	manrui	bases loaded	201

1811

粛

0a11.8

丷 米 ヨ
2o 62 39

粛 肅

SHUKU – quietly, softly, solemnly

静粛	seishuku	stillness, quiet, hush	674
厳粛	genshuku	solemnity, austerity, gravity	841
自粛	jishuku	self-discipline, self-control	62
粛清	shukusei	(political) purge	671
粛党	shukutō	purge disloyal elements from a party	504

1812

庸

3q8.2

广 月 ヨ
/18 43 39

庸

YŌ – mediocre, ordinary

中庸	chūyō	middle path, golden mean	28
凡庸	bon'yō	mediocre, run-of-the-mill	1153
登庸	tōyō	appointment, promotion	991

1813

唐

3q7.3

广 ヨ 口
/18 39 24

唐

TŌ – Tang (Chinese dynasty); foreign **Kara** – China, Cathay; foreign

唐突	tōtotsu	abrupt	920
毛唐（人）	ketō(jin)	hairy barbarian, foreigner	287, 1
遣唐使	kentōshi	Japanese envoy to Tang China	1231, 331
唐様	karayō	Chinese style	407

1814 糖

TŌ – sugar

6b10.3

米 ヨ 口
/62 39 24

糖

砂糖	satō	sugar	1204
製糖	seitō	sugar manufacturing	434
糖分	tōbun	sugar content	38
果糖	katō	fruit sugar, fructos	176
血糖	kettō	blood sugar	803

1815 粧

SHŌ – adorn (one's person)

6b6.1

米 土 厂
/62 22 18

粧

化粧	keshō	makeup	254
化粧品	keshōhin	cosmetics	254, 230
化粧室	keshōshitsu	dressing room; lavatory	254, 166
厚化粧	atsugeshō	heavy makeup	649, 254
薄化粧	usugeshō	light makeup	1542, 254

1816 粒

RYŪ, tsubu – a grain; drop(let)

6b5.1

米 立
/62 54

粒

粒状	ryūjō	granular, granulated	636
粒子	ryūshi	(atomic) particle	103
素粒子	soryūshi	elementary/subatomic particle	271, 103
米粒	kometsubu	grain of rice	224
雨粒	amatsubu	raindrop	30

1817 粉

FUN, kona, ko – flour; powder

6b4.6

米 几 力
/62 16 8

粉

粉末	funmatsu	powder	305
製粉所	seifunjo	flour mill	434, 153
粉飾	funshoku	makeup; embellishment	1013
粉ミルク	konamiruku	powdered milk	
メリケン粉	merikenko	wheat flour	

1818 紛

FUN – confused, tangled **magi(reru)** – be mistaken (for), be hardly distinguishable; get mixed; be diverted **magi(rasu/rawasu)** – divert, distract; conceal; evade **magi(rawashii)** – ambiguous, liable to be confused

6a4.8

糸 几 力
/61 16 8

紛

| 紛争 | funsō | dispute, strife | 302 |
| 紛失 | funshitsu | loss, be missing | 311 |

1819 糾

KYŪ – twist (rope); ask, inquire into

6a3.4

糸 十 丨
/61 12 2

糾 糺

糾弾	kyūdan	impeach, censure	1641
糾明	kyūmei	study, inquiry, investigation	18
糾問	kyūmon	close examination, grilling	162
紛糾	funkyū	complication, entanglement	1818
糾合	kyūgō	rally, muster	159

1820 糧

RYŌ, [RŌ], kate – food, provisions

6b12.1

米 日 土
/62 42 22

糧 粮

食糧	shokuryō	food, foodstuffs	322
糧食	ryōshoku	provisions, food supplies	322
兵糧	hyōrō	(military) provisions	798
日々の糧	hibi no kate	one's daily bread	5
心の糧	kokoro no kate	food for thought	97

墨	**1821** 3b11.4 □ 土 日 火 /22 42 44 墨	**BOKU** – India ink; (short for) Mexico **sumi** – India ink

水墨画　　suibokuga　India-ink painting　　　　　　　　　21, 343
白墨　　　hakuboku　chalk　　　　　　　　　　　　　　　205
墨守　　　bokushu　adherence (to tradition)　　　　　　　499
墨絵　　　sumie　India-ink drawing　　　　　　　　　　　345
入れ墨　　irezumi　tattooing; a tattoo　　　　　　　　　　52

占	**1822** 2m3.2 □ ト 口 /13 24 占	**SEN, shi(meru)** – occupy, hold **urana(u)** – tell fortunes

占有　　　sen'yū　occupancy, possession　　　　　　　　265
占領　　　senryō　occupation, capture　　　　　　　　　853
独占　　　dokusen　monopoly　　　　　　　　　　　　　219
買い占め　kaishime　cornering (the market)　　　　　　　241
星占い　　hoshiuranai　astrology; horoscope　　　　　　　743

貼	**1823** 7b5.2 □ 貝 口 ト /68 24 13 貼	**CHŌ, ha(ru)** – stick on, paste, affix

貼付、貼り付ける　chōfu, haritsukeru　stick, paste, affix
　　　　　　　　　　　　　　　　　　　　　　　　192, 192
貼り紙　　harigami　sticker, poster　　　　　　　　　　　180

粘	**1824** 6b5.4 □ 米 口 ト /62 24 13 粘 黏	**NEN, neba(ru)** – be sticky; stick to it, persevere

粘着（力）　nenchaku(ryoku)　adhesion, viscosity　　668, 100
粘土　　　nendo　clay　　　　　　　　　　　　　　　　24
粘液　　　nen'eki　mucus　　　　　　　　　　　　　　480
粘膜　　　nenmaku　mucous membrane　　　　　　　　1515
粘り強い　nebarizuyoi　tenacious, persistent　　　　　　217

粋	**1825** 6b4.5 □ 米 十 /62 12 粋 粹	**SUI** – purity, essence, elite, choice; elegant, fashionable, chic; considerateness **iki** – chic, stylish

純粋　　　junsui　pure, genuine　　　　　　　　　　　　996
粋人　　　suijin　man of refined tastes, man about town　　　1
粋狂　　　suikyō　whimsical, capricious　　　　　　　　904
精粋　　　seisui　pure, selfless　　　　　　　　　　　　670

酔	**1826** 7e4.3 □ 酉 十 /71 12 酔 醉	**SUI, yo(u)** – get drunk; be intoxicated; feel (sea)sick

麻酔　　　masui　anesthesia; narcosis　　　　　　　　　1630
泥酔　　　deisui　get dead drunk　　　　　　　　　　　1729
心酔　　　shinsui　be fascinated (with), ardently admire　　　97
酔っ払い　yopparai　a drunk　　　　　　　　　　　　　591
船酔い　　funayoi　seasickness　　　　　　　　　　　　377

砕	**1827** 5a4.6 □ 石 十 /53 12 砕 碎	**SAI, kuda(ku)** – break, smash, pulverize **kuda(keru)** – break, be crushed; become familiar

粉砕　　　funsai　pulverize, shatter, crush　　　　　　　1817
砕石　　　saiseki　rubble, broken stone　　　┌efforts　　　78
粉骨砕身　funkotsu-saishin　make one's utmost　1817, 1340, 59
玉砕　　　gyokusai　death for honor　　　　　　　　　　295

1828

酷

酷 7e7.1
酉 土 口
/71 22 24

KOKU – severe, harsh, cruel

残酷	zankoku	cruel	661
冷酷	reikoku	heartless, cruel	851
酷評	kokuhyō	sharp/harsh criticism	1067
酷使	kokushi	work (someone) hard	331
酷暑	kokusho	intense heat, swelter	648

1829

披

披 3c5.13
扌 厂 又
/23 18 9

HI – open

披露	hirō	announcement	981
結婚披露宴	kekkon hirōen	wedding reception	494, 576, 981, 650
披歴	hireki	express (one's opinion)	489
披見	hiken	open and read (a letter)	63

1830

抜 拔

抜 3c4.10
扌 十 又
/23 12 9

BATSU, nu(ku) – pull out; remove; leave out; outdistance, surpass
nu(keru) – come/fall out; be omitted; be gone; escape
nu(karu) – make a blunder **nu(kasu)** – omit, skip over

抜群	batsugun	preeminent, outstanding	808
選抜	senbatsu	selection, picking out	814
骨抜き	honenuki	deboned; emasculated, toothless	1340

1831

握

握 3c9.17
扌 尸 土
/23 40 22

AKU, nigi(ru) – grasp, grip, take hold of

握手	akushu	shake hands	57
掌握	shōaku	hold, seize, grasp	508
一握り	hitonigiri	handful	2
握り飯	nigirimeshi	rice ball	325
握り締める	nigirishimeru	grasp tightly, clench	1239

1832

擁

擁 3c13.5
扌 隹 亠
/23 73 11

YŌ – embrace

抱擁	hōyō	embrace	1359
擁護	yōgo	protect, defend	1391
擁立	yōritsu	support, back	121

1833

窒

窒 3m8.9
宀 土 儿
/33 22 16

CHITSU – plug up, obstruct; nitrogen

窒息	chissoku	suffocation, asphyxiation	1308
窒息死	chissokushi	death from suffocation	1308, 85
窒素	chisso	nitrogen	271

1834

窃 竊

窃 3m6.5
宀 儿 十
/33 16 12

SETSU – steal

窃盗	settō	theft, thief	1151
窃盗罪	settōzai	theft, larceny	1151, 906
窃盗犯	settōhan	thief	1151, 903
窃取	sesshu	steal	65
剽窃	hyōsetsu	plagiarism	

控	**1835** 3c8.11 ⊞ 扌 宀 エ /23 33 38 控	**KŌ, hika(eru)** – hold back, refrain from; note down; wait

控除　*kōjo*　deduct, subtract　　　　　　　　　1112
控訴　*kōso*　(intermediate) appeal (to a higher court)　1491
手控え　*tebikae*　note, memo; holding off/ back　　57
控え室　*hikaeshitsu*　anteroom, lobby　　　　166
控え目　*hikaeme*　moderate, reserved　　　　55

貢	**1836** 7b3.3 貝 エ /68 38 貢	**KŌ, [KU]** – pay tribute **mitsu(gu)** – support (financially)

貢献　*kōken*　contribution, services　　　　1438
年貢　*nengu*　annual tribute　　　　　　　45
貢ぎ（物）　*mitsugi(mono)*　tribute　　　　79

貪	**1837** 2a9.20 亻 貝 一 /3 68 1 貪	**DON, musabo(ru)** – covet, be vocarious; indulge in

貪欲　*don'yoku*　avaricious, rapacious, covetous　　1179
貪婪　*donran*　covetousness, greed

拷	**1838** 3c6.2 ⊞ 扌 耂 一 /23 22 1 拷	**GŌ** – beat, torture

拷問　*gōmon*　torture　　　　　　　　162
拷問具　*gōmongu*　instrument of torture　162, 426

扶	**1839** 3c4.4 ⊞ 扌 大 一 /23 34 1 扶	**FU** – help

扶養　*fuyō*　support (a family)　⌐(someone)　406
扶養義務　*fuyō gimu*　duty of supporting　406, 291, 235
扶養料　*fuyōryō*　sustenance allowance, alimony　406, 319
扶助　*fujo*　aid, support, relief　　　　633
扶持　*fuchi*　rice ration allotted to a samurai　458

搬	**1840** 3c10.2 ⊞ 扌 舟 几 /23 63 20 搬	**HAN** – carry, transport

運搬　*unpan*　transport, conveyance, delivery　445
搬送　*hansō*　convey, carry　　　　　447
搬入　*hannyū*　carry/send in　　　　52
搬出　*hanshutsu*　carry/take out　　53

肥	**1841** 4b4.5 ⊞ 月 尸 l /43 40 2 肥	**HI, koe, ko(yashi)** – manure, dung, night soil **ko(yasu)** – fertilize **ko(eru)** – grow fat; grow fertile; have fastidious taste

肥料　*hiryō*　manure, fertilizer　　　　319
肥満　*himan*　corpulence, fatness, obesity　201
肥大　*hidai*　corpulence, obesity; hypertrophy　26
堆肥　*taihi*　compost, barnyard manure　1749

把	**1842** 3c4.5 ⊞ 扌 尸 丨 /23 40 2 把	**HA** – take, grasp; bundle	

把握　*haaku*　grasp, comprehend　1831
把捉　*hasoku*　grasp, comprehend　1660
把持　*haji*　grasp, clasp　458
一把　*ichiwa*　one bundle　2
十把　*jippa*　ten bundles　12

1843
4k8.5 ⊞
心 大 彡
/51 34 31
惨　惨

SAN, ZAN, miji(me) – piteous, wretched, miserable

悲惨　*hisan*　misery, distress, tragedy　1075
惨事　*sanji*　disaster, tragic accident　80
惨状　*sanjō*　miserable state, disastrous scene　636
惨敗　*sanpai, zanpai*　crushing defeat　520
惨死　*zanshi*　tragic/violent death　85

1844
3r3.1 …
尸 丶
/40 2
尽　盡

JIN, tsu(kusu) – exhaust, use up; render (service), make efforts
tsu(kiru) – be exhausted, be used up, run out, end
tsu(kasu) – exhaust, use up, run out of

尽力　*jinryoku*　efforts, exertions; assistance　100
無尽蔵　*mujinzō*　inexhaustible supply　93, 1360
論じ尽くす　*ronjitsukusu*　discuss fully/exhaustively　293

1845
4j8.2 ⊞
欠 ネ 士
/49 45 22
款

KAN – article, section; goodwill; friendship

借款　*shakkan*　(international) loan　780
長期借款　*chōki shakkan*　long-term loan　95, 456, 780
定款　*teikan*　articles of association/incorporation　356
約款　*yakkan*　agreement, provision, clause　211
落款　*rakkan*　signature (and seal)　858

1846
3p8.1 ⊞
壴 几
/22 20
殻　殻

KAKU, kara – husk, hull, shell

地殻　*chikaku*　the earth's crust　118
地殻変動　*chikaku hendō*　movement of the earth's crust
118, 257, 231
貝殻　*kaigara*　seashell　240
卵の殻　*tamago no kara*　eggshell　1103

1847
5d9.4 ⊞
禾 士 几
/56 22 20
穀

KOKU – grain, cereals

穀物　*kokumotsu*　grain　79
穀類　*kokurui*　grains　226
五穀　*gokoku*　the five grains　7
穀倉　*kokusō*　granary, grain elevator　1386
脱穀機　*dakkokuki*　threshing machine, thresher　1457, 537

1848
3p4.2 ⊟
壴 几 卜
/22 20 13
壱　壹

ICHI – one (in documents)

金壱万円　*kin ichiman en*　10,000 yen　23, 16, 13

	1849	**KETSU** – excel	
傑	2a11.6 ⊞	傑出 *kesshutsu* excel, be eminent	53
	イ 木 夕	傑作 *kessaku* masterpiece	361
	/3 41 30	傑物 *ketsubutsu* great man, outstanding figure	79
	傑 杰	豪傑 *gōketsu* hero, great man	1786
		豪傑笑い *gōketsu warai* broad/hearty laugh	1786, 1299

	1850	**SHUN, matata(ku)** – wink, blink, twinkle	
瞬	5c13.1 ⊞	瞬間 *shunkan* instant, moment	43
	目 小 夕	瞬時 *shunji* moment, instant	42
	/55 35 30	一瞬 *isshun* instant; for an instant	2
	瞬	瞬刻 *shunkoku* instant, moment	1274

	1851	**BI, MI, mayu** – eyebrow	
眉	5c4.9 ▢	眉目秀麗 *bimoku shūrei* handsome (man)	55, 1798, 1740
	目 尸 丨	眉間 *miken* between the eyebrows	43
	/55 40 2	眉唾(物) *mayutsuba(mono)* fake, fishy story, cock-and-bull	
	眉	story	1119, 79

	1852	**DŌ, hitomi** – pupil (of the eye)	
瞳	5c12.2 ⊞	瞳孔 *dōkō* pupil (of the eye)	970
	目 立 里		
	/55 54 42		
	瞳		

	1853	**SHŌ, akoga(reru)** – yearn (for), aspire (to)	
憧	4k12.5 ⊞		
	心 立 里		
	/51 54 42		
	憧		

	1854	**KEI** – yearn for, aspire to	
憬	4k12.7 ⊞	憧憬 *shōkei, dōkei* longing, aspiration	1853
	心 日 儿		
	/51 42 24		
	憬		

	1855	**KAI, ku(iru)** – regret, rue **ku(yamu)** – regret, rue; lament, mourn over; offer condolences **kuya(shii)** – vexatious, vexing	
悔	4k6.12 ⊞	後悔 *kōkai* regret	48
	心 女 𠂉	悔悟 *kaigo* remorse, regret	1528
	/51 25 15	悔やみ状 *kuyamijō* letter of condolence	636
	悔	悔やみ言 *kuyamigoto* words of condolence	66

1856

梅

4a6.27 田
木 女 宀
/41 25 15

梅 楳

BAI, ume – ume, Japanese plum/apricot (tree)

梅雨	*baiu, tsuyu*	the rainy season	30
紅梅	*kōbai*	ume with red/pink blossoms	839
松竹梅	*shō-chiku-bai*	pine-bamboo-plum (auspicious	709, 129
梅酒	*umeshu*	ume brandy	signs; 3 grades) 526
梅干し	*umeboshi*	pickled ume	593

1857

敏

4i6.3 田
攵 女 宀
/49 25 15

敏

BIN – agile, alert

敏速	*binsoku*	promptness, alacrity	511
敏感	*binkan*	sensitive	262
鋭敏	*eibin*	sharp, keen, acute	1458
機敏	*kibin*	smart, astute, alert	537
敏腕	*binwan*	able, capable	1376

1858

侮

2a6.20 田
亻 女 宀
/3 25 15

侮

BU, anado(ru) – despise

軽侮	*keibu*	scorn, contempt	556
侮言	*bugen*	an insult	66
侮蔑	*bubetsu*	scorn, contempt	1564

1859

唇

3d7.12 日
口 衤 厂
/24 57 18

唇 脣

SHIN, kuchibiru – lip

口唇	*kōshin*	lips	54
紅唇	*kōshin*	red lips	839
唇音	*shin'on*	a labial (sound)	347
上唇	*uwa-kuchibiru, jōshin*	upper lip	32
下唇	*shita-kuchibiru, kashin*	lower lip	31

1860

辱

2p8.2 日
厂 衤 寸
/18 57 37

辱

JOKU, hazukashi(meru) – humiliate, disgrace

侮辱	*bujoku*	insult	1858
恥辱	*chijoku*	disgrace, dishonor	1805
汚辱	*ojoku*	disgrace, dishonor	706
国辱	*kokujoku*	national disgrace	40
雪辱	*setsujoku*	vindication; revenge	979

1861

賄

7b6.1 田
貝 月 十
/68 43 12

賄

WAI, makana(u) – provide board, supply, furnish; pay for, finance

贈賄	*zōwai*	giving a bribe, bribery	1451
収賄	*shūwai*	accepting a bribe, bribery	770
賄い付き	*makanai-tsuki*	with meals	192

1862

賂

7b6.2 田
貝 夂 口
/68 49 24

賂

RO – gift, present, bribe

賄賂	*wairo*	bribe, bribery	1861

1863

髄

4b14.3

月 门 十
/43 20 12

髄 髓

ZUI – marrow

骨髄	*kotsuzui*	bone marrow	1340
脊髄	*sekizui*	spinal cord	1339
脳髄	*nōzui*	brain	1352
真／神／心髄	*shinzui*	essence, quintessence, soul	428, 310, 97
精髄	*seizui*	essence, quintessence, soul	670

1864

随

2d8.10

阝 月 十
/7 43 12

随 隨

ZUI – follow

追随	*tsuizui*	follow (someone)	1232
随意	*zuii*	voluntary, optional	132
随筆	*zuihitsu*	essay, miscellaneous writings	130
付随現象	*fuzui genshō*	concomitant	192, 298, 752
随一	*zuiichi*	most, greatest, first ⌐phenomenon	2

1865

堕

3b8.14

土 月 阝
/22 43 7

堕 墮

DA – fall

堕落	*daraku*	depravity, corruption	858
堕胎	*datai*	abortion	1371

1866

惰

4k9.6

心 月 工
/51 43 38

惰

DA – lazy, inactive

怠惰	*taida*	laziness, idleness, sloth	1372
惰性	*dasei*	inertia; force of habit	98
惰気	*daki*	inactivity, dullness	134
惰眠	*damin*	idle slumber, lethargy	868

1867

佐

2a5.9

亻 工 十
/3 38 12

佐

SA – help

補佐	*hosa*	aid; assistant, adviser	910
少佐	*shōsa*	major; lieutenant commander (in the navy)	144
大佐	*taisa*	colonel; captain (in the navy)	26
佐官	*sakan*	field officer	326
土佐	*Tosa*	(city and region in Shikoku)	24

1868

婿

3e9.3

女 月 一
/25 43 14

婿 壻

SEI, muko – son-in-law, bridegroom

花婿	*hanamuko*	bridegroom	255
婿養子	*mukoyōshi*	son-in-law taken into the family	406, 103
婿選び	*mukoerabi*	looking for a husband for one's daughter	814

1869

姓

3e5.3

女 土 宀
/25 22 15

姓

SEI, SHŌ – surname, family name

姓名	*seimei*	(one's full) name	82
同姓	*dōsei*	same surname; namesakes	198
改姓	*kaisei*	change one's surname	523
旧姓	*kyūsei*	one's former/maiden name	1279
百姓	*hyakushō*	farmer	14

如	**1870** 3e3.1 ⊞ 女 口 /25 24 如	**JO, NYO** – equal, like, as, if
		突如 *totsujo* suddenly, unexpectedly 920 躍如 *yakujo* vivid, lifelike 1663 欠如 *ketsujo* lack, deficiency 384 如実 *nyojitsu* true to life, realistic 203 如何 *ikaga* how 392

姻	**1871** 3e6.8 ⊞ 女 口 大 /25 24 34 姻	**IN** – marriage
		婚姻 *kon'in* marriage, matrimony 576 婚姻法 *kon'inhō* the Marriage Law 576, 123 姻族 *inzoku* relatives by marriage, in-laws 221 姻戚 *inseki* relatives by marriage, in-laws 488

咽	**1872** 3d6.14 ⊞ 口 大 /24 34 咽	**IN** – throat
		咽頭 *intō* pharynx 276

嫁	**1873** 3e10.6 ⊞ 女 宀 豕 /25 33 27 嫁	**KA** – marry (a man); blame **totsu(gu)** – get married **yome** – bride, young wife; daughter-in-law
		転嫁 *tenka* remarriage; impute (blame) 439 花嫁 *hanayome* bride 255 嫁入り *yomeiri* marriage, wedding (of a woman) 52

稼	**1874** 5d10.3 ⊞ 禾 宀 豕 /56 33 27 稼	**KA, kase(gu)** – work, earn (a living)
		稼働 *kadō* operation, work 232 稼業 *kagyō* one's trade/occupation 279 出稼ぎ *dekasegi* work away from home 53 時間稼ぎ *jikan kasegi* playing/stalling for time 42, 43 稼ぎ手 *kasegite* breadwinner; hard worker 57

塚	**1875** 3b9.10 ⊞ 土 豕 冖 /22 27 20 塚	**tsuka** – mound, hillock
		貝塚 *kaizuka* heap of shells 240 蟻塚 *arizuka* anthill 一里塚 *ichirizuka* milepost, milestone 2, 142

娘	**1876** 3e7.2 ⊞ 女 食 /25 77 娘	**musume** – daughter, girl
		孫娘 *magomusume* granddaughter 932 娘婿 *musumemuko* son-in-law 1868 一人娘 *hitori musume* an only daughter 2, 1 箱入り娘 *hakoiri musume* girl who has led a sheltered 1142, 52 田舎娘 *inaka musume* country girl ⌊life 35, 805

浪	**1877** 3a7.5 □ 氵 食 /21 77 浪	**RŌ** – waves; wander 波浪　*harō*　waves, high seas　　677 浮浪　*furō*　vagrancy, vagabondage　　968 流浪　*rurō*　vagrancy, wandering　　247 浪人　*rōnin*　lordless samurai; unaffiliated person　　1 浪費　*rōhi*　waste, squander　　762
朗	**1878** 4b6.11 □ 月 食 /43 77 朗 脿	**RŌ, hoga(raka)** – clear, bright, cheerful 明朗　*meirō*　bright, clear, cheerful　　18 朗々　*rōrō*　clear, sonorous 朗詠　*rōei*　recite (a Japanese/Chinese poem)　　1272 朗読　*rōdoku*　read aloud, recite　　244 朗報　*rōhō*　good news, glad tidings　　698
恨	**1879** 4k6.2 心 食 /51 77 恨	**KON** – resent, regret **ura(mu)** – bear a grudge, resent, reproach **ura(meshii)** – reproachful, resentful, rueful 遺恨　*ikon*　grudge, rancor, malice, enmity　　1230 悔恨　*kaikon*　remorse, contrition　　1855 痛恨　*tsūkon*　great sorrow, bitter regret　　1402 恨み言　*uramigoto*　grudge, grievance, reproach　　66
痕	**1880** 5i6.2 疒 食 /60 77 痕	**KON, ato** – scar, mark 痕跡　*konseki*　traces, vestiges, evidence　　1673 血痕　*kekkon*　bloodstain　　803 爪痕　*tsumeato*　scratch; pinch mark　　1320
妃	**1881** 3e3.2 女 弓 /25 28 妃	**HI** – (married) princess 王妃　*ōhi*　queen, empress　　294 皇太子妃　*kōtaishihi*　the crown princess　　297, 639, 103 妃殿下　*hidenka*　Her Imperial Highness　　1182, 31
姫	**1882** 3e7.11 女 門 丨 /25 20 2 姫	**hime** – princess 姫君　*himegimi*　princess　　807 舞姫　*maihime*　dancing girl, dancer　　829 歌姫　*utahime*　songstress　　395 姫路　*Himeji*　(city with a famous castle, 100 km west of Ōsaka)　　151
媛	**1883** 3e9.4 女 小 フ /25 35 14 媛	**EN** – princess 才媛　*saien*　talented woman　　560 愛媛県　*Ehime-ken*　Ehime Prefecture　　259, 194

1884

妖

3e4.4
女 大 ノ
/25 34 2
妖

YŌ, aya(shii) – eerie; bewitching, enchanting

妖艶	yōen	voluptuous charm, bewitching beauty	990
妖婦	yōfu	enchantress, siren	316
妖怪	yōkai	ghost, apparition	1573
妖精	yōsei	fairy, sprite, elf	670

1885

沃

3a4.10
氵 大 ノ
/21 34 2
沃

YOKU – fertile

肥沃	hiyoku	fertile	1841
沃土	yokudo	fertile land/soil	24

1886

竜

5b5.3
立 日 ｜
/54 42 2
竜 龍

RYŪ, tatsu – dragon

飛竜	hiryū	flying dragon	539
竜宮	ryūgū	Palace of the Dragon King	734
恐竜	kyōryū	dinosaur	1709
竜骨	ryūkotsu	keel	1340
竜巻	tatsumaki	tornado	516

1887

滝

3a10.8
氵 立 日
/21 54 42
滝 瀧

taki – waterfall

滝口	takiguchi	top/crest of a waterfall	54
滝壺	takitsubo	bottom/basin of a waterfall	
滝登り	takinobori	(salmon) climbing a waterfall	991
華厳の滝	Kegon no Taki	(waterfall near Nikkō)	1122, 841

1888

籠

6f16.1
⺮ 立 月
/66 54 43
籠

RŌ, kago – basket, (bird) cage, case **ko(moru)** – seclude oneself, hole up

灯籠	tōrō	(hanging/garden) lantern	1416
籠城	rōjō	be under siege, hole up, be confined	733
引き籠り、引っ籠り	hikikomori, hikkomori	social withdrawal; a shut-in	216, 216
鳥籠	torikago	bird cage	285

1889

亀

2n9.1
⺈ 日 ｜
/15 42 2
亀

KI, kame – turtle, tortoise

亀甲	kikkō	tortoise shell	1016
亀裂	kiretsu	crack, fissure	1413
海亀	umigame	sea turtle	117
鶴亀	tsurukame	crane and tortoise (as symbols of longevity); congratulations	950

1890

縄

6a9.1
糸 日 ｜
/61 42 2
縄 繩

JŌ, nawa – rope

縄文	jōmon	(ancient Japanese) straw-rope pattern	111
縄張	nawabari	rope off; one's domain	1158
縄跳び	nawatobi	skipping/jumping rope	1666
自縄自縛に陥る	jijō-jibaku ni ochiiru	fall into one's own trap	62, 62, 1541, 1281

	1891	**SHI, ukaga(u)** – visit; ask, inquire; hear, be told	
伺	2a5.23	伺候　shikō　wait upon, attend; make a courtesy call	974
	イ　口　一	奉伺　hōshi　attend, serve	1643
	/3　24　1	暑中伺い　shochū ukagai　hot-season greeting	648, 28
	伺	進退伺い　shintai ukagai　informal resignation	443, 865

	1892	**SHI, ka(u)** – raise, keep (animals)	
飼	8b5.4	飼育　shiiku　raising, breeding	246
	食　口　一	飼料　shiryō　feed, fodder	319
	/77　24　1	飼い主　kainushi　(pet) owner, master	155
	飼	羊飼い　hitsujikai　shepherd	288
		飼い犬　kaiinu　pet dog	280

	1893	**HŌ** – satiated; tired **a(kiru)** – get (sick and) tired of, have had enough of **a(kasu)** – satiate; bore	
飽	8b5.1	飽食　hōshoku　gluttony, engorgement	322
	食　弓　宀	飽和　hōwa　saturation	124
	/77　28　15	見飽きる　miakiru　get tired of seeing	63
	飽	…に飽かして　… ni akashite　regardless of …	

	1894	**HŌ** – gun, cannon	
砲	5a5.3	大砲　taihō　cannon	26
	石　弓　宀	鉄砲　teppō　gun	312
	/53　28　15	砲撃　hōgeki　shelling, bombardment	1054
	砲	砲兵　hōhei　artillery; artilleryman, gunner	798
		(十字)砲火　(jūji) hōka　(cross)fire	12, 110, 20

	1895	**HŌ, awa** – bubble, foam, froth, suds	
泡	3a5.18	気泡　kihō　(air) bubble	134
	氵　弓　宀	水泡　suihō　foam, bubble	21
	/21　28　15	発泡　happō　foaming	96
	泡	泡立つ　awadatsu　bubble, foam, lather up	121
		泡を食う　awa o kuu　be flurried, lose one's head	322

	1896	**KYŪ** – mortar, hand mill; grind **usu** – mortar, hand mill	
臼	0a6.4	臼歯　kyūshi　molar	486
	ヨ　厂　一	臼砲　kyūhō　mortar (cannon)	1894
	39　18　1	脱臼　dakkyū　become dislocated	1457
	臼	石臼　ishiusu　stone mill/mortar	78

	1897	**KI** – damage, censure	
毀	3b10.14	毀損　kison　damage, injure	351
	土　ヨ　厂	名誉毀損(罪)　meiyo kison(zai)　defamation of character, libel, slander	82, 816, 351, 906
	/22　39　18	誹毀　hiki　defamation, libel	
	毀		

庶	**1898**	**SHO** – various; illegitimate (child); the (common) people
	3q8.7	庶務　　shomu　general affairs ……………………………………… 235
	广 火 艹	庶務課　shomuka　general affairs section …………………… 235, 497
	/18 44 32	庶民　　shomin　the (common) people ………………………… 177
		庶民的　shominteki　popular, common, democratic …… 177, 210
	庶	庶子　　shoshi　illegitimate child …………………………… 103

遮	**1899**	**SHA, saegi(ru)** – interrupt, obstruct, block
	2q11.4	遮断　　shadan　interception, isolation, cutoff ……………… 1063
	辶 火 艹	遮断機　shadanki　railroad-crossing gate …………… 1063, 537
	/19 44 32	遮断器　shadanki　circuit breaker ……………………… 1063, 536
	遮	

礁	**1900**	**SHŌ** – sunken rock
	5a12.2	暗礁　　anshō　sunken rock, unseen reef, snag …………… 348
	石 隹 火	岩礁　　ganshō　(shore) reef ………………………………… 1428
	/53 73 44	環礁　　kanshō　atoll …………………………………………… 884
		珊瑚礁　sangoshō　coral reef
	礁	離礁　　rishō　get (a ship) off the rocks, refloat ………… 1355

諮	**1901**	**SHI, haka(ru)** – consult, confer, solicit advice
	7a9.4	諮問　　shimon　question, inquiry …………………………… 162
	言 攵 口	諮問機関　shimon kikan　advisory body …………… 162, 537, 402
	/67 49 24	諮問委員会　shimon iinkai　advisory committee/panel
	諮	162, 474, 163, 158

諾	**1902**	**DAKU** – consent, agree to
	7a8.10	承諾　　shōdaku　consent, agreement ………………………… 972
	言 艹 口	許諾　　kyodaku　consent, approval, permission …………… 750
	/67 32 24	受諾　　judaku　acceptance (of an offer) …………………… 260
		内諾　　naidaku　informal consent …………………………… 84
	諾	諾否　　dakuhi　acceptance or refusal, definite reply …… 1316

匿	**1903**	**TOKU** – shelter, hide
	2t8.2	匿名　　tokumei　anonymity; pseudonym ………………… 82
	匚 艹 口	隠匿　　intoku　conceal, stash away, cover up …………… 887
	/20 32 24	隠匿者　intokusha　hoarder, concealer ………………… 887, 164
	匿	隠匿物資　intoku busshi　secret cache of goods … 887, 79, 763

衝	**1904**	**SHŌ** – collision
	3i12.1	衝撃　　shōgeki　shock, impact ⌐collision ………………… 1054
	彳 車 二	(正面)衝突　(shōmen) shōtotsu　(head-on) ……… 275, 274, 920
	/29 69 4	緩衝地帯　kanshō chitai　buffer zone ………… 1140, 118, 994
		折衝　　sesshō　negotiations ………………………………… 1483
	衝	衝動　　shōdō　impulse, urge, drive …………………………… 231

1905

勲

4d11.3
火 車 力
/44 69 8

勲 勲

KUN – merit

勲功	*kunkō*	distinguished service, merits	837
勲章	*kunshō*	order, decoration, medal	876
勲一等	*kun ittō*	First Order of Merit	2, 578
殊勲	*shukun*	distinguished service, meritorious deeds	1604
偉勲	*ikun*	brilliant exploit, great achievement	1096

1906

薫

3k13.17
艹 車 火
/32 69 44

薫

KUN, kao(ru) – be fragrant, smell good

薫香	*kunkō*	incense; fragrance	1797
薫風	*kunpū*	balmy breeze	29
薫陶	*kuntō*	discipline, training; education	1763
風薫る五月	*kaze kaoru gogatsu*	the balmy month of May	29, 7, 17

1907

芳

3k4.1
艹 方
/32 48

芳

HŌ – fragrance; (honoric prefix) **kanba(shii)** – sweet-smelling, favorable, fair

芳香	*hōkō*	fragrance, perfume, aroma	1797
芳名	*hōmei*	good name/reputation; your name	book 82
(来客)芳名録	*(raikyaku) hōmeiroku*	visitor's	69, 651, 82, 547
秋芳洞	*Akiyoshi-dō*	Akiyoshi Cave (Japan's largest)	470, 1380

1908

倣

2a8.7
亻 方 攵
/3 48 49

倣

HŌ, nara(u) – imitate, follow

模倣	*mohō*	imitation	1514
先例に倣う	*senrei ni narau*	follow precedent	50, 622

1909

昇

4c4.5
日 艹 丨
/42 32 2

昇

SHŌ, nobo(ru) – rise, be promoted

上昇	*jōshō*	rise, ascent; upward trend	32
昇進	*shōshin*	promotion, advancement	443
昇格	*shōkaku*	promotion to a higher status, upgrading	653
昇給	*shōkyū*	pay raise	346
昇級	*shōkyū*	promotion to a higher grade	577

1910

驚

10a12.4
馬 攵 艹
/78 49 32

驚

KYŌ, odoro(ku) – be surprised, astonished, be frightened
odoro(kasu) – surprise, astonish, frighten

驚嘆	*kyōtan*	admiration, wonder	1313
驚異	*kyōi*	wonder, miracle, marvel	1106
驚愕	*kyōgaku*	astonishment; alarm, consternation	

1911

謄

4b13.1
月 言 火
/43 67 44

謄

TŌ – copy

謄写	*tōsha*	copy, duplication	549
謄写器	*tōshaki*	mimeograph machine	549, 536
謄写版	*tōshaban*	mimeograph	549, 1089
謄本	*tōhon*	transcript, copy	25

1912

騰

2 1 3 4 5 6 7 8 9 10 11 16 17 18 19 20

4b16.3 ⊞
月 馬 火
/43 78 44
騰

TŌ – rise (in prices)

(物価)騰貴	(bukka) tōki	rise (in prices)	79, 427, 1228
暴騰	bōtō	sudden/sharp rise	1052
高騰	kōtō	sudden rise, jump (in prices)	190
騰勢	kōsei	rising/upward trend	656

1913

幣

3f12.4 ⊞
巾 攵 小
/26 49 35
幣 幣

HEI – Shinto zigzag paper offerings; money

紙幣	shihei	paper money	180
貨幣	kahei	money; coin, coinage ⌐currency	765
貨幣価値	kahei kachi	the value of money/	765, 427, 431
造幣局	Zōheikyoku	Mint Bureau	704, 170
幣制	heisei	monetary system	433

1914

弊

4i11.3 ⊞
攵 小 廾
/49 35 32
弊

HEI – evil; abuse, vice; (as prefix) our (humble)

弊害	heigai	an evil, ill effect	527
疲弊	hihei	impoverishment, exhaustion	1403
旧弊	kyūhei	an old evil; old-fashioned	1279
弊社	heisha	our company, we	308

1915

却

2e5.3 ⊞
卩 土 ム
/7 22 17
却 卻

KYAKU – pull back, withdraw

却下	kyakka	reject, dismiss	31
返却	henkyaku	return, repay	448
退却	taikyaku	retreat	865
売却	baikyaku	sale, disposal by sale	239
忘却	bōkyaku	forget, lose sight of	1461

1916

脚

4b7.3 ⦀
月 土 阝
/43 22 7
脚

KYAKU, [KYA], ashi – leg

橋脚	kyōkyaku	bridge pier	607
失脚	shikkyaku	lose one's position/standing	311
脚注	kyakuchū	footnote	358
脚本	kyakuhon	play, script	25
脚色	kyakushoku	dramatization, stage/film adaption	204

1917

膝

4b11.4 ⊞
月 木 氵
/43 41 21
膝

hiza – knee; lap

膝掛け	hizakake	lap robe/blanket	1559
膝小僧	hizakozō	kneecap	27, 1453
膝元	hizamoto	near one's knee; at the knees of	137
膝詰め談判	hizazume danpan	face-to-face talk,	1195, 603, 1065
膝栗毛	hizakurige	go on foot, hike it ⌐direct negotiations	287

1918

慎

4k10.4 ⊞
心 目 十
/51 55 12
慎 愼

SHIN, tsutsushi(mu) – be discreet, careful, restrain oneself, refrain from

謹慎	kinshin	good behavior; house arrest	1314
慎重	shinchō	cautious	227
慎み深い	tsutsushimibukai	discreet, cautious	545

1919 鎮

8a10.6

鎮 目 十
/72　55　12

鎮 鎭

CHIN – calm, quell; weight **shizu(meru)** – calm, quell
shizu(maru) – calm down

鎮静剤	chinseizai	a sedative	674, 559
鎮痛剤	chintsūzai	pain-killer	1402, 559
鎮圧	chin'atsu	suppression, quelling	1425
鎮魂曲	chinkonkyoku	requiem	1626, 367

1920 塡

3b10.5

土 目 卜
/22　55　13

塡 填

TEN – fill in

充塡	jūten	fill (up), plug	847
装塡	sōten	a charge (of gunpowder)	1411
塡補	tenpo	fill up, compensate (for), replenish	910

1921 軌

7c2.1

車 十
/69　12

軌

KI – wheel track, rut, railway, orbit

軌道	kidō	railroad track; orbit	149
狭軌鉄道	kyōki tetsudō	narrow-gauge railway	1436, 312, 149
常軌	jōki	normal course of action	506
軌範	kihan	model, example	1143
軌跡	kiseki	track, rut; locus (in geometry or metaphorical)	1673

1922 軟

7c4.1

車 攵
/69　49

軟

NAN, yawa(rakai/raka) – soft

柔軟	jūnan	soft, pliable	788
軟化	nanka	become soft; relent	254
軟弱	nanjaku	weak, weak-kneed	218
軟骨	nankotsu	cartilage	1340
軟着陸	nanchakuriku	soft landing	668, 657

1923 斬

7c4.2

車 斤
/69　50

斬

ZAN, ki(ru) – cut/kill (with a sword)

斬殺	zansatsu	kill with a sword	585
斬新	zanshin	novel, original, latest	174

1924 羨

2o11.4

王 攵 氵
46　49　21

羨

SEN, uraya(mu), uraya(mashii) – envy, be envious (of)

羨望	senbō	envy	685

1925 窯

3m12.5

宀 王 火
/33　46　44

窯 窰

YŌ, kama – kiln

窯業	yōgyō	ceramic industry, ceramics	279
窯元	kamamoto	place where pottery is made	137

	1926	**RO** – furnace, hearth	
炉	4d4.2	暖炉　*danro*　fireplace	645
	火　尸	溶鉱炉　*yōkōro*　smelting/blast furnace	1481, 1711
	/44　40	原子炉　*genshiro*　atomic reactor	136, 103
	炉　爐	核反応炉　*kaku hannōro*　nuclear reactor	1275, 324, 846
		増殖炉　*zōshokuro*　breeder reactor	725, 1607

	1927	**SUI, ta(ku)** – boil (rice), cook	
炊	4d4.1	炊事　*suiji*　cooking	80
	火　攵	自炊　*jisui*　do one's own cooking	62
	/44　49	炊飯器　*suihanki*　rice cooker	325, 536
	炊	雑炊　*zōsui*　porridge of rice and vegetables	584
		炊き出し　*takidashi*　emergency group cooking	53

	1928	**FUTSU, wa(ku)** – boil, seethe **wa(kasu)** – (bring to a) boil	
沸	3a5.3	沸騰　*futtō*　boiling; excitement, agitation	1912
	氵　弓　儿	沸（騰）点　*fut(tō)ten*　boiling point	1912, 169
	/21　28　16	沸き立つ　*wakitatsu*　boil up, seethe	121
	沸	湯沸かし（器）　*yuwakashi(ki)*　hot-water heater	642, 536

	1929	**tsu(keru)** – soak, immerse, pickle, preserve **tsu(karu)** – soak, steep, be submersed, be well seasoned	
漬	3a11.12	漬物　*tsukemono*　pickled vegetables	79
	氵　貝　土	漬物石　*tsukemono-ishi*　weight stone (used in making pickles)	
	/21　68　22		79, 78
	漬	塩漬　*shiozuke*　food preserved with salt	1152

	1930	**JŪ, shiru** – juice, sap, soup, broth, gravy	
汁	3a2.1	（天然）果汁　*(tennen) kajū*　(natural) fruit juice	141, 662, 496
	氵　十	肉汁　*nikujū*　meat juices, gravy	223
	/21　12	墨汁　*bokujū*　India ink	1821
	汁	汁粉　*shiruko*　adzuki-bean soup with rice cake	1817
		みそ汁　*misoshiru*　miso soup	

	1931	**SHA, ni(eru)** – (intr.) boil, cook **ni(ru), ni(yasu)** – (tr.) boil, cook, simmer	
煮	4d8.9	煮沸　*shafutsu*　boiling	1928
	火　日　土	雑煮　*zōni*　rice-cake soup with vegetables	584
	/44　42　22	生煮え　*namanie*　half-cooked, underdone	44
	煮	業を煮やす　*gō o niyasu*　become exasperated	279

	1932	**hashi** – chopsticks	
箸	6f9.1	割り箸　*waribashi*　(wooden) half-split chopsticks	528
	⺮　日　土	塗り箸　*nuribashi*　lacquered chopsticks	1121
	/66　42　22	箸置き　*hashioki*　chopstick rest	432
	箸	火箸　*hibashi*　tongs	20

煎	**1933** 2o11.2 　□ 月 火 几 43 44 16 煎	**SEN, i(ru)** – roast; boil

煎餅　　senbei　(rice) cracker　　　　　　　　　　　　　　1219
煎茶　　sencha　green tea　　　　　　　　　　　　　　　　251
二番煎じ　niban senji　second brew of tea; rehash　　　3, 185
煎り豆腐　iridōfu　bean curd boiled dry and seasoned
　　　　　　　　　　　　　　　　　　　　　　　　　　　988, 1312

弔	**1934** 0a4.41 　… 弓 丨 28 2 弔	**CHŌ, tomura(u)** – mourn, condole

弔意　　chōi　condolence, sympathy　　　　　　　　　　132
弔辞　　chōji　words/message of condolence　　　　　　701
弔電　　chōden　telegram of condolence　　　　　　　　108
弔問　　chōmon　visit of condolence　　　　　　　　　　162
慶弔　　keichō　congratulations and condolences　　　1742

忌	**1935** 4k3.4 　□ 心 弓 /51 28 忌	**KI** – mourning **i(mu)** – loathe, hate; avoid, shun **i(mawashii)** – abominable, disgusting, scandalous

忌中　　kichū　in mourning　　　　　　　　　　　　　　　28
忌避　　kihi　evasion, shirking; (legal) challenge　　1590
忌み言葉　imikotoba　taboo word　　　　　　　　　66, 253

迅	**1936** 2q3.5 　□ 辶 十 一 /19 12 1 迅	**JIN** – fast

迅速　　jinsoku　quick, rapid, speedy　　　　　　　　　511
迅雷　　jinrai　thunderclap　　　　　　　　　　　　　　982
奮迅　　funjin　roused to powerful action　　　　　　　1388

殉	**1937** 4c6.9 　□ 日 夕 𠂇 /42 30 15 殉	**JUN** – follow (someone) into death, dutiful death

殉教者　junkyōsha　martyr　　　　　　　　　　　　245, 164
殉難　　junnan　martyrdom　　　　　　　　　　　　　　566
殉職　　junshoku　die in the line of duty　　　　　　　386
殉国　　junkoku　dying for one's country　　　　　　　　40
殉死　　junshi　kill oneself on the death of one's lord　85

拘	**1938** 3c5.28 　□ 扌 口 𠂇 /23 24 15 拘	**KŌ** – seize, arrest, adhere to

拘束　　kōsoku　restriction, restraint　　　　　　　　　510
拘留　　kōryū　detention, custody　　　　　　　　　　　774
拘置　　kōchi　keep in detention, confine, hold　　　　432
拘置所　kōchisho　house of detention, prison　　432, 153
拘泥　　kōdei　adhere (to), be a stickler (for)　　　　1729

拙	**1939** 3c5.11 　□ 扌 屮 凵 /23 36 20 拙	**SETSU, tsutana(i)** – unskillful, clumsy

拙劣　　setsuretsu　clumsy, bungling, unskillful　　　1203
稚拙　　chisetsu　artless, crude, naive　　　　　　　　1294
拙策　　sessaku　poor policy, imprudent measure　　　901
拙速　　sessoku　not elaborate but fast, rough-and-ready　511
巧拙　　kōsetsu　skill, dexterity　　　　　　　　　　　1737

	1940	**KUTSU** – bend, yield	
	3r5.2	屈曲　*kukkyoku*　crookedness; refraction; curvature	367
	尸 凵 凵	屈折　*kussetsu*　refraction (in physics)	1483
	/40　36　20	屈辱　*kutsujoku*　humiliation, indignity	1860
		卑屈　*hikutsu*　lack of moral courage, servility	1622
	屈	退屈　*taikutsu*　tedious, monotonous, boring	865

	1941	**KUTSU, ho(ru)** – dig	
	3c8.32	採掘　*saikutsu*　mining, digging	960
	扌 尸 凵	発掘　*hakkutsu*　excavation; exhumation	96
	/23　40　36	掘り抜く　*horinuku*　dig through, bore	1830
		掘り返す　*horikaesu*　dig up　bargain	448
	掘	掘り出し物　*horidashimono*　treasure trove; lucky find;	53, 79

	1942	**hori** – moat, canal, ditch	
	3b8.11	堀割　*horiwari*　canal, waterway	528
	土 尸 凵	堀江　*horie*　canal	840
	/22　40　36	堀川　*horikawa*　canal	33
		内堀　*uchibori*　inner moat	84
	堀	外堀　*sotobori*　outer moat	83

	1943	**KUTSU** – cave, den	
	3m10.6	洞窟　*dōkutsu*　cave, cavern	1380
	宀 尸 凵	岩窟　*gankutsu*　cave, cavern	1428
	/33　40　36	巣窟　*sōkutsu*　den, hangout, home	1640
		貧民窟　*hinminkutsu*　slums	766, 177
	窟		

	1944	**HEI** – wall, fence	
	3b9.11	板塀　*itabei*　board fence	1090
	土 尸 艹	石塀　*ishibei*　stone fence	78
	/22　40　32	土塀　*dobei*　mud/earthen wall	24
	塀		

	1945	**RŌ, mo(ru/reru)** – leak, slip from **mo(rasu)** – let leak, divulge	
	3a11.19	漏電　*rōden*　electric leakage, short circuit	108
	氵 雨 尸	脱漏　*datsurō*　be omitted, left out	1457
	/21　74　40	遺漏なく　*irōnaku*　without omission, exhaustively	1230
		雨漏り　*amamori*　leak in the roof	30
	漏	聞き漏らす　*kikimorasu*　fail to hear, miss (a word)	64

	1946	**ZOKU** – robber; rebel	
	7b6.3	盗賊　*tōzoku*　thief, burglar, robber	1151
	貝 戈 十	海賊　*kaizoku*　pirate	117
	/68　52　12	海賊版　*kaizokuban*　pirate edition	117, 1089
		国賊　*kokuzoku*　traitor	40
	賊	烏賊　*ika*　squid, cuttlefish	

1947 賦

7b8.4
貝 戈 ⼘
/68 52 13
賦

FU – tribute, payment, installment; prose poem

月賦	geppu	monthly installment	17
賦税	fuzei	taxation	403
賦課	fuka	levy, assessment	497
賦役	fueki	compulsory labor, corvée	376
天賦	tenpu	inherent nature; inborn, natural	141

1948 禍

4e9.4
ネ 口 冂
/45 24 20
禍

KA – calamity, misfortune

禍根	kakon	root of evil, source of calamity	314
災禍	saika	accident, disaster	1418
戦禍	senka	the ravages of war, war damage	301
禍福	kafuku	fortune and misfortune	1466
舌禍	zekka	unfortunate slip of the tongue	1331

1949 渦

3a9.36
氵 口 冂
/21 24 20
渦

KA, uzu – swirl, vortex, whirlpool, eddy

渦流	karyū	eddy, whirlpool	247
渦中	kachū	maelstrom, vortex	28
戦渦	senka	the confusion of war	301
渦巻き	uzumaki	eddy, vortex, whirlpool; spiral	516

1950 鍋

8a9.13
金 口 冂
/72 24 20
鍋

nabe – pot, saucepan

中華鍋	chūkanabe	wok, Chinese pan	28, 1122
土鍋	donabe	earthen pot	24
鍋物	nabemono	food served in the pot	79
鍋焼き	nabeyaki	baked in a casserole	942
鍋底景気	nabezoko keiki	prolonged recession	571, 872, 134

1951 梨

4a7.24
木 禾 儿
/41 56 16
梨

nashi – pear, pear tree

梨花	rika	pear blossoms	255
洋梨	yōnashi	Western pear	289
山梨県	Yamanashi-ken	Yamanashi Prefecture	34, 194

1952 痢

5i7.2
疒 禾 儿
/60 56 16
痢

RI – diarrhea

下痢	geri	diarrhea	31
赤痢	sekiri	dysentery	207
疫痢	ekiri	children's dysentery, infant diarrhea	1401

1953 痩

5i9.1
疒 日 又
/60 42 9
痩

SŌ, ya(seru) – become thin, get lean, lose weight

痩身	sōshin	slender body, thin build	59
痩躯	sōku	lean figure	
痩せこける	yasekokeru	get all thin, get too skinny	
夏痩せ	natsuyase	loss of weight in summer	469
痩せ我慢	yasegaman	endure for sake of pride	1381, 1499

1954

疾

5i5.12

疒 大 亠
/60　34　15

疾

SHITSU – illness, disease; fast

疾患	*shikkan*	disease, ailment	1395
悪疾	*akushitsu*	malignant disease	304
廃疾	*haishitsu*	disablement, disabiltiy	992
疾走	*shissō*	run at full speed	435
疾風	*shippū*	strong wind, gale	29

1955

嫉

3e10.8

女　疒 大
/25　60　34

嫉

SHITSU – jealousy, envy

嫉視	*shisshi*	envy	616

1956

妬

3e5.1

女　石
/25　53

妬

TO, neta(mu) – be jealous/envious (of)

嫉妬（心）	*shitto(shin)*	jealousy, envy	1955, 97

1957

痴

5i8.1

疒 大 日
/60　34　24

痴　癡

CHI – foolish

白痴	*hakuchi*	idiocy; idiot	205
痴漢	*chikan*	molester of women, masher	565
痴情	*chijō*	foolish passion, blind love; jealousy	209
音痴	*onchi*	tone-deaf	347
愚痴	*guchi*	idle complaint, grumbling	1755

1958

瘍

5i9.3

疒 日 犭
/60　42　27

瘍

YŌ – ulcer

潰瘍	*kaiyō*	ulcer	1229
胃潰瘍	*ikaiyō*	stomach ulcer	1342, 1229

1959

怖

4k5.6

心 巾 十
/51　26　12

怖

FU – fear **kowa(i)** – frightening, scary

恐怖	*kyōfu*	fear, terror	1709
恐怖政治	*kyōfu seiji*	reign of terror	1709, 492, 502
恐怖症	*kyōfushō*	phobia, morbid dread	1709, 1400
高所恐怖症	*kōsho kyōfushō*	acrophobia	190, 153, 1709, 1400

1960

畏

5f4.5

田 礻
/58　57

畏

I – awe, reverence **oso(reru)** – fear, be overawed

畏怖	*ifu*	awe, fear, dread	1959
畏敬	*ikei*	awe and respect, reverence	718
畏縮	*ishuku*	cower, quail, be awestruck, shrink from	1162
畏れ多い	*osoreōi*	gracious, august, awe-inspiring	229

憾	**1961** 4k13.3 ⊞ 心 弋 口 /51 52 24 憾	**KAN** – regret 遺憾　*ikan*　regrettable　　　　　　　　　　　　　　1230
冶	**1962** 2b5.4 ⊞ 冫 口 厶 /5 24 17 冶	**YA** – smelting, casting 冶金（学）　*yakin(gaku)*　metallurgy　　　　　　　23, 109 陶冶　*tōya*　training, cultivation, education　　　　1763
慄	**1963** 4k10.5 ⊞ 心 木 口 /51 41 24 慄	**RITSU** – fear; shudder, shiver 戦慄　*senritsu*　shudder, tremble, shiver　　　　301 慄然　*ritsuzen*　with horror, with a shudder　　　662
惧	**1964** 4k8.3 ⊞ 心 目 儿 /51 43 16 惧	**GU** – fear, misgivings 危惧　*kigu*　fear, misgivings, apprehension　　　　543
錬	**1965** 8a8.3 ⊞ 金 木 日 /72 41 42 錬	**REN** – forge, temper, refine; train, drill 精錬所　*seirensho*　refinery　　　　　　　　　670, 153 錬金術　*renkinjutsu*　alchemy　　　　　　　　　23, 187 錬成　*rensei*　training　　　　　　　　　　　　　261 修錬　*shūren*　training, discipline　　　　　　　975
鍛	**1966** 8a9.5 ⊞ 金 厂 冂 /72 18 20 鍛	**TAN, kita(eru)** – forge; train, drill, discipline 鍛工　*tankō*　metalworker, smith　　　　　　　139 鍛錬　*tanren*　temper, anneal; train, harden　　1965 鍛え上げる　*kitaeageru*　become highly trained　32
錠	**1967** 8a8.12 ⊞ 金 宀 龸 /72 33 14 錠	**JŌ** – lock, padlock; pill, tablet 錠前　*jōmae*　a lock　　　　　　　　　　　　　47 組み合わせ錠　*kumiawasejō*　combination lock　424, 159 手錠　*tejō*　handcuffs　　　　　　　　　　　　57 錠剤　*jōzai*　tablet, pill　　　　　　　　　　　559 一錠　*ichijō*　one tablet/pill　　　　　　　　　2

1968

鎖

8a10.2	田
金 貝 小	
/72 68 35	

鎖

SA – chain; close, shut **kusari** – chain

封鎖	*fūsa*	blockade	1558
閉鎖	*heisa*	closing, shutdown, lockout	401
鎖国	*sakoku*	national isolation	40
連鎖反応	*rensa hannō*	chain reaction	446, 324, 846
金鎖	*kingusari*	gold chain	23

1969

鉢

8a5.4	田
金 木 一	
/72 41 1	

鉢

HACHI, [HATSU] – bowl, pot; brainpan; crown

火鉢	*hibachi*	hibachi, charcoal brazier	20
植木鉢	*uekibachi*	flowerpot	430, 22
衣鉢	*ihatsu*	the mantle, secrets (of one's master)	690
すり鉢	*suribachi*	(conical) earthenware mortar	
鉢巻き	*hachimaki*	cloth tied around one's head	516

1970

鐘

8a12.6	田
金 立 日	
/72 54 42	

鐘

SHŌ, kane – bell

晩鐘	*banshō*	evening bell	749
警鐘	*keishō*	alarm bell	719
半鐘	*hanshō*	fire bell	88
鐘乳洞	*shōnyūdō*	stalactite cave	969, 1380

1971

鈴

8a5.11	田
金 イ 一	
/72 3 1	

鈴

REI, RIN, suzu – bell

電鈴	*denrei*	electric bell	108
呼び鈴	*yobirin*	doorbell, (hotel) service bell	1325
風鈴	*fūrin*	wind-bell	29
鈴虫	*suzumushi*	"bell-ring" insect	893
鈴木	*Suzuki*	(surname)	22

1972

零

8d5.4	日
雨 イ 一	
/74 3 1	

零

REI – zero

零点	*reiten*	(a score of) zero	169
零時	*reiji*	12 o'clock	42
零度	*reido*	zero (degrees), the freezing point	378
零下	*reika*	below zero, subzero	31
零細	*reisai*	small, trifling	708

1973

雰

8d4.2	日
雨 儿 力	
/74 16 8	

雰

FUN – fog

雰囲気	*fun'iki*	atmosphere, ambience	1257, 134

1974

棺

4a8.25	田
木 宀 戸	
/41 33 40	

棺

KAN – coffin

棺桶	*kan'oke*	coffin	
石棺	*sekkan*	stone coffin, sarcophagus	78
納棺	*nōkan*	placing in the coffin	771
出棺	*shukkan*	start of a funeral procession	53

	1975	**MAI** – bury **u(meru)** – bury; fill up **u(maru)** – be buried (under); filled up **u(moreru)** – be buried; sink into obscurity
埋	3b7.2	
	土 日 /22 42	埋葬 *maisō* burial, interment 831
		埋没 *maibotsu* be buried; fall into oblivion 963
	埋	埋蔵 *maizō* buried stores, underground reserves 1360
		埋め立て *umetate* land reclamation 121

	1976	**SHŌ** – manifest, acknowledge
彰	3j11.1	
	彡 立 日 /31 54 42	顕彰 *kenshō* manifest, exhibit, exalt 1227
		表彰 *hyōshō* official commendation 272
	彰	表彰状 *hyōshōjō* certificate of commendation, citation 272, 636

	1977	**BAI, tsuchika(u)** – cultivate, foster
培	3b8.6	
	土 立 日 /22 54 24	栽培 *saibai* cultivation, culture, growing 1177
		培養 *baiyō* cultivation, culture 406
	培	培養液 *baiyōeki* culture fluid/solution 406, 480
		純粋培養 *junsui baiyō* pure culture 996, 1825, 406

	1978	**BAI** – indemnify
賠	7b8.1	
	貝 立 日 /68 54 24	賠償 *baishō* reparation, indemnification 1003
		損害賠償 *songai baishō* compensation for damages 351, 527, 1003
	賠	賠償金 *baishōkin* indemnities, reparations, damages 1003, 23

	1979	**BŌ** – divide, cut up
剖	2f8.1	
	刂 立 日 /16 54 24	解剖 *kaibō* dissection, autopsy, analysis 482
		解剖学 *kaibōgaku* anatomy 482, 109
	剖	生体解剖 *seitai kaibō* vivisection 44, 61, 482

	1980	**SHI, tamawa(ru)** – grant, bestow, confer
賜	7b8.2	
	貝 日 彡 /68 42 27	下賜 *kashi* imperial grant, donation 31
		恩賜 *onshi* imperial gift 564
	賜	賜暇 *shika* leave of absence, furlough 1110

	1981	**TO, ka(keru)** – bet, wager, stake, gamble
賭	7b8.8	
	貝 日 土 /68 42 22	賭博 *tobaku* gambling 611
		賭け事 *kakegoto* betting, gambling 80
	賭	賭け金 *kakekin* stakes, bet 23

	1982	**su(eru)** – set, place, put into position **su(waru)** – sit, be set	
据	3c8.33 ⯐	据え付ける *suetsukeru* set into position, install	192
	扌 尸 ⼝	据え置く *sueoku* leave as is, let stand	432
	/23 40 24	腹を据える *hara o sueru* decide, make up one's mind	1345
	据		

	1983	**TAKU** – open, clear, break up (land)	
拓	3c5.1	開拓 *kaitaku* reclamation, clearing	400
	扌 石	開拓者 *kaitakusha* settler, pioneer	400, 164
	/23 53	拓殖 *takushoku* colonization, settlement	1607
	拓	干拓 *kantaku* land reclamation by drainage	593
		拓本 *takuhon* a rubbing (of an inscription)	25

	1984	**GO** – (the board game) go	
碁	5a8.9 ⯐	囲碁 *igo* (the game of) go	1257
	石 艹 二	碁石 *goishi* go stone	78
	/53 32 4	碁会所 *gokaisho, gokaijo* go club	158, 153
	碁	碁盤 *goban* go board ⌐layout 1149	
		碁盤の目 *goban no me* go-board grid, checkerboard 1149, 55	

	1985	**KI** – go, shōgi, Japanese chess	
棋	4a8.14	将棋 *shōgi* shogi, Japanese chess	637
	木 艹 儿	将棋盤 *shōgiban* shogi board	637, 1149
	/41 32 16	棋譜 *kifu* record of a game of go/shogi	1224
	棋 棊	棋士 *kishi* (professional) go/shogi player	581
		将棋倒し *shōgidaoshi* fall down (like dominoes)	637, 927

	1986	**JŌ** – daughter, young lady	
嬢	3e13.1	お嬢さん *ojōsan* (your) daughter; young lady	
	女 衤 艹	(御)令嬢 *(go)reijō* (your) daughter; young lady	721, 850
	/25 57 32	愛嬢 *aijō* one's dear/favorite daughter	259
	嬢 嬢		

	1987	**JŌ, kamo(su)** – brew; bring about, give rise to	
醸	7e13.1	醸造所 *jōzōsho* brewery, distillery	704, 153
	酉 衤 艹	醸成 *jōsei* brew; cause, bring about	261
	/71 57 32		
	醸 醸		

	1988	**SO** – modeling, molding	
塑	3b10.8	塑像 *sozō* modeling, molding	753
	土 月 儿	可塑性 *kasosei* plasticity	390, 98
	/22 43 16	彫塑 *chōso* carving and (clay) modeling, plastic arts	1202
	塑		

1989 遡 2q10.6 月 辶 儿 /19　43　16 遡	**SO, sakanobo(ru)** – go upstream; go back to 遡行　*sokō*　go upstream　68 遡及的　*sokyūteki*　retroactive　1328, 210
1990 壇 3b13.5 土 日 日 /22　42　24 壇	**DAN, [TAN]** – rostrum, dais, podium 演壇　*endan*　(speaker's) platform, rostrum　344 祭壇　*saidan*　altar　627 文壇　*bundan*　the literary world　111 花壇　*kadan*　flower bed　255 土壇場　*dotanba*　last/critical moment; place of ⌐execution　24, 154
1991 塔 3b9.9 土 艹 日 /22　32　24 塔	**TŌ** – tower: stupa, pagoda; monument 監視塔　*kanshitō*　watchtower　1777, 616 管制塔　*kanseitō*　control tower　328, 433 広告塔　*kōkokutō*　poster column, advertising pillar　707, 703 象げの塔　*zōge no tō*　ivory tower　752 五重の塔　*gojū no tō*　5-story pagoda　7, 227
1992 楼 4a9.10 木 米 女 /41　62　25 楼 樓	**RŌ** – tower, turret, lookout 鐘楼　*shōrō*　bell tower, belfry　1970 楼閣　*rōkaku*　many-storied building, castle　856 楼門　*rōmon*　two-story gate　161 摩天楼　*matenrō*　skyscraper　1631, 141
1993 栓 4a6.26 木 王 亻 /41　46　3 栓	**SEN** – stopper, cork, plug, spigot 消火栓　*shōkasen*　fire hydrant　864, 20 給水栓　*kyūsuisen*　water tap, hydrant　346, 21 水道栓　*suidōsen*　hydrant, tap　21, 149 塞栓　*sokusen*　an embolism　465 栓抜き　*sennuki*　bottle opener　1830
1994 詮 7a6.14 言 王 亻 /67　46　3 詮	**SEN** – inquiry, investigation 詮索　*sensaku*　search, inquiry　1104 詮議　*sengi*　discussion, examination　292 所詮　*shosen*　after all　153
1995 附 2d5.4 阝 寸 亻 /7　37　3 附	**FU** – attach, accompany 附属　*fuzoku*　belonging to, accessory　1750 寄附　*kifu*　contribution, donation　1445 附近　*fukin*　neighborhood, vicinity　452 附録　*furoku*　supplement, appendix　547 附随　*fuzui*　accompany, be entailed by　1864

陵	**1996**	**RYŌ, misasagi** – imperial tomb, mausoleum
	2d8.5 ⊞	丘陵　*kyūryō*　hill　1441
	阝 夂 土	丘陵地帯　*kyūryō chitai*　hilly area　1441, 118, 994
	/7　49　22	御陵　*goryō*　tomb of the emperor/empress　721
	陵	

俊	**1997**	**SHUN** – excellence, genius
	2a7.10 ⊞	俊才　*shunsai*　genius, outstanding talent　560
	亻 夂 厶	俊傑　*shunketsu*　great man　1849
	/3　49　17	俊敏　*shunbin*　keen, quick-witted　1857
	俊	

唆	**1998**	**SA, sosonoka(su)** – tempt, entice; incite, abet
	3d7.8 ⊞	示唆　*shisa*　suggestion　625
	口 夂 厶	教唆　*kyōsa*　instigation, incitement　245
	/24　49　17	
	唆	

頻	**1999**	**HIN** – frequently, repeatedly
	9a8.2 ⊞	頻度　*hindo*　frequency, rate of occurrence　378
	頁 小 卜	頻発　*hinpatsu*　frequency, frequent occurrence　96
	/76　35　13	頻繁　*hinpan*　frequency, rapid succession　1367
	頻	頻々と　*hinpin to*　frequent, in rapid succession

頬	**2000**	**hō** – cheek
	9a7.2 ⊞	頬骨　*hōbone*　cheekbones　1340
	頁 火 二	頬張る　*hōbaru*　stuff one's mouth with food　1158
	/76　44　4	
	頬	

頑	**2001**	**GAN** – stubborn, obstinate
	9a4.6 ⊞	頑固　*ganko*　stubborn, obstinate　1004
	頁 二 儿	頑迷　*ganmei*　bigoted, obstinate　998
	/76　4　16	頑強　*gankyō*　stubborn, obstinate, unyielding　217
	頑	頑健　*ganken*　strong and robust, in excellent health　914
		頑張る　*ganbaru*　persist in, stick to it, hang in there　1158

顎	**2002**	**GAKU, ago** – jaw, chin
	9a9.2 ⊞	顎骨　*gakkotsu*　jawbone　1340
	頁 口 二	上顎　*uwaago*　upper jaw; the palate　32
	/76　24　4	下顎　*shitaago*　lower jaw　31
	顎	顎ひげ　*agohige*　chin beard, goatee

	2003	**GAN** – play, toy, trifle (with)	
玩	4f4.1 ⊞	玩具　　omocha, gangu　toy	426
	王 | 儿 /46　2　16	玩具屋　omochaya　toy shop	426, 167
	玩	愛玩　　aigan　cherish, treasure, prize	259

	2004	**RŌ, moteaso(bu)** – play, trifle, tamper (with)	
弄	4f3.2 ⊟	愚弄　gurō　make a fool of, ridicule, mock	1755
	王 艹 /46　32	翻弄　honrō　trifle with, make sport of	606
	弄		

	2005	**HAN, [BON], wazura(u)** – worry about, be troubled by	
煩	4d9.1 ⊡	**wazura(wasu)** – trouble, bother, annoy	
	火 頁 /44　76	煩雑　hanzatsu　complicated, troublesome	584
	煩	煩忙　hanbō　busy, pressed with business	1460
		煩悩　bonnō　evil passions, carnal desires	1353
		煩わしい　wazurawashii　troublesome, tangled	

	2006	**HAN** – divide, distribute	
頒	9a4.3 ⊞	頒布　hanpu　distribute, circulate	688
	頁 儿 力 /76　16　8		
	頒		

	2007	**KA** – alone, widowed; few, small	
寡	3m11.2 ⊟	多寡　taka　quantity, number, amount	229
	宀 月 一 /33　43　14	寡婦　kafu　widow	316
	寡	寡聞　kabun　little knowledge, ill-informed	64
		寡黙　kamoku　taciturn, reticent	1684
		寡占　kasen　oligopoly	1822

	2008	**HIN** – guest	
賓	3m12.3 ⊟	賓客　hinkaku, hinkyaku　honored guest, visitor	651
	宀 貝 小 /33　68　35	貴賓　kihin　distinguished guest, guest of honor	1228
	賓	主賓　shuhin　guest of honor	155
		来賓　raihin　guest, visitor	69
		迎賓館　geihinkan　reception hall; guest mansion	1098, 327

	2009	**SHŌ** – further; value, respect	
尚	3n5.2 ⊟	高尚　kōshō　lofty, noble, refined	190
	⺌ 口 冂 /35　24　20	尚武　shōbu　militaristic, martial	1071
	尚	尚早　shōsō　premature, too early	248
		時機尚早　jiki-shōsō　too soon, time is not ripe	42, 537, 248
		和尚　oshō　Buddhist priest	124

宵 2,3 (1) (4 strokes) 宵	**2010** 3m7.7 宀 月 小 /33 43 35 宵

SHŌ, yoi – evening

春宵	shunshō	spring evening	468
徹宵	tesshō	all night long	1511
宵の口	yoi no kuchi	early evening	54
宵っ張り	yoippari	staying up till late; night owl	1158
宵越し	yoigoshi	(left over) from the previous evening	1038

硝 5a7.6 石 月 小 /53 43 35 硝	**2011**

SHŌ – saltpeter

硝酸	shōsan	nitric acid	525
硝石	shōseki	saltpeter	78
硝煙	shōen	gunpowder smoke	941

硫 5a7.3 石 亠 ム /53 11 17 硫	**2012**

RYŪ – sulfur

硫酸	ryūsan	sulfuric acid	525
硫化水素	ryūka suiso	hydrogen sulfide	254, 21, 271
硫黄	iō	sulfur	794
硫黄泉	iōsen	sulfur springs	794, 1253
硫黄島	Iōtō, Iōjima	Iwo Jima	794, 286

肪 4b4.2 月 方 /43 48 肪	**2013**

BŌ – (animal) fat

脂肪	shibō	fat	1083
皮下脂肪	hika shibō	subcutaneous fat	1008, 31, 1083
脂肪ぶとり	shibōbutori	fat, obese	1083
脂肪層	shibōsō	layer of fat	⌈fat 1083, 1454
植物性脂肪	shokubutsusei shibō	vegetable	430, 79, 98, 1083

坊 3b4.1 土 方 /22 48 坊	**2014**

BŌ, [BO'] – priest's residence; Buddhist priest/monk; boy

坊主	bōzu	Buddhist priest, bonze	155
三日坊主	mikka bōzu	one who can stick to nothing	4, 5, 155
朝寝坊	asanebō	a late riser	477, 1127
赤ん坊	akanbō	baby	207
坊ちゃん	botchan	(your) son, young master, boy	

紡 6a4.1 糸 方 /61 48 紡	**2015**

BŌ, tsumu(gu) – spin, make yarn

紡績	bōseki	spinning	1169
紡績工場	bōseki kōjō	spinning mill	1169, 139, 154
紡織	bōshoku	spinning and weaving	693
混紡	konbō	mixed/blended spinning	813

緻 6a10.1 糸 攵 土 /61 49 22 緻	**2016**

CHI – fine, close, minute

緻密	chimitsu	fine, close, minute, exact	822
精緻	seichi	minute, fine, subtle	670

2017 羅

5g14.1

罒 隹 糸
/55 73 61

羅

RA – silk gauze, thin silk; (bird-capturing) mist net; in rows

羅列	*raretsu*	enumerate, cite	621
羅針	*rashin*	compass needle	341
羅針盤	*rashinban*	compass	341, 1149
網羅	*mōra*	be all-inclusive, comprehensive	1720
一張羅	*itchōra*	one's best/only clothes	2, 1158

2018 綻

6a8.13

糸 宀 疋
/61 33 14

綻

TAN, hokoro(biru) – come apart at the seams, unravel; begin to open

破綻	*hatan*	failure, breakdown, bankruptcy	676

2019 罷

5g10.2

罒 月 厶
/55 43 17

罷

HI – end, discontinue, stop; leave, withdraw

罷免	*himen*	dismissal (from one's post)	746
罷業	*higyō*	strike, walkout	279

2020 釣

8a3.5

釒 ⺈ 丶
/72 15 2

釣

CHŌ, tsu(ru) – fish, angle; decoy, allure, take in

釣り道具	*tsuridōgu*	fishing tackle	149, 426
釣り針	*tsuribari*	fishhook	341
釣り堀	*tsuribori*	fishing pond	1942
釣り銭	*tsurisen*	(make) change	659
釣り合い	*tsuriai*	balance, equilibrium, proportion	159

2021 醒

7e9.2

酉 日 丨
/71 42 22

醒

SEI – wake up, awaken

覚醒	*kakusei*	awakening, revival; disillusionment	615
覚醒剤	*kakuseizai*	stimulant drugs	615, 559
半醒半睡	*hansei-hansui*	be half-asleep	88, 88, 1118
警醒	*keisei*	warn, arouse, awaken	719

2022 酌

7e3.3

酉 ⺈ 丶
/71 15 2

酌

SHAKU – pour (saké), drink; take into consideration

媒酌	*baishaku*	matchmaking	1595
媒酌人	*baishakunin*	matchmaker, go-between	1595, 1
晩酌	*banshaku*	evening drink	749
独酌	*dokushaku*	drinking alone	219
酌量	*shakuryō*	consideration, extenuation	417

2023 酎

7e3.1

酉 寸
/71 37

酎

CHŪ – double-fermented saké

焼酎	*shōchū*	(a low-grade liquor)	942

2024 7e6.2 酉 儿 /71　16 酬州	**SHŪ** – reward, compensation

報酬　*hōshū*　remuneration　698
無報酬　*muhōshū*　without remuneration, free of charge　93, 698
応酬　*ōshū*　reply, response, retort　846

2025 7e6.4 酉 夂 口 /71　49　24 酪	**RAKU** – whey; dairy products

酪農（場）　*rakunō(jō)*　dairy, dairy farm　370, 154
酪製品　*rakuseihin*　dairy products　434, 230
酪農家　*rakunōka*　dairy farmer, dairyman　370, 165

2026 7e6.1 酉 土 子 /71　22　6 酵	**KŌ** – fermentation; yeast

酵母　*kōbo*　yeast　112
酵母菌　*kōbokin*　yeast fungus　112, 1285
酵素　*kōso*　enzyme　271
発酵　*hakkō*　fermentation　96

2027 7e5.3 酉 宀 十 /71　15　13 酢 醋	**SAKU, su** – vinegar

酢酸　*sakusan*　acetic acid　525
酢漬け　*suzuke*　pickling in vinegar　1929
酢の物　*su no mono*　vinegared dish　79
甘酢　*amazu*　sweet vinegar　1591

2028 3r4.2 尸 十 一 /40　12　1 尾	**BI, o** – tail

末尾　*matsubi*　the end　305
首尾　*shubi*　beginning and end; result, outcome　148
尾行　*bikō*　shadow, tail (someone)　68
尾灯　*bitō*　taillight　1416
徹頭徹尾　*tettō-tetsubi*　thoroughly　1511, 276, 1511

2029 3r2.1 尸 十 /40　12 尻	**shiri** – buttocks, rear end

尻尾　*shippo*　tail; end　2028
尻餅　*shirimochi*　falling on one's butt, pratfall　1219
尻押し　*shirioshi*　push from behind; instigation; backing　1021
尻取り　*shiritori*　(game: taking the last syllable of a word
　　　forming a word that begins with that syllable)　65

2030 3r4.1 尸 氵 /40　21 尿	**NYŌ** – urine

尿素　*nyōso*　urea　271
尿酸　*nyōsan*　uric acid　525
排尿　*hainyō*　urination　1077
夜尿症　*yanyōshō*　nocturnal enuresis, bedwetting　479, 1400
糖尿病　*tōnyōbyō*　diabetes　1814, 381

2031

泌

3a5.10

氵 必 丿
/21 51 2

沁

HITSU, HI – flow, secrete

分泌	*bunpitsu, bunpi* secretion	38
内分泌	*naibunpi* internal secretion	84, 38
分泌物	*bunpibutsu* a secretion	38, 79
泌尿器	*hinyōki* urinary organs	2030, 536
泌尿器科	*hinyōkika* urology	2030, 536, 320

2032

柳

4a5.17

木 厂 阝
/41 18 7

栁

RYŪ, yanagi – willow tree

川柳	*senryū* humorous 17-syllable Japanese poem	33
花柳界	*karyūkai* demimonde, red-light district	255, 461
柳眉	*ryūbi* beautiful eyebrows	1851
枝垂れ柳	*shidare yanagi* weeping willow	889, 1117
柳腰	*yanagi-goshi* slender graceful hips	1373

2033

杉

4a3.2

木 彡
/41 31

杉

sugi – Japanese cedar

杉並木	*suginamiki* avenue of sugi trees	1222, 22
杉並区	*Suginami-ku* Suginami Ward (Tokyo)	1222, 183

2034

柿

4a5.25

木 巾 亠
/41 26 11

柿

kaki – persimmon (tree/fruit)

渋柿	*shibugaki* puckery persimmon	1809
干し柿	*hoshigaki* dried persimmons	593

2035

桑

2h8.1

又 木
/9 41

桑

SŌ, kuwa – mulberry tree

桑門	*sōmon* Buddhist priest/monk	161
桑園	*sōen* mulberry farm/orchard	454
桑田	*sōden* mulberry orchard	35
桑畑	*kuwabatake* mulberry field	36
桑原桑原	*kuwabara-kuwabara* Heaven forbid! 「Thank God!	136, 136

2036

栃

4a5.28

木 厂 万
/41 18 14

栃

tochi – horse chestnut

栃木県	*Tochigi-ken* Tochigi Prefecture	22, 194

2037

昆

4c4.10

日 比
/42 13

昆

KON – insect; multitude

昆虫	*konchū* insect	893
昆虫学	*konchūgaku* entomology	893, 109
昆虫採集	*konchū saishū* insect collecting	893, 960, 442
昆布	*konbu, kobu* sea tangle, tang, kelp	688
昆布茶	*konbucha, kobucha* tang tea	688, 251

2038

鹿

3q8.5 □
厂 儿 冂
18 16 20
鹿

shika, ka – deer

大鹿	ōjika	large deer, moose, elk	26
馬鹿	baka	fool, idiot, stupid; to a ridiculous degree	283
親馬鹿	oyabaka	overfond parent	175, 283
馬鹿安い	bakayasui	dirt-cheap, ridiculously cheap	283, 105
鹿児島県	Kagoshima-ken	Kagoshima Prefecture	1280, 286, 194

2039

麓

4a15.9 凹
木 厂 儿
/41 18 16
麓

ROKU, fumoto – foot/base of a mountain

山麓	sanroku	the foot of a mountain	34

2040

蛇

6d5.7 □
虫 宀 匕
/64 33 13
蛇

JA, DA, hebi – snake

蛇の目	janome	bull's-eye design (on oilpaper umbrella)	55
蛇腹	jabara	accordion-like folds, bellows; cornice	1345
蛇行	dakō	meander, zigzag, fishtail	68
蛇足	dasoku	superfluous (like legs on a snake)	58
長蛇の列	chōda no retsu	long queue/line of people	95, 621

2041

蚊

6d4.5 田
虫 亠 十
/64 11 12
蚊

ka – mosquito

蚊帳	kaya	mosquito net	1159
蚊取り線香	katori senkō	mosquito-repellent incense	65, 299, 1797
蚊柱	kabashira	column of swarming mosquitoes	608

2042

蚕

6d4.8 ...
虫 大 一
/64 34 1
蚕 蠶

SAN, kaiko – silkworm

養蚕	yōsan	sericulture, silkworm raising	406
蚕糸	sanshi	silk thread/yarn	242
蚕食	sanshoku	encroachment, inroads	322

2043

蛍

3n8.2 日
⺌ 虫 冂
/35 64 20
蛍 螢

KEI, hotaru – firefly, glowworm

蛍光灯	keikōtō	fluorescent lamp	138, 1416
蛍光塗料	keikō-toryō	fluorescent paint	138, 1121, 319
蛍雪の功	keisetsu no kō	the fruits of diligent study	979, 837
蛍狩り	hotarugari	firefly catching	1687

2044

蛮

2j10.1 日
亠 虫 儿
/11 64 16
蛮 蠻

BAN – barbarian

(野)蛮人	(ya)banjin	barbarian, savage	236, 1
南蛮	nanban	southern barbarian, European (hist.)	74
蛮風	banpū	barbarous ways/customs	29
蛮行	bankō	act of barbarity, brutality	68
蛮勇	ban'yū	recklessness; brute force	1474

虹	**2045** 6d3.1 ☐ 虫 工 /64 38 虹	***niji*** – rainbow	
		虹彩　*kōsai*　iris (of the eye)	959
		虹色　*nijiiro*　rainbow colors	204
		虹鱒　*nijimasu*　rainbow trout	

駄	**2046** 10a4.1 ☐ 馬 大 丨 /78 34 2 駄	***DA*** – pack horse; of poor quality	
		駄賃　*dachin*　reward, recompense, tip	764
		駄菓子　*dagashi*　cheap candy	1636, 103
		駄作　*dasaku*　poor work, worthless stuff	361
		無駄　*muda*　futile, useless, in vain	93
		下駄　*geta*　geta, Japanese wooden clogs	31

騎	**2047** 10a8.3 ☐ 馬 大 口 /78 34 24 騎	***KI*** – horse riding; (counter for horsemen)	
		騎手　*kishu*　rider, jockey	57
		騎士　*kishi*　rider, horseman	581
		騎兵　*kihei*　cavalry soldier	798
		騎馬　*kiba*　on horseback, mounted	283
		一騎打ち　*ikkiuchi*　single combat, man-to-man fight	2, 1059

椅	**2048** 4a8.27 ☐ 木 大 口 /41 34 24 椅	***I*** – chair	
		椅子　*isu*　chair, seat, couch	103
		車椅子　*kurumaisu*　wheelchair	133, 103

駆	**2049** 10a4.5 ☐ 馬 門 丨 /78 20 12 駆　驅	***KU, ka(keru)*** – gallop, run, rush ***ka(ru)*** – drive, spur on	
		先駆　*senku*　forerunner, pioneer	50
		駆逐　*kuchiku*　drive away, expel, get rid of	1186
		駆除　*kujo*　exterminate	1112
		（後輪）駆動　*(kōrin) kudō*　(rear) drive	58
		駆け回る　*kakemawaru*　run around	90

駒	**2050** 10a5.5 ☐ 馬 口 宀 /78 24 15 駒	***koma*** – colt; chessman, piece (in board games)	
		手駒　*tegoma*　captured shōgi piece (kept in reserve)	57
		駒鳥　*komadori*　Japanese robin	285
		駒込　*Komagome*　(area of Tōkyō)	790
		駒場　*Komaba*　(area of Tōkyō)	154

篤	**2051** 6f10.1 ☐ ⺮ 馬 /66 78 篤	***TOKU*** – serious; cordial	
		危篤　*kitoku*　critically ill	543
		篤行　*tokkō*　good deed, act of charity	68
		篤志家　*tokushika*　benefactor, volunteer	582, 165
		篤農家　*tokunōka*　exemplary farmer	370, 165
		篤学　*tokugaku*　love of learning, diligence in studies	109

罵

2052

5g10.1

目 馬
/55 78

罵

BA, nonoshi(ru) – speak ill of, revile

罵声	*basei*	jeers, boos, hisses	759
罵倒	*batō*	denunciation, condemnation, severe criticism	927
罵言	*bagen*	abuse, revilement, invective	66
罵詈	*bari*	abuse, vilification	
罵詈雑言	*bari zōgon*	abusive language	584, 66

溪

2053

3a8.16

氵 小 大
/21 35 34

渓 溪

KEI – mountan stream, gorge

渓谷	*keikoku*	ravine, gorge, valley	664
渓流	*keiryū*	mountain stream, torrent	247
雪渓	*sekkei*	snowy valley/ravine	979
渓間	*keikan*	ravine; in the valley	43

淫

2054

3a8.17

氵 壬 小
/21 46 35

淫

IN – lewd, indecent; excessive **mida(ra)** – lewd, obscene

淫売	*inbai*	prostitution	239
淫猥	*inwai*	indecent, obscene	
姦淫	*kan'in*	illicit sexual intercourse, adultery, fornication	

詔

2055

7a5.10

言 口 力
/67 24 8

詔

SHŌ, mikotonori – imperial edict

大詔	*taishō*	imperial rescript	26
詔書	*shōsho*	imperial edict/rescript	131

勅

2056

2g7.1

力 木 口
/8 41 24

勅 敕

CHOKU – imperial decree

勅語	*chokugo*	imperial message, speech from the throne	67
勅命	*chokumei*	imperial order/commission	587
詔勅	*shōchoku*	imperial proclamation	2055
勅使	*chokushi*	imperial messenger/envoy	331

璽

2057

4f14.2

王 雨 儿
/46 74 16

璽

JI – imperial seal

国璽	*kokuji*	great seal, seal of state	40
御璽	*gyoji*	imperial/privy seal	721
玉璽	*gyokuji*	imperial seal	295
璽書	*jisho*	document with the imperial seal	131

旺

2058

4c4.2

日 王
/42 46

旺

Ō – flourishing

旺盛	*ōsei*	flourishing, in prime condition	732
旺然	*ōzen*	flourishing	662

爽	**2059** 0a11.7 ⬚ 夾 十 34 12 爽	**SŌ, sawa(yaka)** – refreshing, clear
		爽快　　*sōkai*　thrilling, exhilarating　　　　　　　1498 颯爽　　*sassō*　dashing, smart, elegant

僕	**2060** 2a12.1 ⬚ 亻 王 儿 /3 46 16 僕	**BOKU** – I, me (in masculine speech); manservant
		従僕　　*jūboku*　servant, attendant　　　　　　　　1579 家僕　　*kaboku*　manservant　　　　　　　　　　　165 僕ら　　*bokura*　we (in masculine speech)

俺	**2061** 2a8.25 ⬚ 亻 日 大 /3 42 34 俺	***ore*** – I, me (used by men)
		俺様　　*oresama*　I　　　　　　　　　　　　　　　407 俺たち　*oretachi*　we

撲	**2062** 3c12.1 ⬚ 扌 王 儿 /23 46 16 撲	**BOKU** – hit, strike
		打撲傷　　*dabokushō*　bruise, contusion　　　1059, 643 撲滅　　　*bokumetsu*　eradication, extermination　　1421 相撲　　　*sumō*　sumo wrestling　　　　　　　　　146 相撲取り　*sumōtori*　sumo wrestler　　　　　　146, 65 大相撲　　*ōzumō*　grand sumo tournament; exciting bout　26, 146

俵	**2063** 2a8.21 ⬚ 亻 衤 二 /3 57 4 俵	**HYŌ, tawara** – straw bag/sack
		土俵　　*dohyō*　sandbag; sumo ring　　　　　　　　24 米俵　　*komedawara*　straw rice-sack; bag of/for rice　224 炭俵　　*sumidawara*　sack for charcoal　　　　　1427 一俵　　*ippyō*　one bag/sack　　　　　　　　　　　2

仙	**2064** 2a3.1 ⬚ 亻 山 /3 36 仙	**SEN** – hermit, wizard
		仙人　　*sennin*　mountain wizard; hermit, settler　　　1 仙女　　*sennyo*　fairy, nymph　　　　　　　　　　102 酒仙　　*shusen*　heavy drinker　　　　　　　　　526 水仙　　*suisen*　narcissus　　　　　　　　　　　21 仙台　　*Sendai*　(city in Tōhoku)　　　　　　　　501

嵐	**2065** 3o9.4 ⬚ 山 虫 冂 /36 64 20 嵐	***arashi*** – storm, tempest
		大嵐　　*ōarashi*　big storm　　　　　　　　　　　26 雪嵐　　*yukiarashi*　snowstorm　　　　　　　　　979 砂嵐　　*sunaarashi*　sandstorm　　　　　　　　　1204 嵐山　　*Arashiyama, Ranzan*　(hill in the western section of Kyōto)　34 五十嵐　*Igarashi*　(familiy name)　　　　　　　7, 12

傲	**2066** 2a11.2 亻 方 攵 /3 48 49 傲	**GŌ** – be proud 傲慢 *gōman* proud, arrogant, haughty 1499 傲慢無礼 *gōman-burei* arrogant and insolent 1499, 93, 630 傲然たる *gōzentaru* proud, arrogant, haughty 662
遜	**2067** 2q9.4 辶 糸 子 /19 61 6 遜	**SON** – humble; inferior 謙遜 *kenson* modesty, humility 1802 不遜 *fuson* arrogant, presumptuous ⌐presumptuous 94 傲岸不遜 *gōgan-fuson* arrogant, insolent, 2066, 595, 94 遜色ない *sonshokunai* compare farorably, stand comparison with 204
凸	**2068** 0a5.13 一 丨 1 2 凸	**TOTSU** – convex, protrusion, bulge 凸レンズ *totsurenzu* convex lens 凸面 *totsumen* convex (surface) 274 両凸 *ryōtotsu* biconvex 200 凸版（印刷）*toppan (insatsu)* letter(press), relief (printing) 1089, 1086, 1087
凹	**2069** 0a5.14 一 丨 1 2 凹	**Ō** – concave, indentation, depression 凹凸 *ōtotsu, dekoboko* bumps and depressions, uneven, jagged, rough 2068 凹面鏡 *ōmenkyō* concave mirror 274, 882 凹レンズ *ōrenzu* concave lens
寸	**2070** 0a3.17 寸 37 寸	**SUN** – short, small; measure; (unit of length, about 3 cm) 寸法 *sunpō* measurements; plan 123 寸評 *sunpyō* brief comment 1067 寸暇 *sunka* a moment's leisure, spare moments 1110 寸前 *sunzen* immediately/right before 47 寸断 *sundan* cut/tear to pieces 1063
尺	**2071** 3r1.1 尸 丶 /40 2 尺	**SHAKU** – (unit of length, about 30 cm); measure, length 尺貫法 *shakkanhō* old Japanese system of weights and measures 936, 123 巻き尺 *makijaku* tape measure, surveying tape 516 縮尺 *shukushaku* reduced scale (map) 1162 尺八 *shakuhachi* Japanese end-blown bamboo flute 10
坪	**2072** 3b5.4 土 干 儿 /22 14 16 坪	**tsubo** – (unit of area, about 3.3 square meter) 坪数 *tsubosū* number of tsubo, area 225 延べ坪（数）*nobetsubo(sū)* total area (of all floors) 1167, 225 建坪 *tatetsubo* floor space/area 913 坪二万円 *tsubo niman en* 20,000 yen per tsubo 3, 16, 13 坪当たり *tsuboatari* per tsubo 77

斤	**2073** 0a4.3 斤 50 斤	**KIN** – (unit of weight, about 600 g); ax
		一斤　*ikkin*　one kin — 2
		斤量　*kinryō*　weight — 417

升	**2074** 0a4.32 ... 丗 ｜ 32　2 升	**SHŌ** – (unit of volume, 1.8 liters) ***masu*** – measure; (square, wooden) measuring cup; box (seat); square, box
		一升　*isshō*　one shō — 2
		一升瓶　*isshōbin*　1.8-liter bottle — 2, 1217
		升目　*masume*　square box — 55

斗	**2075** 0a4.17 ... 十 、 12　2 斗	**TO** – (unit of volume, 18 liters)
		一斗　*itto*　one to — 2
		斗酒　*toshu*　kegs of sakè — 526
		北斗（七）星　*hokuto(shichi)sei*　the Big Dipper — 73, 9, 743

厘	**2076** 2p7.1 厂 日 土 /18　42　22 厘	**RIN** – (old unit of currency, 1/1000 yen), (unit of length, about 0.3 mm)
		二銭五厘　*nisen gorin*　2 sen 5 rin, 2.5 sen — 3, 659, 7
		一分一厘　*ichibu ichirin*　1 bu 1 rin, 1.1 bu; some, little, slight — 2, 38, 2
		厘毛　*rinmō*　a trifle; unimportant, insignificant — 287

畝	**2077** 5f5.5 田 亠 厶 /58　11　15 畝 畝	**une** – ridge (between furrows); rib (in fabric)
		畝間　*unema*　space between ridges, furrow — 43
		畝織　*uneori*　rep, ribbed fabric — 693

桟	**2078** 4a6.1 木 戈 一 /41　52　1 桟 棧	**SAN** – crosspiece, frame; beam, spar; bolt (of a door)
		桟橋　*sanbashi*　wharf, jetty — 607
		sankyō　wharf; bridge
		桟道　*sandō*　plank bridge — 149

枠	**2079** 4a4.19 木 卆 /41　12 枠	**waku** – frame, framework; limit, confines; spool
		窓枠　*madowaku*　window frame — 711
		枠内　*wakunai*　within the limits — 84
		枠組　*wakugumi*　frame, framework; framing — 424

2080

棚

4a8.10

木 月
/41 43

棚

tana – shelf

本棚	*hondana*	bookshelf	25
戸棚	*todana*	cupboard	152
棚上げ	*tanaage*	put on the shelf, shelve	32
大陸棚	*tairikudana*	continental shelf	26, 657
棚卸	*tanaoroshi*	inventory, stock taking	720

2081

芋

3k3.1

艹 二 一
/32 14 1

芋

imo – potato

じゃが芋	*jagaimo*	(white) potato	
焼き芋	*yakiimo*	baked sweet potato	942
里芋	*satoimo*	taro	142
芋掘り	*imohori*	potato-digging	1941
薩摩芋	*satsumaimo*	sweet potato	1631

2082

萎

3k8.18

艹 禾 女
/32 56 25

萎

I, na(eru) – wither, droop

萎縮	*ishuku*	wither, atrophy; be dispirited	1162

2083

薪

3k13.3

艹 立 木
/32 54 41

薪

SHIN, takigi – firewood

薪水	*shinsui*	firewood and water	21
薪炭	*shintan*	firewood and charcoal, fuel	1427

2084

芯

3k4.2

艹 心
/32 51

芯

SHIN – pith of a rush; inner part

鉛筆の芯	*enpitsu no shin*	lead (of a pencil)	1713, 130
ろうそくの芯	*rōsoku no shin*	wick (of a candle)	

2085

蔽

3k12.1

艹 攵 小
/32 49 35

蔽

HEI – cover, conceal

遮蔽	*shahei*	cover, shelter, shield, screen	1899
隠蔽	*inpei*	conceal, suppress, cover up	887
隠蔽色	*inpeishoku*	concealing coloration (with animals)	
			887, 204

2086

繭

3k15.7

艹 糸 虫
/32 61 64

繭

KEN, mayu – cocoon

繭糸	*kenshi*	cocoon and (silk) thread; silk thread	242
繭玉	*mayudama*	(type of New Year's decoration)	295

藤	**2087** 3k15.3 艹 月 火 /32 43 44 藤	**TŌ, fuji** – wisteria

藤色　*fuji-iro*　light purple, lilac, lavender　　204
佐藤　*Satō*　(surname)　　1867
伊藤　*Itō*　(surname)
藤田　*Fujita*　(surname)　　35
藤沢　*Fujisawa*　(city, Kanagawa Pref.)　　1031

壌	**2088** 3b13.4 土 衤 艹 /22 57 32 壌 壌	**JŌ** – soil

土壌　*dojō*　soil　　24

堪	**2089** 3b9.1 土 艹 二 /22 32 4 堪	**KAN, ta(eru)** – endure, withstand

堪忍　*kannin*　patience, forbearance; forgiveness　　1503
堪弁　*kanben*　pardon, forgive　　724
堪え忍ぶ　*taeshinobu*　bear patiently　　1503
堪えかねる　*taekaneru*　cannot bear

抹	**2090** 3c5.9 扌 木 一 /23 41 1 抹	**MATSU** – pulverize; powder

抹殺　*massatsu*　expunge; deny; ignore　　585
抹消　*masshō*　erase, cross out　　864
一抹　*ichimatsu*　a tinge of　　2
抹茶　*matcha*　　251
抹香　*makkō*　incense powder, incense　　1797

挫	**2091** 3c7.15 扌 土 亻 /23 22 3 挫	**ZA** – sprain, dislocate

挫傷　*zashō*　sprain, wrench　　643
挫折　*zasetsu*　setback, fail, failure　　1483

搭	**2092** 3c9.10 扌 艹 口 /23 32 24 搭	**TŌ** – board/load (a vehicle)

搭乗　*tōjō*　board, get on　　532
搭乗券　*tōjōken*　boarding pass　　532, 515
搭載　*tōsai*　load, embark　　1176

拐	**2093** 3c5.21 扌 口 力 /23 24 8 拐	**KAI** – kidnap

誘拐　*yūkai*　kidnap　　1799
拐帯　*kaitai*　abscond with money　　994

	2094	**NEN** – twist; pinch	
	3c8.25 ⊞	捻挫　*nenza*　sprain, wrench	2091
	扌 心 亻 /23 51 3	腸捻転　*chōnenten*　twist in the intestines, volvulus	1344, 439
	捻	捻出　*nenshutsu*　contrive, work out, raise (money)	53

	2095	**SHI** – grab, grasp	
	3c11.8 ⊞	真摯　*shinshi*　ernest, sincere	428
	扌 立 十 /23 54 12	摯実　*shijitsu*　ernest, sincere	203
	摯		

	2096	**CHOKU** – make progress/headway, make great strides	
	3c7.10 ⊞	進捗　*shinchoku*　progress, advance	443
	扌 小 卜 /23 35 13	進捗状況　*shinchoku jōkyō*　state of progress	443, 636, 869
	捗		

	2097	**SHI** – heir	
	3d10.13 ⊞	嗣子　*shishi*　heir	103
	口 艹 冂 /24 32 20	後嗣　*kōshi*　heir	48
	嗣		

	2098	**KAKU** – threaten, menace	
	3d14.1 ⊞⊞	威嚇　*ikaku*　threat, menace	1422
	口 土 儿 /24 22 16		
	嚇		

	2099	**CHŌ** – mockery **azake(ru)** – ridicule	
	3d12.2 ⊞⊞	嘲笑　*chōshō*　scornful laugh, derisive smile, ridicule	1299
	口 日 月 /24 42 43	嘲弄　*chōrō*　ridicule	2004
	嘲	自嘲　*jichō*　self-scorn	62

	2100	**YU** – compare, liken	
	3d9.15 ⊞	比喩　*hiyu*　simile, metaphor, allegory	812
	口 月 亻 /24 43 3	比喩的　*hiyuteki*　figurative	812, 210
	喩	直喩　*chokuyu*　simile	429
		引喩　*in'yu*　allusion	216

2101

喝

KATSU – scold

3d8.8

口 日 亠
/24 42 15

恐喝	kyōkatsu	threaten, blackmail	1709
喝破	kappa	declare, proclaim	676
喝采	kassai	applause, cheers	957

2102

謁

ETSU – audience (with someone)

7a8.6

言 日 亠
/67 42 15

謁見	ekken	have an audience (with)	63
拝謁	haietsu	have an audience (with)	1264
謁する	essuru	have an audience (with)	

2103

葛

KATSU, kuzu – kudzu (trailing vine)

3k9.22

艹 日 亠
/32 42 15

| 葛藤 | kattō | entanglements, discord, conflict | 2087 |

2104

朕

CHIN – (imperial) we

4b6.6

月 大 儿
/43 34 16

| 朕思うに | Chin omou ni | We, the emperor, think: | 99 |

2105

爵

SHAKU – peerage, court rank

5g12.1

罒 食 小
/55 77 35

男爵	danshaku	baron	101
公爵	kōshaku	prince, duke	126
伯爵	hakushaku	count, earl	1234
爵位	shakui	peerage, court rank	122
授爵	jushaku	elevate to the peerage, create a peer	612

2106

腫

SHU – tumor, swelling **ha(reru)** – swell, become swollen
ha(rasu) – cause to swell, inflame

4b9.1

月 車 一
/43 69 1

腫瘍	shuyō	swelling, boil	1958
癌腫	ganshu	cancer tumor, carcinoma	
水腫	suishu	dropsy; edema	21

2107

侯

KŌ – marquis

2a7.21

亻 大 亠
/3 34 15

王侯	ōkō	royalty	294
諸侯	shokō	feudal lords	880
侯爵	kōshaku	marquis	2105

2108

喉

3d9.6 ▥

口 大 イ
/24 34 3

喉

KŌ, nodo – throat

咽喉	inkō	throat	1872
耳鼻咽喉科	jibiinkōka	ear, nose, and throat specialty	
			56, 832, 1872, 320
喉頭	kōtō	larynx	276
喉仏	nodobotoke	Adam's apple	592

2109

矯

3d14.5 ▥

口 大 イ
/24 34 15

矯

KYŌ, ta(meru) – straighten, correct

矯正	kyōsei	correct, reform	275
矯激	kyōgeki	radical, extreme	1056
奇矯	kikyō	eccentric conduct	1444
矯め直す	tamenaosu	set up again, correct, reform, cure	429

2110

且

0a5.15 ▤

日 一
/42 1

且

ka(tsu) – and, furthermore

| 且つ又 | katsumata | and | 1700 |

2111

旦

4c1.2 ▤

日 一
42 01

旦

TAN, DAN – morning, dawn

元旦	gantan	New Year's Day	137
一旦	ittan	once	2
旦那（様）	danna(-sama)	master, husband, gentleman	
			826, 407

2112

但

2a5.14 ▥

イ 日 一
/3 42 1

但

tada(shi) – but, however, provided

| 但し書き | tadashigaki | proviso | 131 |

2113

偵

2a9.15 ▥

イ 貝 卜
/3 68 13

偵

TEI – spy, investigate

探偵	tantei	detective	544
探偵小説	tantei shōsetsu	detective story, whodunit	
			544, 27, 404
偵察	teisatsu	reconnaissance	629
内偵	naitei	scouting; private inquiry	84

2114

曹

4c7.10 ▤

日 艹
/42 32

曹

SŌ – officer; comrade

| 法曹 | hōsō | the legal profession; lawyer | 123 |
| 法曹界 | hōsōkai | legal circles, the bench and bar | 123, 461 |

2115	**Ō** – old man	
2o8.6	老翁　*rōō*　old man	552

翁

2116	**BA** – old woman	
3e8.9	老婆　*rōba*　old woman	552
	産婆　*sanba*　midwife	278
	お転婆　*otenba*　tomboy	439
	塔婆　*tōba*　wooden grave tablet	1991

婆

2117	**CHAKU** – legitimate (wife, child, heir)	
3e11.5	嫡(出)子　*chaku(shutsu)shi*　legitimate child	53, 103
	嫡嗣　*chakushi*　legitimate heir	2097
	嫡流　*chakuryū*　lineage of the eldest son	247
	嫡男　*chakunan*　eldest son, heir, legitimate son	101
	嫡孫　*chakuson*　eldest son of one's son and heir	932

嫡

2118	**DO** – servant, slave; fellow	
3e2.2	守銭奴　*shusendo*　miser	499, 659
	農奴　*nōdo*　serf	370
	売国奴　*baikokudo*　traitor	239, 40

奴

2119	**REI** – servant, slave, prisoner	
4e11.1	奴隷　*dorei*　slave	2118
	隷従　*reijū*　slavery	1579
	隷属　*reizoku*　be subordinate (to)	1750
	隷書　*reisho*　(ancient squared style of kanji)	131

隷 隷

2120	**SUI** – leading troops	
3f6.1	元帥　*gensui*　field marshal, admiral	137
	総帥　*sōsui*　commander in chief	710
	統帥　*tōsui*　supreme/high command	849

帥

2121	**TON** – barracks	
0a4.35	駐屯　*chūton*　be stationed	609
	駐屯地　*chūtonchi*　military post	609, 118

屯

頓	**2122** 9a4.1 頁 十 门 /76 12 20 頓	**TON** – sudden halt; stumble; be in order 頓死　*tonshi*　sudden death　　85 頓知　*tonchi*　ready/quick wit　　214 頓着　*tonchaku*　be mindful (of), care, heed　　668 無頓着　*mutonchaku*　indifferent/unattentive to　　93, 668 整頓　*seiton*　in proper order, neat　　512
遞	**2123** 2q7.5 辶 帅 厂 /19 26 18 遞 遞	**TEI** – successive; relay, send 遞信　*teishin*　communications　　157 遞送　*teisō*　convey, send by mail, forward　　447 遞減　*teigen*　successive diminution　　728 遞増　*teizō*　gradual increase　　725
遵	**2124** 2q12.8 辶 酉 寸 /19 71 37 遵	**JUN** – follow, obey 遵守　*junshu*　obey, comply with　　499 遵奉　*junpō*　observe, adhere to, abide by　　1643 遵法　*junpō*　law abiding; work-to-rule (tactics)　　123
骸	**2125** 4b12.7 月 门 亠 /43 20 11 骸	**GAI** – body 骸骨　*gaikotsu*　skeleton　　1340 死骸　*shigai*　corpse　　85 遺骸　*igai*　one's remains, corpse　　1230 残骸　*zangai*　remains, corpse, wreckage　　661
劾	**2126** 2g6.1 力 亠 厶 /8 11 17 劾	**GAI** – investigate, prosecute 弾劾　*dangai*　impeachment　　1641
勃	**2127** 2g6.3 力 十 子 /8 12 6 勃	**BOTSU** – sudden; active 勃発　*boppatsu*　outbreak, sudden occurrence　　96 勃興　*bokkō*　sudden rise to power　　369 勃起　*bokki*　an erection　　374
殴	**2128** 2t6.1 匚 十 又 /20 12 9 殴 毆	**Ō, nagu(ru)** – beat, hit, strike 殴打　*ōda*　assault (and battery)　　1059 殴り殺す　*nagurikorosu*　beat to death, strike dead　　585 殴り付ける　*naguritsukeru*　strike, beat, thrash　　192 殴り込み　*nagurikomi*　an attack, raid　　790 ぶん殴る　*bunnaguru*　give a good whaling/thrashing

| 虞 | **2129**
2m11.1
厂 口 十
18 24 12
虞 | **osore** – fear, concern, risk |

痘	**2130** 5i7.8 疒 口 儿 /60 24 16 痘	**TŌ** – smallpox
		種痘　*shutō*　vaccination　228
		痘苗　*tōbyō*　vaccine　1565
		天然痘　*tennentō*　smallpox　141, 662
		水痘　*suitō*　chickenpox　21

陪	**2131** 2d8.3 阝 立 口 /7 54 24 陪	**BAI** – follow, accompany, attend on
		陪審　*baishin*　jury　1471
		陪審員　*baishin'in*　member of the jury, juror　163
		陪席　*baiseki*　sitting as an associate (judge)　380
		陪食　*baishoku*　dining with a superior　322

濫	**2132** 3a15.3 氵 皿 刂 /21 59 20 濫	**RAN** – overflow; excessive, indiscriminate
		濫用　*ran'yō*　abuse, misuse, misappropriation　107
		濫費　*ranpi*　waste, extravagance　762
		濫作　*ransaku*　overproduction　361
		濫伐　*ranbatsu*　reckless deforestation　1610
		濫獲　*rankaku*　overfishing, overhunting　1392

籃	**2133** 6f15.2 ⺮ 皿 冂 /66 59 20 籃	**RAN** – basket **ai** – indigo (plant, color)
		揺籃　*yōran*　cradle　1761
		揺籃期　*yōranki*　infancy　1761, 456
		伽藍　*garan*　Buddhist temple, monastery
		藍色　*aiiro*　indigo blue, deep blue　204
		藍染め　*aizome*　indigo-dyeing　793

畔	**2134** 5f5.1 田 十 儿 /58 12 16 畔	**HAN** – rice-paddy ridge, levee
		湖畔　*kohan*　lakeshore　475
		河畔　*kahan*　riverside　391

貌	**2135** 4c10.6 豸 犭 儿 /42 27 16 貌	**BŌ** – form, appearance
		全貌　*zenbō*　the full picture/story　89
		容貌　*yōbō*　looks, personal appearance　665
		美貌　*bibō*　good looks　405
		変貌　*henbō*　transformation　257

	2136	**HAN** – spread out	
氾	3a2.3 ⬚	氾濫　*hanran*　flooding, inundation	2132
	氵阝		
	/21　7		
	氾		

2137 – 2141

The following five characters 2137 to 2141 used to be among the 1,945 officially recognized list of Jōyō Kanji. But when the list was revised in 2010, these characters were dropped and other characters were added, raising the count to 2,136 characters.

	2137	**monme** – (unit of weigth, about 3.75 g)	
匁	0a4.38 …		
	𠂉 十		
	15　12		
	匁		

	2138	**SHAKU** – (unit of volume, about 18 ml)	
勺	0a3.5 ⬚		
	𠂉 丶		
	15　2		
	勺		

	2139	**SUI** – spindle; plumb bob, sinker **tsumu** – spindle	
錘	8a8.2 ⬚	紡錘　*bōsui*　spindle	2015
	金 土 ⺾	錘状　*suijō*　spindle-shaped	636
	/72　22　32		
	錘		

	2140	**SEN** – pig iron	
銑	8a6.6 ⬚	銑鉄　*sentetsu*　pig iron	312
	金 土 儿		
	/72　22　16		
	銑		

	2141	**CHŌ** – swell	
脹	4b8.1 ⬚	膨脹　*bōchō*　expansion	1198
	月 衤		
	/42　57　13		
	脹		

Index by Radicals

– 0a –

1: 一 2 · 乙 1017
2: 二 3 · 入 52 · 丁 184 · 七 9 · 九 11
3: 三 4 · 川 33 · 乞 1020 · 勺 2138 · 工 139 · 久 1273 · 万 16 · 乏 767 · 己 371 · 夕 2070 · 寸 26 · 大 1502 · 刃 548 · 与 1328 · 及 1408 · 丈 560 · 才 654 · 丸 94
4: 不 2073 · 斤 137 · 元 1291 · 幻 1730 · 匂 1734 · 勾 1320 · 爪 397 · 予 929 · 互 2075 · 斗 639 · 太 1354 · 凶 141 · 天 84 · 内 575 · 氏 7 · 五 1548 · 牙 315 · 夫 2074 · 升 287 · 毛 1144 · 丹 2121 · 屯 2137 · 匂 28 · 中 (—)
弔 1934 · 井 1255
5: 以 46 · 北 73 · 矛 787 · 巧 1737 · 包 819 · 瓦 1216 · 丘 1441 · 凸 2068 · 凹 2069 · 且 2110 · 必 529 · 斥 1490 · 矢 213 · 左 75 · 丙 1018 · 出 53 · 民 177 · 半 88 · 本 25 · 末 305 · 未 306 · 失 311 · 生 44 · 弁 724 · 甘 1591 · 央 352 · 甲 1016 · 由 364 · 母 112 · 世 252 · 史 332 · 申 309 · 丼 1256 · 冊 1213
6: 臼 1896 · 多 229 · 死 85 · 気 134 · 両 200 · 朱 1602 · 年 45 · 西 72 · 吏 1044 · 毎 116 · 再 796 · 曲 367
7: 良 321 · 身 59 · 来 69
承 972 · 束 510 · 里 142 · 我 1381 · 更 1045 · 串 1394 · 亜 1724 · 寿 1652
8: 非 507 · 長 95 · 表 272 · 画 343 · 果 496 · 東 71 · 垂 1117 · 奉 1643 · 毒 531 · 事 80
9: 飛 539 · 発 96 · 衷 1792 · 甚 1600 · 巻 516 · 専 610 · 奏 1646 · 重 227 · 乗 532
10: 既 1552 · 殊 1604 · 射 922 · 残 661 · 耗 1260 · 耕 1259
11: 疎 1615 · 野 236 · 爽 2059 · 粛 1811
13: 業 279
15: 舞 829

– 2a –
亻

0: 人 1
2: 仏 592 · 化 254 · 仁 1727 · 介 460 · 今 51
3: 仙 2064 · 仕 333 · 代 256 · 他 120 · 付 192 · 令 850
4: 伏 1439 · 休 60 · 件 745 · 伐 1610 · 仲 1430 · 任 334 · 仰 1099 · 伎 890 · 伝 440 · 仮 1092 · 全 89 · 企 490 · 合 159 · 会 158 · 肉 223
5: 位 122 · 伸 1160 · 伴 1066 · 体 61 · 伯 1234 · 佐 1867 · 似 1583 · 但 2112 · 低 570 · 住 156 · 何 392 · 伺 1891 · 余 1109 · 含 1317
6: 依 691 · 使 331 · 価 427 · 例 622 · 佳 1557 · 侍 580 · 供 197 · 併 1218 · 侮 1858 · 舎 805 · 念 588 · 命 587
7: 信 157 · 促 1659
便 330 · 係 931 · 俊 1997 · 保 498 · 侶 1397 · 侵 1125 · 俗 1178 · 侯 2107
8: 倒 927 · 傲 1908 · 俳 1076 · 候 974 · 修 975 · 倍 87 · 俸 1644 · 俵 2063 · 借 780 · 俺 2061 · 倹 899 · 倫 1220 · 値 431 · 健 914 · 個 1005 · 倉 1386
9: 偶 1752 · 側 619 · 停 1244 · 偵 2113 · 偏 1214 · 貪 1837 · 斜 1116
10: 備 782 · 偉 1096 · 傍 1242 · 傘 804 · 僅 1315
11: 働 232 · 傲 2066 · 傾 1533 · 傑 1849 · 僧 1453 · 傷 643 · 債 1170 · 催 1399
12: 僕 2060 · 僚 1406 · 像 753
13: 儀 740 · 億 383
14: 儒 1506
15: 優 1074 · 償 1003

– 2b –
冫

4: 次 385 · 壮 1409 · 兆 1665 · 羽 600
5: 状 636 · 冷 851 · 治 1962 · 求 737
8: 准 1296 · 凍 1268 · 将 637 · 凄 683
14: 凝 1619

– 2c –
子

0: 子 103 · 了 971
1: 孔 970
3: 存 269
6: 孤 1577
7: 孫 932

– 2d –
阝

4: 防 522 · 阪 450 · 那 826 · 邦 825
5: 阻 1135 · 附 1995 · 邪 1551 · 邸 572
6: 限 866 · 郎 1014
郊 836
7: 陣 1493 · 陸 599 · 降 977 · 院 624 · 除 1112 · 陥 1281 · 郡 193 · 郭 1788
8: 陳 1494 · 陪 2131 · 陛 657 · 陵 1996 · 隆 976 · 陰 886 · 険 542 · 随 1864 · 陶 1763 · 郵 533 · 都 188 · 郷 874 · 部 86
9: 隅 1753 · 陽 640 · 階 597 · 隊 809
10: 隔 1696 · 隙 1111
11: 際 628 · 障 877 · 隠 887
13: 隣 828

– 2e –
卩

4: 印 1086
5: 即 471 · 卵 1103 · 却 1915
7: 卸 720

– 2f –
刂

0: 刀 37
2: 刈 1356

切 39
3 刊 594
召 1032
4 州 195
刑 908
列 621
5 判 1065
別 267
6 制 433
刺 902
到 926
刻 1274
利 827
刷 1087
券 515
7 削 1718
契 574
8 剖 1979
剥 1719
剣 900
剤 559
剛 1717
帰 317
9 剰 1115
副 727
10 割 528
創 1387
13 劇 811

– 2g –
力
0 力 100
3 加 722
功 837
幼 1293
5 助 633
励 1423
努 1702
6 劾 2126
効 835
勃 2127
7 勅 2056
勇 1474
8 脅 1335
9 動 231
勘 1601
10 勤 568
11 勧 1094

勢 656

– 2h –
又
0 又 1700
2 双 1701
収 770
友 264
3 皮 1008
6 叔 1782
受 260
7 叙 1114
8 桑 2035

– 2i –
冖
2 冗 1722
3 写 549
7 軍 444
冠 1723
8 冥 1522
11 彙 1637

– 2j –
亠
1 亡 684
2 六 8
文 111
片 1088
3 市 181
玄 1289
4 交 114
充 847
妄 1463
5 享 1787
忘 1461
6 夜 479
卒 801
京 189
育 246
斉 1574
盲 1462

版 1089
7 帝 1237
変 257
哀 1790
亭 1243
8 衰 1791
恋 258
高 190
畜 1287
9 率 802
斎 1575
商 418
10 蛮 2044
11 裏 273
棄 993
12 豪 1786
13 襄 818

– 2k –
十
0 十 12
1 干 593
千 15
支 318
午 49
3 古 172
平 202
4 孝 551
考 550
老 552
缶 1762
5 克 1459
6 協 234
直 429
卓 1448
奔 1773
7 南 74
8 真 428
索 1104
10 博 611
11 準 792

– 2m –
卜
1 上 32

下 31
2 止 485
3 外 83
占 1822
正 275
比 812
6 卓 1794
虎 1677
7 貞 1796
点 169
虐 1680
9 虚 1678
11 虞 2129
虜 1473
12 疑 1617
13 膚 1343
慮 1472

– 2n –
夕
4 色 204
争 302
危 543
5 角 481
免 746
6 負 519
急 303
8 勉 748
9 亀 1889
10 象 752

– 2o –
丶
0 八 10
2 分 38
公 126
父 113
4 羊 288
5 弟 409
谷 664
兵 798
呉 1526
6 並 1222
典 368
7 首 148

前 47
美 405
盆 1150
8 兼 1129
差 669
益 729
翁 2115
釜 1131
9 曽 1450
羞 1806
貧 766
瓶 1217
10 着 668
善 1191
尊 717
普 1223
11 慈 1649
煎 1933
義 291
羨 1924
養 406
14 興 369
15 翼 1107

– 2p –
厂
2 反 324
厄 1424
3 圧 1425
灰 1426
6 厚 649
厘 2076
7 原 136
辱 1860
11 農 370
暦 1635
歴 489

– 2q –
辶
2 辺 789
込 790
3 巡 791
迅 1936
4 廷 1163

近 452
迎 1098
返 448
5 迭 1608
述 1000
延 1167
迫 1233
6 迷 998
建 913
退 865
追 1232
逃 1669
逆 451
送 447
7 連 446
速 511
逓 2123
逐 1186
逝 1485
透 1800
造 704
途 1120
8 進 443
逮 912
遊 1040
逸 747
週 92
9 遇 1754
達 455
運 445
遂 1185
道 149
遍 1215
遅 715
過 419
10 遣 1231
遜 2067
遠 453
違 833
11 遭 1756
適 421
遮 1899
遡 1989
12 遷 943
選 814
遺 1230
遵 2124
13 避 1590
還 885

– 2r –
冂
2 円 13
3 用 107
4 同 198
周 91
岡 1440
7 耐 1504

– 2s –
几
1 凡 1153
7 風 29
段 363

– 2t –
匚
2 区 183
巨 1368
匹 1599
4 匠 1443
臣 854
5 医 220
6 殴 2128
匿 1903
15 臨 855

– 3a –
氵
0 水 21
1 永 1270
氷 1269
2 汁 1930
氾 2136
3 池 119
汚 706
汗 1247
江 840
汎 1155

4	冲	1429		渓	2053		濃	987	10	塊	1625	
	決	357		淫	2054		濁	1735		塩	1152	
	汰	1206		清	671	14	灌	1664		塡	1920	
	沈	964		渋	1809	15	濫	2132		塾	1789	
	沃	1885		渉	438	16	瀬	1614		塑	1988	
	沙	1205		深	545					塗	1121	
	没	963		添	1523		**– 3b –**			毀	1897	
	汽	135		液	480		土		11	境	883	
	沢	1031		済	558					増	725	
5	泣	1300		涼	1267	0	土	24		墨	1821	
	沸	1928		涯	1555	2	去	420		墜	1184	
	油	365	9	測	620	3	地	118	12	墳	1776	
	波	677		湖	475		寺	41		舗	1536	
	泌	2031		港	680		至	924	13	壊	1496	
	泳	1271		湾	681		先	50		壌	2088	
	泊	1235		温	644		在	268		壇	1990	
	注	358		湿	1226	4	坊	2014		墾	1188	
	泡	1895		湯	642		坑	1721		壁	1587	
	法	123		満	201		坂	449				
	況	869		滋	1651		均	820		**– 3c –**		
	沿	1714		湧	1475		走	435		扌		
	沼	1033		渡	379		赤	207				
	治	502		渦	1949	5	坪	2072	0	手	57	8	推	1297
	泥	1729		減	728		幸	697	2	払	591		掛	1559
	河	391	10	溺	966	6	城	733		打	1059		排	1077
	泉	1253		滑	1341		垣	1350	3	扱	1329		接	495
	泰	1647		滝	1887		型	909	4	扶	1839		控	1835
6	津	679		溝	1050		封	1558		把	1842		掲	1733
	浅	660		滞	995		赴	1560		折	1483		採	960
	浮	968		溶	1481	7	埋	1975		抜	1830		授	612
	洗	705		漢	565		起	374		抄	1208		探	544
	洪	1525		漠	1516	8	堆	1749		抑	1100		措	1263
	活	237		源	589		域	1002		批	1068		描	1566
	浄	675		滅	1421		培	1977		抗	843		掃	1128
	洋	289	11	漁	712		埼	1446		技	891		捻	2094
	海	117		漸	1489		堀	1942		投	1060		捨	1537
	派	934		漂	946		基	457		択	1030	9	掘	1941
	洞	1380		漆	1648		堕	1865	5	拓	1983		据	1982
7	酒	526		漫	1500		執	699		拉	1301		提	638
	浦	1534		漬	1929	9	堪	2089		拝	1264		揚	641
	浪	1877		演	344		場	154		押	1021		援	1139
	浜	799		滴	1539		堤	1699		抽	1022		揺	1761
	流	247		漏	1945		塔	1991		抹	2090		搭	2092
	消	864	12	潮	476		塚	1875		拙	1939		揮	1766
	浸	1126		潜	967		塀	1944		披	1829		換	1693
	浴	1180		潟	1736		堅	1363		拍	1236		握	1831
	涙	1305		潔	1307		報	698		抱	1359	10	搬	1840
8	淑	1783		澄	1417		超	1037		抵	569		携	1801
	渇	1731		潰	1229		喪	1793		担	1348		摂	1808
	混	813		潤	1266									
	淡	1420	13	激	1056									

	拐	2093		搾	1596	7	唄	396
	招	462		損	351		哺	1535
	拡	1165	11	摘	1540		唆	1998
	拠	1190		撃	1054		員	163
	拘	1938		摯	2095		唇	1859
	拒	1370	12	撲	2062		哲	1486
6	挟	1437		撤	1512	8	唯	1298
	拷	1838		撮	1621		唾	1119
	挑	1667	13	操	1769		喝	2101
	持	458		擁	1832		唱	1759
	括	1332	14	擬	1618		啓	1487
	挫	1102		擦	1620	9	喉	2108
	拾	1538					喫	1306
	指	1082		**– 3d –**			喩	2100
	拭	1072		口			喚	1694
	拳	817					就	961
7	捉	1660	0	口	54		登	991
	挿	1765	2	叱	1323		短	215
	捕	911		兄	410		尋	1132
	捜	1026		号	266	10	嗅	1311
	捗	2096		台	501		嘆	1313
	挨	1101		可	390		嗣	2097
	振	984		句	337		群	808
	挫	2091		司	861		豊	989
8	推	1297		右	76	11	鳴	948
			3	吐	1322	12	嘲	2099
				叫	1321		噴	1774
				吸	1327		嘱	1751
				舌	1331		器	536
				向	199	14	嚇	2098
				后	1171		矯	2109
				名	82	16	艶	990
			4	吹	1326			
				吟	1318		**– 3e –**	
				呈	1697		女	
				呂	1396			
				告	703	0	女	102
				否	1316	2	好	104
				乱	702		奴	2118
				豆	988	3	如	1870
				君	807		妃	1881
			5	味	307	4	妨	1241
				呼	1325		妊	985
				呪	1324		妖	1884
				知	214		妙	1209
				奇	1444		妥	956
			6	咲	951	5	姑	1956
				咽	1872		姓	1869
				品	230		妹	412

姉 411	7 猛 1685	12 衝 1904	黄 794	定 356	労 233	4 志 582
始 503	8 猫 1567	徹 1511	萎 2082	宛 1374	乳 969	壱 1848
妻 682	猟 1686	13 衡 1692	菜 958	突 920	5 尚 2009	売 239
6 姻 1871	9 猶 1689	衛 834	菊 483	空 140	歩 437	声 759
姿 953	献 1438		菌 1285	6 宣 635	6 栄 736	8 殻 1846
要 425	10 猿 1690	**– 3j –**	9 落 858	客 651	単 300	9 喜 1196
7 娘 1876	11 獄 905	彡	葬 831	室 166	県 194	10 鼓 1200
娯 1527	12 獣 1688		蒸 973	窃 1834	7 挙 815	
娠 986	13 獲 1392	4 形 399	葉 253	7 家 165	党 504	**– 3q –**
姫 1882		5 参 723	葛 2103	宰 1586	8 巣 1640	广
8 婚 576	**– 3h –**	8 彩 959	募 1519	宴 650	蛍 2043	
婦 316	弓	彫 1202	10 夢 830	害 527	常 506	2 広 707
婆 2116		9 須 1531	蓋 1286	宮 734	堂 505	庁 777
9 媒 1595	0 弓 212	11 彰 1976	蓄 1288	案 106	9 営 735	4 床 845
婿 1868	1 引 216	髪 1201	墓 1518	宵 2010	覚 615	応 846
媛 1883	5 弦 1290	12 影 873	幕 1521	容 665	掌 508	序 784
10 嫁 1873	弥 1012		靴 1124	8 寂 1784	10 誉 816	5 府 513
嫌 1803	6 弧 1578	**– 3k –**	11 蔑 1564	宿 179	奨 1415	底 571
嫉 1955	7 弱 218	艹	慕 1520	密 822	12 賞 509	店 168
11 嫡 2117	8 張 1158		暮 1517	窓 711	14 厳 841	6 度 378
13 嬢 1986	強 217	2 芝 250	12 蔽 2085	寄 1445		庭 1164
	9 弾 1641	芋 2081	蔵 1360	窒 1833	**– 3o –**	7 庫 844
– 3f –		共 196	13 薪 2083	9 寒 464	山	座 800
巾	**– 3i –**	4 芳 1907	薄 1542	富 726		唐 1813
	彳	芯 2084	薬 360	10 寝 1127	0 山 34	席 380
0 巾 687		花 255	薫 1906	塞 465	4 岐 892	8 康 916
2 布 688	3 行 68	芸 441	薦 1741	寛 1093	岬 1449	庸 1812
3 帆 1154	4 役 376	5 苗 1565	15 藤 2087	窟 1943	岩 1428	麻 1630
4 希 689	5 彼 1010	英 354	藩 1470	11 寡 2007	岸 595	廊 1015
6 帥 2120	征 1166	茂 1563	繭 2086	察 629	6 峡 1435	鹿 2038
7 帯 994	径 1572	芽 1549	16 藻 1771	蜜 823	峠 1434	庶 1898
師 415	往 940	若 553		寧 1501	炭 1427	9 廃 992
8 帳 1159	6 律 678	茎 1571	**– 3m –**	12 審 1471	幽 1292	10 廉 1804
9 帽 1157	待 459	苦 554	宀	寮 1405	7 峰 1433	11 腐 1312
幅 1467	後 48	昔 778		賓 2008	島 286	12 摩 1631
12 幣 1913	7 徒 436	苛 394	2 字 110	窮 919	8 崎 1447	慶 1742
	徐 1113	6 革 1123	穴 921	窯 1925	崩 1174	13 磨 1632
– 3g –	従 1579	茨 955	3 安 105	13 憲 530	崇 1513	16 麗 1740
犭	8 術 187	荘 1410	守 499		崖 1556	18 魔 1629
	得 375	草 249	宇 1027	**– 3n –**	9 嵐 2065	
0 犬 280	9 御 721	荒 1464	宅 178	⺌		**– 3r –**
2 犯 903	街 186	茶 251	4 究 917		**– 3p –**	尸
4 狂 904	復 939	7 華 1122	完 623	0 小 27	吉	
5 狙 1136	循 1576	荷 393	5 宗 626	1 少 144		1 尺 2071
6 独 219	10 微 1508	恭 1524	宝 296	3 光 138	0 士 581	2 尻 2029
狭 1436	11 徴 1509	8 菓 1636	実 203	当 77	3 吉 1194	尼 1728
狩 1687	徳 1079	著 878	官 326	劣 1203		3 尽 1844
				宜 1137	4 肖 863	
					学 109	

4	尿	2030
	尾	2028
	局	170
5	届	1029
	屈	1940
	居	171
6	屋	167
7	展	1181
9	属	1750
10	殿	1182
11	層	1454
12	履	1745

– 3s –

口

2	囚	1258
	四	6
3	回	90
	因	563
	団	500
4	困	567
	囲	1257
	図	339
5	国	40
	固	1004
6	面	274
9	圏	517
10	園	454

– 4a –

木

0	木	22
1	札	1212
2	朴	1562
	机	1384
	朽	1738
3	杉	2033
	材	561
	村	191
4	林	127
	枚	1211
	枕	965
	杯	1210
	析	1482
	松	709

枝	889
枠	2079
板	1090
枢	1062
采	957
5 相	146
柵	1330
柄	1019
柱	608
柳	2032
柿	2034
枯	1007
栃	2036
査	634
某	1593
柔	788
染	793
架	768
6 桟	2078
株	754
根	314
桁	1691
桃	1670
桜	952
格	653
核	1275
校	115
栓	1993
梅	1856
殺	585
7 梗	1047
械	538
梨	1951
8 椎	1748
棟	1495
棚	2080
極	336
棋	1985
棒	1645
棺	1974
椅	2048
検	540
植	430
森	128
9 楼	1992
楷	598
楽	359
10 概	1553
構	1048
模	1514
様	407

11 槽	1757
標	945
横	795
権	335
12 機	537
樹	1197
橋	607
15 麓	2039
16 欄	1265
25 鬱	1764

– 4b –

月

0	月	17
2	肌	1385
	有	265
3	肝	1346
	肘	1377
4	肥	1841
	服	696
	肢	1199
	股	1055
	青	208
	肯	1334
5	胞	1358
	胆	1347
	肺	1351
	胎	1371
	背	1338
6	脇	1336
	朕	2104
	脂	1083
	脈	935
	胸	1357
	胴	1379
	朗	1878
	脊	1339
	骨	1340
	能	387
7	豚	810
	脚	1916
	脳	1352
	脱	1457
8	脹	2141
	勝	518
	腕	1376
	期	456

朝	477
9 腫	2106
腰	1373
腹	1345
腺	1254
腸	1344
腎	1365
10 膜	1515
静	674
11 膝	1917
12 膨	1198
膳	1193
骸	2125
13 膽	1911
臆	1378
14 髄	1863
15 臓	1361
覇	1743
16 騰	1912

– 4c –

日

0	日	5
1	旧	1279
	旦	2111
	白	205
2	早	248
	旨	1081
	百	14
	旬	338
3	児	1280
4	明	18
	旺	2058
	昇	1909
	易	772
	昆	2037
	的	210
	者	164
5	映	353
	昧	413
	昨	362
	昭	1034
	冒	1156
	星	743
	是	1698
	春	468
	皆	596
	昼	478

6 時	42
書	131
殉	1937
曹	2114
習	601
乾	1249
8 暁	1772
晴	673
晩	749
暑	648
晶	1758
景	872
量	417
最	263
替	757
9 暇	1110
暗	348
暖	645
幹	1248
10 貌	2135
11 暴	1052
暫	1488
12 曇	647
13 曖	414
曜	19
14 韓	1250
覆	1744
15 響	875

– 4d –

火

0	火	20
2	灯	1416
3	災	1418
4	炊	1927
	炉	1926
	炎	1419
5	畑	36
	為	1581
6	烈	1414
7	黒	206
8	焼	942
	煮	1931
	然	662
9	煩	2005
	煙	941
	照	1035

10 熟	700
熊	389
11 勲	1905
熱	655
12 黙	1684
燃	663
13 燥	1770
15 爆	1053

– 4e –

礻

0	示	625
1	礼	630
3	社	308
	奈	947
4	祉	1479
	祈	631
5	神	310
	祖	632
	祝	870
6	祥	1682
	票	944
	祭	627
	尉	1725
	視	616
8	禁	491
	福	1466
	禅	1642
	禍	1948
11	隷	2119

– 4f –

王

0	王	294
	玉	295
1	主	155
3	弄	2004
	玩	2003
4	珍	1278
	皇	297
6	珠	1603
	班	1468
7	理	143
	球	739
	現	298

望	685
8 斑	1469
琴	1319
9 聖	686
10 瑠	1605
璃	1606
13 環	884
璧	1588
14 璽	2057

– 4g –

牛

0	牛	281
	牧	744
	物	79
5	牲	742
6	特	282
9	解	482
13	犠	741

– 4h –

方

0	方	70
4	放	521
5	施	1041
6	旅	222
7	旋	1042
	族	221
10	旗	1043

– 4i –

攵

2	冬	467
	処	1189
3	改	523
	攻	838
	各	652
4	条	573
	麦	270
5	政	492
	故	173
6	教	245
	致	925

敏 1857
7 救 738
赦 1675
夏 469
務 235
8 散 781
敬 718
敢 1807
9 数 225
10 愛 259
11 敷 1544
敵 422
弊 1914
12 憂 1073
整 512
13 麺 1302

– 4j –
欠
0 欠 384
4 欧 1061
7 欲 1179
8 欺 1598
款 1845
10 歌 395
11 歓 1095

– 4k –
心
0 心 97
3 忙 1460
忌 1935
忍 1503
4 快 1498
忠 1431
5 性 98
怖 1959
怪 1573
怒 1703
怨 1375
怠 1372
6 恨 1879
恒 1349
悔 1855
恵 1282

息 1308
恐 1709
恣 954
恩 564
7 悟 1528
悩 1353
悦 1455
悪 304
患 1395
悠 1704
8 惧 1964
惨 1843
情 209
惜 779
悼 1795
惑 1001
悲 1075
9 惰 1866
慌 1465
愉 1705
愚 1755
愁 1708
想 147
感 262
10 慨 1554
慎 1918
慄 1963
態 388
11 憎 1452
慢 1499
慣 937
慰 1726
12 憧 1853
憤 1775
憬 1854
憩 1309
13 憾 1961
憶 382
懐 1497
14 懇 1187
懲 1510
16 懸 933

– 4m –
戸
0 戸 152
3 戻 1304
4 肩 1337

房 1303
所 153
6 扇 1657
8 雇 1655
扉 1658

– 4n –
戈
2 成 261
3 戒 896
式 534
弐 1070
5 威 1422
武 1071
栽 1177
7 戚 488
越 1038
幾 897
9 戦 301
歳 487
11 戯 1679

– 5a –
石
0 石 78
4 研 918
砂 1204
砕 1827
5 破 676
砲 1894
硬 1046
硫 2012
硝 2011
8 碁 1984
碑 1623
磁 1650
10 確 613
礁 1900
13 礎 1616

– 5b –
立
0 立 121

2 辛 1584
4 音 347
5 竜 1886
6 章 876
産 278
翌 602
7 童 416
8 意 132
新 174
辞 701
9 端 1507
辣 1585
11 親 175
15 競 871

– 5c –
目
0 目 55
1 自 62
2 見 63
3 具 426
4 臭 1310
看 1398
省 145
盾 786
眉 1851
5 眠 868
6 眼 867
眺 1668
規 617
7 殖 1607
睡 1118
8 睦 658
督 1785
9 瞳 716
12 瞭 1407
覧 1366
13 瞬 1850
観 614

– 5d –
禾
2 利 329

私 125
季 473
秀 1798
3 和 124
委 474
4 秋 470
秒 1207
科 320
香 1797
5 秩 1609
秘 824
租 1133
称 1011
6 移 1173
7 程 423
税 403
8 稚 1294
9 種 228
稲 1283
穀 1847
10 穂 1284
稼 1874
稿 1172
11 稽 1084
穏 888
積 667
13 穫 1393

– 5f –
田
0 田 35
2 町 182
男 101
4 胃 1342
思 99
畏 1960
界 461
卑 1622
5 畔 2134
畝 774
畜 2077
畿 1624
鬼 860
略 1105
累 1106
異 1810
塁 1138
畳 185
番 1626
9 魂 832
魅 1627
10 幾 898
奮 1388
12 戴 1108

– 5e –
衤
0 衣 690
2 初 692
5 袖 1024
被 1009
袋 1412
6 裂 1413
装 1411
裁 1175
7 補 910
裕 1480
8 裸 1638
褐 1732
裾 1025
9 製 434
複 938
13 襟 1639
16 襲 1681

– 5g –
罒
7 買 241
8 署 879
罪 906
置 432
9 罰 907
10 罵 2052
罷 2019
12 爵 2105
14 羅 2017

– 5h –
皿
0 皿 1148

1 血 803
6 盛 732
盗 1151
7 衆 806
8 盟 730
10 監 1777
盤 1149

– 5i –
疒
4 疫 1401
5 疲 1403
病 381
症 1400
疾 1954
痕 1880
痢 1952
痛 1402
痘 2130
痴 1957
痩 1953
瘍 1958
12 療 1404
癖 1589
癒 1707

– 6a –
糸
0 糸 242
1 系 930
3 級 577
糾 1819
紀 373
紅 839
約 211
4 紡 2015
純 996
紙 180
納 771
紛 1818
紋 1547
素 271
5 細 708
紳 1161
紺 1592

組 424　終 466　紹 463　経 557
6 結 494　絡 859　給 346　絵 345　絞 1545　統 849　絶 755　紫 1478
7 絹 1333　続 243　継 1064
8 維 1295　練 756　緒 881　綿 1251　綻 2018　緑 546　総 710　綱 1716　網 1720
9 縄 1890　線 299　緩 1140　縁 1183　締 1239　編 695　縫 1432　緊 1364
10 緻 2016　縦 1580　縛 1541　緯 1097　繁 1367
11 繊 1676　績 1169　縮 1162
12 繕 1192　織 693
13 繰 1768

– 6b –
米
0 米 224　4 料 319

粋 1825　粉 1817
5 粒 1816　粗 1134　粘 1824　釈 605　断 1063
6 粧 1815　奥 484　歯 486
8 精 670　10 糖 1814　11 齢 852　12 糧 1820　翻 606

– 6c –
舟
0 舟 1145　4 航 842　般 1147　5 舶 1146　船 377　舷 1781　6 艇 1780　15 艦 1779

– 6d –
虫
0 虫 893　3 虹 2045　4 蚊 2041　蚕 2042　5 蛇 2040　7 蜂 821　触 894　10 融 1695

– 6e –
耳
0 耳 56　2 取 65

4 恥 1805　9 趣 1039　11 聴 1080　12 職 386

– 6f –
⺮
0 竹 129　4 笑 1299　5 第 408　笛 1568　符 514
6 筆 130　策 901　筋 1141　等 578　答 160　筒 1569
7 節 472　8 算 760　箋 1672　管 328　箇 1570　9 箸 1932　範 1143　箱 1142
10 篤 2051　築 1710　12 簡 1634　13 簿 1543　14 籍 1261　15 籃 2133　16 籠 1888

– 7a –
言
0 言 66　2 計 340　訂 1561　託 1746　討 1057　記 372　訓 785　4 訪 1240

許 750　訟 1492　設 586　訳 604
5 訴 1491　評 1067　証 493　詐 1597　診 1277　詔 2055　詠 1272　詞 862
6 誠 731　詩 579　詰 1195　話 238　誇 1739　該 1276　詳 1683　詣 1085　詮 1994　試 535
7 誤 928　誘 1799　語 67　誌 583　認 751　説 404　誕 1168　誓 1484
8 誰 1747　課 497　諸 880　謁 2102　談 603　請 672　諾 1902　論 293　調 342
9 諮 1901　謀 1594　謡 1760　諧 1069　諭 1706　諦 1238　謎 999
10 謝 923　講 797　謹 1314　謙 1802

12 譜 1224　識 694　警 719
13 譲 1051　護 1391　議 292

– 7b –
貝
0 貝 240　2 則 618　3 財 562　貢 1836
4 販 1091　貫 936　責 666　貨 765
5 貯 775　貼 1823　費 762　貴 1228　貿 773　賀 769
6 賄 1861　賂 1862　賊 1946　賃 764　資 763
8 賠 1978　賜 1980　賦 1947　賛 758　質 176　賭 1981
9 賢 1362　10 購 1049　11 贈 1451　12 韻 350

– 7c –
車
0 車 133　2 軌 1921

3 軒 1246　4 軟 1922　斬 1923　転 439
5 軸 1023　軽 556　6 較 1546　載 1176　8 輪 1221　輩 1078　輝 1767　9 輸 555　10 轄 1245

– 7d –
足
0 足 58　5 距 1369　践 1671　跳 1666　路 151　跡 1673　7 踊 1661　8 踏 1662　踪 1674　12 蹴 962　14 躍 1663

– 7e –
酉
3 酎 2023　配 524　酌 2022　4 酔 1826　5 酢 2027　6 酵 2026　酬 2024　酪 2025　7 酷 1828　酸 525　9 醒 2021　10 醜 1628　13 醸 1987

– 8a –
金
0 金 23　2 針 341　3 釣 2020　鈍 997
4 鉢 1969　鉄 312　鈴 1971　鉛 1713　鉱 1711
6 銭 659　銀 313　銘 1654　銑 2140　銃 848　銅 1712
7 鋳 1653　鋭 1458
8 錘 2139　錬 1965　錦 1252　錯 1262　錠 1967　録 547　鍵 915　鋼 1715　鍋 1006
9 鍛 1966　鍋 1950　10 鎖 1968　鎮 1919　鎌 1130
11 鏡 882　12 鐘 1970　15 鑑 1778

– 8b –
食
0 食 322　2 飢 1383　4 飲 323　飯 325　5 飽 1893　飾 1013

	飼	1892
6	餌	776
	餅	1219
7	餓	1382
8	館	327

– 8c –
隹

2	隻	1390
4	雄	1476
	集	442
	焦	1036
5	雅	1550
6	雌	1477

	雑	584
	奪	1389
10	難	566
	離	1355

– 8d –
雨

0	雨	30
3	雪	979
4	雲	646
	雰	1973
5	雷	982
	電	108
	零	1972

6	需	1505
7	霊	1225
	震	983
9	霜	978
11	霧	980
13	露	981

– 8e –
門

0	門	161
3	問	162
	閉	401
4	閑	1633
	間	43

	開	400
6	聞	64
	閣	1611
	閥	856
	関	402
7	閲	1456
9	闇	349
10	闘	1612

– 9a –
頁

2	頂	1530
	頃	1532
3	項	1529

	順	783
4	頓	2122
	頒	2006
	預	398
	頑	2001
5	領	853
7	頼	1613
	頻	2000
	頭	276
8	頬	1999
9	類	226
	顎	2002
	顔	277
	顕	1227
	額	857
	題	355
10	願	590

12	顧	1656

– 10a –
馬

0	馬	283
4	駄	2046
	駅	284
	駆	2049
5	駐	609
	駒	2050
8	騎	2047
	験	541
	騒	895
12	驚	1910

– 11a –
魚

0	魚	290
6	鮮	714
8	鯨	713

– 11b –
鳥

0	鳥	285
8	鶏	949
10	鶴	950

Index by Stroke Count

– 1 –

一 2
乙 1017
了 971

– 2 –

二 3
入 52
丁 184
七 9
九 11
人 1
子 103
刀 37
力 100
又 1700
十 12
八 10

– 3 –

三 4
川 33
乞 1020
勺 2138
工 139
久 1273
万 16
己 371
夕 81
寸 2070
大 26
刃 1502
与 548
及 1328
丈 560
才 654
丸 970
孔 684
干 593
于 15
千 32
上 31
下 1153
凡 24
土

口 54
女 102
巾 687
弓 212
小 27
山 34
士 581

– 4 –

乏 767
不 94
斤 2073
元 137
幻 1291
匂 1730
勾 1734
爪 1320
予 397
互 929
斗 2075
太 639
凶 1354
天 141
内 84
氏 575
五 7
牙 1548
夫 315
升 2074
毛 287
丹 1144
屯 2121
匁 2137
中 28
弔 1934
井 1255
仏 592
化 254
仁 1727
介 460
今 51
刈 1356
切 39
双 1701
収 770
友 264
冗 1722
六 8
文 111

片 1088
支 318
午 49
止 485
比 812
分 38
公 126
父 113
反 324
厄 1424
円 13
区 183
匹 1599
水 21
手 57
犬 280
引 216
少 144
尺 2071
木 22
月 17
日 5
火 20
王 294
牛 281
方 70
欠 384
心 97
戸 152

– 5 –

以 46
北 73
矛 787
巧 1737
包 819
瓦 1216
丘 1441
凸 2068
凹 2069
且 2110
必 529
斥 1490
矢 213
左 75
丙 1018
出 53
民 177
半 88

本 25
末 305
未 306
失 311
生 44
弁 724
甘 1591
央 352
甲 1016
由 364
母 112
世 252
史 332
申 309
丼 1256
仙 2064
仕 333
代 256
他 120
付 192
令 850
存 269
刊 594
召 1032
加 722
功 837
幼 1293
皮 1008
写 549
市 181
玄 1289
古 172
平 202
外 83
占 1822
正 275
圧 1425
辺 789
込 790
用 107
巨 1368
永 1270
氷 1269
汁 1930
氾 2136
去 420
払 591
打 1059
叱 1323
兄 410

号 266
台 501
可 390
句 337
司 861
右 76
奴 2118
布 688
犯 903
穴 921
広 707
庁 777
尻 2029
尼 1728
囚 1258
四 6
札 1212
旧 1279
且 2111
白 205
示 625
礼 630
玉 295
主 155
冬 467
処 1189
石 78
立 121
目 55
田 35
皿 1148

– 6 –

臼 1896
多 229
死 85
気 134
両 200
朱 1602
年 45
西 72
更 1044
毎 116
再 796
曲 367
伏 1439
休 60
件 745
伐 1610

仲 1430
任 334
仰 1099
伎 890
伝 440
仮 1092
全 89
企 490
合 159
会 158
肉 223
次 385
壮 1409
兆 1665
羽 600
印 1086
州 195
刑 908
列 621
交 114
充 847
妄 1463
老 550
缶 1762
争 302
危 543
羊 288
灰 1426
巡 791
迅 1936
同 198
匠 1443
池 119
汚 706
汗 1247
江 840
汎 1155
地 118
寺 41
至 924
先 50
在 268
扱 1329
吐 1322
叫 1321
吸 1327
舌 1331
向 199
后 1171

名 82
好 104
如 1870
妃 1881
帆 1154
行 68
芝 250
芋 2081
共 196
字 110
安 105
守 499
宇 1027
宅 178
光 138
当 77
劣 1203
吉 1194
尽 1844
回 90
因 563
団 500
朴 1562
机 1384
朽 1738
肌 1385
有 265
早 248
旨 1081
百 14
旬 338
灯 1416
各 652
忙 1460
成 261
式 534
弐 1070
自 62
衣 690
血 803
米 224
舟 1145
虫 893
耳 56
竹 129

– 7 –

良 321

身 59	迎 1098	芸 441	**– 8 –**	直 429	味 307	居 171
来 69	返 448	究 917		阜 1448	呼 1325	国 40
束 510	臣 854	完 623	承 972	奔 1773	呪 1324	固 1004
里 142	医 220	肖 863	非 507	卓 1794	知 214	林 127
我 1381	沖 1429	労 233	長 95	虎 1677	奇 1444	枚 1211
更 1045	決 357	岐 892	表 272	免 746	妬 1956	枕 965
串 1394	汰 1206	志 582	画 343	並 1222	姓 1869	杯 1210
亜 1724	沈 964	壱 1848	果 496	典 368	妹 412	析 1482
寿 1652	沃 1885	売 239	東 71	迭 1608	姉 411	松 709
位 122	沙 1205	声 759	垂 1117	述 1000	始 503	枝 889
伸 1160	没 963	床 845	奉 1643	延 1167	妻 682	枠 2079
伴 1066	汽 135	応 846	毒 531	迫 1233	狙 1136	板 1090
体 61	沢 1031	序 784	事 80	周 91	弦 1290	枢 1062
伯 1234	坊 2014	尿 2030	依 691	岡 1440	弥 1012	采 957
佐 1867	坑 1721	尾 2028	使 331	段 2128	彼 1166	肪 2013
作 361	坂 449	局 170	価 427	泣 1300	征 1572	肥 1841
似 1583	均 820	困 567	例 622	沸 1928	径 940	服 696
但 2112	走 435	囲 1257	佳 1557	油 365	往 723	肢 1199
低 570	赤 207	図 339	侍 580	波 677	参 1565	股 1055
住 156	扶 1839	杉 2033	供 197	泌 2031	苗 354	青 208
何 392	把 1842	材 561	併 1218	泳 1271	英 1563	肯 1334
伺 1891	折 1483	村 191	侮 1858	泊 1235	茂 1549	明 18
余 1109	抜 1830	肝 1346	舎 805	注 1895	芽 553	旺 2058
含 1317	抄 1208	肘 1377	念 588	泡 123	若 1571	昇 1909
状 636	抑 1100	児 1280	命 587	法 869	茎 554	易 772
冷 851	批 1068	災 1418	孤 1577	況 1714	苦 778	昆 2037
治 1962	抗 843	社 308	阻 1135	沿 1033	昔 394	的 210
求 737	技 891	弄 2004	附 1995	治 502	苟 626	者 164
防 522	投 1060	改 523	邪 1551	沼 1729	宗 626	炊 1927
阪 450	択 1030	攻 838	邸 572	泥 391	宝 296	炉 1926
那 826	吹 1326	条 573	制 433	河 2072	宙 203	炎 1419
邦 825	吟 1318	麦 270	刺 902	坪 697	実 1028	奈 947
即 471	呈 1697	忍 1503	到 926	幸 1983	官 326	祉 1479
卵 1103	呂 1396	忌 1935	刻 1274	拓 1264	宜 1137	祈 631
却 1915	告 703	快 1498	刹 827	拝 1021	定 356	玩 2003
判 1065	否 1316	戻 1304	刷 1087	押 1022	宛 1374	牧 744
別 267	乱 702	辛 896	券 515	抹 2090	突 920	物 79
助 633	豆 988	利 1584	劾 2126	拙 1939	空 140	放 521
励 1423	君 807	私 63	劫 835	披 1829	学 109	欧 1061
努 1702	妨 1241	秀 329	叔 1782	拍 1236	乳 969	忠 1431
忘 1461	妊 985	初 125	受 260	抱 1359	尚 2009	性 98
対 366	妖 1884	町 1798	享 1787	抵 569	歩 437	怖 1959
孝 551	妙 1209	男 692	夜 479	担 1348	岬 1449	怪 1573
克 1459	妥 956	系 182	卒 801	拐 2093	岩 1428	肩 1337
角 481	希 689	言 101	京 189	招 462	岸 595	房 1303
弟 409	狂 904	貝 930	育 246	拡 1165	岳 1442	所 153
谷 664	役 376	車 66	斉 1574	拠 1190	府 513	武 1071
兵 798	形 399	足 240	盲 1462	拘 1938	底 571	具 426
呉 1526	芳 1907	133	版 1089	拒 1370	店 168	季 473
廷 1163	芯 2084	58	協 234		届 1029	和 124
近 452	花 255				屈 1940	委 474

8 – 10 Strokes

耳 取 65
金 金 23
釒 雨 30
門 門 161

– 9 –

飛 539
発 96
衰 1792
甚 1600
巻 516
専 610
奏 1646
重 227
乗 532
亻 信 157
促 1659
便 330
係 931
俊 1997
保 498
侶 1397
侵 1125
俗 1178
侯 2107
孑 孫 932
阝 限 866
郎 1014
阝 卸 720
刂 削 1718
契 574
力 勃 2127
勅 2056
勇 1474
又 叙 1114
一 軍 444
冠 1723
帝 1237
変 257
哀 1790
亠 亭 1243
南 74
卜 貞 1796
点 169
虐 1680
負 519
⺈ 急 303

首 148
前 47
美 405
盆 1150
厚 649
厘 2076
廴 迷 998
建 913
退 865
追 1232
逃 1669
逆 451
送 447
門 耐 1504
几 風 29
氵 泉 363
泉 1253
津 679
浅 660
洗 705
洪 1525
活 237
浄 675
洋 289
海 117
派 934
洞 1380
土 城 733
垣 1350
型 909
封 1558
赴 1560
扌 挟 1437
拷 1838
挑 1667
持 458
括 1332
拾 1538
指 1082
拭 1072
口 咲 951
咽 1872
品 230
姻 1871
女 姿 953
要 425
帥 2120
独 219
狭 1436
狩 1687

引 弧 1578
律 678
待 459
後 48
革 革 1123
茨 955
荘 1410
草 1464
荒 251
宀 茶 635
宣 651
客 166
室 1834
窈 736
単 300
山 峡 1435
峠 1434
炭 1427
幽 1292
广 度 378
尸 屋 167
面 274
木 相 146
柵 1330
柄 1019
柱 608
柳 2032
柿 2034
枯 1007
栃 2036
査 634
某 1593
柔 788
染 793
架 768
月 胞 1358
胆 1347
肺 1351
胎 1371
背 1338
日 映 353
昧 413
昨 362
昭 1034
冒 1156
星 743
是 1698
皆 468
春 596

昼 478
畑 36
火 為 1581
神 310
祖 632
祝 870
珍 1278
王 皇 297
牛 牲 742
方 施 1041
政 492
故 173
心 怒 1703
怠 1375
恨 1372
恒 1879
悔 1349
威 1855
研 1422
砂 918
石 砕 1204
音 1827
臭 347
看 1310
省 1398
盾 145
眉 786
秋 1851
秒 470
科 1207
香 320
胃 1797
思 1342
田 畏 99
界 1960
疫 461
糸 級 1622
糾 1401
紀 577
紅 1819
約 373
虫 虹 839
計 211
訃 2045
訂 340
車 軌 1561
食 則 1058
618
1921
食 322

– 10 –

既 1552
殊 1604
射 922
残 661
耗 1260
耕 1259
亻 倒 927
俳 1908
候 1076
修 974
倍 975
俸 87
俵 1644
借 2063
俺 780
倹 2061
值 899
個 1220
倉 431
准 1005
凍 1386
凄 1296
阝 陣 637
陛 683
降 1493
院 599
除 977
陥 624
郡 1112
刂 剖 1281
剣 193
剤 1979
剛 559
帰 1717
力 脅 1335
桑 2035
又 衰 1522
一 恋 1791
高 258
畜 190
真 1287
索 428
⺈ 勉 1104
748

兼 1129
差 669
益 729
翁 2115
釜 1131
原 136
厂 辱 1860
廴 連 446
速 511
逓 2123
逐 1186
逝 1485
透 1800
造 704
途 1120
通 150
匚 匿 1903
氵 泰 1647
浮 968
酒 526
浦 1534
浪 1877
浜 799
流 247
消 864
浸 1126
浴 1180
涙 1305
土 埋 1975
起 374
扌 拳 817
捉 1660
挿 1765
捕 911
搜 1026
捗 2096
挨 1101
振 984
挫 2091
口 唄 396
哺 1535
唆 1998
員 163
唇 1859
哲 1486
女 娘 1876
娯 1527
娠 986
姫 1882
巾 帯 994
師 415

弱 218
徒 436
徐 1113
従 1579
華 1122
荷 393
恭 1524
宀 家 165
宰 1586
宴 650
害 527
宮 734
案 106
宵 2010
容 665
挙 815
党 504
峰 1433
島 286
庭 1164
庫 844
座 800
唐 1813
席 380
尸 展 1181
桟 2078
株 754
根 314
桁 1691
桃 1670
桜 952
核 653
校 115
栓 1993
梅 1856
殺 585
月 脇 1336
朕 2104
脂 1083
脈 935
胸 1357
胴 1379
朗 1878
脊 1339
骨 1340
能 387
日 時 42
書 131
殉 1937
火 烈 1414

字	番号	字	番号	字	番号	字	番号	字	番号	字	番号	字	番号
祥	1682	笑	1299	虚	1678	喝	2101	習	601	釈	605	着	668
珠	1603	託	1746	亀	1889	唱	1759	乾	1249	断	1063	善	1191
班	1468	討	1057	曽	1450	啓	1487	黒	206	舶	1146	尊	717
特	282	記	372	羞	1806	婚	576	票	944	船	377	普	1223
旅	222	訓	785	貧	766	婦	316	祭	627	舷	1781	遊	1040
致	925	財	562	瓶	1217	婆	2116	尉	1725	蛇	2040	遇	1754
敏	1857	貢	1836	進	443	帳	1159	視	616	第	408	遜	2067
夏	469	軒	1246	逮	912	猛	1685	理	143	笛	1568	達	455
恵	1282	酎	2023	逸	747	猫	1567	球	739	符	514	運	445
息	1308	配	524	週	92	猟	1686	現	298	訪	1240	遂	1185
恐	1709	酌	2022	遜	2067	張	1158	望	685	許	750	道	149
恣	954	針	341	淑	1783	強	217	旋	1042	訟	1492	遍	1215
恩	564	飢	1383	渇	1731	術	187	族	221	設	586	遅	715
悟	1528	隻	1390	混	813	得	375	教	245	訳	604	過	419
悩	1353	馬	283	淡	1420	彩	959	救	738	敗	520	遡	1989
悦	1455			渓	2053	彫	1202	赦	1675	販	1091	測	620
扇	1657	**– 11 –**		淫	2054	菓	1636	務	235	貫	936	湖	475
栽	1177			清	671	著	878	欲	1179	責	666	港	680
破	676	野	236	渋	1809	黄	794	悪	304	貨	765	湾	681
砲	1894	爽	2059	渉	438	萎	2082	患	1395	軟	1922	温	644
竜	1886	粛	1811	深	545	菜	958	悠	1704	斬	1923	湿	1226
眠	868	健	914	添	1523	菊	483	惧	1964	転	439	湯	642
秩	1609	偶	1752	液	480	菌	1285	惨	1843	酔	1826	満	201
秘	824	偽	1582	済	558	寂	1784	情	209	釣	2020	滋	1651
租	1133	側	619	涼	1267	宿	179	惜	779	雪	979	湧	1475
称	1011	停	1244	涯	1555	密	822	悼	1795	問	162	渡	379
袖	1024	偵	2113	堆	1749	窓	711	戚	488	閉	401	渦	1949
被	1009	偏	1214	域	1002	寄	1445	章	876	頂	1530	減	728
畔	2134	貪	1837	培	1977	窒	1833	産	278	頃	1532	堕	1865
留	774	斜	1116	埼	1446	巣	1640	翌	602	魚	290	堪	2089
畝	2077	郭	1788	堀	1942	蛍	2043	眼	867	鳥	285	場	154
鬼	1624	陳	1494	基	457	常	506	眺	1668			堤	1699
疲	1403	陪	2131	執	699	堂	505	規	617	**– 12 –**		塚	1875
病	381	陸	657	推	1297	崎	1447	移	1173			塀	1944
症	1400	陵	1996	掛	1559	崩	1174	袋	1412	疎	1615	堅	1363
疾	1954	隆	976	排	1077	崇	1513	略	860	備	782	報	698
紡	2015	陰	886	接	495	崖	1556	累	1105	偉	1096	超	1037
純	996	険	542	控	1835	殻	1846	異	1106	傍	1242	喪	1793
紙	180	陶	1763	揭	1733	康	916	盛	732	傘	804	提	638
納	771	郵	533	採	960	庸	1812	盗	1151	随	1864	揚	641
紛	1818	都	188	授	612	麻	1630	痕	1880	隅	1753	援	1139
紋	1547	郷	874	探	544	鹿	2038	細	708	陽	640	揺	1761
素	271	部	86	措	1263	庶	1898	紳	1161	階	597	搭	2092
料	319	剰	1115	描	1566	梗	1047	組	424	隊	809	揮	1766
粋	1825	副	727	掃	1128	械	538	終	466	割	528	換	1693
粉	1817	動	231	捻	2094	梨	1951	紹	463	創	1387	握	1831
航	842	勘	1601	捨	1537	豚	810	経	557	勤	568	喉	2108
般	1147	率	802	掘	1941	脚	1916	粒	1816	蛮	2044	喫	1306
蚊	2041	斎	1575	据	1982	脳	1352	粗	1134	博	611	喻	2100
蚕	2042	商	418	唯	1298	脱	1457	粘	1824	象	752	喚	1694
恥	1805			唾	1119	曹	2114						

391

12 – 14 Strokes

就 961
登 991
短 215
尋 1132
女 媒 1595
婿 1868
媛 1883
巾 帽 1157
幅 1467
犭 猶 1689
弓 弾 1641
彳 御 721
街 186
復 939
循 1576
彡 須 1531
艹 落 858
葬 831
葉 253
葛 2103
募 1519
宀 寒 464
富 726
営 735
覚 615
掌 508
山 嵐 2065
喜 1196
广 廊 1015
廃 992
尸 属 1750
口 圏 517
木 椎 1748
棟 1495
棚 2080
極 336
棋 1985
棒 1645
棺 1974
椅 2048
検 540
植 430
森 128
月 脹 2141
勝 518
腕 1376
期 456
朝 477
日 暁 1772
晴 673
晩 749

暑 648
晶 1758
景 872
量 417
最 263
替 757
火 焼 942
無 93
煮 1931
然 662
王 斑 1469
琴 1319
攵 散 781
敬 718
敢 1807
欠 欺 1598
款 1845
心 惑 1001
悲 1075
惰 1866
慌 1465
愉 1705
雇 1655
扉 1658
越 1038
幾 897
石 硬 1046
硫 2012
硝 2011
立 童 416
殖 1607
程 423
税 403
裂 1413
装 1411
裁 1175
補 910
裕 1480
田 塁 1810
畳 1138
番 185
買 241
衆 806
扩 痢 1952
痛 1402
痘 2130
糸 結 494
絡 859
給 346
絵 345
絞 1545

統 849
絶 755
紫 1478
粧 1815
奥 484
歯 486
竹 筆 130
策 901
筋 1141
等 578
答 160
筒 1569
訴 1491
評 1067
証 493
詐 1597
診 1277
詔 2055
詠 1272
詞 862
貯 775
貼 1823
費 762
貴 1228
貿 773
貸 761
賀 769
車 軸 1023
軽 556
距 1369
酉 酢 2027
鈍 997
食 飲 323
飯 325
隹 雄 1476
集 442
焦 1036
雲 646
雰 1973
門 閑 1633
間 43
開 400
頁 項 1529
順 783

– 13 –

業 279
亻 僅 1315
働 232

傲 2066
傾 1533
傑 1849
僧 1453
傷 643
債 1170
催 1399
阝 隔 1696
隙 1111
力 勧 1094
勢 656
一 彙 1637
裏 273
棄 993
準 792
虍 虞 2129
虜 1473
慈 1649
煎 1933
義 291
羨 1924
厂 農 370
遣 1231
遠 453
違 833
遡 1989
氵 溺 966
滑 1341
滝 1887
溝 1050
滞 995
溶 1481
漢 565
漠 1516
源 589
滅 1421
土 塊 1625
塩 1152
填 1920
塑 1988
塗 1121
扌 搬 1840
携 1801
摂 1808
搾 1596
損 351
口 嗅 1311
嘆 1313
嗣 2097
群 808

豊 989
女 嫁 1873
嫌 1803
嫉 1955
犭 献 1438
猿 1690
彳 微 1508
蒸 973
夢 830
蓋 1286
蓄 1288
墓 1518
幕 1521
靴 1124
宀 寝 1127
塞 465
寛 1093
窟 1943
誉 816
奨 1415
鼓 1200
广 廉 1804
尸 殿 1182
口 園 454
木 楼 1992
楷 598
楽 359
虫 腫 2106
腰 1373
腹 1345
腺 1254
腸 1344
腎 1365
日 暇 1110
暗 348
暖 645
幹 1248
火 煩 2005
煙 941
照 1035
禾 禁 491
福 1466
禅 1642
禍 1948
王 聖 686
斈 解 482
攵 数 225
愛 259
心 愁 1708
想 147

感 262
慨 1554
慎 1918
慄 1963
戦 301
歳 487
石 碁 1984
立 意 132
新 174
辞 701
睡 1118
睦 658
督 1785
稚 1294
裸 1638
褐 1732
裾 1025
罒 署 879
罪 906
置 432
盟 730
扩 痴 1957
糸 絹 1333
続 243
継 1064
艇 1780
虫 蜂 821
触 894
⺮ 節 472
誠 731
詩 579
詰 1195
話 238
誇 1739
該 1276
詳 1683
詣 1085
詮 1994
試 535
賄 1861
賂 1862
賊 1946
賃 764
資 763
車 較 1546
載 1176
足 践 1671
跳 1666
路 151
跡 1673
酉 酬 2024

酪 2025
釒 鉢 1969
鉄 312
鈴 1971
鉛 1713
鉱 1711
食 飽 1893
飾 1013
飼 1892
隹 雅 1550
雷 982
電 108
零 1972
頁 頓 2122
頒 2006
預 398
頑 2001

– 14 –

亻 僕 2060
僚 1406
像 753
阝 際 628
障 877
隠 887
豪 1786
疑 1617
厂 暦 1635
歴 489
辶 遭 1756
適 421
遮 1899
氵 漁 712
漸 1489
漂 946
漆 1648
漫 1500
漬 1929
演 344
滴 1539
漏 1945
土 塾 1789
境 883
増 725
墨 1821
扌 摘 1540
鳴 948
女 嫡 2117
獄 905

彳 徴 1509
德 1079
彡 彰 1976
髪 1201
艹 蓑 1564
慕 1520
暮 1517
宀 寡 2007
察 629
蜜 823
寧 1501
广 腐 1312
尸 層 1454
木 概 1553
構 1048
模 1514
様 407
月 膜 1515
静 674
日 貌 2135
火 熊 389
王 瑠 1605
方 旗 1043
欠 歌 395
心 態 388
憎 1452
慢 1499
慣 937
石 碑 1623
磁 1650
立 端 1507
辣 1585
種 228
稲 1283
穀 1847
製 434
複 938
田 魂 1626
鼻 832
罰 907
疒 痩 1953
瘍 1958
糸 維 1295
練 756
緒 881
綿 1251
綻 2018
緑 546
総 710
綱 1716
網 1720

精 670
⺮ 算 760
箋 1672
管 328
箇 1570
誤 928
誘 1799
語 67
誌 583
読 244
認 751
説 404
誓 1484
⻊ 踊 1661
酉 酵 2026
酷 1828
酸 525
金 銭 659
銀 313
銘 1654
銑 2140
銃 848
銅 1712
食 餅 1219
雌 1477
雑 584
奪 1389
⻗ 需 1505
門 聞 64
閥 1611
閣 856
関 402
頁 領 853
馬 駄 2046
駅 284
駆 2049

– 15 –

舞 829
亻 儀 740
億 383
刂 劇 811
衤 褒 818
⺼ 膚 1343
⺝ 慮 1472
養 406
辶 遷 943
選 814
遺 1230

辶 遵 2124
潮 476
氵 潜 967
潟 1736
潔 1307
澄 1417
潰 1229
潤 1266
土 墜 1184
墳 1776
舗 1536
扌 撃 1054
摯 2095
撲 2062
撤 1512
撮 1621
嘲 2099
口 噴 1774
嘱 1751
器 536
巾 幣 1913
彳 衝 1904
徹 1511
彡 影 873
艹 蔽 2085
蔵 1360
宀 審 1471
寮 1405
賓 2008
窮 919
窯 1925
⺌ 賞 509
广 摩 1631
慶 1742
尸 履 1745
木 槽 1757
標 945
横 795
権 335
月 膝 1917
日 暴 1052
暫 1488
火 熟 700
勲 1905
熱 655
黙 1684
王 璃 1606
敷 1544
攵 敵 422
弊 1914
憂 1073

欠 歓 1095
心 慰 1726
憧 1853
憤 1775
憬 1854
戯 1679
石 確 613
日 導 716
穂 1284
稼 1874
稿 1172
稽 1084
田 魅 1627
畿 898
罵 2052
罷 2019
監 1777
盤 1149
糸 縄 1890
線 299
緩 1140
縁 1183
締 1239
編 695
緊 1364
趣 1039
⺮ 箸 1932
範 1143
箱 1142
誕 1168
誰 1747
課 497
諸 880
謁 2102
談 603
請 672
諾 1902
論 293
調 342
賠 1978
賜 1980
賦 1947
賛 758
質 176
車 輪 1221
輩 1078
輝 1767
⻊ 踏 1662
踪 1674
金 鋳 1653
鋭 1458

食 餌 776
餓 1382
⻗ 霊 1225
震 983
門 閲 1456
頁 頬 2000
馬 駐 609
駒 2050

– 16 –

亻 儒 1506
冫 凝 1619
阝 隣 828
興 369
辶 避 1590
還 885
氵 激 1056
濃 987
濁 1735
土 壊 1496
壌 2088
壇 1990
墾 1188
壁 1587
扌 操 1769
擁 1832
女 嬢 1986
獣 1688
獲 1392
彳 衡 1692
衛 834
艹 薪 2083
薄 1542
薬 360
薫 1906
薦 1741
宀 憲 530
广 磨 1632
機 537
樹 1197
橋 607
月 膳 1193
骸 2125
日 曇 663
火 燃 647
隶 隷 2119
攵 整 512
麦 麺 1302

心 憩 1309
憾 1961
憶 382
懐 1497
立 親 175
穏 888
積 667
奮 1388
糸 縫 1432
緻 2016
縦 1580
縛 1541
緯 1097
繁 1367
糖 1814
虫 融 1695
⺮ 篤 2051
築 1710
言 諮 1901
謀 1594
謡 1760
諧 1069
諭 1706
諦 1238
賭 1981
賢 1362
車 輸 555
醒 2021
酉 錘 2139
錬 1965
錦 1252
錯 1262
錠 1967
録 547
鋼 1715
鋼 1006
食 館 327
頼 1613
頭 276

– 17 –

亻 優 1074
償 1003
⺍ 翼 1107
氵 濯 1664
擬 1618
擦 1620
口 嚇 2098

矯 2109
⺍ 厳 841
月 謄 1911
臆 1378
日 曖 414
韓 1250
火 燥 1770
王 環 884
牛 犠 741
懇 1187
石 礁 1900
目 瞳 1852
瞭 1407
覧 1366
田 戴 1108
爵 2105
疒 療 1404
糸 繊 1676
績 1169
縮 1162
齢 852
聴 1080
言 謎 999
謝 923
講 797
謹 1314
謙 1802
購 1049
車 轄 1245
酉 醜 1628
鍵 915
鍛 1966
鍋 1950
⻗ 霜 978
門 闇 349
頁 頻 1999
魚 鮮 714

– 18 –

匚 臨 855
氵 濫 2132
藤 2087
藩 1470
繭 2086
日 曜 19
覆 1744
王 璧 1588
心 懲 1510

Index by Readings

– A –

Reading	Kanji	No.
A	亜	1724
	(悪)	AKU
aba(ku)	暴	1052
aba(reru)	暴	1052
a(biru)	浴	1180
a(biseru)	浴	1180
abu(nai)	危	543
abura	油	365
	脂	1083
ade(yaka)	艶	990
a(garu)	挙	815
	揚	641
	上	32
a(geru)	挙	815
	揚	641
	上	32
ago	顎	2002
AI	哀	1790
	(衷)	SUI
	愛	259
	曖	414
	挨	1101
ai	藍	2133
ai-	相	146
-aida	間	43
aji	味	307
aji(wau)	味	307
aka	赤	207
aka(i)	赤	207
aka(rameru)	赤	207
aka(ramu)	赤	207
	明	18
a(kari)	明	18
aka(rui)	明	18
aka(rumu)	明	18
a(kasu)	明	18
	飽	1893
akatsuki	暁	1772
a(keru)	空	140
	明	18
	開	400
aki	秋	470
akina(u)	商	418
aki(raka)	明	18
akira(meru)	諦	1238
a(kiru)	飽	1893
akoga(reru)	憧	1853
AKU	握	1831
	(屋)	OKU
	悪	304
	(亜)	A
a(ku)	空	140
	明	18
	開	400
a(kuru)	明	18
ama	天	141
	尼	1728
	雨	30
ama(eru)	甘	1591
ama(i)	甘	1591
ama(ru)	余	1109
ama(su)	余	1109
ama(yakasu)	甘	1591
ame	天	141
	雨	30
ami	網	1720
	(綱)	tsuna
a(mu)	編	695
AN	安	105
	案	106
	(宴)	EN
	暗	348
	(音)	ON
	行	68
ana	穴	921
anado(ru)	侮	1858
ane	姉	411
ani	兄	410
ao	青	208
ao(gu)	仰	1099
ao(i)	青	208
ara(i)	荒	1464
	粗	1134
arashi	嵐	2065
araso(u)	争	302
a(rasu)	荒	1464
ara(ta)	新	174
arata(maru)	改	523
arata(meru)	改	523
ara(u)	洗	705
arawa(reru)	表	272
	現	298
arawa(su)	表	272
	著	878
	現	298
a(reru)	荒	1464
a(ru)	在	268
	有	265
aru(ku)	歩	437
asa	朝	477
	麻	1630
asa(i)	浅	660
ase	汗	1247
ase(ru)	焦	1036
ashi	足	58
	脚	1916
aso(bu)	遊	1040
ata(eru)	与	548
atai	価	427
	値	431
atama	頭	276
atara(shii)	新	174
ata(ri)	辺	789
a(taru)	当	77
atata(ka)	温	644
	暖	645
atata(kai)	温	644
	暖	645
atata(maru)	温	644
	暖	645
atata(meru)	温	644
	暖	645
a(teru)	当	77
	充	847
	宛	1374
ato	後	48
	跡	1673
	痕	1880
ATSU	圧	1425
	(庄)	SHŌ
atsu(i)	厚	649
	暑	648
	熱	655
atsuka(u)	扱	1329
atsu(maru)	集	442
atsu(meru)	集	442
a(u)	合	159
	会	158
	遭	1756
awa	泡	1895
awa(i)	淡	1420
awa(re)	哀	1790
awa(remu)	哀	1790
awa(seru)	併	1218
a(waseru)	合	159
a(wasu)	合	159
awa(tadashii)	慌	1465
awa(teru)	慌	1465
aya(bumu)	危	543
ayama(chi)	過	419
ayama(ru)	誤	928
	謝	923
	過	419
aya(shii)	怪	1573
	妖	1884
aya(shimu)	怪	1573
ayatsu(ru)	操	1769
aya(ui)	危	543
ayu(mu)	歩	437
aza	字	110
azake(ru)	嘲	2099
azamu(ku)	欺	1598
aza(yaka)	鮮	714
azu(karu)	預	398
azu(keru)	預	398

– B –

Reading	Kanji	No.
BA	馬	283
	罵	2052
	婆	2116
	(波)	HA
ba	場	154
BACHI	罰	907
BAI	倍	87
	陪	2131
	培	1977
	賠	1978
	(部)	BU
	(剖)	BŌ
	買	241
	(貝)	kai
	梅	1856
	(毎)	MAI
	(海)	KAI
	(敏)	BIN
	媒	1595
	(某)	BŌ
	(謀)	BŌ
	売	239
ba(kasu)	化	254
ba(keru)	化	254
BAKU	漠	1516
	幕	1521
	(漢)	KAN
	(募)	BO
	(墓)	BO
	(暮)	BO

	Kanji	No.	
	(模)	MO	
	(膜)	MAKU	
	博	611	
	縛	1541	
	(専)	SEN	
	暴	1052	BO
	爆	1053	
	麦	270	
BAN	伴	1066	
	判	1065	
	(半)	HAN	
	番	185	
	(審)	SHIN	
	(藩)	HAN	
	板	1090	
	(反)	HAN	BO'
	蛮	2044	BŌ
	(変)	HEN	
	晩	749	
	(免)	MEN	
	盤	1149	
	(般)	HAN	
	万	16	
BATSU	伐	1610	
	閥	1611	
	抜	1830	
	(友)	YŪ	
	(髪)	HATSU	
	末	305	
	罰	907	
-be	辺	789	
BEI	米	224	
BEN	便	330	
	(更)	KŌ	
	弁	724	
	勉	748	
beni	紅	839	
BETSU	別	267	
	蔑	1564	
BI	尾	2028	
	(毛)	MŌ	
	微	1508	
	(徴)	CHŌ	
	美	405	
	眉	1851	BOKU
	備	782	
	鼻	832	
BIN	敏	1857	
	(毎)	MAI	
	(繁)	HAN	
	便	330	

	Kanji	No.	
	(更)	KŌ	
	貧	766	
	(分)	BUN	BON
	(瓦)	GA	
	瓶	1217	
	募	1519	
	墓	1518	
	暮	1517	BOTSU
	慕	1520	
	模	1514	BU
	(漠)	BAKU	
	薄	1543	
	(専)	SEN	
	(薄)	HAKU	
	母	112	
	坊	2014	BO'
	防	522	
	坊	2014	
	妨	1241	
	肪	2013	
	紡	2015	
	房	1303	
	傍	1242	
	(方)	HŌ	BUN
	亡	684	
	妄	1463	
	忘	1461	buta
	忙	1460	BUTSU
	望	685	
	某	1593	
	謀	1594	BYAKU
	冒	1156	BYŌ
	帽	1157	
	剖	1979	
	(倍)	BAI	
	(部)	BU	
	乏	767	
	(之)	SHI	
	棒	1645	
	(奉)	BU	
	貿	773	
	暴	1052	
	膨	1198	
	貌	2135	
	木	22	CHA
	朴	1562	CHAKU
	目	55	
	睦	658	
	僕	2060	CHI
	撲	2062	
	墨	1821	

	Kanji	No.	
	(黒)	KOKU	
	牧	744	
	凡	1153	
	帆	HAN	
	盆	1150	
	(分)	BUN	
	煩	2005	
	没	963	BOTSU
	勃	2127	
	無	93	BU
	舞	829	
	奉	1643	
	(俸)	HŌ	
	(棒)	BŌ	
	部	86	
	(剖)	BŌ	chi
	(倍)	BAI	
	侮	1858	
	(毎)	MAI	
	不	94	chichi
	分	38	
	歩	437	chiga(eru)
	武	1071	chiga(u)
	分	38	chigi(ru)
	文	111	chii(sai)
	聞	64	chiji(maru)
	豚	810	chiji(meru)
	仏	592	chiji(mu)
	(払)	FUTSU	chiji(rasu)
	物	79	chiji(reru)
	白	205	chika(i)
	苗	1565	chikara
	描	1566	chika(u)
	猫	1567	CHIKU
	秒	1207	
	(少)	SHŌ	
	(砂)	SA	
	病	381	
	(内)	HEI	CHIN
	平	202	

– C –

	茶	251	CHA
	着	668	CHAKU
	(差)	SA	
	嫡	2117	
	知	214	CHI
	痴	1957	
	池	119	

Kanji	No.	
地	118	
値	431	
置	432	
(直)	CHOKU	
致	925	
緻	2016	
(至)	SHI	
治	502	
(台)	DAI	
(冶)	YA	
(始)	SHI	
恥	1805	
遅	715	
稚	1294	
質	176	
血	803	
(皿)	sara	
千	15	
乳	969	
父	113	
乳	969	
違	833	
違	833	
契	574	
小	27	
縮	1162	
縮	1162	
縮	1162	
縮	1162	
縮	1162	
近	452	
力	100	
誓	1484	
竹	129	
築	1710	
畜	1287	
蓄	1288	
逐	1186	
陳	1494	CHIN
(東)	TŌ	
(棟)	TŌ	
(陣)	JIN	
珍	1278	
(診)	SHIN	
朕	2104	
(咲)	saku	
賃	764	
(任)	NIN	
鎮	1919	
(真)	SHIN	
沈	964	

chi(rakaru)	散	781
chi(rakasu)	散	781
chi(rasu)	散	781
chi(ru)	散	781
CHITSU	秩	1609
	(失)	SHITSU
	窒	1833
	(室)	SHITSU
CHO	著	878
	緒	881
	(者)	SHA
	(署)	SHO
	(諸)	SHO
	(都)	TO
	貯	775
	(丁)	CHŌ
CHŌ	丁	184
	庁	777
	町	182
	頂	1530
	(貯)	CHO
	(項)	KŌ
	(傾)	KEI
	兆	1665
	挑	1667
	眺	1668
	跳	1666
	(逃)	TŌ
	(桃)	TŌ
	長	95
	帳	1159
	張	1158
	脹	2141
	朝	477
	潮	476
	嘲	2099
	彫	1202
	調	342
	(周)	SHŪ
	徴	1509
	懲	1510
	腸	1344
	(湯)	TŌ
	(場)	JŌ
	鳥	285
	(島)	TŌ
	(微)	BI
	澄	1417
	(豆)	TŌ
	(登)	TŌ
	弔	1934
	(弓)	KYŪ
	超	1037
	(召)	SHŌ
	聴	1080
	(徳)	TOKU
	重	227
	釣	2020
	貼	1823
CHOKU	直	429
	(値)	CHI
	勅	2056
	(束)	SOKU
	捗	2096
	(歩)	HO
CHŪ	中	28
	仲	1430
	沖	1429
	忠	1431
	虫	893
	注	358
	柱	608
	駐	609
	(主)	SHU
	抽	1022
	宙	1028
	(由)	YŪ
	衷	1792
	(哀)	AI
	昼	478
	(旦)	TAN
	鋳	1653
	(寿)	JU
	酎	2023
-CHŪ	中	28

– D –

DA	堕	1865
	惰	1866
	(随)	ZUI
	(髄)	ZUI
	打	1059
	(丁)	TEI
	(灯)	TŌ
	(訂)	TEI
	妥	956
	(桜)	Ō
	駄	2046
	(太)	TAI
	唾	1119
	(垂)	SUI
	蛇	2040
DAI	弟	409
	第	408
	代	256
	(袋)	TAI
	(貸)	TAI
	大	26
	(太)	TAI
	台	501
	(胎)	TAI
	内	84
	題	355
DAKU	諾	1902
	(若)	JAKU
	濁	1735
	(独)	DOKU
da(ku)	抱	1359
dama(ru)	黙	1684
DAN	暖	645
	(援)	EN
	(緩)	KAN
	男	101
	(田)	DEN
	弾	1641
	(単)	TAN
	談	603
	(炎)	EN
	旦	2111
	団	500
	段	363
	断	1063
	壇	1990
dare	誰	1747
da(su)	出	53
DATSU	脱	1457
	(悦)	ETSU
	(説)	SETSU
	(閲)	ETSU
	奪	1389
	(奮)	FUN
DE	弟	409
	(第)	DAI
DEI	泥	1729
	(尼)	NI
DEKI	溺	966
	(弱)	JAKU
DEN	田	35
	電	108
	殿	1182
	(展)	TEN
	伝	440
de(ru)	出	53
DO	奴	2118
	努	1702
	怒	1703
	度	378
	(席)	SEKI
	(渡)	TO
	土	24
	(吐)	TO
DŌ	同	198
	洞	1380
	胴	1379
	銅	1712
	(筒)	TŌ
	童	416
	瞳	1852
	動	231
	働	232
	(重)	CHŌ
	道	149
	導	716
	(首)	SHU
	堂	505
	(党)	TŌ
DOKU	読	244
	(売)	BAI
	(続)	ZOKU
	毒	531
	(母)	BO
	独	219
	(触)	SHOKU
DON	鈍	997
	(屯)	TON
	(純)	JUN
	曇	647
	(雲)	UN
	貪	1837
	(貝)	kai
don	丼	1256
donburi	丼	1256
-dono	殿	1182
doro	泥	1729

– E –

E	会	158
	絵	345
	依	691
	(衣)	I

Reading	Kanji	No.
	回	90
	恵	1282
e	江	840
	柄	1019
	餌	776
-e	重	227
eda	枝	889
ega(ku)	描	1566
EI	永	1270
	泳	1271
	詠	1272
	(水)	SUI
	(氷)	HYŌ
	英	354
	映	353
	(央)	Ō
	栄	736
	営	735
	(宮)	KYŪ
	鋭	1458
	(悦)	ETSU
	(税)	ZEI
	(説)	SETSU
	影	873
	(京)	KEI
	(景)	KEI
	衛	834
	(偉)	I
EKI	役	376
	疫	1401
	液	480
	(夜)	YA
	易	772
	益	729
	駅	284
e(mu)	笑	1299
EN	遠	453
	猿	1690
	園	454
	援	1139
	媛	1883
	(暖)	DAN
	(緩)	KAN
	沿	1714
	鉛	1713
	(船)	SEN
	宴	650
	(安)	AN
	(案)	AN
	延	1167
	(正)	SEI

Reading	Kanji	No.
	(延)	TEI
	炎	1419
	(火)	KA
	縁	1183
	(緑)	RYOKU
	円	13
	塩	1152
	煙	941
	演	344
	艶	990
	怨	1375
era(bu)	選	814
era(i)	偉	1096
eri	襟	1639
e(ru)	得	375
	獲	1392
esa	餌	776
ETSU	悦	1455
	閲	1456
	(脱)	DATSU
	(説)	SETSU
	謁	2102
	(渇)	KATSU
	(掲)	KEI
	(喝)	KATSU
	(褐)	KATSU
	越	1038

– F –

Reading	Kanji	No.
FU	付	192
	附	1995
	府	513
	符	514
	腐	1312
	夫	315
	扶	1839
	普	1223
	譜	1224
	(晋)	SHIN
	布	688
	怖	1959
	(巾)	KIN
	赴	1560
	訃	1561
	富	726
	(副)	FUKU
	(幅)	FUKU
	(福)	FUKU
	婦	316

Reading	Kanji	No.
	(帰)	KI
	(掃)	SŌ
	父	113
	(交)	KŌ
	浮	968
	(乳)	NYŪ
	膚	1343
	(胃)	I
	敷	1544
	(激)	GEKI
	賦	1947
	(武)	BU
	不	94
	歩	437
	負	519
	風	29
	阜	1448
FŪ	富	726
	(副)	FU
	(幅)	FU
	(福)	FU
	夫	315
	(扶)	FU
	(芙)	FU
	封	1558
	(圭)	KEI
	風	29
	(虫)	CHŪ
fuchi	縁	1183
fuda	札	1212
fude	筆	130
fue	笛	1568
fu(eru)	殖	1607
	増	725
fuji	藤	2087
fuka(i)	深	545
	深	545
fuka(maru)	深	545
fuka(meru)	更	1045
fu(kasu)	老	552
fu(keru)	更	1045
FUKU	復	939
	腹	1345
	複	938
	覆	1744
	(履)	RI
	副	727
	幅	1467
	福	1466
	(富)	FU

Reading	Kanji	No.
	伏	1439
	(犬)	KEN
	服	696
	(報)	HŌ
fu(ku)	吹	1326
	噴	1774
	拭	1072
fuku(meru)	含	1317
fuku(mu)	含	1317
fuku(ramu)	膨	1198
fuku(reru)	膨	1198
fukuro	袋	1412
fu(maeru)	踏	1662
fumi	文	111
fumoto	麓	2039
fu(mu)	踏	1662
FUN	分	38
	紛	1818
	粉	1817
	雰	1973
	墳	1776
	噴	1774
	慣	1775
	奮	1388
	(奪)	DATSU
funa	舟	1145
	船	377
fune	舟	1145
	船	377
fu(reru)	触	894
	振	984
fu(ru)	降	977
	振	984
furu(eru)	震	983
furu(i)	古	172
furu(su)	古	172
furu(u)	震	983
	奮	1388
fu(ruu)	振	984
fusa	房	1303
fusa(garu)	塞	465
fusa(gu)	塞	465
fuse(gu)	防	522
fu(seru)	伏	1439
fushi	節	472
fu(su)	伏	1439
futa	双	1701
	蓋	1286
futa-	二	3
futata(bi)	再	796
futa(tsu)	二	3

futo(i)	太	639		楽	359		眼	867		呉	1526
futokoro	懐	1497		(薬)	YAKU		(恨)	KON		娯	1527
futo(ru)	太	639		顎	2002		(根)	KON		誤	928
FUTSU	払	591	GAN	元	137		(銀)	GIN		午	49
	仏	592		玩	2003		(眠)	MIN		御	721
	沸	1928		頑	2001		原	136		(卸)	oroshi
fu(yasu)	殖	1607		願	590		源	589		(許)	KYO
	増	725		(完)	KAN		(願)	GAN		期	456
fuyu	冬	467		(原)	GEN		験	541		碁	1984
				含	1317		(倹)	KEN		(基)	KI
– G –				(今)	KON		(険)	KEN		護	1391
				(吟)	GIN		(検)	KEN		(隻)	SEKI
GA	牙	1548		丸	654		減	728		(獲)	KAKU
	芽	1549		(九)	KYŪ		(惑)	WAKU		(穫)	KAKU
	雅	1550		岩	1428		(感)	KAN		互	929
	(邪)	JA		(石)	SEKI		厳	841	GŌ	後	48
	我	1381		岸	595		(敢)	KAN		合	159
	餓	1382		(干)	KAN		元	137		(拾)	JŪ
	(義)	GI		眼	867		(完)	KAN		(給)	KYŪ
	賀	769		(眠)	MIN		言	66		(答)	TŌ
	(加)	KA		顔	277		(信)	SHIN		拷	1838
	瓦	1216		(産)	SAN		現	298		(考)	KŌ
	画	343	gara	柄	1019		(見)	KEN		号	266
GA'	合	159	GATSU	月	17		嫌	1803		郷	874
GAI	劾	2126	gawa	側	619		(謙)	KEN		剛	1717
	該	1276	GE	下	31	GETSU	月	17		強	217
	骸	2125		外	83	GI	義	291		業	279
	(刻)	KOKU		夏	469		儀	740		豪	1786
	(核)	KAKU		解	482		犠	741		傲	2066
	涯	1555		牙	1548		議	292	GOKU	極	336
	崖	1556	GEI	迎	1098		(我)	GA		獄	905
	街	186		(仰)	GYŌ		疑	1617	GON	厳	841
	(術)	JUTSU		(抑)	YOKU		擬	1618		(敢)	KAN
	概	1553		(卯)	U		技	891		言	66
	慨	1554		(柳)	RYŪ		(支)	SHI		勤	568
	(既)	KI		芸	441		宜	1137		権	335
	外	83		(伝)	DEN		(且)	ka(tsu)	GU	愚	1755
	(夕)	SEKI		(雲)	UN		偽	1582		(偶)	GŪ
	害	527		鯨	713		(為)	I		(隅)	GŪ
	(割)	KATSU		(京)	KEI		欺	1598		具	426
	蓋	1286	GEKI	激	1056		(期)	KI		惧	1964
gake	崖	1556		(敷)	FU		戯	1679		(真)	SHIN
GAKU	岳	1442		撃	1054		(虚)	KYO	GŪ	偶	1752
	(丘)	KYŪ		劇	811	GIN	吟	1318		隅	1753
	(兵)	HEI		隙	1111		(今)	KIN		遇	1754
	額	857	GEN	幻	1291		(含)	GAN		(愚)	GU
	(各)	KAKU		玄	1289		銀	313		宮	734
	(客)	KYAKU		弦	1290		(金)	KIN		(営)	EI
	学	109		舷	1781	GO	五	7	GUN	郡	193
	(字)	JI		(幼)	YŌ		悟	1528		群	808
				限	866		語	67		(君)	KUN

Reading	Kanji	No.
	軍	444
(車)		SHA
(運)		UN
(揮)		KI
GYAKU	逆	451
(朔)		SAKU
(塑)		SO
	虐	1680
GYO	魚	290
	漁	712
(鯨)		GEI
	御	721
(卸)		oroshi
(午)		GO
(許)		KYO
GYŌ	仰	1099
(卯)		U
(迎)		GEI
(抑)		YOKU
(柳)		RYŪ
	暁	1772
(焼)		SHŌ
	凝	1619
(疑)		GI
	行	68
	形	399
	業	279
GYOKU	玉	295
(王)		Ō
GYŪ	牛	281

– H –

Reading	Kanji	No.
HA	波	677
	破	676
(皮)		HI
(披)		HI
(彼)		HI
(被)		HI
(疲)		HI
(婆)		BA
	把	1842
(肥)		HI
	派	934
(脈)		MYAKU
	覇	1743
HA'	法	123
ha	刃	1502
	羽	600
	葉	253

Reading	Kanji	No.
	歯	486
	端	1507
haba	幅	1467
haba(mu)	阻	1135
habu(ku)	省	145
HACHI	八	10
	鉢	1969
hachi	蜂	821
hada	肌	1385
hadaka	裸	1638
ha(e)	栄	736
ha(eru)	生	44
	栄	736
	映	353
hagane	鋼	1715
ha(gareru)	剥	1719
ha(gasu)	剥	1719
hage(masu)	励	1423
hage(mu)	励	1423
ha(geru)	剥	1719
hage(shii)	激	1056
ha(gu)	剥	1719
haguku(mu)	育	246
haha	母	112
HAI	俳	1076
	排	1077
	輩	1078
(非)		HI
(悲)		HI
	敗	520
(貝)		kai
	背	1338
(北)		HOKU
	廃	992
(発)		HATSU
	拝	1264
	杯	1210
	肺	1351
	配	524
hai	灰	1426
hai(ru)	入	52
haji	恥	1805
haji(maru)	始	503
haji(me)	初	692
haji(meru)	始	503
haji(mete)	初	692
ha(jirau)	恥	1805
ha(jiru)	恥	1805
haka	墓	1518
haka(rau)	計	340
haka(ru)	図	339

Reading	Kanji	No.
	計	340
	測	620
	量	417
	諮	1901
	謀	1594
hako	箱	1142
hako(bu)	運	445
HAKU	白	205
	伯	1234
	迫	1233
	泊	1235
	拍	1236
	舶	1146
	博	611
	薄	1542
(簿)		BO
(縛)		BAKU
	剥	1719
(録)		ROKU
(緑)		RYOKU
(縁)		EN
ha(ku)	吐	1322
	掃	1128
	履	1745
hama	浜	799
HAN	反	324
	阪	450
	坂	449
	版	1089
	板	1090
	販	1091
	飯	325
(仮)		KA
(返)		HEN
	半	88
	伴	1066
	判	1065
	畔	2134
	凡	1153
	汎	1155
	帆	1154
	般	1147
	搬	1840
(盤)		BAN
	氾	2136
	犯	903
	範	1143
	班	1468
	斑	1469
(王)		Ō
	煩	2005

Reading	Kanji	No.
	頒	2006
	藩	1470
(番)		BAN
(審)		SHIN
	繁	1367
(敏)		BIN
hana	花	255
	華	1122
	鼻	832
hanaha(da)	甚	1600
hanaha(dashii)		
	甚	1600
hana(reru)	放	521
	離	1355
hanashi	話	238
hana(su)	放	521
	話	238
	離	1355
hana(tsu)	放	521
hane	羽	600
ha(neru)	跳	1666
hara	原	136
	腹	1345
ha(rasu)	晴	673
	腫	2106
hara(u)	払	591
ha(reru)	晴	673
	腫	2106
hari	針	341
haru	春	468
ha(ru)	張	1158
	貼	1823
hasa(maru)	挟	1437
hasa(mu)	挟	1437
hashi	端	1507
	橋	607
	箸	1932
hashira	柱	608
hashi(ru)	走	435
hata	畑	36
	旗	1043
	端	1507
	機	537
hatake	畑	36
hatara(ku)	働	232
ha(tasu)	果	496
ha(te)	果	496
ha(teru)	果	496
HATSU	発	96
(廃)		HAI
	髪	1201

Reading	Kanji	No.
	(友)	YŪ
	鉢	1969
hatsu-	初	692
haya(i)	早	248
	速	511
haya(maru)	早	248
	速	511
haya(meru)	早	248
	速	511
hayashi	林	127
ha(yasu)	生	44
ha(zukashii)	恥	1805
hazukashi(meru)		
	辱	1860
hazu(mu)	弾	1641
hazu(reru)	外	83
hazu(su)	外	83
hebi	蛇	2040
heda(taru)	隔	1696
heda(teru)	隔	1696
HEI	丙	1018
	柄	1019
	病	381
	併	1218
	塀	1944
	餅	1219
	幣	1913
	弊	1914
	蔽	2085
	兵	798
	(丘)	KYŪ
	陛	599
	(階)	KAI
	閉	401
	(才)	SAI
	平	202
	並	1222
HEKI	壁	1587
	璧	1588
	癖	1589
	(避)	HI
HEN	偏	1214
	遍	1215
	編	695
	変	257
	(恋)	REN
	(蛮)	BAN
	片	1088
	(版)	HAN
	辺	789
	(刀)	TŌ
he(rasu)	減	728
he(ru)	経	557
	減	728
HI	皮	1008
	披	1829
	彼	1010
	被	1009
	疲	1403
	(破)	HA
	(婆)	BA
	非	507
	悲	1075
	扉	1658
	(輩)	HAI
	泌	2031
	秘	824
	(必)	HITSU
	卑	1622
	碑	1623
	(鬼)	KI
	比	812
	批	1068
	避	1590
	(壁)	HEKI
	(癖)	HEKI
	妃	1881
	(己)	KI
	否	1316
	(不)	FU
	罷	2019
	(能)	NŌ
	肥	1841
	飛	539
	費	762
hi	火	20
	灯	1416
	氷	1269
	日	5
hibi(ku)	響	875
hidari	左	75
hi(eru)	冷	851
higashi	東	71
hii(deru)	秀	1798
hiji	肘	1377
hika(eru)	控	1835
hikari	光	138
hika(ru)	光	138
hi(keru)	引	216
hiki	匹	1599
hiki(iru)	率	802
hi(ku)	引	216
	弾	1641
hiku(i)	低	570
hiku(maru)	低	570
hiku(meru)	低	570
hima	暇	1110
hime	姫	1882
hi(meru)	秘	824
HIN	賓	2008
	頻	1999
	(少)	SHŌ
	(歩)	HO
	品	230
	(口)	KŌ
	浜	799
	(兵)	HEI
	貧	766
	(分)	BUN
hira	平	202
hira(keru)	開	400
hira(ku)	開	400
hiro(garu)	広	707
hiro(geru)	広	707
hiro(i)	広	707
hiro(maru)	広	707
hiro(meru)	広	707
hiro(u)	拾	1538
hiru	昼	478
hi(ru)	干	593
hirugae(ru)	翻	606
hirugae(su)	翻	606
hisa(shii)	久	1273
hiso(mu)	潜	967
hitai	額	857
hita(ru)	浸	1126
hita(su)	浸	1126
hito	人	1
hito-	一	2
hitomi	瞳	1852
hito(ri)	独	219
hito(shii)	等	578
hito(tsu)	一	2
HITSU	必	529
	泌	2031
	(秘)	HI
	匹	1599
	(四)	yo(tsu)
	筆	130
	(書)	SHO
hitsuji	羊	288
hi(ya)	冷	851
hi(yakasu)	冷	851
hi(yasu)	冷	851
hiza	膝	1917
HO	捕	911
	哺	1535
	舗	1536
	補	910
	(甫)	FU
	歩	437
	(止)	SHI
	(少)	SHŌ
	(渉)	SHŌ
	(頻)	HIN
	保	498
ho	火	20
	帆	1154
	穂	1284
	法	123
HO'	包	819
HŌ	泡	1895
	抱	1359
	胞	1358
	砲	1894
	飽	1893
	方	70
	芳	1907
	放	521
	倣	1908
	訪	1240
	(防)	BŌ
	(坊)	BŌ
	(妨)	BŌ
	(肪)	BŌ
	(紡)	BŌ
	奉	1643
	俸	1644
	(奏)	SŌ
	(棒)	BŌ
	峰	1433
	縫	1432
	報	698
	(幸)	KŌ
	(服)	FUKU
	豊	989
	(曲)	KYOKU
	(豆)	TŌ
	崩	1174
	(棚)	tana
	法	123
	(去)	KYO

reading	kanji	no.	reading	kanji	no.	reading	kanji	no.	reading	kanji	no.
	宝	296		俵	2063		為	1581		印	1086
	(玉)	GYOKU		兵	798		彙	1637		陰	886
	封	1558		(丘)	KYŪ	I-	以	46		飲	323
	(佳)	KA		(岳)	GAKU	i	井	1255		淫	2054
	褒	818		氷	1269	ibara	茨	955		否	1316
	(保)	HO		(永)	EI	ICHI	一	2	ina	稲	1283
	邦	825		拍	1236		壱	1848	ina-	稲	1283
	蜂	821		(白)	HAKU	ichi	市	181	ine	命	587
hō	頬	2000		評	1067	ichijiru(shii)	著	878	inochi	祈	631
hodo	程	423		(平)	HEI	ida(ku)	抱	1359	ino(ru)	犬	280
hodoko(su)	施	1041				ido(mu)	挑	1667	inu	入	52
hoga(raka)	朗	1878	**– I –**			ie	家	165	i(reru)	色	204
hoka	外	83				ie(ru)	癒	1707	iro	彩	959
	他	120		偉	1096	ika(ru)	怒	1703	irodo(ru)	入	52
hoko	矛	787		違	833	i(kasu)	生	44	i(ru)	居	171
hokoro(biru)				緯	1097	ike	池	119		要	425
	綻	2018		(衛)	EI	i(keru)	生	44		射	922
hoko(ru)	誇	1739		胃	1342	IKI	域	1002		鋳	1653
HOKU	北	73		異	1106		(惑)	WAKU		煎	1933
homa(re)	誉	816		畏	1960	iki	息	1308		潔	1307
ho(meru)	褒	818		(累)	RUI		粋	1825	isagiyo(i)	勇	1474
hōmu(ru)	葬	831		唯	1298	ikidō(ru)	憤	1775	isa(mu)	石	78
HON	翻	606		維	1295	ikio(i)	勢	656	ishi	礎	1616
	(番)	BAN		(准)	JUN	i(kiru)	生	44	ishizue	忙	1460
	反	324		(推)	SUI	iko(i)	憩	1309	isoga(shii)	急	303
	本	25		(稚)	CHI	iko(u)	憩	1309	iso(gu)	板	1090
	奔	1773		委	474	IKU	育	246	ita	頂	1530
hone	骨	1340		萎	2082	iku	幾	897	itadaki	頂	1530
honō	炎	1419		(季)	KI	i(ku)	行	68	itada(ku)	痛	1402
hora	洞	1380		衣	690		逝	1485	ita(i)	痛	1402
hori	堀	1942		依	691	ikusa	戦	301	ita(meru)	傷	643
horo(biru)	滅	1421		尉	1725	ima	今	51		悼	1795
horo(bosu)	滅	1421		慰	1726	imashi(meru)			ita(mu)	痛	1402
ho(ru)	掘	1941		位	122		戒	896		傷	643
	彫	1202		(立)	RITSU	i(mawashii)	忌	1935	ita(ru)	至	924
hō(ru)	放	521		医	220	imo	芋	2081	ita(su)	致	925
hoshi	星	743		(矢)	SHI	imōto	妹	412	ito	糸	242
ho(shii)	欲	1179		囲	1257	i(mu)	忌	1935	itona(mu)	営	735
hoso(i)	細	708		(井)	SEI	IN	員	163	ITSU	一	2
hoso(ru)	細	708		移	1173		韻	350		逸	747
hos(suru)	欲	1179		(多)	TA		音	347	itsu-	五	7
ho(su)	干	593		意	132		(損)	SON	itsuku(shimu)		
hotaru	蛍	2043		(音)	IN		因	563		慈	1649
hotoke	仏	592		遺	1230		姻	1871	itsu(tsu)	五	7
HOTSU	発	96		(貴)	KI		咽	1872	itsuwa(ru)	偽	1582
HYAKU	百	14		椅	2048		(囚)	SHŪ	i(u)	言	66
	(白)	HAKU		(奇)	KI		院	624	iwa	岩	1428
HYŌ	票	944		易	772		(完)	KAN	iwa(u)	祝	870
	漂	946		威	1422		隠	887	iya	嫌	1803
	標	945					(穏)	ON	iya(shii)	卑	1622
	表	272					引	216	iya(shimeru)	卑	1622

403

iya(shimu)	卑	1622
iya(su)	癒	1707
izumi	泉	1253

– J –

JA	邪	1551
	蛇	2040
JAKU	若	553
	(右)	YŪ
	弱	218
	(弓)	KYŪ
	寂	1784
	(叔)	SHUKU
	着	668
	(差)	SA
JI	寺	41
	侍	580
	持	458
	時	42
	(待)	TAI
	(等)	TŌ
	(詩)	SHI
	滋	1651
	慈	1649
	磁	1650
	耳	56
	餌	776
	治	502
	(台)	DAI
	(冶)	YA
	(始)	SHI
	次	385
	(欠)	KETSU
	(吹)	SUI
	除	1112
	(余)	YO
	(徐)	JO
	示	625
	(元)	GEN
	仕	333
	(士)	SHI
	字	110
	(子)	SHI
	地	118
	(池)	CHI
	自	62
	(目)	MOKU
	似	1583
	(以)	I
	児	1280
	(旧)	KYŪ
	辞	701
	(辛)	SHIN
	事	80
	璽	2057
JI'	十	12
-ji	路	151
JIKI	直	429
	食	322
JIKU	軸	1023
JIN	人	1
	仁	1727
	(入)	NYŪ
	陣	1493
	(車)	SHA
	(陳)	CHIN
	刃	1502
	(刀)	TŌ
	臣	854
	腎	1365
	(巨)	KYO
	尽	1844
	(尺)	SHAKU
	神	310
	(申)	SHIN
	迅	1936
	甚	1600
	尋	1132
JITSU	日	5
	実	203
JO	除	1112
	叙	1114
	徐	1113
	(余)	JO
	女	102
	如	1870
	序	784
	(予)	YO
	助	633
JŌ	壌	2088
	嬢	1986
	譲	1051
	醸	1987
	浄	675
	静	674
	情	209
	(青)	SEI
	(清)	SEI
	(精)	SEI
	(請)	SEI
	(争)	SŌ
	成	261
	城	733
	盛	732
	(誠)	SEI
	乗	532
	剰	1115
	(垂)	SUI
	定	356
	錠	1967
	場	154
	(湯)	TŌ
	(腸)	CHŌ
	(暢)	CHŌ
	蒸	973
	(承)	SHŌ
	常	506
	(党)	TŌ
	(堂)	DŌ
	状	636
	(犬)	KEN
	畳	1138
	(且)	ka(tsu)
	縄	1890
	(亀)	KI
	丈	1408
	上	32
	冗	1722
	条	573
JOKU	辱	1860
	(唇)	SHIN
JU	受	260
	授	612
	需	1505
	儒	1506
	樹	1197
	(膨)	BŌ
	(鼓)	KO
	従	1579
	(縦)	JŪ
	就	961
	(京)	KYŌ
	寿	1652
	呪	1324
JŪ	十	12
	汁	1930
	(計)	KEI
	(針)	SHIN
	充	847
	銃	848
	(統)	TŌ
	従	1579
	縦	1580
	住	156
	(主)	SHU
	(注)	CHŪ
	(駐)	CHŪ
	拾	1538
	(合)	GŌ
	柔	788
	(矛)	MU
	渋	1809
	(止)	SHI
	獣	1688
	(犬)	KEN
	重	227
-JŪ	中	28
JUKU	塾	1789
	熟	700
	(享)	KYŌ
	(熱)	NETSU
JUN	准	1296
	準	792
	(推)	SUI
	(唯)	YUI
	(集)	SHŪ
	(稚)	CHI
	(維)	I
	旬	338
	殉	1937
	(句)	KU
	盾	786
	循	1576
	遵	2124
	(尊)	SON
	(導)	DŌ
	純	996
	(鈍)	DON
	順	783
	(訓)	KUN
	巡	791
	潤	1266
JUTSU	述	1000
	術	187

– K –

KA	可	390
	何	392
	河	391
	苛	394

Reading	Kanji	No.
	荷	393
	歌	395
	化	254
	花	255
	貨	765
	靴	1124
	(革)	KAKU
	果	496
	菓	1636
	課	497
	家	165
	嫁	1873
	稼	1874
	過	419
	渦	1949
	禍	1948
	加	722
	架	768
	(賀)	GA
	佳	1557
	(圭)	KEI
	(奎)	KEI
	(封)	FŪ
	科	320
	(斗)	TO
	(料)	RYŌ
	箇	1570
	(固)	KO
	(個)	KO
	仮	1092
	(反)	HAN
	下	31
	火	20
	価	427
	夏	469
	暇	1110
	華	1122
	寡	2007
KA'	合	159
ka	蚊	2041
	(虫)	mushi
	香	1797
	鹿	2038
-ka	日	5
kabe	壁	1587
kabu	株	754
kado	角	481
	門	161
kaeri(miru)	省	145
	顧	1656
ka(eru)	代	256

Reading	Kanji	No.
kae(ru)	変	257
	換	1693
	替	757
	返	448
	帰	317
kae(su)	返	448
	帰	317
kagami	鏡	882
kagaya(ku)	輝	1767
kage	陰	886
	影	873
kage(ru)	陰	886
kagi	鍵	915
kagi(ru)	限	866
kago	籠	1888
ka(gu)	嗅	1311
KAI	皆	596
	楷	598
	諧	1069
	階	597
	(陛)	HEI
	海	117
	悔	1855
	(侮)	MAI
	(侮)	BU
	(梅)	BAI
	介	460
	界	461
	会	158
	絵	345
	戒	896
	械	538
	壊	1496
	懐	1497
	怪	1573
	(径)	KEI
	(茎)	KEI
	(経)	KEI
	(軽)	KEI
	塊	1625
	(鬼)	KI
	(魂)	KON
	(魅)	MI
	灰	1426
	(火)	KA
	(炭)	TAN
	街	186
	(術)	JUTSU
	(圭)	KEI
	潰	1229
	(貴)	KI

Reading	Kanji	No.
	快	1498
	(決)	KETSU
	解	482
	(角)	KAKU
	回	90
	改	523
	拐	2093
	開	400
kai	貝	240
kaiko	蚕	2042
kaka(eru)	抱	1359
kaka(geru)	掲	1733
kakari	係	931
	掛	1559
ka(karu)	架	768
	掛	1559
	懸	933
kaka(ru)	係	931
kaka(waru)	関	402
ka(keru)	欠	384
	架	768
	掛	1559
	駆	2049
	懸	933
	賭	1981
kaki	垣	1350
	柿	2034
kako(mu)	囲	1257
kako(u)	囲	1257
KAKU	各	652
	客	651
	格	653
	閣	856
	(略)	RYAKU
	(絡)	RAKU
	(額)	GAKU
	獲	1392
	穫	1393
	(隻)	SEKI
	(護)	GO
	核	1275
	(亥)	GAI
	(刻)	KOKU
	(劾)	GAI
	(該)	GAI
	拡	1165
	(広)	KŌ
	郭	1788
	(享)	KYŌ
	殻	1846
	(穀)	KOKU

Reading	Kanji	No.
	隔	1696
	(融)	YŪ
	覚	615
	(見)	KEN
	較	1546
	(交)	KŌ
	嚇	2098
	(赤)	SEKI
	角	481
	画	343
	確	613
	革	1123
ka(ku)	欠	384
	書	131
	描	1566
kaku(reru)	隠	887
kaku(su)	隠	887
kama	窯	1925
	鎌	1130
	釜	1131
kama(eru)	構	1048
kama(u)	構	1048
kame	亀	1889
kami	上	32
	神	310
	紙	180
	髪	1201
kaminari	雷	982
kamo(su)	醸	1987
KAN	干	593
	刊	594
	汗	1247
	肝	1346
	幹	1248
	乾	1249
	韓	1250
	(岸)	GAN
	(軒)	KEN
	官	326
	棺	1974
	管	328
	館	327
	閑	1633
	間	43
	関	402
	簡	1634
	監	1777
	艦	1779
	鑑	1778
	(濫)	RAN
	(覧)	RAN

	個	1005
	鋼	1006
	(居)	KYO
	戸	152
	湖	475
	雇	1655
	顧	1656
	孤	1577
	弧	1578
	虎	1677
	虚	1678
	拠	1190
	(処)	SHO
	己	371
	去	420
	呼	1325
	庫	844
	鼓	1200
	誇	1739
	股	1055
ko	子	103
	木	22
	粉	1817
	黄	794
ko-	小	27
KŌ	口	54
	向	199
	后	1171
	拘	1938
	高	190
	格	653
	稿	1172
	興	369
	交	114
	郊	836
	効	835
	校	115
	絞	1545
	(父)	FU
	(紋)	MON
	工	139
	巧	1737
	功	837
	攻	838
	項	1529
	江	840
	紅	839
	貢	1836
	控	1835
	(空)	KŪ
	溝	1050
	構	1048
	講	797
	購	1049
	公	126
	広	707
	鉱	1711
	勾	1734
	更	1045
	梗	1047
	硬	1046
	(便)	BEN
	孔	970
	好	104
	厚	649
	孝	551
	考	550
	酵	2026
	行	68
	後	48
	衡	1692
	坑	1721
	抗	843
	航	842
	侯	2107
	候	974
	喉	2108
	洪	1525
	港	680
	(共)	KYŌ
	(供)	KYŌ
	綱	1716
	鋼	1715
	(剛)	GŌ
	荒	1464
	慌	1465
	耗	1260
	耕	1259
	仰	1099
	(仰)	YOKU
	(仰)	BŌ
	恒	1349
	(宣)	SEN
	降	977
	(隆)	RYŪ
	康	916
	(逮)	TAI
	甲	1016
	光	138
	幸	697
	香	1797
	肯	1334
	黄	794
	皇	297
kō	神	310
koba(mu)	拒	1370
kobushi	拳	817
koe	声	759
	肥	1841
ko(eru)	超	1037
	越	1038
	肥	1841
ko(gareru)	焦	1036
ko(gasu)	焦	1036
ko(geru)	焦	1036
kogo(eru)	凍	1268
koi	恋	258
ko(i)	濃	987
koi(shii)	恋	258
kokono-	九	11
kokono(tsu)	九	11
kokoro	心	97
kokoro(miru)	試	535
kokoroyo(i)	快	1498
kokorozashi	志	582
kokoroza(su)	志	582
KOKU	告	703
	酷	1828
	(造)	ZŌ
	刻	1274
	(亥)	GAI
	(劾)	GAI
	(核)	KAKU
	国	40
	(玉)	GYOKU
	黒	206
	(里)	RI
	穀	1847
	(殻)	KAKU
	石	78
	克	1459
	谷	664
koma	駒	2050
koma(ka)	細	708
koma(kai)	細	708
koma(ru)	困	567
kome	米	224
ko(meru)	込	790
ko(moru)	籠	1888
ko(mu)	込	790
	混	813
kōmu(ru)	被	1009
KON	根	314
	恨	1879
	痕	1880
	(限)	GEN
	(眼)	GAN
	(銀)	GIN
	昆	2037
	混	813
	墾	1188
	懇	1187
	困	567
	(木)	BOKU
	(因)	IN
	魂	1626
	(鬼)	KI
	(塊)	KAI
	建	913
	(健)	KEN
	紺	1592
	(甘)	KAN
	献	1438
	(犬)	KEN
	今	51
	金	23
	婚	576
kona	粉	1817
kono(mu)	好	104
ko(rashimeru)	懲	1510
ko(rasu)	凝	1619
	懲	1510
kōri	氷	1269
ko(riru)	懲	1510
koro	頃	1532
koro(bu)	転	439
koro(garu)	転	439
koro(gasu)	転	439
koro(geru)	転	439
koromo	衣	690
koro(su)	殺	585
ko(ru)	凝	1619
	凍	1268
koshi	腰	1373
ko(su)	超	1037
	越	1038
kota(e)	答	160
kota(eru)	答	160
	応	846
koto	事	80
	琴	1319

	望	685	MU	矛	787		名	82		(内)	NAI
	毛	287		務	235		明	18		軟	1922
	耗	1260		霧	980		冥	1522		(軌)	KI
	網	1720		(予)	YO					難	566
	(綱)	KÔ		夢	830					(漢)	KAN
	猛	1685		(夕)	YŪ		**– N –**			南	74
mochi	餅	1219		謀	1594					男	101
mochi(iru)	用	107		(某)	BÔ	NA	奈	947	nan	何	392
mō(deru)	詣	1085		武	1071		(捺)	NATSU	nana-	七	9
modo(ru)	戻	1304		無	93		納	771	nana(me)	斜	1116
modo(su)	戻	1304	mu-	六	8		(内)	NAI	nana(tsu)	七	9
mo(eru)	燃	663	mugi	麦	270		那	826	nani	何	392
mogu(ru)	潜	967	mui-	六	8		南	74	nano-	七	9
mō(keru)	設	586	muka(eru)	迎	1098	NA'	納	771	nao(ru)	直	429
MOKU	木	22	mukashi	昔	778		(内)	NAI		治	502
	目	55	mu(kau)	向	199	na	名	82	nao(su)	直	429
	黙	1684	mu(keru)	向	199		菜	958		治	502
momo	桃	1670	muko	婿	1868	nabe	鍋	1950	nara(beru)	並	1222
MON	門	161	mu(kō)	向	199	nae	苗	1565	nara(bi ni)	並	1222
	問	162	mu(ku)	向	199	na(eru)	萎	2082	nara(bu)	並	1222
	聞	64	muku(iru)	報	698	naga(i)	永	1270	na(rasu)	鳴	948
	文	111	muna	胸	1357		長	95		慣	937
	紋	1547		棟	1495	naga(meru)	眺	1668	nara(u)	倣	1908
	(絞)	KÔ	mune	旨	1081	naga(reru)	流	247		習	601
monme	匁	2137		胸	1357	naga(su)	流	247	na(reru)	慣	937
mono	者	164		棟	1495	nage(kawashii)			na(ru)	成	261
	物	79	mura	村	191		嘆	1313		鳴	948
moppa(ra)	専	610		群	808	nage(ku)	嘆	1313	nasa(ke)	情	209
mo(rasu)	漏	1945	murasaki	紫	1478	na(geru)	投	1060	nashi	梨	1951
mo(reru)	漏	1945	mu(rasu)	蒸	973	nago(mu)	和	124	na(su)	成	261
mori	森	128	mu(re)	群	808	nago(yaka)	和	124	natsu	夏	469
	守	499	mu(reru)	蒸	973	nagu(ru)	殴	2128	natsu(kashii)		
mo(ru)	盛	732		群	808	nagusa(meru)				懐	1497
	漏	1945	muro	室	166		慰	1726	natsu(kashimu)		
mo(shikuwa)			musabo(ru)	貪	1837	nagusa(mu)	慰	1726		懐	1497
	若	553	mushi	虫	893	NAI	内	84	natsu(keru)	懐	1497
mo(su)	燃	663	mu(su)	蒸	973	na(i)	亡	684	natsu(ku)	懐	1497
mō(su)	申	309	musu(bu)	結	494		無	93	nawa	苗	1565
moteaso(bu)			musume	娘	1876	naka	中	28		縄	1890
	弄	2004	mu(tsu)	六	8		仲	1430	naya(masu)	悩	1353
moto	下	31	mut(tsu)	六	8	naka(ba)	半	88	naya(mu)	悩	1353
	元	137	muzuka(shii)			na(ku)	泣	1300	nazo	謎	999
	本	25		難	566		鳴	948	ne	音	347
	基	457	MYAKU	脈	935	nama	生	44		値	431
motoi	基	457		(派)	HA	nama(keru)	怠	1372		根	314
moto(meru)	求	737	MYŌ	妙	1209	namari	鉛	1713	neba(ru)	粘	1824
MOTSU	物	79		(抄)	SHÔ	name(raka)	滑	1341	nega(u)	願	590
mo(tsu)	持	458		(砂)	SA	nami	並	1222	NEI	寧	1501
motto(mo)	最	263		(秒)	BYÔ		波	677	ne(kasu)	寝	1127
mo(yasu)	燃	663		命	587	namida	涙	1305	neko	猫	1567
moyō(su)	催	1399		(念)	NEN	NAN	納	771	nemu(i)	眠	868

Reading	Kanji	No.
nemu(ru)	眠	868
NEN	念	588
	捻	2094
	(今)	KON
	(命)	MEI
	然	662
	燃	663
	粘	1824
	(占)	SEN
	年	45
nengo(ro)	懇	1187
nera(u)	狙	1136
ne(ru)	寝	1127
	練	756
neta(mu)	妬	1956
NETSU	熱	655
NI	二	3
	仁	1727
	弐	1070
	児	1280
	(旧)	KYŪ
	尼	1728
ni	荷	393
nibu(i)	鈍	997
nibu(ru)	鈍	997
NICHI	日	5
ni(eru)	煮	1931
niga(i)	苦	554
niga(ru)	苦	554
ni(gasu)	逃	1669
ni(geru)	逃	1669
nigi(ru)	握	1831
nigo(ru)	濁	1735
nigo(su)	濁	1735
nii-	新	174
niji	虹	2045
NIKU	肉	223
niku(i)	憎	1452
niku(mu)	憎	1452
niku(rashii)	憎	1452
niku(shimi)	憎	1452
NIN	任	334
	妊	985
	(賃)	CHIN
	忍	1503
	認	751
	(刃)	JIN
	人	1
nina(u)	担	1348
nio(u)	匂	1730
ni(ru)	似	1583
nise	偽	1582
nishi	西	72
nishiki	錦	1252
niwa	庭	1164
niwatori	鶏	949
ni(yasu)	煮	1931
no	野	236
NŌ	悩	1353
	脳	1352
	農	370
	濃	987
	能	387
	(態)	TAI
	納	771
	(内)	NAI
no(basu)	伸	1160
	延	1167
no(beru)	述	1000
	伸	1160
	延	1167
no(biru)	伸	1160
	延	1167
nobo(ru)	上	32
	昇	1909
	登	991
nobo(seru)	上	32
nobo(su)	上	32
nochi	後	48
nodo	喉	2108
noga(reru)	逃	1669
noga(su)	逃	1669
noki	軒	1246
noko(ru)	残	661
noko(su)	残	661
no(mu)	飲	323
nonoshi(ru)	罵	2052
noro(u)	呪	1324
no(ru)	乗	532
	載	1176
no(seru)	乗	532
	載	1176
nozo(ku)	除	1112
nozo(mu)	望	685
	臨	855
nu(geru)	脱	1457
nu(gu)	脱	1457
nugu(u)	拭	1072
nu(karu)	抜	1830
nu(kasu)	抜	1830
nu(keru)	抜	1830
nu(ku)	抜	1830
numa	沼	1033
nuno	布	688
nu(ru)	塗	1121
nushi	主	155
nusu(mu)	盗	1151
nu(u)	縫	1432
NYAKU	若	553
NYO	女	102
	如	1870
NYŌ	尿	2030
	(水)	SUI
	女	102
NYŪ	入	52
	(人)	JIN
	乳	969
	(浮)	FU
	柔	788

– O –

Reading	Kanji	No.
O	悪	304
	(亜)	A
	汚	706
	和	124
o	緒	881
	尾	2028
	雄	1476
o-	小	27
Ō	王	294
	旺	2058
	皇	297
	殴	2128
	欧	1061
	(区)	KU
	黄	794
	横	795
	往	940
	(主)	SHU
	(注)	CHŪ
	(柱)	CHŪ
	応	846
	(心)	SHIN
	押	1021
	(甲)	KŌ
	翁	2115
	(公)	KŌ
	凹	2069
	央	352
	桜	952
	奥	484
ō-	大	26
obi	帯	994
o(biru)	帯	994
obiya(kasu)	脅	1335
obo(eru)	覚	615
obo(reru)	溺	966
ochii(ru)	陥	1281
o(chiru)	落	858
oda(yaka)	穏	888
odo(kasu)	脅	1335
odo(ri)	踊	1661
odoro(kasu)	驚	1910
odoro(ku)	驚	1910
odo(ru)	踊	1661
	躍	1663
odo(su)	脅	1335
o(eru)	終	466
oga(mu)	拝	1264
ōgi	扇	1657
ogina(u)	補	910
ogoso(ka)	厳	841
ō(i)	多	229
ō(i ni)	大	26
o(iru)	老	552
oka	丘	1441
	岡	1440
oka(su)	犯	903
	侵	1125
	冒	1156
	沖	1429
oki	起	374
	行	68
oko(ru)	興	369
	怒	1703
	起	374
oko(su)	興	369
o(kosu)	起	374
okota(ru)	怠	1372
OKU	億	383
	憶	382
	臆	1378
	(意)	I
	屋	167
oku	奥	484
o(ku)	置	432
oku(rasu)	遅	715
oku(reru)	後	48
	遅	715
oku(ru)	送	447

Reading	Kanji	No.
	贈	1451
omo	主	155
	面	274
omo(i)	重	227
omomuki	趣	1039
omomu(ku)	赴	1560
omote	表	272
	面	274
omo(u)	思	99
ON	恩	564
	(因)	IN
	遠	453
	(園)	EN
	温	644
	(湯)	TŌ
	穏	888
	(隠)	IN
	音	347
	怨	1375
on-	御	721
ona(ji)	同	198
oni	鬼	1624
onna	女	102
onoono	各	652
onore	己	371
ore	俺	2061
o(reru)	折	1483
ori	折	1483
o(riru)	下	31
	降	977
oro(ka)	愚	1755
oroshi	卸	720
oro(su)	卸	720
o(rosu)	下	31
	降	977
o(ru)	折	1483
	織	693
osa(eru)	抑	1100
o(saeru)	押	1021
osa(maru)	収	770
	治	502
	修	975
	納	771
osa(meru)	収	770
	治	502
	修	975
	納	771
osana(i)	幼	1293
ō(se)	仰	1099
oshi(eru)	教	245
o(shii)	惜	779

Reading	Kanji	No.
o(shimu)	惜	779
oso(i)	遅	715
osore	虞	2129
oso(reru)	恐	1709
	畏	1960
oso(roshii)	恐	1709
oso(u)	襲	1681
oso(waru)	教	245
osu	雄	1476
o(su)	押	1021
	推	1297
oto	音	347
otoko	男	101
otoro(eru)	衰	1791
oto(ru)	劣	1203
otoshii(reru)	陥	1281
o(tosu)	落	858
otōto	弟	409
otozu(reru)	訪	1240
OTSU	乙	1017
otto	夫	315
o(u)	生	44
	追	1232
	負	519
ō(u)	覆	1744
o(waru)	終	466
oya	親	175
ōyake	公	126
oyo(bi)	及	1328
oyo(bosu)	及	1328
oyo(bu)	及	1328
oyo(gu)	泳	1271

– R –

Reading	Kanji	No.
RA	裸	1638
	(果)	KA
	(課)	KA
	羅	2017
	(維)	I
	拉	1301
	(立)	RITSU
RAI	礼	630
	来	69
	雷	982
	頼	1613
RAKU	落	858
	絡	859
	酪	2025

Reading	Kanji	No.
	(各)	KAKU
	(略)	RYAKU
	楽	359
	(薬)	YAKU
RAN	覧	1366
	濫	2132
	籃	2133
	卵	1103
	(卯)	U
	乱	702
	(舌)	ZETSU
	欄	1265
RATSU	辣	1585
	(束)	SOKU
	(辛)	SHIN
REI	令	850
	冷	851
	鈴	1971
	零	1972
	齢	852
	(領)	RYŌ
	隷	2119
	(逮)	TAI
	(康)	KŌ
	(款)	KAN
	礼	630
	(札)	SATSU
	戻	1304
	(涙)	RUI
	例	622
	(列)	RETSU
	励	1423
	霊	1225
	麗	1740
	暦	1635
REKI	歴	489
REN	練	756
	錬	1965
	連	446
	(車)	SHA
	廉	1804
	(兼)	KEN
	恋	258
	(変)	HEN
RETSU	列	621
	烈	1414
	裂	1413
	(例)	REI
	劣	1203
RI	里	142
	理	143

Reading	Kanji	No.
	裏	273
	(厘)	RIN
	利	329
	痢	1952
	璃	1606
	離	1355
	吏	1044
	(史)	SHI
	履	1745
	(復)	FUKU
RICHI	律	678
RIKI	力	100
RIKU	陸	657
RIN	倫	1220
	輪	1221
	(論)	RON
	臨	855
	(臣)	SHIN
	(品)	HIN
	林	127
	(木)	BOKU
	厘	2076
	(里)	RI
	鈴	1971
	(令)	REI
	隣	828
RITSU	律	678
	(津)	SHIN
	率	802
	(卒)	SOTSU
	立	121
	慄	1963
RO	賂	1862
	路	151
	露	981
	(各)	KAKU
	(足)	SOKU
	炉	1926
	(戸)	KO
	呂	1396
	(侶)	RYO
RŌ	郎	1014
	浪	1877
	朗	1878
	廊	1015
	(良)	RYŌ
	(郷)	KYŌ
	漏	1945
	露	981
	(雨)	U
	(路)	RO

	楼	1992
	(桜)	Ō
	(数)	SŪ
	老	552
	(考)	KŌ
	労	233
	(力)	RYOKU
	糧	1820
	(量)	RYŌ
	弄	2004
	籠	1888
ROKU	緑	546
	録	547
	(緑)	EN
	六	8
	麓	2039
RON	論	293
	(倫)	RIN
	(輪)	RIN
RU	留	774
	瑠	1605
	流	247
RUI	累	1105
	塁	1810
	涙	1305
	(戻)	REI
	類	226
RYAKU	略	860
	(各)	KAKU
	(絡)	RAKU
RYO		
	虜	1473
	慮	1472
	旅	222
	(族)	ZOKU
	侶	1397
	(呂)	RO
RYŌ	僚	1406
	寮	1405
	瞭	1407
	療	1404
	量	417
	糧	1820
	料	319
	(斗)	TO
	(科)	KA
	陵	1996
	(陸)	RIKU
	領	853
	(令)	REI
	涼	1267
	(京)	KYŌ
	漁	712
	(魚)	GYO
	猟	1686
	(犬)	KEN
	了	971
	両	200
	良	321
	霊	1225
RYOKU	緑	546
	(録)	ROKU
	(縁)	EN
	力	100
RYŪ	立	121
	粒	1816
	竜	1886
	柳	2032
	留	774
	(貿)	BŌ
	流	247
	硫	2012
	隆	976
	(降)	KŌ

– S –

SA	左	75
	佐	1867
	差	669
	(着)	CHAKU
	作	361
	詐	1597
	(昨)	SAKU
	(酢)	SAKU
	沙	1205
	砂	1204
	唆	1998
	(俊)	SHUN
	(酸)	SAN
	再	796
	茶	251
	査	634
	鎖	1968
SA'	早	248
saba(ku)	裁	1175
sabi	寂	1784
sabi(reru)	寂	1784
sabi(shii)	寂	1784
sachi	幸	697
sada(ka)	定	356
sada(maru)	定	356
sada(meru)	定	356
saegi(ru)	遮	1899
sa(garu)	下	31
saga(su)	捜	1026
	探	544
sa(geru)	下	31
	提	638
sagesu(mu)	蔑	1564
sagu(ru)	探	544
SAI	栽	1177
	裁	1175
	歳	487
	載	1176
	采	957
	採	960
	彩	959
	菜	958
	斎	1575
	済	558
	(斉)	SEI
	(剤)	ZAI
	才	560
	財	562
	(材)	ZAI
	祭	627
	際	628
	(察)	SATSU
	砕	1827
	(枠)	waku
	(粋)	SUI
	(酔)	SUI
	債	1170
	(責)	SEKI
	(積)	SEKI
	(績)	SEKI
	切	39
	(刀)	TŌ
	宰	1586
	(辛)	SHIN
	最	263
	(取)	SHU
	西	72
	再	796
	災	1418
	妻	682
	殺	585
	細	708
	催	1399
	塞	465
sai	埼	1446
saiwa(i)	幸	697
saka	坂	449
	逆	451
	酒	526
saka(eru)	栄	736
sakai	境	883
saka(n)	盛	732
sakana	魚	290
sakanobo(ru)		
	遡	1989
saka(rau)	逆	451
saka(ru)	盛	732
sakazuki	杯	1210
sake	酒	526
sake(bu)	叫	1321
sa(keru)	裂	1413
	避	1590
saki	先	50
	崎	1447
SAKU	作	361
	昨	362
	酢	2027
	搾	1596
	(詐)	SA
	冊	1213
	柵	1330
	錯	1262
	(昔)	SEKI
	(借)	SHAKU
	(措)	SO
	(惜)	SEKI
	削	1718
	(肖)	SHŌ
	索	1104
	(糸)	SHI
	策	901
	(刺)	SHI
sa(ku)	咲	951
	裂	1413
	割	528
sakura	桜	952
sama	様	407
-sama	様	407
sa(masu)	冷	851
	覚	615
samata(geru)		
	妨	1241
sa(meru)	冷	851
	覚	615
samu(i)	寒	464
samurai	侍	580

Reading	Kanji	No.
SAN	参	723
	惨	1843
	桟	2078
	(浅)	SEN
	(残)	ZAN
	(銭)	SEN
	産	278
	(生)	SEI
	(彦)	GEN
	酸	525
	(俊)	SHUN
	(唆)	SA
	散	781
	(昔)	SEKI
	賛	758
	(替)	TAI
	三	4
	山	34
	蚕	2042
	傘	804
	算	760
sara	皿	1148
	更	1045
saru	猿	1690
sa(ru)	去	420
sasa(eru)	支	318
sa(saru)	刺	902
saso(u)	誘	1799
sa(su)	指	1082
	挿	1765
	刺	902
	差	669
sato	里	142
sato(ru)	悟	1528
sato(su)	諭	1706
SATSU	察	629
	擦	1620
	(祭)	SAI
	(際)	SAI
	刹	827
	殺	585
	撮	1621
	(取)	SHU
	(最)	SAI
	札	1212
	(礼)	REI
	冊	1213
	刷	1087
	拶	1102
sawa	沢	1031
sawa(gu)	騒	895

Reading	Kanji	No.
sawa(ru)	障	877
	触	894
sawa(yaka)	爽	2059
sazu(karu)	授	612
sazu(keru)	授	612
SE	施	1041
	(旋)	SEN
	世	252
se	背	1338
	瀬	1614
seba(maru)	狭	1436
seba(meru)	狭	1436
SECHI		
SEI	青	208
	清	671
	情	209
	晴	673
	静	674
	精	670
	請	672
	生	44
	姓	1869
	性	98
	星	743
	醒	2021
	牲	742
	(産)	SAN
	正	275
	征	1166
	政	492
	整	512
	(延)	EN
	(症)	SHŌ
	(証)	SHŌ
	成	261
	盛	732
	誠	731
	逝	1485
	誓	1484
	(折)	SETSU
	制	433
	製	434
	省	145
	(少)	SHŌ
	勢	656
	(熱)	NETSU
	凄	683
	(妻)	SAI
	井	1255
	世	252
	西	72

Reading	Kanji	No.
sei	声	759
	斉	1574
	婿	1868
	聖	686
	歳	487
	背	1338
	昔	778
	惜	779
SEKI	籍	1261
	(借)	SHAKU
	(措)	SO
	(錯)	SAKU
	責	666
	積	667
	績	1169
	(債)	SAI
	赤	207
	跡	1673
	(亦)	YAKU
	戚	488
	寂	1784
	(淑)	SHUKU
	斥	1490
	(斤)	KIN
	析	1482
	(折)	SETSU
	席	380
	(度)	DO
se(ru)	夕	81
SETSU	石	78
	脊	1339
	隻	1390
	関	402
seki	狭	1436
sema(i)	迫	1233
sema(ru)	責	666
se(meru)	攻	838
	浅	660
SEN	践	1671
	銭	659
	(残)	ZAN
	(桟)	SAN
	先	50
	洗	705
	銑	2140
	泉	1253
	線	299
	腺	1254
	栓	1993
SHA	詮	1994
	(全)	ZEN

Reading	Kanji	No.
	鮮	714
	羨	1924
	(羊)	YŌ
	潜	967
	(替)	TAI
	(賛)	SAN
	宣	635
	(恒)	KŌ
	仙	2064
	(山)	SAN
	旋	1042
	(施)	SE
	選	814
	(巽)	SON
	川	33
	千	15
	占	1822
	染	793
	専	610
	扇	1657
	船	377
	箋	1672
	遷	943
	繊	1676
	煎	1933
	戦	301
	薦	1741
	競	871
	利	827
	殺	585
	設	586
	切	39
	窃	1834
	(刀)	TŌ
	接	495
	摂	1808
	説	404
	(悦)	ETSU
	(税)	ZEI
	(鋭)	EI
	折	1483
	(析)	SEKI
	(誓)	SEI
	拙	1939
	(出)	SHUTSU
	節	472
	(即)	SOKU
	雪	979
	舎	805
	捨	1537

SHA	者	164	士	581	shiawa(se)	幸	697		寝	1127
	煮	1931	仕	333	shiba	芝	250		真	428
	射	922	志	582	shiba(ru)	縛	1541		慎	1918
	謝	923	誌	583	shibo(ru)	絞	1545		(鎮)	CHIN
	斜	1116	市	181		搾	1596		心	97
	(斗)	TO	姉	411	shibu	渋	1809		芯	2084
	(余)	YO	師	415	shibu(i)	渋	1809		(必)	HITSU
	(科)	KA	(帥)	SUI	shibu(ru)	渋	1809		請	672
	(料)	RYŌ	支	318	SHICHI	七	9		(青)	SEI
	砂	1204	枝	889		質	176		(清)	SEI
	(少)	SHŌ	肢	1199	shige(ru)	茂	1563		(情)	SEI
	写	549	旨	1081	shi(iru)	強	217		(晴)	SEI
	(与)	YO	指	1082	shiita(geru)	虐	1680		(静)	SEI
	赦	1675	脂	1083	shika	鹿	2038		(精)	SEI
	(赤)	SEKI	史	332	shika(ru)	叱	1323		森	128
	遮	1899	使	331	SHIKI	織	693		(木)	BOKU
	(庶)	SHO	(吏)	RI		識	694		(林)	RIN
	社	308	氏	575		色	204		臣	854
	車	133	紙	180		式	534		(巨)	KYO
SHAKU	尺	2071	示	625	shi(ku)	敷	1544		津	679
	釈	605	視	616	shima	島	286		(律)	RITSU
	(沢)	TAKU	詩	579	shi(maru)	絞	1545		針	341
	(訳)	YAKU	(寺)	JI		締	1239		(計)	KEI
	(駅)	EKI	(侍)	JI		閉	401		深	545
	昔	778	(持)	JI	shime(ru)	湿	1226		(探)	TAN
	借	780	(時)	JI	shi(meru)	絞	1545		診	1277
	(錯)	SAKU	私	125		締	1239		(珍)	CHIN
	(惜)	SEKI	(仏)	BUTSU		占	1822		審	1471
	(措)	SO	(払)	FUTSU		閉	401		(番)	BAN
	勺	2138	始	503	shime(su)	示	625		身	59
	酌	2022	(台)	TAI		湿	1226		信	157
	(釣)	tsu(ru)	(治)	JI	shi(mi)	染	793		進	443
	石	78	思	99	shi(miru)	染	793	shina	品	230
	赤	207	(恩)	ON	shimo	下	31	shino(baseru)		
	爵	2105	子	103		霜	978		忍	1503
SHI	次	385	(了)	RYŌ	SHIN	辛	1584	shino(bu)	忍	1503
	姿	953	刺	902		新	174	shi(nu)	死	85
	恣	954	(策)	SAKU		薪	2083	shio	塩	1152
	資	763	施	1041		親	175		潮	476
	諮	1901	(旋)	SEN		(幸)	KŌ	shira	白	205
	(欠)	KETSU	試	535		振	984	shira(beru)	調	342
	止	485	(式)	SHIKI		唇	1859	shiri	尻	2029
	祉	1479	賜	1980		娠	986	shirizo(keru)	退	865
	紫	1478	(易)	EKI		震	983	shirizo(ku)	退	865
	歯	486	矢	213		(辱)	JOKU	shiro	代	256
	雌	1477	四	6		申	309		白	205
	司	861	死	85		伸	1160		城	733
	伺	1891	至	924		神	310	shiro(i)	白	205
	詞	862	自	62		紳	1161	shiru	汁	1930
	嗣	2097	糸	242		侵	1125	shi(ru)	知	214
	飼	1892	摯	2095		浸	1126	shirushi	印	1086

	(示)	SHI
	(完)	KAN
	拾	1538
	(合)	GŌ
	(拾)	SHA
	終	466
	(冬)	TŌ
	修	975
	(悠)	YŪ
	収	770
	(又)	mata
	囚	1258
	(人)	JIN
	臭	1310
	(息)	SOKU
	執	699
	(幸)	KŌ
	集	442
	(隼)	JUN
	衆	806
	(血)	KETSU
	舟	1145
	秀	1798
	祝	870
	習	601
	襲	1681
	袖	1024
	羞	1806
SHUKU	叔	1782
	淑	1783
	(寂)	JAKU
	(督)	TOKU
	宿	179
	縮	1162
	祝	870
	(兄)	KEI
	(況)	KYŌ
	粛	1811
SHUN	俊	1997
	(唆)	SA
	(酸)	SAN
	旬	338
	春	468
	瞬	1850
SHUTSU	出	53
SO	阻	1135
	狙	1136
	祖	632
	租	1133
	組	424
	粗	1134
	(且)	ka(tsu)
	(助)	JO
	塑	1988
	遡	1989
	素	271
	(麦)	BAKU
	(表)	HYŌ
	措	1263
	(昔)	SEKI
	(惜)	SEKI
	疎	1615
	(束)	SOKU
	訴	1491
	(斥)	SEKI
	想	147
	(相)	SŌ
	礎	1616
SŌ	曽	1450
	僧	1453
	層	1454
	贈	1451
	(増)	ZŌ
	壮	1409
	荘	1410
	装	1411
	相	146
	想	147
	霜	978
	曹	2114
	遭	1756
	槽	1757
	操	1769
	燥	1770
	藻	1771
	挿	1765
	捜	1026
	痩	1953
	宗	626
	踪	1674
	(示)	SHI
	(完)	KAN
	窓	711
	総	710
	(公)	KŌ
	双	1701
	桑	2035
	(又)	mata
	倉	1386
	創	1387
	早	248
	草	249
	走	435
	送	447
	巣	1640
	(果)	KA
	(単)	TAN
	(菓)	KA
	掃	1128
	(帰)	KI
	(婦)	FU
	奏	1646
	(奉)	HŌ
	葬	831
	(死)	SHI
	争	302
	爽	2059
	喪	1793
	騒	895
soda(teru)	育	246
soda(tsu)	育	246
sode	袖	1024
so(eru)	添	1523
soko	底	571
soko(nau)	損	351
-soko(nau)	損	351
soko(neru)	損	351
SOKU	則	618
	側	619
	測	620
	足	58
	促	1659
	捉	1660
	束	510
	速	511
	息	1308
	(臭)	SHŪ
	(憩)	KEI
	即	471
	塞	465
so(maru)	染	793
so(meru)	染	793
-so(meru)	初	692
somu(keru)	背	1338
somu(ku)	背	1338
SON	孫	932
	遜	2067
	(系)	KEI
	(係)	KEI
	村	191
	尊	717
	(寸)	SUN
	存	269
	(在)	ZAI
	損	351
	(員)	IN
sona(eru)	供	197
	備	782
sona(waru)	備	782
sono	園	454
sora	空	140
so(rasu)	反	324
sōrō	候	974
so(ru)	反	324
soso(gu)	注	358
sosonoka(su)		
	唆	1998
soto	外	83
SOTSU	卒	801
	率	802
so(u)	沿	1714
	添	1523
SU	素	271
	(麦)	BAKU
	(表)	HYŌ
	子	103
	(了)	RYŌ
	主	155
	(王)	Ō
	守	499
	(寸)	SUN
	数	225
	(楼)	RŌ
	須	1531
su	州	195
	(川)	SEN
	巣	1640
	酢	2027
SŪ	枢	1062
	(区)	KU
	崇	1513
	(宗)	SHŪ
	数	225
	(楼)	RŌ
sube(ru)	滑	1341
su(beru)	統	849
sube(te)	全	89
sude (ni)	既	1552
sue	末	305
su(eru)	据	1982
sugata	姿	953
sugi	杉	2033
su(giru)	過	419
su(gosu)	過	419

sugu(reru)	優	1074	su(ru)	刷	1087	大	26	tamago	卵	1103
SUI	垂	1117		擦	1620	太	639	tamashii	魂	1626
	睡	1118	surudo(i)	鋭	1458	対	366	tamawa(ru)	賜	1980
	錘	2139	suso	裾	1025	耐	1504	ta(meru)	矯	2109
	(郵)	YŪ	susu(meru)	進	443	帯	994	tame(su)	試	535
	吹	1326		勧	1094	滞	995	tami	民	177
	炊	1927		薦	1741	隊	809	tamo(tsu)	保	498
	(欠)	KETSU	susu(mu)	進	443	(遂)	SUI	TAN	旦	2111
	粋	1825	suta(reru)	廃	992	(墜)	TSUI		担	1348
	酔	1826	suta(ru)	廃	992	態	388		胆	1347
	(砕)	SAI	su(teru)	捨	1537	(能)	NŌ		壇	1990
	推	1297	su(u)	吸	1327	(熊)	YŪ		(但)	tada(shi)
	(准)	JUN	suwa(ru)	座	800	待	459		(昼)	CHŪ
	(唯)	YUI	su(waru)	据	1982	(寺)	JI		単	300
	(維)	I	suzu	鈴	1971	体	61		(巣)	SŌ
	遂	1185	suzu(mu)	涼	1267	(本)	HON		(弾)	DAN
	(逐)	CHIKU	suzu(shii)	涼	1267	替	757		(禅)	ZEN
	(墜)	TSUI				戴	1108		(戦)	SEN
	帥	2120				泰	1647		炭	1427
	(師)	SHI	**– T –**			堆	1749		(灰)	KAI
	衰	1791				平	202		(岩)	GAN
	(哀)	AI	TA	太	639	tai(ra)			淡	1420
	穂	1284		汰	1206	taka	高	190		(炎)	EN
	(恵)	KEI		他	120	taka(i)	高	190		(談)	DAN
	水	21		(也)	YA	taka(maru)	高	190		探	544
	出	53		多	229	taka(meru)	高	190		(深)	SHIN
su(i)	酸	525	ta	手	57	takara	宝	296		嘆	1313
suji	筋	1141		田	35	take	丈	1408		(漢)	KAN
su(kasu)	透	1800	taba	束	510		竹	129		誕	1168
suke	助	633	ta(beru)	食	322		岳	1442		(延)	EN
su(keru)	透	1800	tabi	度	378	taki	滝	1887		鍛	1966
suki	隙	1111		旅	222	takigi	薪	2083		(段)	DAN
suko(shi)	少	144	tada(chi ni)	直	429	TAKU	沢	1031		綻	2018
suko(yaka)	健	914	tada(shi)	但	2112		択	1030		(定)	TEI
su(ku)	好	104	tada(shii)	正	275		(尺)	SHAKU		丹	1144
	透	1800	tada(su)	正	275		宅	178		反	324
suku(nai)	少	144	tadayo(u)	漂	946		託	1746		短	215
suku(u)	救	738	ta(eru)	耐	1504		度	378		端	1507
su(masu)	済	558		堪	2089		(席)	SEKI	tana	棚	2080
	澄	1417		絶	755		(庶)	SHO	tane	種	228
su(mau)	住	156	taga(i)	互	929		濯	1664	tani	谷	664
sumi	炭	1427	tagaya(su)	耕	1259		(躍)	YAKU	tano(moshii)		
	隅	1753	tagu(i)	類	226		(曜)	YŌ		頼	1613
	墨	1821	TAI	台	501		卓	1794	tano(mu)	頼	1613
sumi(yaka)	速	511		胎	1371		拓	1983	tano(shii)	楽	359
su(mu)	済	558		怠	1372	ta(ku)	炊	1927	tano(shimu)		
	澄	1417		代	256	taku(mi)	巧	1737			
	住	156		袋	1412	takuwa(eru)	蓄	1288		楽	359
SUN	寸	2070		貸	761	tama	玉	295	tao(reru)	倒	927
suna	砂	1204		退	865		球	739	tao(su)	倒	927
su(reru)	擦	1620		逮	912		弾	1641	ta(rasu)	垂	1117
							霊	1225	ta(reru)	垂	1117

419

ta(riru) 足 58	廷 1163	哲 1486	(場) JŌ
ta(ru) 足 58	庭 1164	(折) SETSU	党 504
tashi(ka) 確 613	艇 1780　TO	登 991	(常) JŌ
tashi(kameru)	(延) EN	頭 276	(堂) DŌ
確 613	定 356	(豆) TŌ	読 244
ta(su) 足 58	堤 1699	(豊) HŌ	(売) BAI
tasu(karu) 助 633	提 638	途 1120	(続) ZOKU
tasu(keru) 助 633	(是) ZE	塗 1121	統 849
tataka(u) 戦 301	帝 1237	(余) YO	(充) JŪ
闘 1612	締 1239	都 188	筒 1569
tatami 畳 1138	諦 1238	賭 1981	(同) DŌ
tata(mu) 畳 1138	貞 1796	(者) SHA	投 1060
tate 盾 786	偵 2113	度 378	(没) BOTSU
縦 1580	呈 1697	渡 379	透 1800
tatematsu(ru)	程 423	土 24	(秀) SHŪ
奉 1643	体 61	吐 1322	陶 1763
ta(teru) 立 121	(本) HON	斗 2075	(缶) KAN
建 913	弟 409	図 339	悼 1795
tato(eru) 例 622	(第) DAI	徒 436	(卓) TAKU
TATSU 達 455	逓 2123	(走) SŌ	等 578
竜 1886　TEKI	適 421	妬 1956	(寺) JI
ta(tsu) 立 121	滴 1539	(石) SEKI	島 286
建 913	摘 1540　to	戸 152	(鳥) CHŌ
裁 1175	敵 422　to-	十 12	刀 37
断 1063	的 210　TŌ	豆 988	当 77
絶 755	(約) YAKU	登 991	冬 467
tatto(bu) 尊 717	笛 1568	痘 2130	灯 1416
貴 1228　TEN	店 168	頭 276	討 1057
tatto(i) 尊 717	点 169	闘 1612	納 771
貴 1228	(占) SEN	(豊) HŌ	盗 1151
tawamu(reru)	天 141	塔 1991	道 149
戯 1679	添 1523	搭 2092	稲 1283
tawara 俵 2063	展 1181	答 160	踏 1662
ta(yasu) 絶 755	殿 1182	(合) GŌ	藤 2087
tayo(ri) 便 330	典 368	東 71	tō 十 12
tayo(ru) 頼 1613	(曲) KYOKU	凍 1268	to(basu) 飛 539
tazu(neru) 訪 1240	転 439	棟 1495	tobira 扉 1658
尋 1132	(伝) DEN	到 926	tobo(shii) 乏 767
tazusa(eru) 携 1801	墳 1920	倒 927	to(bu) 飛 539
tazusa(waru)	(県) KEN	(至) SHI	跳 1666
携 1801	寺 41　tera	(致) CHI	tochi 栃 2036
te 手 57	照 1035　te(rasu)	逃 1669	todo(keru) 届 1029
TEI 低 570	照 1035　te(reru)	桃 1670	todokō(ru) 滞 995
邸 572	照 1035　te(ru)	(兆) CHŌ	todo(ku) 届 1029
抵 569	撤 1512　TETSU	唐 1813	tōge 峠 1434
底 571	徹 1511	糖 1814	to(geru) 遂 1185
(氏) SHI	(微) BI	謄 1911	to(gu) 研 918
丁 184	(徴) CHŌ	騰 1912	to(i) 問 162
亭 1243	迭 1608	湯 642	tō(i) 遠 453
訂 1058	鉄 312	(陽) YŌ	to(jiru) 閉 401
停 1244	(失) SHITSU	(揚) YŌ	to(kasu) 溶 1481

	解	482	tori	鳥	285	tsuka(maeru)			tsu(ru)	釣	2020
to(keru)	溶	1481	to(ru)	取	65		捕	911	tsurugi	剣	900
	解	482		撮	1621	tsuka(maru)			tsuta(eru)	伝	440
toki	時	42		捕	911		捕	911	tsutana(i)	拙	1939
toko	床	845		採	960	tsuka(reru)	疲	1403	tsuta(u)	伝	440
toko-	常	506		執	699	tsu(karu)	漬	1929	tsuta(waru)	伝	440
tokoro	所	153	tō(ru)	通	150	tsu(kasu)	尽	1844	tsuto(maru)	務	235
TOKU	特	282	toshi	年	45	tsuka(u)	使	331		勤	568
	(寺)	JI	tō(su)	通	150		遣	1231	tsuto(meru)	努	1702
	(持)	JI	tōto(bu)	尊	717	tsuka(wasu)	遣	1231		務	235
	読	244		貴	1228	tsu(keru)	付	192		勤	568
	(売)	BAI	tōto(i)	尊	717		着	668	tsutsu	筒	1569
	(続)	ZOKU		貴	1228		就	961	tsutsumi	堤	1699
	匿	1903	totono(eru)	調	342		漬	1929	tsutsu(mu)	包	819
	(若)	JAKU		整	512	tsuki	月	17	tsutsushi(mu)		
	徳	1079	totono(u)	調	342	tsu(kiru)	尽	1844		慎	1918
	(聴)	CHŌ		整	512	tsu(ku)	付	192		謹	1314
	篤	2051	TOTSU	凸	2068		突	920	tsuya	艶	990
	(馬)	BA		突	920		着	668	tsuyo(i)	強	217
	得	375	totsu(gu)	嫁	1873		就	961	tsuyo(maru)	強	217
	督	1785	to(u)	問	162	tsukue	机	1384	tsuyo(meru)	強	217
to(ku)	溶	1481	to(zasu)	閉	401	tsukuro(u)	繕	1192	tsuyu	露	981
	解	482	TSU	通	150	tsuku(ru)	作	361	tsuzu(keru)	続	243
	説	404		都	188		造	704	tsuzu(ku)	続	243
to(maru)	止	485	tsu	津	679		創	1387	tsuzumi	鼓	1200
	泊	1235	TSŪ	通	150	tsu(kusu)	尽	1844			
	留	774		痛	1402	tsuma	妻	682	**– U –**		
to(meru)	止	485	tsuba	唾	1119		爪	1320			
	泊	1235	tsubasa	翼	1107	tsu(maru)	詰	1195	U	右	76
	留	774	tsubo	坪	2072	tsume	爪	1320		羽	600
tomi	富	726	tsubu	粒	1816	tsu(meru)	詰	1195		宇	1027
tomo	共	196	tsubu(reru)	潰	1229	tsume(tai)	冷	851		有	265
	供	197	tsubu(su)	潰	1229	tsumi	罪	906		雨	30
	友	264	tsuchi	土	24	tsu(moru)	積	667	uba(u)	奪	1389
-tomo	共	196	tsuchika(u)	培	1977	tsumu	錘	2139	ubu	産	278
tomona(u)	伴	1066	tsudo(u)	集	442	tsu(mu)	詰	1195	uchi	内	84
to(mu)	富	726	tsu(geru)	告	703		摘	1540	ude	腕	1376
tomura(u)	弔	1934	tsugi	次	385		積	667	ue	上	32
TON	屯	2121	tsu(gu)	次	385	tsumu(gu)	紡	2015	u(eru)	飢	1383
	頓	2122		接	495	tsuna	綱	1716		植	430
	団	500		継	1064		(網)	ami	ugo(kasu)	動	231
	豚	810	tsuguna(u)	償	1003	tsune	常	506	ugo(ku)	動	231
ton	問	162	TSUI	墜	1184	tsuno	角	481	u(i)	憂	1073
tona(eru)	唱	1759		(隊)	TAI	tsuno(ru)	募	1519	ui-	初	692
tonari	隣	828		対	366	tsura	面	274	uji	氏	575
tona(ru)	隣	828		追	1232	tsura(naru)	連	446	u(kaberu)	浮	968
tono	殿	1182		椎	1748	tsura(neru)	連	446	u(kabu)	浮	968
tora	虎	1677	tsui(eru)	費	762	tsuranu(ku)	貫	936	ukaga(u)	伺	1891
tora(eru)	捉	1660	tsui(yasu)	費	762	tsu(reru)	連	446	u(kareru)	浮	968
to(raeru)	捕	911	tsuka	塚	1875	tsuru	鶴	950	u(karu)	受	260
to(rawareru)	捕	911	tsuka(eru)	仕	333		弦	1290			

Reading	Kanji	No.
u(keru)	受	260
	請	672
uketamawa(ru)		
	承	972
u(ku)	浮	968
uma	馬	283
u(mareru)	生	44
	産	278
u(maru)	埋	1975
ume	梅	1856
u(meru)	埋	1975
umi	海	117
u(moreru)	埋	1975
u(mu)	生	44
	産	278
UN	運	445
(軍)		GUN
	雲	646
(曇)		DON
unaga(su)	促	1659
une	畝	2077
uo	魚	290
ura	浦	1534
	裏	273
ura(meshii)	恨	1879
ura(mu)	恨	1879
urana(u)	占	1822
uraya(mashii)		
	羨	1924
uraya(mu)	羨	1924
ure(e)	憂	1073
ure(eru)	愁	1708
	憂	1073
ure(i)	愁	1708
	憂	1073
u(reru)	売	239
	熟	700
u(ru)	売	239
	得	375
uru(mu)	潤	1266
uruo(su)	潤	1266
uruo(u)	潤	1266
urushi	漆	1648
uruwa(shii)	麗	1740
ushi	牛	281
ushina(u)	失	311
ushi(ro)	後	48
usu	臼	1896
usu(i)	薄	1542
usu(maru)	薄	1542
usu(meru)	薄	1542
usu(ragu)	薄	1542
usu(reru)	薄	1542
uta	唄	396
	歌	395
utaga(u)	疑	1617
utai	謡	1760
uta(u)	歌	395
	謡	1760
uto(i)	疎	1615
uto(mu)	疎	1615
UTSU	鬱	1764
u(tsu)	打	1059
	討	1057
	撃	1054
utsuku(shii)	美	405
utsu(ru)	写	549
	映	353
	移	1173
utsu(su)	写	549
	映	353
	移	1173
utsuwa	器	536
utta(eru)	訴	1491
uwa-	上	32
u(waru)	植	430
uyama(u)	敬	718
uyauya(shii)	恭	1524
uzu	渦	1949

– W –

Reading	Kanji	No.
WA	話	238
(舌)		ZETSU
(活)		KATSU
	和	124
wa	我	1381
	輪	1221
WAI	賄	1861
(有)		YŪ
waka(i)	若	553
waka(reru)	別	267
wa(kareru)	分	38
wa(karu)	分	38
wa(kasu)	沸	1928
wa(katsu)	分	38
wake	訳	604
wa(keru)	分	38
waki	脇	1336
WAKU	惑	1001
(域)		KI
waku	枠	2079
wa(ku)	湧	1475
	沸	1928
WAN	腕	1376
	湾	681
warabe	童	416
wara(u)	笑	1299
ware	我	1381
wa(reru)	割	528
wari	割	528
wa(ru)	割	528
waru(i)	悪	304
wasu(reru)	忘	1461
wata	綿	1251
watakushi	私	125
wata(ru)	渡	379
watashi	私	125
wata(su)	渡	379
waza	技	891
	業	279
wazawa(i)	災	1418
wazu(ka)	僅	1315
wazura(u)	患	1395
	煩	2005
wazura(wasu)		
	煩	2005

– Y –

Reading	Kanji	No.
YA	治	1962
(治)		JI
(台)		DAI
	夜	479
ya	野	236
	矢	213
	弥	1012
	屋	167
	家	165
ya-	八	10
yabu(reru)	破	676
	敗	520
yabu(ru)	破	676
yado	宿	179
yado(ru)	宿	179
yado(su)	宿	179
yakata	館	327
ya(keru)	焼	942
YAKU	役	376
	疫	1401
	訳	604
ya(ku)	焼	942
yama	山	34
yamai	病	381
ya(meru)	辞	701
yami	闇	349
ya(mu)	病	381
yanagi	柳	2032
yasa(shii)	易	772
	優	1074
ya(seru)	痩	1953
yashina(u)	養	406
yashiro	社	308
yasu(i)	安	105
yasu(maru)	休	60
yasu(meru)	休	60
yasu(mu)	休	60
yato(u)	雇	1655
ya(tsu)	八	10
yat(tsu)	八	10
yawa(rageru)		
	和	124
yawa(ragu)	和	124
yawa(raka)	柔	788
	軟	1922
yawa(rakai)	柔	788
	軟	1922
YO	予	397
	預	398
(矛)		MU
	誉	816
(言)		GEN
	与	548
	余	1109
yo	世	252
	代	256
	夜	479
yo-	四	6
YŌ	羊	288
	洋	289
	様	407
	養	406
	窯	1925
	陽	640
(尺)		SHAKU
	厄	1424
(危)		KI
	薬	360
(楽)		GAKU
	約	211
	益	729
	躍	1663

Table 18. The 79 Radicals (without variants)

2	亻 a	冫 b	孑 c	阝 d	卩 e	刂 f	力 g	又 h	宀 i	亠 j
	十 k	卜 m	夂 n	丷 o	厂 p	辶 q	冂 r	几 s	匚 t	

3	氵 a	土 b	扌 c	口 d	女 e	巾 f	犭 g	弓 h	彳 i	彡 j
	艹 k	宀 m	丷 n	屮 o	耂 p	广 q	尸 r	囗 s		

4	木 a	月 b	日 c	火 d	衤 e	王 f	牛 g	方 h	攵 i	欠 j
	心 k	戸 m	戈 n							

5	石 a	立 b	目 c	禾 d	礻 e	罒 f	罒 g	皿 h	疒 i

6	糸 a	米 b	舟 c	虫 d	耳 e	竹 f

7	言 a	貝 b	車 c	𧾷 d	酉 e

8	金 a	食 b	隹 c	雨 d	門 e

9	頁 a		10	馬 a		11	魚 a	鳥 b

A version of the table of the 79 radicals with variants appears on page 57.